W9-BUE-230

# CHILDREN'S ILLUSTRATED DICTIONARY

# CHILDREN'S ILLUSTRATED DICTIONARY

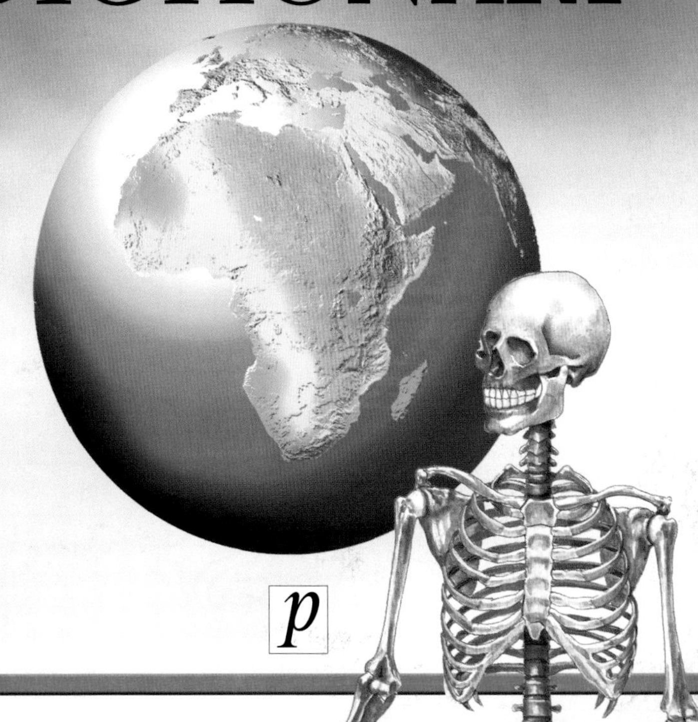

Authors
John Grisewood, Neil Morris, Ting Morris

Artists
The Maltings Partnership, Andrew Clark, Julie Banyard, Gill Platt, Sally Launder, Wayne Ford, Guy Smith, Mike Saunders, Simon Girling Associates.

This is a Parragon Publishing book
This edition published in 2006

Parragon Publishing
Queen Street House
4 Queen Street
Bath BA1 1HE, UK



This edition designed and edited by
Starry Dog Books Limited



ISBN 1-40545-900-X

Printed in Indonesia

# Introduction

Have you ever played the game in which you try to describe something in words only—without using any gestures—and other people have to work out what you are describing? How would you describe an elephant or a television?

This dictionary describes an elephant as follows: "the largest living land animal, with big ears, a trunk, and tusks." The television is described as "a box-shaped instrument that receives programs which have been broadcast and shows them on a screen as moving pictures with sound."

That is exactly what a dictionary does. It tells us what words mean. A good dictionary should describe things well by being clear and concise. If a word has two or more meanings, it should tell us. "Pine," for example, has two quite different meanings: the noun "pine" is an evergreen tree with needles, but the verb means "to become weak and sad because of wanting something very much." The noun "bear" is an animal, but the verb means "to carry," "to support the weight of something," "to produce" (as in fruit), or "to accept or tolerate."

A good dictionary has certain other features:

It tells you how words are spelled ("accommodation" has two "c's" and two "m's").

It tells you how awkward words are pronounced ("gnome," "handkerchief," "suede," "qualm," and "typhoon," for example).

It tells you what the part of speech is. Is it a noun, verb, adjective, or adverb? This is useful. For instance, the noun "object," meaning "a thing," is pronounced "**ob**-ject," but the verb, meaning "to protest," is pronounced "ob-**ject**."

It provides example sentences or phrases to help you understand how a word should be used. For instance, for the word "just", there are various meanings, including: "This is just (exactly) the right color" and "There's just (almost not) enough food for us both to eat."

To be really useful, a dictionary must be up-to-date. New words enter the language and old words may die or acquire a new meaning. If you looked at a dictionary that is only a few years old, you probably would not find the word "cursor," for example, meaning "a small, movable point on a computer screen."

This dictionary has some other features that make it rather special:

- Throughout the book, many superb drawings and photographs complement the definitions and add more visual information.
- At the back of the book, you can find lots of useful information about spelling, so you need never think twice about those tricky words that have "i" and "e" next to each other, like "siege" and "ceiling."
- Also at the back of the book, you will find a collection of fun word games that will turn you into a spelling wizard!

We hope you will find this dictionary both useful and interesting. How would you describe it – without using gestures?

*John Grisewood, Neil Morris, Ting Morris*

# How to use this dictionary

All the entries are in alphabetical order. A color band at the top of each page and a thumb-index at the side show you the pages on which all the entries beginning with the same letter appear. A guide word at the top outside corner of each page also helps you find the word you're looking for. The guide word on the left-hand page gives the first word on that page and the guide word on the right gives the last word.

## Headwords

Headwords or entries are printed in **bold**, black type. Other forms of the same word (related words) are also in bold type, for example: **grace** *noun*. **graceful** *adjective*.

## Derivatives

Derivatives or other irregular forms of the headword are shown in parentheses, as in the verb **give** (gives, giving, gave, given), the noun **genus** (genera), and the adjective **grubby** (grubbier, grubbiest). Regular forms are not given, for example, **dog** (dogs).

## Pronunciation

For some of the more difficult words, there is a guide to how to say it correctly, for example: **gnash** *verb* (say nash).

## Definition

This tells you what a word means. If a word has more than one meaning, each meaning is numbered. For example: **graphic** *adjective* 1 clear and vivid... 2 relating to painting and drawing...

governor

Gg

**governor** *noun* 1 a person elected to manage or govern; a ruler. 2 the head of each state in the US. 3 a person who directs an organization.

**grace** *noun* 1 a beautiful and easy way of moving. 2 the love and favor of God. 3 a short prayer of thanks said before meals. **graceful** *adjective*.

**gracious** *adjective* full of grace and charm.

**grade** *noun* 1 a scale that arranges people or things according to quality, rank, or size. *They only sell vegetables of the highest grade.* 2 marks given in a test. 3 one of the 12 years of school in the US. *He's in the fourth grade.* **grade** *verb*. *The hens' eggs were graded according to size.*

**gradient** *noun* a measure of how steep a slope is. *That hill has a gradient of one in seven. It rises one foot for every seven feet along the horizontal.*

**gradual** *adjective* changing or happening slowly. *A gradual improvement.*

**graduate** *noun* a person who has finished a course of studies and taken a university degree. **graduate** *verb*.

**graffiti** *plural noun* (say gra-**fee**-tee) drawings and writing scribbled on buildings or trains.

**grain** *noun* 1 the seed of cereal plants like corn, rice, and wheat. 2 tiny bits of something. *Grains of salt, sand, and sugar.* 3 the pattern of lines in wood.

**gram** *noun* a unit for measuring weight in the metric system. There are 1,000 grams in a kilogram.

**grammar** *noun* the rules of a language and how the words are put together properly.

**grandparent, grandfather, grandmother** the parent of one of a person's parents.

**granite** *noun* (say **gran**-it) a very hard rock produced by volcanic action, used in building.

**grapefruit** (grapefruit or grapefruits) *noun* a round fruit like a big orange, but with a yellow or pink skin.

**graph** *noun* (rhymes with half) a diagram or chart that shows how numbers or amounts compare or are related.

**graphic** *adjective* 1 clear and vivid. *A graphic account of the murder.* 2 relating to painting and drawing. *The graphic arts.*

**graphics** *plural noun* pictures and patterns.

**grasshopper** *noun* a small jumping insect with long back legs. It makes a chirping sound by rubbing its legs together.

grasshopper

**gravity** *noun* 1 seriousness. 2 the natural force that draws things to the Earth so that they stay there and do not float away.

**graze** *verb* 1 when animals graze, they eat grass as it grows. 2 to scrape and cut your skin by rubbing it against something rough, as when you fall over.

**grease** *noun* a thick, oily substance. **greasy** *adjective*.

**great** *adjective* 1 big or heavy. 2 important, famous, or clever. *A great composer.* 3 very good. *It's great to be here.* **greatness** *noun*.

**Great Britain** *noun* the main island and small islands of England, Scotland, and Wales.

**great-grandparents, great-grandfather great-grandmother** the grandparents of a person's father or mother.

**Greece** *noun* a country in southeast Europe.

**Greek** *noun* 1 a person who comes from Greece. 2 the language spoken in Greece. **Greek** *adjective*. *Greek civilization.*

Greece's flag

**greenhouse** *noun* a building made of glass, used for growing plants in a warm atmosphere. **greenhouse effect** the effect of the atmosphere around the Earth warming up; this happens because gases such as carbon dioxide trapped in the atmosphere by pollution are heated by the Sun.

**Grenada** *noun* a country in the Caribbean.

**grayhound** *noun* a slim breed of dog that can run very fast and is used in racing.

grayhound

**grief** *noun* (rhymes with leaf) great sorrow or sadness, especially after a death or misfortune. **grieve** *verb*. *He is grieving for his dead wife.*

**grievance** *noun* a reason to complain or be angry about something, real or imagined.

**grievous** *adjective* very serious or harmful. *He receiv a grievous injury when he fell from the ladder.*

**grind** (grinds, grinding, ground) *verb* to crush someth into very small pieces or into a powder. *Coffee beans smell delicious when they have just been ground.* **gri** **to a halt** to come slowly to a complete stop.

**groceries** *plural noun* food items such as flour, te coffee, jam, milk, and sugar that you buy from a gr or supermarket.

**groin** *noun* the place where the top of your legs

104

**oom** *verb* to clean and brush an animal, particularly horse. **groom** *noun* **1** a person who looks after horses. a man who is about to get married; a bridegroom.

**rotesque** *adjective* (say grow-**tesk**) weird and unnatural; monstrous.

**ground** *noun* **1** the solid surface of the Earth. **2** a sports field. **gain ground** to make progress. **break new ground** to do something new or discover something for the first time. **ground** *verb* past tense of grind.

**grovel** (grovels, groveling, groveled) *verb* to behave in an over-humble way to somebody because you think they are important.

grow

**grow** (grows, growing, grew, grown) *verb* **1** to become larger and taller; to develop. **2** to plant in the ground. *We are growing seedlings in trays.* **grown-up** *noun* an adult. **grown-up** *adjective. He has a grown-up son.* **grow up** to become an adult. **grow out of** *She'll grow out of sucking her thumb in the next year or so.*

**growl** *verb* to make a deep, low, and angry sound. *The dog growled when I tried to take her bone.*

**grub** *noun* **1** a larva or worm-like creature that will grow into an insect. **2** (slang) food.

**grubby** (grubbier, grubbiest) *adjective* dirty. *Wash your grubby hands before dinner.*

**grudge** *noun* a long-lasting feeling of dislike or resentment toward somebody because they harmed or annoyed you in the past.

**grueling** *adjective* very tiring; severe. *It was a long, grueling journey across the mountains.*

**gruesome** *adjective* revolting and shocking, very unpleasant to see, usually involving violence and death.

**guarantee** *noun* **1** a promise by a manufacturer that something is of a certain quality and that it will be repaired or replaced if it goes wrong within a certain time. *The computer has a year's guarantee.* **2** a promise that something will definitely happen. *They guaranteed that they would win the game.* **guarantee** *verb.*

**guard** *verb* to watch over and protect somebody or something. *Police officers guarded the building.* **guard** *noun* **1** a person or group that guards. *A security guard.* **2** some device or thing that protects. *A fire guard.* **on guard** prepared to defend and protect. **off guard** unprepared; not watching or ready.

**guarded** *adjective* **1** protected. **2** cautious and careful not to say too much. *A guarded reply.*

**Guatemala** *noun* a country in Central America.

**Guatemala City** *noun* the capital of Guatemala.

**guess** *verb* **1** to say what you think is the answer without having enough information to know for certain. *Joe guessed the weight of the cake.* **2** to think. *I guess I'd better be going.* **guess** *noun. My guess is that she is older than she looks.* **guesswork** making guesses or the result of guesses. *He cooked the cake by guesswork.*

**guest** *noun* **1** a person who has been invited to stay for a short time in somebody's house; a visitor. **2** a person staying in a hotel. **3** someone who takes part in an event or entertainment by invitation.

**guide** *noun* somebody who leads or shows the way; a person who helps or advises. *A guide showed us around the magnificent cathedral.* **guide** *verb.*

**guide-dog** *noun* a dog that has been trained to help a blind person find his or her way around a house or town.

**guideline** *noun* advice or a rule about how something should be done.

**guilt** *noun* **1** the miserable feeling you have when you know you have done something wrong. **2** the fact that you have done something wrong.

**guilty** *adjective* **1** having done something wrong or committed a crime. *She was guilty of shoplifting.* **2** concerning guilt or shame. *A guilty secret.*

**Guinea** *noun* a country in West Africa.

**Guinea-Bissau** *noun* a country in West Africa.

**Gujurati** *noun* the language spoken in the state of Gujurat in western India.

**gulf** *noun* a bay or large area of the sea almost surrounded by land.

**gunpowder** *noun* a powder that explodes easily. Gunpowder is used in fireworks.

**gust** *noun* a strong and sudden rush of wind. **gusty** *adjective.*

**Guyana** *noun* a country in South America.

**gym** short for gymnasium and gymnastics.

**gymnasium** *noun* a room with special equipment for doing physical exercises. *Sarah goes to the gymnasium at least once a week to keep fit.*

**gymnast** *noun* a person who is trained in gymnastics.

**gymnastics** *noun* **1** highly skilled physical exercises, such as rings and parallel bars. **2** physical or mental agility.

gymnast

Gg



## Phrasal verbs

Phrasal verbs are included as a distinct part of many definitions. They are simple verbs, such as "make," "get," or "go," together with an adverb or preposition (as in "get up," "get away," "get on" etc.). They function like a single word, but the meaning cannot be worked out from the literal meaning of the words. The ability to use and understand phrasal verbs is very important in writing and speaking clearly.

## Examples of use

A sentence or phrase may be given to show how to use the word correctly.

## Parts of speech

These show how words behave in a sentence. They are: adjective, adverb, conjunction, noun, preposition, pronoun, verb. Some of these parts of speech are themselves defined in the dictionary.

## Gazetteer

The dictionary is also a useful mini-gazetteer. It includes as "definition" all the countries of the world and their capitals, from Abu Dhabi, capital of the United Arab Emirates, to Zimbabwe, a country in Africa.

## Illustrations

The illustrations have been carefully selected to extend and complement the definitions. All the pictures have labels to point you to the accompanying definition. "A good picture," they say, "is worth a thousand words."

Aa

**aardvark** *noun* an African mammal with a long snout and a long sticky tongue that it uses for catching insects.

**abacus** (abacuses) *noun* a frame with rows of beads that slide along wires or bars, used for counting.

**abandon** *verb* **1** to leave someone or something without returning. *They abandoned the sinking boat.* **2** to stop doing something. *She abandoned her search when it got too dark to see.*

**abbey** *noun* a church and a group of buildings where monks or nuns live, work, and pray.

abbey

**abbot** *noun* the head of an abbey of monks.

**abbreviation** *noun* a short way of writing a word or group of words. *Mr. is an abbreviation for Mister.* **abbreviated** *adjective*. **abbreviate** *verb*.

**abdicate** *verb* to give up a position, especially that of king or queen, or refuse responsibility. **abdication** *noun*.

**abdomen** *noun* **1** the part of the body that contains the stomach. **2** the back part of an insect's body.

**abhor** (abhors, abhorring, abhorred) *verb* to hate something. **abhorrent** *adjective*. **abhorrence** *noun*.

**ability** *noun* the power or skill to do something. *Cats have the ability to see in the dark.*

**able** *adjective* **1** having the power, time, or opportunity to do something. *I wasn't able to leave work early.* **2** clever or skilled. *An able cook.* **ably** *adverb*.

**abnormal** *adjective* peculiar and not normal. *It's abnormal for it to snow in summer.* **abnormality** *noun*.

**aboard** *adverb, preposition* in or on a ship, bus, train, or airplane. *The ferry is leaving. All aboard!*

**abolish** (abolishes, abolishing, abolished) *verb* to get rid of or to officially end a law or system. *Capital punishment was abolished in the UK.* **abolition** *noun*.

**abominable** *adjective* bad and very unpleasant. **abominably** *adverb*. *He behaved abominably.*

**aborigine** (say ab-or-**ij**-in-ee) *noun* the people who have lived in Australia from the earliest times. **aboriginal** (say ab-or-**ij**-in-ul) *adjective*.

**abortion** *noun* ending a woman's pregnancy by removing the fetus from her womb. **abort** *verb*.

**abortive** *adjective* unsuccessful. *An abortive attempt was made to seize power.*

Aboriginal

**about** *preposition* concerning, in connection with. *The movie is about space travel.* **about** *adverb* **1** approximately. *I live about a mile from here.* **2** almost. *Dinner's about ready.*

**above** *preposition* **1** higher than. *A bee is buzzing above my head.* **2** more than. *Above normal temperature.* **above** *adverb* overhead. *The sky above is turning red in the sunset.*

**abreast** *adverb* side by side and facing the same way. *The boys marched four abreast.*

**abridge** *verb* to make a book or play shorter. **abridged** *adjective*. *The abridged novels of Dickens.* **abridgement** *noun* a shortened version of a book or play.

**abroad** *adverb* in or to a foreign country. *I love to go on vacation abroad.*

**abrupt** *adjective* **1** sudden and unexpected. *The bus came to an abrupt stop at the traffic lights.* **2** rude and unfriendly. *An abrupt answer.*

**abscess** *noun* (say **ab**-sess) a swelling on the body containing a yellow liquid called pus.

**abseil** *verb* (say **ab**-sail) to lower yourself down a vertical surface such as a tall building or cliff using ropes fixed at a higher point.

**absent** *adjective* not present, but away from somewhere. *Anne was absent from school because she had a cold.* **absence** noun. **absent-minded** *adjective* forgetful or not paying attention. *The absent-minded professor left the house without his lecture notes.*

**absolute** *adjective* **1** complete. *I'm telling the absolute truth.* **2** unlimited. *Dictators have absolute power to do what they want.* **3** definite and not likely to change. *I can't give you an absolute answer.*

**absorb** *verb* **1** to soak up a liquid. *Sponges absorb water.* **2** to be deeply interested. *She is absorbed in her work.* **absorbent** *adjective*. **absorbing** *adjective*.

**abstain** *verb* **1** to keep yourself from doing something. *She abstained from eating chocolate for the whole of Lent.* **2** to choose not to vote in an election. **abstention** *noun*. **abstinence** *noun*.

**abstract** *adjective* concerned with thoughts and ideas rather than material things or events. **abstract** *noun* a short written statement of the most important ideas in a piece of writing. The opposite of 'abstract' is 'concrete'.

**absurd** *adjective* stupid and ridiculous. **absurdity** *noun.*

**Abu Dhabi** *noun* the capital of the United Arab Emirates in southwest Asia.

**Abuja** *noun* the capital of Nigeria in west Africa.

**abundant** *adjective* available in large amounts, plentiful, more than enough in quantity. *Abundant supplies of fruit.* **abundance** *noun.* **abundantly** *adverb.*

**abuse** *verb* (say a-**bewz**) **1** to treat a person or an animal in an unkind or violent way. **2** to misuse or use in a wrong way. **abuse** *noun* (say a-**bewss**) **1** rude or cruel words. **2** the wrong and harmful use of something. *Drug abuse.* **abusive** *adjective.*

**abysmal** *adjective* very bad. *What an abysmal film!*

**abyss** *noun* a bottomless pit.

**academic** *adjective* concerned with education and learning. *Academic studies such as law or politics.* **academic** *noun* a teacher or scholar in a university or college of higher education.

academic

**academy** *noun* a school or college that trains people in a particular subject, like: *The Academy of Speech and Drama.*

**accelerate** *verb* to go faster and faster. **acceleration** *noun.*

**accelerator** *noun* a pedal inside a car that you press to increase its speed.

**accent** *noun* (say **ak**-sent) **1** a way of pronouncing a language used by people in a particular region or country. *An English accent.* **2** a mark that is put above or below a letter of the alphabet in some languages to show you how to pronounce it. **3** the part of a word that you emphasize when you say the word. **accent** *verb* (say ak-**sent**) to pronounce a syllable in a word with more force or emphasis. *You accent the second syllable in "tomato."*

**accentuate** *verb* to emphasize.

**accept** *verb* **1** to take something that is offered. **2** to say yes to something. **3** to believe something to be true. *You must accept that abseiling is dangerous.* **acceptance** *noun.*

**acceptable** *adjective* satisfactory.

**access** *noun* a way to get into a place. *The access to the castle is over the drawbridge.*

**accessible** *adjective* easy to approach, understand or reach. *An accessible book.*

**accessory** *noun* **1** something extra that completes the thing it is added to. **2** somebody who helps in or knows the details of a crime, without taking part.

**accident** *noun* an unexpected and usually unpleasant happening. *She was hurt in a car accident.*

**accidental** *adjective* by chance and not on purpose. **accidentally** *adverb.*

**accommodate** *verb* **1** to provide a place for somebody to live. **2** to have enough space for a number of people or things. **3** to do what someone wants or needs. **accommodation** *noun.*

**accompany** (accompanies, accompanying, accompanied) *verb* **1** to go along with somebody or something. **2** to play a musical instrument while somebody else sings or dances. **accompanist** *noun.*

**accomplice** *noun* a person who helps somebody carry out a crime.

**accomplish** *verb* to succeed in completing something. *He accomplished his aim.* **accomplishment** *noun.*

**accomplished** *adjective* talented or skillful.

**according** *adverb* (followed by *to*) as shown by something or said by or in the opinion of somebody. *According to Jack, the visit has been postponed.* **2** in a corresponding way. *You will be paid according to how much work you do.*

accordion

**accordingly** *adverb* therefore; as a result; suitably.

**accordion** *noun* a portable musical instrument that you play by pressing keys and squeezing bellows to force air through reeds.

**account** *noun* **1** a description of something. **2** the money that a person keeps in a bank. **3** a bill or a record of money received or owed. **account** *verb* to give an explanation or reason for something. *How do you account for this broken window?* **on account** an agreement that lets you pay for goods later. **on no account** used to emphasize that someone must not do something for any reason.

**accountant** *noun* a person whose job it is to look after money and the accounts of businesses or people.

**Accra** *noun* the capital of Ghana in West Africa.

**accumulate** *verb* gradually to increase in quantity. **accumulation** *noun.*

**accurate** *adjective* correct and exact. **accuracy** *noun.*

**accuse** *verb* to blame and say that somebody has done something wrong. **accusation** *noun.*

**accustomed** *adjective* used to something. *It will take a little time to get accustomed to your new computer.*

**ace** *noun* **1** a playing card with a single symbol on it. *The ace of spades.* **2** a first hit in tennis or volleyball that cannot be hit back.

**ache** *noun* a pain that goes on hurting for a long time. **ache** *verb* to have a dull pain. *I ache badly all over.*

**achieve** *verb* to succeed in doing or getting something, as a result of your actions. **achievement** *noun.*

**acid** *adjective* a sharp, sour taste. *Lemons have an acid taste.* **acid** *noun* a chemical substance that can dissolve metals and turn blue litmus paper pink. **acid rain** chemicals in the atmosphere (caused by burning coal and oil) that fall with rain and damage trees, other plants, and rivers.

acid rain

**acknowledge** *verb* to admit or accept that something is true. *She acknowledged that she had been mistaken.* **acknowledgment** *noun.*

**acne** *noun* a skin condition in which a lot of red pimples appear on the face, especially common in young people.

**acorn** *noun* the nut or seed of the oak tree.

**acoustics** *plural noun* **1** the science of sound. **2** the qualities of a room that affect the way sounds are heard in it. **acoustic** *adjective. An acoustic guitar does not have its sound made louder electronically.*

**acquaintance** *noun* **1** a person you know, but not well. **2** a knowledge of something. *I have some acquaintance with the Japanese language.*

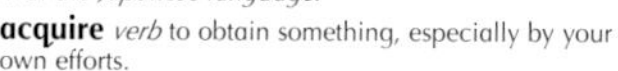

acorn

**acquire** *verb* to obtain something, especially by your own efforts.

**acre** *noun* an area of land equal to 4,047 square meters or 4,840 square yards.

**acrobat** *noun* a person who does difficult physical or gymnastic actions (acrobatics), as in a circus. **acrobatic** *adjective.*

**acronym** *noun* a word made from the first letters of other words, such as FDA (Food and Drug Administration).

**acrophobia** *noun* a great fear of heights.

**across** *adverb, preposition* from one side of something to the other. *The road's too busy to walk across.*

**act** *noun* **1** something that somebody does. *A kind act.* **2** (**Act**) a main division of a play or opera. *Act Two, Scene One.* **3** a law passed by the government. **act** *verb* **1** to do something. *She acted quickly to pick up the child that had fallen over.* **2** to perform as a character in a play or movie. **3** to behave. *He acts shy.*

**action** *noun* **1** something that is done. *His action stopped an explosion from happening.* **2** a gesture or physical movement. **3** a lawsuit. **4** a battle. *My grandfather was killed in action.* **take action** to do something. **out of action** not working.

**active** *adjective* **1** busy and full of energy. **2** able or ready to operate.

**activity** *noun* **1** action and movement. *The city is full of activity.* **2** something that people do, for fun or to achieve something.

**actor** *noun* someone who performs in plays or movies, or on television.

**actually** *adverb* really, in fact. *Did you actually talk to the President?*

**acute** *adjective* **1** severe and great. *An acute shortage of water.* **2** sharp. *Acute hearing.* **acute accent** a sloping mark placed over a vowel in some languages to show how it is pronounced, e.g. é in café. **acute angle** an angle of less than 90°.

actor

**AD** *abbreviation* Anno Domini, the Latin words meaning "in the year of our Lord," used for all dates after the birth of Jesus Christ (e.g. AD 630). CE, or Common Era, is now also used. Compare **BC**.

**adamant** *adjective* determined not to change one's mind. *He's adamant that he will go.*

**adapt** *verb* to change or make something suitable for a new situation or purpose. *We adapted the old shed into an office.* **adaptable** *adjective.*

**adapter** *noun* a device that can connect two or more electrical pieces of equipment.

**add** *verb* to put two or more things together. *If you add four and three, you get seven.* **addition** *noun.* The opposite of "add" is "subtract."

**adder** *noun* any of various small snakes, including the common viper.

**addict** *noun* someone who is unable to stop a habit (often a harmful one, such as drug-taking) without exerting great physical and mental effort.

**addiction** *noun* the condition of being addicted to something like drugs or alcohol. **addictive** *adjective.*

**Addis Ababa** *noun* the capital of Ethiopia in East Africa.

**additional** *adjective* extra, more than usual. *It was so cold she put on an additional sweater.*

**address** *noun* the name of the house, street, and town where somebody lives. **address** *verb* to write an address on an envelope or parcel.

**adenoids** *plural noun* soft lumps of flesh at the back of the nose that sometimes swell and make it difficult to breathe or speak.

**adequate** *adjective* just enough. *We have adequate food supplies for the sheep this winter.*

**adhere** *verb* to stick. *Please adhere strictly to the rules.*

**adhesive** *noun* a substance, like glue, that sticks things together. **adhesive** *adjective* sticky. *Adhesive tape.*

**adjacent** *adjective* very close to or next to. *The playing fields are adjacent to the school.*

**adjective** *noun* a word that tells us something about nouns. In the phrase "big, brown bear," the words "big" and "brown" are adjectives that describe the noun "bear."

**adjust** *verb* to arrange or change something slightly so as to improve it. *She adjusted the curtains so that they hung better.* **adjustment** *noun.*

**administer** *verb* **1** to be in charge of and manage. *She administers the company's finances.* **2** to give out. *The nurse who was on duty always administered the medicine at the correct time.*

**administration** *noun* **1** the management of a company. **2** the government of a country. *The last Liberal administration.* **administrate** *verb* to administer.

**admirable** *adjective* very good and worthy of being admired. *An admirable achievement.*

**admiral** *noun* a very senior officer in the navy.

**admire** *verb* **1** to like and to think somebody or something is very good, to respect. *They admired him for his courage.* **2** to look at something with pleasure. *We admired the view.* **admiration** *noun.*

admiral

**admission** *noun* **1** permission to enter somewhere. *Admission is by invitation only.* **2** the price charged to enter a place. *Admission is free.* **3** a statement that something is true. *By her own admission she was sad.*

**admit** (admits, admitting, admitted) *verb* **1** to agree or say that something is true. *They admitted they were wrong.* **2** to let somebody enter.

**adobe** *noun* **1** a clay brick hardened in the sun. **2** a building made of such brick.

**adolescent** *noun* a young person between childhood and adulthood. **adolescence** *noun.*

**adopt** *verb* to take somebody else's child into your home and make him or her legally your own son or daughter. **adoption** *noun.*

**adore** *verb* to love and admire another person very much. **adoration** *noun.*

**adorn** *verb* to decorate something with ornaments to make it look more attractive.

**adrift** *adverb* floating and drifting without being secured. *The boat was adrift.*

adrift

**adult** *noun* a grown-up person or animal. **adult** *adjective* grown-up. **adulthood** *noun.*

**adulterate** *verb* to spoil something, especially food, by adding to it something harmful or of a lower quality. **adulteration** *noun.*

**advance** *noun* **1** progress. *Medicine has made great advances.* **2** a loan of money. **advance** *verb* **1** to move forward. *The army advanced toward the enemy.* **2** to suggest an idea. *The detective advanced a new theory.* **in advance** before a certain date or event.

**advantage** *noun* something that helps you to succeed and do better than others. *It's a great advantage to be able to speak Japanese.* **take advantage of** to make use of a person or situation to help yourself.

**advent** *noun* **1** the beginning or arrival of something. *The advent of television.* **2 Advent** the four weeks before Christmas in the Christian Church.

**adventure** *noun* an enterprise or activity that is exciting and possibly dangerous and unusual. **adventurous** *adjective. She led an adventurous life in Africa.*

**adverb** *noun* a word that tells us more about a verb, an adjective or another adverb, and answers "how, when, or where?" In the sentence "My grandmother talks very quickly," the words "very" and "quickly" are adverbs.

**advertise** *verb* to inform the public of services offered or goods for sale.

**advertisement** *noun* a notice in a newspaper, as a billboard or on television that gives information about a product, to persuade people to buy or use it.

Aa

aerial

**advice** *noun* a helpful suggestion made to somebody about what they should do.

**advisable** *adjective* sensible and worth doing. *It's advisable to get an early night before going on vacation.*

**advise** *verb* to suggest to somebody what you think they ought to do. *The dentist advised me to brush my teeth twice a day.* **adviser** *noun.*

**aerial** *adjective* from the air or happening in the air. **aerial** *noun* an antenna used to transmit or receive radio or television signals.

**aerobics** *plural noun* energetic physical exercises that increase the body's intake of oxygen.

**aerodynamics** *plural noun* the science of objects moving through the air. **aerodynamic** *adjective.*

**aerosol** *noun* a container that holds a liquid such as paint under pressure and lets it out as a fine spray.

**aerospace** *adjective* involving the designing and building of aircraft and space vehicles.

**affair** *noun* **1** an event. *A barbecue is usually an informal affair.* **2** a relationship between two people, usually temporary. *A passionate love affair.*

**affairs** *plural noun* **1** business dealings. **2** public matters. *He was reporting on current affairs.*

**affect** *verb* to influence or to cause a change in something. *The cold weather affects her health badly.*

**affected** *adjective* not sincere. *An affected smile.*

**affection** *noun* a feeling of gentle love or caring for somebody. **affectionate** *adjective.*

**affluent** *adjective* wealthy. **affluence** *noun.*

**afford** *verb* **1** to have enough money to buy something. **2** to be able to let something happen or do something without risk or damage to yourself.

**afforestation** *noun* the covering of land by forest. The opposite of "afforestation" is "deforestation."

**Afghanistan** *noun* a country in central Asia.

**afloat** *adjective, adverb* floating on a liquid or in the air. *The boat was afloat on the river.*

**afraid** *adjective* **1** frightened. *Are you afraid of the dark?* **2** apologetic. *I'm afraid you'll have to wait outside.* **3** worried. *I'm afraid the pain in my leg may return.*

**Africa** *noun* one of the Earth's seven continents.

Africa

**African** *noun* a native of Africa. **African** *adjective. An African elephant.*

**aft** *adverb* towards the back or stern of a ship or an aircraft. *The captain went aft.*

**after** *preposition* **1** later, when a time or event has happened and is past. *Come here after school.* **2** following someone or something. *The lamb ran after her.* **after** *adverb* later. *I met her the day after.*

**afternoon** *noun* the part of the day between midday and the evening.

**afterward** *adverb* later. *We swam first and had breakfast afterward.*

**again** *adverb* once more. *Please would you sing that song again?*

**against** *preposition* **1** touching or next to something. *She propped the ladder against the wall.* **2** opposed to. *They are against all hunting.* **3** in opposition to. *Who are you playing against tomorrow?*

**agate** *noun* a semiprecious stone with colored stripes.

**age** *noun* **1** the length of time that somebody has lived or that something has existed. *What age are you?* **2** a length of time in history. *The Iron Age.* **age** *verb* to become old. *She aged with dignity.*

**aged** *adjective* **1** (say **ay**-jid) very old. *An aged witch.* **2** (rhymes with 'paged') having a certain age. *A woman aged 50.*

**ageism** *noun* unfair treatment of somebody because of their age.

**ageless** *adjective* **1** showing no signs of getting old. **2** timeless, eternal.

**agenda** *noun* list of topics to be discussed at a meeting.

**agent** *noun* a person who organizes things and does business for other people. *A travel agent.* **secret agent** a spy, such as the fictional character James Bond.

**aggression** *noun* forcefulness, angry or threatening behavior, or an attack without being provoked.

**aggressive** *adjective* forceful or violent and likely to attack people. *An aggressive dog.* **aggressor** *noun.*

**agile** *adjective* nimble. Moving quickly and easily. **agility** *noun.*

**agitate** *verb* **1** to make someone feel nervous or worried. *She was agitated because she was late.* **2** to campaign or argue strongly for something. **agitator** *noun.*

**agitation** *noun* **1** a strong feeling of worry. **2** a protest or campaign.

**ago** *adverb* in the past. *Napoleon lived many years ago.*

**agonize** *verb* to think carefully and with great effort. **agonizing** *adjective verb* painful or difficult.

**agony** *noun* great pain or suffering.

**agoraphobia** *noun* (say agra-**foh**-bee-uh) a great fear of open spaces.

**agree** *verb* **1** to say "yes" to something. **2** to share the same ideas or opinions about something. *We all agree that cruelty is wrong.* **agree with** to be good for or to suit someone. *Curry doesn't agree with him.*

**agreeable** *adjective* pleasant. *Agreeable weather.* The opposite of "agreeable" is "disagreeable."

**agreement** *noun* a promise or an understanding between two or more people or countries.

agriculture

**agriculture** *noun* the science or practice of farming, especially of growing crops. **agricultural** *adjective. Agricultural machinery.*

**ahead** *adverb* **1** in front of. *She walked ahead of me.* **2** in the future. *Plan ahead.*

**aid** *noun* **1** help or support, something that helps you do something. *He walks with the aid of a stick.* **2** money, food, or services given to people in need. **aid** *verb* to help.

**Aids** *noun* (short for or an acronym for Acquired Immune Deficiency Syndrome), a serious illness that destroys the body's natural defenses (immunity) against disease and infection.

**ailment** *noun* an illness that is not very serious.

**aim** *noun* line of sight. *He took aim.* **aim** *verb* **1** to point at something, especially with a weapon. *He aimed the gun at the target.* **2** to plan or try to do something. *Alan aims to be the finest athlete in his school.*

**aimless** *adjective* without any aim or purpose. *An aimless existence.*

**air** *noun* **1** the invisible mixture of gases that surrounds the Earth and which we breathe. **2** general appearance or impression. *You have an air of calm about you.* **air** *verb* **1** to broadcast or make known your views. **2** to make things or a room smell fresh by letting air flow through them. **air conditioning** a system of controlling a building's temperature and keeping it cool in summer. **air conditioner** *noun.* **air-conditioned** *adjective.* **air force** *noun* the part of a country's forces that uses aircraft for fighting (e.g. the US Air Force).

**aircraft** any machine that flies, such as an airplane, glider, or helicopter. **aircraft-carrier** *noun* a warship with a large deck from which aircraft can take off and land.

**airfield** *noun* a place where aircraft take off and land.

**airline** *noun* a company that owns aircraft and provides a regular service.

**airplane** *noun* a machine with wings, driven by one or more engines, that flies through the air carrying passengers or freight.

**airport** *noun* a place you leave from or arrive at when travelling by airplane.

**airtight** *adjective* **1** tightly sealed so that no air can get in or out. *Food can be preserved in airtight containers.* **2** having no mistakes or weaknesses.

**airy** (airier, airiest) *adjective* full of fresh air.

**aisle** *noun* (rhymes with "pile") **1** a passage between rows of seats where you can walk, as in an airplane or a theater, or between the rows of shelves in a supermarket.

**ajar** *adverb, adjective* slightly open. *He left the window ajar to air the room.*

**alarm** *noun* **1** a sudden fear or danger. **2** a loud noise that warns people of danger. *A fire alarm.* **alarm** *verb* to become suddenly afraid or anxious that something bad will happen. *They were alarmed to see smoke pouring out of their house.*

**Albania** *noun* a country in southeastern Europe.

Albania's flag

**Albanian** *noun* a person who comes from Albania. **Albanian** *adjective. Albanian wine is a local product.*

**albatross** (albatrosses) *noun* a large white sea bird with long wings.

**album** *noun* **1** a blank book in which to keep photographs or stamps. **2** a CD, tape or record with a collection of songs.

**alchemy** *noun* (say **al**-kem-ee) the medieval science of trying to turn metals into gold. **alchemist** *noun.*

**alcohol** *noun* **1** a colorless chemical liquid that catches fire quickly. **2** drinks such as beer, whiskey, and wine that contain alcohol, which can make people drunk if imbibed in excess.

**alcoholic** *adjective* containing alcohol. *Wine is an alcoholic drink.* **alcoholic** *noun* a person who is addicted to alcohol and needs to drink it regularly.

**alcove** *noun* a recess in a wall or a small part of a room in which the wall is set farther back.

**ale** *noun* a kind of beer with a slightly bitter taste.

**alert** *verb* to warn people of a possible danger. *The doctor alerted her to the danger of eating too much.* **alert** *adjective* quick-thinking and watchful of what is going on. **on the alert** ready for any possible danger.

**algae** *plural noun* (say **al**-ghee) water-plants such as seaweed that have no roots or stems.

**algebra** *noun* a branch of mathematics that uses symbols and letters to represent numbers and values; x - 5 = 10 is an example of an algebraic formula.

Algeria's flag

**Algeria** *noun* a country in northern Africa.

**Algiers** *noun* the capital of Algeria.

**alias** *noun* (say **ail**-ee-uss) a false name, often used by a criminal. **alias** *adverb* also known as. *Ron Chalky, alias Ronald White.*

**alibi** *noun* (say **al**-ih-by) a proof or claim that a person charged with a crime was somewhere else when the crime was committed.

**alien** *noun* **1** a foreigner or stranger. **2** a creature from space. **alien** *adjective* different or strange. *An alien being.*

**alight** *adjective* on fire, burning. **alight** *verb* to come down from a vehicle. *She alighted from the train.*

**alike** *adjective* similar. *The brothers are very alike.* **alike** *adverb* equally. *She treats them all alike.*

**alive** *adjective* living, not dead. **alive** *adverb* full of life.

**alkali** (alkalis) *noun* a substance that forms a chemical salt when combined with acid and turns pink litmus paper blue.

**all** *adjective* the whole amount or number. *All babies sleep a lot.* **all** *adverb* completely. *He was dressed all in black.* **all along** all the time. **all at once 1** suddenly. *All at once the house shook.* **2** all at the same time. *Try not to spend it all at once.* **all right** *adjective* not ill, hurt or in difficulties. **all right!** *interjection* a phrase you can say when you agree to do something. *"Will you wash the dishes?" "Oh, all right."* **after all** all things considered. *After all, he's only young.*

**Allah** *noun* the name of God in the Islamic religion.

**allege** *verb* (say al-**edge**) to say that something is true or that somebody has done something, without showing proof. **allegation** (say al-eg-**ay**-shun) *noun.*

**allergy** *noun* an illness caused by substances such as dust, fur, or certain foods, which do not normally make people ill. **allergic** *adjective* reacting badly to.

**alley** (alleys) *noun* **1** a passageway between buildings. *The alley provided a shortcut to the shops.* **a blind alley** a situation in which there is no way out.

**alliance** *noun* a union or friendly agreement to cooperate between two or more countries, political parties, or groups of people.

**alligator** *noun* a large reptile with a long body and tail, sharp teeth, and strong jaws. Alligators are similar to crocodiles and live in rivers in the south of the USA.

alligator

**alliteration** *noun* the repetition of the same sound at the beginning of each word in a phrase, e.g. *the sun sank slowly.*

**allocate** *verb* to share or set aside time or money for a particular purpose. *The charity allocated $1,000 for the building of a new children's home.* **allocation** *noun.*

**allotment** *noun* a small grant of something like land or money.

**allow** *verb* to permit or let somebody do something. *Running is allowed in the playground but not in the corridors.*

**allowance** *noun* a fixed amount of money that is paid to somebody regularly. **make allowances for** to take someone's circumstances into account.

**alloy** (alloys) *noun* a metal made by mixing other metals. **alloy** *verb* to mix metals together. **alloy wheel** a lightweight wheel made from a mix of metals.

alloy wheel

**allude** *verb* to talk about something in an indirect way or to mention it in passing. **allusion** *noun.*

**alluring** *adjective* very attractive, appealing, and charming.

**ally** *noun* (say **al**-eye) a country or person that helps and supports another. *America, France, and Great Britain were allies in World War II.*

**almanac** *noun* an annual calendar of months and days containing information about the movements of the Moon and stars or a particular subject or activity.

**almighty** *adjective* **1** having the power to do anything. **2** very important or powerful.

**almond** *noun* the oval nut-like seed of the stone-fruit that grows on the almond tree.

**almost** *adjective* nearly but not quite.

**alone** *adjective, adverb* with no other people, by yourself. *She was alone in the house.*

**along** *preposition, adverb* **1** from one end to the other. *They drove along the road.* **2** in the company of. *He brought his sister along.*

**alongside** *preposition, adverb* next to and by the side of. *He put the bench alongside the wall.*

**aloud** *adverb* in a voice loud enough to be heard. *Archie read the letter aloud.*

**alphabet** *noun* a set of letters in a particular order, used in writing a language. *The English alphabet begins with A and ends with Z.*

**alphabetical** *adjective* in the order of the letters of the alphabet. *The words in this dictionary are arranged in alphabetical order.*

**already** *adverb* before a particular time. *I have already eaten my lunch.*

**Alsatian** *noun* a large wolf-like breed of dog, also called a German shepherd, often used as a guard dog.

**also** *adverb* in addition, too. *He can play and also sing.*

**altar** *noun* a table or raised structure used in religious ceremony.

**alter** *verb* to change in some way. *The village has altered a lot since my grandmother was a child in the 1920s.*

altar

**alternate** *verb* (say awl-ter-**nate**) to happen by turn or to change first one way and then the other. *Barbara alternates between being happy and sad.* **alternate** *adjective* (say awl-**ter**-nat) *Alternate weeks of good weather and bad weather.* **alternately** *adverb.*

**alternative** *noun* **1** a choice between two or more things or possibilities. *The alternative to flying is to travel by train.* **2** different from what is usual. *Alternative medicine can involve using herbs to cure illness.*

**although** *conjunction* even if, in spite of the fact. *Although it was snowing, we drove across the mountains.*

**altitude** *noun* the height above sea level.

**altogether** *adverb* **1** completely. *He has disappeared altogether.* **2** counting everybody or everything. *There are eight of us altogether.*

**aluminum** *noun* a lightweight silver-colored metal.

**always** *adverb* something that happens all the time or very often. *Sally is always smiling.*

**a.m.** *abbreviation* the initial letters of the Latin words 'ante meridiem', which mean before noon. *7 a.m. is 7 o'clock in the morning.*

**amalgam** *noun* **1** a mixture. **2** an alloy of mercury with one or more other metals.

**amalgamate** *verb* combine to make something, such as an organization, bigger. *The two companies have amalgamated.* **amalgamation** *noun.*

**amateur** *noun* a person who does something, such as sports or painting, for pleasure and not for payment. **amateur** *adjective. Amateur dramatics.*

**amateurish** *adjective* not professional or skillful. *Debbie turned in a very amateurish design job.*

**amaze** *verb* to surprise somebody very much. **amazement** *noun* the state of being amazed. *We watched the bungee jumping with fear and amazement.* **amazing** *adjective* surprising. *What amazing tricks!*

**ambassador** *noun* an important official who represents his or her country abroad.

**amber** *noun* **1** a hard, yellowish-red fossil substance that is see-through, and used for jewelry. **2** the yellowish-red color of amber.

**ambi-** *prefix* meaning "both." **ambidextrous** *adjective* able to use both hands equally well.

**ambiguous** *adjective* not clear, having more than one possible meaning. "They are eating apples" is an ambiguous sentence. It could mean "the apples are for eating," or "those people are eating apples." **ambiguity** *noun* of uncertain meaning.

amber

**ambition** *noun* a very strong wish to do something well or to have success and fame. *Her burning ambition is to be a vet.* **ambitious** *adjective.*

**amble** *verb* to walk slowly. **amble** *noun.*

**ambulance** *noun* a vehicle for carrying people who are ill or injured.

**ambush** *verb* to wait in hiding in order to attack somebody by surprise. **ambush** *noun.*

**amend** *verb* to alter or correct something slightly in order to improve it. *Some laws are out of date and need amending.* **amendment** *noun.*

**American** *noun* a person who comes from the United States. **American** *adjective* belonging to or characteristic of the United States.

**amiable** *adjective* pleasant and friendly. **amiably** *adverb.*

**Amman** *noun* the capital of Jordan in southwest Asia.

Aa

**ammonia** *noun* a strong-smelling gas that dissolves in water.

**ammonite** *noun* the fossilized, flat spiral shell of an extinct mollusk.

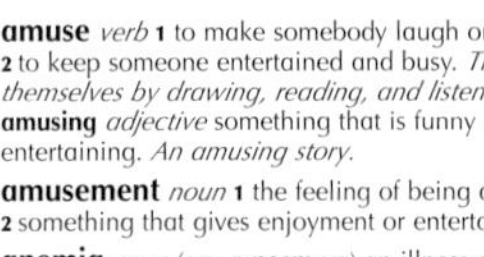

ammonite

**ammunition** *noun* **1** things such as bullets and shells that can be fired from a gun or other weapon. **2** information that can be used against someone.

**amnesia** *noun* loss of memory.

**amnesty** *noun* a general pardon, usually for political offenses, given by the state to prisoners.

**amoeba** *noun* a microscopic, one-celled animal.

**among** *or* **amongst** *preposition* **1** in the middle of, surrounded by. *She lived among the islanders.* **2** one of. *Canada is among the biggest countries in the world.* **3** between. *Share these candies among your friends.*

**amount** *noun* the quantity of something, or how much there is. *A large amount of money was spent on renovating the mansion.* **amount** *verb* to add up to or be equal to. *Her debts amount to over $50.*

**ampersand** *noun* the sign "&" that means "and."

**amphibian** *noun* an animal that, as an adult, can live on land and in water, and breathes air. Frogs, toads, and newts are amphibians. **amphibious** *adjective.*

amphibian

**amphitheater** *noun* a circular, unroofed building with tiers of seats that partly curve around a central open space. Amphitheaters were used for sporting events and plays in Greek and Roman times.

**ample** *adjective* more than enough, plenty. *The car has ample room for five passengers.*

**amplifier** *noun* an electronic device for making sounds louder, used, for example, in radio equipment.

**amplify** (amplifies, amplifying, amplified) *verb* to make louder. **amplification** *noun.*

**amputate** *verb* to cut off a limb for medical reasons. *His leg was amputated after he was hit by a bullet during the civil war.* **amputation** *noun.*

**amputee** *noun* a person who has had a limb amputated. *The amputee was in hospital for weeks after the operation while he learned how to walk again.*

**Amsterdam** *noun* the capital of the Netherlands.

**amuse** *verb* **1** to make somebody laugh or smile. **2** to keep someone entertained and busy. *They amused themselves by drawing, reading, and listening to CDs.* **amusing** *adjective* something that is funny and entertaining. *An amusing story.*

**amusement** *noun* **1** the feeling of being amused. **2** something that gives enjoyment or entertainment.

**anemia** *noun* (say a-**neem**-ya) an illness caused by a shortage of red cells in the blood. **anemic** *adjective. Anemic people are often tired and look pale.*

**anesthetic** *noun* (say an-ess-**thet**-ik) a substance that is given to patients before an operation to stop them feeling pain. **anesthetize** *verb.*

**anagram** *noun* a word made by changing the order of the letters of another word. For example, "horse" is an anagram of "shore."

**analyze** *verb* to examine something in great detail, in order to understand it. *She analyzed the water and found that it was polluted.* **analysis** *noun.*

**analyst** *noun* a person whose job it is to analyze something.

**anarchist** *noun* a person who believes there should be no government and no laws.

**anarchy** *noun* **1** a situation in which no one obeys rules or laws. **2** lack of government in a society.

**anatomy** *noun* **1** the structure of the body of a living thing. **2** the study of the organization or social group and how it works.

**ancestor** *noun* a member of your family who lived in past times. **ancestral** *adjective.*

**ancestry** *noun* all your ancestors, the people from whom you are descended. *Families of noble ancestry often have their own coat of arms.*

**anchor** *noun* a heavy metal object that is lowered on a long chain into the water to stop a boat from moving. *They threw the anchor overboard.* **anchor** *verb* to lower the anchor or fasten securely so something cannot move.

ancestry

**ancient** *adjective* (say **ane**-shunt) **1** (humerous) very old. *My ancient car.* **2** of a time long ago. *Ancient Rome was the center of a great empire.*

**Andorra** *noun* a small country in southwest Europe.

**Andorra la Vella** *noun* the capital of Andorra.

**anecdote** *noun* a short account of an often amusing or interesting incident.

**anemone** *noun* (say a-**nem**-oh-nee) a small woodland or garden plant, usually red, blue, white, or purple.

**angel** *noun* **1** a spiritual being and messenger of God. **2** a very kind person. *Thanks, you're an angel.* **angelic** *adjective.*

angel

**anger** *noun* a strong feeling of wanting to criticize or hurt others when you are not pleased with somebody or something.

**angle** *noun* **1** the space between two straight lines or surfaces that meet. **2** not upright or straight.

**angler** *noun* a person who fishes using a rod.

**Angola** *noun* a country in southwest Africa.

**angry** (angrier, angriest) *adjective* annoyed and feeling full of anger. *I'm angry with her for throwing away my old toys.* **angrily** *adverb.*

**anguish** *noun* an intense feeling of sorrow or pain. **anguished** *adjective.*

**animal** *noun* **1** any living creature that is not a plant. **2** all mammals except human beings. **animal kingdom** one of the three basic groups into which all things in nature are divided; the other two are the mineral kingdom and the plant kingdom.

**animate** *adjective* (say **anny**-mut) alive. Animals and plants are animate. The opposite is "inanimate." Stones and metals are inanimate. **animate** *verb* to make alive.

**animation** *noun* a cartoon movie in which photographs of a series of slightly different drawings are shown in quick succession and appear to move.

**Ankara** *noun* the capital of Turkey, in Asia and Europe.

**ankle** *noun* the joint that connects your leg to your foot.

**annex** *verb* to seize or take possession of. **annexation** *noun* the act of annexing, or taking possession of, a territory. *The annexation of Poland.*

**annexe** *noun* a separate building added to a larger one. *We stayed in the hotel annexe.*

**annihilate** *verb* to destroy completely. *The volcano annihilated all the nearby farms.* **annihilation** *noun.*

**anniversary** *noun* a date on which you remember something special that happened on the same date in an earlier year. *A wedding anniversary.*

**announce** *verb* to make known publicly something important. *The king announced his abdication over the radio.* **announcement** *noun.*

**announcer** *noun* a person who makes an announcement. *A radio announcer.*

**annoy** *verb* to irritate or make somebody angry. *The dog annoyed her by not behaving.* **annoyance** *noun.*

**annual** *adjective* happening every year or once a year. *Annual medical appointment.* **annual** *noun* **1** a plant that lives for one year or season only. **2** a book or magazine that appears once a year. **annually** *adverb.*

**anoint** *verb* to put water or oil on somebody during a religious ceremony.

**anonymous** *adjective* **1** not known by name. *An anonymous author.* **2** without features or qualities. **anonymity** *noun.*

**anorexia** *noun* an illness that makes the sufferer afraid of becoming fat and so makes them not want to eat anything. **anorexic** *adjective.*

**another** *adjective* **1** one more. *He ate another cookie.* **2** different. *Please could you find me the same style dress in another color?*

**answer** *noun* **1** reply. *Have you had an answer to your letter?* **2** a solution. *I can't find an answer to this problem.* **answer** *verb* **1** to speak or write in reply to a question or to something that somebody has said. *"Where are you going?" "To the stables," she answered.* **2** to respond to a signal or telephone. **answer back** to give a rude reply to somebody.

**answerable** *adjective* responsible for.

**answering machine** *noun* a machine that records telephone messages from people who call when you are not able to, or do not want to, answer your telephone.

**ant** *noun* a small sociable black or red insect that lives with other ants in an underground colony. **anthill** *noun* a heap of earth made by ants above their nest.

ants

**antagonist** *noun* an enemy or opponent.

**antagonize** *verb* to make somebody feel angry with you. **antagonism** *noun.* **antagonistic** *adjective.*

**Antananarivo** *noun* the capital of Madagascar.

**Antarctic** *noun* the area of land surrounding the South Pole. **antarctic** *adjective. An antarctic expedition with sledges and husky dogs.*

**Antarctica** *noun* one of the Earth's seven continents, the region surrounding the South Pole.

Aa

**ante-** *prefix* before. **antenuptial** *adjective* means before marriage. **antenatal** *adjective* means before birth.

**anteater** *noun* a toothless mammal from South America that uses its long snout and long sticky tongue to catch the ants and other small insects on which it feeds.

antelope

**antelope** *noun* any one of several kinds of deer-like animals from Africa and Asia. They include gazelles, impala, and springboks.

**antenna** (antennae) *noun* **1** one of the feelers on an insect's head. **2** a metal aerial.

**anthem** *noun* a hymn or song written for a special occasion, or a song of importance to a group of people. *"The Star-Spangled Banner" is the national anthem of the USA.*

**anther** *noun* the part of a flower's stamen where pollen matures.

**anthology** *noun* a collection of poems or stories.

**anthropology** *noun* the study of human beings, especially their customs and beliefs.

**anti-** *prefix* against, opposed to, opposite. *Anti-Communist demonstrations.*

**antibiotic** *noun* a powerful medicine that kills harmful bacteria which cause diseases.

**anticipate** *verb* to look forward to or expect something to happen. *We anticipated that these books would sell well, so we stocked our store with them.* **anticipation** *noun.*

**anticlockwise** *adjective, adverb* moving in the opposite direction to the hands of a clock. Not clockwise.

**anticyclone** *noun* air moving away from an area of high pressure, usually bringing calm weather. The opposite of "anticyclone" is "cyclone."

**antidote** *noun* a medicine that acts against the harmful effects of a poison.

**antifreeze** *noun* a chemical that you put in a car's radiator to stop the water from freezing.

**Antigua and Barbuda** *noun* a country in the Caribbean.

Antigua and Barbuda's flag

**antiquated** *adjective* old-fashioned and out of date. *Antiquated rules.*

**antique** *noun* something that is old and valuable. *His grandfather's watch was a valuable antique.* **antique** *adjective* valuable, old.

**antiquity** *noun* ancient times, especially the times of Ancient Greece and Rome.

**antiseptic** *noun* a substance that kills harmful germs and prevents infection and disease. **antiseptic** *adjective* clean and germ-killing. *Antiseptic soap.*

**antler** *noun* one of the branching horns on a stag's or other deer's head.

**antonym** *noun* a word that has the opposite meaning to another word. "Hot" is the antonym of "cold."

**anus** *noun* the opening at the end of the bowels through which solid food waste leaves the body.

antler

**anxious** *adjective* **1** worried, concerned. **2** eager. *Annie is anxious to help her mother look after her little sister.* **anxiety** *noun.*

**any** *adjective* **1** one of. *Take any of these clothes that you like.* **2** some. *Is there any coffee left?* **3** at all. *Are you any happier?* **4** every. *Any athlete could jump that fence.* (**anybody, anyhow, anyone, anything, anytime, anyway, anywhere**).

**apart** *adverb* **1** separate and at a distance away from each other. *The two villages are about a mile apart.* **2** into parts or pieces. *Andrea took her bike apart.* **apart from** except for. *Apart from a few rain showers, the weather is beautiful at this time of year.*

**apartment** *noun* a set of rooms in a larger building.

**apathy** *noun* a lack of interest or feeling.

**ape** *noun* an animal like a monkey but having no tail, for example the gorilla, chimpanzee, orangutang, and gibbon. **ape** (apes, aping, aped) *verb* to imitate how somebody behaves, usually in a silly way.

**aperture** *noun* a small hole or opening.

**apex** (apexes or apices) *noun* the highest point.

**aphid** or **aphis** *noun* a tiny insect that damages or kills plants by sucking juices from them.

**Apia** *noun* the capital of Samoa in the South Pacific.

**apologize** *verb* to say that you are sorry for doing something. *We apologized sincerely for causing so much trouble.* **apology** *noun.* **apologetic** *adjective.*

**apostle** *noun* one of the original followers of Jesus Christ.

**apostrophe** *noun* (say a-**poss**-tra-fee) a punctuation mark (') that shows that letters have been left out of a word (*we've* for *we have*) or to show the ownership of something (*Margaret's pencil*).

**appall** (appalls, appalling, appalled) *verb* to cause horror or shock. *I was appalled by the lack of behavior in class today.* **appalling** *adjective.*

**apparatus** *noun* the tools or equipment needed for a particular purpose.

**apparent** *adjective* **1** obvious and easily seen. *It was quite apparent that she was bored.* **2** seeming to be true or real.

**apparition** *noun* a ghost or something that has appeared to you.

**appeal** *verb* **1** to ask for something urgently and seriously. *They appealed for help for the orphans.* **2** to be interesting or attractive. **3** to ask for a legal decision to be changed by going to a higher court. **appeal** *noun*. **appealing** *adjective*.

**appear** *verb* **1** to come into view. *He suddenly appeared from behind the wall.* **2** to seem. *Fiona appears to be quite ill.* **3** to take part in. *Actors appear in movies and plays.*

**appearance** *noun* **1** the act of coming into view. *The sudden appearance of the bull frightened everybody.* **2** the way somebody or something looks.

**appendicitis** *noun* painful inflammation of the appendix.

**appendix** (appendixes or appendices) *noun* **1** a small tube inside the body at the end of the intestines. **2** additional information at the end of a book.

**appetite** *noun* **1** hunger or a desire for food. **2** a desire or enthusiasm.

**appetizing** *adjective* smelling and looking so good that you want to eat it.

**applaud** *verb* to show that you like something by clapping your hands. **applause** *noun*.

**apple** *noun* the hard, round, red, green, or yellow fruit of the apple tree.

**appliance** *noun* a tool or piece of electrical equipment designed to do a specific job, especially in the home, such as a vacuum cleaner.

**applicant** *noun* a person who applies or asks for something. *There were lots of applicants for the job.*

**apply** (applies, applying, applied) *verb* **1** to ask for something formally. *She applied for the job.* **2** to be relevant or suitable to a person or situation. *These rules apply to everyone.* **3** to spread or stick on. *She applied the ointment to the burn.* **application** *noun*.

**appoint** *verb* to choose somebody to do a job. *Mrs Bartholomew has been appointed Chief Accountant.*

**appointment** *noun* **1** the act of choosing someone for a job. **2** a meeting that has been arranged.

aqueduct

**appreciate** *verb* **1** to know about and understand the value or good points of something. *She appreciates good food.* **2** to be grateful for something. *I appreciate all the valuable help you've given me.* **3** to rise in value. *House prices have appreciated.* **appreciation** *noun*. **appreciative** *adjective* showing gratitude.

**approach** *verb* **1** to come nearer. *She approached the stray dog.* **2** to speak to somebody about a request or an offer. *Dean approached his uncle about some money for a new car.* **approach** *noun* **1** a road or path leading somewhere. *The approach to the house was bumpy.* **2** the course followed by an airplane before landing.

**approachable** *adjective* easy to talk to and willing to listen. The opposite of "approachable" is "unapproachable."

**appropriate** *adjective* suitable for a certain place or event. *Trainers are appropriate footwear for running.*

**approval** *noun* **1** good opinion. *Does this plan meet with your approval?* **2** permission. *You have to get approval from the council to build a summerhouse.*

**approve** *verb* to agree to, to be in favor of something. *She doesn't approve of my clothes.* The opposite of "approve" is "disapprove."

**approximate** *adjective* near the actual, but not exact. *What is the approximate length of the Nile?*

**apricot** *noun* a soft, yellowish-orange fruit.

**April** *noun* the fourth month of the year. April has 30 days. **April fool** somebody who has been fooled by a trick played on them on the morning of 1 April, which is April Fools' Day.

**apron** *noun* a piece of clothing you wear around the front of your body to protect the clothes underneath when you are cooking or cleaning.

**apt** *adjective* **1** suitable. *An apt quotation to use.* **2** likely to do something. *He's apt to fall asleep when he's bored.* **3** able to learn things quickly.

**aptitude** *noun* an ability to learn and do something well.

**aqualung** *noun* the equipment worn by divers that enables them to breathe underwater.

**aquarium** *noun* a glass tank for keeping fish and other water animals, or a building (in a zoo) where many such tanks are kept.

**aquatic** *adjective* living or growing in water, or having to do with water. *Aquatic plants.*

**aqueduct** *noun* a structure like a bridge that incorporates a canal or pipes for carrying water across a valley.

**Arab** *noun* a member of a group of people originally from Arabia and other parts of southwest Asia and North Africa. **Arabian** *adjective.*

**Arabic** *noun* the language spoken by the Arabs. **arabic numerals** the numerical figures 0 to 9.

**arable** *adjective* plowed and suitable for growing crops. *Arable land.*

**arbitrary** *adjective* decided by a person's random opinion and not according to reason or rules. *An arbitrary decision.*

**arc** *noun* **1** a curved line. **2** in geometry, a section of the circumference of a circle.

**arcade** *noun* **1** a row of arches supported by columns. **2** a covered passageway, usually with small shops on either side. **3** a place where there are slot machines for games. *An amusement arcade.*

**arch** *noun* a curved part of a building, bridge, or wall. **arch** *verb* to form the shape of a curve. *The rainbow arches across the sky.*

**arch-** *prefix* chief or most important. *archbishop.*

**archeology** *noun* (say ar-kee-**ol**-oh-jee) the study of the past and how people lived, by the examination of remains of buildings and tools. **archeological** *adjective. An archeological dig for Roman remains.* **archeologist** *noun.*

**archaic** *adjective* (say ar-**kay**-ik) very old or antiquated.

archer

**archer** *noun* a person who shoots with a bow and arrow.

**archery** *noun* a sport in which people shoot at a target with a bow and arrow.

**archipelago** *noun* (say ar-kee-**pel**-agoh) a group of small islands.

**architect** *noun* a person who designs and plans buildings.

**architecture** *noun* **1** the art or activity of designing buildings. **2** the style and design of a building or buildings. *The architecture of Venice.*

**Arctic** *noun* the region around the North Pole. **arctic** *adjective* (especially of weather) very cold.

**arduous** *adjective* difficult and tiring to do.

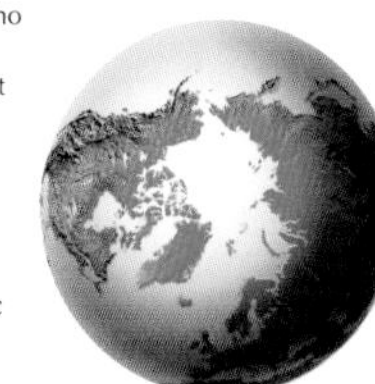

Arctic

**area** *noun* **1** the size of a flat surface. *The barn has an area of 25 square meters.* **2** a part of a place. *The residential area of Boston.* **3** a part of somewhere used for a special purpose. *A non-smoking area.*

**arena** *noun* a large area surrounded by seats where you can watch sports and other entertainments.

**Argentina** *noun* a country in South America.

**Argentinian** *noun* a person who comes from Argentina. **Argentinian** *adjective.*

**argue** *verb* **1** to talk angrily with somebody you disagree with, to quarrel. **2** to give your reasons for or against something. *Mrs Earnshaw argued against building the new road.* **argument** *noun.*

**argumentative** *adjective* often arguing and tending to disagree for the sake of it.

**arid** *adjective* very dry and having little rainfall. Deserts are arid environments.

**aristocracy** *noun* the nobility, the social class to which aristocrats belong, traditionally having wealth and land.

**aristocrat** *noun* someone of the highest social class, who has a title; a nobleman or noblewoman.

**arithmetic** *noun* the study and use of numbers, especially addition, subtraction, division, and multiplication.

ark

**ark** *noun* in a story from the Bible, Noah built an ark, a large, covered vessel that floated, for his family and all kinds of animals to live in during the Great Flood.

**arm** *noun* **1** the part of your body between your shoulder and your hand. **2** anything shaped like an arm. *The arm of a chair.* **arm in arm** two or more persons with arms linked in friendship. **arms** *plural noun* **1** weapons. **2** a coat of arms, a design on a shield, used as the badge of a noble family or city. **up in arms** very angry and ready to fight. *He was up in arms about the decision to ban skating in the park.* **arm** *verb* to supply with weapons (arms) or information. **armed** *adjective* carrying weapons. *The armed forces.*

**armada** *noun* **1** a fleet of ships. **2** the fleet sent from Spain to attack England in 1588. *The Spanish Armada.*

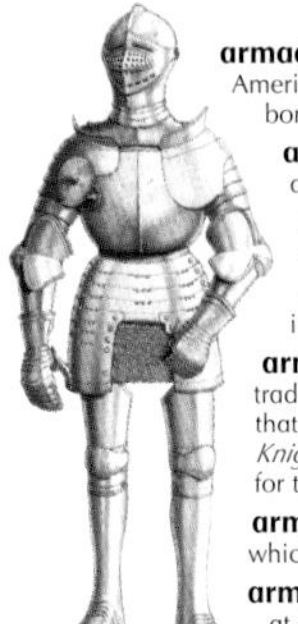
armor

**armadillo** (armadillos) *noun* a South American mammal covered with a shell of bony plates.

**armaments** *plural noun* weapons, ammunition, and military equipment.

**armchair** *noun* a comfortable chair with supports for the arms.

**Armenia** *noun* a country in western Asia.

**armor** *noun* **1** a defensive covering, traditionally of strong metal or leather, that protects a soldier's body in battle. *Knights in armor.* **2** a metal protection for tanks or ships. **armored** *adjective.*

**armory** (armories) *noun* a place in which to store arms (weapons).

**armpit** *noun* the hollow under your arm at the shoulder.

**army** *noun* a large number of soldiers composing an organized force trained to fight on land.

**aroma** *noun* a pleasant, distinctive smell. **aromatic** *adjective. The chef liked to use plenty of aromatic herbs.*

**around** *adverb* on all sides. *He looked around but there was nobody there.* **around** *preposition* in all directions, in a circle. *She walked around the room.*

**arouse** *verb* **1** to stir up or excite feelings. *The terrible news aroused great anger in everybody.* **2** to wake somebody up.

**arrange** *verb* **1** to put in a certain order or position. *He arranged his books in alphabetical order.* **2** to plan or prepare something. *Can you arrange a meeting for next week?* **arrangement** *noun.*

**arrest** *verb* **1** to hold somebody as a prisoner. *The police arrested her for shoplifting.* **2** to stop or prevent. *Progress removing the snow was arrested because Richard did not bring the shovel.* **arrest** *noun.* **arresting** *adjective* attractive, holding your attention.

**arrival** *noun* **1** the act of arriving at or reaching a place. **2** a person or thing that has arrived. *The new arrivals were welcomed by the committee.*

**arrive** *verb* to reach somewhere. *They arrived home last night after their vacation overseas.*

**arrogant** *adjective* having an unpleasantly high opinion of yourself. **arrogance** *noun.*

**arrow** *noun* **1** a stick with a point at one end that you shoot from a bow. **2** a sign that tells you which way to go.

**arsenic** *noun* a very powerful poison used in some weed-killers and to kill rats.

**arson** *noun* the crime of deliberately setting fire to property such as a house. **arsonist** *noun* someone who intends criminal damage by fire. *The arsonist was caught.*

**art** *noun* **1** beautiful paintings, sculpture, music or poetry. *His collection of art was on display in the gallery.* **2** an activity requiring great skill. *The art of good conversation.* **artful** *adjective* **1** skillful. **2** cunning.

**artery** *noun* one of the thick-walled tubes that carries blood from your heart to other parts of your body.

**arthritis** *noun* a disease that makes joints painful and swollen. **arthritic** *adjective.*

**arthropod** *noun* an animal such as an insect, spider, or crab, with a skeleton on the outside of its body.

**article** *noun* **1** an object of some kind. *A belt is an article of clothing.* **2** a piece of writing published in a newspaper or magazine. **3** the words "a" or "an" (indefinite articles) and "the" (definite article).

**articulate** *adjective* **1** able to express thoughts and feelings clearly in words. **2** having joints. **articulate** *verb* to pronounce words clearly.

**artificial** *adjective* not found in nature but made by people. *These plastic flowers look real, but are artificial.*

**artillery** *noun* large guns used by the army.

**artist** *noun* someone who produces or performs any kind of art, including painting, music, and dance.

**artiste** *noun* a professional entertainer, in a circus or theater, for example.

**artistic** *adjective* liking art or showing skill in creating art. *An artistic family.*

**artistry** *noun* the skill of an artist. *The pianist's artistry was much admired.*

**a.s.a.p.** *abbreviation* as soon as possible.

**ascend** *verb* (say az-**send**) to go or move up, to climb. *The plane ascended quickly after takeoff.* The opposite of "ascend" is "descend." **ascent** *noun.*

**ASCII** *abbreviation* American Standard Code for Information Interchange (a computer term).

**ash** (ashes) *noun* **1** the gray powder that is left after something has burned completely. *Wood ash is good for the garden.* **2** a tree with silver-gray bark. *A forest of ash trees.*

**ashamed** *adjective* feeling guilty or embarrassed about something.

**Ashkhabat** *noun* the capital of Turkmenistan in Central Asia.

**ashore** *adverb* on shore or land. *We jumped ashore.*

ash

**Asia** *noun* one of the Earth's seven continents.

**Asian** *noun* a person from Asia. **Asian** *adjective. Asian countries include India and Sri Lanka.*

**ask** *verb* **1** to speak in order to get the answer to a question. **2** to make a request or to say that you would like somebody to do something for you. *She asked him to pass her the potatoes.* **3** to invite. *Ask him to the meeting on Monday.*

**asleep** *adjective* sleeping. *He was still asleep when I called, although it was after lunch.* The opposite of "asleep" is "awake."

**Asmera** *noun* the capital of Eritrea in East Africa.

**asp** *noun* a small poisonous snake.

**aspect** *noun* a side, feature, or look of something. *Let's consider every aspect of the problem before making a final decision.*

**asphalt** *noun* a black, sticky, tar-like substance that hardens when dry and is used for making road surfaces.

**aspiration** *noun* an ambition or strong desire to achieve a goal in life.

**aspirin** *noun* a medicine that helps to ease pain and reduce fever.

**ass** (asses) *noun* **1** a wild donkey. **2** a stupid person.

**assassin** *noun* a person who assassinates or murders. *The assassin was arrested.*

**assassinate** *verb* to murder somebody, especially an important person like a president. **assassination** *noun.*

ass

**assault** *verb* to attack someone violently. **assault** *noun.*

**assemble** *verb* **1** to bring or collect together in one place. *A small crowd assembled in the square.* **2** to put or fit the parts of something together.

**assembly** *noun* **1** a meeting, often regular like a school assembly. **2** the putting together of different parts of something to make a whole. *A car assembly plant.*

**assent** *noun* agreement. *He gave his assent.* **assent** *verb* to agree to something.

**assert** *verb* to declare or state something forcefully so people pay attention. **assertion** *noun* a forthright statement. *He made a false assertion about me.*

**assess** *verb* to judge the quality or value of something. *He assessed the artwork.* **assessment** *noun.*

**asset** *noun* somebody or something that is useful or valuable. *She is good at mathematics so she is a great asset to the finance company.*

**assist** *verb* to help. **assistance** *noun. Can I be of any assistance to you?*

**assistant** *noun* **1** a person who helps. *My aunt is a nursing assistant.* **2** a person who serves at a store. *A counter clerk must be polite to customers.*

**associate** *verb* **1** to spend time with a group, to work together. *He associates mainly with lawyers and students.* **2** to connect two things in your mind. *He associates snow with skiing.*

**association** *noun* **1** a club or a group of people working together, an organization. **2** a connection made in your mind.

**assorted** *adjective* of different kinds. Mixed. *We found assorted items of clothing strewn around the bedroom.* **assortment** *noun.*

**assume** *verb* **1** to accept something as true without question, to suppose. *We assumed she had no money because she dressed so badly.* **assumption** *noun.* **2** to take over. *The Vice President assumed absolute control of the country.*

**assurance** *noun* **1** a confident statement or promise. *He gave every assurance that the bridge was safe.* **2** confidence. *She is playing the piano now with more assurance.* **3** insurance.

**assure** *verb* to tell somebody something confidently and definitely. *The nurse assured him that he would soon be better.*

**Astana** *noun* the capital of Kazakhstan in Central Asia.

**asterisk** *noun* a small star (*) used in printing.

**astern** *adverb* toward the stern or back of a boat.

**asteroid** *noun* any of the small planets that orbit the Sun, mainly between Mars and Jupiter.

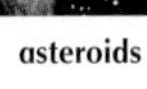

asteroids

**asthma** *noun* a chest illness that makes it difficult to breathe. **asthmatic** *adjective.*

**astonish** *verb* to surprise somebody very much, to amaze. **astonishment** *noun.*

**astound** *verb* to surprise or shock somebody very much. *She was astounded to hear that he had failed the exam.*

astronaut

**astride** *preposition* with one leg on each side of something. *He sat astride the horse.*

**astrologer** *noun* a person who studies the stars to try to predict the future. *The astrologer predicted she would have good fortune that week.* **astrology** *noun.*

**astronaut** *noun* a man or woman who is trained to travel in a spacecraft, often so they can perform scientific operations in space.

**astronomical** *adjective* **1** concerned with astronomy. **2** very large. *The house prices were astronomical.*

**astronomy** *noun* the scientific study of the planets and stars. **astronomer** *noun* a person who scientifically studies the planets and stars.

**astute** *adjective* clever and quick of mind, shrewd. *She is an astute businesswoman.*

**Asuncion** *noun* the capital of Paraguay in South America.

**asylum** *noun* **1** a place to shelter from persecution. *The refugees sought asylum in France.* **2** in the past, a place for treating people who suffered from mental illnesses.

**atheism** *noun* the rejection of a belief in God or gods.

**atheist** *noun* a person who declares they do not believe in God or gods.

**Athens** *noun* the capital of Greece in southern Europe.

**athlete** *noun* a person who performs track and field events. **athletic** *adjective.*

**athletics** *plural noun* competitive sports such as running, jumping, vaulting, and throwing the javelin or the discus.

**atlas** (atlases) *noun* a book of maps.

**atmosphere** *noun* **1** the air that surrounds and protects the Earth. **2** the air in a particular place. *The atmosphere in this city is badly polluted.* **3** the general feeling of a place. *The hotel has a warm and friendly atmosphere, but is very expensive.*

**atoll** *noun* a coral reef in the shape of a ring surrounding a lagoon.

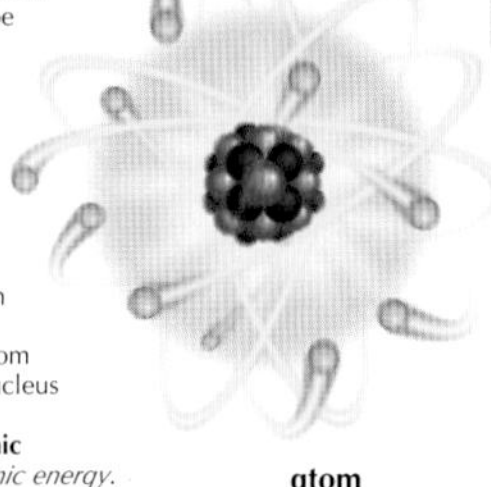

atom

**atom** *noun* the smallest possible part of a chemical element that can take part in a chemical reaction. An atom consists of a nucleus surrounded by electrons. **atomic** *adjective. Atomic energy.*

**atrocious** *adjective* very bad, terrible. *Atrocious spelling mistakes.*

**atrocity** *noun* a very cruel act, a crime.

**attach** *verb* to fasten or join two things together. *She attached another link to the chain.* **to be attached to** to be very fond of somebody or something.

**attachment** *noun* **1** something extra that can be attached. *The vacuum cleaner has a special attachment for cleaning upholstery.* **2** fondness or friendship.

**attack** *noun* **1** a violent attempt to hurt someone or something. **2** a fit or sudden illness. *An asthma attack.* **attack** *verb* **1** to use violence against a person or place. *The army attacked the village.* **2** to criticize or speak strongly against. *The architects were attacked for their bad design.*

**attain** *verb* to reach or achieve something, to succeed. *She attained the ripe old age of ninety.* **attainment** *noun.* **attainable** *adjective.*

attend

**attempt** *verb* to try to do something. *Josephine attempted to climb the tree.* **attempt** *noun. She failed in the attempt.*

**attend** *verb* to be present at a place or happening. *We all attended the protest meeting.* **attendance** *noun.* **attend to** **1** to concentrate. *Please attend to what I'm saying.* **2** to deal with or look after. *He attended to the accident victims.*

**attention** *noun* thought or care given or interest taken in something. *She gave all her attention to her work.* **attract attention** to make somebody notice something.

**attentive** *adjective* **1** being careful to notice or listen. **2** kind and gentle. *He was very attentive to his grandfather's needs and looked after him well.*

Aa

**attic** *noun* a room just under the roof of a house, often used for storage. *We kept our old toys in the attic.*

attic

**attitude** *noun* an opinion or a way of thinking about somebody or something, a way of behaving. *She has a positive attitude about work.*

**attract** *verb* **1** to like and find somebody or something interesting. *Katie was attracted to the boy next door.* **2** to catch the attention of. *The teddy bear attracted the baby's attention and made him laugh.* **3** to make something come nearer. *Brightly colored flowers attract butterflies and bees.* **attraction** *noun.*

**attractive** *adjective* **1** interesting and pleasing. *An attractive idea.* **2** good-looking. *An attractive boy.*

**auburn** *adjective* a red-brown color. *Esmerelda had long auburn hair.*

**auction** *noun* a public sale in which goods are sold to the person who bids (offers to pay) the highest price. **auction** *verb.*

auctioneer

**auctioneer** *noun* someone who conducts an auction.

**audible** *adjective* loud enough to be heard. The opposite of "audible" is "inaudible."

**audience** *noun* a group of people who have come together to watch or listen to an event such as a play or concert. *The new play that has just opened on Broadway is attracting huge audiences.*

**audiovisual** *adjective* recorded sound and pictures, often used as an aid by teachers. *The school's audiovisual equipment includes CDs and cassettes.*

**audition** *noun* a short test piece performed by an actor, singer, dancer, or musician to establish whether he or she is suitable for a part in a group or performance. *Sally was very nervous at the audition and forgot her words, but despite this was given the part.*

**auditorium** *noun* the place in a theater or concert hall where the audience sits.

**August** *noun* the eighth month of the year. August has 31 days.

**aunt** *noun* Your aunt is the sister of your father or mother, or the wife of your uncle.

**au pair** *noun* a young foreign person, usually a young woman, who lives for a short time with a family to learn a language and in return looks after its children and does light housework. *Our Finnish au pair is looking after our three children for the summer.*

**austere** *adjective* **1** simple and without luxury. **2** severe or harsh. **austerity** *noun.*

**Australasia** *noun* one of the Earth's seven continents, consisting of Australia and the islands of the southwest Pacific Ocean.

**Australia** *noun* a country in Australasia.

**Australian** *noun* a person who comes from Australia. **Australian** *adjective. The Australian outback.*

**Austria** *noun* a country in Central Europe.

Austria's flag

**Austrian** *noun* a person from Austria. **Austrian** *adjective. The Austrian Alps.*

**authentic** *adjective* real, genuine, and not a copy. *An authentic painting by Picasso.* **authenticity** *noun.*

**author** *noun* a person who writes a book, article, poem, film script, or play.

**authoritative** *adjective* **1** showing power and authority. **2** reliable and trusted as being correct. *An authoritative atlas contains up-to-date information on its maps and in its glossary.*

**authority** *noun* **1** the power to tell others what to do. *The police have the authority to breathalyze people.* **2** a group or organization that has the power to control what is going on. *The city council refused our application.* **3** an expert. *She's an authority on antiques.*

**authorize** *verb* to give somebody power or permission to do something.

**autism** *noun* an abnormal condition in children, in which they are unable to respond to or communicate with people. **autistic** *adjective.*

**auto-** *prefix* self, self-caused, or same.

**autobiography** *noun* a book that somebody writes about her or his own life. **autobiographical** *adjective.*

**autograph** *noun* a person's name written in their own handwriting, a signature. **autograph** *verb.*

**automatic** *adjective* **1** working by itself without the control of a human being. *An automatic central-heating system.* **2** done without thinking about it. *Breathing is automatic.* **automatically** *adverb.*

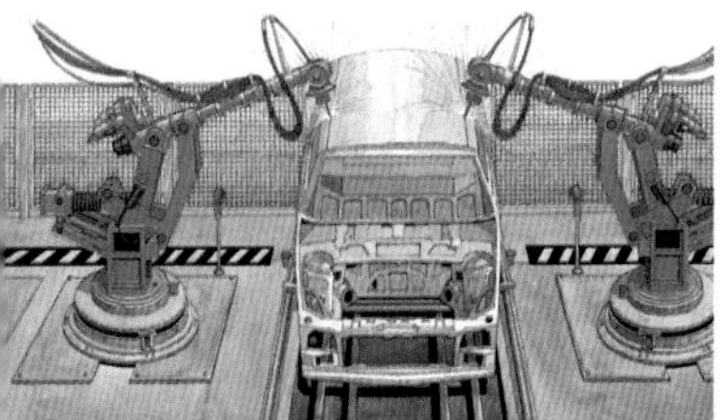

automation

**automation** *noun* the use of machines instead of people to do monotonously repetitive jobs in factories.

**automobile** *noun* a car.

**autopsy** *noun* an examination of a dead body, a post-mortem, in order to determine the cause of death.

**autumn** *noun* the season of the year between summer and winter; fall.

**available** *adjective* **1** obtainable and ready to be used. *Raspberries are not available all year.* **2** free to see people. *She'll be available to interview you in about an hour.* **availability** *noun.*

**avalanche** *noun* a large mass of snow and ice suddenly falling down a mountain.

**avenge** *verb* to harm or punish somebody in return for a wrong they have done to somebody else. *He avenged his father's murder.* **avenger** *noun.*

**average** *noun* in arithmetic, the sum of several amounts divided by the number of amounts. The average of 4+6+9+13 = 8. (4+6+9+13 = 32 divided by 4 = 8.) **average** *adjective* **1** normal, ordinary. *It's been an average week.* **2** not extreme or special. *Her work is average.*

**averse** *adjective* opposed to or disliking. *Averse to hard work.*

**aversion** *noun* a strong dislike or unwillingness. *He has an aversion to jellyfish.*

**aviary** *noun* a large cage for keeping birds.

**aviation** *noun* the science of building and flying aircraft.

**aviator** *noun* (old-fashioned) an aircraft pilot. *The aviator wore flying goggles and a leather hat.*

**avid** *adjective* **1** keen, enthusiastic. *An avid reader.* **2** greedy. *The pupil was avid for the teacher's attention.*

axis

**await** *verb* to wait for, to expect. *We are awaiting the arrival of the new president.*

**awake** *adjective* not sleeping. **awake** (awakes, awaking, awoke, awoken) *verb* to wake up. *I always awake at dawn.*

**award** *noun* something, such as a prize or money, given to somebody for doing well. **award** *verb* to present. *She was awarded an Oscar for her performance in the movie.*

**aware** *adjective* knowing about. *Andy wasn't aware of the dangers of mountaineering in bad weather.* **awareness** *noun.*

**away** *adverb* **1** not here, not at home. *He's away for a few weeks.* **2** at a distance. *The next town is miles away.* **3** into the distance. *The music faded away.* **4** ceaselessly. *She worked away at her exercises.* **do away with** *verb* to get rid of.

award

**awe** *noun* a mixture of wonder, fear, and respect. *She is in awe of her teacher.* **awe-inspiring** *adjective* causing a feeling of awe. *An awe-inspiring poem.*

**awful** *adjective* **1** bad or unpleasant. *What an awful smell!* **2** excessive, a large amount. *She's done an awful lot of knitting in the last hour.*

**awfully** *adverb* very. *I'm awfully sorry.*

**awkward** *adjective* **1** clumsy and embarrassed. *The boy feels awkward among adults.* **2** not convenient. *We are eating, so this is an awkward time to visit.* **awkwardness** *noun.*

**ax** *noun* a tool with a sharp blade on a long handle used for chopping logs or felling trees. *John swung the ax over his head and brought it down with a thud onto the log.*

**axiom** *noun* a rule or principle that everyone generally agrees to be true.

**axis** *noun* **1** a real or imaginary line through the middle of an object around which the object spins. *The Earth rotates on its axis, which passes through the North and South Poles.* **2** a line along the side or bottom of a graph.

**axle** *noun* the rod or bar that goes through the center of a wheel and on which it turns.

**Azerbaijan** *noun* a country in western Asia.

Bb

**babble** *verb* to chatter and talk in a confused and excited way.

**babe** *noun* a baby. *A babe in arms.*

**baboon** *noun* a large African or south Asian monkey.

**baby** *noun* a very young child. *The baby's first smile brought the parents great joy.* **babyish** *adjective.*

**babysitter** *noun* a person who is paid to look after children when their parents are out for the evening. **babysit** (babysits, babysitting, babysat) *verb.*

**bachelor** *noun* a man who has never been married. *Simon's bachelor pad was untidy but comfortable.*

**back** *adjective* at the rear. *The back door was wide open and the dog had run outside.* **back** *adverb* to an earlier place or time. *He thought back to when he was young.* **back** *noun* **1** the part of your body along the spine between your shoulders and buttocks, also the top part of an animal. *She climbed onto the horse's back.* **2** the opposite side to the front, the part situated behind. **back** *verb* **1** to move backward. *She backed away from the growling dog.* **2** to support or help. *Will you back me?* **3** to put money (bet) on an animal. *Uncle Ben backed the winning horse in the race.* **back-breaking** very tiring. *Back-breaking work.* **back down** to give up or change your mind. **back out** to decide not to keep an agreement. *You can't back out of coming to the party.* **put your back into** to work hard.

backbone

**backbone** *noun* the set of joined bones along the back; the spine.

**backfire** *verb* to have the opposite result to the one intended. *The plan backfired when the getaway vehicle refused to start.*

**background** *noun* **1** the part of a scene or picture that is behind the main objects or people. *The picture shows a lake with mountains in the background.* **2** the different facts that surround an event and which help to explain it. **3** a person's past experience or family history and education. *She comes from a farming background.*

**backpack** *noun* a large bag, also called a rucksack, that climbers and hikers carry on their backs. **backpacker** *noun* someone who carries a backpack, such as a young person traveling abroad.

**backward, backwards** *adjective* **1** toward the back. *She left without a backward glance.* **2** slow to learn or develop. *The boy is good at English but backward at arithmetic.* **backward** *adverb* **1** toward the back. *She took a step backward and bumped into the table.* **2** in the reverse way from normal. *As the announcer counted backward, 5, 4, 3, 2, 1, the rocket prepared for liftoff.*

**backyard** *noun* the area of land behind a house. *We are holding a barbecue in the backyard tonight, under the trees near the pond.*

**bacon** *noun* thin slices of salted or dried meat from a pig. *Please bring me a bacon, lettuce, and tomato sandwich with fries.*

**bacteria** *plural noun* microscopic living things. Some bacteria cause diseases.

**bad** (worse, worst) *adjective* **1** not good; unpleasant. *I've got some bad news.* **2** naughty, wicked. *You're a bad girl to tell so many lies.* **3** harmful. *Eating too much candy is bad for you.* **4** hurt or in poor health. *I've got a bad leg.* **5** severe. *A bad accident.* **6** low in quality. *He was a bad teacher.* **badly** *adverb. The test went badly.*

**badge** *noun* a piece of cloth, metal, or plastic that is sewn or pinned onto clothes, with a picture or message on it. *All the nurses in this hospital must wear an identity badge.*

badger

**badger** *noun* a wild animal with gray fur and a black-and-white striped head. European badgers live in underground holes called setts and are active at night. **badger** *verb* to annoy somebody by repeatedly asking them to do something.

**badminton** *noun* a game that is played by hitting a shuttlecock over a high net with rackets.

**baffle** *verb* to be confused or puzzled. *I was baffled as to which way up the painting should hang.* **baffling** *adjective. A baffling problem.*

**bag** *noun* a container for carrying things. **bag** *verb* to put things in a bag.

**baggage** *noun* bags and suitcases that travelers use to carry their belongings. Also called luggage.

**baggy** *adjective* too large or stretched and so hanging in loose folds. *A baggy chin.*

**Baghdad** *noun* the capital of Iraq in southwest Asia.

**bagpipes** *plural noun* a Scottish musical instrument. Using an arm, the player squeezes air from the windbag into the drone pipes, which each produce a single sustained note, and a melody pipe, on which a tune is played.

bagpipes

**Bahamas** *noun* a country in the Caribbean.

**Bahrain** *noun* a country in Southwest Asia.

**bail** *noun* **1** money left with a court of law so that somebody accused of a crime can go free until their trial. **2** in cricket, one of a pair of pieces of wood placed on top of the stumps. **bail** *verb* to scoop water from a boat to stop it from sinking. **bail out** (also bale out) to jump from an aircraft or to escape from something.

**bait** *noun* **1** food used for attracting fish, birds, or animals so that people can catch them. **2** something that is tempting.

**bake** *verb* to cook in an oven. *He baked a cake for their birthday party.*

**baker** *noun* a person who works in a bakery and makes and sells bread and cakes.

**Baku** *noun* the capital of Azerbaijan in southwest Asia.

**balance** *noun.* **1** an even distribution of weight. *Jack has good balance; he can stand on one leg without falling over.* **2** a weighing apparatus. **3** the amount of money somebody has in the bank. **balance** *verb* **1** to keep something steady and not let it fall over. **2** to equalize.

baker

**balcony** *noun* a platform on the outside wall of a building with a wall or railings around it.

**bald** *adjective* (rhymes with "crawled") with little or no hair on the head. **baldness** *noun.*

**bale** *noun* a large bundle of something. *A bale of hay.*

**ball** *noun* **1** a round object, often used to play games. **2** something that is round in shape. *A cannon ball.* **3** a formal party at which people dance. **ball-bearings** *plural noun* very small steel balls that help different parts of a machine to move smoothly against each other.

**ballad** *noun* a poem or song that tells a story. *He sang a romantic ballad.*

**ballerina** *noun* a female ballet dancer.

**ballet** *noun* (say **bal**-ay) a form of highly artistic dancing, usually telling a story, and performed on a stage. **ballet-dancer** *noun.*

**balloon** *noun* a small bag made of thin material such as plastic or rubber and filled with gas. *The children blew up red and blue balloons.* **hot-air balloon** a large bag made of strong material and filled with gas or hot air, attached to a basket underneath in which people ride. **balloonist** *noun.*

**ballot** *noun* a way of voting secretly in an election. *The ballot was rigged and declared invalid.*

**Bamako** *noun* the capital of Mali in northwest Africa.

**bamboo** *noun* a giant tropical grass-like plant with a hollow, woody stem, used to make furniture.

**ban** (bans, banning, banned) *verb* to forbid or say that something must not be done. *She was banned from driving for six months.* **ban** *noun.*

**Bb**

**banana** *noun* a long, curved, tropical fruit with soft white flesh and a yellow skin when ripe.

**band** *noun* **1** a group of musicians or a group of people who get together for a purpose. *A jazz band.* **2** a narrow strip of material that goes around something. *Her hair was held back by a rubber band.* **band together** *verb* to join others to achieve an aim.

**bandage** *noun* a strip of material used to tie around an injury or to cover a wound. **bandage** *verb.*

**Bandar Seri Begawan** *noun* the capital of Brunei in Southeast Asia.

**bandit** *noun* a robber who works with others in a gang or band. *The travelers were attacked by bandits.*

**bang** *noun* **1** a sudden, very loud noise. *She shut the lid with a bang.* **2** a heavy knock. **bang** *verb. He banged three times on the door.*

**Bangkok** *noun* the capital of Thailand in Southeast Asia.

**Bangladesh** *noun* a country in South Asia.

**Bangui** *noun* the capital of the Central African Republic, in central Africa.

**banish** *verb* to send somebody away, usually from their own country, as a punishment. **banishment** *noun.*

**banister** or **bannister** *noun* the wooden uprights and hand-rail along the side of a staircase.

Bangkok

**Banjul** *noun* the capital of Gambia in West Africa.

**bank** *noun* **1** a place that keeps and lends money for people, and which provides financial services. **2** a place for storing or leaving things for collection. *A blood bank.* **3** the side of a river or lake. **4** a piece of raised, sloping land. *We skateboarded down the bank at high speed.* **bank** *verb. I banked my winnings today.* **bank on** to rely on. *You can bank on me to be there – I wouldn't miss it for anything.*

**bankrupt** *adjective* declared in law to be unable to pay debts. **bankruptcy** *noun.*

**banner** *noun* a large flag decorated with a design or message, hung on a pole or between two poles.

Bb

**banquet** *noun* a large, formal dinner, usually held to celebrate a special occasion. *The Mayor held a banquet in honor of the President.*

**baptize** *verb* in the Christian religion, to sprinkle, pour water over, or immerse a person as a sign that they have become a Christian, accompanied by name-giving. To christen. **baptism** *noun*. **baptismal** *adjective*.

**bar** *noun* **1** a long, straight piece of metal or wood. *A cage with iron bars.* **2** a room or a long table or counter in a bar or hotel at which drinks are served. **3** a solid block of something. *A bar of soap.* **4** the equal sections into which music is divided. **bar** (bars, barring, barred) *verb* **1** to keep out. *Children are barred from the premises.* **2** to block. *She barred the door.*

**Barbados** *noun* a country in the Caribbean.

**barbarian** *noun* a cruel, rough, uncivilized person. In the ancient world, barbarians were people who were not Greek or Roman.

**barbaric** or **barbarous** *adjective* brutally cruel. **barbarity** *noun*.

**barbecue** *noun* an outdoor party at which food is cooked on a metal frame over a charcoal fire. **barbecue** *verb*. *We barbecued the steak.*

**barbed wire** *noun* wire with short, sharp spikes sticking out of it at regular intervals, often used for fencing.

**barber** *noun* a men's hairdresser.

**bar code** *noun* a group of thick and thin lines and spaces printed on a product that a computer in a store is able to read to find information about the price and size of the item.

9 781863 095471

**bar code**

**bare** *adjective* **1** uncovered, naked. *Bare arms.* **2** empty. *The movers have gone and the house is bare.* **3** leafless. *The bare branches of the tree.* **bare** *verb* to expose. *The dog bared its teeth.*

**barely** *adverb* scarcely, only just. *She could barely lift the heavy box, try as she might.*

**bargain** *noun* **1** something that you buy at a price that is cheaper than its full value. *This book is a real bargain!* **2** an agreement between two people in return for something. *They struck a bargain; she would wash the car if he would cook supper.* **bargain** *verb* to haggle or argue over the price of something.

**barge** *noun* a long boat with a flat bottom, used on canals mainly, to carry heavy goods. **barge** *verb* to push your way roughly through a crowd of people; to bump clumsily into people or things. *Jim barged his way through the crowd to get to the front row, so he would have a better view of the pop group.*

**bark** *noun* **1** the sharp sound made by a dog or fox. **2** the rough, hard covering of the trunk and branches of trees. **bark** *verb*. *The dog barked at the mailman.*

**barley** *noun* a grain used for food and to make beer.

**bar mitzvah** *noun* a religious ceremony that takes place on a Jewish boy's 13th birthday to celebrate his becoming an adult. A similar ceremony, held when a girl is 12, is called a **bat mitzvah**.

**barn** *noun* a farm building for housing animals or storing crops.

**barnacle** *noun* a small marine crustacean with a hard shell that fixes itself firmly to rocks and the sides of boats.

**barometer** *noun* an instrument that measures air pressure and indicates changes in the weather.

**barometer**

**baron** *noun* a member of the lowest order of British nobility.

**baroness** *noun* the wife of a baron, or a woman holding the rank of baron.

**baroque** *noun* a highly ornate style of European architecture of the late 16th to early 18th centuries.

**barracks** *plural noun* buildings where soldiers live.

**barrage** *noun* **1** an artificial barrier built across a river. **2** continuous heavy gunfire. **3** a huge number of something. *A barrage of complaints.*

**barrel** *noun* **1** a large container with curved sides for storing liquids. *The beer barrels are in the cellar.* **2** the tube of a gun through which a bullet is fired.

**barren** *adjective* not capable of bearing; the soil of barren land is so poor that crops cannot grow.

**barricade** *noun* a barrier that has been quickly put up to block a road. **barricade** *verb* to block. *The demonstrating students barricaded the streets.*

**barrier** *noun* a fence or some other obstacle designed to stop people or things getting past it.

**barrow** *noun* **1** a cart that you can push or pull. **2** a cart from which fruit, vegetables, and other foods are sold in the street. **3** a prehistoric mound of earth and stones covering a grave.

**barter** *verb* to exchange goods for other goods rather than for money; to swap one thing for something else.

**barrow**

**base** *noun* **1** the lowest part of something, especially the part on which it stands. *The base of the vase.* **2** the headquarters or main place from which things are controlled. *The expedition returned to the base.* **base** *verb.* **1** *The teacher based her lesson on the story of Robin Hood.* **2** to use something as a basis or starting point. *The new musical is based on a famous novel.*

**baseball** *noun* an American game played with a bat and ball by two teams of nine players.

**basement** *noun* a room or an area below the level of the street.

baseball

**bashful** *adjective* shy and lacking in confidence. **bashfulness** *noun.*

**basic** *adjective* **1** the most important and necessary. *The basic rules of grammar.* **2** very simple, essential. *Basic needs.* **basically** *adverb* **1** concerned with what is basic or fundamental. **2** most important.

**basil** *noun* a herb used to flavor food.

**basin** *noun* **1** a large bowl, especially for holding water. **2** a large area of land that is lower in the center than at the edges.

**basis** (bases) *noun* the main principle or idea behind something. *The basis of the argument.*

**basket** a woven container with a handle.

**basketball** *noun* a game for two teams in which five players try to score points by throwing a ball through a high net at each end of the court.

**bass** *adjective* the lowest sounds in music. *Deep bass notes.* **double-bass** a very large violin-shaped instrument that plays very low notes.

**Basseterre** *noun* the capital of St Kitts and Nevis in the Caribbean.

**bat** *noun* **1** a mouse-like animal with wings that flies at night hunting for insects. **2** a piece of wood or metal that players use to hit a ball in games such as baseball. **bat** (bats, batting, batted) *verb. I batted the ball.*

**batch** *noun* a group of things that were made at one time, such as loaves, or have to be dealt with together. *A large batch of birthday cards arrived for my grandmother today.*

bazaar

**bath** *verb* the act of washing your body in a bathtub. **bathtub** *noun.*

**bathe** *verb* **1** to go swimming in the sea. **2** to wash a part of the body very gently. *The nurse bathed the wound.* **3** (US) to take a bath or to bath.

**bathroom** *noun* a room with a bathtub or shower and usually a sink and toilet.

**batik** *noun* an Eastern way of printing designs on cloth by covering parts of the cloth with wax patterns and dyeing the rest.

batik

**baton** *noun* **1** a short, thin stick used by a conductor to beat time for an orchestra or choir. **2** a short stick that is passed from one runner to the next in a relay race.

**battalion** *noun* an army unit made up of smaller units called companies.

**batter** *noun* **1** a mixture of flour, milk, and eggs used especially for making pancakes. **2** the person who hits the ball in baseball and other sports. **batter** *verb* **1** to hit something heavily again and again. *The knight battered on the door of the castle.* **2** to coat in batter. *Battered fish.*

**battered** *adjective* beaten up. *A battered old car.*

**battery** *noun* **1** a container that makes and stores electricity. You put batteries in things such as radios and flashlights to make them work. **2** a number of large guns used together. **3** a large group of small cages in which hens or other animals are kept for the mass production of eggs or meat.

**battle** *noun* a fight between two armies or opposing groups. **battle** *verb. She battled against poor health.*

**battleship** *noun* a large, heavily armed warship. *The battleship was painted gray.*

**bay** *adjective* a red-brown color of a horse. **bay** *noun.* **1** a bay horse. *He chose the bay to ride at the rodeo.* **2** a part of the seashore that curves inward. An inlet. **bay window** a window that forms a recess by sticking out from the wall of a house. **at bay** facing an enemy and fighting them off. *A stag at bay.*

**bayonet** *noun* a knife that can be attached to the end of a rifle.

**bazaar** *noun* **1** a market in many eastern countries. *We bought a large pot at the bazaar in Cairo.* **2** a sale to raise money for something. *A church bazaar.*

**BC** *abbreviation* before Christ, used to show the number of years before the birth of Jesus. *Alexander the Great died in 323 BC.* BCE, before the Common Era, is also used.

**beach** *noun* an area of sand or pebbles where the land meets the sea or an ocean.

**beacon** *noun* a light or fire used as a guide or warning. *A beacon was lit on the hilltop to warn of the approach of an enemy fleet.*

**bead** *noun* a small piece of glass or other material with a hole through it, which can be threaded on string or wire to make a necklace or ornament.

**beaker** *noun* **1** a drinking mug without a handle. **2** a glass vessel used for pouring liquids in chemistry.

**beam** *noun* **1** a large, heavy bar of wood, metal, or concrete used to support the roof or floors of a building. **2** a band or ray of bright light. *The beam from the flashlight dazzled us.* **3** a big smile. **beam** *verb.*

**bean** *noun* a plant that produces seeds (beans) that grow in a pod and are eaten as a vegetable. *Green beans.* **full of beans** lively and full of energy.

**bear** *noun* a large wild animal with thick fur and hooked claws. **bear** (bears, bearing, bore, borne) *verb* **1** to support the weight of something. *That little chair won't bear your heavy weight.* **2** to carry from one place to another. *Seeds borne by the wind.* **3** to produce. *The plum tree bears fruit in the fall.* **4** to accept or tolerate something unpleasant. *She bears the cold without complaint.* **bear with** to be patient with. *Bear with me and I'll tell you.*

**beard** *noun* the hair on a man's chin.

**beast** *noun* **1** a large wild animal.

**beat** (beats, beating, beat, beaten) *verb* **1** to hit somebody or something hard and often. *The hail beat against the window and woke us up.* **2** to mix something rapidly with a whisk or fork. *The chef beat the batter with a whisk to get air into it.* **3** to defeat or win against somebody. *He beats me every time we play chess together.* **4** to make a regular sound or movement. *The bird beat its wings up and down.* **beat** *noun* rhythmic knocking. *The beat of the music.*

**beauty** *noun* a quality of something that makes it attractive to look at or to listen to, or that gives pleasure. *The inspiring beauty of the lakes and mountains overwhelmed us.* **beautiful** *adjective.* **beautifully** *adverb.*

**beaver** *noun* a North American wild animal with thick fur, a broad flat tail, and strong front teeth, which it uses to cut branches for damming streams and making ponds, where it builds a home called a lodge.

beaver

**because** *conjunction* for the reason that. *The tennis match was stopped because it had started to rain.*

**become** (becomes, becoming, became, become) *verb* **1** to come to be. To start feeling. *We became very good friends.* **2** to change into. *Caterpillars eventually become moths or butterflies.*

**bed** *noun* **1** a piece of furniture to sleep on. **2** the bottom of the sea or a river. **3** an area for growing flowers or vegetables. *Dad watered the flower bed.*

bed

**bedding** *noun* **1** blankets, quilts, and sheets for a bed (also **bedclothes**). **2** straw for animals to lie on.

**bedridden** *adjective* permanently in bed because of illness or old age.

**bedroom** *noun* a room to sleep in. *The twins share a bedroom at the top of the house.*

**bedspread** *noun* a large piece of cloth that covers the bed.

**bee** *noun* a flying insect with a yellow and black body that lives in large groups and makes honey. Some bees can sting.

bee

**beech** *noun* a hardwood tree with a smooth bark. Beeches are deciduous; their leaves drop in the fall.

**beef** *noun* the meat of cattle.

**beefy** (beefier, beefiest) *adjective* A beefy person is big and has strong muscles.

**beehive** or **hive** *noun* a small wooden house in which bees live and make honey.

**beeline** *noun* a straight line between two places. **make a beeline for** to go directly and swiftly toward something.

**beer** *noun* an alcoholic drink brewed from grains such as malt, barley, and hops.

**beeswax** *noun* the wax produced by bees to build the combs in which they store honey.

**beet** or **sugarbeet** *noun* a plant with a bulbous root that can be eaten as a vegetable (beetroot) or that can be used to make sugar.

**beetle** *noun* an insect with hard covers for its wings.

**beetroot** *noun* a variety of beet with a red root that is cooked as a vegetable.

**before** *preposition* **1** earlier than or sooner than now. *The day before yesterday.* **2** in front of. *She stood before the mirror and brushed her hair.* **before** *adverb* previously. *We've never met before.*

**beg** (begs, begging, begged) *verb* **1** to ask somebody for money or food, especially in the street. *She begged for enough money to buy a bowl of soup.* **2** to ask for something very earnestly and eagerly. *He begged to be allowed to go swimming.* **beggar** *noun.*

**begin** (begins, beginning, began, begun) *verb* to start. *The meeting began at 7 o'clock. They began by reading the minutes.* The opposite of "begin" is "end."

**beginner** *noun* a person who is just starting to do or learn something.

**beginning** *noun* the start of something, the origin. *At the beginning of the week, we won the game.*

**behave** *verb* **1** the way we act or do things. *She's been behaving in a funny way lately.* **2** to act in a good or proper way. *You can come with me only if you behave.*

**behavior** *noun* a way of behaving.

**behind** *preposition* **1** on the other side of or toward the back. *She hid behind the curtain.* **2** not making good progress. *He's behind with his studies.* **3** supporting or encouraging somebody. *We're behind you in your campaign.* **leave behind** *verb* to leave without something. *Peter was always leaving his keys behind.*

**Beijing** *noun* the capital of China in eastern Asia.

**being** *noun* a living creature. *The first human beings lived in Africa.*

**Beirut** *noun* the capital of Lebanon in southwest Asia.

**Belarus** *noun* a country in eastern Europe.

Belarus

**belch** *verb* **1** to let wind from your stomach come noisily out of your mouth; to burp. *In western countries, it is rude to belch at the table.* **2** to send out gases, fire, or smoke, like a volcano.

**Belfast** *noun* the capital of Northern Ireland, which is part of the United Kingdom.

**belfry** (belfries) *noun* a tower attached to a church where bells are hung.

**Belgian** *noun* a person from Belgium. **Belgian** *adjective.*

**Belgium** *noun* a country in northwest Europe.

**Belgrade** *noun* the capital of Serbia and Montenegro in eastern Europe.

**belief** *noun* **1** the things you believe to be true.

**believe** *verb* **1** to think or feel strongly that something is true or real. *I believe in ghosts.* **2** to think that somebody is telling the truth. **3** to think or have an opinion. *I believe he's coming tomorrow.*

**Bb**

**Belize** *noun* a country in Central America.

**bell** *noun* **1** a hollow metal object shaped like an upside-down cup that makes a ringing sound when struck. **2** any device that makes a ringing sound. *An electric alarm bell.*

**bellow** *noun* a deep roaring sound made by a bull or a loud voice. **bellow** *verb. The bull bellowed when it saw the dog.*

**bellows** *plural noun* an instrument used for pumping air into a fire or a church organ.

bellows

**belly** (bellies) *noun* the abdomen or the part of a person's or animal's body containing the stomach and intestines. *The baby had a soft round belly.* **belly button** the navel. *Alice had a sliver stud in her belly button.*

**Belmopan** *noun* the capital of Belize in Central America.

**belong** *verb* **1** to be the property of somebody. *This book belongs to you, it is yours.* **2** to be a member of a group. *Brian belongs to the yacht club.* **3** to have its right place. *Please put the scissors back in the drawer where they belong.*

**belongings** *plural noun* all the things that are yours and which you own.

**below** *adverb* beneath. *The King looked down at the moat below his window and saw his reflection staring back.* The opposite of "below" is "above." **below** *preposition* **1** lower than. *Your chin is below your mouth.* **2** less than. *The temperature is below freezing.*

**belt** *noun* **1** a long strap of leather or other material that you wear around your waist. *He bought a new belt to hold up his trousers.* **2** a narrow area of land. *The corn belt.* **belt** *verb* to hit. *Toby belted his brother on his leg because he wouldn't give back his toy truck.*

**bench** *noun* a long wooden seat on which two or more people can sit. *We sat on the bench in the park and drank lemonade.*

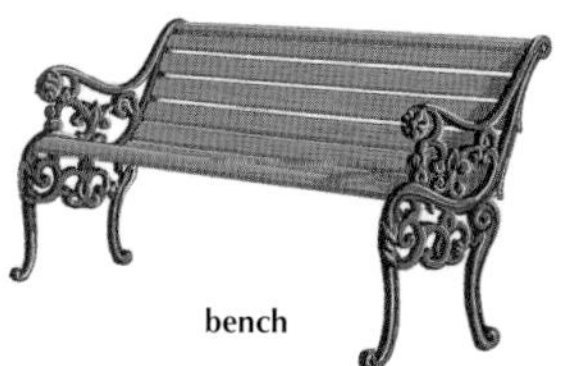

bench

**beneath** *preposition, adverb* **1** under, below. *The cat slept all day beneath the bed.* **2** not worthy or not good enough. *The business executive thought it was beneath her to wash the car.*

**benefit** *noun* **1** an advantage or something that helps you. **2** money that the government pays to people who are ill, unemployed, or very poor. **benefit** (benefits, benefiting, benefited) *verb. She benefited from her vacation and felt much more relaxed afterwards.*

**Benin** *noun* a country in West Africa.

**beret** *noun* (say berr-ay) a soft, round, almost flat hat made of wool, particularly associated with France.

**Berlin** *noun* the capital of Germany in Central Europe.

**Berne** *noun* the capital of Switzerland in Central Europe.

**berry** *noun* a small, roundish, juicy fruit without a stone, such as a strawberry, raspberry, or blueberry.

berry

**berserk** *adjective* to be wild or frenzied.

**berth** *noun* **1** a place to sleep on a boat or a train. **2** a place in a port where a ship or boat can be moored.

**beside** *preposition* at the side of, next to. *My aunt lives in a large house beside the sea.*

**besides** *adverb* in addition to. *Besides playing baseball and hockey, he builds houses.*

**besiege** *verb* to lay siege to a place or surround it with soldiers in order to make it surrender. *The soldiers besieged the castle.*

**best** *adjective, adverb* better than all the others. *The best film I've ever seen.* **best man** a friend of the bridegroom who helps him at his wedding. **best-seller** a book that sells a very large number of copies.

**bet** *noun* money risked on the outcome of forecasting a result. *I made a bet that Amy would beat Sally in the swimming race.* **bet** (bets, betting, bet or betted) *verb* **1** to forecast the result of a race and to risk money on the result. *She bet $3 on the bay horse.* **2** to feel certain. *I'll bet I can swim farther than you.*

**betray** *verb* **1** to let somebody down and hurt them by being disloyal. *She betrayed me by giving away all my secrets.* **2** to show signs of your real feelings. *His face betrayed his sadness when she left for a week.*

**better** *adjective* **1** something that is better has more good about it but is not the best. **2** recovered from an illness. *When you're better, you can go back to school again.*

bicycle

**between** *preposition* **1** in the space or time after one thing and before another. *Between the school and the hospital is a field where we play hockey between suppertime and bedtime.* **2** shared in parts. *They shared the money between them.* **3** used in comparing. *What's the difference between jam and jelly?*

**beverage** *noun* a drink.

**beware** *interjection* be careful and look out for something dangerous. *Beware of the bull!*

**bewilder** *verb* to confuse and worry somebody. *The Frenchman was bewildered by all the street signs in Hong Kong.* **bewildering** *adjective.*

**beyond** *preposition* **1** on the other side or farther than. *Don't drive beyond the crossroads.* **2** outside the limit of, past. *The camera is beyond repair.* **3** too difficult or confusing. *Algebra is beyond me.*

Bhutan

**Bhutan** *noun* a Himalayan country in South Asia.

**bi-** *prefix* two or twice. **biannual** happening twice a year. **bilateral** with two sides. **bilingual** speaking two languages. *Cindy was brought up to be bilingual.*

**biased** *adjective* unfairly preferring one side to another, prejudiced. *She's biased against all foreigners.* **bias** *noun.*

**Bible** *noun* a sacred book that has two main parts: the Old Testament, the holy book of the Jewish religion, and the New Testament, which, with the Old Testament, is the holy book of the Christian religion. **bible** a book of essential information on a subject. **biblical** *adjective.*

**bicker** *verb* to quarrel continuously over trivial things.

**bicycle** *noun* a two-wheeled vehicle that you ride by pushing pedals and steering with handlebars. The short form of bicycle is bike.

**bid** *noun* an attempt to achieve something. *She's going all out in her bid to become ice-dance champion.* **bid** (bids, bidding, bid) *verb* to offer to pay a certain amount of money for something at an auction. **bid** *noun.*

**big** (bigger, biggest) *adjective* **1** large in size. *Elephants are big.* **2** important. *The big game starts today.* The opposites of "big" are "small" and "unimportant."

**bigot** *noun* a bigot is somebody who has strong and usually unreasonable views, which they obstinately refuse to change.

**bike** *noun* a bicycle or motorcycle.

**bill** *noun* **1** a piece of paper on which is written how much you owe for something. *The gas bill.* **2** a written statement of a proposed new law to be discussed by Congress. **3** a piece of paper money. *I gave the taxi-driver a ten-dollar bill.* **4** a wide or long beak on a bird such as a duck.

**billabong** *noun* in Australia, a pool of water that is left when a river has run dry.

**billiards** *noun* a game like pool played with balls and long sticks (cues) on a cloth-covered table with pockets on the sides and corners.

**billion** *noun* **1** in North America and now generally in the UK, a thousand million. **2** previously in the UK, a million million. *There were a billion stars overhead.*

**binary** *adjective* consisting of two parts. **binary system** a number system used in computers in which only two numbers, 0 and 1, are used.

**bind** (binds, binding, bound) *verb* **1** to tie or fasten together. *He bound the magazines into a bundle with string.* **2** to wrap. *She bound the bruise with a bandage.* **3** to join the pages of a book together and put a cover or binding on it. *The book was bound in leather.*

**binder** *noun* a stiff cover or folder for holding papers.

**binoculars** *plural noun* an instrument with lenses that you look through to make distant things seem much nearer.

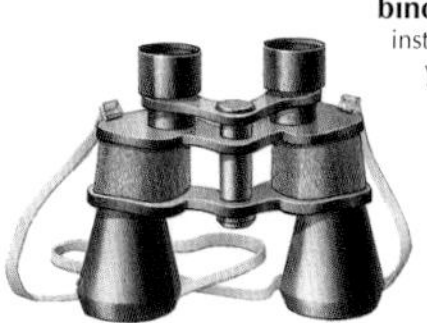

**binoculars**

**biodegradable** *adjective* able to decay naturally. *Paper is biodegradable.*

**biography** *noun* the story of a person's life written by somebody else. **biographical** *adjective.* **biographer** *noun.*

**biologist** *noun* a person who studies biology. *The biologist examined the newt.*

**biology** *noun* the scientific study of living things. *Human biology.* **biological** *adjective.* **biological warfare** the use of germs as weapons in warfare.

**biped** *noun* an animal with only two feet. *Birds and humans are bipeds.*

**biplane** *noun* an airplane with two sets of wings.

**bird** *noun* a creature that is covered with feathers, has two legs, two wings, and a beak. All female birds lay eggs and most birds can fly. **bird of prey** any bird that kills other birds and small animals for food. *Eagles are birds of prey.* **bird-watcher** *noun* a person who studies birds.

**bird**

**birth** *noun* being born, the beginning of anything. *The birth of the baby was a moment of great joy.*

**birth control** *noun* ways of preventing a woman becoming pregnant.

**birthday** *noun* the anniversary or day each year when you celebrate the day you were born. *Birthday cake.*

**biscuit** *noun* a type of bread that is baked in small, round shapes.

**bisect** *verb* to divide into two equal parts.

**Bishkek** *noun* the capital of Kyrgyzstan in Central Asia.

**bishop** *noun* **1** a high-ranking priest in some Christian Churches, in charge of a diocese or group of churches. **2** a chess piece in the shape of a bishop's miter (hat).

**bison** *noun* (*plural* bison) a wild buffalo.

**Bissau** *noun* the capital of Guinea-Bissau, on the west coast of Africa.

**bit** *noun* **1** a very small piece. **2** the metal bar part of a bridle that fits into a horse's mouth. **3** the smallest unit of information, expressed in binary numbers, in a computer.

**bitch** *noun* a female dog.

**bite** (biting, bit, bitten) *verb* **1** to grasp and cut through something with your teeth. **2** to sting. *The gnats have bitten me.* **bite** *noun. The cat's bite has left a red mark.*

**bitter** *adjective* **1** having a sharp, bad taste. *Bitter medicine.* **2** angry and full of hatred. *Bitter enemies.* **3** very cold. *Expect bitter weather in the winter months.*

**bizarre** *adjective* strange and unusual.

**black** *adjective* the darkest of colors. *A black cat is thought to bring bad luck.* **Black** *noun* a person with black skin. **black box** an electronic machine on an aircraft that automatically records details of flights.

**blackberry** *noun* the sweet, black fruit of a wild, prickly bush called a bramble.

**blackbird** *noun* a common European songbird.

**blackboard** *noun* a board painted in a dark color for writing on with chalk.

**blackboard**

**blacken** *verb* to make or become black. *Soot from the fire has blackened the bricks.*

**blackmail** *noun* the crime of trying to get money from somebody by threatening to reveal a secret. *He was arrested for blackmail.* **blackmailer** *noun.* **blackmail** *verb.*

**blacksmith** *noun* a person who makes things out of metal, including horseshoes.

**bladder** *noun* a bag-like organ in your body where urine collects until it leaves your body.

**blade** *noun* **1** the sharp part of an ax, knife, or sword. **2** a narrow leaf. *A blade of grass.* **3** the flat, thin part of an oar or a propeller.

**blame** *verb* to say that somebody has done something wrong and that it is their fault. *She blamed me for spilling paint all over the sofa.* **blame** *noun. My sister took the blame.* **blameless** *adjective.*

**blank** *adjective* **1** unmarked, with nothing on it. *A book of blank pages.* **2** empty. *My mind went blank.*

**blanket** *noun* **1** a thick, warm covering for a bed. **2** any sort of covering. *A thick blanket of snow lay over the fields.*

**blare** *verb* to make a loud, harsh, unpleasant noise. *The taxi horn blared.*

**blaspheme** *verb* (say blass-**feem**) to speak without respect about God and holy things. To swear. **blasphemy** *noun.* **blasphemous** *adjective.*

**blast** *noun* **1** a sudden strong gust of air or wind. **2** a sudden loud noise, especially the noise of an explosion. *He gave a deafening blast on the trumpet.*

**blastoff** *noun* the moment when a rocket or spacecraft takes off. **blast off** *adverb.*

**blaze** *noun* a very bright light or fire. *The blaze of the headlights startled the rabbit.* **blaze** *verb* to give off bright light. *The fire is blazing.*

**blazer** *noun* a suit jacket, without matching pants. *It's a smart restaurant; you better wear a blazer and pants.*

**bleach** *noun* a strong chemical liquid used to kill germs and to make things such as cloth white. **bleach** *verb* to make white. *His white shirt went gray in the wash, so he bleached it.*

**bleak** *noun* **1** cold, bare, and miserable. *The moor is windswept and bleak.* **2** not very hopeful. *Bleak prospects.*

**bleat** *verb* to make a noise like a sheep or goat. *Stop bleating about how hungry you are.* **bleat** *noun.*

**bleed** (bleeds, bleeding, bled) *verb* to lose blood. *A bleeding nose.*

**blend** *verb* **1** to mix things together. *He blended the ingredients into a smooth paste.* **2** When things like colors or sounds come together in a pleasing way, they blend. **blend** *noun. A nice blend of coffee.*

**bless** (blesses, blessing, blessed *or* blest) *verb* to ask God to protect someone or something from harm.

**blind** *adjective* not able to see. *Guide dogs help blind people find their way.* **blind** a screen or covering for a window. *Pull up the blind to let in the sun.* **blindness** *He was struck by blindness in old age.*

**blindfold** *noun* a piece of cloth tied over someone's eyes. **blindfold** *verb.*

**blink** *verb* to close and open your eyes again very quickly. *He blinked in the bright light.*

**blinkers** *plural noun* leather flaps placed on the sides of a horse's eyes so that it can only see forward.

**blinkers**

**blister** *noun* a sore swelling like a bubble on your skin, filled with fluid, caused by a burn or by rubbing. *She got a blister where her shoes rubbed.*

**blizzard** *noun* a heavy snowstorm with strong winds. *They were lost in the blizzard.*

**block** *noun* **1** a lump or solid piece of something with flat sides like a piece of wood. **2** a large building or group of buildings. *Tom lived at the top of apartment block.* **block** *verb* to be in the way of, or to put in the way of something so that nothing can pass. *A broken-down tractor blocked the road and stopped traffic.*

**blockade** *verb* to isolate or cut off a place and stop supplies getting through to it.

**blockage** *noun* something that stops anything passing through. *There was a blockage in the pipe.*

**blond** *adjective* fair hair (of a boy or man).

**blonde** *adjective* pale yellow hair (of a girl or woman).

**blood** *noun* the red liquid that flows around inside the bodies of humans and animals. **blood-curdling** terrifying. **blood donor** a person who gives some of their blood to a blood bank, where it is stored and later given to someone who needs blood during an operation. **blood-vessel** a tube in your body along which blood flows.

**bloodhound** *noun* a large dog with a keen sense of smell, bred for tracking.

**bloodthirsty** *adjective* keen for violence or killing.

**bloom** *noun* a flower. *A rose bloom.* **bloom** *verb.*

**blossom** *noun* the flowers that grow on trees in Spring. **blossom** *verb* **1** to grow blossoms. **2** to grow and improve. *The girl blossomed into a beautiful woman.*

**bloom**

**blot** *noun* **1** a mark or spot made by a spilled drop of ink or paint. **2** a stain or fault that spoils something. **blot** *verb.*

**blouse** *noun* a loose shirt worn by girls and women.

**blow** *noun* **1** a hard hit. *A blow to the head.* **2** a cause of unhappiness or disappointment. *Failing her driving test was a terrible blow.* **blow** (blows, blowing, blew, blown) *verb* **1** to push air quickly through your mouth. **2** to move about in or be moved by the wind. *The wind blew the gate shut.* **blow over** to pass or become forgotten. *The fuss will soon blow over.* **blow up 1** to destroy with an explosion. *Guy Fawkes tried to blow up the Houses of Parliament.* **2** to enlarge. *She blew up the photo on the photocopier.*

**blubber** *noun* the fat from whales. **blubber** or **blub** *verb* to cry.

**blue** *adjective* **1** of the color blue. **2** sad and miserable. *Feeling blue.* **blue** *noun* the pure color of a cloudless sky. **out of the blue** suddenly. *The money arrived out of the blue.*

**blues** *noun* a slow, sad kind of jazz.

**blunder** *noun* a bad and stupid mistake. **blunder** *verb* to stumble or make a clumsy mistake. *He blundered into the room, bumping into the chair as he entered.*

**blunt** *adjective* **1** not sharp. *A blunt knife.* **2** plain and to the point. *His criticism of me was blunt.*

**blur** *noun* a smear, something that is unclear. *In my memory, the accident is a blur.* **blur** (blurs, blurring, blurred) *verb* to make something indistinct or less clear. To smear. *The photograph is blurred.*

**blurb** *noun* a description of a book printed on its cover.

**blurt** *verb* to say something suddenly and without thinking. *She blurted out my age.*

**blush** *verb* to turn red in the face, usually because you are shy, embarrassed, or ashamed.

**boa constrictor** *noun* a large South American snake that crushes its prey to death by winding its body around and squeezing it.

**boar** *noun* **1** a male pig. **2** a wild pig.

**board** *noun* **1** a plank or long flat piece of wood. **2** a piece of wood used for playing games. *A chess board.* **3** a group of people managing an organization. *The company's board of directors met to discuss the merger.* **board** *verb* to get on an aircraft, ship, or train. *We went on board and set sail.*

**boarding school** *noun* a school where pupils live during term time.

**boast** *verb* to talk proudly about what you possess and how good and clever you think you are in order to impress people; to brag. **boast** *noun.* **boastful** *adjective. The boastful girl failed to impress the discerning listener.*

**boat** *noun* a small vessel for carrying people and things on water. **in the same boat** in the same difficult or unpleasant situation.

boat

**body** *noun* **1** all the physical parts of a person or animal, both inside and outside. **2** the main part of a body without the limbs. **3** a dead body, a corpse. **4** the main part of something. **5** a group of people. **bodily** *adjective.*

**bodyguard** *noun* a person (or group of people) who protects someone.

**bog** *noun* soft, wet ground. A marsh. **bogged down** *adjective* stuck and unable to make progress. *Bogged down with work.* **bog down** *verb.*

**Bogota** *noun* the capital of Colombia in South America.

**bogus** *adjective* false, not genuine.

**boil** *noun* a red, painful lump under your skin. *He had a boil on his face.* **boil** *verb* **1** When a liquid boils, it becomes so hot that it bubbles and steams. **2** to cook food in boiling water. **boiling point** the temperature at which a liquid boils.

**boisterous** *adjective* noisy, cheerful, and lively.

**bold** *adjective* **1** showing no fear; brave. **2** clear, easy to see, and impressive. *Bold lettering.* **boldness** *noun.*

**Bolivia** *noun* a country in South America.

**bolster** *noun* a long, firm pillow. **bolster** *verb* to support or make stronger.

**bolt** *noun* **1** a metal bar that slides across to lock a door or window. **2** a metal pin with a screw that fits into a part called a nut to hold things together. **bolt** *verb* **1** to run away suddenly. *The horses bolted.* **2** to eat something quickly. *Don't bolt your food!* **3** to lock a door or window.

bolt

**bomb** *noun* a weapon containing explosive chemicals that is used to destroy buildings. **bomb** *verb. Many cities were badly bombed in World War II.* **bombshell** a surprise. *The news that she had been fired from her job just before Christmas came as a bombshell.*

**bombard** *verb* **1** to attack with gunfire. **2** to attack or overwhelm. *They bombarded the Chairman with difficult questions, but he gave them satisfactory answers.*

**bone** *noun* one of the hard, white pieces that form the skeleton of a person or animal. **bone** *verb* to remove bones.

**bonfire** *noun* an outdoor fire.

**bonnet** *noun* **1** a hat tied under the chin, worn by women or babies.

**bonus** *noun* **1** a reward or extra payment added to your pay. **2** an unexpected extra benefit. *The extra chocolate in the box was a bonus.*

**bony** (bonier, boniest) *adjective* **1** thin and with little flesh. *A bony cow.* **2** having large bones. **3** full of bones. *This fish is very bony.*

**book** *noun* a set of pages, usually printed, bound together in a cover. *My favorite book is a leather-bound book of poems that belonged to my grandmother.* **book** *verb* to reserve or arrange a place in a theater, hotel, or airline for a date in the future. *Let's book a flight to Spain.* **booking** *noun.*

**bookcase** *noun* a piece of furniture fitted with shelves for holding books.

**bookmaker** or **bookie** *noun* a person whose job it is to take bets on, for example, horse-racing.

**bookworm** *noun* a person who likes reading books a lot.

**boom** *noun* **1** a deep, loud sound. *The boom of the bomb.* **2** a period of sudden increase. *A boom in computer sales.*

**boomerang** *noun* a curved stick used by Australian Aborigines as a weapon. It is thrown at its target and returns to the thrower if it misses.

boomerang

**boost** *verb* to increase, push up, or encourage. *The advertisement has boosted sales considerably.* **boost** *noun.*

**boot** *noun* a shoe with high sides covering the ankle and sometimes leg. *Cowboy boots are made of leather and have fairly high heels and pointed toes.* **boot** *verb* to turn on a computer.

**booty** *noun* valuable things stolen after a battle; plunder. *The outlaw made off with a sack full of booty.*

**border** *noun* **1** a frontier or the line along which two countries meet. **border** *verb. Canada borders the United States of America.* **2** a strip along an edge. *A flower border.*

border

**bore** *noun* a dull person who makes you feel weary. *The boss is a real bore.* **bore** *verb* **1** to pierce or drill a hole into something. **2** to tire through lack of interest. **boring** *adjective* dull. *What a boring lesson we had today!*

**boredom** *noun* tiredness caused by dull or monotonous work.

**born** *verb* the moment of birth of a life or activity. *Mom was born in Singapore in 1970.*

**borrow** *verb* to take something belonging to somebody else and use it for a short time before returning it. **borrower** *noun.* The opposite of "borrow" is "lend."

**Bosnia-Herzegovina** *noun* a country in southeastern Europe.

Bosnia-Herzegovina

**bosom** *noun* a woman's chest or breasts. **bosom friend** a very close friend.

**boss** *noun* a person in charge of workers. **boss** *verb* to tell people what to do.

**bossy** *adjective* enjoying giving orders and telling people what to do. *My older sister is very bossy.* **bossiness** *noun.*

**botany** *noun* the scientific study of plants. **botanist** *noun. She's studying to become a botanist.* **botanical** *adjective. The botanical name for this plant.*

**both** *adjective, pronoun* the two together, not only one. *Both Jane's dogs are Labradors.*

**bother** *verb* **1** to feel worried or disturbed about something. **2** to be a nuisance or to worry somebody. **bother** *noun* nuisance. *I'm sorry to be a bother.* **3** to take care, time, and trouble over something. *He won't bother to do his homework as the school term finishes tomorrow.*

**Botswana** *noun* a country in southern Africa.

**bottle** *noun* a container made of glass or plastic for holding liquid. **bottle** *verb. He bottled the delicious homemade lemonade.* **bottle up** *verb* to keep your feelings and thoughts to yourself.

**bottleneck** *noun* **1** a place where a road becomes narrower and traffic cannot flow freely. **2** anything that slows down work or progress.

**bottom** *noun* **1** the lowest part or underside of something. *The bottom of the sea.* **2** the part of your body that you sit on. *She's got a big bottom!* **get to the bottom of** *verb* to solve or explain a mystery. *Let's get to the bottom of the problem.*

**bough** *noun* (rhymes with "how") a large branch of a tree. *An apple bough.*

**bought** past tense of buy.

**boulder** *noun* a large, round rock.

**bounce** *verb* to spring back after hitting something. *The ball hit the floor and bounced back.* **bounce** *noun.* **bouncy** *adjective. A bouncy castle.*

**bound** *verb* to move along by making large leaps. **bound to** certain to. *You're bound to win the competition.* **out of bounds** a place where you are not allowed to go.

**boundary** *noun* a line that marks an edge.

**bouquet** *noun* (say boo-**kay**) a gift of a bunch of flowers.

**bout** *noun* a short period of something. *A serious bout of ill health.*

**bow** *noun* (rhymes with "so") **1** a piece of wood curved by a taut string attached at each end, used for shooting arrows. **2** a long, thin stick used for playing stringed instruments such as violins. **3** a knot with loops. *He tied his shoelaces in a neat bow.* **4 bow** (rhymes with "cow") the front part of a ship. **bow** *verb* (rhymes with "cow") **1** to bend your head or the top part of your body forward. *At the end of the show, the actors bowed.* **2** to give in. *They refused to bow to his unreasonable demands.*

**bouquet**

**bowels** *plural noun* the intestines in the lower part of your body, which carry waste matter from your body.

**bowl** *noun* **1** a deep, round, uncovered dish. *A sugar bowl.* **2** a big, hard, wooden ball used in the game called bowls. **bowl** *verb* to play the game of bowling.

**box** *noun* a wooden or cardboard container with straight sides and usually a lid. **box** *verb* to punch or fight with your fists while wearing heavy leather gloves in a sport called boxing.

**boxer** *noun* **1** someone who practises the sport of boxing. *He is not a heavyweight but a middleweight boxer.* **2** a short-haired breed of dog related to the bulldog. *My boxer looks tough but is really gentle.*

**Boxing Day** *noun* the first weekday after Christmas Day. *We went to a carol concert on Boxing Day.*

**boy** (boys) *noun* a male child. **boyhood** *noun* the childhood of a man. *In my boyhood, there was no such thing as television.*

**boycott** *verb* to refuse to have any dealings with somebody, as a protest or to bring about a change.

**boyfriend** *noun* a person's regular male friend or lover. *She lives with her boyfriend.*

**bra** or **brassiere** *noun* a piece of underwear that supports a woman's breasts.

**brace** *noun* **1** something that straightens or supports. *She will have to wear a wire brace on her teeth for three months to straighten them.* **2** a carpenter's tool for drilling holes. **3** two things of the same kind. *A brace of pheasant.* **4 braces** *plural noun* straps worn over the shoulders to hold up trousers. **brace** *verb* to prepare yourself for something nasty. *He braced himself to go to the dentist and have six fillings.*

**bracelet** *noun* an ornamental band worn around the arm or wrist.

**bracing** *adjective* fresh and strength-giving. *Bracing sea breezes are good for the health.*

**bracket** *noun* **1** a support fixed to a wall for a shelf. **2 brackets** *plural noun* the signs [ ] used in writing or arithmetic to enclose words or symbols. **bracket** *verb* to group together or to fall between given limits.

**brag** (brags, bragging, bragged) *verb* to boast and talk too proudly about yourself. **braggart** *noun* boaster.

**braid** *noun* **1** a narrow strip of decorative material used for trimming. **2** hair or material separated into three stips and woven together. **braid** *verb.*

**Braille** *noun* a system of printing for blind people using raised dots that can be felt and read with the fingers.

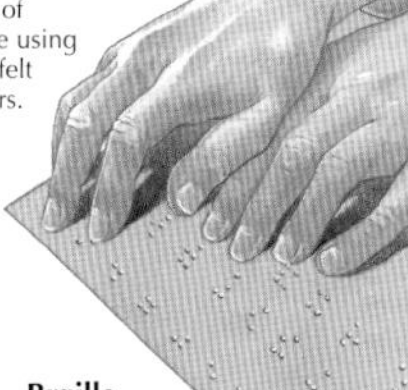

**Braille**

**brain** *noun* the part inside your head that controls how your body works and which enables you to think and feel.

**brainchild** *noun* a person's favorite invention or idea.

**brainteaser** *noun* a difficult problem or puzzle. *This crossword is a real brainteaser.*

**brainwave** *noun* a good idea.

**brainy** (brainier, brainiest) *adjective* clever and intelligent. *A brainy pupil.*

**brake** *noun* the part of a vehicle that you use to slow it down or to stop it. *The brakes failed.* **brake** *verb.*

**bramble** *noun* a prickly bush on which blackberries grow. *A bramble hedgerow.*

**bran** *noun* what is left after flour has been made from the grain of wheat. The husks or outside parts of the seed.

**branch** *noun* **1** part of a tree that sticks out from the trunk. **2** a division of a group or subject. *What branch of science are you studying?* **3** a bank, office, or store belonging to a big organization. *The supermarket has branches in most towns.* **branch** *verb* to divide. *The railroad branches here.* **branch out** to strike out in a new direction. *They've branched out on their own.*

**brand** *noun* a particular kind or make of goods. *An expensive brand.* **brand new** *adjective* unused and completely new.

**brandy** *noun* a strong alcoholic drink.

**Brasilia** *noun* the capital of Brazil in South America.

**brass** *noun* a yellow metal made from mixing two other metals: copper and zinc. **brass band** a group of musicians who play instruments made of brass.

**Bratislava** *noun* the capital of Slovakia in eastern Europe.

Bb

**brave** *adjective* willing to do dangerous things and face danger; fearless. **brave** *noun* an American Indian warrior. **bravery** *noun. He was awarded a medal for bravery.*

**brawl** *noun* a rowdy quarrel or rough fight. *A drunken brawl awoke the neighborhood.* **brawl** *verb.*

**brawn** *noun* great physical and muscular strength. **brawny** *adjective.*

**bray** *noun* the loud sound that a donkey makes. **bray** *verb.*

**brazen** *adjective* **1** made of brass. **2** without shame. *A brazen lie.*

**Brazil** *noun* a country in South America.

**Brazilian** *noun* a person from Brazil. **Brazilian** *adjective. Brazilian coffee.*

**Brazzaville** *noun* the capital of the Republic of the Congo in West Africa.

Brazil

**bread** *noun* a food made from flour, water, and yeast and baked in an oven. *The delicious smell of freshly baked bread.* **breadwinner** the person who earns money for a family to live on.

**breadth** *noun* how wide something is from one side to the other.

**break** *noun* **1** a rest. *You've worked long enough. Take a break.* **2** a sudden change. *Her lucky break was well deserved.* **break** *verb* **1** to split into pieces, to smash. *The glass fell off the table and broke.* **2** to damage something so it does not work. *The radio is broken.* **3** to fail to keep. *He broke his promise.* **breakages** *plural noun* things that are broken. *All breakages must be paid for.* **break down 1** If a car breaks down, it stops going because something has gone wrong. **2** If somebody has a breakdown, they cry and are overcome by nervous exhaustion. **break into** to enter a building by force. **break off** to stop doing something.

bread

**breaker** *noun* a large wave that crashes against the rocks or onto a beach.

**breakfast** *noun* the first meal of the day. *My Dad likes a cooked breakfast.* **breakfast** *verb.*

**breakthrough** *noun* an important achievement or discovery. *A scientific breakthrough.*

**breakwater** *noun* a wall or barrier protecting a harbor or shore from the full force of waves.

**breast** *noun* **1** one of the two soft parts on a woman's chest that produces milk after she has had a baby. The bosom. **2** the chest.

**breath** *noun* the air that you draw in and let out of your lungs. **out of breath** panting. **under your breath** very quietly. *She said it under her breath to her friend so the rest of the people in the room wouldn't hear.*

**breathalyzer** *noun* a device into which the police ask a person to breathe to find out how much alcohol is in their blood. **breathalyze** *verb. He was breathalyzed by the police after he was stopped for speeding.*

**breathe** *verb* to draw air into your lungs through your nose and mouth and send it out again. *Breathe deeply and calm down.*

**breed** *noun* animals that mate and produce others of the same kind. *Bloodhounds and collies are breeds of dog.* **breed** *verb* **1** to mate and produce young. **2** to raise animals to sell. *Tom breeds pigs.*

**breeze** *noun* a soft wind. **breezy** *adjective.*

**brewery** *noun* a place where beer is made (brewed). *Malt is delivered to the brewery.*

**bribe** *noun* a gift or money given to somebody to persuade them to do something unlawful or dishonest. *He gave them a bribe to keep them quiet.* **bribe** *verb.*

**brick** *noun* a small block of hardened clay used for building.

**bride** *noun* a woman who is about to get married. **bridal** *adjective. The bridal suite.*

**bridegroom** *noun* a man who is about to get married. *The bridegroom is usually nervous before the wedding.*

**bridesmaid** *noun* a girl or young woman who helps the bride on her wedding day.

**bridge** *noun* **1** a structure built over a canal, river, or road so that people and vehicles can cross from one side to the other. *A railroad bridge.* **2** a high platform from which a ship is steered. *The captain stands on the bridge.* **3** a piece of wood that holds up the strings stretched along a violin or guitar. **4** a card game for four players. **bridge** *verb. Bridge that gap.*

bridge

**Bridgetown** *noun* the capital of Barbados in the Caribbean.

**bridle** *noun* the leather straps that fit over a horse's head and to which the reins are attached. **bridle** *verb* to show anger. *Paul bridled at the insult.*

**brief** *adjective* lasting or taking only a short time. *We had a brief encounter at the bus station.* **brief** *verb* to give instructions, information, or advice. **briefing** *noun.*

**briefcase** *noun* a flat case for carrying papers.

**briefs** *plural noun* short underwear. *His briefs were too tight for comfort.*

**bright** *adjective* **1** giving out a lot of strong light. **2** a clear, strong color. *Bright orange.* **3** clever. *A bright student.* **brightness** *noun. The brightness of the Sun.* The opposite of "bright" is "dull" or "dim" or "dark."

**brighten** *verb* to make or become brighter.

**brilliant** *adjective* **1** shining brightly. *Brilliant stars.* **2** clever or able. *A brilliant dancer.* **brilliance** *noun.*

**brim** *noun* **1** the top of a container. *The glass is full to the brim.* **2** the part of a hat that sticks out.

**brine** *noun* salty water.

**brink** *noun* the edge of a steep place, such as a cliff.

**brisk** *adjective* **1** lively and efficient. *Brisk manner.* **2** fast. *A brisk walk by the sea.*

**bristle** *noun* a short, stiff hair on an animal or on a man's unshaven face. **bristly** *adjective.*

**British** *adjective* relating to Great Britain and its people.

**brittle** *adjective* hard and easily broken. *Brittle twigs.*

**broad** *adjective* (rhymes with "lord") measuring a lot from one side to the other; wide. **broaden** *verb* to make wider. *They are going to broaden the road.*

**broadcast** (broadcasts, broadcasting, broadcast) *verb* to send out a program to be heard or seen on radio or television. **broadcast** *noun.*

**broadminded** *adjective* tolerant of and accepting people's opinions and behavior that you may not agree with or approve of.

**broadcast**

**broccoli** *noun* a vegetable like a cauliflower with a green stalk and small green flowerheads. *Broccoli is particularly good for you.*

**brochure** *noun* a pamphlet or small book containing information about an organization.

**bronchitis** *noun* an illness of the lungs that makes you cough a lot.

**Bb**

**bronco** *noun* a wild or half-tamed pony. *At the rodeo, the bucking bronco threw off the cowboy who was trying to break him in.*

**bronze** *noun* a reddish-brown metal made by mixing copper and tin. **bronze** *adjective.*

**Bronze Age** *noun* a time in history when people made tools and pots of bronze.

**brooch** *noun* (rhymes with "poach") an ornament that you can pin to your clothes.

**brood** *noun* a family of young birds hatched at the same time. *The mother hen sat on her brood of chicks to keep them warm.* **brood** *verb* **1** to sit on eggs to hatch them. **2** to worry about things for a long time. *Helen was brooding over her poor test result and wondering how she could improve it.*

**Bronze Age**

**brook** *noun* a small stream. *After heavy rainfall, the brook rushed down the mountainside.*

**broom** *noun* a large brush with a long handle for sweeping floors. *Let's sweep the cobwebs out of the hearth with the new broom.*

**broth** *noun* a thin soup containing vegetables and barley. *The doctor recommended a good thick broth.*

**brother** *noun* a boy or man who has the same parents as you. A half-brother has only one parent the same as you. **brotherly** *adjective. Brotherly love.*

**brother-in-law** *noun* the brother of a person's husband or wife, or your sister's husband.

**brought** past tense of bring.

**brow** *noun* **1** the part of your face between your eyes and the top of your head. Your forehead. **2** the arch of hair over each eye. Your eyebrow. **3** the top of a hill.

**brown** *noun, adjective* the color of wood or chocolate. *He came back from his travels as brown as a nut.*

**brownie** *noun* a chewy, fudge-like chocolate cake.

**browse** *verb* to glance at things such as books or goods in a store in a casual way. *He browsed through the catalogs.* **browser** *noun.*

**bruise** *noun* a bluish-black mark on your skin caused by a knock. **bruise** *verb. She bruised her knee when she fell.*

Bb

**Brunei** *noun* a country on the island of Borneo, in Southeast Asia.

Brunei's flag

**Brussels** *noun* the capital of Belgium in Europe.

**brutal** *adjective* cruel, violent, and without feeling. **brutality** *noun*.

**brute** *noun* **1** a cruel person. **2** a wild, savage animal.

**bubble** *noun* a thin ball of liquid filled with air or gas, especially one that floats. *A soap bubble.* **bubble** *verb*. **bubbly** *adjective*. *Bubbly lemonade goes up your nose!*

**buccaneer** *noun* an old word for pirate.

**Bucharest** *noun* the capital of Romania in eastern Europe.

**buck** *noun* **1** a male deer or rabbit. **2** (slang) a dollar. *That will cost you several bucks.* **buck** *verb* When a horse bucks, it leaps into the air with its head down.

**bucket** *noun* a container with a handle for carrying water. *There's a hole in my bucket.*

**bud** *noun* a small, round swelling on a plant that will grow into a leaf or flower. **bud** *verb*. *The trees are starting to bud.* **budding** *adjective*. **nip in the bud** to deal with a problem while it is still small.

**Budapest** *noun* the capital of Hungary in eastern Europe.

Buddhism

**Buddhism** *noun* the religion founded in India by the Buddha in the 500s BC. **Buddhist** *adjective, noun*. *Buddhist monks.*

**budge** *verb* to move a little.

**budget** *noun* a plan of how money should be spent. **budget** *verb*.

**Buenos Aires** *noun* the capital of Argentina in eastern South America.

**buffalo** *noun* **1** one of a variety of wild oxen from Asia and Africa with long curved horns. **2** a bison. *American Indians hunted buffalo.*

**buffet** *noun* (say **buh**-fay) a meal set out on a table from which guests help themselves. *At my sister's wedding, the guests were invited to a buffet in a marquee on the lawn.*

**bug** *noun* **1** an insect, especially an unpleasant one. *Bed bugs.* **2** a germ causing a minor illness. *A tummy bug.* **3** a fault in a computer program. **4** a hidden microphone that records conversations.

**bugle** *noun* a brass musical instrument like a small trumpet, used mainly in the armed forces. **bugler** *noun*.

**build** *noun* the shape and size of a person. *A woman of slender build.* **build** (builds, building, built) *verb* to make something by joining different pieces together. *We intend to build a new house on top of the hill.*

**builder** *noun* a person who earns a living by putting up buildings. *We must get the builder in to mend the roof.*

**building** *noun* a construction such as a house or supermarket with walls and a roof.

**built-up** *adjective* A built-up area is covered with houses, stores, and other buildings and roads.

**Bujumbura** *noun* the capital of Burundi, in east Africa.

**bulb** *noun* the round part of plants such as daffodils and tulips from which the stem grows. **light bulb** the pear-shaped glass part of an electric lamp that gives light.

bulb

**Bulgaria** *noun* a country in eastern Europe.

**bulge** *verb* to swell or stick out. *Santa's sack was bulging with presents for the children.*

**bulk** *noun* **1** great in size. **2** most of. *The bulk of the work has been done.* **bulky** *adjective*. *A bulky package.*

**bull** *noun* a male cow, elephant, seal, or whale. *A bull elephant has big tusks.* **bull's-eye** *noun* the small, round center of a target. *Peter hits the bull's-eye every time.*

**bulldog** *noun* a strong, fearless breed of dog. *The fierce bulldog is unfriendly to other dogs and must be kept on a lead by its owner when it goes for walks.*

**bulldozer** *noun* a powerful vehicle with a big metal blade in front for moving soil and clearing land.

bulldozer

**bullet** *noun* the small, pointed piece of metal that is fired from a gun.

**bullion** *noun* large, heavy bars of gold or silver.

**bully** *noun* somebody who tries to frighten or hurt a weaker or smaller person. **bully** *verb*.

**bump** *verb* to collide or knock into something. *Things that go bump in the night.* **bump** *noun* a round lump caused by something hitting you. **bumpy** *adjective. A very bumpy road.* **bump into** to meet accidentally. *I bumped into Adam.*

**bumptious** *adjective* A bumptious person is full of self-importance. *Our town's bumptious Mayor is a comical figure, always trying to impress.*

**bun** *noun* **1** a small, round cake. **2** a round coil of hair pinned up at the back of a woman's head.

**bunch** *noun* **1** a group of things of the same kind tied or joined together. *The hotel cleaner has to carry the keys for each room, making it an enormous bunch.* **2** a group of people. *A nice bunch of kids.* **bunch** *verb.*

**bundle** *noun* a number of things tied loosely together or wrapped in a cloth. *A bundle of old newspapers.* **bundle** *verb* **1** to tie up loosely. **2** to push or hurry away. *The children were bundled into the bus.*

**bungalow** *noun* a house with all the rooms on the ground floor.

**bungee jumping** *noun* a sport in which a person jumps from a great height, attached by elastic ropes that pull them back up before they hit the ground.

bungalow

**bungle** *verb* to do something awkwardly or badly. **bungler** *noun.*

**bunk** *noun* a narrow bed attached to a wall on a ship or train. **bunkbeds** a bed that has one or more beds above or below it. *The children slept in bunkbeds.*

**buoy** *noun* **1** a floating, anchored marker in the sea that warns ships of danger. **2** a floating, anchored marker in a river to which a boat can be tied.

**buoyant** *adjective* **1** able to float. **2** cheerful.

**burden** *noun* **1** a heavy load. **2** something that is difficult to carry or put up with. *The responsibility is a great burden to him.* **burden** *verb.*

**burglar** *noun* a person who breaks into a building to steal things. **burglary** *noun.* **burgle** *verb.*

**burial** *noun* the act of putting a dead body in a grave. *The burial was a sad affair.*

**Burkina Faso** *noun* a country in West Africa.

**burn** (burns, burning, burned) *verb* **1** to set fire to something. To be destroyed by fire. **2** to hurt or damage with fire. *He burned his hand while cooking.* **burn** *noun.*

**burrow** *noun* a hole made in the ground by an animal as a shelter. **burrow** *verb* to dig or make a tunnel.

**burst** (bursting) *verb* to explode. To break apart suddenly. *The balloons burst in the heat.* **burst into** *He burst into the room. She burst into tears.*

**Burundi** *noun* a country in Central Africa.

**bury** (buries, burying, buried) *verb* **1** to put a dead body or thing in the ground. *The dog buried its bone in the garden.* **2** to hide. *He buried his head in his hands.*

**business** *noun* (say **biz**-ness) **1** the buying and selling of goods and services. A company or organization that makes, buys, or sells things. **2** concerns, events, or situations in general. *What she did is none of your business.* **businesslike** *adjective* efficient, methodical.

**busker** *noun* a singer or musician who performs in the street for money. **busk** *verb.*

**bust** *adjective* (slang) **1** broken. *The television is busted.* **2** bankrupt. *His company has gone bust.* **bust** *noun* **1** a statue of a person's head and the top part of the chest. **2** a woman's breasts. *What is your bust size?*

**bustle** *verb* to hurry because you are busy. *He bustled around putting things away.* **bustle** *noun.*

**busy** (busier, busiest) *adjective* **1** If you are busy, you have a lot to do. *I'm too busy to see you today.* **2** full of people or activity. *A busy office.* **busily** *adverb.* **busybody** a person who interferes with other people's business and gives unwanted advice.

**butcher** *noun* a person who cuts up meat and sells it.

**butler** *noun* the chief male servant in a house. *The butler's pantry.*

**butter** *noun* a soft, yellow food made from cream and milk. **butter** *verb. Please butter the bread for me.*

**buttocks** *plural noun* the fleshy parts of your body on which you sit; your bottom.

**buttress** *noun* a support for an outside wall.

**buy** (buys, buying, bought) *verb* to get something by paying money for it; to purchase. *He bought a new car.*

**buzz** *verb* to make a low humming sound like a bee.

**buzzard** *noun* a large bird of prey that hunts other animals for food.

**bypass** *noun* a road that goes around a town or busy place and not through it. **bypass** *verb. Let's take the longer route and bypass the field with the bull in it.*

buzzard

**bystander** a spectator. *The bystanders cheered loudly as the procession walked past.*

**byte** *noun* a unit of information in a computer's memory, consisting usually of eight bits.

**cab** *noun* **1** a taxi. **2** the front part of a truck, train, or crane in which the driver sits.

**cabbage** *noun* a large, round vegetable with thick green or purple leaves.

**cabin** *noun* **1** a small wooden house. *A log cabin.* **2** a room or compartment in a ship or airplane.

**cabinet** *noun* **1** a piece of furniture with doors and shelves or drawers, used for storing or displaying things. *We keep our documents in a filing cabinet.* **2** a group of politicians who make policy or advise the leader of a government. *A cabinet meeting is in progress.*

**cable** *noun* **1** a thick rope of fibers or wire. **2** a bundle of wires inside a plastic or rubber casing, through which electricity flows. *An electric cable.* **3** a telegram. *He sent a cable.* **cable car** a cabin hanging from a cable that carries people up and down a mountainside or along a road. *The cable car halted suddenly, making everyone gasp.* **cable television** *noun* a system in which TV programs are sent to TV sets along electric cables instead of as radio waves.

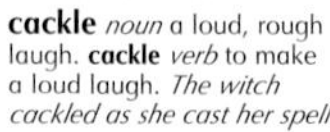

cable car

**cackle** *noun* a loud, rough laugh. **cackle** *verb* to make a loud laugh. *The witch cackled as she cast her spell.*

**cactus** (cacti) *noun* a fleshy, spine-covered plant that grows in hot countries.

**café** *noun* (say **kaf**-ay) a small restaurant that serves refreshments and light meals.

**cafeteria** *noun* (say kaf-it-**eer**-ee-uh) a self-service restaurant where you collect your food before sitting down.

**cage** *noun* a container with wires or bars, often used for keeping animals or birds. *The door of the cage swung open and the parrot stepped out looking surprised.*

**Cairo** *noun* the capital of Egypt in northern Africa.

**cajole** *verb* to persuade somebody into doing something by flattering them. *He cajoled her into giving him the information he needed.*

**cake** *noun* a sweet mixture of flour, eggs, and sugar baked in an oven. *I had a piece of her birthday cake.* **a piece of cake** really easy.

**calamity** *noun* a disaster, such as losing all your money. **calamitous** *adjective.*

**calcium** *noun* a chemical substance found in limestone, teeth, bones, and chalk.

**calculate** *verb* **1** to work out an amount by using numbers. *We calculated that we'd arrive at about 10 o'clock.* **2** to plan. *The advertisements are calculated to attract students.* **calculation** *noun.*

**calculator** *noun* a small electronic machine that can add, subtract, multiply, and divide numbers.

**calendar** *noun* a list that shows the days, weeks, and months of the year, so you can look up the date. Some calendars also list important events in the year.

**calf** (calves) *noun* **1** a young cow, elephant, or whale. **2** the broad, back part of your leg that lies between the knee and the ankle.

calf

**call** *noun* **1** a shout or cry. **2** a visit. **3** a telephone call. **call** *verb* **1** to shout or speak in a loud voice, usually to attract somebody's attention. **2** to ask or order somebody to come to you. *Why don't you come when I call?* **3** to telephone. **4** to give a name to somebody or something. *Her brother is called John.* **5** to describe something or somebody. *I wouldn't call her fat.* **6** to get somebody to come. *We had to call the doctor.* **7** to wake somebody up. *Call me at seven in the morning.* **call for** to demand or need something in a particular situation. *This calls for prompt action.* **call off** to stop something. *The meeting was called off.* **call on** to make a short visit. **call out** **1** to shout. **2** to summon in an emergency. *The fire brigade was called out twice today.*

**calling** *noun* an occupation, especially a profession that involves helping others.

**callous** *noun* hardened skin. *The writer developed a callous on his finger where his pen always rested.* **callous** *adjective* **1** not caring about other people's feelings. *His behavior was selfish and callous.*

**calm** *adjective* **1** not windy. **2** When the sea is calm, it is still and without waves. **3** not excited and not showing any worry. *Please stay calm and leave by the nearest exit.* **calm** *noun. Calm descended after the party.*

**calorie** *noun* **1** a unit for measuring the energy that food produces. *One slice of brown bread has 95 calories, which is less than a slice of cake.* **2** a unit of heat.

**Cambodia** *noun* a country in Southeast Asia.

**camcorder** *noun* a hand-held video camera and recorder all in one. *We recorded Rachel's fifth birthday on the camcorder so she could play it back when she was older.*

**camel** *noun* an animal with a long neck and one or two humps on its back. Camels are used in deserts for riding and carrying goods. *A camel walked slowly across the sand dunes carrying a heavy load.*

**camera** *noun* an apparatus for taking photographs or making movies and television pictures. *Smile at the camera, please!*

**Cameroon** *noun* a country in west Africa.

**camouflage** *noun* (say **kam**-uff-lahzh) a way of hiding things by making them blend in with their surroundings. *A polar bear's white fur is good camouflage in the snow.* **camouflage** *verb. The enemy camp was well camouflaged behind the bushes.*

**camp** *noun* a place where people live in tents, huts, or caravans, usually for a short time. **camp** *verb* to make a camp. **camping** *noun. Scouts and guides go camping.*

camp

**campaign** *noun* a series of planned activities to achieve a particular result. *A successful advertising campaign.* **campaign** *verb. He's campaigning to become president.*

**campus** *noun* the grounds of a university or college. *Most freshmen choose to live on campus in halls of residence rather than in town.*

**can** *noun* a metal container for holding food or drink. **can of worms** a collection of problems. **can** (could) *verb* **1** to be able to. *Can you carry that heavy box?* **2** to know how to do something or have the ability to do it. *She can speak German.* **3** to be allowed to do something. *The teacher says we can go home after the lesson.* **4** a polite way of asking somebody to do something. *Can you tell me the time, please?*

**Canada** *noun* a country in North America.

**Canadian** *noun* a person who comes from Canada. **Canadian** *adjective. We went to see a Canadian film.*

Canada

**canary** (canaries) *noun* a small yellow bird that sings, often kept in a cage or aviary as a pet.

**Canberra** *noun* the capital of Australia.

**cancel** (canceling, canceled) *verb* **1** to say that a planned activity will not take place. *The concert was canceled because the singer had flu.* **2** to stop an instruction for something. *I canceled the booking.* **3** to put a stop on a check so it is no longer valid. **cancellation** *noun.* **cancel out** to balance and have an equal but opposite effect on something. *If I pay for your lunch, it cancels out the debt I owe you.*

**cancer** *noun* **1** a serious disease in which abnormal growths form in the body. *Smoking can cause lung cancer.* **2 Cancer** a sign of the zodiac (21 June to 22 July).

**candid** *adjective* honest, even when unwelcome or unpleasant. **candor** *noun.*

**candidate** *noun* **1** someone who puts themselves forward to be chosen for a job or political position. **2** a person taking an examination.

**candle** *noun* wax with a piece of string (a wick) through it, which gives light when it burns.

**cane** *noun* a long, thin stick. Cane is the hollow stem from a plant such as bamboo. **cane** *verb* to hit with a cane as a punishment for wrongdoing.

**cannabis** *noun* **1** a kind of hemp plant. **2** a drug made from the plant.

**cannibal** *noun* **1** a person who eats other people. *The cannibal shot the man he feared with an arrow and then cooked and ate him.* **2** an animal that eats its own kind. **cannibalism** *noun.*

cannon

**cannon** *noun* a big gun that fires cannon balls.

**cannot** *verb* the negative form of can. *Unfortunately we cannot come to the party.*

**canoe** *noun* a light, long, narrow boat that is moved by using paddles. **canoe** *verb* to go in a canoe. *He canoed down the river.* **canoeing** *noun.*

**can't** short for cannot, see "can." "Can't" is usually spoken rather than written.

**canteen** *noun* **1** a store or restaurant for employees, people in the military, or students. **2** a small container for carrying liquid.

**canter** *noun* the movement of a horse, faster than a trot but slower than a gallop. **canter** *verb.*

**canvas** *noun* **1** a strong, rough cloth used for tents, sails, and bags. *We set up camp and spent the night under canvas.* **2** a stretched piece of cloth on which oil paintings are done. **3** an oil painting on canvas.

Cc

**canvass** *verb* **1** to go to people to ask for their vote, support, or opinion. *They canvassed the neighbors for support.* **2** to ask people for their opinions on a subject. *We canvassed opinion on which brand tastes best.*

**canyon** *noun* a deep, steep valley, usually with a river running through it. *At the bottom of the canyon was a dried up river bed and fresh dinosaur footprints.*

canyon

**cap** *noun* **1** a hat with a peak. **2** a lid or top on a bottle or tube. **3** a piece of paper covered with a tiny amount of explosive that makes a bang when used in a toy gun. **cap** *verb* to cover the top of something.

**capable** *adjective* having the ability to do something. **capability** *noun.*

**capacity** *noun* **1** the amount that can be held. *The stadium has a capacity of 30,000.* If a place is filled to capacity, it is completely full. **2** the ability to do something. *Algebra is beyond my capacity.* **3** a position. *In my capacity as head teacher.*

**cape** *noun* **1** a loose cloak without sleeves and fastened at the neck. **2** a large piece of land surrounded on three sides by water. *When they reached the tip of South Africa, they sailed around the Cape of Good Hope.*

**Cape Town** *noun* the legislative capital of South Africa.

**Cape Verde** *noun* a country in the Atlantic Ocean off West Africa.

Cape Verde's flag

**capital** *noun* **1** a city in which the government of a country is based. *Paris is the capital of France.* **2** a letter written or printed in a large form (A, B, C), used at the beginning of a sentence or a name. *Write your name in capitals please.* **3** a sum of money used to start up a business, as well as money or property used to make more money. *He put up the capital for the new company.* **capital punishment** punishment in which the criminal is killed. *In some states of the US, murderers receive capital punishment.*

**capitalism** *noun* (say **kap**-it-ul-izm) an economic system in which a country's production and distribution of goods (its trade and industry) depend on invested private capital and are run for profit.

**capitalist** *noun* **1** a person who lends his money to businesses, to make more money. **2** a person who supports capitalism. **capitalist** *adjective.*

**capsize** *verb* to overturn in water. *The boat capsized in deep water.*

capsize

**capsule** *noun* **1** a pill containing medicine. **2** the part of a spaceship in which the crew live and work, which can be separated from the rest of the craft in space.

**captain** *noun* **1** the leader of a team or group. *Who's the captain of your football team?* **2** a person in command of a ship or an aircraft. **3** an officer in the army or navy. **captain** *verb* to be captain of a sports team.

**caption** *noun* **1** words put with a picture to explain what it is about. **2** a heading or short title in a newspaper or magazine.

**captive** *adjective* kept as a prisoner. **captive** *noun* taken prisoner. **a captive audience** a group of people who have to listen to somebody. *TV viewers are a captive audience for advertisers.* **captivity** *noun.*

**capture** *noun* **1** the act of capturing. **2** somebody or something that has been taken by force. **capture** *verb* **1** to make a person or an animal a prisoner. **2** to get something by force, skill, attraction, or trickery. *Her beauty captured his heart.* **3** to put data into a computer. **4** to describe something in words or pictures. *The movie captures the beauty of the city.*

**car** *noun* **1** a car has four wheels and an engine and room for a driver and, usually, passengers. Cars drive on roads and highways. *We usually go by car.* **2** a railroad carriage. *This train has a dining car.*

**Caracas** *noun* the capital of Venezuela in South America.

**carat** *noun* **1** a unit for measuring the weight of precious stones such as diamonds, equal to 0.2 grams. **2** a unit for measuring gold. Pure gold is 24 carats.

**caravan** *noun* **1** a home on wheels in which people live or spend their holidays. Caravans are usually pulled by a car. **2** a group of people traveling across a desert.

**carbon** *noun* **1** a substance that is found in all living things. Diamonds and coal are made of carbon. **2** a thin piece of paper with a colored coating on one side which is put between two sheets of paper for making copies of what is written or, historically, typed; also called carbon paper. **3** a copy made by using carbon paper. *A carbon copy.* **carbon dioxide** a gas that is present in the air and is also formed when animals and people breathe out. **carbon monoxide** a poisonous gas, produced especially by car engines.

**carburetor** *noun* the part of a car engine in which gasoline and air are mixed so they can burn to provide power. *The carburetor needs replacing now.*

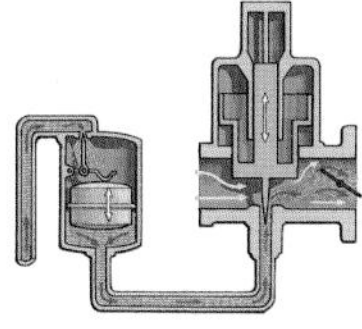

carburettor

**carcass** (carcasses) *noun* the body of a dead animal.

**card** *noun* **1** a folded piece of stiff paper with a picture on the front and a message inside, which you send to people on special occasions. *A birthday card.* **2** a piece of stiff paper on which to write information. **3** a postcard. **4** a small piece of printed plastic that you use if you have an account at a bank or a store. *I paid with my credit card.* **5** one of a pack of 52 playing cards, used for games such as bridge or poker. *We played cards all afternoon.* **on the cards** likely or possible. **put/lay your cards on the table** to make your plans known.

**cardboard** *noun* thick, stiff paper used for making boxes. *A cardboard box.*

**Cardiff** *noun* the capital of Wales, part of the UK.

**cardigan** *noun* a knitted sweater that usually buttons up at the front.

**care** *noun* **1** serious attention, in an effort to avoid making any mistakes. *She plans her essays with great care.* **2** If you take care of somebody or something, you look after them. If you pay for something, do the work, or make the arrangements, you take care of it. **3** worry and sorrow. **care** *verb* to be interested and feel that something is important. *We care about the environment.* If you don't care about something, it doesn't matter to you and you don't worry. **care for 1** to look after somebody or something. **2** to like a person. *Although he's nasty to her, she still cares for him.* If you care for something, you enjoy it. *I don't care for dancing.* **care of** (c/o *abbreviation*) written when sending a letter or parcel to somebody who is living at someone else's address.

**career** *noun* **1** a job or profession that you do for a long time and hope to be successful in. *He's chosen a career in teaching.* **2** the development and progress through a person's working life. **career** *verb* to move very fast and in an uncontrolled way. *The car careered down the street, narrowly missing the oncoming traffic.*

**careful** *adjective* **1** paying attention to what you do in order to avoid danger or damage. *Be careful when crossing the road.* **2** done with care and thought. *A careful report.* **carefully** *adverb*. **carefulness** *noun*.

**careless** *adjective* **1** not paying attention or taking care about something and making mistakes. **2** thoughtless. *Careless driving costs lives.* **3** untroubled and not worried. *She's careless with money.* **carelessly** *adverb*.

**caress** *noun* a loving touch. **caress** *verb* to stroke or kiss somebody to show your love for them.

**cargo** (cargoes) *noun* goods carried in a ship or plane.

**caricature** *noun* an amusing picture or description of somebody, so that parts of his or her character or appearance seem odder or more pronounced than they are in reality. **caricature** *verb* to make a caricature. *He's great at caricaturing all sorts of politicians.*

**carnation** *noun* a scented garden flower.

**carnival** *noun* a public festival with music, dance, and processions of people in elaborate makeup and costumes, usually held during the period before Lent in Roman Catholic countries. *At the Venice carnival, people wear beautiful painted masks and fantastic costumes.*

**carnivore** *noun* an animal that eats meat. Lions and tigers are carnivores. **carnivorous** *adjective*.

**carol** *noun* a Christmas song.

**carpenter** *noun* a person who is skilled at making or repairing wooden things.

carriage

**carpet** *noun* a thick woven covering for floors and stairs. **sweep something under the carpet** to conceal something that happened in the hope that it will be forgotten.

**carriage** *noun* **1** a section of a train for passengers. **2** an old-fashioned passenger vehicle, usually with four wheels, pulled by horses. **3** the movable part of a machine that supports another part. *A typewriter carriage.* **4** the way someone walks and moves his/her head and body.

**carrier** *noun* **1** a person or thing that moves goods or passengers from one place to another. **2** a person who passes on a disease to others without suffering him/herself.

**carrion** *noun* the flesh of dead animals.

**carrot** *noun* a plant with an orange root grown as a vegetable. It can be eaten raw or cooked.

**carry** (carries, carrying, carried) *verb* **1** to hold something or somebody and go from one place to another. *The porter carried my suitcase.* **2** to hold something up, e.g., a roof or ceiling. **3** to pass something like a disease from one person to another. *Mosquitoes can carry dangerous diseases.* **4** to make sound move through the air. *Her voice carried right to the back of the hall.* **5** to win the support of others in a debate when voting is involved. *The motion was carried by 20 votes to 10.* **6** to print something. *The newspapers carried pictures of the funeral.* **7** to have as a result. *In some countries, murder still carries the death penalty.* **8** to keep goods in stock. **9** If somebody's opinion carries weight, people respect it. **get carried away** to become very excited. **carry on 1** to continue. *I tried to speak to him but he just carried on reading.* **2** to manage things in a difficult situation. *Although the theater was nearly empty, the cast carried on.* **3** to complain and make a fuss about something. *My mother carried on all day about the noise.* **4** (informal) If a person is carrying on with somebody, they are having an affair. **carry out** to fulfill, to do what you have promised or have been told to do. *We carried out our plan.*

**cart** *noun* a vehicle for carrying goods, usually drawn by a horse. **cart** *verb* **1** to carry in a cart. *He carted hay to the horses.* **2** to carry something heavy and find it tiring. *I don't want to cart those bags around town.*

**carton** *noun* a plastic or cardboard container for food or drink.

**cartoon** *noun* **1** an amusing drawing or set of drawings, often showing something of interest in the news. *There was a funny cartoon about the strike in the newspaper.* **2** an animated film. *Have you seen the latest Disney cartoon?* **cartoonist** *noun.*

**cartridge** *noun* **1** a container holding film for a camera, a tape, or ink for a pen or printer. **2** a tube holding explosive for a bullet.

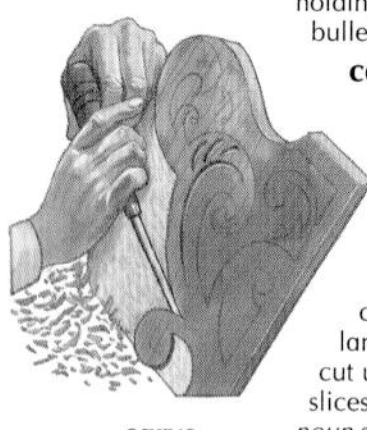

carve

**carve** *verb* **1** to make something by cutting a special shape out of wood or stone. *The statue was carved from marble.* **2** to subdivide. The brothers carved up their father's land between them. **3** to cut up cooked meat into slices. **carving** *noun.* **carver** *noun* someone who carves wood or stone.

**cascade** *noun* a waterfall. **cascade** *verb* to fall in, or like, a cascade. *Her hair cascaded over her shoulders.*

**case** *noun* **1** a container. *A case of wine.* **2** a suitcase. *I packed my case and left.* **3** an event or a situation of a particular kind. *In this case, I wouldn't pay the fine.* **4** an event the police are investigating or a question that will be decided on in court. *A murder case.* **5** an example of something bad, or of a disease. *A case of Asian flu.* **6** a patient, a lawyer's client, or a person looked after by a social worker. **5** facts and arguments for and against a plan used in a discussion. *The case for giving up smoking.* **7** in grammar, the change in the form of a word showing how it relates to other words in the sentence. *"Emma's" is the possessive case of "Emma."* **in case** an action taken in advance referring to a particular thing that might happen. *I've brought a map in case we get lost.* **in any case** anyway. *I'll come, in any case.*

**cash** *noun* money in coins and notes. **cash** *verb* to exchange a check for money. **cash-and-carry** a supermarket that sells goods in bulk, cheaper than other stores. **cash machine** an automatic machine, usually in or outside a bank, from which customers can withdraw cash.

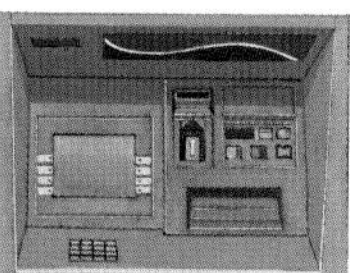

cash machine

**cashier** *noun* a person who takes in or pays money in a bank or store.

**cast** *noun* **1** all the actors in a movie or play. **2** an object made from liquid metal, plastic, or plaster poured into a mold. **3** a hard covering made of plaster that keeps a broken bone in place while it is mending. **cast** *verb* **1** to throw. *The fishermen cast their nets into the sea.* **2** to cast doubt on something means that you're not sure about it. **3** to give your vote in an election. *Have all the votes been cast?* **4** to choose actors for a movie or play. **5** to make an object by pouring liquid into a mold and letting it harden.

**castaway** *noun* a shipwrecked person.

**castle** *noun* **1** a large, strong building with high walls that was built, usually in the Middle Ages, to protect lords and royalty from their enemies. **2** a chess piece. *Joseph made a clever move by taking the pawn with his castle.*

castle

**Castries** *noun* the capital of St Lucia in the Caribbean.

**casual** *adjective* **1** happening by chance, without planning. *A casual conversation.* **2** relaxed and not doing things very seriously, sometimes seeming uninterested. *The teacher didn't like his casual attitude.* **3** informal. *I wear casual clothes at home.* **4** not permanent or regular. *Casual work.* **casually** *adverb.*

**casualty** *noun* a person who is injured or killed in a war or an accident. *There were five casualties in the hospital waiting room.*

**cat** *noun* **1** a small furry pet animal. **2** a large wild animal of the cat family. Lions, tigers, and leopards are all big cats. **cat burglar** a burglar who climbs up a building and enters by a high window or the roof. **cat ice** thin ice over shallow water. **let the cat out of the bag** to tell a secret.

**catalog, catalogue** *noun* a list of names, places, goods, and other things put in a particular order so that they can be found easily. *I buy all my clothes from a catalog.* **catalog** *verb* to list something in a catalog. *The library books have all been cataloged.*

**catalyst** *noun* (say **kat**-uh-list) something that causes a change or speeds up an event. One person's actions can also act as a catalyst to others.

**catamaran** *noun* a sail boat with two separate hulls.

**catapult** *noun* **1** a Y-shaped stick with an elastic band attached between the forks, used to shoot small stones. **2** an ancient military machine used to hurl stones and rocks at an enemy. **catapult** *verb* to launch, as if from a catapult. *The actor was catapulted to stardom after he made his first movie.*

cataract

**cataract** *noun* **1** a large waterfall, especially one that falls over a steep drop. **2 cataract** a growth over the eyeball that blurs a person's vision. *My grandfather had a cataract removed from his left eye.*

**catarrh** *noun* (say kuh-**tar**) an inflammation of the nose and throat similar to a cold.

**catastrophe** *noun* (say ku-**tass**-trof-ee) a disastrous event that causes suffering and damage. **catastrophic** *adjective. Adding acid to the mixture proved to be a catastrophic mistake.* **catastrophically** *adverb. The science experiment went catastrophically wrong and blew the roof off the lab.*

**catch** *noun* **1** to get hold of something like a ball. *He saved the game with a great catch.* **2** something caught or worth having. *She's a good catch; I would marry her.* **3** a trick; a hidden difficulty. *That car's too cheap; there must be a catch.* **4** a hook or another method of fastening something or locking a door. *The catch on the door is broken.* **5** a game in which children throw a ball to each other. **catch** (catches, catching, caught) *verb* **1** to get hold of an object that is moving through the air. *He threw the ball and I caught it.* **2** to capture an animal or a person after chasing them. *You can catch fish in a net and mice in a trap.* **3** to be in time for a bus or train. *Leave now if you want to catch the bus.* **4** to suddenly discover a person doing something wrong. *The teacher caught them smoking in the toilet.* **5** to become stuck. *I caught my shirt on a nail.* **6** to manage to hear. *I didn't catch his name.* **7** to become infected by an illness. *The baby caught a cold.* **8** to reach in time. *He has only just left; you can still catch him.* **9** If you catch sight of somebody or something, you see them for just a moment. **catch fire** to start burning. **catch somebody's eye** to attract their attention. **catch on 1** to become popular. *The new style soon caught on.* **2** to begin to understand. *I didn't catch on at first.* **catch up 1** to reach the same point as somebody or something in front of you. *You go on; I'll catch up with you.* **2** to reach the same standard or level as someone or something else. *I had to catch up on my homework before going out.*

**catching** *adjective* spreading quickly from one person to another. *Is the disease that you are suffering from catching?*

**category** *noun* a division or class of something.

**caterpillar** *noun* a small worm-like creature with many legs. *Caterpillars turn into beautiful butterflies and moths.*

caterpillar

**cathedral** *noun* the main church of a district, containing the bishop's ceremonial chair.

**Catholic** *noun* a member of the Roman Catholic Church. **Catholic** *adjective. Their children go to a Catholic school.* **Catholicism** *noun.*

**cauliflower** *noun* a vegetable with a large head of white flower buds.

**cause** *noun* **1** a person or thing that makes something happen. *Nobody knows the cause of the fire.* **2** reason. *You've got no cause for complaint.* **3** a purpose for which people work, such as a charity. *The money is for a good cause.* **cause** *verb* to make something happen. *The accident was caused by negligence.*

**causeway** *noun* a raised path across wet ground.

**caution** *noun* **1** a warning. **2** the act of taking care to avoid danger or making mistakes. **caution** *verb* to give a warning to somebody. **cautious** *adjective.*

Cc

**cavalry** *noun* soldiers who fight while riding on horses.

**cave** *noun* an underground hollow, sometimes in the side of a cliff or hill. **cave in** *verb* to fall down inwards. *The roof of the tunnel caved in.*

**cave-dweller** *noun* a person living in a cave. *The cave-dweller killed a mammoth.*

**caver** *noun* someone who explores caves.

**cavity** *noun* a hole.

**CD** *abbreviation* Compact Disc.

**CD-ROM** *abbreviation* Compact Disc Read-Only Memory, a CD on which large amounts of information can be stored.

**cease** *verb* **1** to end. **2** to stop doing something. *Cease this idle chat!*

**ceiling** *noun* **1** the top part of a room forming the upper surface. **2** the highest limit of something.

**celebrate** *verb* to do something special to show that a day or an event is important. *We had a party to celebrate Grandma's 80th birthday.* **celebration** *noun.*

**celebrity** *noun* **1** fame. **2** a famous person.

**celery** *noun* a plant with long stems grown as a vegetable and often eaten raw in salad.

**cell** *noun* **1** a small room in which a prisoner is kept. **2** a small room in which a monk or a nun lives. **3** the smallest part of humans, plants, or animals. **4** one of the compartments of a honeycomb. **5** a unit of an apparatus, such as a battery for producing electric current.

**cellar** *noun* an underground room of a building, often used for storing things.

**cello** *noun* (say **chel**-oh) a musical instrument with strings, similar in shape to a violin, but larger. **cellist** *noun.*

**cellular** *adjective* **1** made up of cells. **2** cellular blankets are loosely woven and very warm. **3** a cellular (cell) phone is a small, portable phone.

**Celsius** *adjective* (say **sel**-see-us) from the Celsius scale for measuring temperature. Water boils at 100° Celsius.

**cement** *noun* **1** a gray powder, made from lime and clay, used for building. When cement is mixed with water and left to dry, it becomes hard as stone. **2** a strong glue. **cement** *verb* **1** to cover with cement. *The area in front of our house has been cemented over, so we can park our car there.* **2** to strengthen an agreement or a friendship.

**cemetery** *noun* (say **sem**-e-ter-ee) a place where dead people are buried.

**census** *noun* the official count of population.

**cent** *noun* the 100th part of a dollar.

**centenary** *noun* (say sen-**teen**-u-ree) a 100th anniversary of an event.

**Central African Republic**

**center** *noun* **1** the middle part or the point around which something turns or revolves. **2** an important place of interest and great activity. *Harvard is a center of learning.* **3** in sport, a player in a team who plays near the middle of the field. **center** *verb* **1** to put something near or in the middle. **2** to concentrate your thoughts or ideas on something. **center of attention** a person who attracts a great deal of notice.

**centimeter** *noun* a measure of length. There are 100 centimeters in a meter.

**centipede** *noun* a long crawling creature with a segmented body and many legs.

**central** *adjective* **1** in the middle of something, near the center. **2** most important. *The government's central aim is to improve education.* **central heating** a system of heating buildings from a central boiler through a network of pipes and radiators. **centrally** *adverb.*

**Central African Republic** *noun* a country in central Africa.

**Central America** *noun* a narrow strip of seven countries between Mexico and South America.

**centurion** *noun* (say sent-**yoor**-ee-un) a commander of 100 men in the armies of the ancient Roman empire.

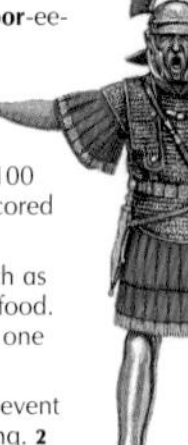

**centurion**

**century** *noun* **1** a period of 100 years. **2** in cricket, 100 runs scored by a batsman.

**cereal** *noun* **1** any grain, such as wheat, rice, or corn, used for food. **2** a breakfast food made from one or more kinds of grain.

**ceremony** *noun* **1** a special event or occasion, such as a wedding. **2** the things said and done during such an occasion. *I love all the ceremony at big church weddings.* **Master of Ceremonies** or **MC** someone who introduces speakers at a dinner. **ceremonious** *adjective.*

**certain** *adjective* **1** sure, having no doubt. *I'm certain that's right.* If you make certain of something, you find out first. **2** not named. *A certain person was involved in the crime.* **3** some but not much. *He seems to get a certain pleasure out of it.*

**certificate** *noun* an official document giving facts about a person. *When a baby is born, he/she is required to have a birth certificate.* **certify** *verb.*

**CFC** *abbreviation* chlorofluorocarbon. A substance used in refrigerators and aerosols. CFCs have caused the ozone layer in the atmosphere to shrink.

**Chad** *noun* a country in Central Africa.

**chaffinch** *noun* a small songbird.

**chair** *noun* **1** a seat with legs and a back for one person to sit on. **2** a person in control of a discussion. *Who is in the chair at tomorrow's meeting?* **chair** *verb* to be in charge of a meeting.

**challenge** (challenging, challenged) *verb* **1** to demand to have a fight, play a game, or run a race to see who is stronger or better. *I challenged my brother to a game of tennis.* **2** to question the truth of something. **challenge** *noun* **1** a demand to see who is stronger or better. **2** a difficult project that demands effort and willpower. *Mountaineering is a great challenge.* **challenger** *noun.*

**champion** *noun* **1** a person or team that wins a race or game. *A tennis champion.* **2** somebody who speaks or fights for other people and defends ideas. *She is a champion of women's rights.* **champion** *verb.*

**champion**

**championship** *noun* a competition to find the best player or team. *Wimbledon is the oldest tennis championship.*

**chancellor** *noun* a high state official. *The Chancellor of the Exchequer is England's finance minister (director).*

**change** *verb* **1** to become, do, or make something different. *She's changed a lot since I last saw her five years ago. When I get home from work I always change my clothes and go for a run across the park. We changed buses in Dallas.* **2** to give something up and do something else. *I've changed my job in Philadelphia for something better paid in Washington D.C.* **change** *noun* **1** the act of changing or the result of changing. *You can tell there is going to be a change in the weather by the way the birds are flying.* **2** the money returned to the payer when the cost of the goods is less than the amount given. *It costs 50 cents and you gave her a dollar, so you get 50 cents change.* **3** the same amount of money in coins or smaller bills. *Have you got change for a dollar?* **4** a change of clothes is a clean set. **change your mind** to come to have another opinion. *I've changed my mind about taking the new job I've been offered in the city.* **change money** to exchange a sum of money for the same amount in coins or notes. **for a change** something different from what usually happens. *Why don't we go out for a change of scene?*

**channel** *noun* **1** a stretch of water that connects two seas. *The English Channel connects the North Sea and the Atlantic Ocean.* **2** a passage along which water flows. **3** a wavelength for television or radio programs. *I often watch Channel 5.* **channel** (channeling, channeled) *verb* **1** to form a channel in something. **2** to direct. *He channeled his energy into the new project.*

**chaos** *noun* a state of disorder and confusion. *The accident caused chaos on the highway when traffic was brought to a standstill in both directions.*

**chapel** *noun* **1** a small sanctuary, sometimes as part of a hospital or school. *A Methodist chapel.* **2** a room, recess, or cell that is part of a church with its own altar.

**chapter** *noun* **1** a main division of a book, usually with its own number or title. **2** a special period in history. **3** a regular assembly of a cathedral's staff. **chapter and verse** the exact place where detailed information can be found.

**char** (charring, charred) *verb* to become black from burning. *The sausages on the barbeque are charred.*

**character** *noun* **1** the qualities that make a person or a place what they are. *The twins have very different characters.* **2** a person in a story, movie, or play. **3** a character is somebody interesting or different from others. *He's a real character.* **4** a letter, number, or other symbol. **characteristic** *adjective.* **characterize** *verb.*

**charade** (say shu-**rayd**) *noun* **1** an act that can easily be seen by others to be a pretense or foolish. *The trial was just a charade.* **2 charades** *plural noun* a game in which players take turns to guess words acted out by others.

**charge** *noun* **1** a price asked or paid for goods or a service. **2** an official written or spoken statement accusing someone of a crime. *He was arrested on a murder charge.* **3** the care and responsibility for a person or thing. **4** a sudden attack. **5** an amount of explosive to be fired. **6** electricity in a battery or other electrical apparatus. **take charge** to be responsible for something or someone. *I'll take charge of the children if you do the dish washing.* **charge** *verb* **1** to ask a price for something. *He charged me for delivery.* **2** to accuse somebody of a crime. **3** to rush forward in an attack. *The cavalry charged across the plain at the enemy.* **4** When you charge a battery, it lasts longer. **5** If you are charged with something or charged to do something, you are given a duty or task.

**chariot** *noun* a horse-drawn vehicle with two wheels, used in battles and races in ancient times. *Cheering filled the Colosseum in Rome as the chariots raced around the stadium.*

**chariot**

**charity** *noun* **1** an organization that helps raise money for people or animals in need. *A charity for stray dogs.* **2** kindness toward others.

**charm** *noun* **1** the ability to be attractive and to please. *He used all his charm to win her over.* **2** an act, saying, or object that has magical powers. **3** an ornament on a bracelet or chain. **charm** *verb* **1** *He charmed her with flattery.* **2** to control something by using magical powers.

**charming** *adjective* delightful, pleasing. *She is a charming person.*

**chart** *noun* **1** a map of the sea and coast or sky and stars. **2** a map with special information in curves and graphs. *A weather chart.* **3** a list of information in a particular order. *The charts list the most popular musical releases.* **chart** *verb. Explorers charted the coastline.*

**chase** *verb* to go after somebody or something in order to try and catch them or make them go away. *The dog chased the squirrel up a tree.* **chase** *noun.*

**chasm** *noun* (say kazm) **1** a deep crack in the ground. **2** a large difference between two things or groups. *The chasm between us widened.*

chauffeur

**chauffeur** *noun* (say **shoh**-fer) a person employed to drive somebody.

**chauvinist** *noun* (say **shoh**-vin-ist) a person who shows great prejudice, especially against women. *He's a real male chauvinist.*

**cheat** *verb* **1** to behave in a dishonest way in order to win or gain something. **2** to lie or to trick somebody. *He cheated on the exams.* **cheat** *noun* a person who cheats.

**check** *noun* **1** an examination to find out if something is correct. **2** keeping somebody or something under control. *We must keep the disease in check.* **3** in chess, the position of the king when under attack. **4** a pattern of squares in different colors. **5** a printed form telling the bank to pay money from your account to the person whose name you have written on the check. **6** a mark you put next to an answer. **check** *verb* **1** to make sure something is correct. *Have you checked the bill?* **2** to stop doing something. *The bad weather checked their progress.* **check in** to register at a hotel or report at an airport. *You have to check in an hour before takeoff.* **check on** to make sure something is happening as it should. **check out** to pay the bill and leave a hotel. **check out counter** a place in a supermarket where goods are packed and paid for. **check-up** a medical examination.

**cheer** *noun* a shout of praise or happiness. *The crowd gave a big cheer.* **cheer** *verb* to encourage with shouts.

**cheerful** *adjective* looking, sounding, and feeling happy. *The cheerful girl sang loudly in the shower.* **cheerfully** *adverb.*

**cheetah** *noun* a big cat with a spotted coat. It is the fastest land animal in the world.

**chef** *noun* a cook in a restaurant.

**chemical** *adjective* used in, made by, or connected with chemistry. **chemical** *noun.* **chemically** *adverb.*

**chemistry** *noun* the study of how substances are made up and how they react with other substances.

**chestnut** *noun* **1** a reddish-brown nut inside a prickly green case. **2** the tree on which these nuts grow. **chestnut** *adjective* a reddish-brown color.

**chest of drawers** *noun* a piece of furniture containing a set of drawers where clothes may be kept.

chestnut

**chew** *verb* to move food about in your mouth and grind it with your teeth, so it is easy to swallow. **chew over** to think about something carefully for a while.

**chicken** *noun* **1** a young bird, especially a hen. **2** the bird's meat used as food. *We had chicken for dinner.* **3** (slang) a coward or frightened person. **chicken out** not to do something because you are frightened.

**chickenpox** *noun* a disease marked by red itchy spots.

**chief** *noun* a leader or highest official. **chief** *adjective* most important. **chiefly** *adverb.*

**child** (children) *noun* **1** a young boy or girl. **2** a son or daughter. *I love my child.*

**childhood** *noun* the time when a person is a child.

**childish** *adjective* behaving like a child, often in a silly way. *It's very childish to shout and scream like that.*

**Chile** *noun* a long, thin country on the west coast of South America.

Chile

**chill** *noun* **1** an unpleasant coldness. *There is a chill in the air.* **chilly** *adjective.* **2** an illness caused by cold in which you might have a temperature, a headache, and feel shivery. **3** a feeling of fear and doom. **chill** *verb* **1** to make something colder. **2** to become cold with fear. **chilling** *adjective. We watched a chilling documentary last night.*

**chimney** *noun* a hollow brick tube on a roof through which smoke goes up into the air.

**chimpanzee** *noun* an African ape.

**chin** *noun* the front of the lower jaw.

**china** *noun* **1** a kind of fine white clay. **2** cups, saucers, plates, and ornaments made of china. *The china cupboard is full.* **3 China** a country in East Asia.

**Chinese** *noun* a person who comes from China. **Chinese** *adjective. We went to an excellent Chinese restaurant for dinner.*

**chipmunk** *noun* a small, striped animal with a long bushy tail, common in North America.

**chirp** *verb* to make a short, sharp sound like a bird or insect.

**Chisinau** *noun* the capital of Moldova in eastern Europe.

chipmunk

**chivalry** *noun* (say **shiv**-ul-ree) good manners, helpfulness, and polite behavior, particularly by men to women. **chivalrous** *adjective.*

**chocolate** *noun* **1** a sweet, edible substance made from cocoa beans. **2** a small candie or bar made of chocolate. *A box of chocolates.* **3** a hot drink made from the powder of crushed cocoa beans. **4** the color brown.

**choice** *noun* **1** a number of things from which you can choose. *We have a choice of three movies.* **2** the thing or things you have decided on. *The French film was my choice.* **3** the right, act, or possibility of choosing. *My friend had no choice but to come.* **choice** *adjective* of high quality, best. *We only sell choice wines.*

**choir** *noun* a group of people who sing together, for example in a church or school.

**choke** *noun* a device controlling the amount of air going into the engine that makes it easier to start a car. **choke** *verb* **1** to be unable to breathe properly because something is blocking the air passages. *He choked on a fish bone.* **2** to stop someone breathing by pressing on the throat or squeezing the neck. *The victim was choked to death.* **3** If a place is choked with cars or people, it is so full that it is impossible to move.

**cholesterol** *noun* (say kol-**est**-er-ol) a white, fatty substance found in the blood and tissues of animals and in egg yolk. Too much cholesterol is bad for the heart.

**choose** (choosing, chose, chosen) *verb* **1** to pick out a person or thing from a greater number. **2** to decide to do something. *We chose to stay a little longer.*

**chop** *noun* **1** a quick, heavy blow with a chopper or an ax. **2** a slice of meat, usually including a rib bone. **chop** (chopping, chopped) *verb* to cut wood or food into small pieces with a chopper, an ax, or a knife. **chop and change** to keep changing your mind about what to do.

**chopper** *noun* a heavy tool, like an ax, used for cutting wood or meat.

**chopsticks** *noun* a pair of sticks held in one hand to eat food, traditionally used in China and nearby countries.

**chord** *noun* (say kord) **1** a number of musical notes sounded at the same time. **2** in geometry, a straight line connecting two points on a curve.

**chore** *noun* (say chor) a small everyday task or duty that is usually fairly boring.

**choreography** *noun* (say ko-ree-**og**-ru-fee) the art of planning and arranging dances for the stage. **choreographer** *noun.*

**chorus** *noun* **1** a group of people who sing together. **2** a part of a song that is repeated after each verse by singers. **3** a group of singers or dancers who act together in a show. *She dances in the chorus.* **in chorus** at the same time. **chorus** *verb* when two or more people sing or say something at the same time.

**chose** past tense of choose.

**chosen** past participle of choose.

**Christian** *noun* a person who believes in Jesus Christ and his teachings. A member of the Christian Church. **Christian** *adjective* believing in the Christian religion. **Christianity** *noun.* The Christian religion, its beliefs, and practices.

**Christmas** (Christmases) *noun* the day when people celebrate the birth of Jesus Christ: 25 December. **Christmas Eve** the day before Christmas Day. **Christmas tree** an evergreen tree decorated at Christmas time.

Christmas tree

**chrome** *noun* (say krohm) a hard, silver-colored metal used for covering objects such as faucets and the handlebars of bikes.

**chronic** *adjective* lasting for a long time. *A chronic illness kept him away from work for several months.*

**chronological** *adjective* arranged in the order in which things happened, according to time. *I've listed the historical events in strict chronological order at the back of the book.* **chronologically** *adverb.* **chronology** *noun.*

**chrysalis** *noun* **1** (also called a pupa) a butterfly or moth in the stage between being a caterpillar and the time when it flies. **2** the hard covering (cocoon) of a chrysalis during that time.

**church** *noun* **1** a building in which Christians hold religious services. **2 the Church** a group of Christian people who believe the same things. *The Pope is head of the Roman Catholic Church throughout the world.*

chrysalis

**cigar** *noun* a roll of dried tobacco leaves that people smoke. *Cigars are usually much bigger than cigarettes.*

**cigarette** *noun* finely cut tobacco wrapped in paper that people smoke. Smoking is bad for the health.

**cinema** *noun* **1** a place where you can watch movies. **2** the art or business of making movies.

**cipher** *noun* (say **sy**-fer) **1** a secret way of writing; a code. *Inscribed with strange ciphers.* **2** empty.

**circa** *preposition* about, approximately, used in front of a date. *He died circa 1850.*

**circle** *noun* **1** a round, flat shape enclosed by a line. Every part of the line is the same distance from the center. **2** a circular form like a ring or a halo. **3** a group of people who like the same thing or have similar interests. *He is well respected in political circles.* **4** seats on the upper floor of a theater. **circle** *verb* to go around in a circle.

civil war

**circular** *adjective* **1** round, shaped like a circle. **2** moving in a circle, starting from one point and ending up in that same place. *We chose a circular route for our walk.*

**circular** *noun* a printed letter, advertisement, or notice sent to a large number of people.

**circulation** *noun* **1** the process of passing something around. *When will the tickets be put into circulation?* **2** the flow of blood through the body. *She's got good circulation.* **3** the movement of any substance around a system. *Air circulation.* **4** the average number of sold copies of a newspaper or magazine. *This magazine has a circulation of 50,000.* **circulate** *verb.*

**circumcision** *noun* cutting off the foreskin of the penis for medical or religious reasons. **circumcise** *verb.*

**circumference** *noun* the distance around a circle or round object.

**circumstance** *noun* the conditions that affect an event, situation, action, or person. *Mysterious circumstances surrounded her disappearance.* **under the circumstances** because of the way things are. *I decided it was the best thing to do under the circumstances.* **under no circumstances** never.

**circus** (circuses) *noun* a show with clowns, animals, and acrobats in a big tent. *The circus travels from one town to another giving performances to families.*

**cistern** *noun* a tank for storing water. *Flush the toilet and the cistern empties.*

**citizen** *noun* **1** a member of a state or country. *She's a British citizen.* **2** the inhabitant of a city.

**citrus fruit** *noun* a fruit with thickish peel and pulpy flesh, such as a lemon, orange, lime, or grapefruit. Many citrus fruits have a sour-sweet taste.

**city** *noun* a large town or its citizens.

**civil** *adjective* **1** belonging to the people, not military or religious. **2** ordinarily polite. *He answered with a civil reply.* **civility** *noun.* **civil rights** the right of citizens to freedom and equality. **Civil Service** in England, all government departments, except the armed forces.

**civilian** *noun* a person who is not a member of the armed forces.

**civilization** *noun* **1** a society that has reached a high level of education and culture. *The Greek civilization.* **2** the state of making or becoming civilized.

**civilize** *verb* to educate and bring culture to people.

**civil war** *noun* a war between people of the same country. *We learn about the American Civil War in school.*

**claim** *verb* **1** to say that something belongs to you. *Who claimed the lost umbrella?* **2** to say that something is a fact. *He claims to have written to me, but I haven't received the letter.* **3** to give as a reason for something. *He claimed he was late because he had missed the bus.* **claim** *noun* **1** a statement of something as a fact. *His claim to have written is a lie.* **2** a demand for something you have a right to. **3** a piece of ground or property belonging to somebody.

**clan** *noun* a large family or a group of families. *The Scottish clans were gathering on the border.*

**clap** (clapping, clapped) *verb* **1** to hit your hands together loudly, to show that you are pleased or to attract attention. *Everybody clapped when the music started.* **2** to hit somebody in a friendly way. *He clapped him on the shoulder and said, 'Hello'!* **clap** *noun* **1** the sound of people clapping. **2** a friendly slap. **3** a clap of thunder.

**clarinet** *noun* a woodwind instrument, shaped like a tube with a flared end. To play it you blow into it and cover the holes.

**clarity** *noun* clearness. *He explained it with such clarity that I understood immediately what he meant.*

**clash** *verb* **1** to fight, argue, or disagree with somebody. *Gangs of hooligans clashed with the police.* **2** When colors clash, they don't look good together, for example pink and orange. **3** to take place at the same time and therefore be difficult. *I can't go to the concert because it clashes with the tennis match.* **4** to make a loud sound, like the noise of metal objects being hit together. **clash** *noun.*

clarinet

**clasp** *noun* **1** a metal fastener for holding two things or the parts of something together. *I can't close my purse because the clasp has broken.* **2** a tight, firm hold with your fingers or arms. **clasp** *verb* to take something in your hands or arms and hold it tightly.

**class** (classes) *noun* **1** a group of pupils or students who are taught together. **2** people of the same social and economic group. **3** people, animals, or things that are similar. **4** an examination result. *A first-class degree in History.* **5** good style. *You can see from the way she dresses that she has class.* **class** *verb* to say that somebody or something belongs in a particular group of things; to put things in a class. *You can class all the books on this shelf as classics.* **in class** during the lesson. *We like to ask the teacher questions in class.*

**classic** *adjective* **1** of very high quality, outstanding. *A classic novel.* **2** well known and serving as a good example for what is expected. *This is a classic case of measles.* **classic** *noun* **1** a book or movie of very high quality. **2** Classics is the study of ancient Greek and Roman customs, language, and literature. *I am reading Classics at university.*

**classical** *adjective* **1** thought of as best, because it follows old traditions; serious and lasting. *I prefer classical ballet to modern dance.* **2** going back to Roman or Greek customs, art, and literature. *In classical times, many people had slaves to work for them.*

**classroom** *noun* a room in a school or college in which children or students are taught. *The geography classroom was full of students studying maps.*

**clause** *noun* **1** a part of a written agreement or legal document. *It was covered by a clause in the contract written in small print.* **2** a group of words with its own verb forming part of a sentence.

**claustrophobia** *noun* an abnormal fear of being in a small, closed space.

**claw** *noun* **1** a sharp nail on the toe of an animal or bird. *Cats have sharp claws.* **2** Crabs and lobsters catch and hold things with their claws. **3** an instrument like a hook fitted to some machines for lifting things. **claw** *verb* to pull and scratch with a claw or hand. *The cat clawed a hole in my armchair.*

Cc

**clay** *noun* a kind of earth that is soft when it is wet and hard when it is dry. Bricks and pots are made from clay.

**clean** *adjective* **1** without any dirt or marks. *I put on clean clothes.* **2** not yet used. *Can I have a clean sheet of paper?* **3** fair. *A clean fight.* **4** morally pure, not dirty or involving sex, drugs, or anything illegal. *He only tells clean jokes when there are girls around.* **clean** *adverb* entirely, absolutely, free from qualification. **clean** *verb* to make something clean from dirt or dust. *I cleaned the car for you.* **come clean** to decide to be honest and admit something you've kept secret. **clean up 1** to make an area or a person clean and tidy again. *Before my parents came back, we cleaned up the mess.* **2** You clean up when you win a bet and take all the money.

**clear** *adjective* **1** easy to see through. *The crystal is so clear, you can see through it.* **2** not cloudy. *A clear sky.* **3** easy to understand or hear. *A clear description.* **4** empty, free from blockages, unwanted things, or dangers. *A clear road ahead.* **5** free from doubt, guilt, or difficulty. *I'm very clear about my plans.* **6** free from obstruction. *Allow three clear days for your cold to pass.* **clear** *adverb* **1** easily heard or seen. *He said it loud and clear.* **2** out of the way, not near or touching. *Stand clear of the doors.* **clear** *verb* **1** to be or make free of something like clouds, murkiness, traffic, or unwanted objects. *The mist has cleared. The tablets will clear your headache.* **2** to get past something without touching it. *The horse cleared the fence.* **3** to state that somebody is not guilty. *The jury cleared him of all charges.* **4** to get somebody's permission for something. *You'll have to clear your plans with the manager.* **clearly** *adverb.* **clear away** to take away things that are no longer needed. **clear off** to go away. **clear up 1** to stop raining or being cloudy. **2** to make tidy. **3** to solve or settle a mystery or misunderstanding. **make yourself clear** to say something so that it is understood and there is no doubt about your wishes.

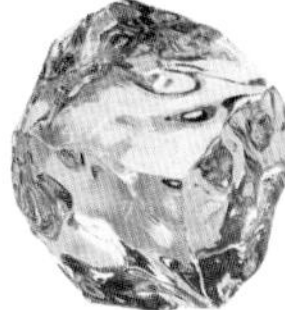

clear

**clench** *verb* to close tightly, especially your teeth or fist.

**clergy** *noun* ministers of the Christian Church. *The clergy wear surplices in church.*

**clerk** *noun* (rhymes with Dirk) a person who works in an office, bank, retail store, or law court and may look after accounts, records, and paperwork.

**cliché** *noun* (say **klee**-shay) a phrase that has been used so much that it has become meaningless.

**cliff** *noun* a steep rock or piece of land. *It was a long drop to the sea from the top of the cliff.*

**climate** *noun* the weather conditions of a place. *Oranges grow best in countries with a hot climate.*

**climax** *noun* the most important or exciting moment in a story, situation or experience, usually near the end. *The play built up to a climax.*

**cliff**

**climb** *verb* **1** to go up, down, or across something. *We climbed over the wall.* **2** to go higher. *Prices have climbed.* **3** to grow upward. *A rose climbing up a fence.* **climb** *noun. It was a hard climb.*

**climber** *noun* a person or plant that climbs.

**clinic** *noun* a place where people go to get specialist medical treatment or advice.

**clip** *noun* **1** a small metal or plastic fastener for holding things together. **2** a short piece of a movie or television program. **clip** *verb* **1** to cut. *Diane clipped the hedge with her shears.*

**cloak** *noun* **1** a loose coat without sleeves that fastens at the neck. **2** a covering. *Under the cloak of snow, the familiar fields looked completely different.* **cloak** *verb* to hide or cover secrets.

**clock** *noun* an instrument that tells the time. **turn the clock back** to go back to things or ideas as they were a long time ago. *The old lady looked at herself in the mirror and knew she couldn't put the clock back.* **clock in/out** *verb* to record the time when you start/stop work. *The workers clocked out at 4 p.m. every day.*

**clockwise** *adjective* moving in the same direction as the hands of the clock. *Turn the knob clockwise.*

**clockwork** *noun* a mechanism with wheels and springs that is wound up. **clockwork** *adjective. Clockwork toys.*

**clog** *noun* a wooden shoe or one with a wooden bottom. *Clogs are part of Holland's traditional dress.* **clog** (clogging, clogged) *verb* to become blocked with grease or dirt. **clog up** *The sink is clogged up.*

**cloister** *noun* **1** a monastery or convent. **2** a covered passage on the side of a court. **cloister** *verb* to confine or seclude from the world.

**clone** *noun* an animal or plant that has been produced in a laboratory from the cells of another animal or plant. A clone looks exactly like the animal from which it was made. **clone** *verb.*

**close** *adjective* (say klohss) **1** near. *My cousins are my close relatives.* **2** trusted and liked. *Sophie is my closest friend.* **3** tight, with little space between, especially in competitions and games. *It was a close contest.* **4** thorough and careful. *A close examination of the document showed that it was a forgery.* **5** warm and airless. **close** *adverb* (say klohss) **1** near. *I live quite close.* **2** almost. *Close to 30 years ago.* **close** *noun* (say klohz) **1** the end of an activity or a period of time. **2** (say klohss) an enclosed area around a cathedral. **3** In England, a short street closed at one end. *The cathedral choristers live in the close.* **close** *verb* (say klohz) **1** to shut. *She closed the door.* **2** to end. *The offer closes at the end of this month.* **closely** *adverb.* **closeness** *noun.* **close down** to stop work. *Most of the coal mines have closed down.* **close in** to come nearer and nearer. *Winter is closing in.* **close-up** *noun* a photograph or movie shot that is taken from very near. *In the close-up, you can see her wrinkles.*

**closed** *adjective* **1** not open. *The windows were closed.* **2** not open to the public, especially a store or museum. *Closed on Mondays.* **behind closed doors** in secret.

**closet** *noun* a small room for storing things. **closet** (closeting, closeted) *verb* to shut away. *They were closeted in the study.*

**closure** *noun* **1** the closing down of a factory, store, or business. **2** a closed condition, the end of a discussion. *Let's go to closure on this deal.*

**cloth** *noun* **1** woven fabric used for making clothes, coverings, and other things. **2** a piece of material for cleaning, for example, a dish cloth.

**clothes** *plural noun* things you wear, such as trousers, shirts, and dresses.

**clothing** *noun* clothes collectively. *You'll need waterproof clothing if you are going mountain biking in this wet weather.*

**cloud** *noun* **1** a mass of small drops of water that floats in the sky. *Clouds usually appear white or gray.* **2** a mass of smoke or dust in the air. **cloud** *verb* to become unclear. **cloudy** *adjective.* **cloud over** *The sky clouded over.* **under a cloud** out of favor, in disgrace. *He had an argument and left under a cloud.*

**clouds**

**clover** *noun* a small plant with three round leaves on each stem, used for fodder.

**clown** *noun* **1** a person in a circus who wears funny clothes and makeup, and says and does silly things to make people laugh. **2** a person who acts like a clown. **clown** *verb. Stop clowning around!*

**club** *noun* **1** a group of people who meet because they have the same interests. *My brother has joined the football club.* **2** the place where the club members meet. **3** a big, heavy stick with a thick end that can be used for fighting. **4** a specially shaped stick for hitting a golf ball. **5** a playing card with black clover leaves on it. *The King of Clubs.* **club** *verb* to hit somebody with a heavy stick. **club together** to give money to share the cost with others. *We all clubbed together to buy a present.*

**clue** *noun* something that helps you find the answer to a question or problem. *The footprints provided a clue.* **not to have a clue** not to know much about something.

**clump** *noun* a group. *A clump of daffodils.* **clump** *verb* to walk with heavy footsteps. *She clumped up the stairs in big heavy boots.*

clump

**clumsy** *adjective* **1** A clumsy person moves around awkwardly, walks into and knocks things over, breaking them. **2** tactless and not very skillful. *A clumsy explanation.*

**cluster** *noun* a small group of people or things close together. *Look at that cluster of bright stars.* **cluster** *verb* to form a tight group. *The sheep clustered together for warmth as the snow fell.*

**clutch** (clutches) *noun* **1** a tight hold. If you are in somebody's clutches, they have control over you. **2** the pedal you press in a car while changing gear. **clutch** *verb* to hold tightly.

**coach** (coaches) *noun* **1** a less expensive type of seat on a plane or train. **2** a train carriage designed to carry passengers. **3** a four-wheeled horse-drawn carriage that was used to carry passengers and mail. **4** a person who trains sportspeople. *The baseball team has a new coach.* **5** a teacher who gives private lessons. **coach** *verb* to train or teach. *She was coached by her dad to become a champion runner.*

**coal** *noun* **1** a hard black or brown mineral substance from under the earth that gives heat when it is burned. Coal is dug out of mines. **2** a piece of coal. **coal-scuttle** a container used to store coal by a fireside in the home.

**coarse** *adjective* **1** rough, not smooth. **2** rude, vulgar. **coarseness** *noun.*

coast

**coast** *noun* land right next to the sea. **coastal** *adjective.* **the coast is clear** when there is nobody around to see or catch you.

**coastline** *noun* the outline of the coast. *The rocky coastline is slowly being worn away.*

**coat** *noun* **1** a piece of clothing with sleeves that you wear over other clothes when you go outdoors. **2** an animal's fur or hair. **3** a layer of paint or varnish. *Let's give the wall another coat of paint.* **coat** *verb.*

**coating** *noun* a thin covering or layer spread over a surface. *The wall has an uneven coating of plaster.*

**coax** *verb* to persuade somebody to do something by speaking kindly and gently to them.

**cobra** *noun* (say **koh**-bruh) a poisonous snake. *A cobra was coiled up in the grass.*

**cobweb** *noun* a spider's web.

**cock** *noun* a male bird.

**cockerel** *noun* a young male fowl.

**Cockney** *noun* **1** a person born in the East End of London. **2** the dialect that Cockneys speak.

**cockpit** *noun* a compartment for the pilot of a plane or the driver of a racing car.

**cocoa** *noun* **1** a brown powder made from crushed cocoa seeds. **2** a hot drink made from cocoa powder and water or hot milk.

**coconut** *noun* **1** a large, round nut with a hard, hairy shell that grows on the coconut palm tree. **2** the white flesh inside the nut, which is used in cooking and baking.

**cocoon** *noun* a covering of silky threads that is produced by many insect larvae for protection.

**cod** (cod) *noun* a large sea fish or its meat.

**code** *noun* **1** a set of signals or a system of words, letters, or numbers used to write messages. *You can only crack a code if you know its system.* **2** a set of laws or rules. *You must know the state driving code if you want to pass your driving test.* **code** *verb* to replace the letters or numbers of a message with other letters or numbers. **coded** *adjective. A coded message.*

**coffee** *noun* **1** a drink made by pouring hot water on to the roasted and ground seeds, called coffee beans, of a tropical plant. *A cup of strong coffee.* **2** the coffee beans or powder the drink is made from.

**coffin** *noun* a box in which a dead person is buried. *A vampire rose from the stone coffin.*

**cog** *noun* one of a number of teeth around the edge of a wheel which moves and is moved by another wheel or part of a machine.

**cogwheel** *noun* a wheel with cogs or teeth.

**coin** *noun* a piece of metal money. **coin** *verb* **1** to manufacture coins. **2** to invent a new word or phrase.

**cogwheels**

**coincide** *verb* to happen at the same time as something else. *Her vacation coincided with his trip to Italy.*

**coincidence** *noun* a remarkable set of events. *By coincidence, the two brothers met on the plane to New York, although neither had known the other was intending to fly that day.*

**cold** *adjective* **1** not warm, having a low temperature. **2** unfriendly or unkind. *She seems very cold and unloving.* If something leaves you cold, you can't get excited about it. **cold** *noun* **1** low temperature, cold weather. *Wrap up warm if you're going out in the cold.* **2** an infectious illness that makes you sneeze and cough. *Dress up warmly, or you'll catch a cold.* **coldness** *noun.*

**cold-blooded** *adjective* **1** Cold-blooded animals have a body temperature that changes according to the temperature around them. Reptiles are cold-blooded. **2** (of a person) cruel and unfeeling.

**colic** *noun* a severe pain in the stomach, common in young babies.

**collaborate** *verb* to work together or with someone else on a job. **collaboration** *noun.*

**collapse** *verb* **1** to fall down suddenly. *The roof of the rickety barn collapsed in the high winds.* **2** If you collapse, you become weak or ill. **3** a sudden failure in the way something works. *The plan collapsed.* **4** to fold up, for example a table or chair. **collapse** *noun* the act of falling down or inward. **collapsible** *adjective. Collapsible chairs are easy to store.*

**collar** *noun* **1** the part of a shirt, dress, or coat that stands up or folds down around the neck. **2** a leather band around the neck of a dog, cat, or horse. **collar** *verb* to catch somebody. *The teacher collared the boy just as he was leaving the room and told him not to run.*

**colleague** *noun* a person you work with.

**college** *noun* **1** a large school where people can study after high school. **2** the part of a university that teaches a particular subject.

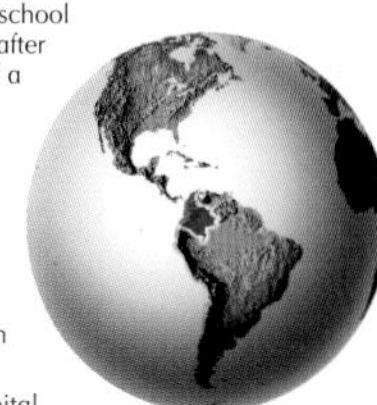

**Colombia**

**collide** *verb* to crash into something. *The two boys collided on the pitch.* **collision** *noun.*

**Colombia** *noun* a country in northern South America.

**Colombo** *noun* the capital of Sri Lanka in southern Asia.

**colon** *noun* **1** a mark (:), often put before listing a number of things. **2** the large part of the intestine.

**colonel** *noun* (say **ker**-nul) an army officer in charge of a regiment.

**colony** *noun* **1** a country that is controlled by another more powerful country. **2** a group of people of the same kind, or who have the same interests, living together. **3** a group of animals living together. *A colony of bees.*

**colossal** *adjective* huge, astonishing.

**color** *noun* **1** Color is what you see when light is broken up into parts. Red, blue, and green are colors. **2** something seen in all its colors, not just in black and white. **3** the quality that makes things interesting or more exciting. *He'll add color to the party.* **color** *verb* **1** to color in a picture, for example with crayons. **2** to influence somebody's opinion or feelings. **3** to blush or turn red in the face. **color-blind** unable to distinguish certain colors. **colored** *adjective.*

**column** *noun* **1** a tall stone holding up part of a building or standing alone; a pillar. *The Parthenon in Athens is surrounded by stone columns.* **2** a long, narrow shape. *A column of smoke.* **3** a daily feature, written by the same person, in a newspaper or magazine. **4** a vertical area of text on a page. *There are two columns on this page.* **5** a group of people or animals that move in a long line. *A column of ants crossed the forest floor.*

**coma** *noun* (say **koh**-muh) a state in which someone is not conscious for a long time, from which it is difficult to wake up, usually due to illness or an accident.

**comb** *noun* a piece of plastic or metal with a row of teeth, used for tidying your hair. **comb** *verb* **1** to brush your hair with a comb. **2** to search thoroughly. *We combed the house for the missing keys.*

**combination** *noun* **1** a mixture of things. *The club members are a good combination of young and old.* **2** a code of numbers or letters for opening a lock.

**combustion** *noun* the act of burning.

**come** (coming, came) *verb* **1** to move toward a place or a person who is speaking. **2** to arrive at a particular place or reach something, like a decision. *I've come to the conclusion that I like skating.* **3** to happen. *How did you come to be invited?* **4** to exist. *The T-shirts come in all colors.* **5** become. *My laces have come undone.* **come about** to happen. **come across** to meet or find. **come by** to get. **come in 1** to enter. **2** to become fashionable. **3** to be received. *A report of the accident has just come in.* **come in for** to get a share of something. *She's come in for some criticism.* **come into** to inherit. **come off 1** to take place or succeed. **2** to become unfastened. **3** to fall from something. *He came off his bike.* **come through** to survive a difficult situation. **come to 1** *The bill came to $20.* **2** to awake from unconsciousness. **come up 1** to come to attention, be mentioned, or discussed. *My question came up at the meeting.* **2** to be attainable. *An interesting job has come up.* **3** to win. *Your number might come up next time.* **come up against** to meet something, such as a difficult situation. **come up with** to think of.

**comedian** *noun* an actor who plays a funny part or a person who makes people laugh.

**comedy** *noun* a funny play, movie, or situation.

**comet** *noun* an object traveling across the sky that looks like a star with a bright tail of light.

**comfortable** *adjective* **1** relaxing and pleasant to be in or on. *A comfortable chair.* **2** having enough money. *We are comfortable and can afford most things now.* **3** free from pain or worry. *I feel comfortable talking to people I know.*

**comma** *noun* a mark (,) used in writing to show a pause or to separate items in a list. *Oranges, apples, and pears are all fruit.*

**comment** *noun* an opinion or explanation about an event, a book, or a person. *I have made a few comments on your essay.* **comment** *verb. She commented on my new tie.*

**commentary** (commentaries) *noun* **1** opinions and descriptions spoken during an event. *I listened to the commentary on the baseball game.* **2** a collection of written opinions and explanations on an event, a book, or a person. *I read the editor's commentary with interest.*

comet

**commerce** *noun* the buying and selling of goods on a large scale.

**commercial** *adjective* **1** used in commerce. **2** profitable, out to make money. *His movie is a commercial success.* **3** Commercial television and radio are paid for by advertisements. **commercial** *noun* an advertisement on television or radio.

**committee** *noun* a group of people chosen by others to carry out special duties.

**common** *adjective* **1** shared by two or more. *It is our common aim to save energy.* If people have something in common, they share the same interest or are somehow the same. **2** ordinary or happening often; familiar. *Smith is a common name.* **3** generally known. *It is common knowledge that smoking is bad for you.* **4** If something is done for the common good, it is done for all people. **common law** unwritten law based on customs. **common sense** good sense and the ability to make the right decision, gained from experience. **common** *noun* a grassy area of land where everybody is allowed to go.

**communicate** *verb* to make news, information, or your feelings known to other people. *The six-month-old baby girl communicates her wishes very clearly.*

**communication** *noun* **1** the act of sharing and exchanging news or information. **2** a message. **3** Communications are the things such as television, radio, telephone, fax, e-mail, roads, and railroads that link people and places.

**communism** *noun* a political system in which production is owned and controlled by the state. **communist** *noun.* **communist** *adjective.*

community

**community** (communities) *noun* **1** people living in one particular place or area. **2** a group of people living together and sharing interests, religion, or nationality.

**commuter** *noun* a person who travels regularly between home and work. **commute** *verb. I commute by train to my office in the city.*

**Comoros** *noun* a country in the Indian Ocean off the coast of East Africa.

**compact** *adjective* closely packed and neatly fitted together. *A compact kitchen.*

**compact disc** *noun* a disc from which recorded sound is reproduced. CD stands for Compact Disc.

**comparative** *adjective* judged by comparing and thinking about things. *Despite the noisy farm next door, they live in comparative peace and quiet.* **comparative** *noun* the form of an adjective or adverb that shows "more." The comparative of "good" is "better." **comparatively** *adverb.*

**compare** *verb* to look at and examine things or people to find out in what ways they are similar or different. *It's cold compared to yesterday.* **comparison** *noun.*

Cc

**compass** (compasses) *noun* (say **kum**-puhss) an instrument used for finding directions. The needle of a compass always points north.

**compasses** *noun* a V-shaped instrument with a sharp point, used for drawing circles.

**compatible** *adjective* able to exist or work well with another. The opposite of "compatible" is "incompatible."

**compel** (compelling, compelled) *verb* to make somebody do something they don't want to do.

**compensate** *verb* to make up for loss, injury, or damage, usually by paying money. **compensation** *noun. They asked for compensation for their ruined holiday.*

**compete** *verb* to take part in a game, race, or examination.

compete

**competent** *adjective* able to do something reasonably well. *She is a competent teacher.*

**competition** *noun* **1** a game, race, or other test that people try to win. **2** the act of trying to win or get something. *I was in competition with two other applicants for the job.* In business, competition means trying to get people to buy one thing rather than another. *Competition helps to keep prices down.*

**competitive** *adjective* **1** keen to take part in tests and enjoying competition. **2** Competitive prices are low prices. *Selling at competitive rates.*

**competitor** *noun* a person, firm, or product competing with others.

**complain** *verb* to say that you are not happy about something. *The neighbors complained about the noise from the boy-next-door's drum kit.*

**complaint** *noun* **1** a statement expressing unhappiness with a particular situation. *He made an official complaint.* **2** an illness.

**complement** *noun* **1** a complete set. *The ship had a full complement of sailors aboard.* **2** something that accentuates the good qualities of another thing.

**complete** *adjective* **1** whole. **2** finished. *When will work on the new house be complete?* **3** total, full. *The party was a complete surprise.* **complete** *verb* to finish doing something or add what is needed. **completion** *noun.*

**complex** *adjective* difficult to understand or explain. *A complex problem.* **complex** *noun* **1** a group of buildings or things connected with each other. *A new housing complex.* **2** an emotional problem that influences a person's behavior. *If you blame me, I'll get a guilt complex.*

**complexion** *noun* the natural color and quality of the skin of your face. *She has a beautiful complexion.*

**complicated** *adjective* difficult. *A complicated problem.* **complication** *noun.*

**compliment** *noun* an expression of praise and admiration. *He paid her a compliment on her new dress.* **compliment** *verb.*

**component** *noun* a part of a larger object or machine. *The bike's components are made in southern Italy.*

**compose** *verb* **1** to make up or form something. *The company is composed of managers, secretaries, and builders.* **2** to write music or poetry. **3** to make yourself calm. *Compose yourself before you speak.*

**composer** *noun* a person who writes music.

**composition** *noun* **1** a piece of music. **2** an essay or story written at school. **3** the various parts that make up something. *A chemical composition.* **4** an artistic arrangement. *The composition of the painting was unbalanced, with all the large elements on one side.*

**comprehend** *verb* to understand. *When she refused to marry him, he simply couldn't comprehend her reasons.* **comprehension** *noun* **1** the capability of understanding. **2** in an examination, an extract from a text about which questions are asked to test your understanding of it. *She made a score on her French comprehension exam.*

**comprehensive** *adjective* including everything needed. *The President gave a comprehensive explanation of his plans.*

compress

**compress** *verb* (say kum-**press**) to squeeze something together so it takes up less space. *Scrap metal is compressed into cubes before being recycled.* **compress** *noun* (say **kom**-press) a soft pad pressed on a wound to stop it bleeding.

**compromise** *noun* the settlement of differences of opinion through each side accepting less than it had asked for. *After a long discussion, we reached a compromise.* **compromise** *verb.* **to compromise yourself** to bring yourself into disrepute.

**compulsive** *adjective* not being able to stop yourself from doing something. **compulsion** *noun.*

**compulsory** *adjective* having to do something. *Education is compulsory for all children in Europe.* The opposite of "compulsory" is "optional."

**computer** *noun* an electronic machine that can make calculations, store information, or control other machines.

**computerize** *verb* **1** to store information on a computer. **2** to equip a business with computers.

**Conakry** *noun* the capital of Guinea.

**concave** *adjective* curved inward, like the inside of a hollow ball. The opposite of "concave" is "convex."

**conceal** *verb* to hide or keep secret. *The box concealed her diary.*

**conceited** *adjective* being too proud of yourself and your abilities; vain. **conceit** *noun.*

**concentrate** *verb* **1** to give all your attention to something. *You must concentrate more on your homework.* **2** to bring or come together. *Industry is concentrated in the north.* **concentrated** *adjective. Concentrated orange juice should be diluted with water.*

**concentration** *noun* **1** If something needs concentration, it requires all your attention. **2** a gathering. *A concentration of troops at the border.*

**concept** *noun* an idea.

**concern** *noun* **1** something that is very important to you. *Her well-being is my main concern.* **2** a business. *A profitable concern.* **concern** *verb.*

**conclude** *verb* **1** to end. **2** to decide or come to believe something after having thought it over. *When they didn't call back, he concluded that they had gone away.*

**conclusion** *noun* **1** an ending. **2** an opinion or judgment. *The jury reached the conclusion that he must be guilty.*

**concrete** *adjective* definite, real. *Can you give me a concrete example?* **concrete** *noun* building material made by mixing together cement, sand, gravel, and water. *A concrete bridge.*

concrete

**condemn** *verb* **1** to say that you find something wrong and unacceptable. *We condemn violence.* **2** to judge a person guilty or sentence a criminal. **3** to force somebody to suffer. *After her husband's death, she was condemned to a life of poverty.*

**condense** *verb* **1** to make a speech or piece of writing shorter. *He condensed his report to a few sentences.* **2** to change from gas or vapor into liquid. **3** to become thicker. **condensed** *adjective. Condensed milk.*

**condition** *noun* **1** the state somebody or something is in. *My bike is in very good condition.* **2** The conditions people live or work in are the surroundings that affect their well-being. *It is impossible to work under these conditions.* **3** something that is dependent on another thing, or necessary for something else. *You can come to stay on condition that you help with the baby.*



**condom** *noun* a rubber covering for the penis used as a means of birth control and to prevent infection.

**conduct** *noun* (say **kon**-dukt) **1** behavior. *His conduct at school has improved.* **2** the manner in which something is managed. **conduct** *verb* (say kun-**dukt**) **1** to behave. *They conducted themselves well.* **2** to lead or guide a person. **3** to control or manage a group. *To conduct a meeting.* **4** to direct. *To conduct an orchestra.* **5** to act as a path for electricity or heat.

**conductor** *noun* **1** a person who conducts musicians in an orchestra. **2** a person who collects fares from passengers on buses and trains. **3** something that conducts heat or electricity. *Copper is a good conductor.*

conductor

**confuse** *verb* **1** to make a person feel puzzled. To make something difficult to understand. *He confused me with his long explanation.* **2** to get things mixed up. *I'm always confusing her with her sister.* **confusion** *noun* **confusing** *adjective. A confusing explanation.*

**Congo** *noun* one of two countries in Africa; the Republic of the Congo is also called Congo-Brazzaville; the Democratic Republic of the Congo was formerly called Zaire.

**conifer** *noun* (say **kon**-if-er) a type of tree that has needle-like leaves and bears its fruit in cones. *A conifer plantation covered the hillside.*

**conjure** (say **kun**-juh) *verb* to do magic tricks. *The magician conjured a large white rabbit out of a hat.* **conjuror** *noun* a person who does magic tricks. **conjure up** to make something appear.

**connect** *verb* **1** to join together. *If we connect this wire with that one, it should work.* **2** to link by telephone. *Don't hang up, I'm trying to connect you.* **3** to be related or linked. *The families are connected.* **connection** *noun.*

**conquer** *verb* **1** to defeat and take over; to conquer a country. **2** to overcome an illness or a difficult situation. **conqueror** *noun.*

**conquest** *noun* **1** the conquering of something. *The conquest of Mount Everest.* **2** overcoming something.

**conscience** *noun* the part of your mind that tells you if what you are doing is right or wrong. *You have a guilty conscience when you do something wrong.*

**conscious** *adjective* **1** noticing what is happening. *He was conscious of everybody looking at him.* **2** awake. *The patient is conscious again.* **consciousness** *noun.*

**consequence** *noun* something that happens as a result of something else.

**conserve** *verb* to store or keep from going bad or being wasted. **conservation** *noun.*

**consider** *verb* **1** to think about something in order to make a decision. *I'm considering changing my job.* **2** to view as. *I consider him an idiot.* **consideration** *noun.* **take into consideration** to allow for something. *I will take your illness into consideration when marking your paper.*

**considerable** *adjective* a lot of. *She earned a considerable amount of money.*

**consist** *verb* to be made of. *Europe (right) consists of many different countries.*

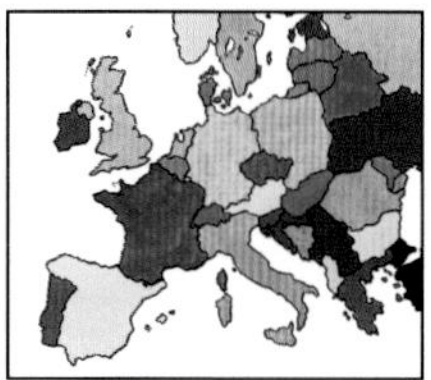

consist

**consonant** *noun* any of the letters of the alphabet except for the vowels a, e, i, o, and u. *How many consonants are there in your name?*

**conspiracy** *noun* a secret plan to do something that is against the law. A plot.

**conspirator** *noun* a person who takes part in a conspiracy.

**constellation** *noun* a group of stars whose outline is regarded as forming a pattern or figure.

**constipated** *adjective* unable to empty your bowels.

**constituency** *noun* a body of constituents, as in the voters in a district or an area represented.

**constitution** *noun* **1** a system of laws that states how a country is governed. *The constitution requires elections to be held every five years.* **2** the general condition of a person's health. **3** the way in which something is made.

**construct** *verb* to build or make by fitting parts together.

construct

**construction** *noun* **1** a building. **2** the process of building. *The bridge is under construction.* **3** words put together to form a phrase or sentence. *The construction of a sentence.* **4** an explanation. *The wrong construction was put on his behavior.*

**constructive** *adjective* helpful.

**consult** *verb* to go to a person or book for information. *You can consult a dictionary to find out how a word is spelled and what it means.*

**consultant** *noun* a person who is paid to give advice.

**consume** *verb* **1** to eat or drink something. **2** to use up. *The car consumes a lot of petrol.* **3** to destroy. *Locusts consumed the entire crop in a matter of hours.*

**consumer** *noun* a person who buys and uses goods and services.

**contact** *noun* **1** the process of touching or coming together; communication. *I'm not in contact with him.* **2** a person. *He's got some useful contacts.* **contact** *verb.*

**contact lens** *noun* a tiny piece of plastic shaped to fit over the eye to help you see clearly. *The supermodel wears disposable contact lenses.*

**contagious** *adjective* spreading from person to person. *A contagious disease.*

**contain** *verb* to hold. *The book contains all the information you need.*

**container** *noun* **1** a box, barrel, or bottle in which to hold things. **2** a metal box used for transporting goods.

**contemporary** *adjective* **1** happening now; modern. *Contemporary design.* **2** happening in the same period of time as something else. *Contemporary politicians were critical of Nixon.* **contemporary** *noun. Our fathers were contemporaries at school.*

**contempt** *noun* lack of respect, thinking that somebody or something is not important. *I hold him in contempt.*

**content** *adjective* (say kun-**tent**) happy, satisfied. *She was content with her life.*

**contents** *plural noun* (say **kon**-tents) things contained. *He emptied the contents of his pocket.*

**contest** *noun* (say **kon**-test) a struggle or fight in which people take part in order to win. *The race was an even contest.* **contest** *verb* (say kun-**test**) to compete or fight for a place. *To contest an election.*

**continent** *noun* one of Earth's huge land masses. *Europe, Asia, and North America are continents.*

**continual** *adjective* frequently recurring. *The continual tapping on the window by the tree branch was driving her crazy.*

**continue** *verb* **1** to go on doing or being something without stopping. **2** to start again after stopping. **continuation** *noun.*

**continuous** *adjective* without a break. **continuously** *adverb.* **continuity** *noun.*

**contract** *noun* (say **kon**-trakt) a written agreement between people. **contract** *verb* (say kun-**trakt**) **1** *We have been contracted to do the music for the wedding.* **2** to get a disease. *My sister has contracted German measles.* **3** to make or become smaller or shorter. *"Has not" is often contracted to "hasn't."* **contraction** *noun.*

**contradict** *verb* to say that something said or written is wrong. *Please don't contradict me.* **contradiction** *noun.*

**contrast** *noun* (say **kon**-trast) the difference seen between things when they are compared. *There was a big contrast between their results.* **contrast** *verb* (say kun-**trast**).

cook

**contribute** *verb* **1** to join with others in doing things or giving money to help make something successful. *She contributed toward my success.* **2** to write an article for a newspaper or magazine. **contribution** *noun. He made a contribution of $100.*

**control** *noun* the power to influence, make decisions, or give orders. **control** *verb* to have control of something. *The teacher can't control the class.*

**convenience** *noun* **1** ease of use. *I always buy frozen food for convenience when I'm busy at work.* **2** a useful appliance, such as a dishwasher. **3** a public toilet.

**convenient** *adjective* **1** easy to use or suitable. **2** easy to get to. *It's a convenient place to shop.*

**convent** *noun* a place where nuns live, work, and pray.

converge

**converge** *verb* to come from different directions and meet. *Let's meet where the roads converge.*

**conversation** *noun* a talk between people.

**converse** *verb* to have a conversation.

**convex** *adjective* curved outward, like the outside of a ball. The opposite of "convex" is "concave."

**convey** *verb* **1** to carry from one place to another. **2** to make known. *I would like to convey my deepest sympathy on the death of your father.*

**convict** *verb* (say kun-**vikt**) to find somebody guilty of a crime. *He was convicted of murder.* **convict** *noun* (say **kon**-vikt) a person who has been found guilty of a criminal offense.

**convoy** *noun* a group of ships or vehicles traveling together.

**cook** *verb* to make food. **cook** *noun. He's a wonderful cook.*

**cookie** *noun* a small, flat, dry, usually sweetened cake.

**cool** *adjective* **1** a temperature between warm and cold. **2** calm. *She keeps cool even when she is annoyed.* **cool** *verb* to make or become cool. *I cooled down in the pool.*

**cooperate** *verb* to work together for a common purpose. **cooperation** *noun.*

**cooperative** *adjective* **1** helpful. **2** owned by its members. *A cooperative business.*

**cope** *verb* to deal with something successfully. *She copes with all of her family's needs.*

**Copenhagen** *noun* the capital of Denmark in Europe.

**copper** *noun* a reddish-brown metal. Wires and some domestic water pipes are made of copper. **copper** *adjective. A copper color.*

**copy** *noun* **1** a thing that looks exactly like another. *Can I have a copy of the picture?* **2** an example of a book, newspaper, or magazine of which there are many others. *His copy of the book was torn.* **copy** *verb* **1** to make a copy of something. **2** to do the same as another person.

**coral** *noun* a hard red, pink, or white stony mass formed from the skeletons of tiny sea animals. *A coral reef is an amazing sight.*

coral

**cord** *noun* **1** a thick string. **2** wires inside a plastic casing for electrical equipment. **3** a part of the body. *We use our vocal cords to make sounds.*

**corduroy** *noun* thick, velvety cotton material with thin ridges raised on one side of the cloth. *A corduroy jacket.*

**core** *noun* **1** in various fruits such as apples or pears, the hard middle that contains the seeds. **2** the central, most important part of anything.

**cork** *noun* the soft, light bark of the cork oak. Cork tiles are used as a floor covering. **2** the cork stopper of glass containers such as wine bottles.

Cc

**corner** *noun* **1** the place where two edges, lines, walls, or streets meet. **2** a region. *The four corners of the world.* **in a corner** in a difficult situation. **corner** *verb* to drive into a corner.

**coronation** *noun* the crowning of a king or queen. *Our family all watched the coronation of the new king on television as we couldn't be there in person.*

**corporal** *adjective* of or relating to the body.

**corpse** *noun* a dead body.

**correct** *adjective* **1** without any mistakes. **2** most suitable in a particular situation. **correct** *verb* **1** to put something right and mark the mistakes. **2** to point out a person's faults in order to improve their behavior. **correction** *noun.*

**correspond** *verb* **1** to write letters to each other. **2** to be the same or in agreement with something. *Her report of the accident corresponds with his.* **3** to be like or match closely. *Our fence corresponds with his boundary.*

**correspondence** *noun* **1** writing and exchanging letters. **2** the letters you receive. *A pile of correspondence.* **3** likeness or relationship between particular things.

**corridor** *noun* a passageway or hall in a building.

**corrode** *verb* to destroy by chemical action or by rust. *Acid corrodes metal.* **corrosion** *noun.* **corrosive** *adjective. He used a corrosive acid to etch his drawing onto metal.*

**corrugated** *adjective* shaped into ridges or folds. *Corrugated paper is used for packing.*

**corrupt** *adjective* immoral or wicked. *The newspaper exposed the corrupt politicians.* **corrupt** *verb* to make somebody change from good to bad. *Power corrupts people.* **corruption** *noun. Corruption at the heart of the government brought about its downfall.*

**cosmetics** *noun* substances such as lipstick and eyeshadow, used to beautify the face.

**cosmic** *adjective* related to the universe. *Cosmic rays from outer space.*

**cosmonaut** *noun* a Russian astronaut.

**cosmos** *noun* (say **koz**-moce) the universe.

**cost** *noun* the price of something. **at all costs** no matter what the cost. **cost** (costing, cost) *verb* **1** to have a certain price. **2** to cause a loss or disadvantage to somebody. *Drunken driving costs lives.* **3** to estimate. *He costed my antiques.*

cosmonaut

Costa Rica's flag

**Costa Rica** *noun* a country in Central America.

**costume** *noun* clothes worn by actors or by people at a particular time in history. *National costume is sometimes worn on historic occasions.*

**cot** *noun* a bed with high sides for a baby.

**cottage** *noun* a small house, especially in the country.

**cotton** *noun* **1** cloth made from the soft white fibers covering the seeds of the cotton plant. **2** a tall tropical plant. **3** cotton thread.

**cotton ball** *noun* soft, fluffy cotton used for putting cream on your skin or cleaning wounds. *She used a cotton ball to remove her makeup.*

**couch** *noun* a sofa. *Please sit on the couch.*

**cough** *verb* to push air out of your throat and make a sudden, harsh noise. **cough** *noun* **1** the sound of coughing. **2** an illness that makes you cough. *The baby had a nasty cough.*

**could** past tense of the verb "can".

**council** *noun* a group of people chosen to make laws and decisions and to run a town or county. *The council gave us permission to stage a week-long music festival in the town square.*

**councilor** *noun* a member of a council.

**counsel** *noun* **1** advice. **2** a group of lawyers acting for somebody in court. **counsel** (counseling, counseled) *verb. She counsels families who have problems.*

**counselor** *noun* a person trained to give advice and help to people in need.

**count** *noun* **1** counting. **2** a number reached by counting. **3** one of a number of crimes somebody is accused of. *He was found guilty on all counts.* **4** a European nobleman equal to an English earl. *The count married a beautiful girl from a neighboring town.* **count** *verb* **1** to say numbers in order. *He counted up to 10.* **2** to say or name objects or people to find the total number in a collection. *The teacher counted the children.* **3** to include. *There are four of us, counting me.* **4** to have importance or value. *It's the thought that counts.* **5** to consider. *I count myself lucky.* **lose count** not know the exact number. *I've lost count of how many times I've been there.*

**counter** *noun* **1** a flat surface like a table on which goods are shown and where customers are served in a store or bank. **2** a small, flat, round piece of plastic or wood used in board games. **counter** *verb* **1** to act against something. **2** to meet an attack by hitting back.

**counterfeit** *noun* a copy of something made in order to deceive, a fake. **counterfeit** *adjective. Counterfeit money.* **counterfeit** *verb. It is illegal to counterfeit money.*

**country** *noun* **1** a land with its own people, government, and language. **2** all the people who live in a particular country. *The President spoke to the country via TV.* **3** land away from towns. *We live in the country.*

**county** (counties) *noun* a region in a state or country that has its own local government. *Orange county.*

**couple** *noun* **1** two people or things. **2** two people who are married or live together. **couple** *verb* to connect or link together.

**coupon** *noun* a ticket or piece of printed paper allowing the holder to receive goods or information or to pay less money than usual for something.

**courage** *noun* the ability to control fear and face danger or difficulty. **courageous** *adjective.*

**courier** *noun* **1** a messenger who takes letters and parcels from one place to another, usually as quickly as possible. **2** a person who works for a travel company and looks after tourists.

courier

**course** *noun* **1** lessons or lectures on a particular subject. **2** a series of events or things you can do in a particular situation. **3** the direction or route in which something goes. **4** part of a meal. *What would you like for your main course?* **5** a ground for certain games. *A golf course.* **in the course of** during. **of course** certainly.

**court** *noun* **1** a place where law cases are heard and judged. **2** a place where a king or queen, their family, and officials live. **3** an area for games. *A tennis court.* **court** *verb* to try to win somebody's love.

**courtesy** *noun* (say **ker**-tuh-see) polite behavior. **courteous** *adjective.*

**cousin** *noun* the child of your uncle or aunt.

**cove** *noun* a small bay on the coast.

cove

**cover** *noun* **1** a thing put on to cover another thing. **2** the binding of a book. **3** something that shelters you from bad weather. *We spent the day under cover.* **4** a guarantee from an insurance company against loss or damage. **cover** *verb* **1** to put something on or around something else to protect or hide it. *I covered my eyes.* **2** to spread over. *Snow covered the fields.* **3** to travel a certain distance. **4** to have enough money for something. *$10 should cover the gasoline.* **5** to deal with or discuss a subject. *The book covers the whole of modern history.* **6** to insure against damage or loss.

**coward** *noun* a person who shows fear and avoids dangerous situations. *Cowards lack courage.* **cowardly** *adjective.*

**cowardice** *noun* cowardly behavior.

cowboy

**cowboy, cowgirl** *noun* a person whose job is to take care of cattle.

**coy** *adjective* pretending to be shy and modest. *She gave him a coy smile.*

**crab** *noun* a sea animal with a shell-covered body and five pairs of legs, the first pair modified as pincers.

**crack** *noun* **1** a thin line on the surface of a glass or plate, for example, where it has cracked but not come apart completely. **2** a narrow gap or split. **3** a sudden loud noise. **crack** *verb* **1** to split or make something split. *The hot water cracked the glass.* **2** to make a sudden loud noise. *To crack a whip.* **3** to break down. *After days of questioning, he finally cracked.* **crack a problem** to finally solve a problem. **crack a joke** to tell a joke. **crack up** to break down. **at the crack of dawn** very early in the morning. *Our flight is leaving at the crack of dawn.* **have a crack at something** to try to perform a difficult task. *He had a crack at hitting the bull's-eye, but missed the target completely.*

**cracker** *noun* **1** a firework that explodes with a crack. *The crowd let off hundreds of crackers to celebrate Chinese New Year.* **2** a thin, dry type of hard, flat bread that is often eaten with cheese.

**cradle** *noun* a baby's small bed, made so that it can be gently rocked. **from the cradle to the grave** from birth to death. **cradle** *verb* to hold gently.

**craft** *noun* **1** a skill, especially in making things with your hands. *Pottery, patchwork, weaving, and woodwork are all crafts.* **2** the skill of tricking people. **3** a ship, boat, plane, or rocket. **crafty** *adjective. I wouldn't trust him; he's very crafty.*

**cram** (cramming, crammed) *verb* **1** to push lots of things or people into a small space. **2** to fill. *His head was crammed with facts.*

**crane** *noun* **1** a machine for lifting and moving heavy objects. **2** a large bird with a long neck and long legs. **crane** *verb* to stretch out your neck in order to see something better.

**crash** *noun* **1** a loud noise made by something falling or breaking. **2** a bad accident. **3** a business failure. **crash** *verb* **1** to make a loud noise when falling, or hitting something violently. **2** to hit and damage something. *She crashed into the car in front of her.* **3** to move noisily or break through something with force. *He crashes through the house like an elephant.* **4** to fail, especially in business or money matters. *The stock market crashed.*

**crate** *noun* a box made of wood for putting goods in. *A crate of oranges.*

**crater** *noun* **1** a round hole in the top of a volcano. **2** a very large round hole in the ground or on the surface of another planet.

**crawl** *verb* **1** to move on your hands and knees with the body close to the ground. **2** to move slowly. *The traffic was crawling along.* **3** to be full of or covered with crawling things. *Don't sit on the grass; it's crawling with ants.* **4** If something makes your skin crawl, it gives you a bad feeling. **crawl** *noun* **1** a slow crawling movement. **2** a fast swimming stroke.

**crawl**

**crazy** *adjective* **1** foolish. **2** very interested or excited. *My brother is crazy about football.* **crazily** *adverb.* **craziness** *noun.*

**creak** *verb* to make a sound, usually when something is moved or moves. **creak** *noun* the sound of wood bending or an unoiled door opening.

**cream** *noun* **1** the fatty part of milk. *We had cream on our strawberries.* **2** food with a texture similar to cream. **3** a soft substance that you put on your skin to make it soft or to soothe it. **4** the best part of something. *The cream of society.* **creamy** *adjective.* **cream** *verb* to mix food until it has the consistency of cream. **cream** *adjective* a whitish color.

**cream**

**crease** *noun* **1** a line made on cloth, paper, or clothes by folding, crushing, or pressing. **2** a wrinkle in skin. **crease** *verb. I creased my dress by sitting for a long time on a fold of the fabric.*

**create** *verb* **1** to make something new. *They have created a garden in the desert.* **2** to produce or cause something to happen. *The new hit musical created a revival of Fifties fashion.*

**creation** *noun* **1** the process of making something. *The creation of great works of art.* **2** a thing created. *The sculpture is all my own creation.*

**creative** *adjective* able to invent and produce new ideas and things; imaginative.

**creator** *noun* a person who makes or invents a thing.

**creature** *noun* a living being.

**crèche** *noun* (say kresh) a day nursery for babies and young children.

**credit** *noun* **1** the practice of allowing somebody to buy something and pay for it later. **2** the money a bank or business has agreed somebody can borrow. **3** the time you are allowed to pay a debt. *They gave us a month's credit.* **4** somebody with a good reputation. *He's a credit to the school.* **5** trust. *Don't give any credit to what he says.* **6** Credits are the list of people who helped to make a movie or TV program. **credit** *verb* **1** to believe. **2** to say that somebody has done something. *She is credited with many achievements.* **3** to increase an account with a sum of money. *We will credit your account with the refund.* **credit card** a plastic card you can use to buy goods on credit.

**creditor** *noun* a person to whom money is owed.

**creed** *noun* a set of beliefs or opinions.

**creek** *noun* **1** a small inlet on the sea coast. **2** a stream of water smaller than a river and larger than a brook.

**creep** (crept) *verb* **1** to move slowly and quietly. *She creeps around the house.* **2** to move slowly toward or across something. **creep** *noun* an annoying person you dislike. *That creep always flatters the boss.* If someone or something gives you the creeps, they make you feel nervous. **creepy** *adjective. A creepy story.*

**cremate** *verb* to burn a dead body to ashes. **cremation** *noun. After the cremation, we buried the ashes.*

**crematorium** *noun* a place where a body is cremated.

**crescent** *noun* **1** a curved shape like a crescent moon. **2** a curved street.

**crevice** *noun* an opening or crack in a rock.

**crew** *noun* **1** all the people working on a ship, plane, or spacecraft. **2** a group of people working together. *The film crew started work at dawn.*

**crib** *noun* **1** a new-born baby's small bed with bars on the sides. **2** a wooden box in a stable where food is left out for animals.

cricket

**cricket** *noun* **1** an insect like a grasshopper. The males produce a chirping sound. **2** an outdoor game played by two teams on a grass pitch with a ball, bats, and two wickets.

**cried** past tense of the verb "cry."

**crime** *noun* **1** an unlawful activity. **2** an action that you feel is wrong, but not a matter for the police. *It would be a crime not to enjoy the sunshine.*

**criminal** *noun* a person who has committed a crime. **criminal** *adjective. A criminal act.*

**crimson** *adjective* a dark purple-red color.

**cringe** *verb* to move back with fear.

**crisis** *noun* a serious situation which is at the point of getting better or worse.

**crisp** *adjective* **1** dry and easily broken. *Crisp pastry.* **2** fresh or newly made. *A crisp shirt.* **3** fresh and cold. *A crisp morning.* **4** quick and clear. *A crisp hello.*

**critic** *noun* **1** a person who gives his opinion about books, movies, music, or art. **2** a person who points out the mistakes in someone or something.

**critical** *adjective* **1** finding faults or mistakes. *He made critical remarks about my work.* **2** very dangerous, coming to a crisis. *A critical illness.* **critically** *adverb.*

**criticism** *noun* **1** pointing out faults and mistakes. **2** a critic's opinion on books, movies, music, or art. **criticize** *verb.*

Croatia's flag

**Croatia** *noun* a country in Southeast Europe.

**crockery** *noun* cups, plates, and other dishes. *He displayed all their crockery on the dresser.*

**croissant** *noun* (say **krwah**-sahn) a crescent-shaped bread roll.

**cross** *noun* **1** a mark that looks like an X. **2** an upright post with another shorter bar going across. The cross is an important Christian symbol. **3** a mixture of two animals or plants. *A mule is a cross between a horse and a donkey.* **cross** *verb* **1** to be angry. **2** to go across something. **3** to draw lines across something. **4** to put one arm, leg, or finger on top of the other. **5** to mix one animal or plant with another. **6** to oppose somebody's wishes. *If you cross me, I'll get angry.*

**crouch** *verb* to lower your body close to the ground by bending your knees and back.

**crowd** *noun* a large group of people in one place. **crowd** *verb* **1** to come together in a large group. **2** to fill completely. *The new museum was crowded with tourists carrying cameras.* **3** to cram in.

**crown** *noun* **1** a headdress like a ring made of gold and jewels, worn by a king or queen. **2** The Crown is the governing power of a monarchy. **3** the top part of your head. **crown** *verb* to put a crown on somebody who has become king or queen. **crown jewels** the magnificent regalia and other jewelry worn by a monarch on certain State occasions.

**crucial** *adjective* (say **kroo**-shuhl) extremely important. *A crucial appointment.*

**crucify** (crucifying, crucified) *verb* to punish by nailing or binding a person to a cross and leaving them to die. **crucifixion** *noun.* **The Crucifixion** the death of Jesus Christ on the Cross, or a picture representing it.

**crude** *adjective* **1** in a raw or natural state. *Crude oil.* **2** rough, not skillfully made. *A crude drawing.* **3** not showing sensitive feeling; vulgar. *Crude jokes.*

**cruel** (crueler, cruelest) *adjective* causing pain or suffering to people or animals. **cruelty** *noun.*

cruise

**cruise** *noun* a vacation on a ship that visits a number of places. **cruise** *verb* to move in a car or ship at a comfortable speed.

**crumb** *noun* a very small piece, especially of bread, cake, or cookie.

**crumble** *verb* **1** to break or fall into lots of small pieces. **2** to lose power or to come to an end or to nothing. *Her hopes soon crumbled.*

**crumple** *verb* to become full of creases and folds. *She crumpled up the envelope.*

**crunch** *verb* **1** to crush hard food noisily with your teeth. *The dog was crunching a bone.* **2** to make a crushing or breaking noise. **crunch** *noun* **1** crunching **2** a crunching noise. *The crunch of footsteps on the gravel drive.* **the crunch** a point when a difficult decision has to be made. *When it came to the crunch, I decided to marry Bill instead of Tom.* **crunch time** a period when you have to make the most effort to achieve something.

**crusade** *noun* **1** any of several expeditions to Palestine made by Christian knights in the Middle Ages. **2** a movement against something bad or for something good. *A crusade against smoking in public places.*

**crustacean** *noun* (say krust-**ay**-shuhn) an animal with a shell. Crabs and lobsters are crustaceans.

**crutch** *noun* a stick with a crosspiece at the top that fits under the arm to support people who have difficulty walking.

**crustacean**

**cry** (cries) *noun* **1** a sound you make when you feel excited or frightened. *A cry of pain.* **2** a shout to attract somebody's attention. **3** weeping. **cry** (cried) *verb* **1** to shed tears. **2** to shout or say something loudly. *She cried for help.*

**crypt** *noun* an underground room in a church.

**crystal** *noun* **1** a natural mineral that looks like ice. **2** a shaped piece of this mineral used in jewelry or decoration. **3** high-quality glass, often cut. **crystal** *adjective. Crystal clear.*

**Cuba** *noun* a country in the Caribbean.

**cube** *noun* **1** an object with six square sides that are all the same size. *A cube of sugar.* **2** the number made by multiplying a number by itself twice. The cube of 2 is 2 x 2 x 2, which makes 8. **cube** *verb* **1** to multiply a number by itself twice. **2** to cut something into cubes. **cubed** *adjective. The cubed cushion made a good footrest.*

**cubicle** *noun* a small room, especially for changing clothes. *A swimming pool cubicle.*

**cuckoo** *noun* **1** a bird that lays its eggs in other birds' nests. **2** the sound a cuckoo makes.

**cud** *noun* the half-eaten food that cows and sheep bring up a number of times, before finally swallowing.

**cue** *noun* **1** a signal for somebody to do or say something. **2** a long stick used to hit the balls in a game of pool.

**culprit** *noun* a person who has done something wrong. *The culprit owned up.*

**cultivate** *verb* **1** to use land for growing crops. **2** to develop something and make it strong. **cultivation** *noun. Rice cultivation in Thailand.*

**cultivate**

**culture** *noun* **1** an understanding of literature, art, music, and other activities of the mind. **2** the shared customs and traditions of a group of people at a particular time. *He studied the Inca culture.* **3** a group of cells grown in a laboratory for medical study. **4** the cultivation of plants and the rearing of bees. **cultural** *adjective.*

**cultured** *adjective* well educated, with good manners and a knowledge of the arts.

**cunning** *adjective* clever in deceiving others. *He's as cunning as a fox.* **cunning** *noun.*

**cupboard** *noun* a piece of furniture with shelves and a door for keeping things in.

**curb** *verb* to keep something under control. *The government has curbed the powers of the police.* **curb** *noun* a border or edging.

**cure** (cured, curing) *verb* **1** to make an illness disappear or a person well again. *There are many diseases that drugs can cure.* **2** to stop something bad. *We are working hard to cure his stinginess.* **3** to preserve something to make it last longer. *Fish and meat can be cured by drying, smoking, or salting.* **cure** *noun. Doctors are searching for a cure for the common cold.*

**curious** *adjective* **1** interested in things and wanting to find out. *I'm curious to know what he said to my mother the other day.* **2** unusual and interesting. *That's a curious story!* **curiosity** *noun.*

**curl** *noun* **1** a twist, wave, or ringlet of hair. *Goldilocks had long golden curls.* **2** a spiral shape. *A curl of butter.* **curl** *verb* to twist hair into curls or be in curls. **curl up** **1** to form curls or twists. *The leaves have turned brown and curled up.* **2** to lie with your arms and legs drawn close to the body. *She curled up in the large armchair in front of the fire.*

**curly** *adjective* full of curls. *My sister has curly hair like my Dad's, but mine is straight.*

**currant** *noun* **1** a small dried grape used in baking and cooking. **2** a soft red, black, or white berry. *Blackcurrant juice.*

**currency** (currencies) *noun* **1** the money used in a country. *The value of foreign currencies is always changing.* **2** the common use of something. If an idea gains currency, more people get used to it and accept it.

**current** *adjective* happening or being used now. *The current craze for body piercing.* **current** *noun* **1** water or air moving in one direction. *The river has a strong current.* **2** the flow of electricity. *An electric current.*

**curry** (curries) *noun* meat or vegetables cooked with hot-tasting spices, often served with rice. *I love to cook Indian curries.*

**curse** *noun* a word, phrase, or sentence asking supernatural powers to harm somebody or something. *There must be a curse on our family, because everything is going wrong.* **curse** *verb* **1** to swear or say rude words because you are angry. **2** to use a curse against somebody. *The witch cursed the princess.*

**cursor** *noun* a small movable point on a computer screen used to identify a position.

**curtain** *noun* **1** a piece of material hung up at a window or door. **2** the heavy sheet of material lowered in front of a theater stage. **3** something that covers or hides. *A curtain of mist descended over the hills.*

**curve** *verb* to bend. *The road curves at the top of the hill.* **curve** *noun* a bending line, like the edge of a circle. *A curve in the road.* **curvy** *adjective.*

**cushion** *noun* **1** a pillow filled with soft material to sit on or lean against. **2** anything soft or springy in the shape of a square. *We floated on a cushion of air.* **cushion** *verb* to protect from shock, a knock, hardship, or change. *The branches must have cushioned his fall.*

**custody** *noun* **1** the legal right of caring and looking after a child. *The mother was given custody of the children.* **2** imprisonment. **take into custody** to arrest.

**custom** *noun* **1** something that is accepted behavior among people or that people of a particular society always do at a certain time. *Different countries have different customs.* **2** regular business given to a store by customers. *The local store lost most of its custom to the new supermarket.*

**custom**

**customer** *noun* a person who buys goods from a store or uses a bank or other business.

**customs** *plural noun* a place where government officers check your luggage for goods on which you need to pay duty (tax) when your enter or leave a country. *We were stopped at customs.*

**cut** *noun* **1** the act of cutting. **2** the result of cutting. *There's a cut in the cloth.* **3** an opening or small wound. **4** a reduction. *A price cut.* **5** a part that is cut out. *I noticed lots of cuts in the movie.* **6** a style or shape. *A good haircut.* **7** a share. *She promised me a cut of her win if I gave her $1.00 to buy a lottery ticket.* **cut** (cutting, cut) *verb* **1** to make an opening in your skin with something sharp. *I cut my finger.* **2** to divide, break, or make something shorter with a knife, scissors, or another sharp instrument. *I've cut some flowers.* **3** to reduce time, size, or quantity. *Stores are cutting prices.* **4** to shorten something. *The movie was cut by twenty minutes.* **5** to make a recording. *We cut a disc.* **cut and dried** already decided and impossible to change. **cut back** to reduce. *Factories are cutting back on staff.* **cut in** to interrupt. **cut off** **1** to stop a person while speaking. *He cut me off when I was in the middle of asking a question.* **2** to stop a telephone connection. *We were cut off and the line went dead.* **3** to remove something from its source, as a flower from a bush. **4** to stop the supply. *The electricity was cut off because we couldn't pay the bill.*

**cute** *adjective* **1** pretty; attractive. *She's a cute little girl.* **2** clever. *That's a cute idea.*

**cutlery** *noun* knives, forks, and spoons.

**cycle** (cycling, cycled) *verb* to ride a bicycle or tricycle. **cyclist** *noun* someone who cycles.

**cyclone** *noun* (say **seye**-klohn) **1** a tropical storm that moves very fast around a calm central area. **2** a violent hurricane with a narrow diameter.

**cygnet** *noun* (say **sig**-nit) a young swan.

**cylinder** *noun* an object or container with a long tubular body.

**cynic** *noun* (say **sin**-ik) a person who sees no good in anything and believes that people always behave in a selfish way. **cynical** *adjective.*

**Cypriot** *noun* a person who comes from Cyprus. **Cypriot** *adjective. A Cypriot dance.*

**Cyprus** *noun* an island country in the eastern Mediterranean Sea. The island is divided into Greek-Cypriot and Turkish-Cypriot areas.

**Cyprus's flag**

**czar** *noun* (say zar) the title of the former emperors of Russia.

**Czech** *noun* (say chek) **1** the language spoken in the Czech Republic. **2** a person who comes from the Czech Republic. **Czech** *adjective. A Czech tennis player won Wimbledon.*

**Czech Republic** *noun* a country in eastern Europe, formerly called Czechoslovakia.

**dab** (dabs, dabbing, dabbed) *verb* to touch quickly and gently with something soft. *She dabbed the dirty mark with a damp cloth.*

**dachshund** *noun* a small black or brown dog with a long body and very short legs.

**dad** *or* **daddy** (daddies) *noun* an informal word for father.

**daddy-long-legs** *noun* also known as a cranefly, a flying insect with very long legs.

**daffodil** *noun* a tall plant with a yellow or white bell-shaped flower that grows from a bulb in spring.

**daft** *adjective* silly or foolish. *You really look daft in those trousers – they're far too short for you!*

**dagger** *noun* a weapon for stabbing that looks like a short, pointed knife.

**Dáil** (say doyle) *noun* the lower house in the parliament (central government) of the Republic of Ireland, the equivalent of the British House of Commons.

**daily** *adjective* happening or done every day. **daily** *adverb.* **daily** (dailies) *noun* a newspaper that is published every day except on Sunday.

**dainty** (daintier, daintiest) *adjective* small, pretty, and delicate. *Dainty feet.* **daintiness** *noun.* **daintily** *adverb.*

**dairy** (dairies) *noun* a place where milk is put into bottles and where milk products such as butter and cheese are made and sold. **dairy** *adjective.*

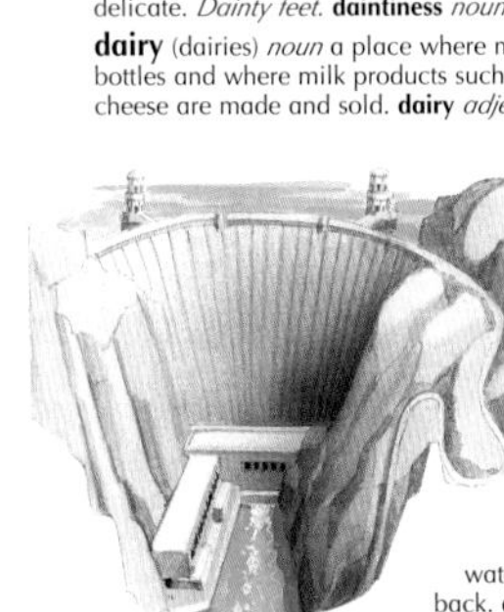

dam

**daisy** *noun* a small wild flower with a yellow center and white petals.

**Dakar** *noun* the capital of Senegal in West Africa.

**dam** *noun* **1** a strong barrier or wall built across a river to hold back water. **2** the water held back. **dam** (dams, damming, dammed) *verb.*

**damage** *verb* to harm or spoil something. **damage** *noun.* **damaging** *adjective.*

**damages** *noun* money that somebody is paid for injury or harm done to them. *She was awarded $100 in damages by the supermarket after she slipped on the wet floor and twisted her ankle.*

**Damascus** *noun* the capital of Syria in southwest Asia.

**damp** *adjective* moist or slightly wet. **dampness** *noun.*

dance

**dance** *verb* to move your feet and body to the rhythm of music. **dance** *noun* **1** a style of dancing with special set steps, e.g., a waltz, a gavotte, or the tango. **2** a party at which there is dancing. **dancer** *noun.*

**dandelion** *noun* a wild plant with a yellow flower and round fluffy seed head.

**dandruff** *noun* small flakes or scales of dead skin found on the scalps of some people.

**danger** *noun* **1** the chance that something may happen that will cause harm or injury. **2** a situation that is not safe. *The tunnel is in danger of collapsing.* **danger** *interjection. Danger! Falling rocks.* **dangerous** *adjective.*

**Danish** *adjective* of Denmark or its people. *A Danish ship.* **Danish** *noun.* The language spoken in Denmark.

**dank** *adjective* damp and cold.

**dappled** *adjective* marked with patches or spots of dark and light colors. *A dappled horse.*

**dare** *verb* **1** to be brave enough or rude enough to do or try to do something. *How dare you contradict me!* **2** to challenge somebody to do something brave. *I dare you to jump.* **dare** *noun.*

**daring** *adjective* brave and not afraid to take chances. **daring** *noun.*

**dark** *adjective* **1** with little or no light. **dark** *noun* darkness. **2** not light or fair in color. *She has dark hair.* **in the dark** not knowing about something. **a dark horse** somebody who may have unexpected, hidden abilities.

**darken** *verb* to make or become dark.

**darn** *verb* to mend a hole in a piece of clothing by sewing threads across it.

**dart** *noun* a small arrow that players throw at a round board marked with numbers in a game called darts. **dart** *verb* to move suddenly and quickly.

**dash** *noun.* **1** a short line (–) used in writing. **2** a small amount. *A dash of salt.* **dash** *verb* to rush somewhere.

**data** *noun* facts and information.

**database** *noun* a large amount of information stored on a computer.

**date** *noun* **1** the day, month, and/or year of a particular event. **2** an appointment to meet somebody, particularly a boyfriend or girlfriend. **3** the brown, sticky fruit of the date palm. **date** *verb* **1** to put a date on a letter. **2** to guess or give a date when something was made. *This church dates from 1400.* **3** to go out with a boyfriend or girlfriend. **out-of-date** **1** old-fashioned. **2** no longer valid. *An out-of-date ticket.* **up-to-date** modern.

**daughter** *noun* somebody's female child.

**daunt** *verb* to feel afraid that you won't be able to do something. *He was daunted by the huge task that lay ahead of him.* **daunting** *adjective.*

**dawdle** *verb* to waste time by moving or doing something slowly.

dawn

**dawn** *noun* the beginning of the day when the Sun rises.

**day** (days) *noun* **1** the 24 hours from one midnight to the next midnight. **2** the part of the day from sunrise to sunset when it is light. **call it a day** to stop doing something, with the intention of returning to it later.

**daydream** *noun* pleasant, distracting thoughts that some people have when they are awake. **daydream** *verb.*

**dazed** *adjective* bewildered and unable to think clearly, perhaps because of a shock.

**dazzle** *verb* **1** to blind briefly or make somebody dazed with a bright light. **2** to amaze or impress somebody. *She was dazzled by his wit.* **dazzling** *adjective.*

**de-** *prefix* adding de- to a noun or verb changes its meaning to its opposite or a negative.

**deadline** *noun* a time or date by which some work or a job must be finished.

**deadlock** *noun* a situation in which people cannot settle a disagreement. *The talks ended in deadlock.*

**deadly** (deadlier, deadliest) *adjective* fatal, likely to kill.

**deaf** *adjective* unable to hear well or unable to hear at all. **deafness** *noun.*

**deafen** *verb* to make unable to hear because the noise is so loud. **deafening** *adjective.*

**deal** *noun* **1** a business agreement. **2** a bargain. **deal** (deals, dealing, dealt) *verb* **1** to do business by buying and selling. **2** to give out cards to people in a card game. **dealer** *noun.* **deal with** **1** to take action to sort out a problem. **2** to be about, concerned with. *This book deals with religion in Africa.*

deal

**dear** *adjective* **1** loved very much. *A dear friend.* **2** the way of beginning a letter before putting the name of the person you are writing to. *Dear Mrs. Smith.* **3** costing a lot of money. The opposite of "dear" is "cheap." **dear** *noun* **1** a person you love or who is lovable. **2** an interjection, used when surprised, upset, or angry. *Oh dear, I'm late!*

**death** *noun* the end of life. **put to death** to kill, execute. **frightened/sick to death** very scared/fed up. **death penalty** the punishment of death for a person who has committed a crime such as murder. **death trap** a building, vehicle, or something else that is very dangerous. *The old mine shaft is a potential death trap.*



**deathly** *adjective, adverb* like death. *He turned deathly cold when he saw the ghost appear.*

**debate** *noun* a discussion, especially at a public meeting. **debate** *verb.*

debris

**debris** *noun* (say **deb**-ree) scattered pieces of things that have been destroyed, or garbage. *Lots of debris was left on the beach after the vacationers had gone home.*

**debt** *noun* (say det) **1** money you owe somebody. *Pay off your debts before you buy a new car.* If you are in debt, you owe money. **2** a feeling that you owe somebody for something they have done for you. *A debt of gratitude.*

**debtor** *noun* a person who owes money. The opposite of "debtor" is "creditor."

**debug** (debugging, debugged) *verb* **1** to remove faults or problems from a computer. **2** to remove a listening device.

**decade** *noun* a period of ten years. *The first decade of the 21st century.*

**decaffeinated** *adjective* with the caffeine removed. *Decaffeinated tea and coffee are better for your health.*

**decapitate** *verb* to cut off someone's head. *During the French Revolution, many aristocrats were decapitated.*

**decathlon** *noun* a competition in which athletes take part in ten different events, involving running, jumping, hurdling, shot put, discus, pole vault, and javelin.

**decay** *verb* **1** to go bad. *Your teeth can decay if you eat too much sugar.* **2** to lose health or power, to become weak. **decay** *noun. The building is falling into decay.* **decayed** *adjective.*

**deceased** *noun* a person who has recently died.

**deceit** *noun* the fact of being dishonest by making people believe a lie. **deceitful** *adjective.*

**deceive** *verb* to make somebody believe something that is not true. *He deceived everybody with his terrible lies.*

**December** *noun* the twelfth month of the year. December has 31 days.

**decent** *adjective* **1** socially acceptable, honest, and respectable. **2** acceptable, good. *A decent salary.* **decency** *noun. He had the decency to apologize.*

**deception** *noun* the fact of deceiving somebody or being deceived. **deceptive** *adjective. The outside of the house is deceptive; inside, it is in need of much repair.*

**decibel** *noun* (say **dess**-ib-el) a unit for measuring the loudness of sound.

**decide** *verb* **1** to do something after thinking about it; to make up your mind. *I've decided to have a vacation in Italy.* **2** to settle something or bring it to an end. *Lack of money decided the issue.*

**decided** *adjective* clear and definite; easily seen. *You have a decided advantage because you are tall.*

**deciduous**

**deciduous** *adjective* (say dis-**id**-yoo-us) deciduous trees shed their leaves every fall. (Trees that never shed their leaves, such as holly, are called evergreen.)

**decimal** *adjective* counting units in tens. *Decimal currency.* The dot in a decimal fraction (e.g. 1·5) is called a decimal point. **decimal** *noun.*

**decipher** *verb* (say di-**seye**-fer) to work something out that is difficult to read or understand. *I can't decipher his writing.*

**decision** *noun* **1** a choice made about what should be done. Deciding. *She made the right decision.* **2** the ability to decide and act quickly.

**decisive** *adjective* **1** acting quickly. **2** having a definite result or making certain that there will be a particular result. *A decisive victory.* **decisively** *adverb.*

**deck** *noun* **1** a floor on a ship or bus. **2** a piece of equipment for playing records on or tapes in. *A tape deck.* **3** a pack. *A deck of playing cards.*

**declare** *verb* **1** to make known or to say something clearly. *I have declared my support for the Democrats.* **2** to tell Customs that you have bought goods abroad or to tell the tax office about your income. **declaration** *noun* something declared, such as war.

**decline** *verb* **1** to refuse politely. *We declined the invitation to the party because we already had a prior engagement.* **2** to become smaller, weaker, or worse. *Her health is declining rapidly.* **decline** *noun* a gradual loss of strength or importance, or a lowering of standards.

**decode** *verb* to work out the meaning of a code. *He tried to decode the message.*

**decompose** *verb* to rot or decay after having died. **decomposition** *noun.*

**decorate** *verb* **1** to make something look more attractive by adding things to it. *The cake was decorated with sugar flowers.* **2** When you decorate a room, you paint or wallpaper the walls. **3** to give somebody a medal. *The soldier was decorated for bravery.* **decoration** *noun.*

**decorator** *noun* a person who paints houses or paints and wallpapers rooms.

**decrease** *verb* to become smaller or weaker. *Sadly, the number of voluntary workers is decreasing.* **decrease** *noun.* **decreasing** *adjective.*

**decree** *noun* an official order or decision, especially by a ruler or a government. **decree** *verb. The king decreed an end to the war.*

**decrepit** *adjective* very old and in bad condition. *A decrepit old house.*

**dedicate** *verb* **1** to give a lot of time and effort to something. *She dedicates her life to prayer.* **2** to declare a book or performance to be in honor of somebody. *I dedicate this book to my mother.* **dedication** *noun.*

**dedicated** *adjective* devoted to something or somebody. *Dedicated to her job.*

**deduce** *verb* to work something out by looking at the facts and reaching a conclusion. *There has been no sign of them all year, and from this I deduce that they must have moved away.* **deduction** *noun.*

**deed** *noun* **1** something done, especially something good. **2** The deeds of a house are official documents detailing its history. They are given to new owners upon the transfer of ownership.

**deep** *adjective* **1** going a long way down from the surface. *A deep hole.* **2** measured from back to front. *The drawers are 20 inches deep.* **3** serious, to a great extent. *Deep feelings.* **4** low. *A deep voice.* **deeply** *adverb.*

**deep-freeze** *noun* a refrigerator for storing frozen food; a freezer.

**deer** (*plural* deer) *noun* a large, four-hoofed, grazing animal. Males usually have antlers.

**deer**

**deface** *verb* to spoil something, especially a wall or a notice, by scribbling on it. *The white wall was defaced with graffiti.*

**default** *verb* to fail to do something you have agreed to do. **default** *noun.* If you win a game by default, you have won because the other player has not arrived.

**defeat** *verb* **1** to beat. *The Dallas Cowboys were defeated in the final quarter.* **2** to cause to fail. *My plan was defeated.* **3** to be too difficult to solve. *The problem defeated me.* **defeat** *noun.*

**defect** *noun* (say **dee**-fekt) a fault or imperfection. *His keyboard had a defect and would not type the letter "a."* **defect** *verb* (say di-**fekt**) to leave your own country, party, or army to join the opposing side. **defector** *noun. The defector slipped across the border at night.*

**defective** *adjective* having faults, not working properly.

**defend** *verb* **1** to protect, guard, or speak in support of, especially when attacked. *She is always defending her little brother.* **2** to try to prove in court that an accused person is not guilty. **3** in sports, to play in a position that stops an opponent from scoring points or goals. If a champion defends her title, she wants to win to keep it. **defender** *noun.*

**defendant** *noun* a person who is on trial, having been accused of committing a crime.

**defense** *noun* **1** something used for defending or protecting. *The trees act as a defense against the wind.* **2** the act or action of defending. **3** the arguments put forward by a defendant in court. **4** the lawyers representing an accused person in a trial. **5** a group of players in a sports team who try to stop the opposition from scoring.

**defensive** *adjective* **1** used for defending. *Defensive weapons.* **2** behaving in an unsure or threatened way. *She is defensive about her friends.* **on the defensive** behaving as if expecting an attack.

**defer** (defers, deferring, deferred) *verb* **1** to arrange that something will take place at a later date. *She deferred her studies for a year.* **2** to agree with a person or an opinion out of respect. *She deferred to the teacher, even though she wanted to argue the point.*

**defiance** *noun* openly refusing to obey. If you act in defiance of an order, you do something forbidden. **defiant** *adjective. The defiant teenager stayed out late, despite his mother's wishes.*

**deficient** *adjective* lacking in a particular thing, short of something. **deficiency** *noun. A deficiency in vitamin C.*

**define** *verb* to say exactly what something is or to explain what a word means. *Let's define the problem.* **definition** *noun.*

**definite** *adjective* firm and unlikely to change. *I need a definite answer.* **definite article** the word "the" is the definite article. ("A" and "an" are indefinite articles.) **definitely** *adverb.*

**deforestation** *noun* the cutting down of forests.

**deformed** *adjective* abnormally shaped. **deformity** *noun.*

**defrost** *verb* **1** to get rid of ice or frost, especially in a refrigerator or on a windshield. **2** When you defrost food, it becomes unfrozen.

**defuse** *verb* **1** to remove the fuse from an unexploded bomb so it cannot explode. **2** to make a situation less dangerous. *He defused the situation by apologizing.*

deforestation

Dd

**defy** (defies, defying, defied) *verb* **1** to refuse to obey. *Criminals defy the law.* **2** to challenge somebody to do something that seems impossible. *I defy you to swim across the river.* **3** to be impossible to understand or solve. *The problem defies solution.*

**degree** *noun* **1** a unit for measuring temperature, usually written with a degree sign (°). **2** a unit of measurement of angles. *A right angle is a 90° angle.* **3** the extent or amount of feeling. *I admire him, to a degree.* **4** an academic grade given by a university or a college to a person who has finished a course or passed an examination. *A degree in German.* **by degrees** gradually.

**deity** (deities) *noun* (say **day**-it-ee) a god or goddess. *They worshiped several deities.*

**delay** *verb* **1** to put something off until later. *We have decided to delay the meeting until the middle of this afternoon.* **2** to make somebody or something late.

**delete** *verb* to cross out something written or printed.

**deliberate** *adjective* (say dil-**ib**-er-ut) **1** planned; done on purpose. *A deliberate lie.* **2** slow and careful, especially when moving or speaking. **deliberately** *adverb.* **deliberate** *verb* (say dil-ib-er-**ayt**) to think carefully. **deliberation** *noun* careful consideration of a subject.

**delicacy** (delicacies) *noun* **1** something soft, fine, and graceful. **2** something that needs careful and tactful handling. *He didn't appreciate the delicacy of the situation.* **3** delicious and often expensive food.

**delicate** *adjective* **1** soft, fine, and graceful. *Lace is strong but delicate fabric.* **2** fragile, easily broken, or becoming ill easily. *A delicate child.* **3** not strong, especially when talking about color, taste, or smell. *A delicate flavor.* **4** needing careful treatment or tactful handling. *Don't mention her old boyfriend; it's a delicate subject.*

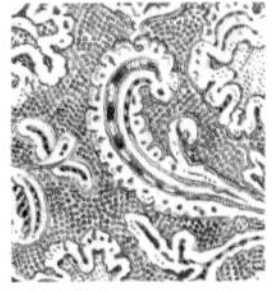

delicate

**delicatessen** *noun* a store or section of a supermarket selling cooked meats, cheeses, and other prepared foods.

**delicious** *adjective* giving great pleasure, having a pleasant taste or smell. *The food was delicious.*

**delight** *noun* great pleasure. *To our delight, the test was canceled.* **delight** *verb* to give or feel a lot of pleasure. **be delighted** *I'd be delighted to come to Marianne's party.* **delightful** *adjective.*



**deliver** *verb* **1** to take something, especially goods or messages, to somebody's house or office. *The mailman delivered the letters.* **2** to give a speech. **3** to help with the birth of a baby. *The baby was delivered this morning.* **delivery** *noun.*

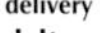

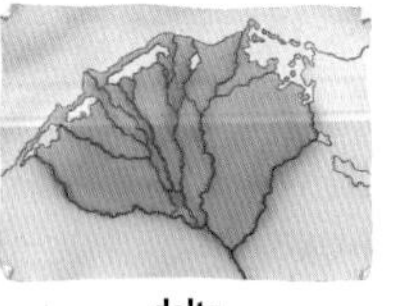

delta

**delta** *noun* **1** the low, fan-shaped area at the mouth of a river, where it splits up into many channels. *The Nile delta.* **2** the Greek letter "D" (written Δ).

**deluge** *noun* **1** a heavy fall of rain; a great flood. *After the deluge, the river subsided.* **2** things arriving in large numbers. *We had a deluge of applications for the job we advertised.* **deluge** *verb.*

**demand** *noun* **1** a firm request. **2** a desire to buy or get something. **demand** *verb* **1** to ask for something firmly, as if ordering it. *I demand an explanation.* **2** to need. *Teaching demands a lot of patience.* **in demand** wanted. *Fast cars are in great demand, even though they are expensive to run.*

**demanding** *adjective* needing attention, time, or energy. *Looking after small children is very demanding.*

**demo** (demos) *noun* a demonstration; sample example.

**democracy** *noun* **1** a system of government in which a country's people elect the leaders of their country. **2** a country governed by democracy. **democrat** *noun.* **democratic** *adjective. A democratic decision.*

**demolish** *verb* to pull down old buildings or destroy something. **demolition** *noun. The demolition work began as soon as the sun was up.*

**demon** *noun* a devil or evil spirit.

**demonstrate** *verb* **1** to show how something works or prove a point by giving examples. **2** to take part in a march or meeting, to show support for a cause. *The students are demonstrating against higher course fees.* **demonstration** *noun.*

**demonstrative** *adjective* showing your feelings. *She often kisses her children; she is a demonstrative mother.* "This," "that," "these," and "those" are **demonstrative adjectives**. They are used to point out a person or a thing.

**den** *noun* **1** the home of a fox or wolf. **2** a person's private room or a child's outdoor play area. *The boys made a den underneath some overhanging branches.*

**denial** *noun* **1** the denying or refusing of something. *A denial of justice.* **2** saying that an accusation is not true. *He printed a denial in the newspaper.*

**Denmark** *noun* a country in northern Europe, part of the region known as Scandinavia.

**denounce** *verb* to speak or write against somebody. *He was denounced as a traitor.* **denunciation** *noun.*

**dense** *adjective* **1** thick, crowded together, or difficult to see through. *A dense forest.* **2** stupid. **density** *noun.*

**dent** *noun* a hollow in a hard surface made by a collision or by pressure. *There was a dent in the side of the can.* **dent** *verb* to make a dent.

dent

**dental** *adjective* of or for the teeth. *Free dental treatment for children.* Dental floss is a thin string.

**dentist** *noun* a person trained to treat people's teeth.

**dentures** *plural noun* false teeth.

**depart** *verb* to go away, leave. *The train to Paris is about to depart from platform three.* **departure** *noun.*

**department** *noun* a part of a large business, government, college, or store. **department store** *noun* a large store in which all sorts of goods, for example perfume and clothing, are sold in different departments.

**depend** *verb* **1** If you depend on somebody or something, you need them. *Our group depends on your leadership.* **2** to trust somebody or to rely on something. *You can always depend on me.* **3** to vary according to circumstances. *The success of the trip will depend on the weather.* **it depends** said when you are not sure about what will happen. *"Are you going to the movie?" "I don't know. It depends."*

**deport** *verb* to send an unwanted person out of a country. **deportation** *noun.*

**deposit** *noun* **1** a sum of money paid into a bank account. *I'd like to make a deposit, please.* **2** money paid as part payment for something. *If you want to order the goods, you will have to pay a deposit.* **3** a layer of a substance left somewhere. *There were deposits of sugar at the bottom of the bottle.* **4** a natural layer of sand, coal, or rock. **deposit** *verb* **1** to put something down. *Sand was deposited by the wind.* **2** to pay money as a deposit.

**depot** *noun* (say **dee**-poh) **1** a place for storing goods. **2** a place where buses or trains are parked and repaired.

**depressed** *adjective* sad, dispirited. **depression** *noun.*

**deprive** *verb* to take or keep something away from somebody. *The garden has been deprived of rain.*

**depth** *noun* the distance from the top of something to the bottom of it or the distance from the front to the back of something. How deep something is. **in depth** thoroughly, including all aspects. **out of your depth** **1** to be in water that is too deep to stand in. **2** to try and do something that is too difficult.

**derive** *verb* **1** to get from. *She derives great pleasure from her children.* **2** to come from. *The word "democracy" derives from the Greek word for "people."*

descend

**descend** *verb* to go down. **be descended from** to be related to and come from a certain family. **descent** *noun.*

**descendant** *noun* a person or an animal related to another who lived a long time ago. *She is a descendant of George Washington.*

**describe** *verb* **1** to say what something or somebody is like. **2** to mark out. *To describe a circle.* **description** *noun.* **descriptive** *adjective.*

**desert** (say **dez**-urt) *noun* a large, often sand-covered area of land where very little rain ever falls. *The Arizona desert.* **desert** (say diz-**ert**) *verb* **1** to go away with no intention of returning; to abandon. **2** to run away from military service. **desertion** *noun. The soldier was accused of desertion.* **deserter** *noun.* **deserted** *adjective* empty; abandoned.

desert

**deserts** *plural noun* what somebody deserves. *He got his just deserts.*

**deserve** *verb* to be worthy of something. *He deserves to win after all the hard training he has done.*

**desiccate** *verb* to dry or dry up. *Desiccated coconut.*

**design** *noun* **1** a drawing that shows how something is to be made or built. *He showed the designs for his new fashion collection.* **2** the way something is made or built. *I love the design of this car.* **3** a pattern of shapes to decorate something. *Curtains with a floral design.* **4** a thought-out plan. **design** *verb* **1** to invent the look of something. *He designs for a jeweler.* **2** to plan. *This dictionary is designed for children.* **designer** *noun.*

**desire** *noun* a strong wish for something. *I have a great desire to meet the President.* **desire** *verb.*

**desk** *noun* a table, often with drawers, at which you sit to read, write, and work.

**despair** *noun* a complete loss of hope. **despair** *verb. He despaired of ever seeing her again.*

**despatch** (British variant of dispatch) see **dispatch**.

**despise** *verb* If you despise somebody, you think that they are worthless.

**dessert** *noun* (say di-**zert**) sweet food eaten at the end of a meal.

**destination** *noun* the place to which a person or thing is going.

**destiny** *noun* **1** Your destiny is what will happen to you in your life. *It was her destiny to marry the King.* **2** the force that controls your life. Fate. **destined** *verb. They were destined to meet again.*

**destroy** *verb* to ruin something, or break it to pieces. *The enemy soldiers destroyed the walls of the castle.* **destruction** *noun.* **destructive** *adjective.*

**detail** *noun* a small point or fact. *The drawing showed the details of the bird's markings.* **detailed** *adjective.*

**detective** *noun* a person, especially a police officer, whose job it is to find out what has happened in a crime.

**deteriorate** *verb* to become worse. *The roof of the barn deteriorated that winter.* **deterioration** *noun.*

**determined** *adjective* having firmly decided to do something in order to be successful. *She is determined to win the tennis tournament.* **determination** *noun.*

**devastate** *verb* **1** to destroy or damage. *The hurricane devastated the whole area.* **2** to shock. *I was devastated when he gave me the terrible news.* **devastation** *noun.*

**develop** *verb* **1** to grow or become bigger. *Her small company soon developed into a major business.* **2** to come into existence, to become more serious. *The baby has developed a big appetite now that she is eating solids.* **3** to make prints from a photographic film. **4** to use an area of land for building houses, stores, and factories. **development** *noun.*

devastate

**device** *noun* something made or built for a particular purpose. *She has invented an unusual listening device.*

**devise** *verb* to invent or think up. *The inventor devised a new kind of flying machine.*

**devour** *verb* to eat greedily.

**dew** *noun* tiny drops of water that form during the night on the ground or cool surfaces. *Dew lay on the grass.*

**Dhaka** *noun* the capital of Bangladesh in southern Asia.

**diabetes** *noun* (say die-uh-**bee**-teez) an illness in which there is too much sugar in a person's blood. **diabetic** *adjective* (say die-uh-**bet**-ik). *Diabetic marmalade.*

**diagnose** *verb* to find out what is wrong with a person and what illness they might have. *The doctor diagnosed a case of measles.* **diagnosis** *noun.*

**diagonal** *adjective* (say die-**ag**-un-ul) A diagonal line goes in a slanting direction, joining opposite corners. **diagonal** *noun.*

**dialect** *noun* a form of language spoken in a particular region, which has different words and pronunciation from other forms of the same language.

**dialysis** *noun* (say die-**al**-ih-siss) a process of removing harmful products from the blood, especially when the kidneys are not functioning properly.

**diameter** *noun* (say die-**am**-it-er) the length of a straight line that runs from one side of a circle or sphere to the other side, passing through the center.

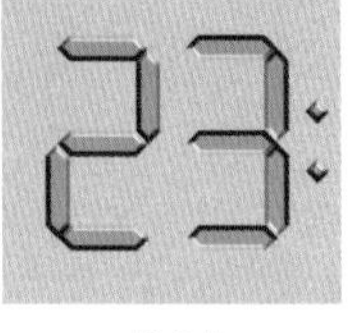

**digital**

**diaper** *noun* a piece of thick, soft paper or cloth that is put around a baby's bottom.

**diaphragm** *noun* (say **die**-uh-fram) **1** a large, dome-shaped muscle that rises and falls when you breathe in and out. **2** a holed plate that limits the amount of light passing through a camera lens.

**diary** (diaries) *noun* **1** a book divided into separate sections for each day of the year, used for writing down appointments. **2** a book for recording daily events.

**dictate** *verb* **1** to say aloud what somebody should write down. *She dictated a letter to her secretary.* **2** to give orders. *I won't be dictated to.* **dictation** *noun.*

**dictator** *noun* a ruler who has total power over a country. Most dictators take power by force. *A ruthless dictator ran the country.*

**diesel** *noun* **1** a vehicle that has a diesel engine. **2** fuel for a diesel engine.

**diet** *noun* **1** the sort of food usually eaten by a person or an animal. *A healthy diet.* **2** special kinds of food eaten in order to be healthy or to lose weight. *I'm on a strict low-fat diet.* **diet** *verb.*

**difference** *noun* **1** the fact of being different; being unlike each other. *The difference between boys and girls.* **2** the amount left between two numbers when one is subtracted from the other. *The difference between 10 and 4 is 6.* **3** When people have their differences, they have a disagreement. **4** When something makes a difference, it is important. *The clothes I wear make a big difference to the way I feel and behave.*

**different** *adjective* **1** not the same. **2** various. *The dress comes in different colors.*

**difficult** *adjective* **1** not easy, hard to do or understand. **2** a difficult person is somebody who is not easily pleased and is hard to get along with. **difficulty** (difficulties) *noun.*

**digest** (say die-**jest**) *verb* **1** to make food change so the body can use it. *Fruit is easy to digest.* **2** to take in information and think it over. **digestion** *noun.*

**digest** (say **die**-jest) *noun* a summary of information.

**digit** *noun* **1** any of the numbers 0, 1, 2, 3, 4, 5, 6, 7, 8, and 9. **2** a finger, thumb, or toe.

**digital** *adjective* **1** a reading displayed as numbers rather than by the movement of a dial. *A digital clock.* **2** using a system in which information is represented in the form of changing electrical signals. *He made a digital recording of his new song.*

**dilemma** *noun* a difficult situation in which you have to choose between two or more possible actions.

**dilute** *verb* to make a liquid weaker or thinner by mixing it with water or other liquid. *I like to dilute my orange juice.*

**dime** *noun* a coin worth 10 cents.

**dimension** *noun* **1** a measurement, especially of length, height, or width. *The exact dimensions of the room.* **2** The dimensions of a problem are its extent and importance.

**diminish** *verb* to become smaller.

**din** *noun* a loud, annoying noise. *What a din!*

**dine** *verb* to have dinner. **dine out** to eat in a restaurant or at a friend's house.

**dinghy** (dinghies) *noun* (say **ding**-ee) **1** a small, open sailing boat. **2** an inflatable rubber boat.

**dingy** (dingier, dingiest) *adjective* (say **din**-jee) dark, depressing, and dirty-looking. *He's got a dingy little room.*

**dinghy**

**dinner** *noun* the main meal of the day.

**dinosaur** *noun* one of many types of extinct reptiles that lived in prehistoric times.

**diplomacy** *noun* **1** the building of relations between different countries and people. **2** the skill of doing and saying the right thing at the right time. *She handled the delicate situation with tact and diplomacy.*

**diplomat** *noun* **1** a government official who represents his/her country in another country, usually from an embassy. **2** a tactful person. **diplomatic** *adjective.*

**direct** *adjective* **1** going straight to a point. *A direct flight.* **2** honest and frank. *Please give me a direct answer.* **3** exact. *The direct opposite.* **directly** *adverb.* **direct** *verb* **1** to tell somebody the way. *Can you direct me to the bus station?* **2** to order somebody to do something. **3** to organize people doing something. *Who is directing the new Batman film?* **director** *noun.*

**direction** *noun* **1** the course or line along which a person moves or looks, or which must be taken to reach a destination. *In which direction is Tokyo?* **2** control or management. *The movie was made under his direction.* **directions** *plural noun* instructions on how to do, use, or find something. *Can you give me directions?*

direction

**dirt** *noun* earth, soil, or anything that is not clean.

**dirty** (dirtier, dirtiest) *adjective* **1** not clean. *My hands are dirty.* **2** vulgar. *Dirty jokes.* **3** mean, unfair. *Putting acorns in your brother's bed was a dirty trick.*

**dis-** *prefix* forming the opposite of a word. "Dishonest" is the opposite of "honest."

**disabled** *adjective* physically or mentally unable to do something. *There are special parking spaces reserved for disabled people.* **disability** *noun.*

**disadvantage** *noun* a condition that causes problems and makes success difficult. The opposite of "disadvantage" is "advantage." *You are at a disadvantage as an accountant if you can't use a computer.*

**disagree** *verb* **1** to have different opinions and so not agree. **2** If food disagrees with you, it makes you feel ill. *The avocado disagreed with her.* **disagreement** *noun.*

**disappear** *verb* to stop being seen; to go out of sight. **disappearance** *noun.*

**disappoint** *verb* to fail to come up to somebody's hopes or expectations. *I was disappointed by my test results.* **disappointment** *noun.*

**disaster** *noun* **1** an unexpected event that causes great damage and suffering. *Floods and earthquakes are natural disasters.* **2** a failure, something unsuccessful. *Our vacation was a disaster because the hotel was still a building site.* **disastrous** *adjective.*

**disciple** *noun* a person who follows the teachings of a leader. *Jesus and his disciples.*

**discontinue** (discontinues, discontinuing, discontinued) *verb* to stop something. *Unfortunately my favorite brand of breakfast cereal has been discontinued.*

**discover** *verb* **1** to find or find out. **2** to be the first person to find something. *The Vikings were the first Europeans to discover America.* **discovery** *noun.*

**discreet** *adjective* **1** tactful in what you say or do. **2** not attracting a lot of attention. *She made a discreet enquiry to find out if he already had a girlfriend.* **discretion** *noun.*

**discriminate** *verb* **1** to notice a difference between two or more things. *We must discriminate between right and wrong.* **2** to treat things or people differently. If you discriminate against somebody, you treat them unfairly. **discrimination** *noun. Racial discrimination is a crime.*

Dd

**discuss** *verb* to talk about something. *I often discuss politics while drinking coffee with my friends.* **discussion** *noun.*

**disguise** *verb* to make somebody or something look or sound different so they are not recognized by other people. **disguise** *noun.* a different appearance, worn to hide the original. *He wore a mask with a false moustache as a disguise.* **in disguise** disguised.

disguise

**disheveled** *adjective* (say di-**shev**-uld) messy, especially somebody's hair or clothes.

**dishonest** *adjective* not honest. *It is dishonest to cheat.* **dishonestly** *adverb.*

**disinfectant** *noun* a substance used to destroy germs.

**dislike** *verb* to not like. *I dislike long car journeys intensely.* **dislike** *noun.*

**disloyal** *adjective* not loyal. *He was disloyal to his regiment.* **disloyally** *adverb.*

**dismay** *noun* a feeling of worry and disappointment. **dismay** *verb.* **dismayed** *adjective. I was dismayed at the way she never did as she was told.*

**dismiss** *verb* **1** to send somebody away or remove someone from their job. *He was dismissed for constantly being late for work.* **2** to stop thinking about something or somebody or to refuse to consider an idea. *We dismissed the idea.* **dismissal** *noun.*

**disobedience** *noun* not doing what you are told to. Not obeying. **disobedient** *adjective.*

**dispatch** *verb* to send somebody or something to a destination. *The message was dispatched early this morning.* **dispatch** *noun* an official report or message.

**dispense** *verb* to give something. *The volunteers helped to dispense gifts.* **dispenser** *noun.*

**display** *verb* **1** to put something in a place it can easily be seen. *The gallery displayed Tibetan masks in the window.* **2** to show. *He displayed his ignorance when he said Paris was the capital of Italy.* **display** *noun.*

Dd

**dissatisfied** *adjective* not satisfied or content.

**dissect** (say die-**sekt**) *verb* to cut something up in order to examine it, especially a dead animal or plant. **dissection** *noun*.

**distance** *noun* the amount of space between two places. *My new house is within walking distance of my office.* **in the distance** far away. **from a distance** a long way away from something in space or time. **distant** *adjective. The distant hills.*

**distinct** *adjective* **1** easily heard or seen. *I noticed a distinct bruise on his leg.* **2** clearly different. **distinctly** *adverb*.

**distinction** *noun* **1** a clear difference. **2** excellence, or an award for excellence. *She had the distinction of being the first woman to win.*

**distinguish** *verb* **1** to establish or notice differences between things. *I can't distinguish one from the other.* **2** to show excellence. *He distinguished himself by winning the first prize in the competition.*

**disturb** *verb* **1** to spoil somebody's rest or to interrupt what they are doing. *That noise disturbs my concentration.* **2** to make somebody upset or worried. **3** to move things from their position. *Nothing in the room had been disturbed.* **disturbance** *noun*.

**dive** (dived or dove, diving) *verb* **1** to plunge headfirst into water. *She dived into the pool.* **2** to swim under water. *They went diving for pearls.* **3** to go down steeply. *The eagle dove from a great height.* **4** to move quickly and suddenly. **diver** *noun*.

dive

**divert** *verb* **1** to change the direction or purpose of something. *Traffic has been diverted because of the accident.* **2** to turn someone's attention away from something else. **3** to amuse or entertain. **diversion** *noun*.

**divide** *verb* **1** to split up or be separated into smaller parts. *We divided the candies between us.* **2** in arithmetic, to find out how many times one number is contained in another. *Divide 12 by 3 and you get 4.*

**division** *noun* **1** the process or result of dividing or being divided. *We have a fair division of work in our family.* **2** in arithmetic, the act of dividing one number by another. **3** a disagreement among members of a group. **4** a group having a special purpose within an organization. *The publicity team belonged to the public relations division of the company.*

Diwali

**divorce** *noun* the legal ending of a marriage. **divorce** *verb* **1** to end a marriage. **2** to detach or separate things. *He is a dreamer and his ideas are divorced from reality.*

**Diwali** (say di-**vah**-lee) *noun* a Hindu religious festival of light.

**dizzy** (dizzier, dizziest) *adjective* feeling that everything is going around and around; the sensation of being unbalanced. *Skipping makes me feel dizzy.*

**Djibouti** *noun* a country in Africa, and its capital city, also Djibouti.

Djibouti's flag

**do** (does, doing, did, done) *verb* **1** to carry out or deal with something; to perform an action or activity. *I'm doing the cooking.* **2** to be enough. *That will do.* **3** in questions with another verb. *Do you know him?* **4** in statements, with "not" forming the negative. *I do not know him.* **5** to stress something. *He hasn't received the invitation, but I did send him one.* **6** instead of repeating a verb that has already been used. *We earn as much money as they do.* **7** at the end of a statement to form a question. *He won the game, didn't he?* **do away with** to get rid of. **do up** to repair or improve. *They are doing up the house.*

**dock** *noun* **1** a place where ships are loaded and unloaded or repaired. **2** the place in a court where the accused person stands or sits. **3** a plant with broad leaves that grows as a weed. **docker** *noun* a worker at the wharves. **dock** *verb* **1** (of a ship) to come or go into dock. **2** to join with another spacecraft in space. **3** to reduce the amount of money that you pay someone.

**doctor** *noun* **1** a person who treats people who are ill. **2** an academic title, a high university degree. *A Doctor of Law.* **just what the doctor ordered** obtaining something desirable. *This warm bath is just what the doctor ordered after that long walk in the snow.*

**document** (say **dock**-you-munt) *noun* an official piece of paper giving proof or information about something. **document** (say **dock**-you-ment) *verb. To document the past, we have used records from the library.*

**dodge** *verb* to move away quickly in order to avoid being struck or seen.

**Dodoma** *noun* the capital of Tanzania in eastern Africa.

**doe** *noun* a female deer, rabbit, or hare.

**Doha** *noun* the capital of Qatar in southwest Asia.

**doll** *noun* a child's toy that looks like a girl or boy. *The girls in my class like to swap their Barbie dolls' clothes and accessories.*

**dolphin** *noun* a sea animal like a small whale with a long nose. Dolphins are mammals that breathe through a blowhole.

**dome** *noun* a round roof on a building. A dome is shaped like half a ball.

**Dominica** *noun* a country in the Caribbean.

**Dominican Republic** *noun* a country in the Caribbean; the eastern part of the island of Hispaniola.

**dolphin**

**domino** *noun* a small rectangular piece of wood or plastic marked with two sets of spots used for playing a traditional game called dominoes. *She beat me at dominoes.*

**donate** *verb* to give something, especially money, to a good cause. *I donated some money to charity.* **donation** *noun. He made a generous donation to the church restoration fund.*

**done** past tense of do. **done** *adjective.*

**donkey** (donkeys) *noun* an animal like a small horse, with long ears.

**door** *noun* a movable frame or barrier that is moved to open or close the entrance to a building, room, or cupboard. **answer the door** to open the door to a visitor. **door-to-door** *adjective* visiting homes to sell something. *We bought our children's encyclopedia from a door-to-door salesman.*

**dormant** *adjective* not active. *A dormant volcano is no longer dangerous.*

**dormitory** (dormitories) *noun* a room or building containing several or many beds, as used by kids when they go to summer camp or stay overnight in a youth hostel.

**dormouse** (dormice) *noun* a woodland animal like a large mouse with a long furry tail. It hibernates in winter. *Our baby son is as sleepy as a dormouse.*

**DOS** *abbreviation* Disk Operating System; software used in a computer system to manipulate information.

**dormouse**

**dose** *noun* the amount of medicine to be taken at one time. *We must increase the dose from one to two pills a day to make sure she gets better quickly.* **dose** *verb. I dosed myself with aspirin to help me get over the flu.*

**dot** *noun* a small spot. **dot** *verb* to mark or cover with dots. **dotted** *adjective.*

**double** *adjective* **1** twice as much or twice as many. *A double portion of spaghetti.* **2** for two people or things. **3** having two parts that are exactly the same. **4** having two different uses or meanings. **double** *noun* **1** an amount or size that is twice as large as the original amount or size. *I paid $5 for it and sold it for double that.* **2** a person who looks exactly like somebody else. *He's his father's double.* **double** *verb* **1** to become twice as large, strong, or fast. *Sales doubled last year since we started selling on the internet.* **2** to have a second use. *My bedroom doubles as a study.* **doubly** *adverb.*

**doubt** *noun* a feeling of not being sure about something. *We have no doubt that he will pass the test.* **doubt** *verb* to feel doubt. **doubtful** *adjective. It is doubtful whether he will get here on time.*

**doughnut** *noun* a round cake or ring, fried in hot fat and covered with sugar.

**dove** *noun* a bird like a pigeon.

**dowdy** (dowdier, dowdiest) *adjective* not fashionable, dull. *Dowdy clothes.*

**down** *adverb, preposition* **1** toward, at, or in a lower position. *Please get the book down from the shelf.* **2** in a lower place or from one place to another. *We walked down to the shore.* **3** to a smaller size, grade, or standard. *Prices are down.* **4** to put something in writing. *To take down notes.* **5** move on to a surface. *Sit down.* **down** *noun* **1** a bird's soft feathers. **2** fine soft hair. *The down on the baby's head was red.* **down** *verb.*

**downcast** *adjective* **1** sad, depressed. **2** looking downward, especially when feeling sad. *With downcast eyes, he told her he was leaving the country.*

**downfall** *noun* **1** a fall from power; ruin. *Drink was his downfall.* **2** a fall of rain; a downpour.

**downstairs** *adverb, adjective* to, at, or on a lower floor. *I'll wait for you downstairs.*

**doze** *verb* to sleep lightly or be half asleep.

**dozen** *noun* twelve. *A dozen eggs.*

**Dr** *abbreviation* doctor.

**drab** (drabber, drabbest) *adjective* not colorful; dull. *My aunt wears drab clothes.*

**drag** (drags, dragging, dragged) *verb* **1** to pull a heavy load along or pull somebody roughly. *He dragged the suitcase across the street.* **2** to go on slowly; to seem to last a long time. *The meeting dragged.* **3** to move along while touching the ground. *Her dress dragged in the mud.* **4** to search for something by pulling a heavy net along a river or lake bed. *The police dragged the lake looking for the stolen car.*

**dragon** *noun* an imaginary animal or monster in children's stories that has scales and wings and breathes fire.

**dragonfly** (dragonflies) *noun* an insect with a long body and two pairs of large, thin wings. *The dragonflies darted and hovered over the pond in the warm summer sun.*

dragon

**drain** *noun* **1** a pipe that carries away water or other unwanted liquid. **2** something that uses up time, money, or energy. *Her sons are a drain on her finances.* **drain** *verb* **1** to flow away slowly. **2** to make weak or take away strength. **3** to empty or become dry or empty. *He drained the glass in one gulp, then threw it in the hearth and made a wish.*

**drake** *noun* a male duck.

**drama** *noun* **1** a play for the theater, television, or radio. **2** the study of plays, their writing, presentation, and performance. **3** exciting real-life events or an emotional situation. *Our visit turned into a drama after we locked the keys in the car.*

**dramatic** *adjective* **1** impressive, exciting. *The new music teacher has made some dramatic changes.* **2** showing feeling in a lively way. *His speech was dramatic, and the audience applauded loudly.*

**drastic** *adjective* having a strong and often violent effect. *We made the drastic decision to return home at once.*

**draw** (draws, drawing, drew, drawn) *verb* **1** to make pictures, patterns, or diagrams with a pencil or pen. **2** to pull something heavy. *Two horses drew the carriage.* **3** to pull something out of a place; to take out. *To draw money out of the bank.* **4** to attract. *The concert drew a large crowd.* **5** to come or move in the direction mentioned. *Our vacation is drawing to an end.* **6** to end a game or contest with the same points on both sides; to tie. **7** to form an idea. *To draw a conclusion.* **draw** *noun* **1** equal marks in a game or contest. *The game ended in a draw.* **2** the drawing of lottery tickets. *Luck of the draw.* **draw ahead** to move in front of somebody. **draw the curtains** to open or close the curtains. **draw up 1** to come near and stop. *A car drew up outside my door.* **2** to prepare, especially a report or document.

draw

**drawback** *noun* a disadvantage, something that can cause trouble or difficulty. *The high cost of printing the leaflets is a drawback because the advertising budget is very small.*

**drawbridge** *noun* a bridge over a moat or river that can be pulled up by chains to protect a castle or to let ships pass by underneath.

**drawing** *noun* **1** the making of pictures with a pen or pencil. **2** a picture made by drawing.

**dread** *noun* great fear. *I watched the soldiers approach with dread.* **dread** *verb* to fear something greatly. *I dread the court hearing.* **dreadful** *adjective* bad, disagreeable. *She has a dreadful haircut.*

**dreadlocks** *plural noun* hair worn in tight braids that look like rope. *Bob Marley wore his hair in dreadlocks.*

**dredge** *verb* to remove mud or sand from the bottom of a river. **dredger** *noun* a large boat or barge used for dredging a river.

**dress** (dresses) *noun* **1** a piece of clothing that covers the top part of the body and extends into a skirt. *For my wedding I wore a full length white dress decorated with pearls.* **2** clothing in general. *The children wore Tibetan national dress.* **dress** *verb* **1** to put on clothes. *"Get dressed quickly or you will be late!"* **2** to wear clothes. *She was dressed in black.* **3** to add sauce to food. *I have dressed the salad.* **4** to cover with a bandage. *Let me dress that wound for you.* **5** to arrange goods for display. *We dressed the window of the store for Christmas.* **dress up 1** to put on smart clothes. **2** to wear something odd for fun or put on clothes in a game. *The children dressed up as pirates.* **get dressed** to put on clothes.

**dresser** *noun* **1** a chest of drawers or bureau, with a mirror **2** a person who is employed to help actors dress for the stage. **3** a cupboard to hold dishes and cooking utensils. **4** a table or bench on which meat and other things are dressed.

**dressing** *noun* **1** a bandage for covering a wound. **2** a sauce for food. *Salad dressing.* **dressing gown** *noun* a robe worn loose while dressing or lounging.

**drew** past tense of draw.

**dribble** *verb* **1** to let drops of spit (saliva) trickle out of your mouth. *Babies dribble when their teeth are coming through.* **2** to move a ball forward with short kicks (in various games).

**drift** *noun* **1** sand or snow that the wind has blown into a pile. *A drift of snow is blowing across the garden.* **2** a general movement or the direction in which something is moving. *There is a drift away from higher education.* **3** the meaning of something, especially a speech. **drift** *verb* **1** to float or be carried along by the wind or waves. **2** to move without a plan or purpose. *She just drifts from one job to another.*

drive

**drive** *noun* **1** a journey in a car or bus. **2** energy and enthusiasm. *People with a lot of drive are often very successful.* **3** the act of hitting a ball or the force with which it is hit, especially in golf or cricket. **4** a planned effort by a group for a particular purpose. *We are having a sales drive.* **drive** (drives, driving, drove, driven) *verb* **1** to travel in a vehicle or make it move. *My brother drives a tractor.* **2** to take somebody somewhere in a car. *I'll drive the children home.* **3** to force to go. *She drives all the customers away.* **4** to make somebody do something. *His illness has driven him to drink.* **5** to direct force into or on to something. *To drive a nail into a wall. The engine is driven by steam.* **driver** *noun.*

**drizzle** *noun* light rain. **drizzle** *verb.*

**drone** *noun* **1** a male bee. **2** a low humming sound. **drone** *verb* **1** to make a low humming sound. **2** to talk in a low, boring voice. *He droned on and on.*

**drowsy** *adjective* sleepy. **drowsiness** *noun.*

**drug** *noun* **1** a medicine. **2** a substance that affects your mind and feelings and is addictive. *In some countries, it is illegal to take addictive drugs for pleasure.* **drug** (drugs, drugging, drugged) *verb.*

**drum** *noun* **1** a musical instrument made of a hollow round frame with a skin stretched tightly over it. *He beat the drum in the procession.* **2** a round container for liquids. *A large drum full of oil.* **drum** (drums, drumming, drummed) *verb* **1** to play a drum. **2** to tap. *He drummed his fingers on the table.* **drummer** *noun.*

duel

**dryer** *noun* a device for drying hair or clothes. *The hair dryer blows hot or cold.*

**dual** *adjective* having two parts or two functions. *The driving instructor's car has dual controls, luckily!*

**Dublin** *noun* the capital of Ireland in western Europe.

**duel** *noun* a fight with guns or swords between two people. **duel** *verb.* **duellist** *noun.*

**duet** *noun* **1** a performance by two singers or musicians. **2** a piece of music written for two singers or players.

**dumb** (say dum) *adjective* **1** unable to speak. **2** unwilling to speak, silent. *He remained dumb throughout the trial.* **3** stupid. *You aren't really that dumb.*

**dune** *noun* a hill made of sand piled up by the wind on a seashore or in the desert.

Dd

**dung** *noun* solid waste matter from the bowels of large animals, especially cattle.

dungeon

**dungeon** *noun* (say **dun**-jun) a dark underground prison cell found in a castle.

**duplicate** *adjective* exactly the same. *Duplicate keys.* **duplicate** *noun* something that is exactly the same as something else; an exact copy. *Luckily I had a duplicate of the missing photograph.* **duplicate** *verb* to make or be a duplicate.

**during** *preposition* **1** throughout. *During the week.* **2** at some point. *He phoned twice during the morning.*

**Dushanbe** *noun* the capital of Tajikistan in Central Asia.

**dusk** *noun* the time when it is not completely dark, just before nightfall.

**Dutch** *adjective* relating to or coming from the Netherlands or related to the Dutch language. *Dutch cheese.* **Dutch** *noun* the language spoken in Holland. **go Dutch** to share expenses. *We always go Dutch when I go out with my boyfriend.*

**duty** (duties) *noun* **1** something a person must do because they think it is right. *It's my duty to look after my sick uncle.* **2** something you have to do as part of your job. *He told me what my duties would be.* **3** a tax on certain goods. *A duty on cigarettes.* **on duty** at work. *The doctor is on duty tonight.* **off duty** not at work.

**duvet** *noun* (say **doo**-vay) a thick, soft bed covering.

**dye** (dyes, dyeing, dyed) *verb* to color something, especially hair or cloth, by soaking it in a colored liquid. *I want to dye my hair red.* **dye** *noun* the substance used for dyeing things.

**dynamo** *noun* a machine that turns mechanical power into electricity.

**dynasty** (dynasties) *noun* (say **din**-a-stee) a line of rulers of a country who all belong to the same family. *Note Britain's Tudor dynasty.*

**dyslexia** *noun* (say dis-**lek**-see-a) a condition that makes it difficult to read and spell. **dyslexic** *adjective.*

**each** *adjective, pronoun* **1** every single one of two or more things. *Each student.* **2** for one. *The tickets are $10 each.* **each other** one another. *They loved each other.*

**eager** *adjective* wanting to do something very much; keen. **eagerly** *adverb.*

**eagle** *noun* any of various large meat-eating birds, or birds of prey, with very good eyesight.

**ear** *noun* **1** the organ of hearing. You have two ears, one on either side of your head. **2** the part at the top of a cereal plant that contains seeds or grain. *Ears of corn stood in a vase on the windowsill.* **all ears** listening with great interest. *Tell us what she did, we're all ears.* **go in one ear and out the other** heard but forgotten immediately. **play it by ear** to act from moment to moment, without making plans in advance. **up to your ears** incredibly busy.



ear

**earn** *verb* **1** to get money in return for working. *I earned $40 for one hour's work.* **2** to get something, especially praise, because you deserve it. *That will earn him respect.* **earnings** *plural noun.*

**eardrum** *noun* a thin, tight membrane over the inside of the ear that vibrates when reached by sound waves.

**earnest** *adjective* serious and sincere. **in earnest** serious. *"Is your offer of a free vacation made in earnest?"*

**earring** *noun* a piece of jewelry worn on the ear.

**Earth** *noun* the planet on which we live. *The spacecraft has returned to Earth.* **earth** *noun* **1** the soil in which plants thrive and grow. **2** the ground. **3** a wire that passes from electrical equipment to the ground and makes the equipment safe. **earth** *verb* to connect a piece of electrical equipment to the ground with a wire to make it safe. *Have you earthed the appliances?*

**earthquake** *noun* a sudden violent shaking of the Earth's surface.

**earwig** *noun* a crawling insect with pincer-like appendages at the tail end.

**easily** *adverb* without difficulty or very likely.

**east** or **East** *adjective, adverb* toward the east, or in the direction in which the sun rises (the opposite of west). *An east wind.* **east** *noun* **1** *The sun rises in the east.* **2** the eastern part of a country or continent.

**Easter** *noun* a religious festival when Christians remember the death and resurrection of Jesus Christ.

**easy** (easier, easiest) *adjective, adverb* **1** not difficult, not needing much effort. *It was easy to persuade him to come.* **2** without any problems. *She has an easy life.* **take it/things easy** to relax and not do or work too much. **go easy on something** to avoid using too much of it.

**easygoing** *adjective* not easily worried or upset. *My parents are very easygoing; they don't mind what I do.*

**eavesdrop** (eavesdrops, eavesdropping, eavesdropped) *verb* to listen secretly to somebody else's conversation.

**ebony** *noun* a hard, black wood. **ebony** *adjective.*

**eccentric** (say ek-**sen**-trik) *adjective* behaving strangely, having odd habits or an unusual appearance. **eccentric** *noun* an eccentric person. **eccentricity** *noun.*

**echo** (echoes) *noun* a sound that is heard again as it bounces back from a wall or the inside of a cave. **echo** (echoes, echoing, echoed) *verb* **1** to make an echo. *Our footsteps echoed in the tunnel.* **2** to repeat somebody else's words or actions.

**eclipse** *noun* when the Moon or Earth passes in front of the Sun or Moon, hiding their light. *A total eclipse of the Sun.* **eclipse** *verb* to do or be much better than anyone or anything else. *His paintings eclipsed all the other exhibits.*

eclipse

**ecology** *noun* the pattern of relationships between plants, animals, and people to each other and their surroundings. **ecologist** *noun.* **ecological** *adjective.*

**economic** *adjective* **1** relating to economics. **2** making a profit. *It's not economic to run buses to the village.*

**economical** *adjective* using money, time, or goods carefully; not wasteful. *He's very economical with the stationery, if nothing else.* **economically** *adverb.*

**economics** *plural noun* the science of the production and distribution of wealth.

**economy** (economies) *noun* **1** the system by which a country spends its money and organizes its industry and trade. **2** the careful spending of money or use of goods in order to save money.

**ecosystem** *noun* a system relating all the plants, animals, and people in an area to their surroundings.

**ecstasy** (say **ek**-stuh-see) *noun* a feeling of rapture and happiness. **ecstatic** *adjective.* **ecstatically** *adverb.*

Ecuador

**Ecuador** *noun* a country in northern South America.

**edge** *noun* **1** the thin cutting part of a knife or another cutting tool. **2** the place or line where something stops and something else begins. The side of something. *The edge of the cliff.* **on edge** nervous. **edge** *verb* **1** to form the edge of something or put an edge on something. *The lawn was edged with flowers.* **2** to move slowly and carefully. *He edged toward me.*

**edible** *adjective* fit to be eaten, eatable.

**edifice** (say **ed**-if-iss) *noun* a large, imposing building.

**Edinburgh** *noun* the capital of Scotland, part of the UK.

**edit** *verb* **1** to prepare a newspaper, magazine, or book, and improve the way it is written. *This manuscript needed a lot of editing.* **2** to choose, arrange, and put parts of a movie or recording together.

**edition** *noun* **1** the form in which a book or magazine is printed. *He bought the paperback edition instead of the hardback.* **2** the number of copies of a book or magazine printed. *The first edition has already sold out.*

**editor** *noun* **1** a person who edits a book, magazine, or newspaper. **2** the person who is in charge of a newspaper.

**educate** *verb* to teach or train somebody for a prolonged period of time. **education** *noun.*

**eel** *noun* a long, thin fish that looks like a snake.

**effect** *noun* **1** a condition caused by something; a result. *He felt the effects of the alcohol the next morning.* **2** an impression produced on the mind. *Sound effects are very important in a film.* **effect** *verb* to produce or make something happen. *The changes in the law will be effected soon.* **in effect** really. *In effect, the reply told her nothing.* **take effect** to start happening.

**effective** *adjective* **1** impressive. **2** producing the result you set out to achieve. *Gasoline can be an effective stain remover.* **3** actual or real. *She took effective control.* **to become effective** to come into force. *The new opening hours become effective on Tuesday.* **effectiveness** *noun.* **effectively** *adverb.*

**efficient** *adjective* working well without wasting time or effort. *He's very efficient at his job, doing his work quickly and effectively.* **efficiency** *noun.*

**e.g.** *abbreviation* for example. *In certain countries, e.g., Italy, France, and Holland, local cheeses are delicious.*

**egg** *noun* **1** an oval object laid by female birds, fish, and reptiles that contains new life. **2** a hen's egg used as food. *Would you like your egg fried or scrambled?* **3** a female reproductive cell in humans, animals, and plants. The scientific term for a human egg is an ovum.

**Egypt** *noun* a country in northern Africa.

**Eid** (say eed) *noun* a Muslim festival celebrating the end of the fast of Ramadan (Eid ul-Fitr), or the end of a journey to Mecca (Eid ul-Adha).

eel

**either** *adjective, pronoun* **1** one or the other of two. *Both computers work, you can use either.* **2** one and the other of two. *"Which do you prefer?" "I don't like either."* **either** *adverb* also (used in negative statements). *I don't like cats and I don't like dogs either.* **either** *conjunction* the first of two or more possibilities. *I'll either write or phone you when I feel better.*

**eject** *verb* **1** to throw somebody out of a place. *They were forcibly ejected from the stadium for causing a disturbance.* **2** to push out with force. *The machine ejected the coins.*

**elaborate** (say i-**lab**-uh-rut) *adjective* full of detail with a number of complicated parts. *The curtains had an elaborate pattern of flowers.* **elaborate** (say i-**lab**-uh-rate) *verb* when you elaborate on something, you describe or explain it in detail.

**elapse** *verb* (of time) to pass by. *Three months have elapsed since the wedding.*

**elastic** *adjective* able to stretch and go back to its original shape. *An elastic band.* **elastic** *noun* material that stretches. **elasticity** *noun.*

**elder** *adjective* older. *My elder sister.* **elder** *noun* **1** the older of two people. **2** an older person. *We should respect our elders.* **3** a tree with white flowers and red or black berries.

**elect** *verb* **1** to choose by voting. *A new government was elected.* **2** to decide to do something. *They elected to stay.*

**election** *noun* the process of voting to choose a person or party to hold an official position, especially a political one. *She stood for President in the election, but was defeated by the rival candidate.*

**electric** *adjective* **1** producing or produced by electricity. *An electric toaster.* **2** very exciting. *The atmosphere at the concert was electric.*

**electrical** *adjective* **1** relating to electricity. *An electrical fault.* **2** operating by electricity.

**electrician** *noun* a person whose job is to fit and repair electrical equipment. *The electrician installed the electric cables in the new house.*

**electricity** *noun* **1** a form of energy that is used for heating and lighting or for driving machines. This kind of electricity is produced by generators or batteries. **2** energy resulting from charged particles. *Static electricity.*

**electrode** *noun* the point where an electric current enters or leaves a battery.

**electron** *noun* a tiny particle of matter with a negative electric charge.

**electronic** *adjective* produced or worked by the flow of electrons, usually using microchips. *He recorded his electronic music onto a CD.* **electronics** *noun.*

**elegant** *adjective* showing good taste in design and style. Graceful and pleasing. *She looked very elegant in her new dress.* **elegance** *noun.*

**element** *noun* **1** a single part that combines with others to make a whole. *Listening is an important element of her job.* **2** a part of something. *There is an element of truth in what she said.* **3** the heating part of an electrical appliance. **4** the most important parts or the basics of a subject. *The elements of mathematics.* **5** in science, an element is a substance that consists of only one type of atom. Gold and oxygen are elements. **6** a suitable surrounding. *The director was in his element when talking about films.* **the elements** the weather; wind and rain.

**elementary** *adjective* easy, simple, or basic. *I took an elementary course in computing last month.* **elementary school** US grade school or the first six to eight years of a child's education.

**elephant** *noun* the largest living land animal, with big ears, a trunk, and tusks.

**elevator** *noun* a box-like machine that takes people from one level of a building to another.

**eligible** *adjective* **1** entitled to be chosen. *You are eligible for a grant.* **2** desirable or suitable.

**elite** (say uh-**leet**) *noun* the most important or powerful group of people in a community.

**eloquent** *adjective* able to make good speeches that persuade and influence others. **eloquence** *noun.*

**El Salvador** *noun* a country in Central America.

**elusive** *adjective* difficult to catch or find. *Success as a film star proved elusive.*

**e-mail** *noun* electronic mail.

**emancipate** *verb* to free someone from rules that limit their activity. **emancipated** *adjective. Today's women are more emancipated than their grandmothers.* **emancipation** *noun.*

**embankment** *noun* a wall of stones or earth that holds back a river or supports a road or railroad.

**embarrass** *verb* to make somebody feel awkward or self-conscious. *The questions embarrassed me so much that I blushed.* **embarrassment** *noun.*

**embroider** *verb* to sew a design or picture on to cloth. **embroidery** *noun.*

**embryo** (say **em**-bree-oh) *noun* an unborn baby or animal as it starts to grow in its mother's womb. **embryonic** *adjective* undeveloped.

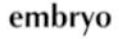
**embryo**

**emerald** *noun* **1** a green precious stone. **2** a clear green color. *She had emerald green eyes.*

**emergency** (emergencies) *noun* an unexpected dangerous event that needs immediate action. *Phone for the police in an emergency.*

**emigrate** *verb* to leave your own country to live in another country. **emigration** *noun.* **emigrant** *noun.*

**emotion** *noun* a strong feeling such as love, jealousy, fear, or grief. *She was overcome with emotion.* **emotional** *adjective. He made an emotional speech of thanks.*

**emotive** *adjective* causing emotion. *The war was a very emotive issue.*

**emperor** *noun* the ruler of an empire. If the ruler is a woman, she is called an empress.

**emphasize** *verb* to give special importance to something. *He emphasized to his mother that he wanted to go out on his birthday.* **emphasis** *noun.*

**empire** *noun* **1** a group of countries controlled by one ruler. *The former British Empire.* **2** a large group of companies or stores controlled by one person. *She has built up a giant fashion empire.*

**employ** *verb* **1** to pay somebody to do work for you. *The company employs 20 people.* **2** to make use of something or somebody. *He employed all his charm to win her over.*

**employee** *noun* a person who is paid a salary to work for somebody else.

**employer** *noun* a person who employs people. *The staff were in dispute with their employer over wages.*

**employment** *noun* **1** having a paid job; employing or being employed. *He's still looking for employment.* **2** a person's regular job.

**emu** *noun* a large, flightless, Australian bird, like an ostrich.

**emu**

**enamel** *noun* **1** a shiny substance that is put on metal, glass, or pottery to decorate and protect it. **2** the outer covering of a tooth. **enamel** *adjective. Enamel paint.*

**enchant** *verb* **1** to charm and delight somebody. *She enchants him with her gentle manner.* **2** to put somebody or something under a magic spell. **enchanted** *adjective* magic. *An enchanted forest.*

**encounter** *verb* **1** to meet unexpectedly. **2** to be faced with something bad, especially danger or prejudice. *We encountered many difficulties.* **encounter** *noun.*

**encourage** *verb* **1** to give courage or hope to somebody. *I encouraged her to start painting.* **2** to support or help develop. *Don't encourage his laziness.* **encouragement** *noun.* **encouraging** *adjective. We received encouraging news from the hospital.*

end

**end** *noun* **1** the point or place where something stops; the last part of something. *At the end of the street.* **2** finish. *It was the end of our friendship.* **3** a small piece left. *There were lots of crayon ends on the floor.* **4** death. *His was a cruel end.* **5** purpose. *He is doing this for his own selfish ends.* **in the end** finally. **make ends meet** to have just enough money to live on. **end** *verb* to finish or stop. *How did the play end?*

**endeavor** (say in-**dev**-uh) *verb* to try. **endeavor** *noun.*

**endure** *verb* **1** to put up with, to bear, especially pain or suffering. *She was forced to endure great hardship.* **2** to last. *His love for me will endure forever.* **endurance** *noun*

**enemy** (enemies) *noun* **1** somebody who hates or wants to hurt another person. When two people hate each other, they are enemies. **2** a country or army that is at war with another. *The enemy attacked at night.*

**energetic** *adjective* full of energy.

**energy** *noun* **1** the strength and ability to do a lot. **2** the effort put into work. *She concentrated all her energy on her job.* **3** the power that works and drives machines.

**engage** *verb* **1** to employ. **2** to attract somebody's attention. **3** to fit into or lock together parts of a machine. **4** to bind with a promise of marriage.

**engagement** *noun* **1** an agreement to marry. **2** the period of time during which two people are engaged. **3** an arrangement to meet somebody or do something.

engine

**engaging** *adjective* attractive, interesting.

**engine** *noun* **1** a machine that produces the power which makes a vehicle move. **2** a machine that pulls a railroad train; also called a locomotive.

**engineer** *noun* **1** a person who designs machines, roads, or bridges. **2** a person who repairs machines or electrical devices. **engineer** *verb* to make happen. *He engineered an interview with the boss.*

**England** *noun* one of the countries of Britain and the United Kingdom.

**English** *noun* **1** the people of England. **2** the language spoken in Great Britain, America, Canada, Australia, and many other parts of the world. **English** *adjective.*

**enormous** *adjective* extremely large is size or amount.

**enough** *adverb* having the right amount or to the right degree. *He's not old enough to understand.* **enough** *adjective* as much as necessary. **enough** *pronoun. Not enough is known about the universe.*

**enquire, enquirer, enquiry**. See inquire, inquirer, inquiry.

**entertain** *verb* **1** to give food and drink to guests at your home. **2** to amuse and interest. *He entertained us with stories.* **3** to think about. *I didn't entertain the idea.*

**entertainment** *noun* **1** the act of being entertained or being entertaining. **2** a performance.

**Ee**

**enthusiasm** *noun* a strong feeling of interest, liking, and excitement. **enthusiast** *noun.* **enthusiastic** *adjective.*

**entire** *adjective* whole. **entirely** *adverb.*

**entry** (entries) *noun* **1** The act of coming or going in. **2** the right to enter. **3** something entered in a list or book.

**envelop** (say in-**vel**-up) *verb* to cover or surround completely. *The hills were enveloped in mist.*

**envelope** (say en-vel-**ope**) *noun* a paper wrapper in which you place a letter before sending it.

**envious** *adjective* feeling envy. *He was envious of his successful brother.*

**environment** *noun* the surroundings and conditions in which people, animals, and plants live. **environmental** *adjective. Environmental pollution.*

**envy** (envies, envying, envied) *verb* wishing you had something that somebody else has. *I envied her her beauty.* **envy** *noun* a feeling of resentment toward someone who has something that you would like.

**epic** *noun* **1** a long poem about heroes and heroic deeds. **2** a historic or long book or movie. **epic** *adjective.*

**epidemic** *noun* a large number of cases of an infectious disease in one area at the same time. *A flu epidemic has been forecast.*

**episode** *noun* **1** one separate and important event. *That vacation was one of the funniest episodes in my life.* **2** one of several parts of a radio or TV series.

**epoch** (say **ee**-pok) *noun* a period of time in history or life during which an important event happened.

**equal** *adjective* the same amount, size, or degree. **equally** *adverb.* **equal** *noun* a person or thing with the same qualities as another. **equal** *verb* **1** to be the same as another one in amount, size, or value. *His salary doesn't equal mine.* **2** to be as good or do as well as somebody else. *I've equaled the record.*

**equality** *noun* being equal, having the same rights and opportunities.

**equator** *noun* an imaginary circle around the middle of the Earth.

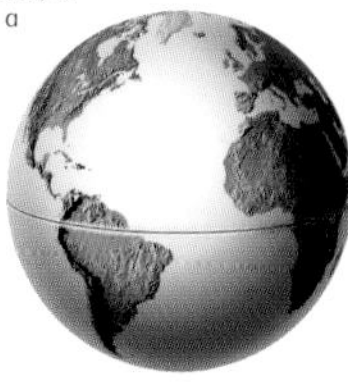
equator

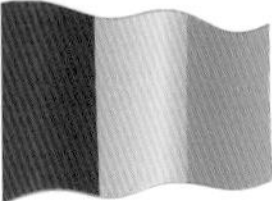
Equatorial Guinea's flag

**Equatorial Guinea** *noun* a country in West Africa.

**equestrian** *adjective* to do with horses and horseriding. *An equestrian event.*

**equinox** *noun* the time of the year when day and night are equal in length, about 20 March and 22 September.



**equip** *verb* to supply with what is needed. *The gym is fully equipped with weights and exercise machines.*

**equivalent** *adjective* same, equal in value or meaning. *The sum of money he was paid was equivalent to a full week's work.* **equivalent** *noun.*

**era** *noun* a period of time that starts from a particular event or date. *The Christian era.*

**eradicate** *verb* to get rid of something or destroy it completely. *We are determined to eradicate crime.*

**erase** *verb* **1** to rub out. **2** to wipe out a recording. *I erased the tape by mistake.*

**eraser** *noun* a piece of rubber used to erase marks or writing on paper.

**erect** *adjective* upright. *He stood erect.* **erect** *verb* to build or set up. *They erected a statue of the famous poet in the town square.* **erection** *noun.*

**Eritrea** *noun* a country in northeast Africa.

**error** *noun* a mistake.

**erupt** *verb* **1** to explode and spurt out lava. *The volcano erupted.* **2** to break out or happen suddenly. *Violence erupted after the baseball game.* **eruption** *noun.*

**escalate** *verb* to increase by stages. *The violence soon escalated.*

**escalator** *noun* a moving staircase that goes up or down, often found in subway stations.

**escape** *verb* **1** to get away from a person or place; to get out. *Three prisoners escaped last night.* **2** to avoid, especially something unpleasant. *They escaped the accident unhurt. The criminal escaped punishment because there were no witnesses to his crime.* **escape** *noun. They had planned the escape for weeks.*

erupt

**especially** *adverb* specially, in particular. *I love chocolate, especially milk chocolate.*

**espionage** *noun* the act of spying.

**essential** *adjective* **1** absolutely necessary. *A knowledge of languages is essential for foreign correspondents.* **2** most important. *I only read the essential books on the reading list.* **essential** *noun. Just tell me the bare essentials, not the minor details.*

**establish** *verb* **1** to set up, especially a new government or business. **2** to place or settle yourself or somebody else. *Once he has established himself in the company, he'll make progress very quickly.* **3** to find out or make certain. *We must establish the truth first.*

**estate** *noun* **1** a large piece of land in the country owned by one person, usually holding a large house. **2** an area of land with houses or factories on it. **3** everything, including money and property, that someone leaves when they die.

**esthetics** (say **ess**-theh-tics) *noun* the study of beauty, especially beauty in art.

**Estonia** *noun* a Baltic country in Europe.

**estuary** (estuaries) (say **ess**-tew-er-ee) *noun* the wide mouth of a river where it flows into the sea or ocean.

**etc.** *abbreviation* et cetera (Latin for "and other things"); and so on.

**Ethiopia** *noun* a country in northeast Africa.

**ethnic** *adjective* relating to people's race or culture. *Ethnic minorities must have equal rights.*

**etymology** (etymologies) *noun* (say et-i-**mol**-uh-jee) **1** the history and source of a word. **2** the study of the origins and meanings of words. **etymological** *adjective.*

**EU** *abbreviation* European Union.

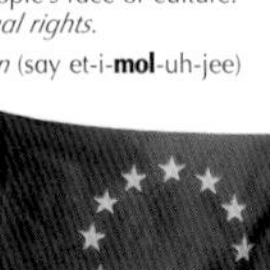
EU flag

**Europe** *noun* one of the Earth's seven continents.

**European** *adjective* coming from or relating to Europe. *A common European currency.*

**evacuate** *verb* to leave a place or move people out of a place, especially because of a crisis. *You must evacuate the building immediately. Thousands were evacuated after the earthquake.* **evacuation** *noun.*

**evade** *verb* to avoid a person or thing. *He cleverly evaded the question of money.* **evasion** *noun. He was fined for tax evasion.*

**evaporate** *verb* **1** to change from a liquid into a gas called water vapor. *Water evaporates in the heat of the sun.* **2** to disappear. *My hopes evaporated.* **evaporation** *noun. Evaporation made the puddle disappear.*

**even** *adjective* **1** flat, smooth, level. *The floor is not very even.* **2** regular, unchanging. *Indoor plants do best in an even temperature.* **3** equal, especially when talking about things that can be measured. *An even distribution of wealth. We both won a game; now we're even.* **4** Even numbers are numbers that can be divided by two. *Four, ten, and 26 are all even numbers.* **evenly** *adverb.* **evenness** *noun.* **even** *adverb* **1** used to stress a word or statement. *Even the teacher was surprised how difficult the test was.* **2** used before a comparison, meaning "still." *He is even taller than his father.* **even so** nevertheless. *She says she doesn't get along with her parents, but even so, she doesn't want to leave home.* **even though** despite the fact that. *Even though she's upset, she won't say anything.* **even out** to make or become even. *Things even themselves out in the end.*

**evening** *noun* the end of the day, before nightfall. *We usually go out on Saturday evening.*

**event** *noun* **1** something that happens, especially something unusual or important. **2** one of the races or other sporting activities in a competition. **in any event** whatever happens.

**eventual** *adjective* happening at last. *He deserved his eventual success.*

**ever** *adverb* **1** at any time. *Getting a computer was the best thing I ever did.* **2** all the time; forever. *They lived happily ever after.* **ever since** since continuously. *Ever since I've known him, he has never been late.*

**evergreen** *adjective* having green leaves all year. *Evergreen trees such as holly keep their leaves in winter, while deciduous trees like oak drop theirs in the fall.*

evergreen

**every** *adjective* **1** each one. *Every word she says is true.* **2** happening at regular intervals. *Every time I have asked her to marry me, she has refused.* **3** all possible. *He has every reason to be unhappy.* **every now and then** sometimes. *I see my parents every now and then.* **every other** *I go there every other day, on Tuesday, then Thursday, then Saturday.*

**everybody** *pronoun* each person or all people. *Everybody wants to come to Sandy's birthday party.*

**everyone** *pronoun* everybody.

**everything** *pronoun* each thing or all things. *Money isn't everything.*

**everywhere** *adverb* in, at, or to every place. *I've looked everywhere for my keys.*

**evidence** *noun* proof; something that makes a matter or statement clear. *The thieves destroyed the evidence by burning their clothes.* **give evidence** to tell what is known about somebody or something in a court of law.

**evil** *adjective* very bad, wicked, usually causing harm. *He's an evil man to treat her that way.* **evil** *noun.* The opposite of "evil" is "good."

**evolution** *noun* the change and development that takes place over a long period of time, during which animals and plants evolve. **evolutionary** *adjective.*

evolution

**evolve** *verb* to develop gradually.

**ewe** (rhymes with "boo") *noun* a female sheep. *Ewe's milk.*

**ex-** *prefix* former, no longer the thing the noun refers to. *An ex-minister is no longer a minister. Harry's ex-wife moved to the city after their divorce.*

**exaggerate** *verb* to say that something is bigger, better, or worse than it really is. *You can't believe his stories; he always exaggerates the truth.* **exaggeration** *noun.*

**examine** *verb* **1** to test somebody's knowledge. **2** to look at a person or thing carefully. *The doctor examined the patient.* **examination** *noun.*

**example** *noun* **1** something that shows how a rule works or what others of the same kind are like. *The penguin is an example of a bird that does not fly* **2** a person or thing worth copying. *Her courage is an example to us all.* **for example** *Some birds can't fly – penguins and emus, for example.*

**exasperate** *verb* to annoy or make angry. *I was exasperated by the child's refusal to sit down.* **exasperation** *noun.*

**excavate** *verb* to dig out. *Archeologists are excavating an ancient Roman site.* **excavation** *noun.*

excavate

**exceed** *verb* to be greater than something. *The whole cost of the expedition must not exceed $1,000.*

**excel** (excels, excelling, excelled) *verb* to be extremely good. *He excels at music.*

**excellent** *adjective* extremely good.

**except** *preposition* not including. *The apples all look delicious, except that bruised one.* **except** *verb* to leave out. *No one can be excepted.*

**exception** *noun* somebody or something that does not follow the general rule. *Dogs were not permitted, but they made an exception for mine because it's a guide dog.*

**exceptional** *adjective* **1** very unusual. *Only in exceptional circumstances.* **2** unusually or extremely good. *Her grades were exceptional.*



**excess** (excesses) *noun* more than is needed; too much of something. *There is an excess of sugar in the cake.* **excess** *adjective. You will have to pay for excess baggage.*

**exchange** *verb* to get something else for something. *I exchanged my dollars for euros. We exchanged addresses.* **exchangeable** *adjective.*

**excite** *verb* to arouse strong feelings. *We were very excited when we got tickets for the concert.* **exciting** *adjective. An exciting adventure.* **excitable** *adjective. He is very nervous and excitable.* **excitement** *noun.*

**exclaim** *verb* to shout with strong feeling. *"No!" he exclaimed. "You are never to go there again."* **exclamation** *noun.* **exclamation mark** *noun* the punctuation mark (!) which shows an exclamation.

**exclude** *verb* to keep or leave somebody or something out. *If you are not a member, you will be excluded from the meeting.* **exclusion** *noun.*

**exclusive** *adjective* **1** excluding many people and so catering for just a few. *An exclusive club.* **2** not appearing anywhere else. *The newspaper contains an exclusive interview with the American movie star.*

**excursion** *noun* a short journey. *We went on an excursion to the country.*

**excuse** *noun* (say eks-**kewss**) the reason given or an explanation for something that has been done. **excuse** (say iks-**kewz**) *verb* **1** to forgive. You excuse a person for doing something wrong or inconvenient. *Please excuse me for being late.* **2** to free somebody from a duty. *He asked to be excused from basketball training because of injury.* **excuse me** used as an apology or when asking for something or interrupting somebody.

**execute**

**execute** *verb* **1** to kill somebody as a punishment for a crime. *The murderer was executed with an ax.* **2** to perform or carry out something, especially a plan or an order. *This task is not very easy to execute.* **execution** *noun.* **executioner** *noun.*

**executive** *noun* a senior person with managerial authority in a business.

**executor** *noun* somebody appointed to carry out a person's instructions in their will. *Her son was the executor of her will.*

**exercise** *noun* **1** movements done to keep healthy or train for a particular sport. *Cycling and swimming are good forms of exercise. Gymnastic exercises.* **2** a short piece of work, especially a set of questions for practise at school. *We had to complete an exercise to improve our grammar.* **exercise** *verb* **1** to do exercises to become fit and healthy. *I try to exercise every day.* **2** If a problem exercises your mind, you think a lot about it.

**exercise**

**exert** *verb* to use power or influence in order to achieve something. If you exert yourself, you make an effort. **exertion** *noun.*

**exhaust** *verb* **1** to tire out. *I'm exhausted.* **2** to use up completely. *Our food supplies were soon exhausted.* **exhausting** *adjective.* **exhaust** *noun* **1** the waste gas produced by an engine. **2** the pipe through which waste gas escapes, also called an exhaust pipe (as on a car).

**exhaustion** *noun* the state of being tired out. *Physical and mental exhaustion set in after a hard day's work.*

**exhaustive** *adjective* thorough, comprehensive. *His exhaustive report covered every detail.*

**exhibit** *verb* **1** to show in public in a museum or a gallery. *The gallery exhibited the artist's latest paintings.* **2** to show your feelings to other people. *His manner exhibited signs of distress.* **exhibit** *noun* a painting, sculpture, or artifact exhibited in a museum or gallery. *Please do not touch the exhibits.*

**exhibition** *noun* a collection of things shown in a public place.

**exile** *noun* **1** a person who has been forced to leave his country, usually for political reasons. **2** having to live away from your own country. *He died alone and in exile.* **exile** *verb. I exile you; you may never return!*

**exist** *verb* **1** to be real. *Do you think ghosts really exist?* **2** to stay alive. **existence** *noun.*

**exit** *noun* **1** a way out. *Where's the exit?* **2** leaving a room or the stage. *She made a quick exit.* **exit** *verb* to leave. *Let's exit the building before the fire spreads.*

**exorcize** *verb* to get rid of an evil spirit. *They had special rituals to exorcize ghosts.* **exorcism** *noun.*

**exotic** *adjective* unusual and interesting. *There are many exotic flower species in the botanical gardens.*

exotic

**expand** *verb* **1** to become larger. *Scientists say the universe is expanding.* **2** to tell a story in more detail. **expansion** *noun.*

**expect** *verb* **1** to think that something will happen. *I never expected to win the race. She expects them to make their own beds.* **2** to believe that somebody will come. *We are expecting them at five o'clock.* **expectation** *noun. Unfortunately the hotel didn't live up to our expectations.*

**expel** (expels, expelling, expelled) *verb* **1** to send somebody away, usually for doing wrong. *He was expelled from school for serious misconduct.* **2** to force out. *When you breathe out, air is expelled from your lungs.* **expulsion** *noun.*

**expend** *verb* to spend or use up. *She expended a lot of energy climbing the hill.*

**expenditure** *noun* the spending of money or effort.

**expense** *noun* the spending of money. If you spare no expense, you don't worry about the cost of something. *I've had a lot of expenses during this past month.*

**expensive** *adjective* costing a lot of money. *She wears expensive clothes.* **expensively** *adverb.*

**experiment** *noun* a test made in order to learn or prove something. *A scientific experiment.* **experiment** *verb* to try things out and make experiments. *It's dangerous to experiment with drugs.* **experimental** *adjective.*

**explode** *verb* **1** to blow up, as a bomb does. **2** to burst out suddenly or show violent feelings. *She exploded with laughter at my joke.* **explosion** *noun.* **explosive** *adjective. Explosive materials.*

**exploit** (say **eks**-ploit) *noun* a brave or adventurous deed. **exploit** (say iks-**ploit**) *verb* **1** to use or develop, especially a country's natural resources. **2** to use unfairly and selfishly for your own profit. *The poor were exploited.* **exploitation** *noun.*

**explore** *verb* **1** to travel to places in order to find out what they are like. **2** to examine a subject. *Have you explored all the possibilities?*

**explorer** *noun* a traveler to unvisited territory. *The maritime explorer sailed west.*

explorer

**export** *verb* to transport or send goods to another country for sale. **export** *noun* **1** the process of exporting goods. *The export of ivory has been banned.* **2** exported goods. Exports are products sold in another country. *Exports have risen this year.*

**exterior** *noun* the outside of something. **exterior** *adjective. The exterior walls are crumbling.*

**exterminate** *verb* to destroy or kill. *Many insects were exterminated by the pesticide.* **extermination** *noun.* **exterminator** *noun.*

**extinct** *adjective* **1** not existing any more. *Dinosaurs have been extinct for millions of years.* **2** no longer active. *An extinct volcano.*

**extra** *adjective, adverb* more than usual; additional. *She says that exercising gives her extra strength.*

**extraordinary** *adjective* **1** very strange or unusual. *Sarah's hat was an extraordinary sight.* **2** unusually great. *She has an extraordinary musical talent.*

**extravagance** *noun* **1** spending more money than is reasonable or than you can afford. **2** something that is very expensive. *A sports car is a real extravagance.* **extravagant** *adjective. She has extravagant tastes.*

**exuberant** *adjective* full of energy and cheerfulness. *They greeted us noisily with lots of exuberant shouting and waving.* **exuberance** *noun.*

**eye** *noun* **1** one of two organs in the face that we see with. *We close our eyes when we go to sleep.* **2** the power of seeing. *You have sharp eyes.* **3** the hole in a needle through which thread passes. **4** a dark spot on a vegetable, such as a potato, from which a new plant grows. **eye** *verb* to watch or look at closely. *He eyed her keenly.* **keep an eye on** to watch somebody or something. *Please keep an eye on the house while we're away.*

**eyeball** *noun* the whole of the eye that is shaped like a ball, including the part concealed behind the eyelids.

**eyebrow** *noun* the line of hairs growing above the eyes.

**eyelid** *noun* either of the two pieces of covering skin that move down when you close your eyes or blink.

**eyesight** *noun* the power to see. *He wears glasses because he has poor eyesight.*

**eyewitness** *noun* a person who has seen an accident or a crime happen and can describe it. *Will eyewitnesses to the accident please contact the police?*

**eyrie** (rhymes with "weary") *noun* an eagle's nest. *The eagle builds its eyrie from large twigs and sticks.*

eyrie

Ee

**fable** *noun* a short story, usually one with animals, that teaches a lesson about human behavior or truth.

**face** *noun* **1** the front part of the head. **2** a look or expression on the face. *A happy face.* **3** the front, upper side, or surface of something. *The north face of the mountain.* **face** *verb* **1** to have the front pointing in, or to turn it toward, a certain direction. *Our house faces the park.* **2** to be brave enough to deal with something unpleasant or dangerous. **3** to cover a surface, such as a wall, with a layer of different material. **face to face** two people or animals looking straight at each other.



**facsimile** (say fak-**sim**-il-ee) *noun* an exact copy or reproduction of something.

**fact** *noun* something that is true or has actually happened. **in fact** really.

**factor** *noun* **1** one of the things that influences an event and brings about a result. *Money was an important factor in the decision.* **2** a number by which a larger number can be divided. *2 and 4 are factors of 8.*

factory

**factory** (factories) *noun* a large building where goods are made, usually by machines.

**factual** *adjective* based on facts. *She gave a factual account of events.*

**faculty** *noun* **1** any of the powers of the mind or body, such as speech or understanding. *Although she is 90 years old, her faculties are still in good shape.* **2** a large department in a university.

**Fahrenheit** *adjective* a measurement of temperature on a scale where water freezes at 32° and boils at 212°.

**fail** *verb* **1** to try to do something and not succeed. *All my plans failed.* **2** not to do or remember something. *You failed to warn me that she doesn't like eggs.* **3** not to produce the expected result or work as expected. *The brakes failed.* **4** If a teacher fails you, she grades you as not having passed a test. **failed** *adjective* unsuccessful.

**failing** *noun* a weakness or fault.

**failure** *noun* **1** lack of success, failing to do something. **2** an unsuccessful person.

**faint** *adjective* weak, not clear. *The writing was very faint.* **faint** *verb* to lose consciousness suddenly.

**fair** *adjective* **1** honest and just. **2** pale or light in color. **3** fine, especially when talking about the weather. **4** reasonable. *After living in France for a year, he has a fair knowledge of French.* **fair** *noun* **1** an outdoor event with machine rides and amusements. **2** a market or exhibition where goods are displayed and sold. *Children's books are sold at the Bologna book trade fair.* **fairness** *noun.*

**fairground** *noun* the place where a fair is held. *We had a fantastic time on the rides at the fairground.*

fairground

**fairy** (fairies) *noun* a small, imaginary person with wings and magical powers.

**faith** *noun* **1** a strong belief or trust. **2** a particular religion. *The Christian faith.*

**faithful** *adjective* trustworthy and loyal.

**fake** *noun* a person or thing that is not what it appears to be. *The painting is a fake.* **fake** *verb* **1** to make something look better or more valuable in order to deceive people. **2** to pretend. *He faked a limp.*

**falcon** *noun* a bird of prey that can be trained to hunt other birds and animals. **falconry** *noun.*

**fall** (falls, falling, fell, fallen) *verb* **1** to go down or drop to a lower place. **2** to become lower. *The temperature fell.* **3** to happen. *Silence fell.* **4** to pass into another state. *I have fallen in love.* **5** to die in battle. **fall** *noun* **1** a drop from a higher to a lower place. **2** getting lower or less in quantity, quality or level. **3** autumn, the season between summer and winter. **fall for 1** If you fall for somebody, you are attracted to them. **2** to be deceived by. *I don't fall for his tricks.* **falls** *plural noun* a waterfall. *Niagara Falls.*

**false** *adjective* **1** not true, wrong. *She gave a false name.* **2** artificial. *False teeth.*

**familiar** *adjective* **1** well known. **2** knowing something well. *Are you familiar with this play?* **3** in close friendship with someone.

**family** *noun* **1** parents and their children, grandparents, and other relations. **2** a group of related things, especially animals or plants. *Lions belong to the cat family.*

**famine** *noun* a severe lack of food in a region for a long time.

**fan** *noun* **1** something that moves the air to make you or a room cooler. **2** an admirer or supporter. **fan** (fans, fanning, fanned) *verb* to make the air move.

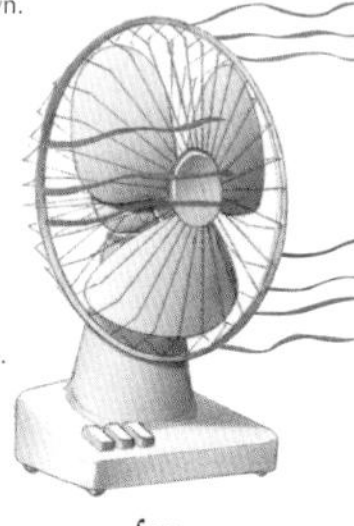

fan

**fancy** *adjective* **1** brightly colored and decorated. **2** expensive and of high quality. **fancy** (fancies) *noun* (old fashioned) a feeling of liking something or someone. *I have taken a fancy to that restaurant.* **fancy** (fancies, fancying, fancied) *verb* to imagine or consider something is true. *He fancies himself a dancer.* **fanciful** *adjective.*

**fantasy** (fantasies) *noun* a situation that exists only in your imagination. **fantastic** *adjective.*

**far** *adjective* distant, a long way off. **far** (farther/further, farthest/furthest) *adverb* **1** at or to a great distance. *Do you live far from here?* **2** much. *That's far too expensive.* **far-fetched** *adjective* unlikely or impossible, especially an idea or example. *His story was too far-fetched for us to believe.* **far-reaching** *adjective* having wide influence or effect over a long period of time. *Far-reaching reforms.*

**fare** *noun* **1** the money paid by passengers for a journey. **2** food and drink. **fare** *verb* to get along. *Because we had learned some Italian, we fared well when we got to Italy.*

farm

**farm** *noun* **1** a place where crops are grown and animals are kept. **2** a farmhouse. **farm** *verb* to grow and harvest crops or raise animals.

**farmer** *noun* a person who owns or works on a farm. *The farmer kept pigs and chickens.*

**fascinate** *verb* to attract and be very interesting. *Space travel always fascinated him as a boy, and now he is an astronaut.* **fascination** *noun.* **fascinating** *adjective.*

**fast** *adjective* **1** quick. *He has bought a fast car.* **2** firmly fixed. *Wash the shirt separately as the color is not fast and may run.* **3** showing a time that is later than the real time. *My watch is fast.* **fast** *adverb* **1** quickly. *He was driving too fast.* **2** fully. *She was fast asleep.* **fast** *verb* to eat no food. *Ramadan is a time of fasting in the Islamic world.* **fast** *noun.* **fast food** inexpensive food that is cooked and served quickly.

**fasten** *verb* **1** to fix one thing to another. **2** to close or lock. *Fasten your seatbelts before takeoff.* **fastener** *noun.* **fastening** *noun.*

**fatal** *adjective* bringing or ending in death. *A fatal accident.* **fatally** *adverb.*

**fate** *noun* **1** the power that is believed to control events. *Fate was against us.* **2** what will happen or has happened to somebody. *It was her fate.*

**fatigue** *noun* **1** a feeling of extreme tiredness. **2** weakness in metal that may make it break.

fault

**fault** *noun* **1** a large crack in the surface of the Earth. *Earthquakes usually occur along faults.* **2** a mistake or imperfection. *An electrical fault.* **3** a bad point about a person or thing. *He's always finding fault with me.* **fault** *verb* to find fault with something or somebody. *His attitude can't be faulted.* **faulty** *adjective.*

**fauna** *noun* all the wild animals of a region or period. *She was studying the flora and fauna of the Alps.*

**favor** *noun* **1** a liking of somebody or something. *He is trying to win her favor.* **2** If you are in favor of something, you like the idea of it. If somebody is in favor, he/she is liked. If he/she is out of favor, he/she is not liked. **3** a kind act. *Would you do me a favor and take me to the station?* **favor** *verb* **1** to like or support, especially a plan or an idea. *The government favors free school meals.* **2** to prefer or be kinder to one person over another. *Our teacher tends to favor the girls.*

**favorable** *adjective* good, approving. *The teacher gave her a favorable report.*

**favorite** *adjective* liked more than all others. *What is your favorite book?* **favorite** *noun* **1** a person or thing preferred over others. *This toy is my favorite.* **2** in sport, the competitor expected to win.

**favoritism** *noun* the act of unfairly treating one person or group better than another. *Favoritism is not fair.*

**fear** *noun* **1** an unpleasant feeling that something bad, dangerous, or painful might happen. *She has a fear of flying.* **2** danger. *She has no fear of failure.* **fear** *verb* to be afraid or to worry about something or somebody. *They feared for their lives.* **for fear of** because of worry about something. *I didn't ring the doorbell last night for fear of disturbing you.* **never fear** there is no danger of that.

**fearful** *adjective* **1** causing fear or being afraid. *A fearful storm shook the house.* **2** bad, terrible. *Your room is always in a fearful mess.*

**fearless** *adjective* without fear, not afraid. *She was fearless in the face of danger.* **fearlessly** *adverb.*

**fearsome** *adjective* terrible or frightening. *The monster was a fearsome sight.*

**feasible** *adjective* possible.

**feast** *noun* **1** a large and very good meal. *The wedding feast lasted many hours.* **2** a religious festival. **feast** *verb* to eat and drink very well.

**feat** *noun* a courageous or skillful action that is difficult to do. *His survival was a feat of endurance.*

**feature** *noun* **1** an important part. *Sand is a feature of the desert.* **2** an important part of your face. *Your eyes, mouth, and nose make up your features.* **3** an article in a newspaper or a special program on radio or TV. **feature** *verb* to be an important part of.



**February** *noun* the second month of the year. February has 28 days, but in leap years it has 29.

**fee** *noun* a sum of money paid for services.

**feeble** *adjective* weak, having very little power. *He made a rather feeble attempt to climb up.* **feebly** *adverb.*

**feedback** *noun* comments made about something that you have done, so that possible changes can be made.

**feel** (feels, feeling, felt) *verb* **1** to touch something with your fingers or hold it. *Just feel the quality of the fabric.* **2** to have a certain sensation – wet, dry, soft, or sticky, for example. *My clothes feel soft.* **3** to be aware of a mood or to know that something is happening to your body. *I'm not feeling well.* **4** to think something or have an opinion. *I feel strongly that the action is right.* **5** to search, usually with your hands, feet, or a stick. *He felt in his pockets for money.* **feel** *noun. I like the feel of silk.* **feel like** to want. *I feel like a swim.*

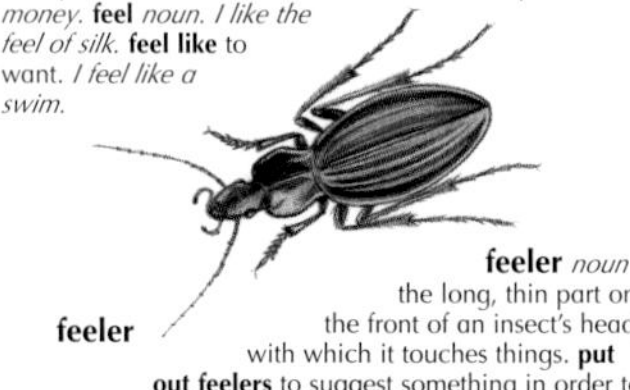

**feeler**

**feeler** *noun* the long, thin part on the front of an insect's head, with which it touches things. **put out feelers** to suggest something in order to find out what others think or want to do.

**feeling** *noun* **1** the power to feel things. *I'm so cold, I've lost all feeling in my hands.* **2** an emotion or physical sensation. *An itchy feeling.* If you have a feeling for somebody or something, you like them. **3** what you think; an idea. *I have a feeling that he'll do very well in the test.* **4** sympathy and understanding. *He read the poem with great feeling.*

**feet** plural of foot. **fall on one's feet** to have good luck. *He's fallen on his feet with that new job.*

**feint** (say faynt) *noun* a pretend attack that is intended to deceive an opponent, as in fencing or boxing. **feint** *verb.*

**feline** (say **fee**-line) *adjective* like a cat.

**female** *adjective* **1** a woman or girl. **2** an animal or plant that can have babies, lay eggs, or produce fruit. *A bitch is a female dog.* **female** *noun* a person or animal that belongs to the sex that can have babies or lay eggs.

**feminine** *adjective* **1** with the qualities of a woman. *She designs very feminine clothes.* **2** in grammar, referring to words that are classed as female. *French nouns are either masculine or feminine.* **femininity** *noun.*

**feminist** *noun* a person who believes that women should have the same rights and opportunities as men. **feminism** *noun.*

**fence** *noun* a barrier made of wood or wire around an area or used to divide two areas of land. **fence** *verb* **1** to build a fence around an area or along something. *We fenced in the garden to keep the cows out.* **2** to fight with a long thin sword as sport. **fencing** *noun.*

**ferment** (say fer-**ment**) *verb* **1** to turn liquid into an alcoholic drink by the action of yeast. **2** to excite and stir up. **fermentation** *noun.*

**fern** *noun* a woodland plant with green, feathery leaves and no flowers.

**ferocious** *adjective* fierce, savage. *A ferocious dog guards the entrance to the house.* **ferocity** *noun.*

**ferret** *noun* a small animal with a pointed nose. Ferrets are used for catching rats and rabbits. **ferret out** to search for something or find out information.

**ferry** (ferries) *noun* a boat that goes across a river or other narrow channel of water carrying people and cars. **ferry** (ferries, ferrying, ferried) *verb* to transport people or goods. *She ferries the children to school each day.*

**fertile** *adjective* **1** Land or soil is fertile when plants grow well in it. *Silt from the river makes the land fertile.* **2** able to produce babies or seeds. **3** full of ideas. *My brother has a fertile imagination.* **fertility** *noun.*

**fertilize** *verb* **1** to put pollen into a plant or sperm into an egg to make a new plant, animal, or person grow. **2** When you fertilize soil, you add things to it to make it more fertile. **fertilization** *noun.*

**fertilizer** *noun* a natural substance or chemical added to soil to make it more fertile. *Organic fertilizers are best for the environment.*

**fertilize**

**fester** *verb* **1** to become infected, especially a wound or cut. **2** to poison the mind, causing bitterness over a period of time. *Hatred still festers between the brothers.*

**festival** *noun* **1** a time for special celebration. *Christmas is a Christian festival.* **2** when a number of events, such as concerts, are held in one place at a stated time.

festival

**festive** *adjective* joyful and suitable for a festival. *It was Christmas and all the family were in a festive mood.* **festivity** *noun.*

**fetch** *verb* **1** to get and bring back. *We must fetch a doctor.* **2** to be sold for a certain price. *These old books might well fetch a lot of money.*

**fetus** (fetuses) *noun* (say **fee**-tus) a developing animal or human embryo; a human baby three or more months old inside its mother.

**feud** *noun* (say fewd) a long-lasting quarrel, especially between families.

**few** *adjective, pronoun* not many; a small number. *A few of the children went home early.* **fewer than** not as many as. *Fewer than ten students passed the test.*

**fiasco** *noun* (say fee-**ass**-koh) an absurd failure. *The vacation was a complete fiasco: the car broke down, the roof of the chalet leaked, and Sue broke her leg.*

**fiber** *noun* **1** a very thin thread, especially one used to make cloth or rope. **2** parts of plants or seeds that the body cannot digest. *A high fiber diet cuts out most processed foods.* Wholewheat bread and beans are high in fiber. **3** a thin piece of flesh, like thread, in the body. *Muscles are made of fibers.* **fibrous** *adjective.*

**fiction** *noun* writing or stories about something that is a fantasy. *Is it fact or fiction?* **fictional** *adjective.*

**fictitious** *adjective* not true; invented. *The man gave the police a fictitious name.*

**fiddle** *noun* **1** a violin. *Paul played us many tunes on the fiddle, and we danced until dawn.* **2** a dishonest action; a swindle. **fiddle** *verb* **1** to play the violin. **2** to get or change something, especially accounts, dishonestly. *He fiddled the figures.* **3** to touch or move things around with your fingers. *Please stop fiddling with the matches.* **as fit as a fiddle** in very good health. **play second fiddle** to be less important. **fiddler** *noun.*

**fidget** *verb* to move around restlessly and never sit still. *Some children fidget a lot.* **fidget** *noun. Rebecca is a terrible fidget.*

**field** *noun* **1** a piece of land with grass or crops growing on it. **2** an area of grass marked out for a game. *A football field.* **3** a battlefield. **4** a piece of land where oil, coal, gold, or other things may be found. **5** a subject, an area of study, or an activity. *She is an expert in the field of medical research.* **6** a magnetic field. **field** *verb* to catch the ball after it has been hit in baseball or other games. **field a question** to answer a difficult question. **field of vision** the whole area you can see. *Her large, floppy hat restricted her field of vision.*

**fierce** *adjective* **1** angry and violent. **2** very strong. *The camels crossed the desert in the fierce heat.*

**fiery** *adjective* flaming, like fire. *He has a fiery temper.*

**fig** *noun* a soft, pear-shaped fruit full of seeds that grows on trees in hot countries. It can be eaten fresh or dried. **to not give a fig** not to care at all about something.

fig

**fight** (fights, fighting, fought) *verb* **1** to use your hands, weapons, or words against another in order to win. When people fight, they try to hurt each other. **2** to try to overcome or stop something. *We must fight crime.* **3** to quarrel. **fight** *noun* **1** the act of fighting somebody, using hands or weapons. **2** a struggle to overcome something. *The fight against poverty.*

**fighter** *noun* **1** a person who fights. **2** a fast military aircraft. *The jet fighter thundered overhead.*

**figure** *noun* **1** a sign that stands for a number. 1, 3, and 9 are figures. **2** how much something costs. *She sold her house for a huge figure.* **3** a diagram or drawing, usually in a book. **4** the shape of the body. *She has an excellent figure.* **5** a wooden or stone carving of a person or an animal. *The tourist bought a wooden figure of an elephant.* **6** a person. *He was a great figure in the world of pop music.* **figure** *verb* **1** to take part in something. *He doesn't figure much in the article.* **2** to believe or to work something out. *I figure they'll make him boss.* **figure of speech** an expression used to make your meaning stronger, e.g., "As pretty as a picture."

Fiji's flag

**Fiji** *noun* a country composed of many islands in the Pacific Ocean.

**filter** *noun* **1** a device through which liquids are passed to make them clean. **2** a piece of glass or plastic used on a camera lens to hold back light. **filter** *verb* **1** to pass through a filter. *It's good to filter drinking water.* **2** to pass or move slowly, especially of people, traffic, or ideas. *Light filtered through the curtains.*



**filth** *noun* a disgusting amount of dirt. **filthy** *adjective. Your muddy boots have made the carpet filthy.*

**final** *adjective* last, at the end. *The final word on the page.* **final** *noun* the last game in a competition or the last examination. *They are in the NBA finals.* **finalist** *noun.*

**finally** *adverb* **1** lastly or at last. *Finally, I'd like to thank the principal.* **2** after a long time. *I finally found out where he lives.*

**finance** *noun* the control and management of money. **finance** *verb* to provide money for something. *Who is financing the trip?* **finances** *plural noun* money, especially of a business. *How are the company's finances?*

**find** (finds, finding, found) *verb* **1** to get or see somebody or something by searching or by chance. **2** to learn by working, experimenting, or experience. *Doctors are hoping to find a cure.* **find** *noun* something found.

**fine** *adjective* **1** excellent. *We had a fine time on Sunday.* **2** dry, bright, and sunny. *In fine weather.* **3** very thin. *Fine hair.* **fine** *adverb* very well. *That suits me fine.* **fine** *noun* a sum of money to be paid as punishment. *I had to pay a parking fine.* **fine** *verb* to make somebody pay a fine. **cut it fine** to just make it on time.

**finger** *noun* **1** one of the long, thin parts of the hand, especially those other than the thumb. **2** a thin piece of something. **finger** *verb* to touch with your fingers.

**fingerprint** *noun* the mark made by the lines on the skin of the fingertip. *They left no fingerprints.*

**finish** (finishes) *noun* **1** the end or last part of something. *The finish of a race.* **2** the coating, especially of painted articles. **finish** *verb* to reach the end or bring to the end.

**Finland** *noun* a Scandinavian country in northern Europe.

**Finnish** *noun* the language spoken by the Finns, the people of Finland. **Finnish** *adjective.*

Finland

**fir** *noun* an evergreen tree with leaves that look like needles. The seeds are formed in cones. *We walked through the plantation of firs.*

**fire** *noun* **1** burning with flames. *The house is on fire.* If you set fire to something, you light it in order to burn it. **2** burning coal or wood or an apparatus that uses gas or electricity for heating or cooking. **3** the shooting of guns. *The enemy opened fire.* **fire** *verb* **1** to shoot a gun or propel bullets, missiles, or arrows. **2** to shoot off other things. *He fired lots of questions at us.* **3** to bake pottery. *Clay pots are fired in a kiln.* **4** to dismiss somebody from a job. *He was fired for misconduct.* **5** to excite. *His speech fired our enthusiasm.* **catch fire** to begin to burn.

**fire engine** *noun* a large vehicle that carries firefighters and equipment for putting out fires. *The fire engine raced toward the fire.*

**firefighter** *noun* a person who puts out fires. *The firefighter was awarded a medal.*

**firm** *adjective* **1** not completely hard, but not changing shape when pressed. *Firm muscles.* **2** steady; not shaking or moving. *Keep a firm grip on it.* **3** strong and sure; not likely to change. *We need a firm decision.* **firm** *noun* a business or organization. *He works for a computer firm.*

**fist** *noun* a hand with the fingers tightly closed. *In boxing, you fight with your fists.*

**fit** (fitter, fittest) *adjective* **1** right or good enough. *The meal was fit for a king.* **2** healthy. *She goes jogging every day to keep fit.* **fit** *noun* **1** the way something fits. **2** a sudden attack of an illness or loss of consciousness. *The boy had a coughing fit during the concert.* **3** an outburst. *He hit him in a fit of anger.* **fit** (fits, fitting, fitted) *verb* **1** to be the right size or shape. *The shoes don't fit; they're too small.* **2** to make clothes the right size and shape for somebody. *He had a suit fitted.* **3** to put into place. *We had a new lock fitted on the door.* **4** to be or make suitable. *The description fits her well.* **fitness** *noun.* **fit in** **1** to feel comfortable among a group of people. **2** to find time to do something. *We'll fit in an extra lesson before the test.* **have someone in fits** to make someone laugh uncontrollably at something.

**fix** *noun* **1** something arranged, especially by deception. *The election was a fix, which later caused large numbers of voters to protest.* **2** to take an amount of an addictive drug. **fix** *verb* **1** to make something firm, to attach it. **2** to decide or arrange. *We have fixed the date for our vacation.* **3** to repair. *He managed to fix the bike.* **4** to treat colors or a photographic film with chemicals to protect them from light. **5** to prepare or cook, especially food or a drink. *I'll fix myself dinner.* **fix up** to arrange or improve. **in a fix** in a difficult situation.

**fixture** *noun* built-in furniture or equipment in a house or apartment that is left behind when you move. *The bathtub and lights are fixtures of the house.* **be a permanent fixture** to always be present and unlikely to leave. *Sharon's boyfriend seems to be a permanent fixture at present.*

fjord

**fjord** *noun* (say **fee**-ord) a long, narrow inlet of sea between steep cliffs, as in Norway. *We went on a cruise among the Norwegian fjords.*

**flabby** *adjective* soft, loose fat. *He's a bit flabby around the waist.*

**flag** *noun* a piece of cloth with a design on it that represents something, such as a country. *The Texas flag.* **flag** (flags. flagging, flagged) *verb* **1** to become weak. *My interest in this project is flagging.* **2** to signal with a flag. **flag down** to wave, as at a car to make it stop.

**flagstone** *noun* a smooth, flat stone slab used for paving floors.

**flair** *noun* instinctive talent. *That design student has a real flair for fashion.*

**flake** *noun* **1** a small, thin piece of something. **2** a piece of falling snow. **flake** *verb* to come off in flakes. *The paint is flaking off.*

**flame** *noun* hot, bright burning gas, seen when something is on fire. *The car burst into flames.* **in flames** burning.

**flamingo** (flamingos or flamingoes) *noun* a tropical water bird with long legs and pink feathers.

flamingo

**flammable** *adjective* likely to catch fire or burn easily. Flammable is the same as inflammable. The opposite of flammable is nonflammable.

**flank** *noun* the side of something, especially an animal. **flank** *verb* to be placed on one or both sides. *The princess was flanked by two tall men in dinner suits.*

**flare** *noun* **1** a sudden bright flame or light. **2** a device producing a bright light that is used as a signal. **flare** *verb* to burn with a bright flame for a short time. **flare up** to show sudden anger.

**flared** *adjective* shaped so that something gets wider toward the bottom. *Flared trousers.*

**flash** (flashes) *noun* **1** a sudden bright light. *Flashes of lightning.* **2** a sudden idea or display of wit. *She had a flash of inspiration.* **3** a device producing a sudden bright light for taking photographs in the dark. **4** a short news report. **flash** *verb* **1** to shine brightly once or several times. **2** to suddenly think of something. **3** to move very fast or appear suddenly. *Cars flashed past me.* **4** When you flash a look at somebody, you look at them very quickly. **flash in the pan** a sudden short-lived success. **in a flash** quickly. *The ambulance was there in a flash.*

Ff

**flat** (flatter, flattest) *adjective* **1** not curved; smooth, with no bumps. **2** dull or boring. **3** not deep or high. *Flat shoes.* **4** complete or absolute. *A flat refusal.* **5** without energy. A flat drink is not fizzy. A flat battery no longer produces electricity. **flat** *adverb* **1** exactly. *He arrived in five minutes flat.* **2** If something falls flat, it is unsuccessful. **3** spread out. *Lie flat on the ground.* **flat** *noun* a set of rooms on one floor, smaller than an apartment. **flat out 1** at top speed. **2** using all your energy.

**flatter** *verb* **1** to say that a person or thing is better, more important, or more beautiful than they really are. **2** to show somebody or something as better then they really are. *The picture flatters her.* **flattery** *noun.*

**flaw** *noun* something that makes a person or thing imperfect; something wrong. **flawed** *adjective.*

flea

**flea** *noun* a small jumping insect that bites and sucks blood from people and animals.

**fledgling** *noun* a young bird.

**flee** (flees, fleeing, fled) *verb* to run away from something or somewhere. *We had to flee the country.*

**fleece** *noun* the wool covering of sheep. *She spun the fleece on her spinning wheel.* **fleece** *verb* to trick a person out of their money. *We were fleeced in the market.*

**fleet** *noun* a group of ships, planes, or other vehicles belonging to one country or company. *A fleet of taxis.*

**flesh** *noun* **1** the soft substance that includes fat and muscle between the bones and the skin of people and animals. **2** the soft part of fruit and vegetables. **fleshy** *adjective.* **in the flesh** in real life. *He doesn't look so tall in the flesh.* **flesh out** to give more details.

**flex** (flexes) *noun* a long, flexible, covered wire for electricity. **flex** *verb* to bend or stretch, especially a muscle, leg, or arm. *He flexed his muscles.*

**flexible** *adjective* **1** easily bent. **2** easily changed to suit new conditions; adaptable. *I prefer flexible working hours.* **flexibility** *noun.*

**flicker** *verb* **1** to burn or shine unsteadily. **2** to move lightly or jerkily. *His eyelids flickered.* **flicker** *noun.*

**flight** *noun* **1** flying. **2** a plane journey. **3** a set of stairs. **4** the act of running away and escaping. **5** a group of birds flying together. *A flight of geese.*

**flimsy** (flimsier, flimsiest) *adjective* thin or light and easily damaged. **flimsily** *adverb. The table is very flimsily built.* **flimsiness** *noun.*



**fling** *noun* **1** throwing something quickly. **2** a short, wild time of fun and enjoyment. **3** a dance. **fling** (flings, flinging, flung) *verb* **1** to throw quickly or carelessly. *She flung some clothes in a suitcase and left.* **2** to move quickly and violently. *She flung her head back angrily.*

**flint** *noun* **1** a hard, gray stone, easily shaped into primitive cutting tools or weapons such as arrowheads. **2** a small piece of flint or hard metal that can be struck to produce sparks and light things.

flint

**flip** (flips, flipping, flipped) *verb* **1** to turn something over quickly. **2** to move something into a different position or send it spinning in the air with a quick push or light hit. *She flipped open her diary.* **flip** *noun.*

**flippant** *adjective* not serious, especially when trying to be amusing. *She made some very flippant remarks.* **flippancy** *noun.*

**flipper** *noun* **1** the flat limb of some sea animals used for swimming. **2** Flippers are attachments you can wear on your feet to help you swim more quickly.

**flirt** *verb* to behave in a playful way as if you were attracted to somebody. *She flirts with all the boys.* **flirt** *noun* somebody who flirts a lot. *She's a terrible flirt.* **flirtatious** *adjective.*

**float** *noun* **1** a light object, such as a cork, that is used to help somebody or something float. **2** a vehicle on which people parade through the streets in a festival procession. **3** a sum of money kept, especially by storekeepers, for giving change or paying small bills. **float** *verb* **1** to stay or move in a liquid or in the air. *The leaf floated down the river.* **2** to move aimlessly about. *She floats from one job to another without ever settling down.*

**floating voter** *noun* somebody who does not always vote for the same party.

**floe** *noun* (rhymes with glow) a sheet of floating ice. *The polar bear walked across the ice floe.*

**flog** (flogs, flogging, flogged) *verb* to beat a person or an animal with a whip. *The jockey flogged his horse hard to make it run faster, but the horse came in second and the jockey was later rebuked.* **flogging** *noun.*

flood

**flood** *noun* **1** a large amount of water in a place that is usually dry. *The village was almost destroyed by the flood.* **2** a large amount. *A flood of complaints.* **flood** *verb* **1** to cover with a flood. **2** to arrive in large amounts. *Calls flooded in after the TV program.*

**floor** *noun* **1** the surface, especially of a room, that you walk on. **2** all the rooms that are on the same level in a building. *Our apartment is on the second floor.* **3** The ground at the bottom of the sea, a cave, or a valley. **floor** *verb* **1** to knock down. *The punch floored him.* **2** to confuse. *His question completely floored me.*

**flop** (flops, flopping, flopped) *verb* **1** to sit or lie down suddenly and heavily. **2** to fail or be unsuccessful. *The play flopped.* **flop** *noun* **1** a flopping movement or sound. **2** a total failure. **floppy** *adjective* not firm. *Floppy hats.*

**flora** *noun* all the plants growing in a region. *Flora and fauna.*

flora

**florist** *noun* a person or shop that sells flowers. *The florist's art is arranging flowers.*

**flour** *noun* a powder made from ground grain, especially wheat, used to make bread and cakes. **floury** *adjective. The cook washed her floury hands.*

**flourish** (flourishes, flourishing, flourished) *verb* **1** to grow healthily. *Your new baby is flourishing.* **2** to be well and successful. *Our store is flourishing and we are going to expand the business.* **3** to wave something around for people to notice. *He rushed into the room flourishing a cheque.* **flourish** *noun.*

**flower** *noun* **1** the colored or white part of a plant that produces seeds and fruit. **2** the flower and its stem. **flower** *verb* to produce flowers. *Daffodils flower in spring.*

**flu** *noun* short for influenza, an illness in which you may have a cold, a temperature, and aching muscles.

**fluent** *adjective* able to speak and write a language easily. *She speaks fluent French and German.* **fluently** *adverb.* **fluency** *noun.*

**fluid** *adjective* **1** able to flow, not solid. **2** not fixed, likely to change. *Her ideas were totally fluid.* **3** smooth and graceful. *We watched the dancer's fluid movements.* **fluid** *noun* a substance that can flow, such as a liquid or a gas.

**fluster** *verb* to make somebody nervous; to fuddle and confuse. *I got flustered when they all started asking me questions.*

**flute** *noun* a woodwind musical instrument shaped like a long pipe or tube that you blow into, covering the holes to make notes.

foliage

**flutter** *noun* **1** a quick, irregular movement; vibration. **2** a feeling of agitation, confusion or excitement. *He was in a flutter because he was going on vacation later that day and still had not packed his suitcase.* **flutter** *verb* **1** to move quickly and irregularly, up and down or from side to side. *The flags fluttered prettily in the wind.* **2** to move through the air with small, quick movements. *Ticker tape fluttered down.*

**fly** (flies) *noun* **1** a small flying insect. **2** the front opening on pants. **fly** (flies, flying, flew, flown) *verb* **1** to move through the air like a bird or plane. **2** to control a plane or transport passengers in a plane. **3** to make something fly. *To fly a kite.* **4** to move or pass very quickly. *Time flies when you enjoy your work.* **5** to move or wave about. *Flags were flying.* **send somebody flying** to hit a person so they fall over. **fly at somebody** to attack a person suddenly and violently.

**foal** *noun* a young horse.

**foam** *noun* **1** a mass of small white air bubbles, especially on top of a liquid. **foam rubber** rubber filled with air bubbles, used to fill, for example, pillows.

**focus** (focuses) *noun* **1** a point or distance from an eye or lens where an object is sharpest. *The picture is in focus.* **2** the point at which beams of light or sound waves meet. **3** the center of interest or attention. **focus** (focused, focusing or focussed, focussing) *verb* **1** to adjust a lens so that things can be seen clearly. *He focused the telescope on the Moon.* **2** to concentrate.

**foe** *noun* an enemy.

**fog** *noun* very thick mist.

**foggy** *adjective* thick with fog. **I don't have the foggiest idea.** I have no idea at all.

**foil** *noun* **1** metal sheet as thin as paper, usually used for wrapping up food. **2** somebody or something that makes another person or thing look better. *Richard acted as a foil for his friend.* **3** a long, thin sword with a covered point used in the sport of fencing. **foil** *verb* to stop somebody from carrying out a plan. *The police managed to foil the robbers after hearing of their plan.*

**foliage** *noun* leaves of plants and trees.

**folk** (folks) *noun* people. *Please send it to the folks back home.*

**follow** *verb* **1** to come or go after, or move behind something or someone in the same direction. **2** to go in the same direction. *I followed the route on the map.* **3** to come next on a list. *Tuesday follows Monday.* **4** to do what somebody says or suggests. *I followed his advice.* **5** to take an interest in something. *He follows the news.* **6** to understand. *I couldn't follow his line of thought.* **7** to be true or logical. *It doesn't follow that because you don't like school, you don't have to go.* **follower** *noun.* **following** *adjective.* **following** *noun. She has a large following of fans.*

**font** *noun* **1** a stone water basin that is used for baptisms in a church. **2** a typeface, such as you choose on a computer.

font

**food** *noun* something that is eaten by people or animals, or taken in by plants to help them to grow and live. **food chain** *noun* a way to describe how creatures feed on each other. For instance, plants are eaten by insects, which are caught by small animals, and so on. Humans are at the top of the food chain.

**fool** *noun* **1** a silly person who acts stupidly. If you make a fool of somebody, you make them look stupid. **2** a clown. **3** a sweet made of cream and stewed fruit. *My mother makes a delicious blueberry fool in the summer.* **fool** *verb* **1** to trick somebody. *She fooled me into thinking it was her car.* **2** to behave in a silly way. *Please stop fooling around and listen to me.* **foolish** *adjective* unwise or stupid.

**foolproof** *adjective* something that is easy to use and cannot go wrong. *My plan is absolutely foolproof.*

**foot** (feet) *noun* **1** the part at the end of the leg below the ankle that people and animals stand on. **2** the lowest part or the bottom end. *The church is at the foot of the hill.* **3** a measurement of length (*abbreviation* ft, equal to 12 inches or 30.5 centimeters). **on foot** walking. *What's the quickest way on foot?* **fall on your feet** to be lucky. **have cold feet** to be nervous. **stand on your own two feet** to be financially independent. **have one foot in the grave** to be very old. **put your foot in it** to say the wrong thing; to be tactless or to make an embarrassing mistake.



**for** *preposition* **1** to show that something is intended to be given to somebody. *This giant present is for you.* **2** toward, in order to reach. *This bus is for downtown.* **3** for the purpose of. *The computer is for my office.* **4** in order to have, get, or do something. *I'm doing it for your own good.* **5** to show distance, time, or price. *For the first time.* **6** in favor of. *How many people are for the strike and how many are against it?* **7** because of something. *I was grounded for being late.* **8** as being or meaning. *She looked so old I took her for your grandmother.* **9** with reference to something surprising. *She looks amazingly young for her age.* **10** being suitable. *The right person for the job.* **for ever** emphatically forever.

**forbid** (forbids, forbidding, forbade, forbidden) *verb* to order somebody not to do something. *I forbid you to go out until you've finished your homework.*

**force** *noun* **1** power or strength. *He had to use force to open the door.* **2** a power that produces changes of movement in a body. *The force of gravity.* **3** a person, thing, belief, influence, or idea that causes changes. *The forces of good and evil.* **4** an organized group of police or soldiers. *The police force.* **force** *verb* **1** to make somebody do something against their will. *He forced the children to clean up their rooms.* **2** to use force to do or get something. *I had to force the lock to get in.* **in force** in large numbers. **join forces** to combine efforts. **forced** *adjective. A forced smile.*

**ford**

**ford** *noun* a shallow place in a river where you can walk or drive across it. *The ford was liable to flood.*

**forecast** *noun* a statement that tells you what is likely to happen. *The weather forecast was good.* **forecast** (forecasts, forecasting, forecast) *verb.*

**forehand** *noun* a stroke played in tennis with the palm turned forward. The opposite of "forehand" is "backhand."

**forehead** *noun* (say **for**-hed or for-red) the part of the face above the eyes.

**foreign** *adjective* **1** belonging to a country that is not your own. *Foreign language.* **2** not natural or belonging. *She is such an honest person; lying is foreign to her.*

**foreigner** *noun* a person from another country.

**foresee** (foresees, foreseeing, foresaw) *verb* to know what is going to happen. *I foresee trouble.* **foresight** *noun.*

**forest** *noun* a large area of land covered with trees. *A beech forest.*

**forest**

**forever** *adverb* **1** continually. *He was forever complaining about that.* **2** eternally.

**foreword** *noun* an introduction to a book.

**forfeit** *verb* (say **for**-fit) to lose something because you have done something wrong or broken a rule. *If you don't pay the bill within two weeks, you forfeit your discount.* **forfeit** *noun* **1** something lost, a price to be paid. **2** something you have to do when you lose a game. *She lost the round and was made to pay a forfeit.*

**forge** *noun* a place where metal is heated and shaped. *Horseshoes are made in a forge.* **forge** *verb* **1** to copy things, especially currency, paintings, or documents, in order to deceive people. **2** to shape something by heating and hammering it. *The blacksmith forged an iron staircase and a fire grate.* **3** to form or create something, especially links or a friendship. **forger** *noun.*

**forgery** *noun* **1** a crime of forging things such as currency. **2** something forged. *The painting was discovered to be a forgery.*

**forget** (forgets, forgetting, forgot, forgotten) *verb* **1** to not remember. **2** to stop thinking about. *Let's forget about the money you owe me.* **3** to stop planning to do or get something, because it is no longer possible. *If you don't study, you can forget about college.*

**forgive** (forgives, forgiving, forgave, forgiven) *verb* to say or feel that you are no longer angry with somebody about something. *He still hasn't forgiven his sister for forgetting his birthday.* **forgivable** *adjective. A forgivable error.* **forgiveness** *noun. He begged for forgiveness.*

forklift truck

**fork** *noun* **1** an instrument with prongs at the end of a handle for eating food. **2** a large tool with prongs for digging the garden. **3** a point, especially in the road, which divides into two parts in the shape of a Y. **fork** *verb* **1** to lift, dig, or move with a fork. **2** to divide in a Y-shape. *Turn right where the road forks.* **fork out** to pay money to someone, usually unwillingly. **forklift truck** a truck with a platform or prongs at the front for lifting, lowering, and moving heavy goods.

**form** *noun* **1** the shape or appearance of something or somebody. *A pencil sharpener in the form of a crocodile.* **2** a particular kind, or a particular way of behaving. *Ice and snow are forms of water.* **3** a piece of paper with questions to be answered and filled in. **4** a class in school. **5** a way in which a word may be spoken, written, or spelled. *The irregular forms of verbs are listed in this dictionary.* **form** *verb* **1** to take shape, develop, or come into existence. **2** to shape or create something. *He can hardly form a sentence, he is so upset.*

fossil

**formal** *adjective* correct, according to accepted rules or customs. *I'm expecting a formal apology.* **formally** *adverb. We dressed formally for the dance.* **formality** (formalities) *noun.*

**format** *noun* the shape and size of something, or the way it is presented. *I like the format of this book.*

**former** *adjective* **1** of an earlier period. *Her former husband has married again, to a very wealthy woman.* **2** the first of two people or things just mentioned. *Extra trains and buses are needed. The former will be more expensive.* (The second of two things just mentioned is called the "latter.")

**formerly** *adverb* in earlier times.

**formidable** *adjective* very difficult to overcome. *They faced some formidable problems in their first year of business, but overcame them one by one.*

**formless** *adjective* without shape, not clear.

**formula** (formulas or formulae) *noun* **1** a group of letters, signs, or numbers that make a rule. *The chemical formula for water is $H_2O$.* **2** a list of substances or directions for making or achieving something. *My formula for success is plenty of sleep.* **3** a set of words or behavior used regularly for a particular occasion. *They changed the formula of the meetings.* **4** suggestions organized in a manner that will solve a problem.

**fortnight** *noun* a period of two weeks. *A fortnight's vacation.* **fortnightly** *adverb.*

**fortress** (fortresses) *noun* a castle or other strong building that is difficult to attack.

**fortuitous** *adjective* by chance, especially by lucky chance; accidental.

**fortunate** *adjective* lucky. **fortunately** *adverb.*

**fortune** *noun* **1** (good) luck. **2** fate; what will happen in the future. *The old woman told him his fortune.* **3** a large amount of money. *She earns a fortune.*

**forward** *adjective, adverb* **1** to or toward the front, toward the future. *A step forward.* **2** advanced or early in development. *The boy is very forward for his age.* **3** to be sure or eager in an unpleasant way. *She is too forward for my liking.* **forward** *noun* an attacking player in the front line of a sports team. **forward** *verb* to send a letter, parcel, or information. *Please forward letters to my new address in Spain.*

**fossil** *noun* the remains of an animal or a plant that lived long ago and has hardened into rock. *A fossil of a dinosaur tooth.* **fossilize** *verb.*

**foster** *verb* **1** to bring up a child as if you were her/his father or mother. **2** to help something grow or develop. *France is fostering a good relationship with Germany.*

**fought** past tense of fight.

**foul** *adjective* **1** dirty; having a bad taste. **2** hateful. *She's got a foul temper.* **foul** *noun* an action against the rules in a game. **foul** *verb* **1** to dirty. **2** to go against the rules in a game.

**found** *verb* **1** to establish or give money to start something. **2** to base something on. *Her success was founded on hard work.*

**foundation** *noun* **1** the base on which a building rests. **2** the things that beliefs are based on.

**founder** *verb* **1** to become filled with water and sink. *The ship foundered on the rocks.* **2** to fail. *The company foundered and went bankrupt.*

**foxglove** *noun* a tall, upright plant that has purple flowers with white spots shaped like the fingers of a glove.

foxglove

Ff

**foyer** *noun* (say **foy**-ay) the entrance hall in a theater or hotel. *I'll meet you in the foyer.*

**fraction** *noun* **1** a small part or bit. *For a fraction of a second.* **2** a number that is not a whole number; a part of a whole number. $\frac{1}{2}$ and $\frac{1}{3}$ are fractions.

**fragrance** *noun* a sweet or pleasant smell. **fragrant** *adjective. Fragrant air from the rose garden.*

**France** *noun* a country in western Europe.

**frank** *adjective* honest and direct. *I will be frank with you, I don't think he'll pass the test.* **frankly** *adverb.* **frankness** *noun.* **frank** *verb* to stamp a letter or parcel to show that postage has been paid.



**frantic** *adjective* wild and desperate; extremely anxious. *He was frantic with worry.* **frantically** *adverb.*

**fraud** *noun* **1** getting money by trickery. **2** a person who pretends to be something he/she is not. **fraudulent** *adjective.*

**freak** *noun* an unusual or strange person, animal, thing, or happening. **freak** *adjective. A freak storm.*

**Freetown** *noun* the capital of Sierra Leone in West Africa.

**freezing point** *noun* the temperature at which water freezes into ice. Freezing point is 32°F or 0° C.

freight

**freight** *noun* (say frayt) **1** the transportation of goods over long distances by trucks, ships, trains, or airplanes. **2** goods. **freight** *verb.*

**French** *noun* **1** the people of France. **2** the language of France. **French** *adjective. The French flag is red, white, and blue.* **French fries** *plural noun* thin pieces of potato fried in oil.

**frequent** *adjective* (say **free**-kwunt) happening often. *My brother is a frequent visitor; he comes every day.* **frequently** *adverb.* **frequency** *noun.* **frequent** (say fri-**kwent**) *verb* to be or go somewhere often.

**fresh** *adjective* **1** newly made, picked, grown, or arrived. Not old or stale, canned, or cooked. **2** cool, refreshing, and unused. *She put fresh sheets on the bed.* **3** new. *Let's make a fresh start.* **4** Fresh water is not salty. **freshly** *adverb. Freshly caught fish.* **freshness** *noun.*

**friction** *noun* **1** the rubbing of one thing against another. *Oil is used in machines to stop friction.* **2** disagreement and quarrels. *There is always friction between them.*

**friend** *noun* **1** a person you know and whose company you enjoy. **2** a helpful person. **have friends in high places** to know important people who can help you.

**friendly** *adjective* acting as a friend. *A friendly gesture.* **friendship** *noun.*

**frighten** *verb* to fill with fear. *The big dog frightened the little girl.* **fright** *noun.*

**frisk** *verb* **1** to run and jump around playfully, as children or animals do. **2** to search somebody with your hands for hidden weapons or goods. *The police frisked the man and found a gun on him.* **frisky** *adjective.*

**frivolous** *adjective* **1** not serious; light-heartedly looking for pleasure. *Clubbing is a frivolous way of spending your time.* **2** amusing; not important.

**frock** *noun* a dress.

**frog** *noun* a jumping animal, often brownish-green, that lives in water and on land. The noise a frog makes is called a "croak."

**from** *preposition* **1** showing a starting point in time, place, or number. *We took the train from Paris to Amsterdam.* **2** showing who gave or sent something. *He got the sweater from his aunt.* **3** showing what something is made of, what it is based on, or where you might find it. *The model was cut from cardboard.* **4** out of the possession of, showing separation. *He took the doll from his little sister.* **5** judging by. *From the noise they are making, it must be a party.* **6** showing difference or change. *I can't tell one from the other.* **7** because of, showing the reason for something. *In parts of Africa, people are suffering from famine.*

frog

**front** *noun* **1** the side that is normally seen and faces forward. *The front of the house.* **2** the part that is ahead of others. *He went to the front of the line.* **3** a road beside the sea. *We walked along the front.* **4** the place or line where two armies are fighting in war. **5** a line of separation where masses of cold air meet masses of warm air. *A cold front.* **in front** ahead of others. **in front of** facing somebody or something. *He spends too much time in front of the television.*

**frontier** *noun* the border where one country meets another country.

**froth** *noun* small white bubbles on liquid that look like foam. **frothy** *adjective. A frothy milkshake.*

**frown** *verb* to move your eyebrows toward each other and wrinkle your forehead because you are annoyed or worried. **frown** *noun. He frowned with disapproval.*

**frugal** *adjective* **1** careful with money or food; not wasteful. **2** small and costing little. *The frugal meal consisted of bread and cheese.* **frugally** *adverb.*

fruit

**fruit** (fruits or fruit) *noun* **1** Fruit grows on trees and bushes, contains seeds, and is used for food. *Apples and strawberries are kinds of fruit.* **2** good or bad results of something. *Now you can enjoy the fruit of your hard work.* **fruity** *adjective.*

**fruitful** *adjective* producing good results. *We had a fruitful meeting.*

**frustrate** *verb* **1** to stop you from doing what you would like to do or to stop plans from being carried out. *Our plans for a picnic were frustrated by bad weather.* **2** to feel disappointed and angry. *It's frustrating not to be able to see you when I want to.* **frustration** *noun.*

**fry** (fries, frying, fried) *verb* to cook something in hot fat, usually in a frying pan.

**fudge** *noun* a soft brown sweet made with butter, sugar, and milk. **fudge** *verb* to avoid giving exact figures or facts in order to deceive people. *The government have fudged the issue again.*

**fuel** *noun* something that is burned to produce heat, especially coal and oil. **fuel** (fuels, fueling, fueled) *verb* **1** to supply something with fuel or take in fuel. **2** to make a situation worse or cause an argument. *His annoyance was fueled by the dog's refusal to come when called.*

**fugitive** *noun* (say few-ji-tiv) somebody who is running away from something. *A fugitive from justice.*

**fulcrum** *noun* the point on which a bar (called a lever) is fixed or is supported in lifting something.

**fulfill** (fulfills, fulfilling, fulfilled) *verb* **1** to do what was promised, to carry out what is required. *He fulfilled his promise.* **2** to make true or come true. **fulfillment** *noun.*

**full** *adjective* **1** completely filled, holding as much or as many as possible. **2** containing a large number of people or things. *He is always full of ideas.* **3** complete, with nothing missing. *She wrote down her full name and address.* **4** as much or great as possible. *The ambulance drove at full speed.* **5** rounded. *She has a full figure.* **6** wide and loosely fitting. *A full skirt.* **full bodied** a full taste, sound, color. *We chose a full-bodied red wine to have with the duck.* **full of something** to be talking about something with great enthusiasm. **in full** not leaving out anything. *She told me the story in full.* **fully** *adverb.* **fullness** *noun.*

**fumble** *verb* to handle or search for something clumsily. *He fumbled in his pocket for his keys.*

**fun** *noun* amusement, something enjoyable. **make fun of** to tease or laugh at somebody in an unkind way.

**Funafuti** *noun* the capital of Tuvalu.

**function** *noun* **1** a special duty or purpose. What somebody or something is there to do. *One of the chair's functions is to conduct meetings.* **2** an important party or event. *We were invited to a function at the embassy.* **3** an activity a computer can carry out. **function** *verb* to be in action or work.

**fundamental** *adjective* very important or basic. **fundamentally** *adverb.*

**funeral** *noun* the ceremony of burying or cremating a dead person.

fungus

**fungus** (fungi, say **fung**-gee) *noun* a plant-like organism without flowers, leaves, or green coloring. Mushrooms, toadstools, and mold are all fungi.

**funnel** *noun* **1** a chimney on a steamship or steam engine for letting out smoke. **2** an object with a wide, round top and a narrow tube at the bottom, used for pouring liquids and powders into a container with a narrow opening. **funnel** *verb.*

**furnace** *noun* a container with a very hot fire, used for burning things, melting metal, making glass, or producing steam in a factory. *A burning fiery furnace.*

**furniture** *noun* movable things like tables, chairs, and beds that are put in a room.

**furtive** *adjective* done secretly, hoping not to be seen. *He gave her a furtive glance.* **furtively** *adverb.*

**fury** *noun* great anger, rage. **furious** *adjective. I am furious that you are late.*

**fuse** *noun* **1** a short, thin piece of wire, e.g., in an electric plug, that acts as a safety device by melting if too much electricity is passed through it. *The lights went out when a fuse blew.* **2** a tube or cord on a bomb or firework that is lit to set it off. **fuse** *verb* **1** to stop working because a fuse has melted. *Suddenly all the lights in the house fused.* **2** to melt in great heat or become joined by melting. *The wires have fused together.*

**fuselage** (say **fewz**-uh-ligh) *noun* the main body of an airplane where people sit or goods are carried.

**futile** (say **few**-tile) *adjective* of no use, not successful. *It's futile to argue, because I know I'm right.* **futility** *noun.*

**future** *noun* the time or events still to come. **future** *adjective. What are your future plans?*

**gabble** *verb* to speak so quickly that people cannot understand you, especially when reading aloud.

**gable** *noun* the vertical, triangular part of the end of a house from the level of the eaves to the ridge of the roof. **gabled** *adjective. A row of gabled houses.*

**Gabon** *noun* a country in Central Africa.

**Gaborone** *noun* the capital of Botswana.

**gadget** *noun* any small, useful instrument or tool used for a particular job. *This gadget is called a garlic press.*

**gain** *verb* **1** to win, earn, or obtain something. **2** to increase. *He's gained in height since last year.* **gain** *noun* **1** a profit. **2** an increase.



**galaxy** *noun* a gigantic group of stars and planets. *The Milky Way is a galaxy.*

galaxy

**gallant** *adjective* **1** brave. *A gallant knight.* **2** honorable and polite.

**galleon** *noun* a large sailing ship of the 16th century, usually Spanish. *A galleon in full sail.*

**gallery** *noun* **1** a building or long room for displaying paintings and other works of art. **2** the highest floor of seats in a theater.

**galley** (galleys) *noun* **1** the kitchen of a ship or aircraft. **2** a usually single-decked ship of ancient times that was driven by both sails and oars.

**gallon** *noun* a measure for liquids. There are eight pints or 3.8 liters in a gallon.

**gallop** *verb* the fastest pace of a horse. *We galloped across the moor.*

**gallows** *singular and plural noun* a wooden structure on which criminals were once hanged. *The gallows on the hill.*

**galvanize** *verb* **1** to cover a metal with zinc to protect it from rusting. **2** to shock into doing something. *The threat of flooding galvanized the men into action.* **galvanized** *adjective. A galvanized garbage can.*

**Gambia** *noun* a country in West Africa.

**gamekeeper** *noun* a person who looks after game animals and birds.

**gander** *noun* a male goose.

**gangster** *noun* one of a gang of criminals.

**gaol** *noun* (also spelled jail) a prison.

**gape** *verb* **1** to stare with your mouth wide open, usually in surprise. **2** to be wide open. *A gaping hole.*

**garage** *noun* **1** a place where cars and other motor vehicles are kept. **2** a place that sells gasoline or where cars can be repaired.

**garbage** *noun* waste material including old food.

**gargle** *verb* to wash your throat with a medicinal liquid without swallowing it and then to spit it out.

**gargoyle** *noun* a grotesque carving of a human or animal head, often forming part of a gutter on a building.

gargoyle

**garish** *adjective* (say **gair**-ish) over-colored or decorated; too bright, gaudy.

**garlic** *noun* a strong-tasting bulb like a small onion, used in cooking to add flavor to food.

**garret** *noun* a small, often dismal room in the attic of a house. *The poet lived in a garret.*

**gas** (gases) *noun* **1** any of many substances like air that are neither liquid nor solid. Oxygen and nitrogen are gases. **2** the kind of gas we use as a fuel in our homes for heating and cooking. **3** (short for gasoline) fuel for cars, made from petroleum.

**gasoline** *see* **gas**.

**gastric** *adjective* relating to or belonging to the stomach.

**gate** *noun* **1** a kind of outside door or barrier across an opening in a fence, hedge, or wall. **2** the number of people who pay to see a sports event.

**gatecrash** *verb* to go to a party when you have not been invited. **gatecrasher** *noun* an uninvited guest.

**gaucho** *noun* a cowboy from the pampas of South America.

**gauge** *noun* (rhymes with cage) an instrument for measuring. *A fuel gauge.* **gauge** *verb* measure or estimate. *She tried to gauge the depth of the pond as accurately as she could.*

**gaunt** *adjective* very thin, bony, and haggard. *His gaunt face.*

**gauze** *noun* a thin net-like cloth often used with bandages.

gaucho

**gay** *adjective* **1** homosexual. **2** bright and cheerful. *Gay colors.* **gaiety** *noun.* **gaily** *adverb.*

**gazetteer** *noun* a geographical dictionary that lists and describes places.

**gelding** *noun* a castrated (neutered) male horse.

**gene** *noun* one of the parts of a cell of all living things that controls and passes on characteristics from parents to offspring.

**generate** *verb* **1** to produce electricity. *Electricity is generated in power stations.* **2** to bring into being; to cause. *The Viking exhibition generated a great deal of interest in the history of the town.*

**generation** *noun* all the people who were born at about the same time (the period of time between generations is about 25 years). *My generation.*

**genetic** *adjective* concerning the genes or inherited through the genes. *His red hair was a genetic characteristic inherited from his father.*

**genius** *noun* (say **jee**-nee-us) an exceptionally clever and creative person.

**gentile** *noun* a person who is not Jewish. **gentile** *adjective.*

**gentle** *adjective* careful, soft, not forceful.

**genuine** *adjective* real and not fake or untrue.

geology

**genus** (genera) *noun* a group containing similar species of plants or animals. *Foxes and hyenas are two species of the dog genus.*

**geography** *noun* the study of the Earth, its natural features, its people, resources, and weather. *World geography is a popular subject in school.* **geographer** *noun.* **geographic** *adjective.*

**geology** *noun* the study of the Earth's rocks and layers of soil. **geological** *adjective.* **geologist** *noun.*

**geometry** *noun* a branch of mathematics concerned with the study of angles, lines, shapes, and solids. **geometric** *adjective.*

**Georgetown** *noun* the capital of Guyana in northern South America.

**Georgia** *noun* **1** a country in Southwest Asia. **2** a state in the south of the USA.

**gerbil** *noun* a small desert rodent with long back legs.

**geriatric** *adjective* relating to or concerning old people.

**German** *noun* **1** a person who comes from Germany. **2** the language spoken in Germany, Austria, and parts of Switzerland. **German** *adjective. German music.*

**Germany** *noun* a country in Central Europe.

**germinate** *verb* When seeds germinate, they begin to sprout, bud, or grow shoots.

**gesture** *noun* **1** a movement of the hand or head intended to mean something. *She wrung her hands in a gesture of despair.* **2** an action that expresses feelings. *He invited them to supper as a friendly gesture.*

**get** (gets, getting, got) *verb* **1** to obtain. *I must get a new book from the library.* **2** to receive. *I hope to get a lot of presents this Christmas.* **3** to bring. *Can you get me a glass of water?* **4** to become. *You'll get wet if you stand in the rain.* **5** to prepare. *Dad will get supper.* **6** to catch (an illness). *I hope you don't get my cold.* **7** to cause to happen. *You must get your watch repaired.* **8** to own something. *Have you got a dog?* **9** to understand. *I don't get the joke.* **10** to ask somebody to do something. *We'll get the builders to move the bricks.* **11** to arrive. *We'll get home at midnight.* **get around 1** *How do these stories get around?* **2** *He's over 90 but still manages to get around.* **get ahead** *She got ahead through hard work.* **get along with** *He's friendly and gets along with everybody.* **get at** *The truth is difficult to get at.* **get by** *He gets by on his small pension, but is finding it hard.* **get down to** *She's getting down to some serious work at last.* **get off 1** *Don't get off the bus while it is still moving.* **2** *She got off with a small fine.* **get on** *How are you getting on with your homework?* **get over** *The doctor said it will take a week to get over that illness.* **get up** *He must get up at 5.00 a.m. tomorrow.*

**geyser** *noun* a natural spring from which hot water and steam shoot upward, often at regular intervals.

**Ghana** *noun* a country in West Africa.

**ghastly** *adjective* very unpleasant, horrible. *A ghastly accident.* **ghastliness** *noun.*

**ghost** *noun* the spirit or shape of a dead person that some people believe walks at night. **ghostly** adjective.

**giant** *noun* in myths and fairy tales, a really tall, often cruel, man. **giant** *adjective. We grew a giant marrow.*

**gibberish** *noun* speech that makes no sense at all. *Don't talk gibberish.*

geyser

**gibbon** *noun* a small ape with very long arms.

**giddy** (giddier, giddiest) *adjective* feeling dizzy, light-headed, and about to fall over. **giddiness** *noun.*

**gig** *noun* **1** a public performance of pop music or jazz. *A gig in the park.* **2** a rowing boat for racing at sea.

**gigantic** *adjective* (say jie-**gan**-tik) of more than giant size, enormous. *The gigantic redwood tree towered over them and made them feel dizzy.*

Gg

**gill** *noun* an organ on each side of a fish through which it breathes.

**gimmick** *noun* a clever or unusual trick or device that is done or made to attract attention, especially to advertise something. **gimmicky** *adjective.*

**ginger** *noun* **1** a hot spice made from the root of a tropical plant used to flavor food such as stir-fries or drinks such as ginger ale and ginger beer. **2** an orange-brown color. **ginger** *adjective.*

**gingerbread** *noun* a sweet, flat cookie or cake flavored with ginger.

**gingerly** *adjective, adverb* carefully and gently. *Gingerly he peeled off the label.*



**giraffe** *noun* an African animal with very long legs, a very long neck, and short yellow fur marked with irregular brown patches.

**girl** *noun* a female child. **girlish** *adjective.*

**girlfriend** *noun* **1** a boy or man's usual and regular female friend. **2** the female friend of a woman. **3** the partner of a lesbian.

**gist** *noun* the rough outline or main points of something. *He gave us the gist of the story while we were on the way to the theater.*

**give** (gives, giving, gave, given) *verb* **1** to hand something over to somebody. **2** to bend or collapse. *The fence gave under her great weight.* **3** to organize or present something. *They are giving a concert tonight.* **4** to do something suddenly. *Pat gave a sigh of relief.* **give away** *I'm giving away all my money.* **give back** *Jack gave back the tapes he'd borrowed.* **give in 1** *They gave in their guns to the police.* **2** *He won't give in (succumb) to your threats.* **3** *You don't know the answer, so why don't you give in (admit defeat)?* **give off 1** *The bonfire is giving off a lot of smoke.* **give out 1** *She gave out (distributed) the prizes.* **2** *The engine has finally given out (broken).* **give up 1** *We gave up (renounced) the idea of moving away.* **2** *Mom has given up (stopped) smoking.*

**glacial** *adjective* **1** concerning ice or glaciers.

**glacier** *noun* a large mass of ice that fills a mountain valley and moves very slowly downward.

glacier

**gladiator** *noun* a warrior in Roman times who fought other gladiators or wild animals for the entertainment of spectators in arenas such as the Colosseum in Rome.

**glamorous** *adjective* exciting and charming. *She has a glamorous job in the fashion business.* **glamor** *noun* physical attractiveness often achieved by makeup.

**glance** *verb* **1** to look at something for a brief moment. *She glanced at her watch.* **2** to hit and then bounce off something at an angle. *The ball glanced off the bat and smashed the window.* **glance** *noun.*

**gland** *noun* an organ in the body that produces substances for the body to use or that removes unwanted substances. *Sweat glands.* **glandular** *adjective. She had a glandular fever that made her very tired.*

**glare** *verb* **1** to look at somebody fiercely and angrily. **2** to shine with strong, dazzling light. **glare** *noun.*

**glaring** *adjective* **1** very bright. *Glaring headlights.* **2** obvious. *Glaring gaps in your general knowledge.*

**glass** *noun* **1** a hard, brittle, and usually transparent material used in making windowpanes, bottles, and mirrors. **2** a container made of this material, used for drinking. **3** a mirror. **glassy** *adjective.*

**glasses** *plural noun* a pair of lenses in a metal or plastic frame that people with poor eyesight wear over their eyes to help them see better; also called spectacles.

**glaze** *verb* **1** to put glass into something. *He glazed the window frames.* **2** to cover something with a coating of a shiny substance called glaze. **glazier** *noun.*

**gleam** *verb* to shine softly or briefly. *The polished furniture is gleaming.* **gleam** *noun.*

**glen** *noun* a long, deep, narrow valley. *We visited a Scottish glen.*

**glide** *verb* **1** to move smoothly and silently. **2** to fly smoothly.

**glider** *noun* a small aircraft without an engine that floats on air currents.

glen

**glimmer** *verb* to flicker or to shine very faintly. **glimmer** *noun. A glimmer of hope.*

**glisten** *verb* to shine or gleam, especially because wet or polished.

**glitter** *verb* to sparkle. *From the airplane she saw the glittering lights of the city below.* **glitter** *noun.*

**global** *adjective* relating to the whole world. *Global issues were the subject of the conference.*

**gloom** *noun* **1** near-darkness, dimness. **2** sadness and a feeling of depression. **gloomy** *adjective. A gloomy cave.*

**glorious** *adjective* **1** magnificent, causing great happiness. *A glorious day.* **2** worthy of glory or honor. *A glorious victory was won by the Persians.*

**glory** *noun* **1** great fame, praise. **2** splendor. *The glory of the mountains.* **glory** *verb* be proud of something you have done. *They gloried in their achievements.*

**glossy** *adjective* shiny and smooth. *She enjoyed reading glossy magazines on the bus.* **gloss** *noun.*

**glow** *verb* to shine with a gentle, steady light without flames. **glow** *noun.*

**glowworm** *noun* an insect that gives out a greenish glow from its tail.

glowworm

**glucose** *noun* a natural sugar found in plants. *Glucose gives you a boost of energy.*

**glue** *noun* a thick, sticky substance used for sticking things together. **glue** *verb.*

**glut** *noun* a much greater supply of something than is needed. *A glut of fruit.*

**glutton** *noun* **1** a person who greedily eats too much. **2** someone who is always eager. **gluttonous** *adjective.*

**GMT** *abbreviation* for Greenwich Mean Time.

**gnarled** *adjective* (say narld) twisted and full of lumpy knots. *A gnarled old oak.*

**gnash** *verb* (say nash) to grind or strike your teeth together with anger or pain.

**gnat** *noun* (say nat) any of many small, mosquito-like insects that bite. *A swarm of gnats.*

**gnaw** *verb* (say naw) to chew on something hard for a long time. *A dog gnaws a bone.*

**gnome** *noun* (say nowm) in fairy tales, a little old man who lives underground, guarding the earth's treasures.

**gnu** *noun* (say noo) an African ox-like antelope, also known as a wildebeest.

**go** (goes, going, went, gone) *verb* **1** to move away from or to somewhere; to travel. *Let's go over there and sit under the trees.* **2** to visit. *My sister and I are going to India in December.* **3** to leave. **4** to disappear. *My tools have gone.* **5** to do something. *I'm going to mow the lawn.* **6** to become. *This fruit is going bad.* **7** to work correctly. *The car won't go.* **8** to fit or have a place somewhere. *The knives go in that drawer.* **9** to lead somewhere. *The road goes to the sea.* **10** to make a certain sound. *Cats go "miaow."* **go ahead** *Despite the weather, we'll go ahead with the play.* **go back** *We're going back home.* **go off** *The bomb went off with a bang.* **go on** *We can't go on quarreling like this.* **go with** *Does this tie go with (look good with) this shirt?*

**goal** *noun* **1** the space or net between two posts that players have to kick or hit a ball into in games such as football. **2** something you hope to achieve, an ambition. *Her goal was to become a scientist.*

**god** *noun* **1** any one of many supernatural beings that people believe have power over nature and human fortunes. *In ancient Greece, the gods lived on Mt Olympus.* **2** an idol. **3** the embodiment of some quality or aspect of existence, for example, the god of love. **4 God** the creator and sovereign of the universe in the Christian, Islamic, and Jewish religions.

**godparent** *noun* a friend of the family who, at a child's baptism, promises to help their godchild be brought up as a Christian.

Gg

**gold** *noun* a very valuable yellow metal that is found in rocks and streams, used for making jewelry. **gold** *adjective* colored like gold.

**golden** *adjective* made of gold or shining like gold. *She has beautiful golden hair.* **golden wedding** the 50th anniversary of a wedding.

**gondola** *noun* a long, narrow boat with high, pointed ends used on the canals of Venice.

**gondolier** *noun* someone who paddles a gondola on the canals of Venice, Italy. *The gondolier sang loudly to his passengers.*

**goodbye** *interjection* what we say when we leave somebody.

gondola

**goosebump** *noun* (also goosepimple) tiny bumps on the skin caused by cold or fear.

**gorge** *noun* a deep valley with steep sides. **gorge** *verb* to eat greedily until you are too full.

**gorgeous** *adjective* **1** very pleasant. **2** beautiful. *She looked gorgeous in her new balldress.*

**gorilla** *noun* the largest and strongest of the apes, found in the forests of Central Africa.

**Gospel** *noun* one of the first four books of the New Testament, the part of the Christian Bible that describes the life and teachings of Jesus.

**gossip** *noun* idle, often untrue chat about other people's personal affairs. **gossip** *verb.*

**govern** *verb* to control a country or an organization (from a company to a club), managing and making rules and policy for how it operates.

**government** *noun* a group of people who govern or rule a country.

**governor** *noun* **1** a person elected to manage or govern; a ruler. **2** the head of each state in the US. **3** a person who directs an organization.

**grace** *noun* **1** a beautiful and easy way of moving. **2** the love and favor of God. **3** a short prayer of thanks said before meals. **graceful** *adjective*.

**gracious** *adjective* full of grace and charm.

**grade** *noun* **1** a scale that arranges people or things according to quality, rank, or size. *They only sell vegetables of the highest grade.* **2** marks given in a test. **3** one of the 12 years of school in the US. *He's in the fourth grade.* **grade** *verb. The hens' eggs were graded according to size.*



**gradient** *noun* a measure of how steep a slope is. *That hill has a gradient of one in seven. It rises one foot for every seven feet along the horizontal.*

**gradual** *adjective* changing or happening slowly. *A gradual improvement.*

**graduate** *noun* a person who has finished a course of studies and taken a university degree. **graduate** *verb*.

**graffiti** *plural noun* (say gra-**fee**-tee) drawings and writing scribbled on buildings or trains.

**grain** *noun* **1** the seed of cereal plants like corn, rice, and wheat. **2** tiny bits of something. *Grains of salt, sand, and sugar.* **3** the pattern of lines in wood.

**gram** *noun* a unit for measuring weight in the metric system. There are 1,000 grams in a kilogram.

**grammar** *noun* the rules of a language and how the words are put together properly.

**grandparent, grandfather, grandmother** the parent of one of a person's parents.

**granite** *noun* (say **gran**-it) a very hard rock produced by volcanic action, used in building.

**grapefruit** (grapefruit or grapefruits) *noun* a round fruit like a big orange, but with a yellow or pink skin.

**graph** *noun* (rhymes with half) a diagram or chart that shows how numbers or amounts compare or are related.

**graphic** *adjective* **1** clear and vivid. *A graphic account of the murder.* **2** relating to painting and drawing. *The graphic arts.*

**graphics** *plural noun* pictures and patterns.

**grasshopper** *noun* a small jumping insect with long back legs. It makes a chirping sound by rubbing its legs together.

**grasshopper**

**gravity** *noun* **1** seriousness. **2** the natural force that draws things to the Earth so that they stay there and do not float away.

**graze** *verb* **1** when animals graze, they eat grass as it grows. **2** to scrape and cut your skin by rubbing it against something rough, as when you fall over.

**grease** *noun* a thick, oily substance. **greasy** *adjective*.

**great** *adjective* **1** big or heavy. **2** important, famous, or clever. *A great composer.* **3** very good. *It's great to be here.* **greatness** *noun*.

**Great Britain** *noun* the main island and small islands of England, Scotland, and Wales.

**great-grandparents, great-grandfather great-grandmother** the grandparents of a person's father or mother.

**Greece's flag**

**Greece** *noun* a country in southeast Europe.

**Greek** *noun* **1** a person who comes from Greece. **2** the language spoken in Greece. **Greek** *adjective. Greek civilization.*

**greenhouse** *noun* a building made of glass, used for growing plants in a warm atmosphere. **greenhouse effect** the effect of the atmosphere around the Earth warming up; this happens because gases such as carbon dioxide trapped in the atmosphere by pollution are heated by the Sun.

**Grenada** *noun* a country in the Caribbean.

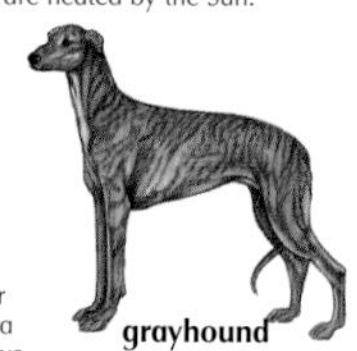

**grayhound**

**grayhound** *noun* a slim breed of dog that can run very fast and is used in racing.

**grief** *noun* (rhymes with leaf) great sorrow or sadness, especially after a death or misfortune. **grieve** *verb. He is grieving for his dead wife.*

**grievance** *noun* a reason to complain or be angry about something, real or imagined.

**grievous** *adjective* very serious or harmful. *He received a grievous injury when he fell from the ladder.*

**grind** (grinds, grinding, ground) *verb* to crush something into very small pieces or into a powder. *Coffee beans smell delicious when they have just been ground.* **grind to a halt** to come slowly to a complete stop.

**groceries** *plural noun* food items such as flour, tea, coffee, jam, milk, and sugar that you buy from a grocer or supermarket.

**groin** *noun* the place where the top of your legs meet.

**groom** *verb* to clean and brush an animal, particularly a horse. **groom** *noun* **1** a person who looks after horses. **2** a man who is about to get married; a bridegroom.

**grotesque** *adjective* (say grow-**tesk**) weird and unnatural; monstrous.

**ground** *noun* **1** the solid surface of the Earth. **2** a sports field. **gain ground** to make progress. **break new ground** to do something new or discover something for the first time. **ground** *verb* past tense of grind.

**grovel** (grovels, groveling, groveled) *verb* to behave in an over-humble way to somebody because you think they are important.

**grow**

**grow** (grows, growing, grew, grown) *verb* **1** to become larger and taller; to develop. **2** to plant in the ground. *We are growing seedlings in trays.* **grown-up** *noun* an adult. **grown-up** *adjective. He has a grown-up son.* **grow up** to become an adult. **grow out of** *She'll grow out of sucking her thumb in the next year or so.*

**growl** *verb* to make a deep, low, and angry sound. *The dog growled when I tried to take her bone.*

**grub** *noun* **1** a larva or worm-like creature that will grow into an insect. **2** (slang) food.

**grubby** (grubbier, grubbiest) *adjective* dirty. *Wash your grubby hands before dinner.*

**grudge** *noun* a long-lasting feeling of dislike or resentment toward somebody because they harmed or annoyed you in the past.

**grueling** *adjective* very tiring; severe. *It was a long, grueling journey across the mountains.*

**gruesome** *adjective* revolting and shocking, very unpleasant to see, usually involving violence and death.

**guarantee** *noun* **1** a promise by a manufacturer that something is of a certain quality and that it will be repaired or replaced if it goes wrong within a certain time. *The computer has a year's guarantee.* **2** a promise that something will definitely happen. *They guaranteed that they would win the game.* **guarantee** *verb.*

**guard** *verb* to watch over and protect somebody or something. *Police officers guarded the building.* **guard** *noun* **1** a person or group that guards. *A security guard.* **2** some device or thing that protects. *A fire guard.* **on guard** prepared to defend and protect. **off guard** unprepared; not watching or ready.

**guarded** *adjective* **1** protected. **2** cautious and careful not to say too much. *A guarded reply.*

**Guatemala** *noun* a country in Central America.

**Guatemala City** *noun* the capital of Guatemala.

**guess** *verb* **1** to say what you think is the answer without having enough information to know for certain. *Joe guessed the weight of the cake.* **2** to think. *I guess I'd better be going.* **guess** *noun. My guess is that she is older than she looks.* **guesswork** making guesses or the result of guesses. *He cooked the cake by guesswork.*

**guest** *noun* **1** a person who has been invited to stay for a short time in somebody's house; a visitor. **2** a person staying in a hotel. **3** someone who takes part in an event or entertainment by invitation.

**guide** *noun* somebody who leads or shows the way; a person who helps or advises. *A guide showed us around the magnificent cathedral.* **guide** *verb.*

Gg

**guide-dog** *noun* a dog that has been trained to help a blind person find his or her way around a house or town.

**guideline** *noun* advice or a rule about how something should be done.

**guilt** *noun* **1** the miserable feeling you have when you know you have done something wrong. **2** the fact that you have done something wrong.

**guilty** *adjective* **1** having done something wrong or committed a crime. *She was guilty of shoplifting.* **2** concerning guilt or shame. *A guilty secret.*

**Guinea** *noun* a country in West Africa.

**Guinea-Bissau** *noun* a country in West Africa.

**Gujurati** *noun* the language spoken in the state of Gujurat in western India.

**gulf** *noun* a bay or large area of the sea almost surrounded by land.

**gunpowder** *noun* a powder that explodes easily. Gunpowder is used in fireworks.

**gust** *noun* a strong and sudden rush of wind. **gusty** *adjective.*

**Guyana** *noun* a country in South America.

**gym** short for gymnasium and gymnastics.

**gymnasium** *noun* a room with special equipment for doing physical exercises. *Sarah goes to the gymnasium at least once a week to keep fit.*

**gymnast** *noun* a person who is trained in gymnastics.

**gymnastics** *noun* **1** highly skilled physical exercises, such as rings and parallel bars. **2** physical or mental agility.

**gymnast**

habit

**habit** *noun* **1** the loose garment worn by a monk or nun. **2** something that you do regularly, usually without thinking about it. A custom. *She has a habit of twisting her hair.* **habitual** *adjective.*

**habitat** *noun* the place where an animal or plant naturally lives or grows.

**hack** *verb* **1** to cut something, roughly, with repeated blows. *He hacked his way through the undergrowth.* **2** to ride a horse in open countryside. **3** to get information from a computer system illegally. **hacker** *noun.*

**haddock** *noun* an edible sea fish, related to cod. *Smoked haddock with poached egg.*

**haggard** *adjective* looking thin, ill, and tired. *Worry has made her look haggard and old.*

**haggle** *verb* to argue over the price of something; to bargain. *We haggled with the stallholder over a carpet.*

**hail** *noun* frozen rain. *The hail beat against the windows.* **hailstone** *noun* a frozen raindrop. **hail** *verb* **1** to call out or wave to get attention. *She hailed a taxi.* **2** a fall of hailstones. *It hailed on Tuesday.*

**hair** *noun* **1** a fine thread that grows on the skin of people and animals. **2** the soft mass of these threads covering a person's head. *Harry has fair hair.* **let your hair down** to behave in a relaxed way and enjoy yourself. **keep your hair on** to stay calm and not get excited, said to someone who is getting agitated or irate. **split hairs** to argue about unimportant details.

**haircut** *noun* **1** the act of cutting somebody's hair. **2** the style in which hair has been cut.

**hairdresser** *noun* a person who cuts and arranges (or styles) your hair.

**hair-raising** *adjective* terrifying.

**hairy** (hairier, hairiest) *adjective* **1** covered in hair. **2** (slang) exciting and risky. *A hairy ride on the roller-coaster made us scream.*

**Haiti** (say **hay**-tee) *noun* a country in the Caribbean, the western part of the island of Hispaniola.

**halal** *noun* meat from animals that have been killed according to Islam's religious laws. *A halal butcher.*

**half** *adjective* one of two equal parts. *A half bottle of wine.* **half** *adverb* partly, not completely. *The meat is still half-frozen.* **half** (halves) *noun. Half an apple.* **half-hearted** *adjective* not very keen or enthusiastic. *She made a half-hearted effort to enjoy the party.*

**half-time** *noun* a short break between two halves of a game such as football or baseball. *During school football matches, both teams sit and rest and have something to drink at half-time.*

**halfmast** *noun* the position half-way down a flagpole at which a flag is flown as a sign that somebody important has died. *The flag was flown at halfmast in every town.*

**hall** *noun* **1** a room or passageway at the entrance to a house. **2** a large room or building for public meetings and concerts.

**Halloween** *noun* All Hallows' Eve, the evening of 31 October (the day before All Saints' Day), when people used to believe that ghosts and witches roamed around. Today, homes are decorated with pumpkin lanterns and children go trick or treating.

Halloween

**hallucinate** *verb* to hear or see things that are not really there. **hallucination** *noun.*

**halt** *verb* to come or bring to a stop. *The train halted.* **halt** *noun. It came to a sudden halt.*

**halve** *verb* **1** to divide or cut something into two equal parts. **2** to reduce by half.

**ham** *noun* **1** salted meat from a pig's back leg. **2** (slang) an actor who is not very good and overacts.

**hamburger** *noun* a bread roll containing a round slab of ground meat.

**hamlet** *noun* **1** a very small village. **2** In England, usually a small village without a church.

hammock

**hammock** *noun* a swinging bed made of strong cloth, net, or rope that is hung up between two supports.

**hamper** *noun* a large basket with a lid, for carrying things. *A picnic hamper.* **hamper** *verb* to prevent or make something difficult to do; to hinder. *Her tight jacket hampered her movements.*

**hamster** *noun* a small, furry, tailless rodent that can store food in its cheeks. Hamsters are often kept as pets. *My hamster likes to eat sunflower seeds.*

**hand** *noun* **1** the part of your body at the end of your arm and below your wrist with four fingers and a thumb. **2** a pointer on a clock. *My watch has an hour hand, a minute hand, and a second hand.* **3** help. *Can you give me a hand, please?* **4** a worker. *A farm hand.* **5** the cards a player holds in his or her hand in a card game. *I had a winning hand.* **hand** *verb* to give. *She handed me the letter.* **at first hand** directly and not through other people. **by hand 1** made by a person, not a machine. **2** delivered by a person, not by mail. **in hand** being dealt with, under control. **hand out** to give out, share. **on hand** ready and available. **out of hand** out of control.

**handbag** *noun* a small bag usually carried by women for money and personal belongings; a purse.

**handcuffs** *plural noun* a pair of metal rings joined by a chain and locked around a prisoner's wrists to stop them from escaping. **handcuff** *verb.*

**handicap** *noun* **1** a disadvantage or something that makes it difficult to do what you want to do. *His lack of experience was a handicap.* **2** a disability of the body or mind. *Being deaf can be a handicap.*

**handiwork** *noun* work such as pottery or weaving that needs skillful use of the hands.

**handkerchief** *noun* (say **hang**-ker-chiff) a piece of cloth used for blowing and wiping your nose.

**handle** *noun* the part of an object that you hold the object by or move to make it work. *Turn the handle to open the door.* **handle** *verb* **1** to hold or move something with your hands. **2** to deal with. *Grooms handle horses.*

**handlebars** *plural noun* the steering bar with a handle at each end at the front of a bicycle or motorcycle that the rider holds. *Hold on to the handlebars.*

**handsome** *adjective* attractive, good-looking.

**hang** (hangs, hanging, hung) *verb* **1** to attach something by its top part so that the lower part is free. *She hung her coat on a hook.* **2** to swing loosely. *The dog's tongue is hanging out of its mouth.* **3 hang** (hangs, hanging, hanged) to kill somebody by putting a rope around their neck and letting them drop from a support. **hang around** to wait around somewhere with nothing to do. **hang back** to be unwilling to say or do something. **hang on 1** to hold tightly. **2** to wait. *Hang on, wait for me!*

**hangar** *noun* a large building where aircraft are kept. *Aircraft hangar.*

**hanger** *noun* curved wire, plastic, or wood on which to hang clothes in a closet.

**hang glider** *noun* a kite-like frame to which a person is strapped as it glides in the sky, propelled by the wind and air currents.

hang glider

**hanker** *verb* to want something badly, to long for. *She is hankering after a ride in the helicopter.*

**Hanoi** *noun* the capital of Vietnam.

**Hanukkah** *noun* the Jewish festival of lights, which is held in December.

**haphazard** *adjective* unplanned, happening by accident. *A haphazard arrangement.*

**happy** (happier, happiest) *adjective* **1** the feeling of being pleased and cheerful. **2** willing. *I'd be happy to go instead of you.* **happiness** *noun.* **happily** *adverb.*

**Harare** *noun* the capital of Zimbabwe in southern Africa.

**harass** *verb* to annoy or threaten somebody repeatedly. **harassment** *noun.* **harassed** *adjective. Sarah feels harassed by her boss.*

**harbor** *noun* a place where boats can moor in shelter, usually part of a small coastal town.

**hard** *adjective* **1** solid and difficult to shape or break; not soft. *Concrete becomes hard when it sets.* **2** difficult. *A hard jigsaw.* **3** severe and tough. *Hard discipline.* **hard** *adverb* with great energy or effort. *Work hard, play hard.* **hardness** *noun.* **hard copy** a printed copy of information created on a computer, also called a printout. **hard disk** *noun* a device that is fixed inside a computer and holds a large amount of data.

**hardback** *noun* a book with a long-lasting, stiff cover. *Novels are usually published in hardback first.*

**harden** *verb* to make or to become hard and stiff. *The clay hardened.*

**hardly** *adverb* almost but not completely; scarcely. *He was so tired he could hardly keep his eyes open.*

**hardship** *noun* suffering or difficulty. *He suffered great hardship.*

**hardware** *noun* **1** all the pieces of machinery that make up a computer, e.g., the printer and VDU (visual display unit, or screen). **2** tools and equipment used in the home and yard.

**hardy** *adjective* strong, robust, and able to endure severe conditions. *Hardy plants.*

**hare** *noun* an animal like a large rabbit.

**harm** *verb* to hurt or damage somebody or something. **harm** *noun. The harm was already done.*

**harmful** *adjective* bad for you. *Too much sugar is harmful to your teeth.*

**harmless** *adjective* safe and not dangerous or harmful. *A harmless insect.*

**harmony** *noun* **1** musical notes played at the same time and which sound pleasant. **2** agreement and cooperation. **harmonious** *adjective.* **harmonize** *verb.*

**harness** *noun* the leather straps and metal fittings used to attach a horse to a cart or carriage that it pulls. **harness** *verb. Please harness the mare.*

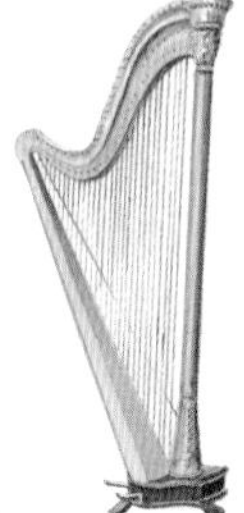

harp

**harp** *noun* a musical instrument that you play by plucking its strings with your fingers. **harpist** *noun* someone who plays a harp.

**harpoon** *noun* a spear with a rope attached that is used to hunt whales. **harpoon** *verb.*

**harpsichord** *noun* a keyboard instrument similar to a piano, but with horizontal strings that are plucked mechanically.

**harsh** *adjective* **1** stern, unkind, and severe. *Harsh treatment.* **2** rough and unpleasant. *A harsh sound.*

**harvest** *noun* the time when grain and other crops are cut and gathered. *Harvest is the busiest time of the year for the farming community.* **harvest** *verb.*



**hassle** *noun* an annoyance or a cause of trouble. *It's too much hassle to go by bus.* **hassle** *verb* (slang) to pester or bother somebody. *Stop hassling me!*

**haste** *noun* a hurry. *She was late and left in great haste.* **hasten** *verb. Radio hastened the end of silent movies.*

**hasty** (hastier, hastiest) *adjective* done quickly, sometimes too quickly and without care. *They made a hasty decision to turn left instead of right.*

**hat** *noun* a covering for the head. *A hat keeps your head warm.* **talk though your hat** to talk nonsense. *He may sound like he knows what he's talking about, but he's actually talking through his hat!*

**hatch** *noun* a movable covering for a hole in a floor, wall, or ceiling. *An escape hatch on an airplane.* **hatch** *verb* **1** An egg hatches when it breaks open and a chick or reptile comes out. **2** to plan. *What scheme are you hatching?* **hatchback car** a car with a door at the back that opens upward.

hatch

**hate** *verb* to dislike somebody or something very much, to loathe. **hate, hatred** *noun.*

**hateful** *adjective* bad, unkind, or unpleasant. *What a hateful person he is!*

**haul** *verb* to pull or drag something heavy with a lot of effort. *We hauled the boat onto the beach.*

**haunt** *verb* If a ghost haunts a place, it visits it regularly. **haunted** *adjective.*

**Havana** *noun* the capital of Cuba in the Caribbean.

**have** (has, having, had) *verb* **1** to own. *She has 20 pairs of shoes.* **2** to experience or enjoy something. *Let's have a party.* **3** to be forced to do something. *I have to go home today.* **4** to receive. *I had a lot of cards on my birthday.*

**havoc** *noun* great damage, chaos.

**hawk** *noun* a bird of prey with good eyesight and sharp talons.

**hay** *noun* grass that has been cut and dried for feeding to animals. **make hay while the sun shines** to do things while you have the opportunity.

**hayfever** *noun* an illness like a bad cold caused by an allergy or bad reaction to breathing in the pollen of grasses or flowers.

**hazard** *noun* a risk or something that can cause harm. *That loose step is a hazard.*

**hazel** *noun* **1** a small tree on which hazelnuts grow. **2** a green-brown color. *Hazel eyes glow with a special warmth.*

hawk

**hazy** (hazier, haziest) *adjective* **1** misty. *A hazy day.* **haze** *noun.* **2** not clear, confused. *I have only a hazy idea of how to get there.*

**head** *noun* **1** the top part of your body above your neck, containing your face, hair, and skull. **2** the leader or person in charge of something. *The head of a department.* **3** the front or upper part of something. *The head of the river.* **head** *verb* **1** to move in a direction. *They headed for the beach.* **2** to be in charge of. *She heads the news team.* **heads** the side of a coin showing somebody's head.

**headache** *noun* **1** a pain in your head. **2** a problem.

**headland** *noun* land jutting out into the ocean.

**headlight** *noun* one of the large, strong lights at the front of a motor vehicle.

**headline** *noun* a title, heading, or words printed in large, bold print at the start of a story in a newspaper. **headlines** *plural noun* the main items of news on the radio or television. *The news headlines in brief.*

**headquarters** *noun* the main place from which a business or organization is controlled. *The headquarters of the bank are in New York.*

**headway** *noun* progress. *He's making some headway in Japanese this term.*

**heal** *verb* to make or become better or healthy again. *Physician, heal thyself.*

**health** *noun* the condition of your body and how well or ill it is.

**healthy** (healthier, healthiest) *adjective* **1** well and not suffering from any illness or injury; fit. **2** something that is good for you. *Healthy exercise.* **healthily** *adverb.*

**heap** *noun* an untidy pile or mass of things. *A heap of dirty dishes.* **heaps** *plural noun* a large amount. *There's heaps of time before the train leaves.* **heap** *verb. She heaped the leaves onto the bonfire.*

**hear** *verb* **1** to receive or pick up sound with our ears, to listen to. **2** to receive information. *We hear you are going away for a few weeks.*

**hearing** *noun* one of the body's five senses. Hearing is the ability to hear. **hearing aid** *noun* a small device that makes sounds louder and which people with poor hearing wear in or behind their ears to help them hear things better.

**hearse** *noun* a vehicle for carrying a coffin to a funeral. *The black hearse drew up outside the church.*

**heart** *noun* **1** the organ inside your chest that pumps blood around your body. **2** the main or most important part. *The heart of the matter.* **3** courage and enthusiasm. *She put her heart into the job.* **4** **hearts** one of the four suits in a pack of playing cards. **heart attack** a serious condition where the heart suddenly stops working properly, sometimes causing death.

**heartbreak** *noun* overwhelming distress. **heartbreaking** *adjective* causing great sadness. *I am so sorry to hear your heartbreaking news.* **heartbroken** *adjective. She was heartbroken when her father died.*

**heartfelt** *adjective* very sincerely. *My heartfelt thanks go to all concerned.*

**heartless** *adjective* cruel and pitiless. *The heartless pirates stripped the enemy ship bare.* **heartlessness** *noun.*

**hearth** *noun* the floor of a fireplace.

**hearty** (heartier, heartiest) *adjective* **1** enthusiastic and friendly. *They gave us a hearty welcome.* **2** strong, big, and healthy. *A hearty meal was enjoyed by all.*

**heat** *adjective* **1** the hotness or warmth of something. *The heat of the fire.* **2** one of a number of races in a competition, the winners of which go forward into the next trial. **heat** *verb* to make something hot. *The fire heated the room.* **heated** *adjective. A heated debate.*

**heath** *noun* a wild and open area of land covered with grass and shrubs.

**heather** *noun* an evergreen shrub with pink, purple, or white flowers that grows on moors and heaths.

**heave** *verb* to lift or move something with great effort.

**heaven** *noun* a place of great happiness where God or the gods are believed to live, and where Christians believe that good people go when they die.

heather

**heavy** (heavier, heaviest) *adjective* **1** having great weight and hard to lift. *A heavy suitcase.* **2** great amount or force. *Heavy rain fell in sheets.* **3** (slang) serious, boring, and complicated. *She gets heavy when she talks about her work.* **heaviness** *noun.* **heavily** *adverb.*

**Hebrew** *noun* the original language of Judaism.

**hectare** *noun* a measure of an area of land, equal to 10,000 square meters or 2,471 acres.

**hectic** *adjective* very busy and full of exciting activity. *We had a hectic day decorating the house for Christmas.*

**hedge** *noun* a fence around a field or garden made of closely planted shrubs or small trees. **hedge** *verb* **1** to surround land with a hedge. **2** to avoid giving a straight answer. *She hedged on the subject.*

**hedgehog** *noun* a small animal covered in needle-like prickles. Hedgehogs come out at night to hunt insects. They roll up into a ball if frightened.

**hedgerow** *noun* a row of bushes forming a hedge around a field or along a country road.

hedgehog

**heel** *noun* **1** the back part of your foot. **2** the part of a sock or shoe that covers or supports the heel. *She's wearing shoes with very high heels.*

**heifer** *noun* (say **heff**-er) a young cow that has not yet had a calf.

**height** *noun* **1** how high something is from top to bottom. *The height of the room is nearly 20 feet.* **2** the highest, best, or most important point or part of something. *The height of fashion.*

**heighten** *verb* to make something higher or become greater. *Their excitement heightened as they approached the fairground in the park.*

**heir** *noun* (say air) an heir is a person who will have (inherit) the money or title of somebody when they die.

**heiress** *noun* (say **air**-ess) a female heir.

**heirloom** *noun* a special or valuable object that is passed down in a family from one generation to the next.

**helicopter** *noun* an aircraft with a fast-turning blade (rotor) on top, which acts as both a propeller and wings.

**helium** *noun* a colorless gas that is lighter than air and does not burn. It is used to fill balloons.

**hell** *noun* **1** a place where some religions claim the devil lives. **2** a state or place of misery. **for the hell of it** for fun. **hell for leather** at full speed.

**hello** *interjection* a word we use to attract somebody's attention or greet somebody, or what we say when we answer the telephone.

**helm** *noun* a ship's steering wheel; a tiller. *Please take the helm while I pull in the sails.*

**helmet** *noun* a strong, hard covering worn to protect the head. *Soldiers, firefighters, and builders wear helmets in dangerous conditions.*

helmet

**helpful** *adjective* useful and willing to help.

**Helsinki** *noun* the capital of Finland in northern Europe.

**hemisphere** *noun* **1** the shape of half a sphere. **2** one half of the Earth. *Europe is in the northern hemisphere.*

**hence** *adverb* **1** for this reason. *There has been no rain, hence the drought.* **2** from now on. *From this day hence.*

**herald** *verb* **1** to say that something is going to happen. **2** to be a sign that something is going to happen. *Dark clouds herald storms.*

**heraldry** *noun* the study of coats-of-arms.

**herb** *noun* a plant used to add flavor in cooking or for making medicines. **herbal** *adjective. Herbal remedies.*

**herbivore** *noun* an animal that eats only plants. Horses and cattle are herbivores. **herbivorous** *adjective.*

**heretic** *noun* (say **hair**-uh-tik) a person who supports an opinion (usually religious or political) that is against the official view or what most people generally accept. **heretical** *adjective.* **heresy** *noun.*

**heritage** *noun* traditions, buildings, or lands that are passed from one generation to the next.

**hero** (heroes) *noun* **1** a man or boy admired for having done something brave or especially good. **2** the most important male character in a book, movie, or play. **heroism** *noun.* **heroic** *adjective. Heroic deeds.*

**heroin** *noun* a strong, addictive drug.

**heroine** *noun* **1** a woman or girl admired for having done something brave or especially good. **2** the most important female character in a book, movie, or play.

**hesitate** *verb* to pause or to stop doing something for a short time because you are uncertain, undecided, or worried. **hesitation** *noun. He agreed to help without any hesitation.* **hesitant** *adjective.*

**heterosexual** *adjective* sexually attracted to people of the opposite sex. **heterosexuality** *noun.*

**hibernate** *verb* When animals hibernate, they spend the winter in a deep sleep. Bears, hedgehogs, and tortoises all hibernate. **hibernation** *noun.*

hibernate

**hiccup** *noun* (say **hik**-up) a repeated sound caused by a muscular spasm, which people may unexpectedly find themselves making.

**hideous** *adjective* very ugly, unpleasant. *The monster in the story had a hideous face.*

**hieroglyphics** *plural noun* (say **hy**-er-uh-glif-iks) the ancient Egyptian system of writing that uses pictures to represent words and sounds.

**high** *adjective* **1** a long way above the ground. *The swallows flew high overhead.* **2** the distance from the top to the bottom of something. *The door is 7 feet high.* **3** greater than normal. *The police car drove at a high speed.* **4** not deep or low. *Children have high voices.* **5** important or above others in rank. **high-pitched** shrill and high in sound. *A high-pitched wail.* **high-rise** very tall, a tall building. **high tech** high technology; the use of advanced computers and electronics.

**highlands** *plural noun* a hilly region, especially the highlands of northern Scotland.

**highlight** *noun* the most interesting part of something. *Seeing the elephants in the game park was the highlight of our vacation in South Africa.* **highlight** *verb* **1** to draw attention to something. *He highlighted the importance of good spelling when he spoke to the class.* **2** to use a colored pen to mark important parts of a document. *He highlighted all the nouns in the paragraph.*

**high-strung** *adjective* sensitive and nervous. *The horse is high-strung and needs careful handling.*

**highway** *noun* a main road.

**highwayman** (highwaymen) *noun* in the past, a robber on horseback who stopped travelers at gunpoint.

**hijack** *verb* to take control of an aircraft, train, or vehicle by force and make it go somewhere. **hijack** *noun. The hijack ended in Moscow where the plane landed and the passengers were released.*

**hijacker** *noun* a person who hijacks.

**hilarious** *adjective* exceedingly funny in a noisy way. **hilarity** *noun. The hilarity of the situation made us laugh.*

**hilt** *noun* the handle of a sword or dagger. **up to the hilt** completely. *I support my team up to the hilt.*

**hinder** *verb* to get in the way and so make things difficult for somebody, to prevent and delay. **hindrance** *noun. You are being a hindrance, not a help.*

**Hindu** *noun* (say hin-**doo**) a follower of Hinduism, an Indian religion which has many gods and teaches that a person's spirit will return to Earth in a different form after death. **Hindu** *adjective.*

**hinge** *noun* a moving metal joint on which such things as doors, gates, windows, and lids to boxes can swing when opened.

**hip** *noun* one of the two joints on either side of your body between the top of your legs and your waist.

hippopotamus

**hippopotamus** (hippopotamuses or hippopotami) *noun* a large African animal with short legs and thick skin that lives in or near lakes and rivers. It is often called a hippo for short. Its name means "river horse."

**hire** *verb* to pay money to employ somebody or use something for a short time. *She hired two men to mend the roof.*

**historian** *noun* a person who studies and analyzes the past, and writes about history.

**historic** *adjective* famous or important in the past. *We can learn a lot from historic houses.*

**historical** *adjective* concerned with events and people in history. *Was Hamlet a historical person?*

**history** *noun* **1** the study of the people and events of the past. **2** a description of the past. *A history of Mexico.*

**hitchhike** *verb* to travel by getting free rides from passing vehicles. A hitchhiker requests a ride by holding up his/her thumb.

**HIV** short for Human Immunodeficiency Virus, a virus that weakens a person's resistance to diseases and may lead to Aids.

**hoard** *noun* a secret store of money, treasure, or food. **hoard** *verb. Squirrels hoard nuts for the winter.*

**hoarding** *noun* a large board or temporary wooden fence covered in advertisements.

**hoarse** *adjective* a rough, low voice caused by a sore throat or by shouting too much.

**hoax** *noun* a practical joke, trick, or deception. *We had to evacuate the building, but the bomb scare was a hoax.* **hoax** *verb.*

**hobby** *noun* an activity such as model-making that you enjoy doing in your spare time.

**hoe** *noun* a garden tool with a long handle and a short blade, used for weeding.

**hog** *noun* a male pig that has been neutered. **hog** (hogs, hogging, hogged) *verb* to take possession of something greedily and not share it. *He hogged the sofa, so the rest of us had to sit on the floor.*

**Hogmanay** *noun* New Year's Eve in Scotland.

**hole** *noun* an opening or gap in something; a hollow space. *There's a hole in the toe of my sock. She hit the golf ball into the hole.*

**hollow** *adjective* not solid; having an empty space inside. *Bottles and pipes are hollow.* **hollow** *noun* **1** a hole. **2** a small valley.

**holly** *noun* an evergreen tree with shiny, spiky leaves and sometimes red berries in winter.

**hologram** *noun* a photograph created by laser beams that appears to be three-dimensional (seeming to have width, depth, and height).

holly

**holy** *adjective* relating to or belonging to God or a religion. Churches and temples are holy places. **holiness** *noun.*

**home** *noun* the place where you usually live or where you were brought up. **feel at home** to feel relaxed with somebody or something.

**homicide** *noun* (say **hom**-uh-side) the killing of a human being.

**homosexual** *adjective, noun* sexually attracted to somebody of the same sex; gay. **homosexuality** *noun.*

**Honduras** *noun* a country in Central America.

**honest** *adjective* (say **on**-est) an honest person is somebody who always tells the truth and whom you can trust. **honesty** *noun. Honesty is always the best policy.*

**honey** *noun* (rhymes with bunny) the sweet, sticky food made by bees from the nectar of flowers. *Yogurt and honey for breakfast.*

**Honiara** *noun* the capital of the Solomon Islands.

**honor** *noun* (say **on**-ur) **1** to give great respect to somebody. *He was honored by everybody for his great achievements.* **2** to praise and reward somebody publicly. **3** to keep an agreement. **honor** *noun* good reputation.

**hoodwink** *verb* to trick somebody.

**hoof** (hooves or hoofs) *noun* the hard covering on the feet of some animals, such as horses, cows, and sheep.

hook

**hook** *noun* **1** a bent piece of metal, often with a feather attached, for catching fish. **2** a bent piece of metal or plastic for hanging things on.

**hooligan** *noun* a violent, noisy person who starts fights and deliberately breaks things. **hooliganism** *noun.*

**hoop** *noun* a large ring made of metal or wood. *At the circus we saw an acrobat jump through a hoop of fire.*

**hope** *noun* a feeling that something you want will happen. *She hopes to pass her test with flying colors.* **hope** *verb* to want something to happen and be expecting it to happen. *I hope you will win first prize.*

**hopeful** *adjective* feeling confident and full of hope. **hopefulness** *noun.*

**hopeless** *adjective* **1** without hope. **2** bad, useless. *He's hopeless at drawing, but very good at science.*

**horde** *noun* **1** a large group or crowd. *Hordes of tourists swarmed into the piazza.* **2** Historically, a troop of Tartars or other nomads. *Mongol hordes rode across the plains.*

horizon

**horizon** *noun* the line in the distance where the sky and land or sea seem to meet.

**horizontal** *adjective* lying flat on the ground, in line with the horizon; going from side to side, not up and down. *Draw a horizontal line across the page.*

**hormone** *noun* a chemical substance produced in your body that controls particular functions of the body. Some hormones control growth and others control digestion, for example.

**horoscope** *noun* a forecast of somebody's future, based on the position of the stars at the time of that person's birth. *Have you read your horoscope in the paper today?*

**horrible** *adjective* terrible, unpleasant. *What a horrible noise that drill is making!*

**horrid** *adjective* revolting, horrible. *Horrid weather.*

**horrify** (horrifies, horrifying, horrified) *verb* to shock or fill with great horror and disgust. *I was horrified to hear that our friend had been killed.*

**horror** *noun* a feeling of shock or fear. *He watched the snake slide toward him with horror.*

**horticulture** *noun* the science of gardening and the growing of fruit, flowers, and vegetables. **horticultural** *adjective. Let's go to the horticultural show tomorrow.*

**hospice** *noun* a hospital where people who are dying or suffering from incurable diseases are looked after by doctors and nurses.

**hospitable** *adjective* friendly and generous to guests and strangers. *We were given a very hospitable welcome.* **hospitality** *noun.*

**hospital** *noun* a place where people who are ill or injured are treated and looked after.

**hostage** *noun* a person who is held prisoner by people who will not release her or him until their demands have been met.

**hostel** *noun* a place where people such as students or hitchhikers can stay overnight cheaply.

**hostile** *adjective* behaving in an unfriendly way. *The President was met by a hostile group of students.*

**hotel** *noun* a building with many bedrooms where people pay to stay and have meals.

**hound** *noun* a breed of dog that is used for hunting and racing. Foxhounds, deerhounds, and bloodhounds are all different kinds of hound. **hound** *verb* to follow or harass somebody. *The actress was hounded by photographers wherever she went.*

**hour** *noun* a period of time consisting of 60 minutes. There are 24 hours in a day. **hourly** *adjective, adverb. The hourly rate for the job is not very impressive.*

**house** *noun* **1** a building where people live. **2** a building used for a particular purpose. *The White House.* **house** (say houze) *verb* to provide a place for somebody to live.

**household** *noun* all the people who live together in one house. **household word** a familiar name, saying, or thing.

**housekeeper** *noun* a person who is paid to look after a house and manage a household.

**housework** *noun* cleaning, washing, cooking, and other work that must be done in a house.

**hovel** *noun* a small, filthy, broken-down house or hut. *The refugee lived in a hovel.*

**hover** *verb* **1** to remain in the air over one spot without moving. **2** to linger or to stay near one place.

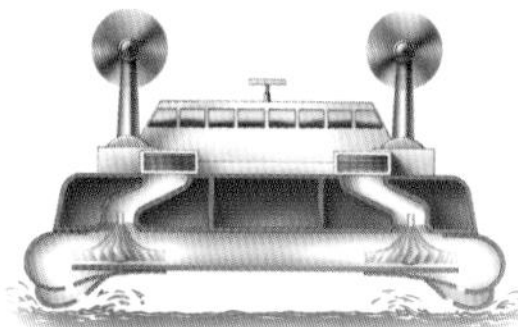

hovercraft

**hovercraft** *noun* a boat that can fly over sea or land, lifted up on a cushion of air as it moves.

**howl** *verb* to make a long, loud, crying sound like the one an animal makes when it is in pain. **howl** *noun.*

**HQ** *abbreviation* Headquarters.

**hue** *noun* a color or shade of color.

**human** *adjective* having natural and understandable feelings. *It's only human to cry when you are upset.* **human** *noun* human being. A man, woman, or child.

**humane** *adjective* kind and gentle, not cruel. *The humane treatment of animals.*

**humanity** *noun* **1** all people. **2** being kind and humane.

**humble** *adjective* modest and not vain or self-important. *He's very clever, but in spite of his achievements, he's humble too.*

**humid** *adjective* damp and sometimes warm. *Humid weather.* **humidity** *noun.*

**humiliate** *verb* to make somebody feel ashamed or appear stupid to other people. **humiliation** *noun.*

**hummingbird** *noun* a very small, brightly colored bird with a long, slender beak. It hovers over flowers to feed on their nectar, beating its wings so fast that they make a humming sound.

**hummingbird**

**humor** *noun* **1** what makes people laugh or smile. **2** a mood. *Is she in a good humor today?* **sense of humor** the ability to see what is funny and to laugh at it. **humor** *verb* to give in to someone's wishes. *I know you don't want to go, but please humor me.*

**humorous** *adjective* funny. *A humorous book.*

**hunch** *noun* a feeling about something, not based on facts. *I had a hunch you would be on this bus.* **hunch** *verb* to lean forward with your shoulders raised and your head bent down.

**Hungarian** *noun* **1** a person who comes from Hungary. **2** the language spoken in Hungary. **Hungarian** *adjective. Hungarian dances.*

**Hungary** *noun* a country in eastern Europe.

**hunger** *noun* a strong wish or need to eat. **hunger** *verb. She hungered for fame and fortune.*

**hungry** (hungrier, hungriest) *adjective* feeling hunger or the need for food. *The hungry dog hurried to eat all its supper.* **hungrily** *adverb. It ate hungrily.*

**Hungary's flag**

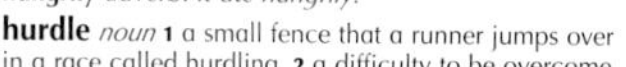

**hurdle** *noun* **1** a small fence that a runner jumps over in a race called hurdling. **2** a difficulty to be overcome.

**hurl** *verb* to throw something as far as you can.

**hurricane** *noun* a violent storm with strong winds. *The hurricane tore off the roof.*

**hurry** (hurries, hurrying, hurried) *verb* to move quickly or do something as fast as you can. **hurry** *noun. Why are you in such a hurry, when we have all day to spare?*

**hurt** *verb* **1** to cause pain or harm to a person or an animal. **2** to feel pain. *My bruised knee hurts.*

**husband** *noun* the man to whom a woman is married.

**husk** *noun* the outer covering of some fruits and cereals. *Don't eat the husk.*

**husky** *adjective* (of a voice) low and rough. **husky** *noun* a strong dog used to pull sleds in Arctic regions.

**hybrid** *noun* a plant or animal produced from two different kinds (species) of plant or animal. A mule is a hybrid of a horse and a donkey. **hybrid** *adjective. A hybrid rose.*

**hydrant** *noun* a water pipe in the street, to which a hose can be attached to draw water from the main water supply to put out fires.

**hydroelectricity** *noun* electricity produced by using water power, at a dam or a waterfall, for example.

**hydrofoil**

**hydrofoil** *noun* a fast, light boat that skims over the surface of water on fin-like foils attached to its hull.

**hydrogen** *noun* the lightest of all gases and the simplest of all chemical elements. It combines with oxygen to make water.

**hyena** *noun* a wolf-like wild animal from India and Africa that hunts in packs and lives off the flesh of dead animals. The howl of a hyena is like hysterical laughter.

**hygiene** *noun* (say **hy**-jeen) the science and practice of cleanliness and good health. **hygienic** *adjective.*

**hymn** *noun* (say him) a religious song of praise. *We sang hymns in church.*

**hyphen** *noun* a mark ( - ) used in writing to join two parts of a divided word at the end of a line or to join two or more words to make a new word, for example: *self-defense, nine-year-old girl, three-car garage.*

**hypocrite** *noun* a person who pretends to have feelings, qualities, or beliefs which he or she does not really have.

**hypodermic needle** *noun* a thin, hollow needle that is used to inject drugs into a vein. *Never re-use a hypodermic needle.*

**hysteria** *noun* uncontrollable excitement or distress. *She had a fit of hysteria when her cat was run over.*

Hh

**ice** *noun* water that has frozen. **ice** *verb* to spread icing on a cake. **ice age** *noun* a time long ago when large areas of the Earth were covered with ice. **ice cream** a smooth, sweet, frozen food usually made with milk or cream. **ice cube** a small block of ice used to cool drinks. **ice hockey** a game played on ice by two teams in which the skaters try to score goals by hitting a rubber puck (ball) with a long stick. **ice skate** *noun* a boot with a metal blade on the bottom for sliding smoothly over ice. **ice skate** *verb* to move on ice wearing ice skates.

**iceberg** *noun* a large lump of ice floating in the sea. Most of an iceberg is hidden under the surface of the sea. **the tip of the iceberg** only a small part of a problem.

iceberg

Iceland's flag

**Iceland** *noun* a Scandinavian country in northwest Europe.

**icicle** *noun* a long, pointed stick of ice formed by water freezing as it drops.

**icon** *noun* **1** a picture of Jesus Christ or a saint painted on wood, seen in many Greek or Russian Christian (Orthodox) churches. **2** a small picture on a computer screen representing a program, which can be selected by clicking the mouse.

**icy** (icier, iciest) *adjective* **1** very cold. *Icy weather.* **2** covered in ice. *Icy roads.*

**idea** *noun* **1** a thought or picture in your mind. **2** a plan. *She had the idea of becoming a vet.* **3** purpose. *The idea of the game is to score as many goals as possible.*

**ideal** *adjective* perfect or suitable. *He's an ideal husband.* **ideal** *noun* the best possible person, thing, situation, or example.

**identical** *adjective* exactly the same in every way.

**identify** (identifies, identifying, identified) *verb* to recognize somebody or something and be able to name them. *His owner identified the dog.* **identification** *noun.*

**identity** *noun* a person's distinguishing characteristics that make them individual.

**idiom** *noun* an expression or special way of saying something in which the words have a meaning different from what they appear to have. For example, the idiom "to drop off" means to fall asleep; and "heads will roll" means that some people will suffer or be fired from jobs.

**idiot** *noun* a stupid person. **idiotic** *adjective. What an idiotic idea!*

**idle** *adjective* **1** lazy and work-shy. **2** not working. *During the strike the machines were left idle.* **3** worthless or not really meant. *Idle threats.* **idleness** *noun.*

**idol** *noun* **1** something, such as a statue, that is worshiped as a god. **2** a famous person who is greatly admired. *A pop idol.*

**igloo** *noun* a house made out of blocks of snow and ice in the shape of a dome by the Inuits of the Arctic region.

igloo

**ignite** *verb* to set fire to or to catch fire. *Petrol ignites with a whoosh of flames.*

**ignition** *noun* a device in a motor vehicle that starts the engine working by igniting the fuel. *Turn the key to start the ignition.*

**ignorant** *adjective* knowing very little about something; badly educated. *She's ignorant about computers.* **ignorance** *noun.*

**ignore** *verb* to take no notice of somebody or something; to disregard. *She totally ignored me when I said hello to her in the street.*

**il-** *prefix* used before many words beginning with "l" to indicate "against" or "not." *illiterate* (not literate).

**ill** (worse, worst) *adjective* **1** not in good health; unwell. **2** bad or harmful. *The ill effects of smoking.* **illness** *noun.*

**illegal** *adjective* not allowed by law. *It is illegal to park there after 8.00 a.m.*

**illegible** *adjective* writing that is so poor that it is difficult or impossible to read.

**illiterate** *adjective* unable to read or write. **illiteracy** *noun.*

**illogical** *adjective* not obeying logic and therefore not making sense. *It is illogical to hope he will come to the party when you haven't invited him.*

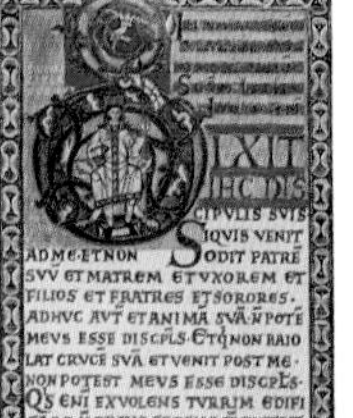


illuminate

**illuminate** *verb* **1** to decorate a book such as a Bible with gold and colored letters and pictures. **2** to light up or shine a light on something. *The castle is illuminated at night.* **illumination** *noun.* A decorated letter in an early handwritten manuscript. **illuminations** *plural noun. The streets are decorated with Christmas illuminations.* **illuminating** *adjective.*

**illusion** *noun* a false idea or image of something that is not really there. *The optical illusion (right) allows you to see a vase or two faces looking at each other.*

**im-** *prefix* like in- , used before certain words beginning with "b," "m," and "p" and meaning "against," "not," or "without." *Immeasurable* (too great to be measured).

illusion

**image** *noun* **1** a picture or statue. **2** any picture in a book, movie, or on television. **3** your reflection in a mirror. **4** a picture of something in your mind. **5** a very close likeness. *He is the image of his twin brother.* **6** a person's image is the general opinion that others have of them.

**imagery** *noun* the descriptive words used by writers to create pictures in the minds of readers. *Beautiful imagery.*

**imaginary** *adjective* not real but existing only in the mind. Goblins and elves are imaginary creatures.

**imagination** *noun* **1** the ability to create pictures in the mind. *Use your imagination and write a story about space travel.* **2** the ability to create new ideas.

**imaginative** *adjective* having a lot of imagination.

**imagine** *verb* **1** to have a picture of something in your mind. *Can you imagine life without cars?* **2** to think you see or hear things that are not really there. *You're just imagining there's a ghost under your bed.*

**imitate** *verb* to copy or behave like somebody or something. *She can imitate her mother's voice perfectly.* **imitation** *noun. He does a good imitation of a dog.*

**immature** *adjective* **1** not fully grown or developed; unripe. **2** behaving childishly and not like an adult. **immaturity** *noun.*

**immediately** *adverb* at once and without delay. **immediate** *adjective.*

**immense** *adjective* very big. *The Sahara is an immense desert in North Africa.* **immensity** *noun.* **immensely** *adjective. Romantic comedies are immensely popular.*

**immerse** *verb* to put something into a liquid until it is completely covered. **immerse yourself in** to give all your attention to something.

**immigrant** *noun* somebody who immigrates to and comes to settle in a country. **immigration** *noun.*

**immigrate** *verb* to come to live and settle in a country. *They immigrated quite recently.*

**imminent** *adjective* Something that is imminent is expected to happen very soon. *The forecast says that snow is imminent.*

**immobile** *adjective* not moving or unable to move. **immobility** *noun.* **immobilize** *verb* to make immobile and unable to move. *All traffic has been immobilized by the heavy fall of snow during the night*

**immoral** *adjective* behaving in a way that is considered wrong. **immorality** *noun.*

**immortal** *adjective* never dying but instead living and lasting for ever.

**immune** *adjective* protected against a disease and so unable to catch it. **immunity** *noun.* **immunize** *verb* to give somebody an injection so that they cannot catch a disease. *All babies should be immunized against diseases such as polio.*

**imp** *noun* a mischievous little creature in fairy tales.

**impact** *noun* **1** the force of one object colliding with another. **2** the strong effect or impression that something has. *Computers have had a great impact on the way we learn, both at home and at school.*

impala

**impala** *noun* a small African antelope that is capable of long, high jumps. It lives in large herds.

**impartial** *adjective* fair and not favoring one person or one side more than another. **impartiality** *noun.*

**impassable** *noun* not able to be passed through or across. *Heavy snowstorms made the mountain roads impassable.*

**impatient** *adjective* unwilling to wait and easily annoyed. **impatience** *noun.*

**impede** *verb* to get in the way of somebody or something and so slow down progress.

**impenetrable** *adjective* **1** impossible to get through. *An impenetrable forest.* **2** impossible to understand. *His foreign accent was impenetrable.*

**imperfect** *adjective* **1** not perfect and having some fault. **2** a verb tense indicating a repeated or incomplete action in the past. *She was sitting in a chair.* **imperfection** *noun. The embroidery teacher would not tolerate imperfection in her students' work.*

**imperial** *adjective* **1** of or having to do with an empire or an emperor or empress. **2** The imperial system is a traditional non-metric British system of weights and measures using inches, feet, yards, and miles; ounces, pounds, and hundredweights; and pints and gallons.

**impersonal** *adjective* unfriendly and showing no personal feelings or warmth. *An impersonal letter.*

**impetuous** *adjective* an impetuous person acts suddenly and without thinking first.

**implement** *noun* a tool or instrument.

**imply** (implies, implying, implied) *verb* to suggest or hint at something without actually saying it directly. **implication** *noun.*

**impolite** *adjective* rude and bad-mannered.

**import** *verb* (say im-**port**) to buy goods from another country to sell in your own country. **import** *noun* (say **im**-port). The opposite of import is export.

**impossible** *adjective* not possible; something that cannot be done or cannot happen.

**impostor** *noun* someone who pretends to be somebody else in order to deceive and get things they want.

**impracticable** *adjective* not possible to use or put into practice. *An impracticable idea.*

**impractical** *adjective* not useful and lacking common sense. *He's quite impractical and couldn't boil an egg.*

**impress** *verb* to cause somebody's admiration or respect. *I was impressed by his knowledge.* **impressive** *adjective.*

Ii

**impression** *noun* **1** the way something appears to you and the effect it has on you. *His kindness made a great impression on us.* **2** a vague idea or belief. *I have the impression I've been here before.* **3** a mark made by something pressing on a surface. *Our cats left the impressions of their paws in the wet concrete.* **4** an impersonation or attempt at copying how somebody talks and behaves, usually in order to entertain people.

**impressionable** *adjective* very easily influenced or impressed by others. *Some young people are very impressionable and easily led astray.*

**imprison** *verb* to put somebody in prison. **imprisonment** *noun. His punishment was imprisonment.*

**improvise** *verb* **1** to do something without planning or rehearsing it beforehand. *She had lost her notes and had to improvise the speech.* **2** to make something quickly with whatever materials are available. *We improvised a table from cardboard boxes.* **improvisation** *noun.*

**impudent** *noun* rude and showing no respect; insolent. **impudence** *noun.*

**in-** *prefix* meaning "not" when added to the beginning of certain words: *inadequate* (not adequate), *inactive* (not active), *inconsistent* (not consistent).

**inarticulate** *adjective* unable to express yourself well when speaking.

**inaudible** *adjective* not loud enough to be heard clearly.

**incapable** *adjective* unable to do things expected of you.

**incentive** *noun* something that encourages you to do something. *He was promised a bike as an incentive to make him work hard.*

**incessant** *adjective* going on and on and never stopping. *The incessant noise of the traffic.*

**inch** *noun* a measurement of length, equal to 2.54 centimeters. There are 12 inches in a foot.

**incident** *noun* a single event or happening.

**incidentally** *adverb* by the way.

**incinerator** *noun* a container for burning trash. *Please put these bandages straight in the incinerator.*

**incision** *noun* a cut into a patient's body made by a surgeon during an operation.

**incite** *verb* to arouse and encourage people to action, good or bad.

**inclination** *noun* a tendency or slight preference to do something. *My inclination is to turn right.* **incline** *verb*

**incoherent** *adjective* speaking in a rambling way that is not easy to follow or understand. **incoherence** *noun.*

**income** *noun* the money a person regularly earns. *She has an income of $30,000 a year.* **income tax** the part of a person's income that must be paid to government.

**incompetent** *adjective* lacking the ability to do a job well. **incompetence** *noun.*

**incomplete** *adjective* unfinished; not complete.

**incongruous** *adjective* strange and out of place. *A skyscraper would look incongruous in a small village.*

**incorrect** *adjective* wrong. *The man always seems to give incorrect answers to my questions.*

**increase** *verb* (say in-**krees**) to make bigger or to become bigger. **increase** *noun* (**in**-krees).

**incredible** *adjective* **1** difficult or impossible to believe. *An incredible adventure story.* **2** amazing; very good. *An incredible film.*

**incriminate** *verb* to prove the guilt of someone.

**incubator** *noun* **1** a container in which premature and weak babies are kept alive and safe until they are strong. **2** a heated container for keeping eggs warm until the chicks hatch. **incubate** *verb* to keep eggs warm until they hatch.

incubator

**incurable** *adjective* not able to be cured or made better. *An incurable disease.*

**indecent** *adjective* shockingly rude and offensive. **indecency** *noun.*

**indefinite** *adjective* vague; not fixed or limited. *He has gone to Mongolia for an indefinite period.* **indefinite article** the adjective "a" (and "an" before a vowel).

**independent** *adjective* free; not controlled by or needing help from others. *Most colonies have become independent.* **independence** *noun. The country finally gained independence from its more powerful neighbor.*

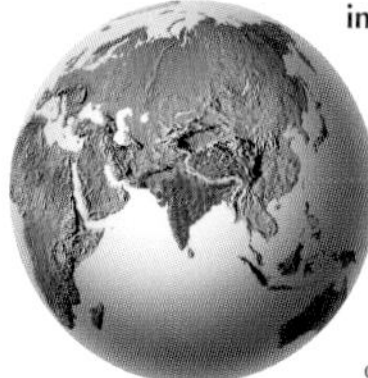

**index** *noun* a section at the end of some books giving an alphabetical list and page number of all the subjects mentioned in the book. *The index in my book is very useful.*

**India** *noun* a large country in South Asia.

**Indian** *noun* **1** a person who comes from India. **2** an American Indian. **Indian** *adjective. An Indian temple.*

India

**indicate** *verb* **1** to show or point out something. *He indicated on the map where the village is.* **2** to be a sign of. *Dark clouds indicate rain.* **3** to show which way you are turning; to signal. *Indicate left.* **indication** *noun. He gave no indication as to what he was feeling.*

**indifferent** *adjective* **1** having no feelings and not caring. *She is indifferent to what people think of her.* **2** not very good. *An indifferent meal.* **indifference** *noun.*

**indigestion** *noun* pain you get in your stomach when you have eaten too much and have difficulty digesting your food. **indigestible** *adjective.*

**indirect** *adjective* not direct or straightforward. *We followed an indirect route on our map that went around the hills.*

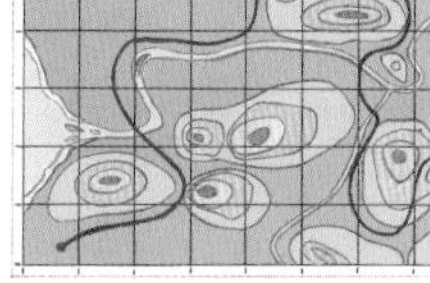

indirect

**individual** *adjective* **1** relating to one person or thing and not to a group. *She has individual tennis coaching from the champion.* **2** having an unusual quality or way of behaving. *He has an individual way of walking: leaning backward with his chin jutting forward!* **individual** *noun* a single person. *She is a highly creative individual.* **individually** *adjective* separately.

**individuality** *noun* a quality that makes a person or thing different and stand out from others. *Her hairstyle is striking in its individuality.*

**Indonesia** *noun* a country in Southeast Asia, made up of Sumatra, Java, and many other islands.

**indulge** *verb* **1** If you indulge in something, you take great pleasure in it, even if it is bad for you. **2** To indulge somebody is to let them have or do what they want; to spoil them. **indulgence** *noun.* **indulgent** *adjective. Jane's daughter has very indulgent grandparents; they bring her presents whenever they visit.*

**industrial** *adjective* concerning industry and factories. *The industrial regions of Italy.* **Industrial Revolution** the name given to the widespread introduction of steam-driven machines in factories during the 18th and 19th centuries, notably in Britain.

Industrial Revolution



**industrious** *adjective* hardworking.

**industry** *noun* **1** work; the making of things in factories. **2** a particular business or branch of industry. *The food industry.* **3** hard work.

**inefficient** *adjective* not working well and wasting time or energy.

**inert** *adjective* without power and unable to move. **inertia** *noun* lack of energy.

**inevitable** *adjective* sure to happen or impossible to stop. **inevitability** *noun.*

**infamous** *adjective* well known or famous for being bad. *An infamous thief.*

**infant** *noun* a very young child. **infancy** *noun* the time in your life when you are an infant.

**infantry** *noun* soldiers who fight on foot; foot-soldiers, collectively.

**infantryman** *noun* a soldier of an infantry regiment.

**infatuated** *adjective* to have such a strong love for somebody that you cannot think sensibly about them. **infatuation** *noun.*

**inferior** *adjective* not so good or important in rank or quality. The opposite of "inferior" is "superior." *An inferior bottle of wine.*

infantryman

**inferiority complex** Somebody who has an inferiority complex always thinks that he or she is less important or less good at doing things than others.

**infertile** *adjective* **1** unable to produce babies. **2** Infertile land is of such poor quality that crops will not grow.

**infested** *adjective* full of pests such as insects or rats. *The house was infested with fleas.*

**infinite** *adjective* endless and without limits; so great that it cannot be measured or imagined. *I loved him for his infinite kindness toward animals.* **infinity** *noun.*

**infinitive** *adjective* the basic form of a verb, having "to" in front of it. *To go, to dream, to plan, to talk, to visit.*

**inflammable** *adjective* catching fire easily.

**inflate** *verb* to make something expand by filling it with air or gas. *They inflated the balloons with a pump.*

**inflation** *noun* a rise in prices.

**inflexible** *adjective* unable to bend or change in any way. *Inflexible rules.*

**influence** *noun* **1** the power to make somebody do something or make something happen. **2** a person who has such power. *His uncle was a great influence on his decision to become an actor.* **influence** *verb.* **influential** *adjective.*



**influenza or flu** *noun* an infectious disease that gives you a headache, fever, and aching muscles.

**informal** *adjective* **1** friendly and relaxed, not following rules. *Informal clothes.* **2** used in ordinary conversation or writing. **informality** *noun.*

**information** *noun* all the facts or details about something. *Can you give me any information about the delay to the trains?*

**information technology** **(IT)** the use of computers to store, arrange, and send information. *I have a new job in IT, installing a company's new computers.*

**informative** *adjective* giving useful or helpful facts. *We watched an informative TV program about endangered animals.*

**ingenious** *adjective* clever and imaginative. *An ingenious invention.* **ingenuity** *noun.*

**ingot** *noun* a lump of metal, usually in the shape of a brick. *The bank robbers escaped with a van full of gold and silver ingots.*

ingot

**ingredient** *noun* any one of a number of things that go into a mixture from which something is made, as in cooking. *Flour, eggs, and milk are the basic ingredients of the batter used for making pancakes.*

**inhabit** *verb* to live in a place.

**inhale** *verb* to breathe in.

**inherit** *verb* **1** to receive something such as money or property from somebody who has died. *She inherited the house from her aunt.* **2** to have the same qualities or characteristics as your parents or ancestors. *He has inherited his father's good looks.* **inheritance** *noun.*

**inhuman** *adjective* cruel, showing no kindness or pity. **inhumanity** *noun.*

**initial** *noun* (say in-**ish**-ul) the first letter of a word or name. *Robin Ashe's initials are R.A.* **initial** *adjective* first or at the beginning. *My initial reaction is good.*

**initiative** *noun* the ability to do things on your own and to lead the way. *Marcus showed a lot of initiative and got the job done without having to be shown how.*

**injure** *verb* to hurt or damage a part of a person's or an animal's body. **injury** *noun.*

innumerable

**innocent** *adjective* **1** without blame or guilt. *The prisoner was innocent.* **2** harmless. *Innocent fun.* **innocence** *noun.*

**innovation** *noun* something that is completely new. A new invention or way of doing things. *Computers were a major innovation in schools.*

**innumerable** *adjective* too many to be counted. *Innumerable stars in the sky.*

**inoculate** *verb* to protect somebody from a disease by injecting them with a weak form of the disease. **inoculation** *noun.*

**input** *noun* information that you put into a computer. **input** *verb. I've input the corrections to the text.*

**inquest** *noun* an official inquiry to find out why somebody suddenly died.

**inquire** *verb* to ask questions to find out about something. *Alice inquired about the times of buses.*

**inquiry** *noun* **1** a question. **2** a detailed and official investigation. *An inquiry into the cause of the fire.*

**inquisitive** *noun* always asking questions.

**inscribe** *verb* to write or carve words on the hard surface of something.

**inscription** *noun* words written or carved on something.

**insect** *noun* a small animal with six legs, no backbone, and usually with wings. An insect has three parts to its body. Beetles, butterflies, and flies are insects.

**insecticide** *noun* a poison that is used to kill insects that are pests.

**insert** *verb* to put something inside something else.

**insight** *noun* a clear understanding of something. *An insight into his behavior.*

**insincere** *adjective* not honest and pretending to have feelings about something. *He said he liked me but I knew he was insincere.*

**insipid** *adjective* **1** without taste; weak. *An insipid cup of coffee.* **2** lacking interest or vigor.

**insolent** *adjective* rude and insulting. *Insolent behavior.* **insolence** *noun.*

**insoluble** *adjective* **1** If something is insoluble, it will not dissolve. **2** incapable of being solved.

**insomnia** *noun* sleeplessness; difficulty in going to sleep.

**inspire** *verb* to influence somebody and encourage them to feel confident and enthusiastic about what they are doing. *The teacher inspired me to practise harder.* **inspiration** *noun.* **inspiring** *adjective.*

**install** *verb* **1** to put something in a place ready to be used. *He installed a new oven in the kitchen.* **2** publicly to give somebody an important position. *She was ceremonially installed as mayor.*

**installment** *noun* **1** one of the parts into which something is divided; an episode. **2** one of a series of regular payments for something.

**instead** *adverb* in place of something or somebody. *May I have milk instead of cream in my coffee?*

**instinct** *noun* behavior that is natural and does not have to be thought about or learned. *Birds build their nests by instinct.* **instinctive** *adjective. Instinctive behavior.*

**institute** *verb* to start something. *To institute reforms.*

**institution** *noun* **1** a large or important organization. *Hospitals, prisons, universities, and other institutions.* **2** an established custom, habit, or tradition. *Putting up decorations at Christmas is an institution.*

**instrument** *noun* **1** a device or tool you use to help you with your work. *Scientific instruments.* **2** A musical instrument is an object such as a piano or a guitar that you play to make music.

**insulate**

**insulate** *verb* to cover something with a material that will not let heat or electricity escape from it. *Electric wires are insulated with rubber or plastic.* **insulation** *noun.*

**insult** *verb* (say in-**sult**) to upset somebody by saying something rude to them or behaving in a bad way. **insult** *noun* (say **in**-sult). *It was an insult to my intelligence.*

**insurance** *noun* small sums of money (premiums) you pay regularly to an organization (an insurance company) that agrees to protect you and give you an amount of money to, for example, replace something of yours when stolen or damaged, or to pay future medical bills.

**intake** *noun* **1** the number of people taken in. *A high intake of students.* **2** the process of taking something in. *The news was greeted by a sharp intake of breath.*

**integrate** *verb* **1** to combine people, often of different races, in one community. **2** to fit different parts together. **integration** *noun.*

**integrity** *noun* complete honesty and trustworthiness. *A woman of integrity.*

**intelligent** *adjective* clever and able to learn and understand things quickly and easily. **intelligence** *noun.*

**intense** *adjective* **1** strong or great. *Intense cold.* **2** serious and with strong feelings. *He gets very intense about his work.* **intensity** *noun.*

**intensive** *adjective* **1** thorough. *Intensive investigations.* **2** concentrated. *The patient is in intensive care.*

**intention** *noun* what you intend or plan to do. *Please state your intentions clearly.* **intend** *verb.*

**intentional** *adjective* intended or done on purpose. *Intentional damage.*

**inter-** *prefix* among or between. *Interplanetary travel.*

**interact** *verb* to have an effect on one another. *All the chemicals in this experiment interact with each other.*

**interaction** *noun* the action or influence of people or things on one another.

**interactive** *adjective* (in computers) the exchange of information between a computer and its user.

**intercept** *verb* to stop somebody or something that is moving from one place to another. *He intercepted the ball with a fine catch.*

**interest** *verb* to want to learn or find out more about something. **interest** *noun* **1** *He has a great interest in geology.* **2** extra money you pay to a bank for money you have borrowed. **interested** *adjective* having a private interest; not impartial. *An interested party.*

**interesting** *adjective* If something is interesting, you want to find out more about it. *Archeology is an interesting subject.*

**interface** *noun* in computing, a connection that allows two pieces of equipment to be operated together.

**interfere** *verb* to meddle or take part in something that has nothing to do with you. **interference** *noun.*

**interior** *noun* the inside of something. **interior** *adjective.*

**interjection** *noun* a word or phrase used to express surprise or pain. *"Ouch! It hurts."*

**internal** *adjective* relating to the inside of something or somebody. *The internal plans of the house.*

**international** *adjective* concerning several countries. *An international peacekeeping force flew into the country.*

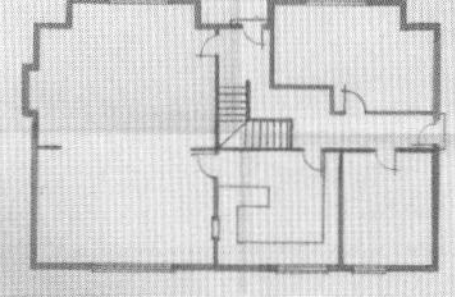

**internal**

Ii

**interpret** *verb* **1** to translate or put the words of one language into another. **2** to decide or explain what something means. *He interpreted her nod as meaning "yes."* **interpretation** *noun.*

**interpreter** *noun* a person who translates from one language into another. *The French reporter worked with an interpreter when he interviewed the Russian President, because he wasn't fluent in Russian himself.*

**interrupt** *verb* **1** to stop somebody while they are talking or doing something. *I'm reading, so please don't interrupt me for half an hour.* **2** to disturb or stop something happening for a short time. *Thunder interrupted the lesson.* **interruption** *noun.*

**interval** *noun* **1** a period of time between two dates or events. **2** a short break in a play or concert. **at intervals** happening sometimes but not regularly.

**intervene** *verb* to become involved in or to join in something such as a quarrel in order to stop it from happening or to prevent it becoming too heated. **intervention** *noun.*



**intervening** *adjective* the time between two events. *The intervening years.*

**interview** *noun* a meeting at which a person is asked questions to see if he or she is suitable for a job; a meeting at which things are discussed. **interview** *verb. He was interviewed three times for the job.*

**intestines** *plural noun* the long tube that is coiled inside the body through which food passes after it has left the stomach and before waste is passed out.

intestines

**intimate** *adjective* (say **in**-tim-ut) **1** very friendly and close. *Intimate relations.* **2** personal and private. *Intimate letters sent by the soldier to his wife back home were published in his biography after his death.*

**intimidate** *verb* to frighten somebody in an attempt to make them do something you want; to threaten. **intimidation** *noun.*

**intolerant** *adjective* not willing to tolerate or accept ideas, beliefs, or behavior different from your own. **intolerance** *noun.*

**intoxicated** *adjective* **1** having drunk too much alcohol. *Peter was intoxicated.* **2** excited beyond control. *She felt intoxicated with happiness.*

**intrepid** *adjective* brave and bold; without fear. *Intrepid astronauts explored the Moon.*

**intricate** *adjective* complicated and hard to follow; detailed. *An intricate pattern.*

intricate

**intrigue** *noun* (say **in**-treeg) a scheme or plot. *Intrigue was rife in the office.* **intrigue** *verb* (say in-**treeg**) to interest or fascinate somebody. *Animal behavior has intrigued Robert since he was a boy.*

**introduce** *verb* **1** to bring people together for the first time and make them known to one another. **2** to bring in something or use it for the first time. *The company introduced a new computer.*

**introduction** *noun* **1** the act of introducing somebody or something. **2** a piece of writing at the beginning of a book, telling you what it is about. **3** a first experience of something. *An introduction to swimming.*

**intrude** *verb* to enter somewhere or join something when you are not wanted or have not been invited; to disturb. **intrusion** *noun.* **intrusive** *adjective.*

**intruder** *noun* somebody who intrudes or breaks in, such as a burglar.

**intuition** *noun* a feeling or understanding about something that you do not have to think about but cannot explain in a logical way. *His intuition told him that his son was in trouble and needed help that night.*

**inundate** *verb* **1** to flood. **2** to receive so much of something that you cannot cope with it; to overwhelm. *She was inundated with job offers.* **inundation** *noun.*

**invade** to send troops into another country or place to fight the people living there and to take control of it. **invasion** *noun.*

**invalid** *adjective* (say in-**val**-id) something that is not legal and so cannot be used. *Your ticket is out of date and therefore invalid.* **invalid** *noun* (say **in**-val-id) a person who is disabled by illness or injury.

**invaluable** *adjective* very valuable or priceless; very useful. *Learning to read is an invaluable skill that makes life easier and is greatly rewarding.*

**invert** *verb* to put something in the opposite position, especially by turning it upside down.

**invertebrate** *noun* any animal without a backbone such as an insect, slug or worm.

invertebrate

**invest** *verb* to buy something in order to sell it at a future date and make a profit.

**investigate** *verb* to try to find out all the facts about something; to examine carefully. *The police were called in to investigate the disappearance of the painting from the museum.* **investigation** *noun.*

**invisible** *adjective* something that cannot be seen. *Air is invisible, and so are smells!*

**invitation** *noun* written or spoken words asking you to come to something, such as a party. *I'd be happy to accept your kind invitation to the ball.*

**invite** *verb* to ask somebody to come to something or to go somewhere. *My uncle invited me to stay at his house for the Easter holidays.*

**inviting** *adjective* tempting or attractive. *An inviting warm fire on a cold day.*

**invoice** *noun* a document asking for payment for goods that have been sent or for work that has been done.

**involve** *verb* **1** to be necessary as part of a job. *The job involves a lot of letter writing.* **2** to be interested in and concerned with. *I don't want to be involved with your problems.* **involvement** *noun.*

**IQ** *abbreviation* Intelligence Quotient, the level of someone's intelligence, with 100 being the average level, assessed by asking questions on a wide range of subjects.

**Iran** *noun* a country in Southwest Asia.

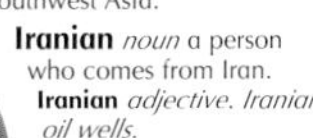

Iran

**Iranian** *noun* a person who comes from Iran. **Iranian** *adjective. Iranian oil wells.*

**Iraq** *noun* a country in Southwest Asia.

**irate** *adjective* (say eye-**rate**) angry and complaining. *She wrote an irate letter to the council.*

**Ireland** *noun* a country in northwest Europe.

**iris** *noun* **1** a tall garden flower. **2** the colored part of your eye.

**Irish** *adjective* connected to or relating to Ireland and its people (the Irish).

**iron** *noun* **1** a heavy gray metal that is one of the chemical elements. **2** a heavy electrical tool that heats up and which you use to smooth creases from clothes. **ironing** *noun. Have you any ironing to do?*

**irony** *noun* the use of words to say the opposite of what they mean. *"That was clever of you to smash my best plate!"* **ironic** *adjective.*

**irregular** *adjective* **1** not regular or usual. *He works irregular hours, so I never know when he'll be home.* **2** not even or smooth. *The irregular surface of the wall made it hard to cover it with wallpaper.*

irrigate

**irrigate** *verb* to supply water for crops on dry land by means of ditches, pipes, or canals. **irrigation** *noun.*

**irritable** *adjective* easily annoyed; in a bad mood.

**irritate** *verb* **1** to make somebody annoyed, cross, and impatient. **2** to make your skin feel itchy. **irritation** *noun.*

**Islam** *noun* the religion followed by Muslims, based on the teachings of the prophet Muhammad. **Islamic** *adjective.*

**Islamabad** *noun* the capital of Pakistan.

**island** *noun* a piece of land surrounded by water.

**isle** *noun* an island, usually used as part of its name. *The Isle of Skye and the Isle of Mull are both in Scotland.*

**isobar** *noun* a line on a weather map that connects places with the same or equal atmospheric pressure.

**isolate** *verb* to place something apart from others and by itself; to separate. *The chemist isolated a previously unknown element.* **isolation** *noun.*

**Israel** *noun* a country in Southwest Asia.

**issue** *noun* **1** an edition of a newspaper or magazine brought out at a particular time. *Today's issue has the latest news.* **2** something that is given out; a supply. **3** a problem or an important topic for discussion. *The issue of bullying.* **issue** *verb* to supply with. *The hikers were issued with special boots.* **take issue with** to disagree.

**isthmus** *noun* a narrow strip of land that joins two larger pieces of land.

**IT** *abbreviation* Information Technology, in which computers are used to store and retrieve information.

**Italian** *noun* **1** a person who comes from Italy. **2** the language spoken in Italy. **Italian** *adjective. Italian opera.*

**Italy** *noun* a country in southern Europe.

**itch** *noun* an uncomfortable, tingling feeling on your skin that makes you want to scratch yourself. **itch** (itches, itching, itched) *verb. A mosquito bite itches.*

**item** *noun* a single thing on a list or in a group of other things. *An item of news.*

**ivory** *noun* the hard, smooth, white material from which the tusks of elephants and walruses are made.

**Ivory Coast** *noun* a country in West Africa.

**ivy** *noun* a climbing evergreen plant with shiny, pointed leaves. *Let's decorate the house with holly and ivy.*

**jab** (jabs, jabbing, jabbed) *verb* to hit or stab with something pointed. **jab** *noun* an injection. *A flu jab.*

**jackal** *noun* a wild animal of the dog family that feeds off the dead bodies of other animals. Jackals come from Asia and Africa.

**jackknife** *verb* when the trailer of a two-part truck suddenly bends around toward the cab or driver's seat. *The truck jackknifed on the black ice.*

**jackpot** *noun* the biggest prize to be won in a game or a lottery.

**jacuzzi** *noun* a bath with underwater jets that make the water swirl. *Having a jacuzzi is very relaxing.*

**jade** *noun* a precious green stone used in making jewelry. *Mom's jade necklace sets off her green eyes.*

**jaded** *adjective* bored and lacking in enthusiasm.

**jagged** *adjective* with many sharp, rough, and uneven points. *A coastline of jagged rocks.*

jaguar

**jaguar** *noun* a South American wild cat with yellow and black spots like a leopard.

Jj

**jail** *noun* another spelling for gaol, a prison where people are kept as a punishment for committing a crime. *The bank robber was sent to jail.*

**Jakarta** *noun* the capital of Indonesia in Southeast Asia.

**Jamaica** *noun* a country in the Caribbean.

**January** *noun* the first month of the year. January has 31 days.

**Japan** *noun* a country in east Asia.

**jargon** *noun* the special technical language used by a particular group of people. *Computer jargon.*

**jaunt** *noun* a trip or short journey made for pleasure. *My grandparents have gone on a jaunt to New Mexico.*

**jaunty** *adjective* cheerful and carefree. *A jaunty walk through the woods.* **jauntiness** *noun.*

**javelin** *noun* a short, light spear thrown by hand, usually in athletic sports.

**jazz** *noun* a type of music with a strong rhythm. Jazz was first played in America.

**jealous** *adjective* unhappy because you want what somebody else has. **jealousy** *noun.*

**jeans** *noun* trousers made from a strong cotton material called denim. *Her new blue jeans look great with her white denim jacket.*

**jeer** *verb* to make fun of somebody in a rude, loud, and unkind way; to mock. *The crowd jeered at the politician who was holding a rally in the park.*

**jellyfish** *noun* a sea animal without a backbone (invertebrate) that looks like an umbrella made of jelly. Jellyfish have tentacles that can sting.

**jeopardy** *noun* (say **jep**-ur-dee) If somebody or something is in jeopardy, they are in danger or somehow threatened.

jester

**Jerusalem** *noun* the capital of Israel in Southwest Asia.

**jester** an entertainer at a royal court during the Middle Ages.

**jet** *noun* **1** a strong stream of liquid or gas forced out under pressure. *The fountain threw up jets of water.* **2** an aircraft that is driven forward by a strong jet of air forced out of the back of the engine.

**jet lag** *noun* great tiredness and a feeling of confusion that some people suffer after a long plane journey that takes them to a place with a different time zone.

**jetty** *noun* a pier or landing stage where boats can moor and unload.

**Jew** *noun* **1** a person of the Hebrew race described in the Old Testament of the Bible. **2** a person who follows the religion of Judaism. **Jewish** *adjective.*

**jewel** *noun* a beautiful and precious stone such as a ruby or emerald.

**jewelry** *noun* rings, bracelets, necklaces, and other ornaments that people wear.

**jigsaw** *noun* a puzzle made of pieces of cardboard or wood cut in different shapes that you fit together to form a picture.

**jingle** *noun* **1** the ringing sound made by small bells or keys knocking together. **2** a simple but catchy tune or song used in radio and TV advertisements. **jingle** *verb.*

**jockey** (jockeys) *noun* a person who rides horses in races.

**jodhpurs** *plural noun* (say **jod**-purz) close-fitting pants from knee to ankle that you wear for riding a horse; riding breeches.

jockey

**join** *verb* **1** to fasten, tie, or somehow connect things together. **2** to become a member of a club or organization. *I'm going to join the tennis club.* **3** to unite or come together.

**joint** *noun* **1** a place where two things are joined together. **2** a place where two bones in your body are joined together, such as your elbow or knee. **joint** *adjective* shared by two or more people. *I can't take all the credit; it was a joint effort.*

**joke** *noun* **1** to say things that are intended to be funny; to jest, make merry with; to banter. Something that you say or do to make people laugh. **2** a laughing stock. **joke** *verb. You must be joking!*

**joker** *noun* **1** somebody who tells a lot of jokes. **2** an extra card in a pack of playing cards which in certain games may have value.

**jolly** (jollier, jolliest) *adjective* happy, cheerful, full of fun.

**Jordan** *noun* a country in Southwest Asia.

**jostle** *verb* to shove or push and bump into people.

**journal** *noun* (say **jer**-nul) **1** a diary or daily record of things you have done. **2** a magazine, especially one that deals with a particular subject. *The Nursing Journal.*

**journalese** *noun* (say jer-nul-**eez**) a style of writing particular to newspapers and magazines, often careless and far-fetched in style.

**journalism** *noun* (say **jer**-nul-izum) the job of gathering news and writing articles for newspapers and magazines.

**journalist** *noun* (say **jer**-nul-ist) a person who writes or edits articles for a newspaper or magazine.

**journey** (journeys) *noun* (say **jer**-nee) the act of traveling from one place to another; a trip. **journey** *verb.*

**joust** *noun* (say **jow**-st) a sporting fight in the Middle Ages between two knights on horseback, using long lances. **joust** *verb.*

**joy** *noun* **1** a feeling of great happiness. **2** success or luck. The opposite of "joy" is "sorrow."

**jubilee** *noun* a celebration to commemorate an important event.

**Judaism** *noun* the religion of the Jewish people.

joust

**judge** *noun* **1** a person who hears cases in a court of law and decides how a guilty person should be punished. **2** a person who decides who is the winner of a competition. **3** a person who forms an opinion about something. *A good judge of character.* **judgment** *noun.*

**juggle** *verb* to keep throwing and catching a number of objects, such as balls, in the air without dropping them. *We learned to juggle at camp last summer and I'm pretty good at it now.* **juggler** *noun.*

**juice** *noun* (rhymes with loose) the liquid you can squeeze from fruit and vegetables. **juicy** *adjective.*

**jumbo** *adjective* very large. **jumbo jet** a large passenger plane, a Boeing 747.

**jump** *verb* **1** to leap or throw your body into the air. **2** to go over something by leaping. **jump** *noun* something you jump over. *The horse is coming to the last jump.*

**jumpy** (jumpier, jumpiest) *adjective* nervous. *The silence in the house made me jumpy.*

**junction** *noun* a place where railroad lines or roads join or cross each other.

**junior** *adjective* **1** of lower rank or importance. *He has been a junior executive for two years.* **2** of or for younger people. *A junior dictionary.*

junk

**junk** *noun* **1** a Chinese sailing boat with a flat bottom. **2** things that are old and useless or worthless. **junk food** food that has a low nutritional value, but may be quick and easy to prepare.

**junkie** *noun* a drug addict.

**jury** *noun* a group of people who are chosen to hear a case in a court of law and decide whether an accused person is guilty or not.

**just** *adjective* fair and right; honest. *A just decision was eventually reached.* **just** *adverb* **1** not long ago. *She just went home.* **2** only. *Just a minute!* **3** exactly. *This is just the right color.* **4** almost not. *There is just enough food for us both to eat.*

**justice** *noun* **1** treatment that is just, fair, and right. **2** a country's system of laws and how they are operated by the law courts. **3** a judge. *A justice of the peace.*

**justify** (justifies, justifying, justified) *verb* to defend or to prove that something is just and fair. *How can you justify hitting the dog when all he did was jump up with excitement?* **justification** *noun.*

**jute** *noun* a plant fiber used to make rope, twine, and burlap, a coarse cloth for sacks, and a hard-wearing floor covering.

**juvenile** *adjective* **1** concerning young people. **2** childish and silly. *Juvenile behavior is inappropriate here; please keep quiet and sit still.*

**Kabul** *noun* the capital of Afghanistan in southern Asia.

**kaleidoscope** *noun* a tube that you turn as you look through to see changing patterns of color made by mirrors and loose pieces of plastic fitted in a compartment at one end.

**Kampala** *noun* the capital of Uganda in eastern Africa.

**kangaroo** *noun* a large Australian animal with strong back legs for jumping. The female has a pouch on her stomach in which she carries her baby, called a joey. Kangaroos belong to a group of animals called marsupials.

**kangaroo**

**karaoke** *noun* (say ka-ree-**ok**-kee) a kind of entertainment from Japan in which people publicly sing pop songs to recorded music, following the words of the song on a screen.



**karate** *noun* a self-defense sport originating in Japan in which two people fight each other with kicks and blows.

**Kathmandu** *noun* the capital of Nepal in southern Asia.

**kayak** *noun* (say **kye**-ak) a canoe covered in canvas, originally used by the Inuit people.

**Kazakhstan** *noun* a country in western Asia.

**kebab** *noun* small pieces of meat or vegetables cooked on a skewer. *A chicken kebab.*

**keel** *noun* the long piece of steel that lies along the bottom of a ship's frame.

**kelp** *noun* a kind of seaweed used as a fertilizer. *Sea otters eat kelp.*

**kennel** *noun* **1** a small shelter or hut in which a dog is kept. **2 kennels** a place where dogs are bred or where dogs can be looked after when their owners are away.

**Kenya** *noun* a country in Central Africa.

**kerb** *noun* the line of stones along the edge of a sidewalk.

**kernel** *noun* the edible middle part of a nut.

**kestrel** *noun* a small falcon. Kestrels eat small animals.

**ketchup, catsup** *noun* a thick sauce made from tomatoes.

**keyboard** *noun* **1** the set of keys on a computer or piano that you press. **2** an electronic musical instrument. *A keyboard player.*

**kestrel**

**keystone** *noun* the brick or stone in the center of an arch that holds the other bricks or stones in place.

**khaki** *noun* (say **kah**-key) a yellow-brown color. *Many soldiers wear khaki uniforms.*

**Khartoum** *noun* the capital of Sudan in North Africa.

**kidnap** (kidnaps, kidnapping, kidnapped) *verb* to capture somebody and keep them prisoner until you get what you demand, e.g., money. **kidnapper** *noun.*

**kidney** (kidneys) *noun* Your kidneys are organs in your body that keep your blood clean by removing waste products and passing them out in the form of urine.

**Kiev** *noun* the capital of Ukraine in eastern Europe.

**Kigali** *noun* the capital of Rwanda in Central Africa.

**kill** *verb* to end the life of a person or animal. **kill** *noun* **1** the act of killing. **2** the animal killed. *The tiger stood over its kill and licked its lips.*

**kiln** *noun* a very hot oven for baking pottery and bricks to make them hard.

**kilogram** or **kilogramme** *noun* a measure of weight equal to 1,000 grams. Also called a kilo. *A kilo of sugar.*

**kilometer** *noun* a measure of length equal to 1,000 meters.

**kilt** *noun* a knee-length, pleated skirt made from tartan cloth, traditionally worn by Scottish men.

**kimono** *noun* a long, loose robe with wide sleeves, traditionally worn by Japanese women.

**kin** *noun* (old-fashioned) your family and relations. **next of kin** your closest relation.

**kind** *adjective* helpful and friendly to people; gentle. *It was kind of you to visit me in the hospital.* **kind** *noun* a group of things that are similar. A type of something. *What kind of dog is that?* **kindness** *noun.*

**kimono**

**kindle** *verb* to set light to something.

**kindergarten** *noun* a school for little children up to age five.

**king** *noun* **1** a male ruler of a country. Kings are not elected but inherit their position by succeeding the previous ruler. **2** a playing card with a picture of a King on it. **3** a chesspiece. Who takes the King wins the game.

**kingdom** *noun* **1** a country that is ruled by a King or Queen. *The United Kingdom.* **2** a division of the natural world. *The animal kingdom.*

**kingfisher** *noun* a bird with bright blue and brown feathers and a dagger-like beak that it uses to catch fish from lakes and rivers.

**Kingston** *noun* the capital of Jamaica in the Caribbean.

**Kingstown** *noun* the capital of St Vincent and the Grenadines in the Caribbean.

**Kinshasa** *noun* the capital of the Democratic Republic of the Congo (formerly Zaire) in Central Africa.

**kiosk** *noun* (say **kee**-osk) a small hut-like building on the street where you can buy things such as newspapers, magazines, and candy.

**Kiribati** *noun* (say keer-ee-bahss) a country of many islands in the Pacific Ocean.

**kitchen** *noun* a room that is used for preparing and cooking food.

**kitten** *noun* a very young cat. **kittenish** *adjective* behaving like a kitten; playful.

kiwi

**kitty** *noun* a sum of money put in by several people for everybody in a group to use.

**kiwi** *noun* (say **kee**-wee) a New Zealand bird that cannot fly.

**knack** *noun* the ability to do something difficult with ease and skill. *He has a knack for skating.*

**knave** *noun* **1** a picture playing card with a value between ten and the Queen. A knave is often called a jack. *The knave of hearts.* **2** a dishonest person.

**knead** *verb* to squeeze and stretch dough with your hands before baking.

**knee** *noun* the joint in the middle of your leg where it bends. *James went down on bended knee when he asked Elizabeth to marry him.*

**kneecap** *noun* the movable bone in front of your knee.

**kneel** *verb* to bend your knees and rest on them. *We kneel to pray.*

**knife** (knives) *noun* a metal tool with a handle and a sharp blade that you use for cutting. **knife** *verb* to stab with a knife. *The escaped convict knifed him in the leg.*

**knight** *noun* **1** in the Middle Ages, a soldier who fought on horseback for his King or lord. **2** a man who has been given the title "Sir" by a monarch. **3** a chesspiece with a horse's head.

**knit** (knits, knitting, knitted) *verb* **1** to make clothes by looping wool together with two long needles. **2** to join closely, e.g., broken bones.

knight

**knob** *noun* a round handle on a door or drawer. *Turn the knob to the right to open the door.*

**knock** *verb* **1** to hit or strike something hard. *Is there somebody knocking at the door?* **2** to hit something so that it falls. *Sue knocked her mug off her desk.* **knock** *noun.* **knock out** to hit somebody so hard that they become unconscious.

**knocker** *noun* a hinged metal ring, knob, or hammer on a door that you use for knocking. *The mailman banged the knocker three times.*

**knot** *noun* **1** a join or fastening made by tying pieces of string, rope, or cloth together. **2** a hard, dark part in wood where a branch joined a tree. **3** a measure of speed for ships. One knot is about 1.85 kph. **knot** (knots, knotting, knotted) *verb* to fasten something by tying its ends into a knot. *Fishermen's knots.*

**know** (knows, knowing, knew, known) *verb* to have learned or have information about something and to recall it easily. *Do you know French?* **2** to remember or to recognize somebody or something. *Yes, I know Sharon; we were at school together.*

**knowing** *adjective* showing that you know something secret. *He gave her a knowing look.*

**knowledge** *noun* the things that you know and understand; things that you learn by studying. *A good knowledge of French.*

**knowledgeable** *adjective* clever and well-informed about a subject.

**knuckle** *noun* the bones at the joint of a finger. *Her knuckles were swollen with arthritis.*

**koala** *noun* an Australian marsupial animal with thick gray fur. It looks like a small bear. Koalas live in eucalyptus trees and feed on the leaves.

koala

**kookaburra** *noun* an Australian bird of the kingfisher family that makes a loud laughing noise.

**Koran** or **Qu'ran** *noun* the holy book of Islam, the religion of Muslims.

**kosher** *adjective* (say **koh**-shur) food that has been specially prepared in accordance with the laws of the Jewish religion.

**Kuala Lumpur** *noun* the capital of Malaysia in southern Asia.

**Kuwait** *noun* a country in Southwest Asia. Its capital is **Kuwait City**.

**Kyrgyzstan** *noun* a country in Central Asia.

**lab** *noun* (abbreviation) a laboratory.

**label** *noun* a piece of paper, cloth, or plastic that is attached to something and that gives information about it. **label** (labels, labeling, labeled) *verb* to put a label on something. *She labeled her son's school clothes.*

**laboratory** *noun* a room or building where scientists do their research and carry out experiments.

**labor** *noun* **1** hard, physical work. **2** workers considered as a group. **3** the pain a woman feels when giving birth. **labor** *verb* to work hard. **laborer** *noun* an unskilled worker. **Labour Party** one of the three main political parties in Great Britain.

**laborious** *adjective* difficult and needing a lot of hard work or effort. *Digging is a laborious job.*

**labyrinth** *noun* a maze of passages or paths.

**lace** *noun* **1** a delicate material made of fine threads woven into a pretty pattern with holes in it. **2** a long, thin cord that is threaded through holes and used, for example, to fasten a shoe or boot. **lace** *verb*. *Lace your boots tightly.*

**labyrinth**

**lack** *verb* to be without something that is needed or wanted. *She lacks the essential ingredient to make a chocolate cake.* **lack** *noun*.

**lacquer** *noun* (say **lack**-ur) a varnish or glossy paint.

**lad** *noun* (old fashioned) a boy or young man.

**ladder** *noun* **1** two long wooden or metal poles with cross-pieces or steps called rungs, used for climbing up or down. **2** the jobs one must do in a company or organization in order to gain power or a better position. *John is climbing the corporate ladder.*

**ladle** *noun* a large, deep spoon with a long handle used for lifting out liquids such as soup. *Grandma gave us all a generous ladle of soup.*

**lady** *noun* **1** a woman, especially one who has refined manners. **2** in Britain, the title of a peeress or a peer's wife or widow. *Sir John and Lady Foxtalbot invite you to a garden party.* **ladylike** *adjective*. *Ladylike behavior.*

**ladybug**

**ladybug** *noun* a small, round, flying beetle, usually with a number of black spots on shiny red wings. Ladybugs eat aphids and other harmful plant pests. *Is it lucky to see a ladybug with six spots?*

**lag** (lags, lagging, lagged) *verb* to move or develop more slowly than others and so be unable to keep up. *Catch up Timothy! You're lagging behind everybody else.* **time lag** the time that passes between an event or cause and its effect.

**lagoon** *noun* a seawater lake separated from the ocean by sandbanks, coral, or rocks.

**laid-back** *adjective* (slang) relaxed and unworried. *A laid-back kind of guy.*

**lair** *noun* a den or hidden place where a wild animal sleeps. *The bear curled up in its lair.*

**lake** *noun* a large area of fresh water surrounded by land. *It took us all day to walk around the lake.*

**lama** *noun* a Buddhist monk in Tibet.

**lamb** *noun* **1** a young sheep. **2** the meat of a young sheep. *We're having roast lamb for dinner.* **lamb** *verb* to give birth to lambs.

**lame** *adjective* **1** unable to walk properly because of an injured leg. *The pony is lame and walks with a limp.* **2** weak and not good enough. *A lame excuse.* **lameness** *noun*. **lame duck** a weak person or company that cannot function without help.

**lamp** *noun* a device that gives light by burning electricity, gas, oil, or a candle. **lampshade** *noun* a cover placed over a lamp to soften its light.

**lance** *noun* a long weapon with a wooden shaft and a pointed steel head, used by knights on horseback in the Middle Ages.

**land** *noun* **1** all the dry surface of the Earth that is above the sea. **2** the ground used for farming, gardening, or building on. **3** a country or nation. **land** *verb* **1** to arrive on land by ship. **2** to bring an aircraft down to the ground. *The plane landed at noon.* **3** to get into trouble. *He landed in prison.*

**landing** *noun* **1** a level area at the top of a flight of stairs. **2** bringing to the ground or to the shore. *The plane made an emergency landing.*

**landlady, landlord** *noun* **1** a person who rents a house or room to someone. **2** someone who runs a public house.

**landmark** *noun* **1** some building or object that you can see clearly from a distance. **2** an event marking a turning point in history. *He won a landmark victory.*

**landscape** *noun* a wide view across an area of land or all that you can see from one place.

**lane** *noun* **1** a narrow country road. **2** one of the strips on a highway that is wide enough for a single line of traffic. **3** the strip of running track used by a runner or the strip of water in a pool used by a swimmer.

**language** *noun* **1** all the words that we use to talk or write to one another; human speech. **2** the system of words used in one or more countries. *Spanish is the language spoken in Spain and in most of South America.* **3** any other system of communicating. *Sign language.*

**lanky** *adjective* tall and thin.

**lantern** *noun* a container, often with glass sides, for holding a candle or oil lamp, which may be carried.

Laos' flag

**Laos** *noun* a country in Southeast Asia.

**lap** *noun* **1** the top, flat part of your legs when you are sitting down. **2** one journey around a race track. **lap** (laps, lapping, lapped) *verb* An animal laps up water by flicking it into its mouth with its tongue.

**La Paz** *noun* the seat of government of Bolivia.

**lapel** *noun* the part below the collar of a jacket that folds back to the chest on both sides.

**lapse** *noun* **1** a small, careless mistake. **2** a period of time that has passed. *A lapse of memory.*

**laptop** *noun* a small, portable computer that you can use on your lap.

**lard** *noun* fat from pigs, used in cooking.

**large** *adjective* big in size or amount; not small. **largeness** *noun.* **at large** free after escaping. *The zoo's lion is still at large.*

**largely** *adverb* mostly.

**lark** *noun* a small, brown bird that flies high in the sky and sings beautifully.

**larva** (larvae) *noun* an insect in its first stage of development after coming out of the egg and before becoming a pupa; a grub. A larva looks like a worm.

laser

**laser** *noun* a device that produces a very narrow and powerful beam of light, used for cutting with precision.

**lash** *noun* **1** a whip. **2** one of the small hairs growing around the eye (eyelash). **lash** *verb* **1** to hit violently, as with a whip. *The waves lashed against the rocks.* **2** to make rapid movements like a whip. *The cat lashed its tail in anger because it wanted to go outside.*

**lasso** *noun* (say lass-**oh**) a long rope with a loop at one end, used to catch cattle and horses. **lasso** *verb.*

**last** *adjective* **1** coming after all others. *The last horse in the race.* **2** the only one remaining. *The last slice of cake.* **3** most recent; just past. *Last night.* **4** previous or one before this one. *Her last job.* **last** *verb* **1** to continue. *The concert lasted for four hours.* **2** to remain in good condition for some time. *These shoes have lasted well.*

**late** *adjective, adverb* **1** not early, but after the usual or expected time. *She was an hour late for her appointment.* **2** near the end of a period of time. *They arrived home late in the evening.* **3** previous; recently dead. *The late preacher.* **lateness** *noun.* **lately** *adverb* recently.

**later** *adverb* after some time.

**lateral** *adjective* concerned with the side; sideways. *Lateral movement.*

**lathe** *noun* a machine that holds and turns wood or metal while it is being shaped with a cutting tool.

**lather** *noun* the bubbles or foam you get when you mix soap or detergent in warm water. *This soap makes a good lather.*

**Latin** *noun* the language spoken by the ancient Romans.

latitude

**latitude** *noun* on a map or globe, a position or distance measured in degrees north or south of the equator.

**latter** *adjective* the second of two things, compared with the former, which is the first of two things. *She went out with both Tom and Fred, and finally married the latter.*

**Latvia** *noun* a country in the Baltic region of Europe.

**laugh** *verb* to make sounds that show that you are very happy or think something is funny. *We laughed at the joke.* **laugh** *noun.* **laughter** *noun.*

**laughable** *adjective* ridiculous and absurd.

**launch** *verb* **1** to send a boat or ship into the water. **2** to send a rocket into space. **3** to start something new or important. *They launched the company with a champagne party.* **launch** *noun.* **launch pad** a place from which rockets are sent into space.

**laundromat** *noun* a place where you pay to use washing machines that wash your dirty clothes.

**lava** *noun* **1** the hot, molten (melted) rock that flows from an erupting volcano. **2** this rock when it cools and becomes solid.

**lavender** *noun* a small shrub with narrow leaves and sweet-smelling, pale purple flowers. *Norfolk lavender.*

**lavish** *adjective* generous and plentiful. *A lavish banquet.*

**law** *noun* **1** all the rules made by a government that everybody in a country must obey. **2** a general rule or principle that explains how something works. *Please review the laws of friction for the test.*

**lawful** *adjective* allowed by law. *He was just doing his lawful business.*

**lawyer** *noun* a person whose job it is to advise people about the law and to represent them in a court of law.

**lay** (lays, laying, laid) *verb* **1** to put something down. *He laid the map on the table.* **2** to put something in a particular position. *She laid her coat over the chair.* **3** (of a bird) to produce an egg. *The chicken laid three brown eggs this morning.*

**layabout** *noun* a lazy person who avoids doing work.

**layby** *noun* an area at the side of a road where vehicles can stop for a while.

**layout** *noun* **1** the way text and pictures are arranged on a page. **2** the way things are arranged on a plan. *The layout of the new supermarket.*

**layer** *noun* a thickness of something that lies between or on top of other pieces. *The cake was covered with a layer of icing and filled with a layer of cream.*

**lazy** (lazier, laziest) *adjective* not liking work, effort, or exercise. *Cats are lazy and sleep a lot.* **laziness** *noun.* **lazily** *adverb.*

**lead** *noun* (rhymes with bed) **1** a soft, gray metal. **2** the substance in the middle of a pencil that makes a mark. **3 lead** (rhymes with need) example. *Follow my lead.* **4** The leading position. *The white horse took the lead.* **lead** (leads, leading, led) *verb* rhymes with need in the present tense **1** to go in front and show the way, to take in a certain direction. *Please lead me out of the maze – I've been in here for hours!* **2** to be in first place. *The gray horse was leading for most of the race.* **3** to be in charge of other people. *The captain led her team bravely.* **4** to live a certain way of life. *Our dog leads a happy life.*

Ll

**leaf** (leaves) *noun* **1** one of the flat, usually green, parts of a plant that grows from a stem. **2** a page of a book.

**leaflet** *noun* a sheet of paper, usually folded, with information printed on it. *The politician pushed the leaflet through the mailbox.*

leap

**leak** *noun* a hole in a container or pipe through which liquid or gas can escape. **leak** *verb* **1** (of a gas or liquid) to escape through a hole or crack. **2** to give away secret information.

**leap** (leaps, leaping, leapt or leaped) *verb* to jump up high or to jump over something. **leap** *noun.* **leap year** every fourth year, in which February has 29 days instead of 28. Leap years have 366 days instead of 365.

**learn** (learns, learning, learned) *verb* to find out about something or how to do something. *Josephine is learning to speak French.*

**learned** *adjective* A learned person knows a lot. *The learned monk studied for many hours each day.*

**learning** *noun* a great deal of knowledge. *His learning is amazing.*

**lease** *noun* an agreement between the owner of a property and a person renting it for a stated period of time. *They signed a two-year lease on the house.*

**least** *adjective* smallest or less than all the others. *This is the least expensive bike.* **at least** the minimum, but likely to be more. *It will cost at least $50.*

**leather** *noun* the skin of animals used to make such things as shoes, handbags, and belts. **leathery** *adjective* tough like leather.

**leave** (leaves, leaving, left) *verb* **1** to go away from somewhere. The opposite of "to leave" is "to arrive." **2** to let something remain where it is. *She left her clothes all over the floor.* **3** to forget to take something with you. *I left my coat indoors.* **4** what remains after the main part has been used or taken away. *Seven from eight leaves one.* **5** to pass on something to somebody after you die. *My uncle left me his gold watch.* **leave out** not to include, to forget to put in. *Did you leave out my coat when you packed the car?* **leave** *noun* **1** a vacation or time away from a job. **2** permission to be absent from duty.

Lebanon's flag

**Lebanon** *noun* a country in Southwest Asia.

**lecture** *noun* **1** a formal talk about a particular subject given to a class or audience. **2** a scolding or warning. *The teacher gave him a lecture on how to behave.* **lecture** *verb.*

**ledge** *noun* a shelf-like space on a cliff, rock, or wall. *The bird nested on the ledge.*

**leek** *noun* a long, white vegetable with green leaves at one end. It tastes similar to an onion.

**leer** *verb* to look and smile at somebody in an unpleasant way. *The old man leered at her.*

**leeward** *adjective* on the sheltered side, turned away from the wind.

**left** *noun* You are reading these words from left to right. **left** *adjective. Close your left eye.* **have two left feet** to be clumsy. **left-wing** *adjective* in politics, supporting more liberal ideas and policies like those of socialism. The opposite of "left-wing" is "right-wing."

**leftovers** *plural noun* food that has not been eaten after a meal. *In winter, my mother usually makes a warming soup from yesterday's leftovers.*

**leg** *noun* **1** one of the parts of the body that animals and humans use for walking, running, and standing on. **2** one of the parts that support a chair or other piece of furniture. **pull somebody's leg** to tease or make a fool of somebody by trying to make them believe something that is not true.

leopard

**legal** *adjective* **1** allowed by the law. *Cock fighting is no longer legal.* **2** concerned with the law. *The legal system.* The opposite of "legal" is "illegal."

**legend** *noun* an old, well-known story that may or may not be true. *In the legend of King Arthur, the boy Arthur is the only person who can pull the great sword Excalibur from a stone.* **legendary** *adjective.*

**legible** *adjective* clear enough to be read easily. *The writing is very faded, but it is just legible.* **legibility** *noun.*

**legion** *noun* a large division of the ancient Roman army (from three to six thousand soldiers).

**legitimate** *adjective* allowed by the law; lawful. *His legitimate son inherited the land.* **legitimacy** *noun.*

**leisure** *noun* free time when you can do what you like and you do not have to work. **leisurely** *adjective. A leisurely life is the life for me.*

**lemon** *noun* a bright yellow, oval citrus fruit with a sour-tasting juice.

**lemonade** *noun* a sweet, and sometimes carbonated, drink with a lemon flavor.

**lend** (lends, lending, lent) *verb* to let somebody have something for a short time, before they give it back to you. *It was raining so I lent him my umbrella.* The opposite of "lend" is "borrow."

**length** *noun* **1** how far it is from one end of something to the other horizontally. *A length of cloth.* **2** how long something lasts. *We were surprised at the length of her stay abroad.*

**lengthen** *verb* to make or become longer. *I'll need to lengthen your trousers now that you've grown so tall.*

**lengthy** (lengthier, lengthiest) *adjective* long; lasting a long time.

**lenient** *adjective* not severe or strict. *The lenient teacher never commented if we were late with our homework.* **lenience** *noun.*

**lens** *noun* **1** a piece of curved glass or plastic that bends light. Lenses are used in cameras to focus images, and in glasses to improve eyesight. **2** a part of the eye that focuses light on the retina.

**Lent** *noun* in the Christian Church, a period of 40 days fasting and penance before Easter. *Sarah gave up chocolate for Lent.*

**leopard** (say **lep**-urd) *noun* a large wild, spotted cat of Africa and Asia.

**lesbian** *noun* a woman who is sexually attracted to other women; a gay woman.

**Lesotho** *noun* a small country in southern Africa.

**-less** *suffix* without. *Colorless, smokeless.*

**less** (lesser, least) *adjective* not so much. *Please make less noise.* **less** *adverb. You should eat less and sleep more.* **less** *preposition* minus. *Six less four equals two.*

**lessen** *verb* to make or become smaller in importance or size. *Your behavior doesn't lessen my regard for you.*

**lesson** *noun* **1** something that is learned or taught; instruction. **2** an experience that is a warning or example. *His accident was a lesson to him to be more careful in the future.*

**lethal** *adjective* able to cause death; deadly. *A lethal weapon was found at the crime scene.*

**lettuce** *noun* a plant with large green leaves that is eaten in salads.

**leukemia** *noun* (say loo-**kee**-mee-uh) a serious, life-threatening, cancer-like disease in which the blood produces too many white cells.



**lever** *noun* **1** a strong bar that you use to lift something heavy by placing one end of it under the object and pushing down on the other end. **2** a long handle that you use to work a machine.

**liable** *adjective* **1** legally responsible for something. *You are liable for damaging the machine.* **2** likely to. *In winter the lake is liable to freeze.*

**liar** *noun* a person who does not tell the truth.

**liberal** *adjective* generous and tolerant. *A liberal attitude.*

**liberate** *verb* to set a country, a person, or an animal free. **liberation** *noun.*

**Liberia** *noun* a country in West Africa.

**liberty** *noun* freedom from control or slavery. **take liberties** to behave rudely and without respect.

**librarian** *noun* a person who is in charge of or who works in a library.

**library** (libraries) *noun* a room or building where a lot of books and records are kept, usually for people to borrow or consult.

librarian

**Libreville** *noun* the capital of Gabon in West Africa.

**Libya** *noun* a country in North Africa.

**lichen** *noun* (say **lie**-kin) a flat, yellowish or green plant that grows in patches on rocks and tree trunks.

**lie** (lies, lying, lied) *verb* **1** to say something that you know is untrue. *She lied to the police about the theft.* **2 lie** (lie, lies, lying, lay, lain) to rest your body in a flat position. *I feel sick so I'm going to lie down.* **3** to remain. *The snow lies thick on the ground.* **4** to be located in a certain place. *The village lies 10 miles north of Newtown.* **lie** *noun. It is dishonest to tell a lie.*

**Liechtenstein** *noun* a small country in Central Europe.

**life** *noun* **1** the time between a person's or an animal's birth and death when they are alive. **2** the ability of plants and animals to grow and develop, unlike such things as rocks and metals. **3** a way of living. *She leads a very exciting life.* **4** liveliness. *He is full of life.* **take somebody's life** to kill somebody.

**lifebelt** *noun* a ring or belt that floats and which a person in the sea holds onto or wears to stop them from sinking or drowning.

lifeboat

**lifeboat** *noun* a boat that rescues people who are shipwrecked or in danger at sea.

**lifeguard** *noun* a person who has been trained to help rescue swimmers in danger.

**lifejacket** *noun* an inflatable jacket that you wear on board a boat. It will keep you afloat if you fall in the water.

**lifeless** *adjective* **1** dead. **2** uninteresting. *Lifeless acting.*

**lifelike** *adjective* looking like a real person or animal. *The artist painted a lifelike portrait of my aunt.*

**lifestyle** *noun* the way that someone lives, including where they live and what their interests are.

**lift** *verb* **1** to pick something up and raise it to a higher place. **2** to rise. *The plane lifted into the air.* **lift** *noun* **1** a higher or better frame of mind. **2** a short ride in a vehicle, like a car or truck. *Would you give me a lift into town so I can go shopping?*

**liftoff** *noun* the launching of a rocket.

**light** *adjective* **1** (of color) pale and not strong. *Light blue.* **2** full of bright light. *A light room.* **3** (of weight) weighing little, not heavy. *As light as a feather.* **4** gentle or small in amount. *We ate a light meal.* **5** not too serious. *Light music on the radio.* **light** *noun* **1** what makes us able to see things; not dark. *The Sun gives us light.* **2** something that gives out light. *She turned on the outside light so he would be able to find his way up the path in the dark.* **light** (lights, lighting, lit or lighted) *verb* **1** to make something start burning. *Let's light the candles.* **2** to give light to a place. **light-hearted** cheerful and without a care. **light-year** the distance in space that light travels in a year. **out like a light** falling asleep quickly, or becoming unconscious. **throw light on** help to explain.

**lighten** *verb* **1** to become brighter or less dark. **2** to make something less heavy.

**lighthouse** *noun* a tower-like building by the sea that sends out a very bright, flashing light to guide ships or warn them about nearby dangerous rocks.

**lighting** *noun* artificial lights such as candles and electric light.

**lightning** *noun* a bright flash of electricity that lights up the sky during a thunderstorm. *Thunder and lightning.*

**likely** (likelier, likeliest) *adverb* probable and expected to happen. *I think it's likely to rain later today.*

**likeness** *noun* a resemblance. *There's a great likeness between the brothers.*

lighthouse

**lilac** *noun* a small tree or shrub with sweet-smelling purple or white flowers.

**Lilongwe** *noun* the capital of Malawi in southeast Africa.

**Lima** *noun* the capital of Peru in South America.

**limb** *noun* an arm or a leg or the wing of a bird.

**lime** *noun* **1** an oval, green citrus fruit similar to a lemon. **2** a substance obtained from limestone and used in making cement.

**limerick** *noun* a humorous five-line poem with the rhyme-scheme: a, a, b, b, a.

**limestone** *noun* a kind of rock from which lime is obtained for making cement.

**limit** *noun* a boundary or some point beyond which you do not go. *A 70 mph speed limit.* **limit** *verb* to set a boundary; to restrict. *She limits herself to one piece of candy in the afternoon.*

**liner** *noun* a large passenger ship.

**linger** *verb* to dawdle or wait around, seeming unwilling to leave.

**lining** *noun* a layer of material that lines the inside of something. *Most jackets have a lining, and in some it is quilted for warmth.*

**linguist** *noun* a person who studies foreign languages and is good at learning and speaking them.

link

**link** *noun* **1** a ring or loop in a chain. **2** a connection between two things. *The bridge is a link between the two islands.* **link** *verb* to join. *They linked arms.*

**lion** *noun* a large wild cat with light brown fur that lives in Africa and Asia. The male has a thick, shaggy mane. Lions live in family groups called prides.

**lioness** *noun* a female lion.

**lip** *noun* Your lips are the soft edges of your mouth. *Luscious lips.*

**lip-read** *verb* (of a deaf person) to understand what somebody is saying by looking carefully at their lips while they are speaking. *Sally learned to lip-read.*

**liquefy** (liquefies, liquefying, liquefied) *verb* to make or become liquid.

**liquid** *noun* **1** any substance that flows, such as water. **2** any substance that is not a gas or a solid. **liquid** *adjective.*

**liquidize** *verb* to crush food like fruit and vegetables into a liquid or purée in a liquidizer.

**Lisbon** *noun* the capital of Portugal in southwest Europe.

**lisp** *verb, noun* a speech problem in which the "s" sound in a word is pronounced "th."

**list** *noun* a series of names or things written down one under the other. *A list of the club's members.* **list** *verb* **1** to write things down on a list. **2** (of a ship) to lean to one side. *As the boat listed, we all grabbed the rail.*

**listen** *verb* to pay attention to what you hear. **listener** *noun* someone who listens. *The priest is a patient man, and a good listener.*

**liter** *noun* a measure of liquids equal to 1,000 milliliters.

**literally** *adverb* exactly as the words state. *He literally knocked me off my feet when he ran past.*

**literate** *adjective* able to read and write.

**literature** *noun* **1** novels, plays, and poetry that are especially good. **2** printed material on a particular subject. *Is there any literature about it in the record file?*

**Lithuania** *noun* a country in the Baltic region, in northwest Europe, to the west of Russia.

Lithuania's flag

**litter** *noun* **1** trash, such as paper and bottles, left lying around on the ground. **2** all the animals born to the same mother at the same time. *The pig had a litter of nine piglets.*

**little** *adjective* **1** small in size or quantity. **2** not much. *There's very little time left.*

**live** *adjective* (rhymes with dive) **1** not dead, but living. *There was a live rabbit under the bed.* **2** full of electricity. *This wire is live.* **3** a performance on radio or television that is happening as you listen or watch. **live** *verb* (rhymes with give) **1** to be alive; to have life. Plants and animals live. **2** to continue to stay alive. *The tortoise lived for 50 years.* **3** to inhabit or have a home somewhere. *My grandma lives in Italy.*

**livelihood** *noun* the way a person earns money to live. *He earns a good livelihood from repairing old houses and selling them.*

**lively** *adjective* full of energy. *He has a very lively mind and is interesting company.*

**liver** *noun* **1** a large and important organ in your body that helps to clean your blood and process food. **2** this organ from an animal, used as food. *Liver served with polenta is a special dish in Venice.*

**livestock** *noun* animals kept on a farm. *John keeps cattle and other livestock.*

**living** *adjective* alive, not dead. **living** *noun* what a person does to earn money to live. *What do you do for a living?*

**lizard** *noun* a small reptile with a long, scaly body, four legs, and a tail. Most lizards live in warm countries.

lizard

**Ljubljana** *noun* the capital of Slovenia in eastern Europe.

**llama** *noun* a South American animal similar to a camel, but without a hump.

**load** *noun* something heavy that is carried. An amount of something to be carried. *A load of wood.* **load** *verb* **1** to put a load on something that will carry it. *He loaded the wood on the truck.* **2** to put bullets in a gun, film in a camera, or data in a computer. **loads of** a lot of something.

**loaf** (loaves) *noun* a whole piece of bread, usually of a standard size or shape. *She took the homemade loaf out of the oven and gave us each a warm slice of it.*

**loan** *noun* something that somebody lends you, usually money, to be returned, usually with interest. *I'll pay back the loan next week, I promise.*

**loathe** *verb* (rhymes with clothe) to hate or dislike something very much.

**lobe** *noun* the soft part of the lower ear. *Her earlobes were pierced and in them she wore long diamond earrings.*

**lobster** *noun* a shellfish or sea animal with a long body covered in a hard shell. It has eight legs and two large claws in front. Lobsters can be eaten.

lobster

**local** *adjective* belonging to or affecting a particular area or place. *The local newspaper carried daily reports of our campaign.* **locally** *adverb.*

**locality** *noun* an area. *This is a friendly locality.*

**locate** *verb* **1** to find the exact position of something. *Joe located the source of the river on the map.* **2** to be situated in a particular place. *The grocery store is located out of town, for the convenience of shoppers.*

**loch** *noun* a Scottish word for lake. *Loch Lomond is beautiful in spring.*

**lock** *noun* **1** a device that fastens a door or lid and that you open and shut with a key. **lock** *verb* to fasten with a lock and key. **2** a section of a canal or river between gates that can be opened and shut to raise or lower boats by altering the level of the water. *The barge went through the lock.*

**locust** *noun* a large kind of grasshopper that travels in swarms and destroys crops. *A plague of locusts.*

**lodge** *noun* **1** a small house, usually at the gates leading to a large house. **2** a beaver's home. **lodge** *verb* **1** to live in a rented room. **2** to become firmly fixed in.

**lodger** *noun* someone who pays to live in a room in another person's house. *Our lodger has been with us for two years.*

**loft** *noun* **1** a room or space under the roof of a building; an attic. *You can get into the loft by lowering the ladder.* **2** a raised level in a barn where hay is kept.

**log** *noun* **1** a length of wood that has been cut from a felled tree. **2** a written record of the journey of a ship or aircraft. *The log book.*

**logic** *noun* the science of careful and correct reasoning.

**logical** *adjective* **1** following the rules of logic. **2** sensible and reasonable.

**logo** *noun* a symbol or lettering that represents a company or organization, an emblem or trademark. *The packaging had the company's logo printed on it.*

**-logy** *suffix* denoting a subject that is studied. *Geology, anthropology, biology.*

**loiter** *verb* to stand around somewhere with nothing to do. *We loitered near the park, waiting for our friends.*

**Lomé** *noun* the capital of Togo in West Africa.

**London** *noun* the capital of England and the UK.

**lonely** (lonelier, loneliest) *adjective* **1** unhappy about being alone. **2** far away and not often visited. *A lonely island in mid ocean.*

**long** *adjective* **1** measuring far from one end to the other. The opposite of "long" is "short." *The longest bridge in the world is in Japan.* **2** taking a lot of time. **3** a certain amount of distance or time. *An hour-long flight.* **long** *verb* to want something very much. *She longed to go home for Christmas.* **longing** *noun.* **longingly** *adverb.*

**longitude** *noun* the position of a place measured as a distance in degrees east or west of a line on a map or globe that runs from the North Pole to the South Poles through Greenwich, in London, England.

longitude

**look** *verb* **1** to move your eyes to see something. **2** to seem or appear to be so. *Dick looks happy today.* **look after** to take care of somebody or something. **look for** to search. *Bridget is looking for her trainers.* **look forward to** to wait for something eagerly. **look into** to investigate. **look out!** Be careful! **look up to** to admire.

**loom** *noun* a machine on which long threads are woven into cloth.

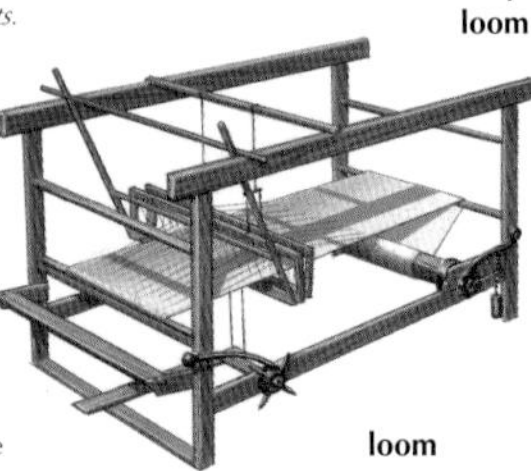

loom

**loop** *noun* a circular shape made in a rope or piece of string. **loop** *verb.*

**loose** *adjective* **1** not held firmly in place. *My loose tooth fell out.* **2** not attached or fastened. *The ponies were loose in the paddock all day.* **3** (of clothes) not fitting tightly, too big. **loosen** *verb* to make or become loose.

**lose** (loses, losing, lost) *verb* **1** If you lose something, you do not have it anymore and cannot find it. *I've lost my glasses again. Have you seen them?* **2** to fail to win. *They lost the game.* **3** to go astray. *We lost our way.*

**loser** *noun* someone who has lost or loses. Someone who seems never to be successful

**loss** *noun* something that has been lost and that you no longer have. *She was very upset by the loss of her precious bracelet.*

**lotion** *noun* a liquid or cream that you put on your skin to clean, soften, or protect it. *Suntan lotion.*

**lottery** *noun* a way of raising money by selling a lot of tickets, only a few of which will win prizes.

**loud** *adjective* **1** making a large amount of sound; not quiet. **2** unpleasantly bright and colorful. *He was wearing a loud purple shirt.* **loudness** *noun.*

**love** *verb* to feel a strong affection for. **lovable** *adjective* easy to love. **lover** *noun* **1** someone with whom you have a physical relationship and whom you love. **2** a person who likes or enjoys something. *A music lover.*

**lovely** (lovelier, loveliest) *adjective* **1** beautiful to look at, listen to, or touch. **2** very pleasant. *We had a lovely day.*

**loyal** *adjective* always faithful and true to your friends. **loyalty** *noun.*

**Luanda** *noun* the capital of Angola in West Africa.

**lubricate** *verb* to put oil or grease on parts of a machine so that they move easily and smoothly. **lubrication** *noun.*

**lucid** *noun* **1** easy to understand. *A lucid explanation.* **2** clear, not confused. *Despite his great age of ninety-eight, his mind was still lucid.*

**luck** *noun* something that happens to you by chance and that you have not planned or cannot control. *Good luck!*

**ludicrous** *adjective* (say **loo**-duh-kruss) very silly; absurd. *You look ludicrous in those baggy trousers.*

luggage

**luggage** *noun* the suitcases and bags that travelers take with them.

**lukewarm** *adjective* **1** A liquid that is lukewarm is only just warm. **2** not enthusiastic. *The movie received only lukewarm praise.*

**lull** *noun* a short period of quiet when little is happening. *There was a lull in the traffic noise.* **lull** *verb* to soothe and make somebody relaxed and calm. *The gentle music lulled the baby to sleep.*

**lullaby** *noun* a gentle song that helps a child go to sleep. *Mother sang the baby a lullaby.*

lumber

**lumber** *noun* rough, partly prepared timber. **lumber** *verb* to walk slowly in a heavy, clumsy way. **lumber with** to give somebody something they do not want. *Lizzie was lumbered with mowing the lawn.*

**lumberjack** *noun* a person who cuts down and saws up trees.

**lunar** *adjective* concerned with the Moon. *A lunar journey.* **lunar month** the time it takes for the Moon to orbit the Earth: 29 days.

**lunatic** *noun* somebody who is foolish or insane. **lunatic** *adjective. A lunatic idea.*

**lung** *noun* one of two organs inside your chest that you use for breathing. The lungs take in oxygen from the air and give out carbon dioxide.

**lunge** *verb* to make a sudden thrust forward. **lunge** *noun* a thrust with a sword, and the basic attacking movement in fencing.

**lure** *verb* to attract and tempt; to lead astray. *They were lured by the bright lights of the fair.* **lure** *noun.*

**lurk** *verb* to wait around unobtrusively, often with a dishonest purpose.

**Lusaka** *noun* the capital of Zambia in Central Africa.

**lush** *adjective* growing thickly and healthily; fertile. *The explorers cut their way through the lush vegetation.*

**lute** *noun* a stringed musical instrument in the shape of half a pear, with a long neck.

**Luxembourg** *noun* a small country in northwest Europe, and its capital city.

**luxury** *noun* **1** something expensive that is very nice to have but that you do not really need. **2** great comfort and having a lot of expensive things. *She grew up in luxury.* **luxurious** *adjective. They lived in a luxurious house.*

**lynx** *noun* a medium-sized wild cat with a short tail and tufts of hair in its ears.

**lyre** *noun* a musical instrument like a small harp. *She played a gentle tune on the lyre.*

**lyrics** *plural noun* the words of a song.

**macabre** *adjective* strange, frightening, and gruesome. *We watched a macabre film.*

**macaroni** *noun* tube-shaped pasta.

**Macedonia** *noun* a country in southeastern Europe. *Macedonia lies to the north of Greece.*

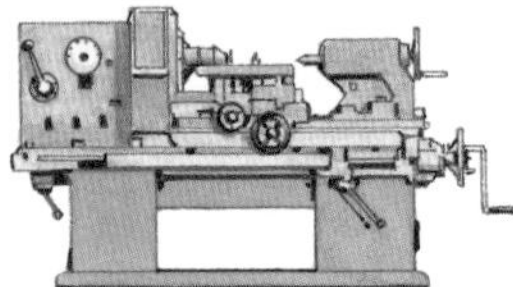

machine

**machine** *noun* a piece of equipment with moving parts that uses electricity or an engine to do a job or make work easier.

**machinery** *noun* **1** the parts of a machine. **2** machines. **3** an organized system of doing something. *The machinery of local government runs very slowly.*

**macho** *adjective* (say **match**-oh) (of a man) aggressively and exaggeratedly masculine; strong and virile.

**mackintosh** *noun* a raincoat or waterproof garment.

**mad** (madder, maddest) *adjective* **1** mentally ill; insane. **2** foolish; not sensible. *He was mad to turn up at the ball uninvited and expect to be allowed in.* **3** very angry. **madness** *noun.*

**Madagascar** *noun* a large island country in the Indian Ocean off East Africa.

**madam** *noun* a formal and polite way of addressing a woman without using her name. *Can I help you, madam?*

**madden** *verb* to annoy. *It maddens me when you bite your nails like that.*

**Madrid** *noun* the capital of Spain in southern Europe.

**magazine** *noun* a publication with a paper cover that is produced, usually every week or month, and which contains articles, photographs, and stories.

**maggot** *noun* the larva or grub of the fly. Maggots look like short worms and live in decaying flesh.

**magic** *noun* **1** in stories, a strange power that makes wonderful or impossible things happen. **2** clever tricks that look as though they happen by magic. **3** enchantment or showing mastery over secret forces in nature.

**magical** *adjective* **1** produced by magic. **2** strange and enchanting. *We had a magical evening.*

**magician** *noun* (say ma-**jish**-un) a person who can do magic tricks; a conjuror.

**magistrate** *noun* a person who acts as a judge in a court of law that deals with less serious offenses.

**magnet** *noun* a piece of metal that has the power to attract (draw toward it) or repel (push away from itself) other metal objects. **magnetic** *adjective. A magnetic compass.* **magnetism** *noun.* **magnetize** *verb.*

**magnificent** *adjective* beautiful and very impressive. *A magnificent castle stood on the hill.* **magnificence** *noun.*

**magnify** (magnifies, magnifying, magnified) *verb* to make something seem larger than it really is by looking at it through a lens in the form of a magnifying glass, a microscope, or a telescope. *Astronomers use telescopes to magnify the stars.* **magnifying glass** a special lens attached to a handle that makes objects look bigger than they really are.

**mahogany** *noun* a very hard, red-brown wood, used in making furniture. *A mahogany table.*

**maid** *noun* a female servant.

**maiden** *noun* (old-fashioned) an unmarried young woman. **maiden name** a woman's surname before she marries. **maiden voyage** a ship's first voyage.

**mail** *noun* **1 the mail** the system of collecting and delivering letters and parcels. **mail** *verb* to send a letter or parcel. **2** a kind of armor made from small metal rings. *The knight wore a coat of mail.*

**maim** *verb* to injure a person or animal so badly that they are disabled for life.

**main** *adjective* the most important.

**mainframe** *noun* a big, powerful computer that can be used by many people at the same time.

**mainland** *noun* the principal and largest mass of land, without its islands, that forms a country.

**mains** *plural noun* the chief cable or pipes that carry electricity, gas, or water to a street.

maiden

**maintain** *verb* **1** to keep in good condition. *The council maintains the building.* **2** to support and look after. **3** to state as true or as a belief. *She maintains that she is innocent.* **4** to continue. *The students have maintained high standards throughout the term.*

**maize** *noun* a tall plant that produces cobs of Indian corn, a cereal with large seeds.

**majesty** *noun* **1** impressive greatness; splendor. *The majesty of the mountains.* **2 Your Majesty** the title people use when speaking to a king or queen. **majestic** *adjective.*

**major** *adjective* important; main. *The new government made major changes.* **major** *noun* an officer in the army, above a captain.

**majority** *noun* **1** more than half of a total. *The majority of people watch television every day.* **2** the number of votes by which somebody wins an election.

**Majuro** *noun* the capital of the Marshall Islands in the North Pacific Ocean.

**make** (makes, making, made) *verb* **1** to put things together to produce something new; to create or build. **2** to prepare. **3** to cause or force something to happen. *The airplane made a forced landing.* **4** to add up or produce. *Three plus six make nine.* **5** to earn or gain. *How much money does the waiter make?* **make** *noun* the name or brand of the company that produced the item. *What make of car is this?* **make somebody's day** to make somebody feel happy by doing something that is the best thing that has happened to them that day. **make do** *verb* to do something with the things you already have, although they are not exactly what you want. *You'll have to make do with my old saucepan, even though it's not as good as yours.* **makeup** special colored creams and powders (cosmetics) that women and actors put on their faces. **make up** *verb* **1** to invent. **2** to become friends again after quarreling. **3** to put on makeup. **make-believe** *verb* to pretend or imagine things. *Let's make-believe we are cowboys.*

mammoth

**makeshift** *adjective* temporary and only meant to last until something better can be used. *The refugees slept in makeshift accommodation.*

**mal-** *prefix* bad or ill. *Malformed, malfunction, malnutrition.*

**Malabo** *noun* the capital of Equatorial Guinea in West Africa, a country with a mainland and five main islands.

**malaria** *noun* a tropical disease that is carried to a person by the bite of a female mosquito.

**Malawi** *noun* a country in southern Africa.

**Malaysia** *noun* a country in Southeast Asia.

**Maldives** *plural noun* a country of many islands in the Indian Ocean.

**Malé** *noun* the capital of the Maldives in the Indian Ocean.

**male** *noun, adjective* a human or animal belonging to the sex that fertilizes the female to produce babies or eggs. *Boys and men are males. A male horse is called a stallion.* The opposite of "male" is "female."

**Mali** *noun* a country in North Africa.

**malicious** *adjective* (say ma-**lish**-us) unkind and wishing to see others hurt or unhappy; spiteful. *She has a malicious tongue.* **malice** *noun.*

**mall** *noun* a very large building with a lot of stores in it.

**mallard** *noun* a kind of wild duck.

**mallet** *noun* a large wooden hammer.

**malnutrition** *noun* illness caused by eating too little or the wrong kind of food.

**malt** *noun* dried barley, used to make beer and whiskey.

**Malta** *noun* an island country of southern Europe, in the Mediterranean Sea.

**Maltese** *noun* **1** a person who comes from Malta. **2** the language of Malta. **Maltese** *adjective. The Maltese Cross.*

**maltreat** *verb* to treat a person or animal roughly or unkindly. *We should never maltreat our pets.*

**mammal** *noun* any animal of which the female feeds her young with milk from her own body. Humans, elephants, and whales are examples of mammals.

**mammoth** *noun* a kind of large, hairy elephant that lived thousands of years ago during the Ice Age. Mammoths are now extinct.

**man** *noun* **1** a fully grown male human. **2** humans in general. *When did Man first appear on Earth?* **mankind** *noun. "One small step for man, one giant leap for mankind."*

**manage** *verb* **1** to control or be in charge of something. *Lucy manages the production department.* **2** to be able to do something, especially something difficult, to succeed. *She managed to solve the crossword puzzle.* **manager** *noun.* **management** *noun.*

**Managua** *noun* the capital of Nicaragua in Central America.

**Manama** *noun* the capital of Bahrain in Southwest Asia.

**mane** *noun* the long, thick hair on the necks of horses and male lions.

**maneuvre** *noun* (say man-**oo**-ver) **1** a skillful or difficult movement or clever trick. **2** a large-scale exercise of troops.

**manger** *noun* a long, narrow container in a barn or stable from which cattle and horses feed. *Jesus was born in a stable and laid gently in a manger.*

manger

**mangle** *verb* to damage by crushing and twisting out of shape.

**manhood** *noun* the state or condition of being a man.

**mania** *noun* a strong desire or enthusiasm for something.

Mm

**maniac** *noun* **1** a person suffering from a mental illness that makes them behave violently. **2** (informal) an over-enthusiastic person. *She drives like a maniac.*

**Manila** *noun* the capital of the Philippines, an archipelago in Southeast Asia.

**manner** *noun* **1** the way in which something is done. *Let's do this in a professional manner.* **2** the way a person behaves or talks. *She has a friendly manner.* **manners** polite behavior.

**manor** *noun* a large, important house in the country with land around it.

**mansion** *noun* a very large, impressive house.

**manslaughter** *noun* the crime of killing somebody without planning or intending it to happen.

**mantelpiece** *noun* the shelf above a fireplace. *We display our family photographs on the mantelpiece.*

**manual** *noun* a book with instructions on how to use or do something. **manual** *adjective* worked with the hands. *Manual controls, manual labor.*

**manufacture** *verb* to make things in large quantities by machine in a factory.

**manuscript** *noun* a handwritten or typed copy of a book before it is printed.

Mm

**Maori** (Maori or Maoris) *noun* (say **mow**-ree) the original people who lived in New Zealand.

**maple** *noun* a tree with large leaves with five points. The maple leaf is the national emblem of Canada.

**Maputo** *noun* the capital of Mozambique in southeastern Africa.

**marathon** *noun* a race in which of people run 26 miles (42 km).

**marble** *noun* **1** a very hard stone that can be polished to show its pattern or color. **2** a small colored glass ball used in children's games. *A game of marbles.*

**mare** *noun* a fully grown female horse. The opposite of a "mare" is a "stallion."

**margarine** *noun* a soft, yellow, butter-like fat made mainly from vegetable oils.

**margin** *noun* blank space on the sides of a printed page.

**marine** *adjective* to do with the sea. *Whales are marine mammals.* **marine** *noun* a soldier who serves on a ship.

**mark** *noun* **1** a stain or scratch on something. **2** a special sign on something. **3** a number or sign grading a test or paper that shows how good it is. **mark** *verb.*

**market** *noun* a place where things are sold, usually from stalls in the open air.

**marmalade** *noun* a jam made from oranges or other citrus fruits, and usually eaten at breakfast.

**maroon** *noun, adjective* dark red-brown. *Maroon socks.* **maroon** *verb* to abandon or leave somebody alone in an isolated place from which there is no escape, such as a desert island.

**marquee** *noun* a very large tent used for summer parties, circuses and wedding receptions.

marquee

**marriage** *noun* **1** a wedding ceremony. **2** the state of being married. *My sister got married last year.*

**marrow** *noun* **1** a long, large, green vegetable like a big cucumber. **2** a soft substance containing blood vessels in the hollow center of bones.

**marry** (marries, marrying, married) *verb* to take somebody as your husband or wife.

**Marshall Islands** *plural noun* a country of many islands in the Pacific Ocean.

**marsupial** *noun* any mammal, the female of which carries her young in a pouch on her stomach. *Kangaroos are marsupials.*

**martial** *adjective* to do with wars, battles, and soldiers. *The band played marches and other kinds of martial music.* **martial arts** systems of self-defense, such as karate, kendo, and judo, that come from China and Japan.

**Martian** *noun* an imaginary alien from the planet Mars.

**martyr** *noun* someone who chooses to suffer or be killed rather than give up their beliefs. **martyrdom** *noun.*

**marvel** (marvels, marveling, marveled) *verb* to be astonished or surprised. **marvel** *noun. A computer is an electronic marvel.*

**marvelous** *adjective* excellent, very good.

**mascot** *noun* an animal or thing that people think brings good luck. *The team's mascot is a rabbit.*

**masculine** *adjective* concerned with men; manly. **masculinity** *noun.* The opposite of "masculine" is "feminine."

**Maseru** *noun* the capital of Lesotho in southern Africa.

**mask** *noun* a covering worn over the face to hide, disguise, or protect it. **mask** *verb* to cover or disguise something.

mask

**mason** *noun* a person who makes or builds things from stone, or carves stone decorations.

**masonry** *noun* stonework, as found on a cathedral.

**mass** *noun* **1** a large number or quantity. *The plant was covered in a mass of flowers.* **2** a large, shapeless lump of something. **3 the masses** the ordinary people. **4** the celebration of the Holy Communion service in Roman Catholic and some other Christian Churches. **mass** *verb* to gather into a group or mass. *The teenagers massed in the park.* **mass media** ways of communicating through such things as newspapers, radio, and television, from which most people get their news and information. **mass-produced** made by machines in very large quantities.

maze

**massacre** *noun* (say **mass**-uh-ker) the brutal killing of a large number of people. **massacre** *verb.*

**masterly** *adjective* showing skill. *The violinist gave a truly masterly performance.*

**masterpiece** *noun* an outstandingly skillful work of art.

**mastery** *noun* **1** having complete control of something. *Mastery over his phobia.* **2** skill. *Mastery of the piano.*

**material** *noun* **1** a substance from which you can make other things. *Wood, glass, bricks, and cement are materials used in building houses.* **2** cloth used for making clothes. *The material I've used is silk.*

**maternal** *adjective* relating to a mother or mothers; motherly. *Maternal feelings.*

**mathematics** *plural noun* the study of the science of numbers, measurements, quantities, and shapes. **mathematical** *adjective.* **mathematician** *noun.*

**matrimony** *noun* marriage or the state of being married. **matrimonial** *adjective.*

**matter** *noun* **1** the substance or material from which all things are made. Matter can be a solid, a gas, or a liquid. **2** a subject or situation. *Financial matters.* **3** a problem. *What's the matter with you today?* **matter** *verb* to be important. *Does it matter?*

**mature** *adjective* **1** fully developed and adult; grown up. **2** ripe. **mature** *verb. Puppies mature into dogs.*

**maul** *verb* to injure somebody badly by attacking or handling them savagely.

**Mauritania** *noun* a country in northwest Africa.

**Mauritius** *noun* an island country in the Indian Ocean off East Africa.

**mauve** *adjective* a pale purple color.

**maxim** *noun* a general rule or wise piece of advice. *"Look before you leap" is an old maxim, and a wise one.*

**maximum** *noun* the greatest number or amount possible. **maximum** *adjective.* The opposite of "maximum" is "minimum."

**mayhem** *noun* general chaos.

**mayor** *noun* a person in charge of the council or government of a town or city.

**maze** *noun* a system of complicated paths, often running between high hedges, or lines on a page, which is difficult to find your way through to its center or exit.

**Mbabane** *noun* the administrative capital of Swaziland.

**meadow** *noun* a grassy field where animals graze.

meadow

**meal** *noun* Breakfast, lunch, tea, and dinner are meals.

**mean** *adjective* unwilling to give; not generous or kind. **mean** (means, meaning, meant) *verb* **1** to intend or plan to do something. *I meant to telephone, but I forgot.* **2** to intend to show or express. *Red means danger.*

**meaning** *noun* **1** what something means. *Dictionaries tell us the meaning of words.* **2** the importance, purpose, or intention of something. *What is the meaning of this?*

**meaningful** *adjective* full of significance; important.

**meaningless** *adjective* without any purpose. *His life seems meaningless.*

**means** *plural noun* **1** a method or way of doing something. *The prisoner found some means of escape.* **2** wealth. *A woman of substantial means.*

**meanwhile** *adverb* at the same time as. *The rain fell; meanwhile, Megan slept.*

**measles** *noun* a mainly children's infectious disease causing a fever and a rash of small, red spots on the skin.

**measure** *verb* to find out or to show how long, tall, wide, or heavy something is. **measure** *noun* **1** a unit of measurement. A meter is a measure of length. **2** an action or law. *The government took measures to reduce crime.*

**measurement** *noun* how much something measures.

medal

**mechanic** *noun* a person who is skilled at mending machines.

**mechanical** *adjective* **1** relating to machinery. **2** worked by a machine. *A funny mechanical mouse.* **3** automatic and done without thought.

**mechanism** *noun* the system of the working parts of a machine.

**medal** *noun* something similar to a large coin with words or a symbol on it, given as a reward.

**media** see mass-media.

**medical** *adjective* concerning doctors and their work in preventing and treating disease. **medical** *noun* a complete examination of your body by a doctor.

**medicine** *noun* **1** the tablets and liquid substances you swallow to try to treat and cure an illness. *The medicine tasted horrible.* **2** the treatment and study of illnesses.

**medieval** *adjective* relating to the Middle Ages, a period in European history that lasted between about AD 1100 and 1450.

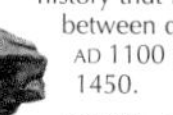

megalith

**mega-** *prefix* very big.

**megabyte** *noun* a unit of memory in a computer (about a million bytes).

**megalith** *noun* a very large, usually upright, stone put up in prehistoric times as a monument or part of one.

**melancholy** *noun, adjective* very sad or gloomy. *A melancholy tale.*

**mellow** *adjective* **1** (of fruit) sweet and juicy. **2** (of light) soft and golden. **3** (of people) older and more pleasant. **mellow** *verb. She has mellowed with age.*

Mm

**melody** (melodies) *noun* a sweet, pleasing tune. *I played a lovely melody on the flute.*

**melon** *noun* a large, round, juicy fruit with a green or yellow skin and lots of seeds inside.

**melt** *verb* to change from a solid to a liquid by heating. *The ice cream melted in the sun.*

**member** *noun* somebody that belongs to a group, team, club, or family. **membership** *noun.*

**memorable** *adjective* worth remembering; famous; easy to remember. *A memorable day at the fair.*

**memorize** *verb* to learn something so well that you can remember it word for word. *Actors must memorize their lines before performing on stage.*

**memory** *noun* **1** the ability to remember things. *He has a good memory for telephone numbers.* **2** a thing that you can remember about the distant past. *I have an early childhood memory of a visit to the sea.* **3** the part of a computer that stores information.

**menace** *noun* somebody or something that is a threat or danger and may cause damage. *Black ice is a menace to drivers because you cannot see it is there.*

**mend** *verb* to repair or to make something that is broken useful again. *When is somebody going to mend the washing machine?*

**menstruation** *noun* blood that comes from a woman's womb about once a month; a period. **menstruate** *verb.*

**mental** *adjective* relating to the mind; done in the head. *John has good mental abilities.*

**mention** *verb* to make a brief remark or use few words about something. *I think she did mention you would be away.* **mention** *noun.*

**menu** (menus) *noun* **1** a list of the dishes from which you can choose in a restaurant. **2** a list of choices displayed on a computer screen.

**MEP** *abbreviation* Member of the European Parliament.

**merchandise** *noun* goods for sale.

**merchant** *noun* a person who buys and sells large quantities of goods of a particular kind. *A coffee merchant.* **merchant navy** a nation's ships that carry goods; commercial shipping.

**merciful** *adjective* willing to forgive somebody and not punish them.

**merciless** *adjective* cruel and showing no pity; ruthless.

**mercury** *noun* a silver metal that is usually liquid. Mercury is used in thermometers.

**mercy** *noun* ready to show kindness and forgiveness to somebody who has done something wrong.

**merge** *verb* to combine or blend together. *The two firms decided to merge.* **merger** *noun.*

**merry** (merrier, merriest) *adjective* **1** cheerful and happy. *Have a merry Christmas.* **2** (informal) very slightly drunk.

**mesmerize** *verb* to be so fascinated by something that you can think of nothing else; to be hypnotized.

**metal** *noun* a hard material that goes soft and can be bent when heated. Metals are usually shiny and conduct heat well. Copper, gold, iron, and silver are all metals.

**metamorphosis** *noun* the complete change in form that some animals go through as they develop. *The metamorphosis of a tadpole into a frog.*

meteor

**metaphor** *noun* an expression in which something or somebody is described as though they were something else. *She has green fingers and he has a heart of gold.*

**meteor** *noun* a large piece of metal or rock that travels through space and normally burns up if it enters Earth's atmosphere.

**meteorite** *noun* a meteor that has fallen to Earth.

**meteorology** *noun* the scientific study of the atmosphere and weather. **meteorologist** *noun* a person who forecasts the weather.

**meter** *noun* **1** an instrument that measures how much electricity, gas, or water has been used. **2** a measure of length equal to 1,000 millimeters.

**metric system** a system of weighing and measuring based on multiples of 10. Kilograms, liters, and meters are all metric measures.

**method** *noun* a certain way of doing something; a system.

**methodical** *adjective* in an orderly, well-organized way, according to plan.

**metropolis** *noun* a large city.

**Mexico** *noun* a country in Central America, south of and bordering the USA.

Mexico

**Mexico City** *noun* the capital of Mexico.

**micro-** *prefix* very small. *Microchip, microfilm, microsecond.*

**microbe** *noun* a living thing that is so tiny that it can be seen only through a microscope. *Swarming with microbes.*

**microchip** or **silicon chip** *noun* a tiny piece of silicon with electronic circuits printed on it, used in computers and other electronic equipment.

**Micronesia** *noun* a country of many islands in the Pacific Ocean.

**microphone** *noun* an electrical instrument used to help record sound, or to make sounds louder.

**microscope** *noun* an instrument with lenses that makes tiny objects look much larger. *We looked at the ant under the microscope.*

**microscopic** *adjective* so tiny that it cannot be seen except through a microscope.

**microwave** *noun* an oven that cooks food very quickly by using energy in short waves (electronic microwaves).

**midday** *noun* the middle of the day, 12 noon.

**middle** *noun, adjective* halfway. **middle age** between the ages of about 40 and 60. **Middle Ages** a period in European history between about 1100 and 1450. **Middle East** (also called Southwest Asia) an area at the eastern end of the Mediterranean, including Egypt and Iran.

**midwife** *noun* a person whose job it is to help women with the birth of their babies.

**migraine** *noun* (say **my**-grane) a very severe, throbbing headache that makes you feel sick.

**migration** *noun* the movement from one area to another of a large group of animals, birds, or people. **migrate** *verb.* **migratory** *adjective.* **migrant** *noun* **1** one who moves from one country to another regularly.

**mildew** *noun* a grayish fungus that grows on plants or decaying matter.

**mile** *noun* a measure of distance equal to 1,760 yards or 1.6 km. **to be miles away** to daydream.

**militant** *adjective* aggressive and ready to fight; very active in support of a cause.

**military** *adjective* relating to the armed forces. *In some countries, all young men have to do military service.*

**millennium** (millennia) *noun* a thousand years.

**milligram** *noun* a very small measure of weight. There are 1,000 milligrams in a kilogram.

**milliliter** *noun* a very small liquid measure. There are 1,000 milliliters in a liter.

**mime** *noun* a kind of acting without words in which the actors use gestures and facial expressions. **mime** *verb.*

**mimic** (mimics, mimicking, mimicked) *verb* to imitate somebody's actions or speech, usually to amuse people. **mimic** *noun. He's a good mimic.*

**minaret** *noun* a tall tower near a mosque from the top of which the muezzin calls people to prayer.

**mince** *noun* meat that has been minced or ground into small pieces.

**mincemeat** *noun* finely chopped apples, dried fruit, and spices, used in making pies.

**mindless** *adjective* stupid and unthinking.

**miner** *noun* a person who works in a mine. *The miners were looking for gold.*

**mineral** *noun* a natural substance such as coal, gold, and salt, which is mined from the earth. **mineral** *adjective* of or containing minerals. *Mineral water.*

**mini-** *prefix* smaller or shorter than normal.

minaret

**miniature** *adjective* very small. **miniature** *noun* a minute but detailed painting.

**minim** *noun* in music, a half note.

**minimum** *noun* the smallest amount or number of something you can have for something to happen. *You need a minimum of ten people for the trip.* The opposite of "minimum" is "maximum."

**minister** *noun* **1** a member of the clergy who holds services in a Protestant Christian church. **2** the head of a government department in Europe.

**minnow** *noun* a tiny fish found in lakes and rivers. *He caught only minnows.*

**minor** *adjective* not serious. *A minor burn.* **minor** *noun* a young person under the age of 18.

minnow

Mm

**minority** *noun* **1** the smaller of two groups of people or things. *Only a minority voted against him.* **2** a small number of people of one race, culture, or religion living among a larger group of people of a different race, culture, or religion. The opposite of "minority" is "majority."

**Minsk** *noun* the capital of Belarus in eastern Europe.

**mint** *noun* **1** a plant whose leaves are used as a flavoring. **2** a place where coins are made.

**minus** *noun* a mathematical term or symbol (–) meaning subtract or take away.

**minute** (**my**-newt) *adjective* **1** very small; tiny. *A minute speck of dirt.* **2** very detailed. *A minute examination.* **minute** *noun* (**min-**it) a period of time consisting of 60 seconds. There are 60 minutes in an hour.

**miracle** *noun* an amazing and unexpected happening for which there is no explanation. *His escape was a miracle.* **miraculous** *adjective.*

**mirage** *noun* something that you imagine you see that is not really there; an optical illusion. *The travelers saw a mirage of an oasis in the desert.*

**mirror** *noun* a piece of special glass, metal, or plastic that reflects light and whatever is in front of it.

**mis-** *prefix* wrongly. *Misbehave, misjudge.*

**misbehave** *verb* to behave badly. **misbehavior** *noun.*

**miscellaneous** *adjective* a mixture or assortment of various things.

Mm

**mischief** *noun* annoying but harmless behavior. **mischievous** *adjective. A mischievous child.*

**miser** *noun* a very mean person who likes to hoard money and not spend it. **miserly** *adjective.*

**misery** *noun* **1** a feeling of great unhappiness, wretchedness. **2** (informal) a person who is always complaining. *She's a real misery.* **miserable** *adjective. Jane is miserable because she can't go to the concert.*

miser

**mislead** *verb* to give somebody a false idea by making them believe something that is untrue. To deceive or give wrong information. **misleading** *adjective. This newspaper article is very misleading.*

**missile** *noun* a weapon that is sent through the air and which explodes when it hits its target.

**mission** *noun* an important job that somebody is sent somewhere to do. *A space mission.*

**missionary** *noun* somebody who is sent to another country to tell its people about a religion.

**mistake** *noun* something that is incorrect; an error.

**misunderstand** (misunderstands, misunderstanding, misunderstood) *verb* to get the wrong idea.

mixer

**mix** *verb* to combine or put different things together. **mixture** *noun. A cake mixture.* **mix-up** *noun* confusion or muddle.

**mixer** *noun* a machine that you use to mix things together. *A noisy cement mixer.*

**mnemonic** *noun* (say ne-**mon**-ik) an aid, such as a rhyme, to help us remember facts.

**moat** *noun* a deep, wide ditch, usually filled with water, surrounding a castle to protect it from attack.

**mob** *noun* a noisy, and often violent, crowd of angry people. **mob** *verb. The fans mobbed the pop star.*

**mobile** *adjective* able to be moved around easily and quickly. *A mobile home.*

**moccasin** *noun* a soft leather shoe without a heel. Moccasins were first worn by American Indians.

**mock** *verb* to make fun of somebody, often by copying them in a cruel and unpleasant way. **mock** *adjective* not real; imitation. *Mock diamonds.* **mockery** *noun.*

**modem** *noun* an electronic device that sends information between one computer and another by telephone.

**moderate** *adjective* neither too big nor too small.

**modest** *adjective* **1** quiet and not boastful. **2** not extreme or very large; moderate. *Her needs are modest.*

**Mogadishu** *noun* the capital of Somalia in eastern Africa, bordering the Gulf of Aden and the Indian Ocean.

**moisture** *noun* dampness; tiny drops of water, such as steam or mist, in the air.

**Moldova** *noun* a country in eastern Europe.

**molecule** *noun* the smallest amount of a substance that can exist on its own. A molecule of water is made up of two hydrogen atoms and one oxygen atom.

**mollusk, mollusc** *noun* any animal with a soft body and no backbone, usually protected by a hard shell, like snails and limpets.

**molten** *adjective* melted, especially by intense heat.

mollusc

monkey

**momentum** *noun* the force gained by an object as it moves. *The sled gained momentum as it sped downhill.*

**Monaco** *noun* a tiny country in southern Europe, bounded by France.

**monarch** *noun* (say **mon**-ark) a king or queen. **monarchy** *noun.*

**monastery** *noun* a group of buildings in which a community of monks lives and works; an abbey. **monastic** *adjective.*

**Mongolia** *noun* a country in Central Asia.

**mongoose** (mongooses) *noun* a small African or Asian animal with a long body that kills poisonous snakes.

**monitor** *noun* **1** a pupil at school who is given special duties by a teacher. **2** a computer screen. **3** an instrument, usually with a screen, that keeps a check on something and records any changes.

**monkey** *noun* an animal with long arms and a long tail that climbs trees. Monkeys are primates and belong to the same group as apes and people. **monkey business** some mischievous or illegal activity.

**mono-** *prefix* one or alone. *Monorail.*

**monopoly** *noun* sole control of the manufacture or supply of a product or service. **monopolize** *verb* to control something completely.

**monotonous** *adjective* dull and lacking any variety. *She has a monotonous voice.* **monotony** *noun.*

**Monrovia** *noun* the capital of Liberia in West Africa.

**monsoon** *noun* a strong prevailing wind around the Indian Ocean that changes direction in winter and summer. The summer monsoon brings heavy rainfall.

**monster** *noun* **1** a huge, terrifying, imaginary creature. **2** a cruel, wicked person. **monster** *adjective* very big or strange. **monstrous** *adjective* huge and atrocious.

**Monte Carlo** *noun* the capital of Monaco in southwest Europe, bordering the Mediterranean Sea.

**Montevideo** *noun* the capital of Uruguay in southern South America.

**month** *noun* a period of time and one of the twelve divisions of the year. **monthly** *adjective* happening once a month or every month. *A monthly magazine.* **calendar month** one of the twelve divisions of the year, e.g., from 1 March to 31 March. **lunar month** a period of about 29 days, the time it takes for the Moon to orbit the Earth.

**monument** *noun* **1** an old and important building or statue. *Ancient monuments.* **2** a building or statue erected so that people will remember an important person or event. **monumental** *adjective.*

**mood** *noun* the way you feel or your state of mind at a particular time. *Winning the game put him in a good mood.* **moody** *adjective* bad-tempered or liable to change mood quickly for no apparent reason. **moodiness** *noun.*

**moon** *noun* **1** a natural satellite or small planet that orbits a larger planet. **2 the Moon** the natural satellite that orbits the Earth once every four weeks (i.e., the lunar month). The Moon is our closest neighbor in space.

**moonlight** *noun* the light from the Sun reflected by the Moon. *Moonlight turned the sea silver.*

**moor** *noun* a large area of open, often high, land, usually covered with heather or gorse. **moor** *verb* to tie up a boat so that it cannot drift away. **mooring** *noun. Our mooring is in a sheltered position near the river mouth.*

**moose** (plural moose) *noun* a large, brown deer found in the forests of North America. The male has enormous, flattened antlers.

moose

**mop** *noun* an implement with soft material such as a sponge attached to a long handle, used for cleaning floors. **mop** (mops, mopping, mopped) *verb* to wipe with a mop or cloth. *He mopped his brow in the midday heat.*

**mope** *verb* to feel gloomy and sorry for yourself.

**moral** *adjective* relating to the goodness or badness of human behavior and what is right and wrong. **moral** *noun* a lesson or point made in a story about what is right and wrong. **morals** *plural noun* the standards of behavior of a society and its beliefs in right and wrong.

**morale** *noun* (say mor-**al**) the spirit of hope, confidence, and enthusiasm among members of a group or team. *After its win, the team's morale was very high.*

**more** *adjective, pronoun* bigger in number, size, or amount. *She has more books than me.* **more** *adverb. Can you say it once more?*

**morgue** *noun* a mortuary or place where corpses are kept until they are buried or cremated.

**Moroccan** *noun* a person who comes from Morocco. **Moroccan** *adjective. A Moroccan mosque.*

**Morocco** *noun* a country in North Africa.

**Moroni** *noun* the capital of the Comoros Islands off the east coast of Africa.

**morning** *noun* the part of the day from sunrise to noon.

**morsel** *noun* a very small piece of food.

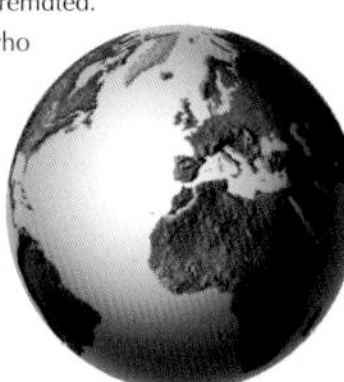

Morocco

**mortal** *adjective* **1** incapable of living for ever. All living things are mortal. **2** causing death. *A mortal illness.* **mortal** *noun* a human being.

**mortgage** *noun* (say **more**-gage) a loan of money from a bank that you use to buy a house, and repay over a period of years. **mortgage** *verb* to transfer the ownership of your house or property to a bank in return for money it lends you.

**mortuary** *noun* a place where dead bodies are kept before they are buried or cremated.

**mosaic** *noun* (say moh-**zay**-ik) a picture or design made from small pieces of colored glass or stone set in concrete. *The inside of the church roof was covered in a stunning mosaic of the twelve Apostles.*

**Moscow** *noun* the capital of Russia, in Europe and Asia.

**Moslem** another spelling for Muslim.

**mosque** *noun* a building in which Muslims pray. *The floor of the mosque was covered in prayer rugs.*

**mosquito** *noun* (say moss-**kee**-toe) a small flying insect that bites animals and people and sucks their blood. Some mosquitoes transmit the disease malaria.

**moss** (mosses) *noun* a small green plant that forms a soft covering on stones in damp places. **mossy** *adjective.*

**most** *noun, adjective* the largest in size, number, or amount. *Most apples are green or red.* **most** *adverb.* *The most intelligent boy in the class.*

Mm

**mostly** *adverb* generally, mainly. *What you are saying is mostly nonsense!*

**motel** *noun* a hotel that caters specially for motorists and their cars.

**moth** *noun* an insect like a butterfly that is usually seen flying at night.

**mother** *noun* a female parent; the woman who gave birth to you. **mother** *verb* to look after like a mother. **motherly** *adjective.* **motherhood** *noun. Motherhood was her greatest joy.*

**motion** *noun* movement; the action of moving. *The motion of the bus sent him to sleep.* **motion** *verb* to signal or make a movement, usually with the hand. *She motioned him to sit down.* **motion picture** *noun* a movie.

moth

**motionless** *adjective* not moving.

**motive** *noun* a reason for doing something. *What was the motive for the crime?*

**motor** *noun* an engine in a machine that uses fuel to make it work or move. **motor** *adjective* having to do with engines and vehicles. *A motor vehicle.*

**motorcycle** *noun* a heavy, two-wheeled vehicle with an engine. *Tom rode his motorcycle every weekend.*

mountain

**mottled** *adjective* marked with patches of different color.

**motto** *noun* a phrase that sums up what is important to a group, or a guiding principle. *"Think before you speak" is a good motto.*

**mountain** *noun* a very high and usually steep hill. *He set out to climb the mountain.*

**mourn** *verb* to feel great sadness because somebody has died; to grieve. **mourning** *noun. They mourned their lost loved ones.*

**movable** *adjective* able to be moved. *The hands of a clock are movable.*

**move** *verb* **1** to go from one position or place to another. *Don't move, I want to take your photograph.* **2** to change your home. *We moved into a new house.* **3** to feel or make you feel something deeply.

**movement** *noun* **1** the act of moving. *She made a sudden movement.* **2** a group of people working for a common cause. **3** a section into which some pieces of classical music are divided. *Most symphonies have a slow movement.*

**movie** *noun* **1** a motion picture. *Let's go to the movies.* **2** the theater where you go to watch a movie.

**moving** *adjective* touching the feelings. *It was a moving film about orphans.*

**Mozambique** *noun* a country in southeast Africa.

**much** *adjective, adverb, pronoun* a large amount. *Did you eat much for lunch?*

**muezzin** *noun* a person who calls Muslims to prayer, usually from a minaret.

**mug** *noun* a tall cup, usually with straight sides, that you use without a saucer. *I'd like a mug of hot chocolate, please.* **mug** (mugs, mugging, mugged) *verb* to attack and rob somebody in the street. *Jane was mugged outside her home.* **mugger** *noun.*

**mule** *noun* an animal that is the offspring of a male donkey and a female horse or pony. *The mule carried us up the mountain.*

**multi-** *prefix* many. *Multicolored.*

**multimedia** *adjective* involving the use of a mixture of different media, such as TV, radio, and video.

**multiple** *adjective* involving more than one; many. *The actress had multiple addresses, as she owned properties around the world.* **multiple** *noun* any number that can be divided exactly by another number. 20, 30, and 40 are multiples of 2, 5, and 10.

**multiply** (multiplies, multiplying, multiplied) *verb* to increase a number by adding the number to itself a given number of times. Three plus three plus three make nine or 3 x 3 = 9. **multiplication** *noun.*

**multitude** *noun* a crowd, a large number of things. *I've a multitude of things to do.*

**mumble** *verb* to speak in a low, indistinct voice that is not easy to understand.

**mummy** (mummies) *noun* **1** a dead body that has been preserved from decay by being rubbed with special oils and wrapped in cloths, as in ancient Egypt. **2** a word used by English children for "mother."

mural

**mumps** *noun* a painful infectious disease that makes your neck and the sides of your face swell.

**munch** *verb* to chew something in a noisy way. *The horse munched a crisp apple.*

**mural** *noun* a picture painted on a wall.

**murder** *verb* to kill somebody on purpose. **murder** *noun.* **murderous** *adjective.*

**murderer** *noun* a person who commits a murder. *The murderer was jailed for life.*

**Muscat** *noun* the capital of Oman in Southwest Asia.

**muscle** *noun* solid tissue inside your body that stretches and relaxes to make parts of it move. *Tennis players need to have strong arm muscles.*

**muse** *noun* in Greek and Roman mythology, one of the nine goddesses who inspire poetry, music, drama, and other things. **muse** *verb* to reflect on something.

**museum** *noun* (say mew-**zee**-um) a place where interesting or rare objects are on display for people to look at.

**mushroom** *noun* a fungus. Some you can eat, but others are poisonous.

**music** *noun* **1** the pattern of sounds made by somebody singing or by playing musical instruments. **2** the written or printed signs and notes that represent musical sounds.

**musical** *adjective* **1** relating to music. *Musical instruments.* **2** good at making or understanding music. **musical** *noun* a play or movie featuring singing and dancing.

muscle

**musician** *noun* **1** a composer of music. **2** a person who plays a musical instrument well.

**musket** *noun* an old-fashioned gun with a long barrel.

**Muslim** or **Moslem** *noun* a person who follows Islam, the religion founded by the prophet Mohammed. **Muslim** *adjective.*

**mussel** *noun* a small shellfish with two black shells. Mussels attach themselves to rocks.

mussel

**must** *verb that strengthens other verbs* **1** to need to; to have to. *I must go to bed now.* **2** to be obliged to. *You must obey the rules.* **3** to be definitely or likely. *You must be happy to have won.*

**mustard** *noun* a hot-tasting yellow paste made from the seeds of the mustard plant and used to flavor food.

**mute** *adjective* **1** unable to speak. **2** silent; speechless. *They stared at each other in mute amazement.*

**mutilate** *verb* to damage somebody or something, usually by cutting off a part of it. *A mutilated letter.*

**mutiny** *noun* a rebellion by sailors or soldiers against officers. **mutiny** *verb.* **mutinous** *adjective. Mutinous troops.* **mutineer** *noun. The mutineers took over the ship and threw the captain overboard.*

**mutter** *verb* to speak in a low voice that cannot be heard clearly; to grumble. *Please don't mutter into your beard, because I can't hear you.*

**mutual** *adjective* **1** shared by two or more people; in common. *We have mutual friends.* **2** done equally to each other. *Mutual respect.*

**muzzle** *noun* **1** the nose and mouth of an animal such as a dog or wolf. **2** straps put over an animal's muzzle to stop it from biting. *The dog had to wear a muzzle after it bit the mailman.* **3** the open end of a gun.

**Myanmar** *noun* a country in Southeast Asia, formerly called Burma.

**mystery** *noun* **1** something strange that has happened and which you cannot explain or understand; puzzling. *It's a complete mystery as to how the king escaped from the castle dungeon without being caught.* **2** a secret; a mystery guest. **mysterious** *adjective* wrapped in mystery. *A mysterious castle loomed out of the forest.*

**myth** *noun* **1** a story from the distant past, usually about gods and heroes and how the world began. **2** a widely held belief that is a false notion. *It's a myth that spinach builds your muscles.* **mythical** *adjective. A mythical dragon saved the princess in the fairy tale.*

**mythology** *noun* a collection of myths. *Norse mythology contains some wonderful stories.*

Mm

**nag** (nags, nagging, nagged) *verb* to annoy somebody by constantly complaining or trying to persuade them to do something. *Mother's always nagging me to clean up my room.* **nag** *noun.*

**nail** *noun* **1** the hard covering that protects the ends of your fingers and toes (fingernails, toenails). **2** a thin piece of metal with one end pointed and the other end flat. Nails are used for fastening pieces of wood together and for hammering into walls to hang things from. **nail** *verb. He nailed a notice to the door.*

**Nairobi** *noun* the capital of Kenya, in East Africa.

**naked** *adjective* with no clothes on; uncovered. **nakedness** *noun.*

**name** *noun* **1** a word by which a person, animal, or place is known. *My cat's name is Archie.* **2** a reputation. *The bank has a good name.* **name** *verb. They named their baby William.* **name after** to give somebody or something the same name as somebody else. *The city of Adelaide in Australia is named after Queen Adelaide.*

**namesake** *noun* somebody with the same name as you.

**Namibia** *noun* a country in southern Africa.

**nanny** *noun* a person who is employed to look after young children in their own home. **nanny goat** a female goat.

Namibia



**nap** *noun* a short sleep.

**nape** *noun* the back of the neck.

**napkin** *noun* a square piece of cloth or paper that you put on your lap to protect your clothes while you eat a meal, or that you use to wipe your lips afterward.

**narrate** *verb* to tell someone, or to broadcast, a story or relate an account of something. *I narrated the tale of the time I got lost in the African jungle and was rescued by an elephant.*

**narrative** *noun* a story or account of things that have happened. *The narrative was well written, but the dialogue was terrible.*

**narrator** *noun* a person who tells a story or delivers a commentary in a movie or on a radio program.

**narrow** *adjective* thin and not measuring very much from one side to the other. *The door is too narrow for the piano to go through.* **narrow** *verb. The road narrowed as it climbed the hill, until it was only just wide enough for our car to pass along.* The opposite of "narrow" is "wide."

**narrow-minded** *adjective* unwilling to understand or even consider ideas that are new or different.

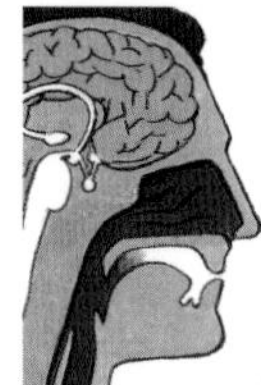

nasal

**nasal** *adjective* relating to the nose. *The nasal passages.*

**Nassau** *noun* the capital of the Bahamas in the Caribbean.

**nasty** (nastier, nastiest) *adjective* **1** a bad appearance, taste, or smell. **2** unkind. *Don't be nasty to your sister.*

**nation** *noun* a community of people living in an area, sharing the same language and customs, and controlled by one government. *The nations of the world.*

**national** *adjective* belonging to a nation. *National dress.* **national anthem** a country's official hymn or song. **national park** an area of countryside under the care and ownership of a nation's government.

**nationalism** *noun* great pride in the culture, history, and success of your own country.

**nationalist** *noun* **1** a person who is very proud of their country. **2** a person who wants their country to be independent. *A Scottish nationalist.*

**nationality** *noun* belonging to a particular nation. *He is of Russian nationality.*

**nationalize** *verb* to place a privately owned company under state control. **nationalization** *noun.* The opposite of "nationalize" is "privatize."

**native** *noun* **1** one of the first inhabitants of a country. *Native American.* **2** a person who was born in a particular place. *She's a native of Canada.* **native** *adjective.*

Native American

**Native American** *noun* (often called American Indians) a member of one of the original tribes of people who lived in North America before the Europeans arrived.

**nativity** *noun* the birth of Jesus Christ.

**natural** *adjective* **1** relating to or concerned with nature. *Earthquakes are natural disasters.* **2** made by nature and not by humans. *The natural beauty of the mountains.* **3** ordinary and not surprising. *It's natural to laugh if you are amused and to cry if you are upset.*

**naturalist** *noun* somebody who studies wildlife. *A naturalist in the field.*

**nature** *noun* (say **nay**-chur) **1** everything in the world around us not made by people, such as plants, animals, oceans, and mountains. **2** characteristics that make up what a person or animal is like; personality. *He has a forgiving and kindly nature.*

**naughty** (naughtier, naughtiest) *adjective* badly behaved, mischievous. *The naughty girl pulled the dog's tail, even though she had been told not to.* **naughtiness** *noun.* **naughtily** *adverb.*

**nautical** *adjective* relating to ships, sailing, and the sea. *A nautical chart.*

**naval** *adjective* relating to the navy or ships of war. *A naval battle is one fought on or in the ocean.*

**navel** *noun* the small, round hollow or small button-shaped dome in your stomach where your umbilical cord was attached when you were born.

**navigate** *verb* to steer a ship or to pilot an aircraft in the right direction with the help of maps and special instruments. **navigation** *noun.*

**navigator** *noun* somebody who navigates or directs the movement of a ship or aircraft.

**navy** *noun* the warships and sailors that help defend a country on the ocean. **navy blue** *noun, adjective* very dark blue.

**N'Djamena** *noun* the capital of Chad in northern Africa.

**n.b.** *abbreviation* Latin words "nota bene," meaning "note well" or "take note."

**nearly** *adverb* almost, but not quite.

**necessary** *adjective* what must be done or is needed, essential, and important. *The climb is dangerous, so please take all necessary precautions.*

**nectar** *noun* sweet juice that bees collect from flowers to make honey.

**nectarine** *noun* a fruit similar to a peach, but with a smoother skin.

**needle** *noun* **1** a thin piece of steel with a sharp point at one end and a hole (or eye) at the other end for putting a thread through, used for sewing. **2** a long, thin, pointed stick made of plastic or steel that is used for knitting. **3** an instrument with a long, thin metal part used for giving injections. **4** a moving pointer on a meter. **5** the narrow, pointed leaf of a coniferous tree. *Pine needle.*

**needless** *adjective* unnecessary. *Needless worry is very destructive.* **needless to say** of course.

**needlework** *noun* sewing and embroidery.

**negative** *adjective* **1** meaning "no." "I will not come" and "I'll never go" are negative answers. **2** a number less than zero. The opposite of "negative" is "positive." **negative** *noun* **1** a photographic film showing dark areas as light and light areas as dark, used to make prints. **2** (in electricity) the opposite charge to positive.

**neglect** *verb* to fail to look after or give enough attention to. *The garden is overgrown because he neglected to weed it.* **neglect** *noun. The house fell into neglect.*

**negotiate** *verb* to discuss something in order to come to an understanding or agreement; to bargain. **negotiation** *noun. The dispute was settled by negotiation.*

**neigh** *noun* the sound that a horse makes. **neigh** *verb. The horse neighed loudly when she saw me coming.*

**neighbor** *noun* (say **nay**-bor) somebody who lives near or next door to you. **neighboring** *adjective* next to one another. *Italy and France are neighboring countries.*

**neighborhood** *noun* the area where you live.

**neighborly** *adjective* friendly and helpful, like a good neighbor.

**neither** *adjective, pronoun* not either; not one and not the other. *Neither answer is right.* **neither** *conjunction. I neither like him nor dislike him.*

**neon** *noun* a chemical gas. Neon is sometimes used in glass tubes to make them glow orange-red when electricity is passed through them (neon light).

**Nepal** *noun* a Himalayan country in southern Asia, north of India.

**nephew** *noun* the son of your brother or sister. *My nephew Tim.*

**nerve** *noun* **1** a long, thin fiber in your body that carries messages and feelings between your brain and body so that your body can feel and move. **2** calm bravery. *You need a lot of nerve to be a paraglider.*

**nervous** *adjective* **1** relating to the nerves. *The nervous system.* **2** timid and easily frightened. *A nervous horse.* **nervousness** *noun.*

nerve

**nest** *noun* a home built by birds, some insects, and some animals, in which to lay eggs and raise young. **nest** *verb. Swallows are nesting in the stable.*

**nestle** *verb* to curl up close together as if in a nest. *The cow and calf nestled together in the hay.*

**net** *noun* **1** a material made of knotted string or rope with a regular pattern of holes between the threads. **2** net material used, for example, as a fishing net, a tennis net, or a hairnet.

**Netherlands** *noun* (usually preceded by **the**) a country in northwest Europe, also called Holland.

Netherlands' flag

**nettle** *noun* (or stinging nettle) a wild plant with large, jagged leaves covered in hairs that sting you if you touch them.

**network** *noun* **1** a widespread organization. *The telecommunications network.* **2** an arrangement looking like a pattern of crisscrossing lines. *A network of underground tunnels.* **3** a system of linked computers that share a storage system.

**neuter** *adjective* (say **new**-ter) neither male nor female, with no sexual organs or with the sexual organs removed.

**neutral** *noun* **1** not taking sides or having strong feelings for or against a disagreement or a war, for example. *A neutral country.* **2** (of colors ) not strong. *Gray and beige are neutral colors.*

**neutron** *noun* one of the particles that make up the nucleus of an atom, but carry no electrical charge.

**New Delhi** *noun* the capital of India.

**news** *noun* information about events that have recently happened. *I heard about it on the news.*

**newt** *noun* an amphibian with short legs and a long tail that lives on land, but lays its eggs in water.

**New Zealand** *noun* a country in Australasia.

**next** *adjective* **1** the nearest. **2** the one immediately after. *I'll catch the next bus.* **next** *adverb. What happens next?*

**Niamey** *noun* the capital of Niger, in West Africa.

**nibble** *verb* to bite off small bits of a food.

**Nicaragua** *noun* a country in Central America.

**nickel** *noun* **1** a silver-colored metal that is mixed with other metals to make coins. **2** a five-cent coin in the US.

**nickname** *noun* a special name that people call you instead of your real name.



**Nicosia** *noun* the capital of Cyprus.

**niece** *noun* the daughter of your brother or sister.

**Niger** *noun* a country in West Africa.

**Nigeria** *noun* a country in West Africa.

**night** *noun* the time between sunset and sunrise, when it is dark. The opposite of "night" is "day."

**nightingale** *noun* a small brown bird whose beautiful singing is often heard at night.

nightingale

**nightly** *adjective, adverb* taking place at night or every night. *The news is broadcast nightly at 9 o'clock.*

**nightmare** *noun* **1** a terrifying dream. **2** a frightening experience or situation.

**nil** *noun* nothing; no score; 0; zero. *The team won the game by three goals to nil.*

**nimble** *adjective* able to move quickly and easily; active. *The nimble deer leapt over the fallen tree.*

**nip** (nip, nipping, nipped) *verb* **1** to give a small, sharp bite; to pinch. *The hamster nipped its owner when she made a sudden move.* **2** to move quickly and for a short time. *I'll just nip out and buy a newspaper.*

**nipple** *noun* the small, bulging, dark part that sticks out on each of a person's breasts and from which a baby sucks breast milk from its mother; a teat.

**nitrogen** *noun* a colorless, tasteless gas that makes up over three-quarters of the Earth's atmosphere and the air we breathe.

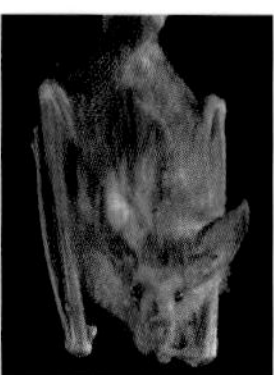

nocturnal

**noble** *adjective* **1** aristocratic, important, and of high social rank. *The Bourbons are a noble French family.* **2** honest and of a good and generous nature. **nobility** *noun*. **nobleman, noblewoman** *noun*.

**nobody** *pronoun* not one person. *There was nobody on the beach except us.* **nobody** *noun* an unimportant person.

**nocturnal** *adjective* concerned with or active during the night. *Bats are nocturnal animals that hunt at night.*

**nod** (nods, nodding, nodded) *verb* to move your head up and down, as a sign of agreement or to say "yes." **nod off** to half fall asleep by letting your head droop.

**noise** *noun* sound, usually one that is harsh, loud, and unwanted. *Cats make a disturbing yowling noise.* **noisily** *adverb*. The opposite of "noise" is "silence."

**noisy** (noisier, nosiest) *adjective* making a lot of unpleasant noise, full of noise. *Noisy streets.*

nomad

**nomad** *noun* a member of a group of people without a permanent home. Nomads often live in tents and wander from place to place with their herds, looking for pasture. **nomadic** *adjective*.

**nominate** *verb* to propose a candidate for election. To put forward somebody's name. *I nominate you three boys to cook the dinner tonight.* **nomination** *noun*.

**non-** *prefix* not, without. *Nonbreakable cups and plates are recommended for babies.*

**none** *pronoun* not one; not any. *You've eaten all the biscuits and there are none left!*

**nonfiction** *noun* books about real events rather than imaginary characters or situations.

**nonsense** *noun* **1** foolish words that are meaningless. *You're talking utter nonsense.* **2** silly behavior. *I'll stand no nonsense.* **nonsense verse** amusing poetry.

**nonstop** *adjective* going on without stopping. *A non-stop flight to San Francisco.*

**noon** *noun* midday; 12 o'clock in the middle of the day.

**nor** *conjunction* and not (used with neither). *I like neither spiders nor snakes.*

**north** *noun* If you face the direction of the Sun as it rises in the morning, north is on your left. The opposite of "north" is "south."

**North America** *noun* one of Earth's seven continents.

**North Korea** *noun* a country in East Asia, officially called the Democratic People's Republic of Korea.

**northern** *adjective* in or of the north.

**Northern Ireland** *noun* a country that is part of the United Kingdom.

**North Pole** *noun* the most northerly point on Earth. The north end of the Earth's axis, in the Arctic region.

**Norway** *noun* a Scandinavian country in northern Europe.

**nostalgia** *noun* a feeling of sadness and affection for the past and the happy times you had.

**nostril** *noun* one of the two holes at the end of your nose.

North Pole

**notable** *adjective* famous or important.

**notice** *noun* **1** a written message or announcement that is put in a public place so everybody can read it. **2** attention. *Don't take any notice of what he says.* **3** warning. *The water may be cut off without notice.* **notice** *verb* to see or hear. *She noticed the hole.*

**noticeable** *adjective* easily seen or noticed. *There's been a noticeable improvement in your handwriting.*

**notion** *noun* a general idea or vague belief or opinion. *I have a notion that he's gone to India.*

**notorious** *adjective* well known for being bad or unpleasant; infamous.

**Nouakchott** *noun* the capital of Mauritania in northwest Africa.

**novel** *adjective* new, different, and original. *A novel design.* **novel** *noun* a long written story about imaginary people and events.

**novelty** *noun* something new, unusual, and different.

**nuclear** *adjective* to do with the nucleus, especially that of an atom, and the power created by splitting it. *Nuclear energy, nuclear missile, nuclear reactor.*

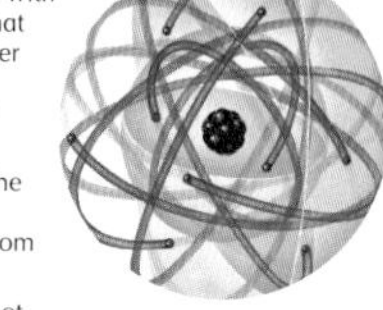

nucleus

**nucleus** (nuclei) *noun* the central part or core of something, such as an atom or a living cell.

**nude** *adjective* naked; not wearing clothes. **nude** *noun* a person not wearing clothes. **nudity** *noun.*

**nudge** *verb* to gently poke or push somebody with your elbow. *Nudge me if I fall asleep during the speech.*

**nugget** *noun* a rough lump of precious metal. *The goldminer found a nugget of gold in the stream.*

**nuisance** *noun* somebody or something that is annoying. *Our neighbor is such a nuisance.*

**numb** *adjective* unable to feel anything. *My fingers are numb with cold.*

**Nuku'alofa** *noun* the capital of Tonga in the South Pacific.

**number** *noun* **1** a word or numeral we use for counting, for example, one, two, three, or 1, 2, 3. **2** a quantity or amount. *She has a large number of CDs.* **number** *verb* **1** count. *The flock numbered 500.* **2** to put a number on. *I numbered the pages of my letter.*

**numeral** *noun* a symbol or group of symbols you use to write a number. 5, 10, and 12 are Arabic numerals and V, X, XII, and C are Roman numerals.

**numerate** *adjective* able to understand numbers and do calculations. **numeracy** *noun.*

**numerical** *adjective* concerning numbers. *Please put the library books back in numerical order.*

**numismatics** *plural noun* the study of coins and medals.

**nun** *noun* a member of a religious community of women who live, pray, and work together in a building called a convent or an abbey.

**nurse** *noun* a person who has been trained to look after ill, injured, or old people, especially in a hospital. **nurse** *verb. Ned nursed his dad when he was sick.*

**nursery** *noun* **1** a place where young children can go to play during the day while their parents are away. **2** a child's bedroom and playroom in a home. **3** a place where plants are grown to be sold.

**nutritious** *noun* nourishing and healthy food. *We try to serve three nutritious meals every day*

**nylon** *noun* a strong artificial fiber made of chemicals, used in making clothes, ropes, and brushes. *The ballet dancer wore pink nylon tights.*

Nn

**oaf** *noun* an insulting word for a stupid or awkward person, usually a man or boy.

**oak** *noun* a large deciduous tree with hard wood. The nut of an oak tree is called an acorn. *Mighty oaks grow from small acorns.*

**oar** *noun* a long pole with a flat part (the blade) at one end, used for rowing a boat.

**oasis** (oases) *noun* an area in a desert where there is water and where plants grow. *At last we arrived at the oasis, where we ate dates and drank water.*

**oath** *noun* a serious promise to tell the truth or be faithful. *I swore an oath on the Bible to tell the truth.*

**oatmeal** *noun* oats that have been ground and are used to make porridge.

**oats**

**oats** *plural noun* a type of cereal grain, used as food. *Porridge oats.*

**obedient** *adjective* obeying; willing to do what you are told to do. *The children were brought up to be obedient to their parents.*

**obese** *adjective* (say oh-**beece**) very fat. **obesity** *noun.*

**obey** *verb* to do what somebody asks or tells you to do. *A sheepdog is quick to obey the commands it is given.* **obedience** *noun.*

**obituary** *noun* an announcement of somebody's death, usually in a newspaper and giving a short account of the person's life and achievements.



**object** *noun* (say **ob**-ject) **1** a nonliving thing that you can see and touch. **2** a purpose. *The object of the meeting is to choose a new team.* **3** in grammar, the person or thing toward which the action of a verb is directed. "Flower" is the object in the sentence "John picked a flower." **object** *verb* (say ob-**ject**) to say that you dislike or disapprove of something. *He objected to being served burned toast.*

**objectionable** *adjective* unpleasant and likely to offend; disagreeable. *What an objectionable man!*

**objective** *noun* the aim or goal you are trying to achieve. *His objective was to win the dance competition.* **objective** *adjective* based on facts and not influenced by feelings, opinions, or prejudice. *She wrote an objective report on the causes of the strike at the factory.*

**obligation** *noun* something that you have to do; a duty. **obligatory** *adjective. Wearing a uniform is obligatory.*

**oblige** *verb* **1** to make somebody do something; to force or compel. *She was obliged to get off the bus because she did not have a ticket.* **2** to help or do a favor for somebody. *Please oblige me by closing the door quietly.*

**obliging** *adjective* willing to help others. *A very obliging young man gave me his seat.*

**oblique** *adjective* **1** sloping. **2** indirect. *The question seemed rather oblique to me.*

**obliterate** *verb* to destroy something completely. *We painted the wall to obliterate the graffiti.*

**oblong** *noun* a shape with two parallel long sides and two parallel short sides, like a brick.

**obnoxious** *adjective* very unpleasant or rude. *He is obnoxious when drunk.*

**oboe** *noun* a woodwind instrument.

**obscene** *adjective* (say ob-**seen**) indecent; foul; sexually offensive. *I will not tolerate obscene language.* **obscenity** *noun.*

**obscure** *adjective* **1** not well known. *An obscure book on astronomy.* **2** not easy to understand. *An obscure problem.* **3** not distinct; faint. **obscurity** *noun.* **obscure** *verb* conceal from sight. *The pillar obscured my view of the stage.*

**oboe**

**observatory**

**observatory** *noun* a building with large telescopes for observing the stars, planets, and the skies.

**observe** *verb* **1** to watch somebody or something carefully. **2** to see and notice something. **3** to obey something such as a law or custom. *Jews observe the festival of Hanukkah in December.* **4** to remark. *Tim observed that the mailman was late.* **observant** *adjective* quick at observing things. **observation** *noun.*

**obsolete** *adjective* out-of-date and no longer used. *Your computer is obsolete.*

**obstacle** *noun* something that blocks the way and makes it difficult for you to do something; a hindrance.

**obstinate** *adjective* refusing to obey or do what somebody wants; stubborn. *The obstinate child would not go to bed.* **obstinacy** *noun.*

**obtain** *verb* to get something by buying, taking, or being given it. **obtainable** *adjective. Tickets are obtainable in the foyer after 6.00 o'clock.*

**obtuse angle** *noun* an angle between 90 and 180 degrees. An obtuse angle is greater than a right angle.

**obverse** *noun* the side of a coin showing the head or principal design. The opposite of "obverse" (heads) is "reverse" (tails).

**obvious** *adjective* easy to see and understand; clear. *It's obvious to me that she has broken her finger by the way she is holding it.*

**occasion** *noun* a particular time when something happens. *Weddings and birthdays are important occasions that we all enjoy celebrating.*

**occasional** *adjective* happening sometimes but not regularly. *An occasional chocolate is nice!*

**occupation** *noun* 1 the work a person does for a living; a job. 2 a hobby or something you like doing in your spare time. 3 the invasion and taking control of a town or country by an army. *The German occupation of France during World War II.*

**occupy** (occupies, occupying, occupied) *verb* 1 to live in. *Who occupies the house next door?* 2 to keep busy. 3 to invade and capture an enemy town or country. **occupant, occupier** *noun.*

**occur** (occurs, occurring, occurred) *verb* to happen. *Thunderstorms occur mainly in summer.* **occur to** to suddenly think about something. **occurrence** *noun.*

**ocean** *noun* any of the great masses of salt water that surround the continents.

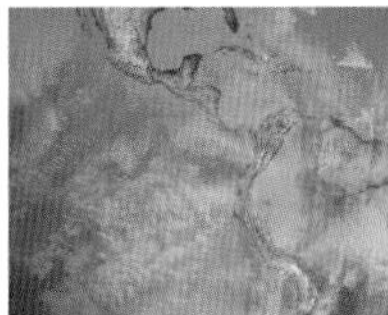
ocean

**o'clock** *adverb* "of the clock," an expression we use when telling the time. *Six o'clock.*

**octagon** *noun* a flat shape with eight sides. **octagonal** *adjective. The octagonal room in the tower.*

**octave** *noun* in music, the eight notes of any scale.

octopus

**October** *noun* the tenth month of the year. October has 31 days.

**octopus** (octopuses) *noun* a sea creature with a round body and eight tentacles.

**odd** *adjective* 1 strange; not ordinary. 2 of numbers, not even and not divisible by two; three, five, and 37 are odd numbers. 3 one of a pair and not matching. *An odd sock.* 4 different; various. *Odd jobs.* 5 **odds** chances or probability of something happening (especially in gambling). **odd one out** the one that is different from the others.

**ode** *noun* a poem, often addressed to somebody or to something. *Ode to a Nightingale, by John Keats.*

**odious** *adjective* very unpleasant.

**odor** *noun* a strong smell, often an unpleasant one.

**odorless** *adjective* without smell.

**offend** *verb* 1 to upset a person's feelings. 2 to do wrong or commit a crime. **offense** *noun. Trespassing is an offense.* **offensive** *adjective. Offensive behavior.*

**offhand** *adjective* 1 unthinking and casual; rude. *An offhand manner.* 2 impromptu and without preparation. *I can't tell you the answer offhand but I'll look it up.*

**offer** *verb* 1 to say that you are willing to do something. 2 to ask somebody if they would like something; to hold out or give. *She offered him a glass of juice.* 3 to say how much money you are willing to give for something. *Harry offered her $100 for the clock.* **offer** *noun.*

**office** *noun* 1 a place where people work and where business is conducted. Offices usually contain desks, telephones, and computers. 2 an important position. *The office of mayor.*

**officer** *noun* a senior person in the armed forces or police who is in charge of other people. *The officer ordered his men to advance.*

**official** *adjective* coming from or done by people in authority. *An official inquiry.* **official** *noun* a person with a position of authority. *Government officials.*

**offspring** *noun* the children or young of humans and animals. *Jack's offspring all have red hair.*

**often** *adverb* frequently; again and again. *We often go swimming in the evening.*

**ogre** *noun* a frightening, cruel giant in fairy tales.

**oil** *noun* Oils are different kinds of smooth, thick liquids that do not mix with water and which burn easily. You can use oil as a fuel for heating and cooking, and for making machines run smoothly. **oil** *verb.*

Oo

**ointment** *noun* a cream that you put on your skin to heal cuts and scratches.

**old** *adjective* 1 having lived, existed, or lasted for a long time. 2 having lived for a certain amount of time. *Owen is 11 years old.* 3 belonging to an earlier time. *My old geography teacher.* 4 worn out and no longer new. *Old clothes.* The opposite of "old" is "new."

**old-fashioned** *adjective* out-of-date, belonging to the past.

**olive** *noun* a small black or green oval fruit that can be crushed to produce olive oil, used in cooking. Olive trees grow in Mediterranean countries.

**Olympic Games** *plural noun* international competitions in sports held in a different country every four years. *The 2004 Olympic Games were held in Greece, where the Games originated.*

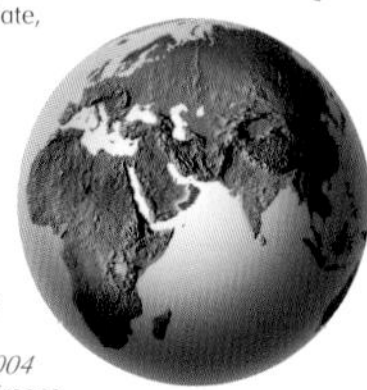
Oman

**Oman** *noun* a country in Southwest Asia bordering the Arabian Sea.

**omelet** *noun* a food made by beating eggs together and frying them into a flat, round shape. Omelets are often served with a savory filling.

**omen** *noun* a sign of good or evil in the future.

**ominous** *adjective* suggesting that something bad is about to happen; threatening. *Those dark clouds look ominous to me.*

**omit** (omits, omitting, omitted) *verb* **1** to leave something out. *Your name has been omitted from the list.* **2** to fail to do something. *She omitted some important details.* **omission** *noun.*

**omnivore** *noun* an animal that eats both plants and meat. **omnivorous** *adjective.*

**once** *adverb* **1** at one time in the past. **2** happening one time only. *She comes here once a day.* **once** *conjunction* when. *Once you understand it, you'll never forget it.*

**onion** *noun* a strong-tasting, round bulb eaten as a cooked vegetable or raw in salads.

**on-line** *adjective, adverb* a service with a direct connection to and interaction with a computer. *On-line shopping is popular in many homes.*

**onlooker** *noun* somebody who watches something happen without taking part; a spectator. *The onlookers cheered as the procession passed by.*

**only** *adverb* **1** no more than. *It'll only take me a minute to get ready.* **2** just. *She wants to play only for an hour.* **only** *adjective* no others of the same kind. *This is the only watch I have.* **only** *conjunction* but. *I'd love to come, only I can't.* **only child** a child with no brothers or sisters.

**ooze** *verb* to flow slowly through a narrow opening. *Mud oozed under the door.*

**opaque** *adjective* If something is opaque, you cannot see through it and it does not let light through.

**open** *adjective* **1** not shut so people or things can go through; not covered. **2** ready for business. *The store is open.* **3** honest. *She was very open about her doubts.* **open** *verb* **1** to make open or no longer shut; to become open and no longer shut. *Omar opened the door and let in the cat.* **2** to begin. *The movie opens in Spain.*

**opening** *noun* **1** a space. *The rabbit squeezed through an opening in the fence.* **2** the beginning of something. *The official opening of the library is next week.* **3** an opportunity. *An opening into the music business would be a dream come true.*

**opera**

**opera** *noun* a play with music to which all or most of the words are sung. **operatic** *adjective.*

**operate** *verb* **1** to make something work. *Can you operate this machine?* **2** to cut open a part of somebody's body to heal a disease or repair an injury. *The surgeon had to operate on Dick's broken leg.* **operation** *noun.*

**opinion** *noun* what you think or believe about something. *What is your opinion of the Arkansas team?*

**opossum**

**opinionated** *adjective* stubbornly believing that your opinions are right.

**opossum** *noun* a small, tree-dwelling American marsupial that can hang from trees by its tail.

**opponent** *noun* somebody who is against you in a contest or fight. *Sam outwitted his opponent.*

**opportunity** *noun* a good time to do something. *Take the opportunity to speak French while you are in France.*

**oppose** *verb* to be against and to try to prevent something. *The town opposed the building of a main road nearby.* **opposition** *noun.*

**opposite** *noun* something that is completely different in every way from another thing. "Happy" is the opposite of "sad." **opposite** *adjective* **1** different. *They drove in opposite directions.* **2** facing; on the other side. *They stood on opposite sides of the street.*

**oppress** *verb* to govern or treat people harshly and unjustly. **oppression** *noun. The country suffered years of oppression under its dictator.* **oppressor** *noun.*

**opt** *verb* to choose. *We opted to go skiing.* **option** *noun. I have two options: to go or to stay.* **opt out** to decide not to take part.

**optical** *adjective* relating to the eyes and eyesight. *An optical illusion.*

**optician** *noun* a person who sells spectacles and who is trained to test people's eyesight and prescribe glasses.

**optimism** *noun* the belief that only the best will happen and all will end successfully. **optimist** *noun. She is always a cheerful optimist in difficult situations.* **optimistic** *adjective.* The opposite of "optimistic" is "pessimistic."

**optional** *adjective* not compulsory; that you can choose or not choose.

**oral** *adjective* relating to the mouth. *Oral hygiene.* **2** spoken, not written. *An oral test.*

**orange** *noun* **1** a round, juicy fruit with a red-yellow skin (peel). **2** the color of this fruit. **orange** *adjective.*

**orangutang** *noun* a large Indonesian ape with shaggy red fur and long arms.

**orator** *noun* a skilled public speaker.

**orbit** *noun* a path followed by an object such as a spacecraft or planet as it moves around a planet or star. **orbit** *verb. The Moon orbits the Earth and the planets orbit the Sun.*

**orchard** *noun* a piece of land on which a lot of fruit trees are grown.

**orchestra** *noun* (say **or**-kess-trah) a large group of people who perform music together, playing different instruments. **orchestral** *adjective.*

**orchid** *noun* (say **or**-kid) one of many varieties of plant that usually has brightly colored, strangely shaped flowers, with one petal larger than the others.

**ordeal** *noun* a difficult, unpleasant, or dangerous experience. *Rescuing the missing sheep was an ordeal.*

**order** *noun* **1** a command given by somebody in control telling people what to do. *The officer gave his order.* **2** a sequence or a way things are arranged. *Alphabetical order.* **3** neatly arranged; tidy. *He put his papers in order.* **order** *verb* **1** to tell somebody firmly to do something. **2** (in a restaurant) to ask for something to be brought to you; to ask for something to be obtained. *We ordered apple pie and ice cream.* **out of order** not working; broken.

organ

**ordinary** *adjective* not special or interesting; usual. *He's an ordinary kind of guy.*

**ore** *noun* rock or earth containing metal that can be extracted.

**organ** *noun* **1** a musical instrument with a keyboard and pipes of different lengths, through which air is pumped to produce sounds. *Rousing chords from the organ.* **2** a part inside the body that does a particular job. The heart, kidneys, liver, and lungs are organs.

**organic** *adjective* grown without using chemicals or pesticides. *Organic food is healthy and delicious.*

**organism** *noun* any living animal or plant.

**organization** *noun* **1** a group of people working together as a club or in business. **2** the act of organizing something so it runs smoothly. *The organization of the conference took a lot of time.*

**organize** *verb* **1** to plan and prepare something in an orderly way. *Wendy organized a party for her brother's birthday.* **2** to put things in order. **organizer** *noun.*

**oriental** *adjective* relating to the countries of eastern and southern Asia, such as China, Japan, and India.

**origami** *noun* the Japanese art of folding paper into beautiful shapes.

**origin** *noun* **1** the start or source of something and why it began. *What is the origin of Halloween?* **2** ancestry or where somebody or something came from. *She's of Jamaican origin.*

**original** *adjective* **1** the first of its kind to exist or to be made. *The original palace was burned down.* **2** not an imitation. *Original paintings.* **3** different and imaginative. *An original design.*

**originate** *verb* to start to exist; to have origins. *Baseball originated in the US.*

**ornament** *noun* a small, pretty object that you wear, put on a shelf or table, or hang up at festival times as a decoration. *Ornaments for a Christmas tree.* **ornamental** *adjective. Ornamental gardens.*

**ornithology** *noun* the scientific study of birds. **ornithologist** *noun.*

**orphan** *noun* a child whose parents are both dead. *They were orphans of World War II.*



**orthodontist** *noun* a dentist who specializes in straightening and adjusting irregular or crooked teeth.

**orthodox** *adjective* what is accepted and generally thought to be right by most people; believing in traditional ideas. *She has very orthodox views.* **orthodoxy** *noun.*

**oscillate** *noun* to swing backward and forward like a pendulum. **oscillation** *noun.*

**Oslo** *noun* the capital of Norway, a Scandinavian country.

**ostrich** *noun* a very large bird with long legs and a long neck. Ostriches can run very fast but cannot fly. They come from Africa.

ostrich

**other** *adjective* 1 different; not the same as. *The other way is shorter.* 2 opposite. *On the other side of the road.* **other** (others) *pronoun* the rest; more. *Jim's here, but the others haven't arrived yet.*

**ought** *verb* must; should.

**Ottawa** *noun* the capital of Canada.

outback

**otter** *noun* a small animal with a long body and brown fur that lives near rivers and eats fish. Otters have webbed feet to help them swim.

**Ouagadougou** *noun* the capital of Burkina Faso in West Africa.

**ounce** *noun* a measure of weight equal to 28.3 grams. There are 16 ounces in a pound.

**out-** *prefix* 1 surpassing; more. *Outclassed.* 2 external; outside. *Outhouse.* 3 longer; beyond. *Outlive.*

**outback** *noun* the large, unpopulated inland areas of Australia.

**outbreak** *noun* a sudden appearance or start of something. *An outbreak of flu.*

**outcome** *noun* the result. *What's the outcome of the singing competition?*

**outdoor** *adjective* in the open air. **outdoors** *adverb, noun. In the summer, we eat outdoors.* The opposite of "outdoors" is "indoors."

**outer space** *noun* everything beyond the Earth's atmosphere; the universe.

outer space

**outfit** *noun* a set of clothes, especially for a particular occasion. *Aunt Masie wanted a new outfit for the wedding.*

**outgrow** (outgrows, outgrowing, outgrew, outgrown) *verb* to grow too large or too old for something. *He has outgrown his shoes already.*

**outing** *noun* a day-trip or short journey somewhere for pleasure. *We went on an outing to the country.*

**outlaw** *noun* a criminal who has not been caught and is hiding. **outlaw** *verb* to make something illegal.

**outline** *noun* 1 a line around the edge of something that shows its shape. 2 the main points rather than a detailed description of something. *An outline of the play's plot.* **outline** *verb. She outlined her plans.*

**outlook** *noun* 1 a view. *A room with a fine outlook.* 2 a person's general attitude or way of looking at things. *Cathy has a cheerful outlook on life.* 3 what is likely to happen with the weather. *The outlook is fine.*

**output** *noun* 1 the amount of something produced in a factory or by a person. 2 data produced by a computer.

**outrage** *noun* a feeling of anger about a shocking or violent act. **outrageous** *adjective* shocking. *Some people wore outrageous costumes for the carnival.*

**outright** *adjective* complete; absolute; direct. *She's the outright winner.* **outright** *adverb* instantly. *I told him the bad news outright.*

**outset** *noun* the beginning. *I knew from the outset that Sue would win the competition.*

**outside** *noun* the exterior or outer part of something; the surface of something farthest from the middle. *Take the peel off the outside of the orange.* **outside** *adjective, adverb, preposition. The outside lane of the highway.* The opposite of "outside" is "inside."

**outskirts** *plural noun* the parts around the outer edges of a town.

**outspoken** *adjective* saying clearly and strongly what you think, even if you offend people. *An outspoken critic of the system.*

**outstanding** *adjective* 1 excellent. *An outstanding performance.* 2 not paid. *An outstanding bill.*

**outwit** (outwits, outwitting, outwitted) *verb* to be too clever for somebody. *The deer outwitted the hunters and made its escape into the woods.*

**oval** *noun* any object with an egg-shaped outline. **oval** *adjective. Oval earrings.*

**oven** *noun* a metal box in which you roast or bake food. *Your supper is in the oven.*

**over** *preposition* 1 above; higher. *She hung the picture over her bed.* 2 across. *The dog jumped over the stream.* 3 more than. *She has over a dozen pairs of shoes.* 4 on top of. *He laid blankets over the bed.* **over** *adverb* 1 ended. *The ordeal is over.* 2 down from being upright. *I fell over.* 3 upside down. *Flip the pancake over.* 4 not used; remaining. *Any cake left over?* **over and over again** many times.

**over-** *prefix* 1 excessive. *Overconfident.* 2 above; in a higher position. *Overlord.* 3 movement or position above. *Overhang.* 4 extra. *Overcoat.*

**overalls** *plural noun* a one-piece garment that you wear over your ordinary clothes to keep them clean when doing a messy job.

overboard

**overboard** *adverb* over a boat's side and into the water. *The containers fell overboard.* **go overboard** to become too enthusiastic about something.

**overcast** *adjective* (of the sky) cloudy and dark. *The sky was overcast and it looked like rain.*

**overcome** (overcomes, overcoming, overcame, overcome) *verb* **1** to conquer or defeat; to get the better of. *She has overcome her fear of flying.* **2** to be affected by very strong emotions. *He was overcome with joy when he heard the news.*

**overdue** *adjective* behind time; late. *I'm afraid your library book is overdue and you'll have to pay a fine.*

**overflow** *verb* to spill or run over the edges of a container. *The river overflowed its banks and flooded the meadows for miles around.*

**overhaul** *verb* to examine something carefully to see if it needs repairing. **overhaul** *noun. She gave her bike a thorough overhaul before going for a ride.*

**overhead** *adjective, adverb* above you. *The lights overhead cast long shadows in front of us.*

**overheads** *plural noun* all the regular costs involved in running a business, such as lighting, heating, insurance, and advertising.

**overhear** (overhears, overhearing, overheard) *verb* to hear accidentally what people are saying when they do not know you are listening.

**overlap** (overlaps, overlapping, overlapped) *verb* to partly cover or lie across something else. *Roof tiles overlap.*

**overlook** *verb* **1** to fail to see or do something; not to notice. *You have overlooked how much it will cost!* **2** to forgive and not punish somebody. *I'll overlook your mistake.* **3** to have a view above something. *Your rooms are at the front of the hotel and overlook the sea.*

**overrated** *adjective* not as good as most people say. *An overrated movie.*

**overrun** (overruns, overrunning, overran) *verb* **1** to spread over; to swarm. **2** to go beyond the time allowed. *The TV program overran by ten minutes.*

**overseas** *adjective, adverb* abroad; across the sea. *Overseas students are welcome at the college.*

**overtake** (overtakes, overtaking, overtook, overtaken) *verb* **1** to come upon suddenly. **2** to catch up with and pass while moving or undertaking a task.

**overthrow** (overthrows, overthrowing, overthrew, overthrown) *verb* to defeat or cause something to fall. *The French Revolution overthrew the monarchy.* **overthrow** *noun.*

**overtime** *noun* extra time spent working outside normal working hours. *If you'll work overtime, I'll pay you double your usual salary.*

**overture** *noun* a short piece of music introducing a ballet, opera, or musical that sets the mood.

**overturn** *verb* **1** to fall over or cause something to fall over so that it is turned upside down. **2** to reverse or invalidate. *The decision to ban skateboarding in the park has been overturned.*

**overwhelm** *verb* **1** to defeat completely; to crush. **2** to cover completely. *The waves overwhelmed the boat and the crew had to abandon the ship.* **3** to put too great a load on. *Paul was overwhelmed with work.*

**owe** *verb* to have to pay or give something to somebody, especially money that you have borrowed. *I owe you $6 for the tickets.*

owl

**owl** *noun* a bird of prey with a flat face and large eyes that hunts for small animals, such as mice, at night. *A wise old owl.*

**own** *verb* to have something that belongs to you; to possess. *Who owns this skateboard?* **own** *adjective* belonging only to you. *Mary has her own computer.* **owner** *noun.* **on your own** by yourself and without help. *He cooked the meal all on his own.*



**ox** (oxen) *noun* a bull that is used in some countries to pull carts and plows.

**oxygen** *noun* a colorless, tasteless gas that makes up about a fifth of the Earth's atmosphere. All life on Earth needs oxygen to live. *Astronauts need to take a supply of oxygen with them into outer space.*

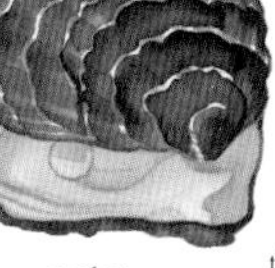
oyster

**oyster** *noun* an edible sea creature that lives inside two shells (a bivalve). Some oysters produce a pearl inside their shell. *David loves to eat oysters.*

**ozone** *noun* a gas that is a form of oxygen with three atoms instead of two. **ozone-friendly** *adjective* not harmful to the layer of ozone around the Earth. *An ozone-friendly spray can.* **ozone layer** *noun* a layer or belt of ozone high in the atmosphere that protects the Earth by absorbing harmful rays from the Sun. *The ozone layer is becoming thinner; as a result, many more people who don't wear protective cream in the sun are contracting skin cancer.*

**pace** *noun* **1** walking or running speed, or the speed at which something happens. *Work at your own pace.* **2** a single step when walking or running. *She took three paces forward.* **keep pace with** to go forward at the same rate. *He kept pace with the latest developments.* **pace** *verb* **1** to walk with regular steps. **2** to set the speed, especially for a runner in a race.

**pacemaker** *noun* **1** a person who sets the speed in a race that others try to keep up with. **2** a machine that is used to correct an irregular heartbeat.

**pacifist** *noun* someone who refuses to fight in a war because they believe war is wrong.

**pacify** (pacifies, pacifying, pacified) *verb* to make calm.

**pact** *noun* an agreement. *The two countries signed a trading pact.*

**pad** *noun* **1** anything filled with soft material used to protect, clean, or stuff something. *Skaters wear knee pads.* **2** a number of sheets of paper fixed together at the top or the side so that they can be torn out. *A writing pad.* **3** the place where a helicopter or rocket takes off. **4** the soft part of an animal's paw. **5** a room or an apartment. *We went back to his pad to watch TV.* **pad** (pads, padding, padded) *verb* **1** to add something extra. **2** to walk softly.

**paddle** *noun* a short pole with a flat blade on one or both ends for moving a small boat in water. **paddle** *verb* **1** to move a boat through water. *They paddled their canoes upriver.* **2** to walk barefoot in shallow water.

**Pp**

**paddock** *noun* a field near a house or stables where horses are kept.

**paddy field** *noun* a field where rice is grown.

**padlock** *noun* a lock that can be put on and taken off, for use on a door, box, or locker. **padlock** *verb. He padlocked the shed.*

**pagan** (say **pay**-gun) *adjective, noun* not believing in the main religions of the world.

**page** *noun* **1** a piece of paper in a book, newspaper, or magazine. **2** a servant in uniform, usually a boy, who works in a hotel, for example, carrying bags. **3** a boy who attends a bride at a wedding. **page** *verb* to call the name of someone over a public address system, as in a hotel or hospital, or to bleep them on their personal pager.

**pageant** *noun* **1** a show, usually outdoors, about the history of a place and its people. **2** a ceremony with a procession of people in costume. **pageantry** *noun.*

**pager** *noun* a small radio device with a bleeper that you can carry around, and that alerts you if someone calls or gives you a message.

pagoda

**pagoda** *noun* a temple, especially Buddhist or Hindu, shaped like a tower with many tiers.

**pail** *noun* a bucket. *A pail of milk.*

**pain** *noun* **1** an unpleasant feeling of hurt when you are injured or ill. **2** a feeling of unhappiness when something upsetting happens. **pain** *verb. It pains me to see you unhappy.* **take pains** to make an effort. *She takes great pains with her homework.* **a pain in the neck** an annoying person. **painful** *adjective.* **painless** *adjective* not causing pain. *The operation was painless.*

**painkiller** *noun* medicine that lessens or stops pain.

**painstaking** *noun* careful and thorough. *A painstaking investigation.*

**paint** *noun* a colored liquid or other substance that can be put on a surface. **paint** *verb* **1** to put paint on something. *He painted the chair red.* **2** to make a picture with paint. **paints** a set of tubes or cakes of paint, usually in a box, for painting pictures.

**painter** *noun* **1** a person whose job is painting and decorating houses or rooms. **2** a person who paints artistic pictures. *The portrait painter painted a good likeness of her.*

**painting** *noun* a painted picture.

paint

**pair** *noun* **1** two things, usually used together. *A pair of shoes.* **2** two people. **3** an object made up of two parts. *A pair of scissors.* **pair** *verb* to form a pair. *I've paired a blue sweater with red shoes.*

**pajamas** *plural noun* a loose top and trousers worn in bed for sleeping in.

**Pakistan** *noun* a country in southern Asia.

**palace** *noun* a large house that is the home of a king or queen or other important person. **palatial** *adjective.*

**palate** *noun* **1** the inside top, or roof, of the mouth. **2** a person's sense of taste.

**pale** *adjective* **1** having little color; you look pale when your face is almost white or lighter than usual. *She turned pale when she heard the bad news.* **2** light; not bright in color. *In the pale light of dawn.*

**palette** *noun* a board on which an artist mixes colors. It is held in one hand, and has a hole for the thumb.

**Palikir** *noun* the capital of Micronesia in the Pacific.

**palindrome** *noun* a word or phrase that reads the same backward or forward. "Deed" is a palindrome.

**palisade** *noun* a fence made of pointed iron or wooden poles, sometimes used to defend wooden forts.

**pallid** *adjective* unhealthily pale.

**palm** *noun* **1** the inner part of the hand between the fingers and the wrist. **2** a tree with large leaves at the top and no branches. Palms grows in hot countries. *Swaying coconut palms.* **palm** *verb* to steal something by picking it up and hiding it in your palm. **palm off** to trick someone into buying or taking something.

**Palm Sunday** *noun* the Sunday before Easter in the Christian religion.

**pampas** *noun* treeless grassy plains in South America. *They herded the cattle on the pampas.*

**pamper** *verb* to overindulge or spoil a person with luxury. *She was pampered with candy and champagne on their wedding anniversary.*

**Panama's flag**

**pamphlet** *noun* a small booklet that gives information about something.

**pan** *noun* **1** a metal container with a handle, used for cooking. **2** a toilet bowl.

**Panama** *noun* a country in Central America.

**Panama City** *noun* the capital of Panama.

**pancake** *noun* a thin, flat cake made of flour, eggs, and milk (a mixture called batter), and fried on both sides.

**pancreas** *noun* a gland near the stomach that produces chemicals to help digestion.

**panda** *noun* **1** (also called a **giant panda**) a large, bear-like animal with black-and-white fur that lives in Chinese bamboo forests. **2** a red panda, a raccoon-like animal from the Himalayas.

**pane** *noun* a piece of glass in a window.

**panel** *noun* **1** a flat piece of wood or other material that is part of a door or larger object. **2** a group of people chosen to discuss or decide something. *An advisory panel.* **3** a piece of material different in color or fabric that is sewn into a dress. **paneled** *adjective. Pamela sat and sewed in a small, paneled room.* **paneling** *noun.*

**pang** *noun* a sudden strong feeling. *She felt a pang of sadness when she left college for the last time.*

**panic** *noun* a sudden, uncontrollable fear. *She got into a panic when she lost her purse.* **panic** (panics, panicking, panicked) *verb* to become suddenly afraid and to do things without thinking carefully or fail to do things that you should. *She panicked when she saw the tree blow down in the storm and couldn't move.*

**panic-stricken** *adjective* afraid and filled with terror.

**panorama** *noun* a complete view of a wide area. *A panorama of hills and lakes spread below.*

**pansy** (pansies) *noun* a small garden flower related to the violet.

**pansy**

**pant** *verb* to breathe quickly with the mouth open, usually after running or when hot. *The dog panted.*

**panther** *noun* a large wild animal of the cat family.

**panties** *noun* underwear worn by girls.

**pantomime** *noun* the art of expressing emotions through physical movement rather than through speech; mime. *The pantomime artist drew a big crowd.*

**pantry** (pantries) *noun* a small room near the kitchen where food is kept.

**pants** *plural noun* a piece of clothing, like jeans, with separate sections covering each leg, and joined at the top.

**papacy** (say **pay**-puh-see) *noun* the power or authority of the Pope or the position of Pope.

**papal** (say **pay**-pul) *adjective* to do with the Pope.

**paparazzi** *plural noun* photographers who pursue famous people to take pictures of them.

**paper** *noun* **1** material made in thin sheets from wood or cloth, used for writing, printing, or drawing on, or for wrapping and covering things. **2** a newspaper. **3** part of a written examination with questions that have to be answered. **paper** *verb* to put wallpaper on a wall. *We want to paper the living room.* **papers** documents showing who or what a person or thing is.

**Pp**

**paperback** *noun* a book with a soft cover.

**papoose** *noun* a bag on a frame, used for carrying a baby on a person's back.

**Papua New Guinea** *noun* a country in Australasia, forming part of the island of New Guinea.

**Papua New Guinea**

**par** *noun* **1** an average or normal amount, degree, or condition. *Her cold made her feel below par.* When something is on a par with something else, both are equally good or equally bad. **2** in golf, the number of strokes a first-class player should take for a hole or course.

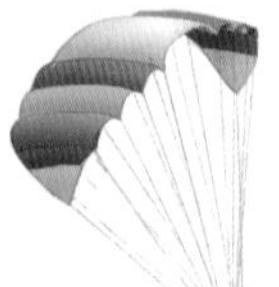

parachute

**parable** *noun* a simple story with a moral point. *He read a parable from the Bible.*

**parachute** *noun* a large piece of fabric attached to a person or thing by long ropes to make them fall slowly when dropped from a plane. **parachutist** *noun.*

**parade** *noun* **1** a procession or gathering of people or things for the purpose of being looked at or to celebrate a special event. *A fashion parade.* **2** soldiers marching together for an inspection or ceremony. **3** a public square, or a row of shops. **parade** *verb*

**paradise** *noun* **1** heaven; a place of perfect happiness. **2** in the Bible, Garden of Eden, home of Adam and Eve.

**paradox** (paradoxes) *noun* **1** a statement that seems wrong or impossible, but has some truth in it. **2** two facts or ideas that are opposite to what is generally believed to be true. **paradoxical** *adjective.*

**paraffin** *noun* a kind of oil used for heating or lighting. *The sailor hung a paraffin lamp on deck.*

**paragliding** *noun* a sport involving cross-country gliding using a parachute shaped like wings.

**paragraph** *noun* a section of a piece of writing consisting of a number of sentences on a subject. A paragraph starts on a new line.

**Paraguay** *noun* a country in central South America.

**parallel** *adjective* lines that run alongside and are the same distance from each other. *The road runs parallel to the railroad.* **parallel** *noun* **1** a line parallel to another. **2** something similar to something else, or a comparison that shows likeness. *She is unique and without parallel.*



**parallelogram** *noun* a four-sided figure with opposite sides parallel.

**paralyze** *verb* **1** to make some or all of the body's muscles unfeeling and unable to move. *A stroke paralyzed his left arm.* **2** to make somebody or something unable to act, move, or work properly. *Paralyzed with fear, she was unable to run away.* **paralysis** *noun.*

**Paramaribo** *noun* the capital of Suriname in northeastern South America.

**parapet** *noun* a low wall at the edge of a bridge or roof.

**paraplegic** *noun* (say par-uh-**plee**-jick) a person whose lower body and both legs are paralyzed. **paraplegia** *noun.*

**parasite** *noun* a plant or animal that lives on or in another and gets food from it. **parasitic** *adjective.*

**parcel** *noun* something wrapped up that can be sent by mail or carried. **parcel** (parcels, parceling, parceled) *verb.* **parcel up** to make into a parcel.

**parchment** *noun* a kind of thick, yellowish paper. In ancient times, parchment was made from the skin of sheep or goats and used for writing on.

**pardon** *noun* forgiveness. *I beg your pardon.* **pardon** *verb* to forgive. **pardonable** *adjective.*

**parenthesis** (parentheses) *noun* (say puh-**ren**-thi-sis) **1** a sentence, or a phrase inserted in a sentence, usually marked off with curved lines: ( ).

**Paris** *noun* the capital of France in southwest Europe.

**parish** (parishes) *noun* In England, an official area such as a village or part of a town.

**Parliament** *noun* an institution made up of a group of people who are elected and make a country's laws. **parliamentary** *adjective.*

parrot

**parody** (parodies) *noun* a piece of writing or music that makes fun of somebody else's style by copying it.

**parrot** *noun* a tropical bird with bright feathers and a hooked beak. Parrots can imitate noises and the human voice. **parrot-style** *adjective* mechanical, without understanding. *The little girl learned her times tables parrot-style, walking round the table.*

**parsley** *noun* a plant with green leaves, used to flavor food.

**parson** *noun* a member of the clergy; a vicar.

**partial** *adjective* **1** not complete. *A partial success.* **2** supporting one person or side more than another, especially in a way that is unfair. **3** liking something very much. *I'm very partial to chocolate.* **partiality** *noun.*

**participate** *verb* to take part in something or have a share in an event. *The audience are asked to participate in the show.* **participation** *noun.*

**particle** *noun* a very small piece or amount. *The scientist was studying subatomic particles.*

**particular** *adjective* **1** relating to one and not any other. *This particular car is faster than the others.* **2** special. *She takes particular care to please her parents.* **3** difficult to please. *She is particular about her food.* **particularly** *adverb.* **particular** *noun* a detail. *He is right in every particular.* **in particular** especially.

**partition** *noun* **1** a thin wall that divides a room. **2** division into two or more parts. **partition** *verb* to divide into two or more parts.

**partner** *noun* one of two people who do things together or share the same activity. *My tennis partner and I have won all the matches we have played together this season.* **partner** *verb.* **partnership** *noun.*

**party** (parties) *noun* **1** a gathering of people who come together to enjoy themselves. *We gave a birthday party for my sister.* **2** a political organization. *The Communist Party.* **3** a group of people who work or travel together. *A party of tourists.* **4** a person who is taking part in a lawsuit. *The guilty party has to pay the costs.* **be party to** be responsible for something. *I was party to the decision.* **party** *verb* to go to parties.

**passion** *noun* a strong attraction or feeling about somebody or something. *She has developed a passion for painting.* **passionate** *adjective.*

**passive** *adjective* **1** not active; showing no feeling or interest in what is said or done to you. **2** in grammar, a form of a verb that describes what is done or will be done to somebody or something. "The car was driven by me" is passive. "I drove the car" is active. **passive** *noun.*

passport

**Passover** *noun* a Jewish festival in memory of the freeing of the Jews from Egypt in the time of Moses.

**passport** *noun* an official document proving you are a citizen of your country, and which allows you to enter other countries.

**password** *noun* a secret word or phrase that you have to know in order to enter a guarded place or to gain access to something such as secure computer files.

**past** *adjective* referring to the time before now. *During the past few hours.* The verbs "went," "called" and "wrote" are in the past tense. **past** *adverb, preposition* **1** up to and beyond a point. *The bus drove past.* **2** after. *It's ten past four.* **past** *noun* the time before the present. **be past it** be no longer active, because you are too old.

**pasta** *noun* an Italian food made of a mixture of flour, eggs, and water. Spaghetti, macaroni, and noodles are all forms of pasta. *Pasta with parmesan cheese.*

**pastel** *noun* **1** a colored crayon. **2** a picture drawn with colored crayons. *He loves working in pastels.* **3** a light or subdued shade of a color such as pale pink.

**pasteurize** *verb* to remove bacteria from milk by heating and then cooling it.

**pastry** (pastries) *noun* a mixture of flour, fat, and water rolled out and baked in an oven.

**pasture** *noun* land covered with grass, suitable for grazing animals such as cattle or sheep. *Lush pasture.*

**patent** *noun* the official right given to an inventor to make or sell their invention and stop others from copying it. **patent** *verb* to get a patent for an invention. **patent** *adjective* **1** protected by a patent. **2** obvious. *It was a patent lie.* **patent leather** leather that has a shiny surface.

**paternal** *adjective* like or relating to a father.

**pathetic** *adjective* sad, weak, or helpless. *What a pathetic joke!* **pathetically** *adverb.*

**patient** *adjective* able to wait calmly without getting annoyed. **patient** *noun* a person who receives medical treatment from a doctor or hospital. **patience** *noun.*

**patriot** *noun* a person who loves and supports his or her country. **patriotic** *adjective.* **patriotism** *noun.*

**patrol** *noun* **1** the time of patrolling. *A soldier on patrol.* **2** a person, group of soldiers, or vehicles patrolling an area. **patrol** (patrols, patrolling, patrolled) *verb* to go at regular times over an area or a building to make sure that there is no trouble. *Soldiers patrolled the border.*

**patron** (say **pay**-trun) **1** somebody important who gives money to or takes an interest in a person, such as an artist. **2** a person who buys things in a store regularly. **patron saint** the protecting saint of a person or place. *Saint Christopher is the patron saint of travelers.*

**patronize** *verb* **1** to behave in a superior manner, as if more important than others. **2** to support and give money to artists.

**pattern** *noun* **1** an arrangement of lines, shapes, or colors, especially a design that is repeated. **2** a particular way in which something is done. *A behavior pattern.* **3** the shape of something to be copied. *A dress pattern.*

pattern

**pauper** *noun* a poor person who has to beg.

**pause** *noun* **1** a moment of silence. **2** a break from doing something. **pause** *verb* to stop for a short while. *Henry paused to think carefully before answering the question.*

**pave** *verb* to put flat stones or bricks on a path or an area. **pave the way** to make something more likely to happen. *Their meeting paved the way to an agreement.*

**pavement** *noun* the hard surface of a road.

**pavilion** *noun* **1** a building next to a sports field for the use of players and spectators. **2** an ornamental building used for dances, concerts, or exhibitions.

**paw** *noun* an animal's foot. **paw** *verb* to feel or touch with a hand or foot. *The bull pawed the ground and lowered its head before charging.*

**pawn** *noun* **1** the smallest and least valuable piece in a game of chess. **2** an unimportant person or country used by others for their own advantage. *He was a pawn in their game.* **pawn** *verb* to leave something, especially valuable articles, with a pawnbroker as a security for money borrowed. *He pawned his watch to pay for a bus ticket to take him home.*

**pawnbroker** *noun* a person who lends money to people in exchange for articles that they leave as security.

**pay** (pays, paying, paid) *verb* **1** to give money for goods bought or work done. *I paid five dollars for his old bike.* **2** to settle a bill or debt. *I'll pay!* **3** to give somebody an advantage; to be worth the trouble or cost. *It pays to be honest.* **4** to give or say something to a person, especially in certain phrases. *He paid her a compliment.* **pay** *noun* money received for work. **pay back** to give back the money that you owe. **pay somebody back** to make somebody suffer for what they did to you. **pay up** to pay fully; to give all the money you owe.

**payee** *noun* a person to whom money is paid or should be paid.

**payment** *noun* **1** paying money or being paid. *When can we expect payment for the work we did for you?* **2** an amount of money paid to somebody.

**PC** *abbreviation* **1** personal computer. **2** politically correct, used of language that is phrased to be inoffensive.

**PE** *abbreviation* physical education, a phrase covering all sports taught in school.

**pea** *noun* the small, round, green seed growing inside a pod, eaten as a vegetable.

**peace** *noun* **1** a time when there is no war between countries, or no trouble, quarreling, or fighting among people. **2** calm and quietness. *Leave us in peace.* **make peace** to end a quarrel. **peaceful** *adjective.*

**peach** *noun* a round, juicy fruit with soft, yellowish-red skin and a large stone.

**peacock** *noun* a large male bird with long, colorful tail feathers that it spreads out like a fan when courting females.

**peahen** *noun* a large brown bird, the female of the peacock.

peacock

**peak** *noun* **1** the pointed top of a mountain. **2** the front part of a cap that sticks out to shade your eyes. **3** the highest level or most successful part of something. *She has reached the peak of her career.* **peak** *verb* to reach the highest point or level of success. *He peaked at rowing when he was twenty.*

**peanut** *noun* a small, round nut that grows in pods under the ground. Peanuts are eaten as a food and also yield oil. **peanut butter** *noun* roasted peanuts crushed into a paste and eaten as a spread on bread. *Peanut butter sandwiches are my favorite snack!*

**pear** *noun* the hard, yellow or green juicy fruit of the pear tree. *Pear and apple pie.* **pear-shaped** rounded at the bottom and tapering toward the top.

pearl

**pearl** *noun* **1** a hard, round, shiny, white object that grows inside the shell of an oyster and is a valuable jewel. *A pearl necklace.* **2** something that looks like a pearl or is a copy of a pearl. **pearly** *adjective.*

**peasant** *noun* a person who works on a farm or owns and lives off a small piece of land.

**peat** *noun* rotted plant material found under the ground. Peat is used for burning instead of coal or to improve soil and make plants grow better.

**pebble** *noun* a smooth, round stone.

**peck** *verb* **1** to hit, tap, or bite with the beak. *The bird pecked a hole in the apple.* **2** to kiss quickly and lightly. **peck** *noun* **1** a quick hit or tap with a beak. **2** a quick kiss.

**peculiar** *adjective* **1** strange, unusual, often in an unpleasant way. *He gave me a peculiar look.* **2** belonging or relating to a particular thing or person only. *That accent is peculiar to the people of this valley.* **peculiarity** *noun.*

**pedal** *noun* a bar that you push or press with your foot to make a bicycle move or a car or machine work. **pedal** (pedals, pedaling, pedaled) *verb* to work something by using pedals. *He had to pedal hard to get up the hill.*

**pedant** *noun* a person who is very strict about unimportant rules and pays too much attention to detail. **pedantic** *adjective.*

**pedestal** *noun* the base on which a statue or pillar stands. *The marble statue stood on a stone pedestal.*

**pedestrian** *noun* (say pi-**dess**-tree-an) a person walking, especially in a town. **pedestrian** *adjective* **1** for the use of people walking. *A pedestrian crossing.* **2** dull, uninspired. *A pedestrian speech.*

**pediatrician** (say pee-dee-uh-**tri**-shun) *noun* a doctor who specializes in diagnosing illnesses in children. **paediatric** *adjective.*

**pedigree** *noun* a list showing the families from which a person or animal has come, especially to show the quality of an animal. *A dog with a fine pedigree.* **pedigree** *adjective.*

**peek** *noun* a quick look. **peek** *verb.*

**peel** *noun* the skin of oranges, apples, potatoes, and other fruit and vegetables. **peel** *verb* **1** to take the skin off fruit and vegetables. **2** to come off in layers, strips, or flakes. *The paint is peeling.*

pedigree

Pp

**peep** *verb* **1** to look quickly, often secretly. **2** to look through an opening. **3** to begin to show. *The ticket peeped out of his pocket.* **peep** *noun* **1** a quick look. **2** a high, weak sound.

**peer** *noun* **1** a member of the nobility. A duke or a baron is a peer. **2** a person who is the same age or has the same rank as yourself. **peer** *verb* to look hard or closely, usually because something is difficult to see. **peer group** a group of people of the same age.

**peevish** *adjective* bad-tempered; stubborn.

**peg** *noun* **1** a piece of wood, metal, or plastic used for fastening things or attaching washing to a line. *A tent peg.* **2** a hook or knob for hanging things on. **peg** (pegs, pegging, pegged) *verb* **1** to fasten with pegs. **2** to strike or pierce with a thrown peg.

**pelican** *noun* a large water bird with a long beak and a pouch for storing fish.

**pellet** *noun* a small ball of metal, paper, or other material.

**pelmet** *noun* a piece of wood or fabric that hides a curtain rod.

pelican

**pelvis** *noun* the round, bony frame and hip bones at the lower end of the spine.

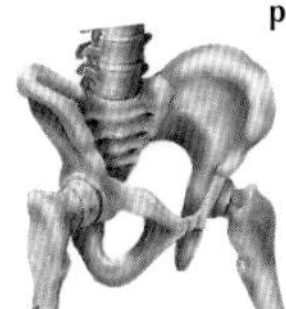

pelvis

**pen** *noun* **1** an instrument for writing with ink. *A fountain pen.* **2** a small place, an enclosure, for farm animals or pets. **pen** (pens, penning, penned) *verb* to shut into a small place. *We penned in the chickens for the night to keep them safe.*

**penal** (say **peen**-ul) *adjective* connected with the punishment of criminals. *Penal laws.*

**penalize** *verb* to punish.

**penalty** *noun* **1** punishment. **2** a point or a chance to score a goal, especially in football, rugby, or hockey, because an opponent has committed a foul.

**pencil** *noun* a wooden instrument containing a core of lead or colored material, used for writing or drawing. **pencil** (pencils, penciling, penciled) *verb* to write or draw with a pencil.

**pendulum** *noun* a weight hanging from a rod that swings from side to side, regulating the movement of many old clocks.

**penetrate** *verb* to force or manage to find a way into something. **penetration** *noun.* **penetrating** *adjective* (of a question or remark) suggesting sensitivity or insight.

**penfriend** *noun* a friend, especially somebody from a foreign country, with whom you exchange letters.

**penguin** *noun* any of a variety of black and white birds that live in the Antarctic and cannot fly.

**penicillin** *noun* an antibiotic used in medicine to destroy bacteria.

**peninsula** *noun* a piece of land almost surrounded by water. *Italy is a peninsula.* **peninsular** *adjective.*

**penis** (penises) *noun* the part of the body that a male human or animal uses for urinating and in reproduction.

**penniless** *adjective* having no money; very poor.

**penny** (pennies) *noun* a coin worth one hundredth of a dollar in the US and Canada; one cent. **the penny has dropped** something has finally been understood.

**pension** *noun* a sum of money paid regularly by the government or a company to a retired person.

**pentathlon** *noun* an athletic competition made up of five different events.

**people** *plural noun* **1** two or more persons. *Only three people came.* **2** all the men, women, and children of a particular place, class, or group. *Young people.*

**pepper** *noun* **1** a hot-tasting powder made from peppercorns and used for making food spicy. **2** a hollow green, red, or yellow vegetable.

**peppermint** *noun* **1** a mint (plant), the leaves of which are used to flavor food. **2** a candy tasting of peppermint.

**per** *preposition* for each. *Ten miles per hour.* **per annum** for each year. **percent** in each hundred.

**perceive** *verb* to notice or see something.

**percentage** *noun* an amount stated as part of a whole or as a share of one hundred parts. *A large percentage of students pass their final exams every year.*

**perceptive** *adjective* quick to notice and understand. *A perceptive guess.* **perception** *noun.*

**percussion** *noun* **1** the striking together of two hard things. **2** musical instruments that are played by being struck, especially drums and cymbals.

**perennial** *adjective* lasting for many years. **perennial** *noun* a plant that lives for more than two years.

**perfect** *adjective* **1** without fault. **2** complete. *A perfect stranger.* **perfectly** *adverb* completely. *I feel perfectly at home here and have no wish to leave.*

**perform** *verb* **1** to do something, especially something difficult. **2** to act in a play or do something in front of an audience. **performer** *noun.*

**performance** *noun* **1** doing something in front of an audience. *Samantha went to the first performance of the new play.* **2** an action performed.

**perhaps** *adverb* it may be; possibly.

**perimeter** *noun* the outer edge of something; the border. *We walked around the perimeter of the grounds.*

**period** *adjective* made at an earlier time in history. *The hotel was full of period furniture, including original four-poster beds.* **period** *noun* **1** a length or portion of time. *For a short period; sunny periods.* **2** a woman's monthly flow of blood or menstruation.

**periodic** *adjective* happening at regular intervals.

**periodical** *noun* a magazine that comes out at regular intervals, for example once a month. *My favorite periodical is* Complete Pony Care, *which I buy every month with my allowance.* **periodical** *adjective.*

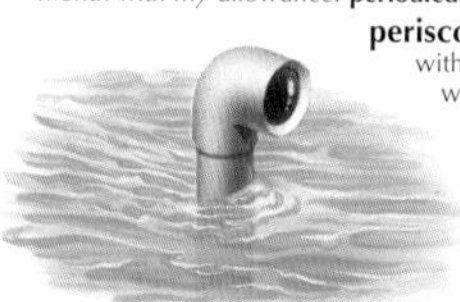

periscope

**periscope** *noun* a tube with mirrors and lenses which, when raised above water, allows somebody in a submarine to see things on the surface.

**perish** *verb* **1** to die or become destroyed. **2** to rot or fall to pieces. *Soft fruit perishes quickly once it has been picked from a tree.* **perishable** *adjective.*

**permanent** *adjective* lasting forever; not expected to change. *My permanent address.* **permanently** *adverb.*

**permissible** *adjective* allowed by the rules.

**permission** *noun* the right to do something; the act of allowing something. *The teacher gave us permission to leave early.*

**permissive** *adjective* allowing too much personal freedom. *Permissive society.*

**Pp**

**permit** (say per-**mit**) (permits, permitting, permitted) *verb* to allow or make something possible. **permit** (say **per**-mit) *noun* an official document stating that somebody is allowed to do something or go somewhere.

**perpendicular** *adjective* pointing straight up. *Perpendicular lines.*

**perpetrate** *verb* to be guilty of something; to do something wrong. **perpetrator** *noun. We caught the perpetrator of the crime.*

**perpetual** *adjective* never ending or changing. *The perpetual sound of the waves.* **perpetually** *adverb.*

**perpetuate** *verb* to preserve from being forgotten. *Let us perpetuate the memory of Martin Luther King by naming this building after him.*

**persecute** *verb* continually to treat a person or group of people cruelly, especially because of their beliefs. **persecution** *noun.*

**persevere** *verb* to continue doing something and not to give up. **perseverance** *noun. Perseverance enabled him to reach the summit of the mountain.*

**persist** *verb* **1** to continue in spite of warning. *If he persists in breaking the rules, he will be expelled.* **2** to continue to exist. *If your headaches persist, take these tablets.* **persistent** *adjective.* **persistently** *adverb.* **persistence** *noun.*

**person** *noun* **1** a human being. *It's too much work for one person.* **2** in grammar, any of the three forms of pronouns or verbs that show who is speaking. "I am" is the first person of the verb "to be." **in person** bodily. *I can't come in person, but I'll send my brother instead.*

**personal** *adjective* **1** belonging, concerning, or done by a particular person. *I'd like your personal opinion.* **2** concerning a person's private life. *There's no need to be personal.* **personally** *adverb. Please don't take it personally.* **personal computer (PC)** *noun* a computer used by a single person, especially at home.

**personality** (personalities) *noun* **1** the character or nature of a person. *He has a good personality.* **2** a famous person. *A well-known television personality.*

**personnel** *noun* the people employed in a business. *All personnel will get a raise today.*

perspective

**perspective** *noun* **1** the apparent relation between objects as to distance and position. *Perspective makes the trees in the background appear smaller than the trees in the foreground.* **2** the art of drawing so that things in the background look farther away than things in the foreground. **3** a particular way of thinking about something. *What happened put everything in perspective.*

**perspire** *verb* to sweat. **perspiration** *noun.*

**persuade** *verb* to make somebody do or believe something. *We persuaded him to buy a new bike.* **persuasion** *noun.* **persuasive** *adjective. The persuasive salesman wouldn't take no for an answer.*

**perturb** *verb* to worry. *News of the invasion of his country perturbed him greatly.*

**Peru** *noun* a country in South America.

**Peruvian** *adjective* of Peru. **Peruvian** *noun.*

**perverse** *adjective* continuing to do something wrong or in a different way from what is wanted. *How perverse of you to like tests.* **perversely** *adverb.* **perversity** *noun.*

**pervert** (say **per**-vert) *noun* a person whose behavior, especially sexual behavior, is not normal and is thought disgusting by others. **pervert** (say per-**vert**) *verb* to turn away from what is right. *He perverted the course of justice by lying to the police.* **perversion** *noun.*

**pessimism** *noun* thinking that whatever happens will be bad. **pessimist** *noun.* **pessimistic** *adjective.*

**pester** *verb* to annoy somebody continually, especially by asking questions or asking for something.

**pet** *noun* **1** an animal kept in the home as a companion. *Dogs are my favorite pets.* **2** a person who is a favorite. *The teacher's pet.* **pet** (pets, petting, petted) *verb* to treat or touch with special love.

**petal** *noun* one of the bright-colored parts that forms a flower. *We made confetti by drying rose petals.*

**petrify** (petrifies, petrifying, petrified) *verb* **1** to make somebody extremely frightened. *The strange noises petrified him.* **2** to turn into stone. *A petrified forest.*

**petrol** *noun* **1** petroleum. **2** (British) gasoline.

**petty** (pettier, pettiest) *adjective* unimportant; trivial. *Petty squabbles.*

**pew** *noun* a long wooden bench in a church. *He sat in the pew and prayed.*

**phantom** *noun* a ghost.

**Pharaoh** (say **fai**-roh) *noun* the ruler of ancient Egypt.

**pharmacy** (pharmacies) *noun* a store where medicines are sold, including those prescribed by a doctor. **pharmacist** *noun.*

**pharaoh**

**phase** *noun* a stage of development. **phase in/out** *verb* to introduce or stop something gradually. *School uniform was phased out in the 1990s, starting with the seniors.*

**pheasant** *noun* a long-tailed bird that is hunted for food. *The hunter shot a pheasant, which was retrieved by his Labrador dog.*

**phenomenal** *adjective* unusual; amazing. *He has phenomenal strength for his age.*

**phenomenon** (phenomena) *noun* an unusual fact, event, or thing. *Summer snow is an almost unknown phenomenon in this country.*

**philately** (say fil-**at**-il-ee) *noun* stamp-collecting. **philatelist** *noun.*

**-phile** *suffix* indicating a person or thing that has a liking for something. *Francophiles like France and everything French.*

**Philippines' flag**

**Philippines** *noun* a country of many islands of Southeast Asia.

**philistine** (say **fil**-ist-ine) *noun* a person who does not like or understand art, music, literature, and beautiful things.

**philology** *noun* the study of the development of language. **philologist** *noun.*

**philosophy** *noun* **1** the study of the meaning of life and right and wrong behavior. **2** the ideas and beliefs that a philosopher has, or your own rules for living your life. *The philosophy of the ancient Greeks.* **philosophical** *adjective.* **philosopher** *noun.*

**Phnom Penh** *noun* the capital of Cambodia in Asia.

**phobia** (say foh-bee-uh) *noun* a great fear of something. *She has a phobia about spiders.*

**phone** *noun, abbreviation* telephone. **on the phone** speaking to someone by phone. **phone** *verb* to telephone. *Please phone home as soon as you can.* **phone-in** *noun* a program on radio or television in which people call and take part in it. *I took part in a phone-in about pets.*

**photo** *noun, abbreviation* photograph.

**photocopier** *noun* a machine that can quickly copy documents and other papers by photographing them.

**photocopy** (photocopies) *noun* a photographic copy of a document or page made by a photocopier. **photocopy** (photocopies, photocopying, photocopied) *verb. Could you photocopy this page for me, please?*

**photogenic** *adjective* looking nice in photographs. *She is very photogenic, and will probably become a model.*

**photograph** *noun* a picture made with a camera and a film sensitive to light. **photograph** *verb* to use a camera to take a photograph. **photography** *noun.* **photographic** *adjective. Photographic equipment.*

**photographer** *noun* somebody who takes photographs. *A wedding photographer.*

**photosynthesis** *noun* the process by which green plants make food in their leaves, using the sun's energy, carbon dioxide, and water.

**phrase** *noun* a group of words used together that form part of a sentence. "In the park" is a phrase in "We went for a walk in the park." **phrase** *verb* to express something in words. *I phrased my letter of complaint carefully.*

**physical** *adjective* **1** connected with a person's body, not their mind. *Physical exercise.* **2** of things that can be touched and seen. *The physical world.* **3** connected with physics. **physically** *adverb.*

**physician** (say fuh-**zih**-shun)*noun* a doctor.

**physics** (say **fiz**-iks) *noun* the study of forces such as heat, light, sound, electricity, and gravity.

**physiotherapy** (say **fiz**-ee-o-ther-uh-pee) *noun* treatment by means of exercise, massage, light, and heat. **physiotherapist** *noun. The physiotherapist devised a program of gentle exercise for the injured player.*

**physique** (say fiz-**eek**) *noun* the shape and size of a person's body, especially a man's.

**piano** *noun* a large musical instrument that a pianist plays by pressing the black and white keys with his/her fingers. **pianist** *noun.*

piano

**piccolo** *noun* a small flute that plays high notes. *A piccolo solo.*

**pick** *verb* **1** to pull or break off part of a plant, especially a flower or fruit. *We picked some strawberries.* **2** to choose carefully. *He always picks the best.* **3** to remove unwanted things or pull pieces off something. *Don't pick your nose!* **4** to take up. *Birds picking at grain.* **pick** *noun* **1** choice. *Take your pick.* **2** the best of many. *The pick of the bunch.* **3** a pickax. **4** a plectrum, used for plucking guitar strings. **pick a lock** to open a lock without a key. **pick a quarrel** to start a quarrel with somebody. **pick somebody's pocket** to steal from somebody. **pick holes in** to find weak points in something. **pick up 1** to lift or take up. **2** to collect. *I'll pick up the children from school.* **3** to take somebody as a passenger. *They picked up a hitchhiker.* **4** to get better. *His health is picking up.* **5** to get to know somebody. *He picked up a girl at the party.* **6** to learn or hear something. *I picked up a few Italian words while on vacation in Tuscany.*

**pickax** *noun* a pointed tool with a long handle used for breaking up rocks or hard ground.

**picnic** *noun* a meal eaten outdoors while sitting on the ground, at the beach or in a field. **picnic** (picnics, picnicking, picnicked) *verb* to have a picnic. **picnicker** *noun.*

**pictorial** *adjective* with pictures.

**picture** *noun* **1** a painting, drawing, or photograph of somebody or something. **2** a movie at a theater or on television. **3** an idea or impression. *She had quite a different picture of the house in her mind.* **4** a perfect example or description of an event. *The baby is a picture of health.* **go to the pictures** to go to the theater to see a movie. **get the picture** to understand a situation somebody is telling you about. **put somebody in the picture** to tell somebody about a situation they need to know about. **picture** *verb* to imagine something.

**picturesque** *adjective* attractive and interesting. *A picturesque mountain village.*

**piece** *noun* **1** a part or bit of something. *A piece of cake.* **2** one single thing, object, or example. *A piece of paper.* **3** something written or composed, especially an article or a play. *A piece of music.* **4** a counter or any object used when playing a board game. *A chess piece.* **5** a coin. *A 50-cent piece.* **piece together** to make something by putting pieces together. *We pieced together the facts.*

**pier** *noun* **1** a bridge-like structure built out into the sea, used as a landing-stage or for people to walk along. **2** a pillar for supporting a bridge or roof.

**pierce** *verb* to make a hole with something sharp or pointed. *She had her ears pierced.* **piercing** *adjective* sharp in an unpleasant way. *A piercing scream.*

**pig** *noun* **1** a pink or black animal with a snout, usually kept on farms for its meat. **2** a dirty or greedy person.

pig

**pigeon** *noun* a gray bird with a round body. **pigeonhole** *noun* a small open box or one of many compartments on a wall for papers and messages. *He left the letter in my pigeonhole, so I could collect it later.*

**pigment** *noun* a substance that gives a particular color to natural things or to paints and dyes. *The green pigment of leaves.* **pigmentation** *noun.*

**pigsty** (pigsties) *noun* **1** a hut for pigs. **2** a dirty room or home.

**pile** *noun* **1** a long wooden, metal, or stone stake that is hammered into the ground as a support for a bridge or building. **2** a number of things lying on top of each other. **3** a large quantity of things or amount of money. **pile** *verb* to put things in or on a pile. **pile in** to come or get into a place in a group quickly and at the same time. **pile out** to leave a place in a group.

pile

**pilfer** *verb* to steal small things. *She used to pilfer from my purse.* **pilferage** *noun.*

**pilgrim** *noun* somebody who travels to a holy place for religious reasons.

**pilgrimage** *noun* a journey made by pilgrims to visit a holy place.

**pillar** *noun* **1** a tall upright stone or wooden post that supports a building. **2** something that looks like a pillar. *A pillar of smoke.* **3** an important member of a group of people. *He's a pillar of society.*

**pilot** *noun* **1** a person trained to fly an airplane. **2** a person who steers a ship in and out of port. **3** a test to find out if something will work. *The TV producers are making a pilot of the series.* **pilot** *verb* **1** to act as a pilot of an airplane or ship. **2** to guide carefully. *He piloted me through the crowd.*

**pincers** *plural noun* **1** an instrument used for gripping or pulling things out. **2** the claws of a crab or lobster.

**pine** *noun* an evergreen tree with leaves that look like needles. **pine** *verb* to become weak and sad because of wanting something very much. *The dog is pining for his master.*

**pineapple** *noun* a large tropical fruit with spiny leaves, a thick skin, and sweet, yellow, juicy flesh.

**pinpoint** *verb* to find or discover exactly what or where something is. *Can you pinpoint the problem?*

**pint** *noun* a unit for measuring liquids.

**pine**

**pioneer** *noun* the first person to go to a place or do or study something new. **pioneer** *verb* to help develop something. *He pioneered the solar car.*

**pious** *adjective* very religious.

**pipe** *noun* **1** a long, hollow, metal or plastic tube through which water or gas can flow. **2** a small tube with a bowl-like container at one end used for smoking tobacco. **3** a tube-like musical instrument, played by blowing. **pipe** *verb* **1** to carry liquid or gas through a pipe. **2** to send music or other sound through a loudspeaker. **3** to play music on a pipe. **4** to add a strip of decoration (called piping). **5** to pipe icing on a cake. **pipe down** be quiet.

**pipeline** *noun* pipes, often underground, for carrying oil, water, or gas a long way. **in the pipeline** being planned or on the way. *Plans for shorter school terms are in the pipeline.*

**piranha** *noun* a small, fierce, meat-eating fish from the rivers of South America.

**piranha**

**pirate** *noun* **1** a sailor who attacks and robs other ships at sea. *Pirate Jack boarded the ship and stole all the gold on board.* **2** someone who copies or broadcasts somebody else's work, such as books, CDs, or DVDs, without permission. *Pirate radio stations do not pay for the music they broadcast.* **pirate** *verb* to copy or broadcast somebody else's work without permission. **piracy** *noun.*

**pirate**

**pitch** (pitches) *noun* **1** a ground marked out and used for playing certain games. *A cricket pitch.* **2** the highness or lowness of a sound. *Her voice dropped to a lower pitch.* **3** the degree or strength of something. *A pitch of excitement.* **pitch** *verb* **1** to set up, as a tent or camp. **2** to throw or fling something. **3** to fall suddenly or heavily. *I tripped and pitched forward.* **4** to give a particular feeling to something; to set a level. *Her stories are pitched so that even the youngest children can easily understand them.* **pitch in** to join in an activity; to get working or eating. **pitch-dark** *adjective* very dark.

**pitfall** *noun* an unexpected difficulty.

**pitiful** *adjective* sad and weak; making you feel pity; not worthy of respect.

**pitiless** *adjective* showing no feeling or pity. *The boss is pitiless; he makes us pay for every error.*

**pity** *noun* **1** feeling sorry for somebody who is suffering or unhappy. *Don't help me out of pity.* **2** a state of disappointment. *It's a pity you can't come to the party tonight.* **take pity on** to feel sorry for somebody and help them. **pity** (pities, pitying, pitied) *verb* to feel sorry for somebody.

**pivot** *noun* **1** a point or pin on which something turns. **2** the most important thing on which everything depends. **pivot** *verb* to turn around as on a pivot. **pivotal** *adjective.*

**placard** *noun* a large poster or notice. *The demonstrators carried placards with slogans on them.*

**place** *noun* **1** a particular position where something belongs or should be. *I put the books back in their place.* **2** any point like a building, an area, a country, a town, or a village. *This is the place where we used to live.* **3** a seat. *He saved me a place.* **4** a house or home. *Come over to my place after school.* **5** a particular point in a story or book. *I lost my place because my bookmark fell out.* **6** a position in a group, race, or competition. *First place.* **7** somebody's role in relation to other people or things. *It's not my place to tell him off.* **8** a position in a team, a school, or at a university. *He got a place on the team.* **9** a point in a series of things, especially in an explanation. *In the first place, I don't want to come, and in the second place, I haven't been invited.* **place** *verb* **1** to put something in a particular place. **2** to say that somebody has achieved a particular position or put somebody in a particular position. *This places him in a difficult position.* **3** When you place an order, you order goods from a firm. **all over the place** everywhere. **in place** in the correct position; suitable. **out of place** not in the correct position; unsuitable. **in place of** instead of. **take place** to happen. *When did the party take place?*

**placid** *adjective* calm; not easily made angry or upset.

**plague** *noun* **1** a dangerous illness that spreads quickly and kills many people. **2** a large number of unpleasant things. *A plague of locusts.* **plague** (plagues, plaguing, plagued) *verb* to annoy or trouble all the time.

Pp

**plaid** *noun* (say plahd) a cloth with a tartan pattern.

**plain** *adjective* **1** simple; not decorated, patterned, or flavored; not complicated. *I prefer plain food.* **2** easy to see, hear, or understand. *It was plain he didn't like her.* **3** honest and open, especially about feelings or opinions. **4** not beautiful or handsome. **plain** *noun* a large, flat area of land. **plainly** *adverb.* **plainness** *noun.*

**plait** (say plaht) *verb* (British for braid) to twist three or more strands, especially hair or rope, under and over one another into one thick length. **plait** *noun* a length of hair or rope that has been braided or plaited.

**plane** *noun* **1** an airplane. **2** a flat surface. **3** a tool with a sharp blade for making wood smooth by shaving small pieces off its surface. **4** a tall tree with big leaves. **plane** *verb* to smooth wood with a plane (tool).

**planet** *noun* any of the large bodies in space that travel around the Sun, such as Earth, Venus, and Mars. **planetary** *adjective.*

**plankton** *noun* tiny plants and animals that live in water and are food for many fish.

**plant** *noun* **1** a living thing that grows in the earth and has leaves and roots. Plants need water and light. **2** large machinery used in industry. **3** a factory. **4** a thing, especially stolen goods, hidden on somebody to make that person look guilty. *The drugs were a plant by the criminal.* **plant** *verb* **1** to put something in the ground to grow. **2** to fix firmly or place in a position. *She planted herself in the chair next to mine.* **3** to hide something or somebody secretly in order wrongly to accuse an innocent person. *He planted the stolen bike in his neighbor's garage.*

**plantation** *noun* **1** a large area of land on which crops, such as tea, sugar, coffee, or cotton, are grown (in the past by slave labor), especially in hot countries. **2** a large area where trees have been planted.

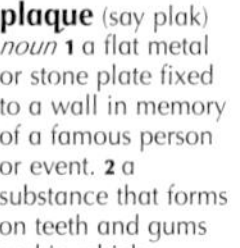

**plantation**

**plaque** (say plak) *noun* **1** a flat metal or stone plate fixed to a wall in memory of a famous person or event. **2** a substance that forms on teeth and gums and in which bacteria can live. *Brushing teeth helps remove plaque.*

**plaster** *noun* **1** a mixture of lime, water, and sand that hardens when dry and is used for covering walls and ceilings. **2** a piece of sticky material with a soft inner pad used to cover a wound. **3** a white paste (plaster of Paris) that dries quickly and is used for making molds or casts around broken bones. **plaster** *verb* **1** to cover with plaster. **2** to cover something thickly, usually too thickly.

**plastic** *noun* an artificial material that can easily be formed into various shapes. Plastic is light and does not break easily. **plastic** *adjective* made of plastic. **plastic surgery** an operation to repair and replace damaged skin or injured or misshapen parts of the body.

**plate** *noun* **1** a flat dish from which food is eaten or served. *A dinner plate.* **2** a flat sheet of metal, glass, or other hard material. **3** a small piece of metal with a person's name on it, usually beside the front door of an office or a house. **4** metal articles, dishes, bowls, and cutlery with a thin covering of gold or silver. **5** a picture or photograph printed on special paper, usually in a book. **6** a piece of plastic with false teeth on it, shaped to fit inside a person's mouth. **plate** *verb* to cover metal objects with a thin layer of gold, silver, or tin. *My best silver plated spoons.*

**plateau** (plateaux) *noun* (say **platt**-oh, **platt**-ohz) a flat area of land high above sea-level.

**plateau**

**platinum** *noun* a very valuable metal used for making jewelry. *Her wedding ring was made of platinum.*

**platypus** (platypuses) *noun* an Australian animal with a beak like a duck and webbed feet.

**platypus**

**play** *noun* **1** a story performed in a theater, on TV, or on the radio; a piece of writing to be performed. *He has written a new play.* **2** playing. *Children learn through play.* **play** *verb* **1** to take part in a sport, a game, or other pleasant amusement. **2** to make music with a musical instrument, perform a musical work, or operate a CD player. *She plays CDs all the time.* **3** to act in a play or movie. *He played a king in the school play.* **4** to behave in a certain way. *She played it very cool when offered the job.* **play along** pretend to agree with somebody. **play around** to spend time having fun, with no particular purpose and no constraints. *The children always play around when their grandmother babysits them.* **play down** to make something seem less important than it is. **play up** to make something seem more important than it is. **play it by ear** to decide what to do as the situation arises, rather than planning in advance.

**player** *noun* a person who plays a game.

**playground** *noun* an outdoor area in a park or school where children can play. *Running in the playground is not allowed.*

**playing card** *noun* one of a set of cards used to play games. *Let's take a pack of playing cards to camp.*

**plea** *noun* **1** a strong request. *She made a plea for help to her mother when she found she could no longer cope with her work and the childcare.* **2** an excuse. *A plea of insanity.* **3** a statement made by the accused in court stating whether they are guilty or not guilty.

**plead** *verb* **1** to make a strong request. *He pleaded with the teacher to give him more time to finish his essay.* **2** to state in court whether one is guilty or not guilty. **3** to offer an excuse.

**pleasant** (say **plez**-ant) *adjective* nice; enjoyable. *We spent a pleasant day on the beach.* A pleasant person is friendly and polite. **pleasantness** *noun.*

**please** *adverb* **1** used when politely asking somebody to do something or asking for something. *Please may I have another cookie?* **2** *verb* to give satisfaction or make somebody happy. *He always tries to please his parents.* **please yourself** do what you want. **as you please** as you think best. *I'll do as I please.*

**pleasure** *noun* **1** a feeling of satisfaction, happiness, and enjoyment. **2** something that is enjoyable and pleases you. *It was a pleasure to meet you.*

**pleat** *noun* a flattened fold in cloth. **pleat** *verb* to make folds. **pleated** *adjective. A pleated skirt.*

**plectrum** *noun* a small piece of plastic or wood, held in the hand and used for plucking the strings of a guitar.

**pledge** *noun* **1** a serious promise or agreement. *He made a pledge of loyalty to the flag of the USA.* **2** something given as a sign of friendship or love. **3** an object given in return for money until that money is repaid. **pledge** *verb* **1** to make a serious promise. *They pledged to meet again next year.* **2** to make a serious promise to give something. *The firm pledged $1,000 to cancer research.*

**plenty** *pronoun, noun* enough; as much or more than is needed. *We've got plenty of time before the next bus.* **plenty** *adverb* quite; more than. *It's plenty big enough for three.*

pliers

**pliers** *plural noun* a gripping tool for holding or pulling out things. *He used a pair of pliers to pull out the nail.*

**plight** *noun* a difficult situation.

**plod** (plods, plodding, plodded) *verb* **1** to walk slowly with a heavy step. **2** to work slowly and without much interest. *David plodded through the textbook he had been told to read for school.*

**plot** *noun* **1** a small piece of ground. *A vegetable plot.* **2** a secret plan. *The police uncovered a plot to shoot the President.* **3** the story structure in a movie or novel. *The director changed the plot.* **plot** (plots, plotting, plotted) *verb* **1** to make a secret plan. **2** to mark the position or course, especially of a ship or plane, on a map.

**plow** *noun* a farming tool with sharp blades for turning over the soil before seeds are planted. **plow** (plowed) *verb* to turn over the soil with a plow; to plow a field. **plow through** to make your way through, usually with difficulty. *He plowed through all the books on the reading list.* **plow back** to put money back into a business. *The company plowed back last year's profits so they could expand.*

plow

**plumber** (say **plum**-mer) *noun* a person who fits and repairs water pipes. **plumbing** *noun.*

**plump** *adjective* slightly fat; round. **plumpness** *noun.*

**plunder** *verb* to rob, especially in a war. *The soldiers plundered the town.* **plunder** *noun.* **plunderer** *noun.*

**plunge** *verb* **1** to suddenly fall or jump downward or forward. **2** to push quickly and forcefully. *She hungrily plunged the knife into the pie.* **3** to fall steeply. *Prices have plunged to rock bottom.* **plunge** *noun* a dive. **take the plunge** to decide to do something risky or difficult.

**plural** *noun* a word that expresses more than one. *Cats is the plural of cat.* **plural** *adjective. Pliers is a plural noun.*



**plus** *preposition* **1** showing that one number is added to another, often written as a plus sign (+). Three plus three, or 3 + 3. **2** with the addition of. *She lost her job plus the company car.* **plus** *noun* **1** a plus sign (+). **2** an advantage. *Knowing lots of languages is a definite plus.*

**plutocrat** *noun* a person who is powerful because he or she is very rich.

**p.m.** *abbreviation* written after a number and used to show the time after midday. *Stores close at 6.00 p.m.*

**pneumatic** *adjective* worked or filled with compressed air. *A pneumatic drill.*

**pneumonia** *noun* an illness in which there is inflammation of one or both lungs.

**poach** *verb* to cook an egg, fish, or fruit in boiling water or other liquid, sometimes in a special pan. *Poached plums.* **poach** *verb* **1** to catch or shoot animals, fish, or birds on somebody else's land, without their permission. **2** to take or use unfairly somebody else's ideas or belongings. **poacher** *noun.*

**poem** *noun* an imaginative piece of writing with short lines, often that rhyme.

**poet** *noun* a person who writes poems. **poetic** *adjective.* **poetry** *noun* poems. *A book of poetry.*

**poison** *noun* a substance that harms or kills animals or plants. **poison** *verb* **1** to put poison in or on something. To kill with poison. *The air is being poisoned by car fumes.* **2** to spoil something or influence somebody in a harmful way. *He poisoned her mind against her friend.* **poisonous** *adjective. A poisonous snake.*

**poke** *verb* to prod or stir something or to pry by asking questions of someone, often annoyingly. *Don't poke into other people's affairs.*

**poky** (pokier, pokiest) *adjective* small; cramped. *It was a poky room.*

**Poland** *noun* a country in Eastern Europe.

Poland

**polar** *adjective* near the North or South Pole. **polar bear** *noun* a white bear that lives near the North Pole.

**pole** *noun* **1** a long, round, usually thin stick or post. *One of the tent poles is missing.* **2** either of the two ends of the Earth's axis; the point as far north as the North Pole or as far south as the South Pole. **3** either of the ends of a magnet. **4** either of the two points of an electric battery. *The positive pole, the negative pole.* **be poles apart** to have completely different opinions on a subject.

**police** *noun* the men and women whose job and duty is to catch criminals and protect people and property. **police** *verb* to keep order by using the police. *Football games are heavily policed.*



**policy** (policies) *noun* **1** a plan of action or statement of aims. *One of our policies is to reduce classroom sizes.* **2** a document that shows an agreement made with an insurance company. **policyholder** *noun.*

**polish** *noun* **1** a substance, like wax, for polishing. **2** a shining surface. **3** elegance and good behavior. *Samantha has real polish.* **polish** *verb* to make things smooth and shiny by rubbing. **polish off** to finish quickly, especially food or work. **polish up** to practice or improve a skill or ability. *I must polish up my French.*

**polite** *adjective* having good manners. **politely** *adverb. The children thanked their grandmother politely.* **politeness** *noun.*

**political** *adjective* concerning the government of a country. *A political party.* **politically correct** complying with ideas of inoffensive behavior or language.

**politics** *noun* the ways in which a country is governed; political affairs. **politician** *noun.*

**polka** *noun* a dance for couples, or the music to which it is danced.

**poll** *noun* (say pole) **1** voting in an election. **2** a questioning of people chosen by chance to find out the general opinion about something; an opinion poll. **poll** *verb* **1** to receive a stated number of votes in an election. **2** to vote in an election.

poll

**pollen** *noun* a fine yellow powder on the male part of a flower that fertilizes other flowers to produce seeds. Bees carry pollen from one flower to another.

**pollinate** *verb* to fertilize with pollen. **pollination** *noun.*

**pollute** *verb* to make dirty and dangerous to live in or use. *Many of our rivers have been polluted.*

**pollution** *noun* **1** polluting the water, air, or atmosphere. **2** substances that pollute.

**poly-** *prefix* many. Polyatomic means having many atoms.

**polygon** *noun* a shape with many sides.

**polythene** *noun* a very light plastic material for making plastic bags and packaging.

**polyunsaturated** *adjective* containing fats that are healthier and more easily digested.

**pompous** *adjective* full of self-importance. *That pompous man behaves as if he owns the place.* **pomposity** *noun.*

**ponder** *verb* to think deeply and carefully.

**ponderous** *adjective* **1** slow and clumsy. *His movements were ponderous.* **2** dull and serious. *He speaks in a ponderous way.* **ponderously** *adverb.*

**pony** (ponies) *noun* a horse of any small breed.

pony

**poodle** *noun* a dog with tightly curled hair.

**pool** *noun* **1** a small amount of water or other liquid. *A pool of water spread across the floor.* **2** a swimming pool. **3** an amount of money used by gamblers. **4** a common supply of workers or goods that can be shared by a number of people. **5** a tabletop game similar to billiards. **pool** *verb* to share. *We pooled our money and rented a villa in Spain last summer.*

**poor** *adjective* **1** having very little money. **2** not good, of low quality, or small in quantity. *She's in poor health.* **3** needing help or sympathy. *The poor little boy was crying.* **poorly** *adverb* badly. *Poorly paid.* **poorly** *adjective* unwell.

**pop** *adjective* popular. *A pop singer.* **pop** *noun* **1** popular music. **2** a short, explosive sound. *The cork came out with a pop.* **3** a soda drink. **pop** *verb* **1** to make a bursting sound. *The balloon went pop.* **2** to put something somewhere quickly. *She popped a candy into her mouth.* **3** to go quickly or suddenly.

**Pope** *noun* the head of the Roman Catholic Church.

**popular** *adjective* **1** liked, enjoyed, or admired by many people. *Katie is a popular name.* **2** of or for the general public. *The popular press.* **popularity** *noun.*

**populate** *verb* to live in; inhabit. *We live in a heavily populated area.*

**population** *noun* the people living in a place, especially a country or town.

**porcelain** *noun* (also called china) a hard, shiny material used for making cups, plates, and other articles. It is produced by baking clay.

**porcupine** *noun* a small animal with long spines or quills over its back and sides.

porcupine

**pork** *noun* meat from pigs.

**porpoise** *noun* a large sea animal similar to a dolphin.

**porridge** *noun* soft food made from cooked oats.

**port** *noun* **1** a harbor where goods are loaded and unloaded. **2** a town with a harbor. **3** the left side of a ship when you are facing the front. **4** a strong, sweet, red Portuguese wine. *Fine ruby port.*

**portable** *adjective* able to be carried. *Our portable TV is small enough to be moved easily from room to room.*

**Port-au-Prince** *noun* the capital of Haiti, a country in the Caribbean.

**portcullis** *noun* a framework of pointed bars above the main entrance to an old castle. The portcullis could be lowered as a protection against attack. *I can see enemy soldiers on horseback approaching the castle – let down the portcullis and prepare to fire!*

**Port Louis** *noun* the capital of Mauritius, an island in the Indian Ocean, east of Madagascar.

**Port Moresby** *noun* the capital of Papua New Guinea in the South Pacific Ocean.

**Port-of-Spain** *noun* the capital of Trinidad and Tobago in the Caribbean.

**Porto-Novo** *noun* the official capital of Benin in West Africa. (The seat of government is at Cotonou.)

**portrait** *noun* a painted picture, drawing, or photograph of somebody.

**portray** *verb* **1** to make a picture of somebody or something. **2** to describe in words. **3** to play the part of a character in a movie or play.

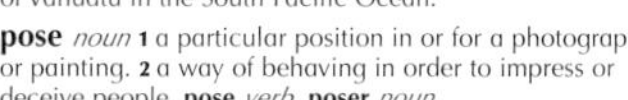

**Portugal** *noun* a country in southwest Europe.

portrait

**Port-Vila** *noun* the capital of Vanuatu in the South Pacific Ocean.

**pose** *noun* **1** a particular position in or for a photograph or painting. **2** a way of behaving in order to impress or deceive people. **pose** *verb.* **poser** *noun.*

**position** *noun* **1** the place where something is or stands. *The house is in a sunny position.* **2** a way of sitting or standing. *He slept in an uncomfortable position.* **3** a situation or condition. *You've put me in a difficult position.* **4** a job. **5** a particular place in a group. **6** an opinion. **position** *verb* to put somebody or something into position. *I positioned the table near the door.*

**positive** *adjective* **1** sure; certain; having no doubt about something. *I am positive it was him.* **2** practical; helpful. *Positive advice.* **3** agreeing; saying yes. *I got a positive reply to my request.* **4** real; noticeable. *It was a positive delight to see you.* **5** greater than zero. *A positive number.* The positive sign is +. **6** If a medical test is positive, it shows that something, usually a disease, is present. **positively** *adverb.*

**possess** *verb* **1** to have or own. **2** to influence somebody's behavior or thinking. *What possessed you to sell your bike?*

**possession** *noun* **1** ownership; possessing. *How did the letter come into your possession?* **2** the things you own. *He left all of his possessions to his son.*

**possessive** *adjective* **1** wanting to keep things for yourself. **2** in grammar, a possessive word shows ownership. "My" and "their" are possessive adjectives. **possessiveness** *noun.*

**possible** *adjective* able to happen, to be done, or that may be true. *Please come as soon as possible.* **possibility** *noun.* **possibly** *adverb.*

**post-** *prefix* later than. *A post-war building.*

**posthumous** *adjective* printed or happening after a person's death. **posthumously** *adverb. The soldier was posthumously awarded a medal.*

**postmortem** *noun* an examination of a dead body to find the cause of death.

**postpone** *verb* to fix a later date or move to a later time. *The game was postponed because of rain.* **postponement** *noun.*

pottery

**potential** *adjective* **1** a natural ability **2** capable of happening or being used. Not yet developed, but able to come into existence. *This movie is a potential success.* **potential** *noun. That boy shows potential.* **potentially** *adverb.*

**potholing** *noun* the sport of exploring underground caves. **pothole** *noun.* **potholer** *noun.*

**pottery** *noun* **1** vases, pots, plates, and other objects that are made from clay and then baked in an oven. **2** a place where pottery is made. **potter** *noun.*

**poultry** *noun* farm birds like chickens and ducks that are kept for eggs and meat.

**pounce** *verb* to leap or swoop down quickly, especially in order to get something. *The cat pounced on the mouse.*

**pound** *noun* **1** a unit of weight equal to 454 grams or 16 ounces. **2** a unit of money used in Britain; one pound is divided into a hundred pence. **3** a place where stray animals and illegally parked cars are taken and kept until collected by their owners. **pound** *verb* **1** to beat or hit loudly and repeatedly. *My heart is pounding.* **2** to crush into a powder or paste.

**pour** *verb* **1** to flow, or to make liquid or another substance flow. *He poured me a drink.* **2** to rain. *It's been pouring all day.* **3** to come or go quickly and in large amounts. *Fan mail has been pouring in.* **pour out** to tell freely and with feeling, especially a story or your troubles.



**poverty** *noun* the state of being very poor.

**power** *noun* **1** the ability to do something or have a certain effect. *He did everything in his power to help.* **2** force; physical strength. *The power of the waves threw shingle up the beach.* **3** energy; the force that makes things work. *Electric power.* **4** authority; the right to do something. *I have the power to arrest you.* **5** a person or organization that has great influence. *America is a world power.* **in power** having the right to govern. **powerful** *adjective.* **powerless** *adjective.*

**practicable** *adjective* that can be done.

**practical** *adjective* **1** good at doing or making things; clever at dealing with difficulties; sensible. **2** useful; convenient; good for a particular purpose. *My practical shoes are not pretty but they are waterproof.* **3** concerned with action and practice, rather than just ideas. *She didn't get the job because she had no practical experience.* **practical joke** a funny trick played on a person. **practicality** *noun.*

**practically** *adverb* **1** in a practical way. **2** almost. *He practically walked into her.*

**practice** *noun* **1** something done regularly or as an exercise. *We have basketball practice twice a week.* **2** doing something; knowledge of a skill. **3** the business of a doctor or lawyer. **practice** *verb* **1** to do something often in order to be good or to get better at it. *I'm practicing this piece on my guitar for the concert.* **2** to take part in an activity or do something actively. *People may practice any religion in this country.* **3** to work as a doctor or lawyer. **out of practice** no longer very good, because of lack of practice.

**pragmatic** *adjective* dealing with things in a practical way, a way which is best under the actual conditions. **pragmatist** *noun.*

prairie

**Prague** *noun* the capital of the Czech Republic in eastern Europe.

**Praia** *noun* the capital of the Cape Verde Islands off West Africa.

**prairie** *noun* a large area of treeless grassland in North America. *Wheat prairies.*

**praise** *verb* to say that somebody or something is very good. *He praised her courage.* **praise** *noun* words that praise somebody or something.

**pray** *verb* to speak to God.

**prayer** *noun* **1** the activity of praying. **2** the words used in praying; a set form of words used during a service. **3** a strong hope. *My prayers were answered when my son got over his illness.*

**pre-** *prefix* before a particular time. *A pre-war building.*

**preach** (preaches, preaching, preached) *verb* to give a talk, especially a moral or religious talk, usually in a church. **preacher** *noun.*

**precaution** *noun* something done in order to avoid a possible known danger or trouble. **precautionary** *adjective.*

**precede** *verb* to go in front.

**precinct** (say **pree**-sinkt) *noun* **1** a specially built shopping area where cars are not allowed. **2** the area around a cathedral or university, often enclosed by walls.

**precious** *adjective* **1** very valuable. **2** much loved by somebody. *My dolls are very precious to me.* **precious little** very little. *He has precious little time for painting because he works so hard.*

**precipice** *noun* a very steep side of a rock, mountain, or cliff. **precipitous** *adjective.*

precipice

**precipitation** *noun* **1** the act of being too hurried; unwise haste. **2** rain or snow that falls. **precipitate** *verb.*

**precise** *adjective* exact; clear. *He gave a precise description of the accident.* **precision** *noun.* **precisely** *adverb. At precisely the moment that the clock struck one, the door opened.*

**precocious** (say pri-**koh**-shus) *adjective* seeming older, having developed earlier than is normal in mind or body. *He is a precocious little boy; he talks like an adult.*

**predecessor** (say **pree**-di-sess-er) *noun* somebody who has had a job before another person, or something that was used before something else. *The new principal is much better than his predecessor.*

**predict** *verb* to say what will or might happen; to forecast. **prediction** *noun. My prediction is that the idea will be very successful.* **predictable** *adjective. A predictable mistake.*

**prefabricated** *adjective* built from parts that have been made in a factory and can be put together quickly. *Prefabricated buildings.* **prefabricate** *verb.*

**preface** *noun* an introduction to a book or speech.

**prefer** (prefers, preferring, preferred) *verb* to like one person or thing better than another. *I prefer coffee to tea.* **preference** *noun. What is your preference?*

**prefix** (prefixes) *noun* a word or group of letters in front of a word that make a new word. The prefix "un-" before "load" makes the word "unload."

**pregnant** *adjective* When a woman or female animal is pregnant, a baby is developing inside her body. **pregnancy** *noun. During her pregnancy, her stomach became enormous.*

**prehistoric** *adjective* of the time before history was written down. *Dinosaurs were prehistoric animals.*

**prejudice** *noun* an unfair opinion or dislike of somebody or something, not based on knowledge or experience. *They were accused of racial prejudice and brought to trial.* **prejudiced** *adjective.*

premature

**premature** *adjective* done or happening earlier than usual or expected. *The premature baby arrived six weeks early and had to be cared for in an incubator.*

**premiere** *noun* the first showing or performance of a movie or play.

**premises** *plural noun* a building and its grounds. *The school premises are well maintained.*

**preoccupied** *adjective* thinking a lot about something and therefore not giving attention to other matters. *She is so preoccupied with plans for her wedding that she can't concentrate on her work.* **preoccupation** *noun.*

**prepare** *verb* to get or make ready. **prepared** *adjective* **1** got ready in advance. **2** willing. *I'm prepared to listen.*

**preposition** *noun* in grammar, a word or group of words used with a noun or pronoun to show its connection with another word with regard to place, position, or time. For example, in "the woman on the stage," "on" is a preposition.

**prescribe** *verb* **1** to advise what medicine or treatment a patient should have. *The doctor prescribed a cough mixture.* **2** to state what must be done. **prescription** *noun. I get the medicine on prescription.*

present

**present** *adjective* (say **pre**-zunt) **1** in this or that place; here. *Is a doctor present?* **2** existing now. *The present government.* **3** being talked or written about now. *We'll make an exception in the present case.* **present** *noun* (say **pre**-zunt) **1** something given; a gift. *Christmas presents.* **2** the time that is taking place now or the things that are happening at the moment. *Try to live in the present, not the past.* **present** *verb* (say pree-**zent**) **1** to give something formally, especially something like a prize. *They presented her with a bouquet of flowers.* **2** to introduce somebody to an important person or introduce a television or radio program. *Professor Bird presented the documentary.* **3** to put on a play or show. **4** to offer, show, or be the cause of. *He loves sailing because it presents such a challenge.* **presentation** *noun.* **presence** *noun. I don't talk about it in her presence.* **at present** now. **presently** *adverb* at this time.

**president** *noun* **1** the leader of a country. *The President of the United States.* **2** someone with a high position in an organization such as a club, college, or company. *The President of our golf club.* **presidency** *noun.* **presidential** *adjective.*

president

Pp

press

**press** (presses) *noun* **1** a machine for printing books and magazines. *A printing press.* **2** a business that prints and makes books and magazines. **3** newspapers, magazines, and all journalists of the media. *He was interviewed by the press.* **4** the action of pushing against something. *At the press of a button.* **5** a device or machine for pressing. *A flower press.* **press** *verb* **1** to push hard against something or push one thing against another. *You have to press harder to make it work.* **2** to squeeze or flatten; to press flowers in a book. **3** to iron. *Please would you press my pants?* **4** to persuade somebody to do something or make demands. *She's always pressing us to stay longer.* **pressed for** short of. *I am pressed for time and money.*

**pressure** *noun* **1** the action of pressing. **2** the force with which something presses. *The water pressure is very low.* **3** a feeling of being forced to do something; a strain. *She was under pressure to do well at school.* **pressure** *verb* forcefully to make someone do something.

**presume** *verb* to think that something is the case or true. *An accused person is presumed innocent until proven guilty.* **presumption** *noun.*

**pretend** *verb* to act as if something is true or real, although in fact it is not, either as a game or to deceive people. *He's just pretending to be asleep, but I know he is really awake.* **pretense** *noun.*

**Pretoria** *noun* the seat of government of South Africa.

**prevailing** *adjective* most common or general, as of a custom or belief. *The prevailing wind is westerly.*

Pp

**prevent** *verb* **1** to stop somebody from doing something. **2** to make sure something does not happen. **prevention** *noun. Crime prevention.* **preventive** *adjective. Preventive medicine.*

**previous** *adjective* happening or being earlier in time, or before the time you are talking about. **previously** *adverb.*

**prey** (say pray) *noun* **1** an animal that is hunted and eaten by other animals. *The lion pounced on its prey.* **2** a victim. **bird of prey** a bird that hunts and eats animals or other birds.

**price** *noun* **1** an amount of money for which something is bought or sold. *We have to fix a price.* **2** something lost in return for something gained. *He paid the price for becoming rich and famous.* **price** *verb* to mark goods in a store with a price. *I've priced the cakes at $2.00 each.*

prey

**priceless** *adjective* worth a lot of money; very valuable. *A priceless painting.*

**pride** *noun* **1** a feeling of delight and pleasure in what you or people you know have done. *She showed him her certificate with pride.* **2** something that makes you feel proud. *The children are her pride and joy.* **3** too high an opinion of yourself, especially because of wealth or position. **4** self-respect. *He swallowed his pride and said sorry.* **pride yourself on** to be proud of. *She prides herself on never having missed a lesson.*

**priest** *noun* **1** a member of the Christian clergy; a clergyman. **2** a specially trained person who performs religious ceremonies. **priestess** *noun.*

**primary** *adjective* extremely important; main. *A peace agreement is our primary aim.* **primarily** *adverb.* **primary colors** red, yellow, and blue, which can be mixed to make up all the other colors.

**prime** *adjective* **1** most important. *Computers are of prime importance in all businesses, hospitals, and schools.* **2** of the very best quality; best. **prime** *noun* the best or most successful stage of something. *She is in her prime.* **prime** *verb* **1** to give somebody information beforehand so that they are prepared. **2** to cover a surface, especially wood, with a coat of paint or oil to prepare it for painting. **3** to get a machine ready for use. **prime minister** the head of a government. **prime number** a number that can be divided only by itself and the number 1, for example, 3, 7, and 11.

**primitive** *adjective* **1** ancient; at an early stage of civilization. *Primitive man made tools from stone.* **2** simple, old-fashioned, or undeveloped.

**prince** *noun* a man or boy in a royal family; the son of a king or queen, or a male ruler in some countries.

**princess** *noun* **1** a woman or girl in a royal family; the daughter of a king or queen. **2** the wife of a prince. *Princess Diana was much loved in England.*

**principal** *adjective* most important. **principal** *noun* **1** the head of a school or college. **2** money lent or put into a business, on which interest is paid.

**principle** *noun* **1** a general rule about how something should be done or how it works. *The principles of grammar.* **2** a rule for behavior. *It was against his principles.* **in principle** in general. *In principle, I agree with you.* **on principle** because of your personal beliefs. *I'm against war on principle.*

**print** *verb* **1** to produce words or pictures on paper with a machine or shapes covered with ink; to make books, magazines, and pictures in this way. *How many copies of this dictionary were printed?* **2** to write words without joining the letters, usually in capitals. *Please print your name and then sign here.* **3** to press a mark onto a surface or make a pattern on cloth. *The pattern has been printed onto the scarf by hand.* **4** to make a photograph from a negative (unprocessed camera film). **print** *noun.*

**printout** *noun* information from a computer printed on a piece of paper.

**prior** *preposition, adjective* earlier or more important than something else. *A prior engagement.* **prior** *noun* a monk who is head of a religious house or priory.

**priority** *noun* something considered more important than other things. *We must make it a priority to tell Sue the news.*

prism

**prism** (say **priz**-um) *noun* **1** a triangular block, usually made of glass, that breaks up light into the colors of the rainbow. **2** a solid shape with a flat base and parallel upright edges.

**privacy** *noun* being private, away from others, and able to do things without other people seeing you.

**private** *adjective* **1** for one person or a small group of people; not public; not shared with others; personal. *A house with a private swimming pool.* **2** secret or kept secret. **3** personal, rather than to do with work or business. *He never talks about his private life.* **4** quiet; not willing to share feelings with other people. **5** independent; not owned by the state. *Private schools.* **in private** without other people hearing. *Can we talk in private?*

**privileged** *adjective* having an advantage over most people. **privilege** *noun* a special honor. *It was a privilege to work with such a famous director.*

**pro** *noun* a professional.

**pro-** *prefix* in favor of. *He is very pro-Italian.* **pro and con** for and against.

**probation** *noun* **1** a period of time during which somebody's abilities at work are tested before they are finally given the job. **2** a system of letting a criminal go free if he behaves well. Somebody on probation is supervised by an official for a period of time.

**probe** *noun* **1** a long, thin, metal instrument used by doctors to search inside the body. **2** an object used for exploring space. **probe** *verb* to search or explore.

**problem** *noun* something difficult; a question for which an answer is needed. **problematic, problematical** *adjective.*

**proboscis** (say pro-**boss**-iss) *noun* **1** the long part of an insect's mouth. **2** an elephant's trunk.

**procedure** *noun* an established way of doing something.

**proceed** *verb* **1** to continue with an action, often after stopping. **2** to go forward in a particular direction.

proboscis

**proceedings** *plural noun* **1** a series of happenings. **2** a lawsuit. *The jury followed the proceedings carefully.*

**process** (processes) *noun* (say **proh**-sess) **1** a series of actions for doing or achieving something. *Packing the car was a slow process.* **2** a series of things that happen naturally. *Chemical processes.* **3** an action in law. **process** *verb* **1** to treat food and other materials in a particular way. *To process (develop) camera film.* **2** to deal with information in an official manner.

**procession** *noun* a group of people or vehicles moving forward, following each other. *A funeral procession.*

**prodigal** *adjective* wasteful, especially of money. *The prodigal son.*

**produce** *verb* **1** to make, grow, or create. *The sun produces heat.* **2** to show or bring out to be seen. *He produced a ticket to prove he had paid.* **3** to make happen. *Good soil will produce good vegetables.* **4** to organize a movie, play, or record. *The movie was directed and produced by the same person.* **produce** *noun* things produced, especially things grown. **producer** *noun.*

**product** *noun* **1** something produced, especially something manufactured. *Cleaning products.* **2** the result of thought or conditions. **3** in arithmetic, the number obtained by multiplying two or more numbers. **production** *noun.*

**profession** *noun* a job that needs special training.

**professional** *adjective* **1** of a particular profession. **2** doing work as a proper job for payment. **3** showing the skill of a professional; competent. **professional** *noun.* **professionally** *adverb.*

professional

**program** *noun* **1** a set of instructions for a computer to carry out. **2** a fixed plan of events, activities, or list of duties. *What is on the program today?* **3** a booklet or list that gives information about what you have come to see or to take part in. *I'll buy a theater program as a souvenir of the play.* **4** a performance, talk, or show on radio or television. *A new music program.* **program** (programs, programing or programming, programed or programmed) *verb. The central heating is programed to come on at six.* **programmer** *noun.*

**progress** (say **prah**-gress) *noun* **1** forward movement; gradually moving nearer something. *We made slow progress up the hill.* **2** development or improvement. *You are making good progress in your work.* **in progress** happening now. *The game is already in progress.* **progress** *verb* (say pruh-**gress**).

**progressive** *adjective* **1** moving forward or happening gradually over a period of time. *The progressive closure of the coal industry.* **2** having modern ideas about how things should be done. *Most progressive schools are against wearing uniforms.*

**prohibit** *verb* to say that something must not be done; to ban. **prohibition** *noun.*

**project** *noun* (say **prah**-jekt) **1** a plan or planned undertaking. **2** a study of a subject by a student. *Our class is doing a project on pop music.* **project** *verb* (say pruh-**jekt**) **1** to stick out above a surface or edge. **2** to cause images to appear on a screen. **3** to throw. **4** to forecast. **projection** *noun.*

**prominent** *adjective* **1** important; well known. **2** standing out; noticeable. *Her rear is the most prominent part of her body.* **prominently** *adverb.* **prominence** *noun.*

**promise** *noun* **1** a statement that you make to somebody to say that you will do or give them something. *She always keeps her promises.* **2** expectation or hope of success. *That singer shows great promise.* **promise** *verb. He promised to buy her a new bike.*

**promising** *adjective* likely to be successful.

**promote** *verb* **1** to give somebody a more important job or higher rank. **2** to bring to notice, especially to increase sales or somebody's popularity. *The company is promoting a new soap.* **promotion** *noun.* **promoter** *noun.*

**prompt** *adjective* without delay; punctual. **promptly** *adverb. He arrived promptly at 9 o'clock.* **prompt** *verb* **1** to make you decide to do something. *Poor results prompted the manager to change the team.* **2** to remind an actor on stage of his next few lines if he has dried up (that is, forgotten the words of the character he's playing).

Pp

**prone** *adjective* lying face downward. **be prone to** be likely to do or have something. *The village is prone to flooding in the winter.*

**prong** *noun* a spike of a fork.

**pronoun** *noun* in grammar, a word that is used in place of a noun that has already been or will be mentioned. "He," "she," "it," "hers," and "them" are pronouns.

**pronounce** *verb* **1** to make the sound of a letter or word. In the word "gnaw," the "g" is not pronounced. **2** to declare formally. *He was pronounced dead.* **pronunciation** *noun* the way words are pronounced. *His French pronunciation has improved greatly since his visit to France.*

**proof** *noun* **1** a thing or fact that shows that something is true. *He has no proof that the car belongs to him.* **2** a trial copy of something printed, made for checking before other copies are printed. **-proof** *suffix* showing that something cannot be damaged or gives protection against something harmful. *A waterproof jacket. A foolproof can-opener. A childproof lid.*

prop

**prop** *noun* **1** a support used to keep something up. **2** (usually plural, props) the furniture and other objects used on stage in a play or on a film set. **prop** (props, propping, propped) *verb* to support or keep something in position by putting something under or against it. *The gardener propped up the branch of the tree with a wooden support.* **prop somebody up** to help and give support to someone.

**propaganda** *noun* information, often false information, put out to influence people. *The extremists handed out leaflets full of propaganda about their cause.*

**proper** *adjective* **1** suitable; correct; right for a situation. *Everything was in its proper place.* **2** respectable or acceptable. *Proper behavior.* **3** inside the limits of an area, like a city. **properly** *adverb. She doesn't eat properly; all she has for lunch is a bag of potato chips.*

**prophecy** (prophecies) *noun* a prediction of future events. **prophesy** *verb.*

**prophet** *noun* **1** a person believed to speak for God; often someone who teaches a religion to people. *Muslims are followers of the Prophet Muhammad.* **2** someone who makes prophecies.

prophet

**proposal** *noun* **1** a plan or suggestion. **2** an offer of marriage.

**propose** *verb* **1** to suggest an idea or plan. **2** to ask somebody to marry you. *Tom proposed to Emma.*

**prosecute** *verb* to accuse somebody of a crime and try to prove it in a court of law. *He was prosecuted for burglary.* **prosecution** *noun* **1** the action of prosecuting somebody. **2** the lawyers who try to prove that an accused person is guilty.

**prospect** (say **pross**-pekt) *noun* **1** a possibility or hope. *What are the prospects of my getting a job?* **2** a wide view. **prospect** (say pruh-**spekt**) *verb* to search in the ground, as for gold, silver, or oil. **prospector** *noun.*

**prosper** *verb* to be successful or rich. **prosperity** *noun.* **prosperous** *adjective.*

**prostrate** *adjective* lying face downward on the ground or on any other flat surface, like a bed.

**protein** *noun* a body-building substance found in living things. Foods rich in protein include meat, eggs, beans, and milk.

**Protestant** *noun* a member of the part of the Christian Church that separated from the Roman Catholic Church in the sixteenth century.

**proton** *noun* a very small piece of matter, an atomic particle, that has a positive electrical charge.

**prototype** *noun* a trial model of a vehicle or machine, from which others have been developed or are copied.

prototype

**proud** *adjective* **1** feeling pleased about something good that you or somebody else has done. *Her mother was proud of her.* **2** having self-respect or having too high an opinion of yourself. *She is too proud to say sorry.* **proudly** *adverb. She proudly showed us her son's medal.*

**prove** *verb* **1** to show that something is true. *Can you prove that you were not in the building on the night that the diamonds were stolen?* **2** to turn out or to be found to be as expected. *He proved to be a bad loser.*

**proverb** *noun* a short, well-known saying, usually giving a general truth. "Too many cooks spoil the broth" is a proverb. **proverbial** *adjective* referred to in a proverb. *The proverbial ill wind blows no one any good.*

**provide** *verb* **1** to give things that are needed or useful. *The hostel provides breakfast.* **2** to state arrangements or make special arrangements that must be fulfilled. **provider** *noun.*

**provided, providing** *conjunction* on the condition that. *I'll lend you some money, provided that you promise to pay me back.*

**province** *noun* **1** a part of a country; a state. *Newfoundland is a province of Canada.* **2** (usually plural, the provinces) all the country outside a capital. **3** special knowledge or learning somebody has or is responsible for. *I work in computing, but games consoles are outside my province.* **provincial** *adjective.*

**provoke** *verb* **1** to make somebody angry, usually on purpose. *That dog bites if provoked.* **2** to cause or force an action. *The boy's rudeness provoked a fight.* **provoking** *adjective* annoying. **provocation** (say proh-vuh-**cay**-shun) *noun.* **provocative** *adjective.*

**prowess** *noun* great ability or skill.

**psalm** *noun* (say sahm) a religious song from the Bible. The Book of Psalms is part of the Old Testament.

**pseudonym** *noun* (say **soo**-do-nim) a false name used by a writer. *Roger Black writes crime fiction under the pseudonym John Smith.*

**psychiatry** *noun* (say sigh-**kie**-uh-tree) the study and treatment of mental illness. **psychiatric** (say sigh-key-**ah**-trik) *adjective.* **psychiatrist** *noun.*

**psychology** *noun* (say sigh-**kol**-oh-jee) the study of the human mind and how it works. **psychological** *adjective. Psychological problems.* **psychologist** *noun.*

**puberty** *noun* (say **pew**-ber-tee) the time in a young person's life when they physically develop into an adult.

**pubic** *adjective* (say **pew**-bic) relating to the area of the body around the sexual organs.

**public** *adjective* belonging to, for, connected with, or known by everyone; not private. *Public transportation.* **public** *noun* all the people. *The castle is open to the public.* **in public** with other people present. *People say different things in public from what they say privately.* **public school** a private school that charges fees.

**publish** *verb* **1** to print and sell books, magazines, newspapers, and other material. *Her first book was published last Spring.* **2** to make known to the public. *The church published the times of the services on its notice board.* **publisher** *noun.*

**puddle** *noun* a small pool of liquid, especially rainwater on the ground.

**puerile** (say **pew**-er-I'll) *adjective* childish.

**puffin** *noun* a small sea bird with a brightly colored beak and black-and-white plumage.

puffin

**pull** *verb* **1** to use force to make something come toward or after you. *He pulled the chair up to the table.* **2** to drive or move a vehicle. **3** to attract interest or support. *Their concerts always pull big crowds.* **4** to injure. *He pulled a muscle in the race.* **pull a face** to make a strange or funny face. **pull apart** to separate by using force. **pull down 1** to make something lower. *Pull down the blind if the sun bothers you.* **2** to demolish a building. **pull in 1** to drive a car somewhere and stop. *We pulled in at the gas station.* **2** to arrive at a station. *The train from Austin has just pulled in.* **pull off 1** to take clothes off quickly. *He pulled off his boots.* **2** to succeed in a difficult situation. *He managed to pull off the trick.* **pull out 1** to take something out. *The dentist pulled out a tooth.* **2** to move or drive out of a place. *The bus pulled out of the station.* **3** to get out of an agreement or situation. **pull through** to recover from a serious illness or accident. *She was very ill, but fortunately she pulled through.* **pull yourself together** to control your feelings and force yourself to be calm, unafraid, and organized.

**pulley** *noun* a wheel over which a rope or chain is moved, used for lifting heavy things.

**pulp** *noun* **1** the soft inner part of a fruit or vegetable. **2** a soft mass of material. *Wood pulp.* **3** cheap books and magazines. **pulp** *verb* to crush.

**pulpit** *noun* a small, raised platform from which the preacher in a church speaks to a congregation.

**pulse** *noun* **1** the regular beating of blood as it is pumped through the body by the heart. You can feel your pulse by touching your wrists. **2** the regular beat or throbbing of music. **pulse** *verb* to beat or shake with strong, regular movements.

**pulverize** *verb* **1** to crush to, or to become, fine powder. **2** to destroy. *The town was pulverized by shelling.*

puma

**puma** (say **pew**-muh) *noun* a large, brown wild cat of western America, also called a cougar or mountain lion.

**pump** *noun* a machine used to force liquid, air, or gas into or out of something through a tube. *A gasoline pump.* **pump** *verb* **1** to force liquid or air into or from something with a pump. *I must pump up my tires.* **2** to get information, usually by asking questions. *He pumped me with questions about my new job.* **3** to force something into somebody or something. *They have pumped a lot of money into the business, and it is now expanding rapidly.*

**pumpkin** *noun* a large, round fruit with a hard orange skin. People hollow out pumpkins and cut faces into the skin to make lanterns at Halloween.



**pun** *noun* an amusing use of words that have the same sound but different meanings.

**punch** (punches) *noun* **1** a hit with a fist. *The boxer had to take a lot of punches before he won the round.* **2** a tool for making holes, especially in paper or leather. **3** a drink made of wine and fruit juice. **punch** *verb* **1** to hit hard with a fist. *He punched him in the stomach.* **2** to make a hole in something.

**punctual** *adjective* doing things at the time appointed. *Josh prides himself on always being punctual and never arriving late for lessons.* **punctually** *adverb.*

**punctuate** *verb* **1** to put periods, commas, and other punctuation marks in a text. **2** to interrupt from time to time, especially a speech. **punctuation** *noun.*

**puncture** *noun* a small hole made by a sharp object, especially in a tire. **puncture** *verb* to make or get a puncture. *A nail in the road punctured my tire.*

**punish** *verb* to make somebody suffer because they have done something wrong. **punishment** *noun.* **punishable** *adjective. Parking here is punishable by a fine.*

**Punjabi** *noun* the language of the Punjab, an area in northwestern India and Pakistan. **Punjabi** *adjective. The Punjabi people.*

**punt** *noun* (chiefly British) a flat-bottomed boat pushed along by a pole. **2** the act of punting a ball. **punt** *verb* **1** to travel in a punt. **2** to kick a ball by dropping it from the hands onto the foot.

punt

**punter** *noun* a person who bets money, especially on horse races.

**pupa** (pupae) *noun* (say **pew**-puh) an insect at the stage of development between a larva (for example, a caterpillar) and an imago (a creature that flies, for example, a butterfly).

**pupil** *noun* **1** somebody, usually a child, who is being taught. **2** the small, round, black opening in the middle of the colored part of your eye. *Susan's pupils dilated when she turned off the light.*

**puppet** *noun* **1** a doll with strings attached, generally to its head, arms, and legs. You make the puppet move by pulling its strings. **2** somebody whose actions are controlled by others. *He is the politicians' puppet.* **glove puppet** a doll that you hold by putting your hand inside its body. **finger puppet** a doll with a tube-shaped body that you put on your finger.

**puppy** (puppies) *noun* a young dog. *My puppy has big feet and is so cute.*

**purchase** *verb* to buy. *I purchased a new coat for the winter when I was in New York.* **purchase** *noun* **1** something bought. **2** the act of buying. *Do you have the receipt showing the date of purchase, madam?* **purchaser** *noun.*

**pure** *adjective* **1** not mixed with anything else; clean and clear. **2** complete; total. *This five-star hotel is pure luxury.* **purity** *noun.*

puppies

**purge** *verb* to get rid of unwanted people or feelings. *I'll purge this town of crime.*

**purple** *adjective, noun* reddish-blue.

**purpose** *noun* **1** a plan; a reason for doing something. *What is the purpose of this machine?* **2** a feeling of having an aim; willpower. *Teaching has given her a sense of purpose.* **on purpose** intentionally; not by accident. *Julie bumped into Jack on purpose.*

**purr** *verb* the low rumbling sound a cat makes when it is pleased. **purr** *noun.*

**purse** *noun* a small bag used for carrying money. **purse** *verb* to draw your lips together into a rounded shape. *She pursed her lips in distaste at the horrible smell.*

**pus** *noun* (say puhss) a thick, yellowish-white, creamy liquid that oozes from an infected wound.

**push** (pushes) *noun* **1** the action of pushing. **2** drive or energy. **push** *verb* **1** to press using force in order to make something or somebody move away or to a different position. *He pushed the window up.* **2** to make your way through something by using force. *Don't push in front of me.* **3** to force somebody to do something or force something on people. *The advertisers are pushing a new drink.* **4** to try to sell something illegal. *To push drugs.* **push ahead** to continue. *We are pushing ahead with the new building.* **push around** to tell someone who is less confident or milder in manner than you what to do in a rude or threatening way. **push for** to try to get. **push on** to continue traveling or trying to achieve something. *We must push on with the journey or we will arrive late.* **push through** to persuade someone to accept a law, policy, plan, or rule, even though there is opposition to it.

**pussyfoot** *verb* to act cautiously. *Don't pussyfoot around; be brave and ask for what you want!*

**put** (puts, putting, put) *verb* **1** to move, place, lay, or fix something or somebody in a certain place or position. *Put your bike in the garage.* **2** to cause something or somebody to be in a particular state. *The news put her in a good mood.* **3** to express something in words or write something down. *She put it very well.* **4** to give money for something, or time or energy to something. *They put $100 into the business.* **put across/over** to describe or explain something to somebody. **put away** to put something into a place where it is usually kept. **put something off** not to do something until later. **put somebody off** **1** not to see somebody until later than planned. **2** to make somebody dislike something or lose interest. *Don't be put off fish because of the smell.* **put on** **1** to turn on a light or a piece of equipment. *She put on a CD.* **2** *He put on his clothes.* **3** to pretend or to behave in an unnatural way. *She only puts on that shy voice.* **4** to add more to something. *She has put on weight.* **put out** **1** to stop a candle or fire from burning. **2** to make something known. *The weatherman put out a bad weather warning.* **3** to place things that are needed somewhere ready to be used. *I put out a clean shirt for you.* **4** to annoy or upset. *I was put out when everybody laughed at me.* **put up** **1** to build. *We put up a new fence.* **2** to give somebody a place to sleep. *We'll put you up for the night.* **3** to raise or unfold. *She put up her hand.* **4** to fix or attach. *To put up a poster.* **5** to provide. *Who is putting up the money for the event?* **put up to** If you put somebody up to something, you tell them to do something foolish. **put up with** to suffer without complaining. *She puts up with a lot from her boyfriend.*

**putrid** (say **pew**-trid) *adjective* rotting and smelling bad. *Putrid vegetation.*

**putty** *noun* a soft paste used to keep glass in window frames or to fill holes.

**puzzle** *noun* **1** a game or toy. *Trying to put the pieces of the wooden puzzle back together kept me occupied for ages.* **2** a difficult question, problem, or something that is hard to understand. *Why she wants to go there is a puzzle to me.* **3** the state of being perplexed or puzzled about something. **puzzle** (puzzles, puzzling, puzzled) *verb* to make somebody feel confused because they do not understand. **puzzle over** to think hard about something confusing. *Dorothy puzzled over the crossword for hours.* **puzzlement** *noun* a puzzled state; perplexity. *She had a look of puzzlement on her face as she read the letter.*

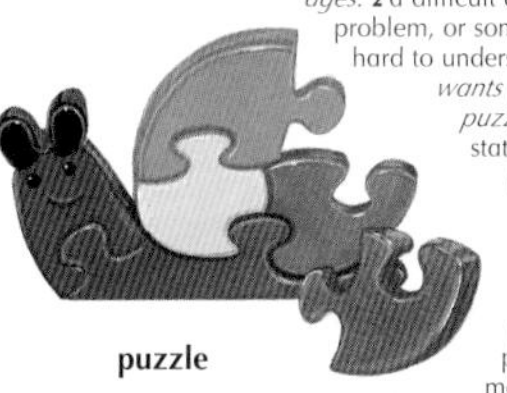

puzzle

**pylon** *noun* a tall metal structure used for holding wires that carry electricity over long distances. *Electricity pylons.*

**Pyongyang** *noun* the capital of North Korea in Asia.

pyramids

**pyramid** *noun* **1** a shape with a flat base and three or four sloping sides that come to a point at the top. **2** an ancient Egyptian stone structure built in a pyramid shape as a tomb for a king or queen.

**pyrotechnics** *noun* **1** the art of making fireworks. **2** a fireworks display.

**python** *noun* a large snake that kills by winding its body around animals and squeezing them to death.

**Qatar** *noun* a country in Southwest Asia.

**quack** *verb* to make the harsh sound that a duck makes. **quack** *noun.*

**quadrangle** *noun* **1** a four-sided shape. **2** a four-sided area or courtyard with buildings all around it.

**quadrant** *noun* **1** a quarter of a circle. **2** an instrument for measuring vertical angles.

**quadri-** *prefix* four.

**quadrilateral** *noun* having four sides.

**quadruped** *noun* any animal with four legs, for example a dog, horse, or elephant.

**quadruple** *verb* to multiply by four. *My allowance has quadrupled in the last ten years.* **quadruple** *noun.*

**quadruplet** *noun* one of four babies born at the same time to the same mother. *The quadruplets are all doing fine, but will stay in hospital for one more day.*

**quagmire** *noun* a soft, marshy area of land. *I got bogged down in a quagmire.*

quail

**quail** *noun* a small, plump bird related to the partridge, often shot as game. **quail** *verb* to show fear by trembling.

**quaint** *adjective* attractively unusual and old-fashioned; charming. *A quaint cottage.* **quaintness** *noun.*

**quake** *verb* to shake; to tremble. *Quentin quaked with fear at the sight of the ghost disappearing through the wall.*

**qualification** *noun* your skills or the training you have had that make you suitable to do a certain job. *The secretary had a qualification in typing.*

**qualify** (qualifies, qualifying, qualified) *verb* **1** to be suitable for a job, especially by passing a test or examination to reach a certain standard. *Karen has qualified as a vet.* **2** to obtain enough points to go on to the next part of a competition. **3** to limit or make a remark less strong. *He qualified his remark that all of his pupils were lazy by adding that only some were lazy.*

**quality** *noun* **1** how good or bad something is. *The sound quality is poor in this theater.* **2** what somebody or something is like; good characteristics. *His best quality is his cheerfulness.*

**qualm** *noun* (sounds like harm) a feeling of unease or misgiving. *Sandra had a qualm of conscience after she lied about who ate the last chocolate candy.*

**quandary** *noun* uncertainty. *I'm in a quandary—should I go or should I stay?*

**quantity** *noun* **1** an amount or number of things. *The quantity of hay in the barn has been reduced because the animals are hungry.* **2** a great amount.

**quantum leap** *noun* a dramatic advance. *We have taken a quantum leap in space research.*

**quarantine** *noun* a period when a person or an animal that may be carrying a disease is kept away from others to prevent the disease from spreading. *Our dog had to be put in quarantine when we brought her back from Mexico in case she had rabies.*

**quarrel** (quarreling, quarreled, quarrels) *verb* to have an angry argument or disagreement with somebody. To stop being friendly. **quarrel** *noun.* **quarrelsome** *adjective. Nobody likes quarrelsome children in the car.*

quarry

**quarry** *noun* **1** a place where sand or stone is dug out of the ground for building. **2** an animal that is being hunted; prey. **quarry** *verb* to dig out sand or stone.

**quart** *noun* a measure of liquid equal to 2 pints or 0.95 liters. *The jug held a quart of milk.*

**quarter** *noun* **1** one of four equal parts into which something can be divided; one-fourth. **2** three months. **3** a 25-cent coin. **4** a district of a city. *The Chinese quarter.* **quarters** a place to stay. *Officers' living quarters.* **quarterly** *adjective* happening every three months. *I take a quarterly magazine.*

**quartet** *noun* **1** a group of four singers or players. **2** a piece of music written for four musicians.

**quartz** *noun* a crystal-like mineral used in pieces of electronic equipment such as quartz clocks or watches.

**quasi-** *prefix* almost or seeming to be. *Quasi-official, quasi-scientific.*

**quaver** *noun* **1** a note in music equal in length to a quarter of a minim or half a crotchet. **2** a tremble in the voice. *A quaver in her voice.* **quaver** *verb* **1** to speak in a trembling voice because of fear or nervousness. **2** to tremble or shake.

quay

**quay** *noun* (say key) an artificial landing place lying alongside or projecting into the water where boats tie up to load and unload.

**queasy** (queasier, queasiest) *adjective* feeling sick; nauseous. **queasiness** *noun.*

**queen** *noun* **1** a female ruler of a country or the wife of a king; a monarch. Queens are not elected but either inherit their position by succeeding the previous ruler or they marry a king. **2** a playing card picturing a queen symbol. **3** a chesspiece that can move in any direction. **4** a large female bee or ant that lays eggs for its colony.

**queer** *adjective* strange; unusual.

**quell** *verb* to crush or put down (a rebellion).

**quench** *verb* **1** to drink enough to satisfy your thirst. **2** to put out a fire. *The firefighters quenched the blaze.*

**query** *noun* a question, a doubt. **query** (queries, querying, queries) *verb* **1** to question. **2** to dispute the accuracy of something.

**quest** *noun* a thorough search.

**question** *noun* **1** what you ask when you want to find out about something. **2** a problem. *The question of finance.* **question** *verb. The teacher questioned her about being late.*

**question mark** *noun* a punctuation mark (?) that is put at the end of a question.

**questionnaire** *noun* a list of questions to be answered by a number of people.

**queue** *noun* (sounds like cue) a waiting line of people or vehicles. **queue** *verb. People are queuing to vote in the election.*

**quibble** *noun* a small, unimportant point not really worth arguing about. *Don't quibble!* **quibbling** *adjective.*

**quiche** *noun* (say **key**-sh) a pastry with a filling of beaten egg and, for example, cheese, ham, or vegetables.

**quick** *adjective* **1** moving rapidly; fast. **2** done in a short time. *A quick snack.* **3** fast to understand; lively. *A quick brain.* **quickness** *noun.*

**quicksand** *noun* dangerously wet sand into which you sink if you walk on it.

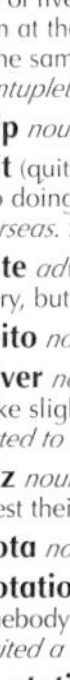

queue

**quicksilver** *noun* the liquid metal called mercury.

**quid** *noun* (British slang) a pound in British money (£1). *Can you lend me a quid?*

**quiet** *adjective* **1** without much noise; silent. **2** calm or without movement. *A quiet life in the country.* **quietness** *noun.*

**quill** *noun* **1** one of the sharp spines on a hedgehog or porcupine. **2** a long, strong feather used as a pen.

**quilt** *noun* a light bed covering filled with warm soft material or feathers.

**quintet** *noun* **1** a group of five singers or players. **2** a piece of music written for five musicians. *A string quintet.*

quintet

**quintuplet** *noun* one of five babies born at the same time to the same mother. *The quintuplets were a surprise.*

**quip** *noun* a witty and often cutting remark.

**quit** (quits, quitting, quitted or quit) *verb* **1** to give up or stop doing something. *She quit her job and moved overseas.* **2** to go away or leave.

**quite** *adverb* **1** totally. *I'm quite sure you are right.* **2** very, but not extremely. *It was quite a good meal.*

**Quito** *noun* the capital of Ecuador.

**quiver** *noun* a long container for arrows. **quiver** *verb* to shake slightly but quickly. *Her lip quivered and she started to cry.*

**quiz** *noun* a game in which people are asked questions to test their knowledge.

**quota** *noun* a share of something.

**quotation** *noun* a person's words repeated exactly by somebody else, particularly from a play or book. *She recited a long quotation from Shakespeare.*

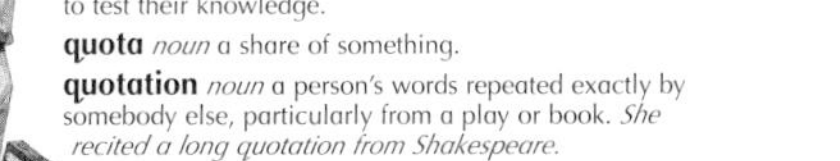

**quotation marks** *plural noun* the punctuation marks ('and') or ("and") used before and after words somebody has said or to highlight words. *"What did you say?" she asked. "Nothing," I replied.*

**quote** *verb* **1** to repeat words that were first said or spoken by somebody else. *He quoted some lines from Shakespeare.* **2** to give a price. *The store quoted me a price for mending my bike.*

**Qu'ran** (alternative to Koran), the Islamic sacred book.

Qq

**Rabat** *noun* the capital of Morocco in North Africa.

**rabbi** *noun* a Jewish religious leader and teacher. *The rabbi prayed in the synagogue.*

**rabbit** *noun* a small, soft, furry animal with long ears that lives in a hole (called a burrow) in the ground.

**rabble** *noun* a crowd of noisy people.

**rabies** *noun* a disease, especially of dogs, passed on by a bite. It makes people and animals go mad and die. **rabid** *adjective* affected with rabies. *The rabid fox.*

**raccoon** (also **racoon**) *noun* a furry animal from North America with a long, banded, bushy tail and sharp snout.

race

**race** *noun* **1** a competition to see who is the fastest. **2** a group of people with the same ancestors and history. **3** a division of people with a type of body or skin color. *The human race.* **race** *verb* **1** to take part in a race. **2** to go quickly. *He raced through his homework.* **race relations** the relationships between people of different races who live in the same country.

**racial** *adjective* of or characteristic of a race or family of human beings. **racially** *adverb. Racially different.*

**racist** *noun* someone who does not like, and discriminates against, people from other races because he thinks his own race is the best or superior. **racist** *adjective. Racist remarks.* **racism** *noun.*

**racket** *noun* **1** a bat with strings across it for playing games such as tennis, squash, or badminton. **2** a loud noise. **3** a dishonest way of making money; a swindle.

**racoon** *noun* see **raccoon**.

**radar** *noun* a way of finding the position or speed of objects by using radio signals that show on a screen. *The plane was last seen on radar.*



**radiant** *adjective* **1** sending out light or heat. *The radiant sun.* **2** looking very happy. *She looked radiant on her wedding day.*

**radiate** *verb* to send out light, heat, or happiness. **radiation** *noun. See* **radioactive**. **radiate from** to spread out from a central point in many directions.

**radiator** *noun* **1** an apparatus, usually connected to a central heating system, used for heating buildings. **2** a device that keeps a car's engine cool.

**radio** (radios) *noun* **1** a method of sending or receiving sound through the air by means of electrical waves. **2** a piece of equipment, a radio set, for listening to radio programs. **3** broadcasting of programs. **radio** *verb. The ship radioed for help.*

**radioactive** *adjective* Something is radioactive if it has atoms that break up and send out radiation in the form of rays that can be harmful to living things. *After the reactor accident, there was radioactive dust in the air.* **radioactivity** *noun.*

**radish** *noun* a small, red vegetable that is eaten raw.

**radius** *noun* **1** the distance, a straight line, from the center of a circle to its outside edge. A circle's radius is half its diameter. **2** the distance from a particular central point where something happens or exists. *All citizens living within a three-mile radius of the town are allowed free bus travel.*

**raft** *noun* **1** logs tied together and used as a boat. **2** an inflatable rubber boat. *The raft saved Jane's life.*

**rage** *noun* **1** a strong, uncontrollable anger. **2** enthusiasm or fervor, especially at its height. **rage** *verb* **1** to be very angry. **2** to be violent. *The storm raged all night.*

**raid** *noun* **1** a sudden attack on an enemy. **2** an unexpected visit by the police. **raid** *verb* to make a raid. *The police raided the man's office.* **raider** *noun.*

**rail** *noun* **1** a fixed bar to hang things on or to hold on to, or forming part of a fence. **2** one of a pair of metal bars along which a train runs. **by rail** in a train.

**railing** *noun* (usually plural, railings) a fence made from metal bars. *I locked my bike to the railings.*

**railroad** *noun* **1** the track or route between two places on which trains run. **2** a system of rail transportation and the organization operating that system.

**rain** *noun* drops of water that fall from clouds. **rain** *verb* **1** to fall as rain. **2** to fall like rain. *Tears rained down her cheeks as the movie came to an end.*

**rainbow** *noun* an arch of colors that appears in the sky when the sun shines through falling raindrops.

**raincoat** *noun* a waterproof coat that is worn in the rain. *Humphrey turned up the collar of his raincoat as he stepped out into the rain.*

**rainfall** *noun* the amount of rain that falls in a place in a certain time. *The Atacama Desert in Chile has the lowest rainfall of any place on Earth.*

**rainforest** *noun* a lush tropical forest with tall trees in which it rains most of the time.

rainforest

**raise** *verb* **1** to move to a higher position. *Raise the flag.* **2** to increase in amount or level. *To raise prices.* **3** to collect or bring together. *To raise money. To raise an army.* **4** to bring up a child or breed animals. **5** to bring up for discussion or attention. *I'm sorry to have to raise the issue of money.* **6** to make appear. *It raised doubts in my mind.* **7** to cause to be heard. *The parade raised a cheer from the crowd.* **raise** *noun* an increase in salary. *They offered me a raise if I would stay in my job, but I didn't accept.*

**rake** *noun* a gardening tool with a row of metal teeth on a bar at the end of a long handle. **rake** *verb* to collect or make smooth with a rake. *He raked the leaves into a pile.* **rake up 1** to collect. **2** to talk about something unpleasant that should be forgotten. *Julie kept raking up the past, asking questions about John's ex-girlfriends.*

**rally** (rallies) *noun* **1** a large public meeting in support of something. *A peace rally.* **2** a car race on public roads. **3** a series of strokes exchanged by players in tennis or badminton. **rally** (rallies, rallying, rallied) *verb* **1** to come together in support of something. *My friends rallied around and helped.* **2** to become stronger; to recover.

ram

**ram** *noun* **1** a male sheep. *The ram with the curly horns can be aggressive.* **2** a device for pushing something. **ram** (rams, ramming, rammed) *verb* to push with great force. *He rammed the coin into the machine.* **RAM** *abbreviation* random access memory. The amount of memory a computer has available that may be used immediately.

**Ramadan** *noun* the ninth month of the Muslim year, when no food or drink is had between sunrise and sunset.

**Ramayana** a Sanskrit epic.

**ramble** *noun* a long walk, often in the country. **ramble** *verb* **1** to walk in the country for pleasure. **2** to talk or write in a confused way. *My grandmother often rambles and says strange things about events that happened during the war.* **rambler** *noun.* **ramble on** to talk for a long time without sticking to the subject. *Lu told us a fairytale before bed, but rambled on so long that we fell asleep before she got to the end.*

**ramp** *noun* **1** a slope built to connect two levels in place of stairs. **2** a slope for driving onto or off a main road or a ferry.

**rampart** *noun* a wide bank of earth, or a barrier, built to protect a fort or city.

**ramshackle** *adjective* badly made and needing repair. *Dad keeps his tools in a ramshackle old shed.*

ranch

**ranch** (ranches) *noun* a cattle-breeding farm in North and South America.

**rancid** *adjective* tasting or smelling unpleasant, especially fatty food.

**random** *adjective* made or done without any plan. *A random selection of CDs.* **at random** without any plan or pattern.

**range** *noun* **1** a connected series of hills or mountains. **2** the distance at which you can see or hear or that a gun can shoot. *Within range, out of range.* **3** a number of different things of the same kind. *We sell a wide range of gardening tools.* **4** the limits that can be measured between two points; the distance between which things vary. *The age range is from 20 to 30.* **5** grassy land in North America for grazing or hunting. **6** an area for shooting practice. **7** a large stove for cooking. **range** *verb* **1** to reach from one limit to another; to vary within limits. *Sizes range from small to extra large.* **2** to place or arrange. **3** to wander.

**ranger** *noun* someone who looks after a park or forest.

**Rangoon** *noun* the capital of Myanmar.

**ransack** *verb* **1** to search a place thoroughly, usually leaving it in a mess. **2** to search and rob a place.

**ransom** *noun* a sum of money that has to be paid to free a kidnapped person. **ransom** *verb* to set somebody free in exchange for a ransom.

**rap** *noun* **1** a quick hit or light knock. **2** blame or punishment. *I'm always taking the rap.* **3** spoken rhymes with a backing of rock music. **rap** *verb* **1** to hit something quickly and lightly. *He rapped him on the knuckles.* **2** to speak in rhymes with a rock music backing.

**rape** *verb* force to perform sexual intercourse with someone against their will. **rape** *noun.* **rapist** *noun.*

**rare** *adjective* **1** uncommon; not often found or happening. *Some orchids are very rare.* **2** lightly cooked. *I like my steak rare.* **rarely** *adverb* not often. **rarity** *noun.*

**Rr**

rat

**raspberry** (raspberries) *noun* a small, soft, red fruit.

**rat** *noun* **1** an animal with a long tail that looks like a large mouse. **2** an untrustworthy person.

**rate** *noun* **1** speed. *We were traveling at a steady rate.* **2** an amount, value, cost, or speed measured by comparing it to some other amount. *The unemployment rate is rising.* **3** a charge. **at any rate** in any case. **at this rate** if things go on in the same way as now. **rate** *verb* to consider, to put a value on something. *The movie is rated as excellent in the newspaper.*

**rather** *adverb* **1** to a slight extent or to a large extent. *It's rather cold today.* **2** more willingly, in preference. *I would rather not say where I've been.* **3** more exactly. *I went to bed late last night – or rather, early this morning.* **4** as an alternative. *I'm looking for something practical rather than fashionable.*

**ratio** (say **ray**-shee-oh) *noun* the relationship between two numbers or amounts which shows how much greater one is than the other. If there are ten applicants for every five jobs, the ratio of applicants to jobs is two to one.

**ration** *noun* a fixed amount allowed to one person. *I've eaten my ration of candies for this week.* **ration** *verb* **1** to limit somebody to a ration. **2** to limit something. *During the hot weather, water was rationed.*

**rational** *adjective* **1** sensible. *There must be a rational explanation.* **2** able to think and make decisions and judgments. *She's usually a very rational person.* **rationally** *adverb.* **rationality** *noun.*

**rattle** *noun* **1** short, sharp sounds. **2** a baby's toy that makes a rattling sound. **rattle** *verb* **1** to make short, sharp sounds. *The windows rattled in the wind.* **2** to make somebody nervous. *She gets rattled if you ask her too many questions.* **rattle off** to say something quickly without thinking. *She rattled off the answers automatically.* **rattle on** to continue to talk quickly and without thinking.

**rattlesnake** *noun* a poisonous American snake that makes a rattling noise with its tail. *He was bitten by a rattlesnake.*

rattlesnake

**raucous** (say **raw**-kus) *adjective* loud and unpleasant, especially of voices. *There was a lot of raucous shouting.*

**rave** *verb* **1** to talk wildly and in an uncontrolled way. *He had a high temperature and was raving all night.* **2** to talk or write enthusiastically about something. **rave** *noun* a large party with loud music.



**raven** *noun* a large black bird. **raven** *adjective* glossy black. *Her raven hair was as black as night.*

**ravenous** *adjective* very hungry.

**ravine** (say ra-**veen**) *noun* a very deep, narrow valley.

**raw** *adjective* **1** not cooked. **2** in the natural state; not treated. *Raw materials.* **3** untrained; new to a job. **4** without skin. *Her fingers were rubbed raw.* **5** of weather, cold and wet. **rawness** *noun.* **raw deal** unfair treatment. *The actor had a raw deal when his lines were cut.*

**ray** *noun* **1** a beam of heat, light, or energy. *Dust floated in the rays of sun that came through holes in the barn roof.* **2** a small amount. *A ray of hope.* **3** one of a number of lines radiating out from the center of something.

**razor** *noun* an instrument used for shaving hair.

**re-** *prefix* again. *He remarried last year.*

**reach** *verb* **1** to arrive at; to get to. *When did the news reach you?* **2** to stretch out a hand to get or touch something. *Can you reach the cup on the top shelf?* **reach** (reaches) *noun* **1** the distance that you can reach. *Put the bottle out of the child's reach.* **2** the length of an arm. *Sebastian has a very long reach.* **3** a straight stretch of a river between two bends.

**react** *verb* to behave in a particular way because of something, to behave differently as a result. *How did your mother react when you told her you wanted to be a model?* **reaction** *noun.* **1** an effect produced by an earlier action. **2** a change in one chemical substance caused by another. *A chemical reaction.*

**reactionary** *adjective* against changes in society. **reactionary** *noun.*

reactor

**reactor** *noun* (in full, **nuclear reactor**) an apparatus or structure in which nuclear energy is produced.

**read** (reads, reading, read) *verb* **1** to look at and understand or say out loud something written or printed. *He plays lots of instruments, but he can't read music.* **2** to guess how somebody feels. *I can read her mind.* **3** to say. *The sign reads "Exit."* **4** to show or register. *The thermometer reads 35 degrees.* **read up on** to find out about something by reading about it. *I'm reading up on the Civil War.* **readable** *adjective* interesting and easy to read. **reader** *noun.* **reading** *noun.*

**real** *adjective* actually existing; not imaginary or artificial. *Real pearls are more beautiful than fake ones.*

**realistic** *adjective* **1** practical, based on actual facts. *Their prices are realistic.* **2** like people or things in real life. *A realistic painting.* **realism** *noun.*

**reality** (realities) *noun* something real; the truth.

**realize** *verb* **1** to understand; to become aware of something. *I never realized that she was your mother.* **2** to make a hope or plan happen. *He realized his dream of becoming a transAtlantic yachtsman.* **3** to get money by selling something. **realization** *noun.*

**realm** *noun* (say relm) **1** a kingdom. **2** an area of thought or knowledge. *Pixies exist only in the realm of fantasy.*

**reap** *verb* **1** to cut and gather. *We reaped the grape harvest.* **2** to gain as a result of something done. *One day she'll reap the benefit of all that hard work.*

reap

**reason** *noun* **1** a cause of an event; an explanation for an action. **2** the ability to think and make judgments; common sense. **reason** *verb* **1** to think carefully and decide. **2** to argue in order to persuade somebody to do something.

**reasonable** *adjective* **1** sensible. **2** fair; not too much. **reasonably** *adverb.*

**rebel** (rebels, rebelling, rebelled) *verb* (say rib-**el**) to fight or protest against anybody in power. **rebel** *noun* (say **reb**-ul) somebody who rebels. *The rebels stormed the castle.* **rebellious** *adjective.* **rebellion** *noun* fighting or opposition to anybody in power.

**recede** *verb* **1** to move back or farther away. *His hair is receding and he will soon be completely bald.* **2** to disappear. *The boat receded into the distance.*

**receipt** *noun* (say ri-**seet**) **1** a piece of paper that states that money or goods have been received. *I will need a receipt for the payment.* **2** the act of receiving. *He rang the school upon receipt of the letter.*

**receive** *verb* **1** to obtain something given or sent to you. *I received the news with joy.* **2** to suffer. *She received a minor blow to the head when the apple fell from the branch.* **3** to welcome a visitor.

receiver

**receiver** *noun* **1** the part of a telephone that you speak into. **2** a person who receives something, especially stolen goods. **3** the part of a radio or television set that receives broadcasts. **4** a person officially appointed to take charge of a bankrupt business.

**reception** *noun* **1** the way somebody or something is received; a welcome. **2** an area in an office, hotel, or large organization where appointments, reservations, and enquiries can be made. **3** a formal party. **4** the quality of receiving sounds or pictures from radio or television.

**recess** (recesses) *noun* **1** a period of time when work or business is stopped. *The judge called a recess.* **2** a space in the wall of a room. *Let's put shelves in the recess.* **3** a hidden part that is difficult to reach.

**recession** *noun* **1** a decline in wealth and economic success. **2** a withdrawal.

**recipe** *noun* instructions on how to cook a particular dish, or make something else.

**recite** *verb* to say something learned out loud. *She recited the poem in class.*

**recognize** *verb* **1** to know what something is or who somebody is. **2** to agree; to see clearly. *The importance of his work has now been recognized.* **3** to accept as real, welcome, or lawful. *The new government was not recognized by the people.* **recognition** *noun.*

**recommend** *verb* to say that somebody or something would be good or useful for a particular job. *I can recommend a good carpenter.* **recommendation** *noun.*

**record** *noun* (say **rek**-ord) **1** information, especially facts, either written down or stored on a computer. *She keeps a record of how much she spends.* **2** in the past, a disk on which sound, especially music, was stored. **3** the best yet done, especially in sports, or the most amazing achievement. *He broke the world record for the 20-yard dash.* **4** facts known about the past or somebody's past life. *This airline has a good safety record.* **record** *verb* (say ri-**kord**) **1** to put something down in writing or on a computer. **2** to store sound or television pictures on disk or tape. *We recorded the new album in the studio.* **recording** *noun.* **for the record** to be reported. **off the record** not to be written down or made known.

record

**recover** *verb* **1** to become well again. **2** to get something back after it has been lost or taken away. **recovery** *noun.*

**recruit** *noun* a new member of an army, group, or society. **recruit** *verb* to get new members. *Lots of people were recruited to put up tents in the field.*

**rectangle** *noun* a long shape with four straight sides and four right angles. **rectangular** *adjective.*

**recuperate** *verb* to get better and become strong again after an illness.

**recur** (recurs, recurring, recurred) *verb* to happen again, either once or many times. **recurrence** *noun.*

**recycle** *verb* to treat things that have already been used so that they can be used again. *In our town, we recycle newspapers and bottles.* **recyclable** *adjective. Some aluminum cans are recyclable.*

**red** *noun* the color of blood. **red** *adjective. Red wine.* **see red** to become very angry. **in the red** to have spent more money than is in your bank account. **red herring** something that takes people's attention away from the important facts of the matter. *The diamond ring that the detective found in the grass was a red herring; it had been dropped by Lady Susan while she was gardening, and did not prove that the robber had escaped across the lawn at all!*

**redundant** *adjective* not necessary or needed because something else means or does the same thing. *"A single, unmarried man" is a redundant phrase.* **redundancy** *noun.*

**refectory** (refectories) *noun* the dining hall in a monastery or convent.

**refer** (refers, referring, referred) *verb* **1** to speak about or mention. **2** to go to for information. *We were not allowed to refer to a dictionary in the test.* **3** to send somebody or something, especially a problem, to somebody else for action. *He was referred to a specialist.*

**reference** *noun* **1** a mention of something. *There were a number of references to the trial in the paper.* **2** referring to somebody or something for information; a note that tells you where information can be found. *I use my computer for quick reference.* **3** a statement, usually a letter, about a person's character. *His professor gave him a good reference.* **with reference to** regarding. **reference book** a book in which you can look things up. *Dictionaries and encyclopedias are useful reference books.*

**referendum** *noun* a vote in which all the people in a country or area are asked to decide on a particular political question.

**Rr**

**refine** *verb* **1** to make substances free from impurities or defects by taking out unwanted substances. *Refined sugar.* **2** to make more cultured. *The lessons refined her understanding of art.*

**refinery** (refineries) *noun* a factory where substances such as oil or sugar are refined.

**reflection** *noun* **1** the sending back of light, heat, or sound from a surface. **2** an image of something in a mirror or shiny surface. *She looked at her reflection in the lake.* **3** a deep thought. *Reflections on old age.* **4** something that makes a bad impression. *Vandalism is a sad reflection on society.* **5** being the result of something. *His meanness is a reflection of his upbringing.* **upon/on reflection** after thinking about something. **reflect** *verb.*

**reform** *verb* to make or become better. *He decided to reform his behavior in the playground after he got into trouble for being too rough.* **reform** *noun. Prison reforms.*

**refrain** *noun* part of a song that is repeated at the end of each verse. *We all sang the refrain at the tops of our voices.* **refrain** *verb* to hold yourself back from doing something. *I refrained from telling John I loved him in case he didn't feel the same way about me.*

**refreshing** *adjective* **1** pleasing and interesting; different from what you are used to. *It was refreshing to meet such helpful people.* **2** giving strength. *I had a most refreshing sleep after the long journey.* **refresh** *verb.*

**refreshments** *plural noun* light food or drink. *Refreshments are served.*

**refrigerator** *noun* a large box or cupboard in which food and drinks are kept cool.

**refuge** *noun* a place that gives shelter and protection from trouble or danger. *The explorers found refuge from the storm in a cave in the hillside.*

**refugee** *noun* a person who has been forced to leave home, usually his or her country, because of war or a natural disaster. *Refugees poured across the border after the earthquake had destroyed their homes.*

**refugee**

**refuse** *noun* (say **reh**-fyooss) waste material, garbage. *There is a weekly refuse collection in our street.* **refuse** *verb* (say rih-**fewz**) to say "no" to something; not to do or accept something. *She refused my offer of help because she was too proud to acknowledge that she needed assistance.* **refusal** *noun.*

**regal** *adjective* (say **ree**-gul) **1** royal; of or by a monarch. **2** suitable for a king or queen; splendid.

**regatta** *noun* an event at which boat races are held.

**region** *noun* a large area, especially of land. **in the region of** about.

**register** *noun* **1** an official list of things or names, such as births, marriages, and deaths. **2** the range of a voice or musical instrument. **register** *verb* **1** to list something in a register. **2** to show on a scale; record. *The thermometer registered 35 degrees.* **3** to make something clear, usually a feeling or an opinion. *Her face registered delight.* **4** to send a letter or parcel by registered mail, whereby compensation is paid for loss or damage.

**regret** (regrets, regretting, regretted) *verb* to feel sorry about something you have done or not done. **regret** *noun.* **regrettable** *adjective.* **regretful** *adjective.*

**regular** *adjective* **1** happening, coming, or doing something again and again at certain times. *Regular meals.* **2** evenly arranged or shaped; not varying. *Regular, white, shining teeth.* **3** normal, standard, or proper. *That's not the regular procedure.* **4** A regular verb is a verb that follows the common pattern. The verb "write" is not a regular verb. **regularly** *adverb.* **regularity** *noun.*

**rehearse** *verb* to practice something, especially a play, speech, or music, before a performance. **rehearsal** *noun.*

**reign** *verb* (say rain) **1** to rule a country as a king or queen. **2** to exist. *Silence reigned.* **reign** *noun. I was born during the reign of Queen Elizabeth II.*

**rein** *noun* a strap for guiding a horse. *Don't let go of the reins!*

**reindeer** (reindeer) *noun* a deer with large antlers that lives in the coldest parts of the world. *The people of Lapland herd reindeer for a living.*

reindeer

**reinforce** *verb* to make stronger. *Reinforced concrete is strengthened with metal bars.* **reinforcement** *noun.*

**reject** *verb* **1** to not accept a person or thing. *The machine rejects bent coins.* **2** to throw away or send back as not good enough. *The oranges were rotten and had to be rejected.* **rejection** *noun.*

**rejoice** *verb* to feel or show great happiness. *The runner rejoiced when he crossed the winning line first.*

**relapse** *verb* to fall back into a worse state, or to return to a previous condition, usually after having been better. **relapse** *noun.*

**relate** *verb* **1** to see or show a connection; to compare one thing with another. *It is difficult to relate these two results.* **2** to tell a story. **3** to get along with. *He cannot relate to cats, but loves dogs.*

rejoice

**relation** *noun* **1** a member of your family. **2** a connection. *There is no relation between her health and her results at school.* **relations** the dealings between people or groups. *Business relations with Germany improved under the new President.*

**relationship** *noun* **1** how people and things are connected. *The relationship between light and heat.* **2** a family connection. *What is your brother's relationship to your aunt's cousin?* **3** a friendship or the way people or groups behave toward each other. *She has never had a better relationship.*

**relative** *adjective* **1** compared to each other or to something else. **2** connected with. **relative** *noun* a person who is related to another; a relation. *My aunt is my only living relative.* **relatively** *adverb.*

**relax** *verb* **1** to become less stiff, tight, or strict. *He relaxed his grip on the wheel.* **2** to be more calm; to rest. *Gwyneth relaxed on the beach.*

**relay** *noun* **1** a relay race; a team race in which each member runs part of the whole distance. **2** a fresh group taking over from a tired one. *We worked all through the night in relays.* **3** a piece of equipment that receives messages by telephone, television, or radio and passes them on to another place. **relay** *verb* to pass on a message or broadcast.

relay

**release** *verb* **1** to set free. *The orphaned lion cub was released into the wild after it had been taught how to hunt for itself.* **2** to let your grip go. *Jeremy released his hold on the rope and let the sail flap in the wind.* **3** to allow to be shown or published. *His new single will be released on Monday.* **release** *noun* **1** being released or something released. **2** a new film, record, or piece of news that has come out. **3** a handle, button, or other device that can be pressed to unfasten something.

**relent** *verb* to become less stern. *She relented after hearing the explanation.*

**relentless** *adjective* without pity.

**relic** *noun* **1** something that was used or made a long time ago. **2** something that belonged to a saint and is usually kept in a church. *The tooth in this silver casket is believed to be a relic of Saint James.*

**relief** *noun* **1** a lessening or ending of pain, worry, or boredom. *It was a relief to know that the mother and baby were both doing well.* **2** help for people in trouble, especially food, money, and clothes. *Famine relief is of vital importance in times of crisis.* **3** a person or group taking over a duty for another.

**relieve** *verb* **1** to lessen pain, trouble, or boredom. **2** to take over a duty from somebody else. *To relieve the guard.* **relieve of** to rob somebody of something.

**religion** *noun* **1** a belief in one god or many gods. **2** the expression of a religious belief in worship. **religious** *adjective. A religious text.*

**reluctant** *adjective* unwilling. **reluctantly** *adverb. He reluctantly agreed to go out in the rain.*

**rely** (relies, relying, relied) *verb* to depend on something happening or to trust somebody or something. *She has always relied on her parents for support.* **reliance** *noun.*

**remain** *verb* **1** to be left behind after other parts have gone. *Two of the guests remained.* **2** to continue to be the same; to stay unchanged. *He remained silent.* **it remains to be seen** we will know later on.

**remainder** *noun* the rest; the part that is left over. *She ate the remainder of her dinner the next day.*

**remains** *plural noun* **1** relics, especially buildings, from ancient times. *The Roman remains are a spectacular sight, especially at dawn.* **2** parts that are left after everything else has gone. *They found some remains of Greek pottery.* **3** a dead body. *The businessman's remains were buried in the family vault.*

**remains**

**remarkable** *adjective* worth speaking about; impressive. **remarkably** *adverb.*

**remember** *verb* **1** to keep in the mind. *I'll always remember the first time we met.* **2** to call to mind, especially after having forgotten it for a while. **remembrance** *noun. The remembrance of her wedding gave her great pleasure.*

**remind** *verb* to tell somebody something they already knew or to make someone recall something. *She reminds me of my mother.* **reminder** *noun.*

**remnant** *noun* **1** a small part of something left over. *We ate the remnants of the meal.* **2** a small piece of fabric.

**remorse** *noun* a feeling of guilt about something you have done wrong. **remorseful** *adjective.*

**remove** *verb* to take something away, off, or out. *How can I remove this stain?* **removal** *noun.*

**renew** *verb* **1** to replace something old with something new of the same kind. *Passports have to be renewed every ten years.* **2** to begin or make again. *After meeting again, we renewed our old friendship.* **3** to put new strength into something; to make as good as new again. **renewal** *noun.*

**renown** *noun* fame; being well known for something good. *A writer of high renown.* **renowned** *adjective.*

**rent** *noun* an amount of money paid for the use of something, like an apartment or house belonging to someone else. **rent** *verb. I rent my house from a landlord.* **rent out** to allow something to be used in return for rent.

Rr

**repair** *verb* to mend or put something right that has broken or gone wrong. **repair** *noun.*

**repay** (repays, repaying, repaid) *verb* to give back, especially money. **repayment** *noun.*

**repeat** *verb* to say or do the same thing again. **repeat** *noun. This TV program is a repeat – I saw it last year.*

**repel** (repels, repelling, repelled) *verb* **1** to drive back. *The army repelled the attack.* **2** to find something horrible or disgusting. *The sight of blood repels him.* **repellent** *adjective, noun. Insect repellent.*

**repel**

**replica** *noun* a copy, especially of a work of art. *This is only a cheap replica of the original statue.*

**reply** (replies) *noun* something said or written as an answer to somebody. *I rang Jane's doorbell, but there was no reply.* **in reply** as an answer. **reply** (replies, replying, replied) *verb* to give an answer.

**report** *verb* **1** to tell or give information about something. *They reported the accident to the police.* **2** to make a complaint against somebody. *The teacher reported the boy to the principal.* **3** to let someone know that you are present. *We have to report to the manager every morning.* **report** *noun* **1** a written or spoken account of an event. **2** a written account of how well or badly a pupil has done during school term. **3** the sound of an explosion.

**reporter** *noun* somebody who writes or broadcasts news reports.

**reporter**

**represent** *verb* **1** to be a picture, sign, or example of something; to show or mean. *Love is often represented by a heart.* **2** to act for another person, especially as a lawyer or leader of a group. *We chose Gregory to represent the class at the school meeting.* **representation** *noun.*

**representative** *noun* somebody chosen to represent others. *Travel representatives welcome and help tourists.* **representative** *adjective* being an example of what others are like. *This picture of water lilies by Monet is representative of Impressionist painting.*

**repress** *verb* to hold back or control. *Steve could hardly repress a grin.* **repression** *noun.*

**reprieve** *noun* a delay before something unpleasant happens or an official cancellation of the punishment of a prisoner, especially a death sentence. **reprieve** *verb.*

**reprimand** *verb* to tell somebody officially that they should not have done a particular thing. **reprimand** *noun.*

**reproduce** *verb* **1** to make a copy of something. To cause something to be seen or heard again. *This painting has been reproduced in many books.* **2** to produce young animals or plants. **reproduction** *noun.*

**reptile** *noun* an animal with scaly skin whose blood changes temperature according to the temperature around it. Snakes, lizards, and crocodiles are all reptiles.

**republic** *noun* a country with an elected president at the head, rather than a king or queen. **republican** *noun.*

**repugnant** *adjective* horrible and disgusting. *The skunk emitted a repugnant smell.*

**repulsive** *adjective* horrible. *Some people find eating snails repulsive.* **repulsion** *noun.*

**reputation** *noun* people's opinion of how good somebody or something is. If you live up to your reputation, you behave in the way people expect you to.

**request** *noun* asking for something or the thing asked for. **request** *verb* to ask politely for something.

**require** *verb* **1** to need. **2** to demand or make somebody do something. *Students are required to bring their own dictionaries.* **requirement** *noun.*

**rescue** *verb* to save from danger; to set free. *The firefighter rescued the child from the burning house.* **rescue** *noun.* **rescuer** *noun.*

**research** (researches) *noun* the study of a subject to find out facts and information. **research** *verb. Luke is researching the feeding habits of monkeys in the African jungle.* **researcher** *noun.*

**resemble** *verb* to be like or similar. *She resembles her aunt; they have the same nose.* **resemblance** *noun.*

**reservation** *noun* **1** an arrangement to keep something for somebody for later use. *I've made a reservation for a table for six.* **2** doubt in your mind. *I've got reservations about going out in such bad weather.* **3** a piece of land kept for a special purpose.

**reserve** *verb* to keep or order something for somebody. *We reserved two hotel rooms.* **reserve** *noun* **1** something kept for later use. *Reserves of food.* **2** an extra player who may replace another player before or during a game. **3** a piece of land set aside for a special purpose. *A nature reserve.* **4** not showing your feelings. **reserved** *adjective.*

reservoir

**reservoir** (say **rez**-uh-vwar) *noun* a place resembling a lake where lots of water is stored.

**resident** *noun* a person who lives in a particular place. *Parking is for residents only.* **resident** *adjective. The resident doctor.*

**resign** *verb* to give up your job or position. *He disagreed with the committee and resigned.* **resign yourself** to accept and put up with something without complaint. *She resigned herself to staying another hour at her desk.* **resignation** *noun.*

**resist** *verb* to fight back against something or not allow yourself to do something. *I can't resist another piece of cake.* **resistance** *noun. Resistance is futile – you'll give up in the end!* **resistant** *adjective.*

**resolution** *noun* **1** being firm. **2** something you make up your mind to do; a promise *My New Year's resolution is to give up candy.* **3** a formal decision taken at a meeting, especially after a vote. **4** the act of resolving.

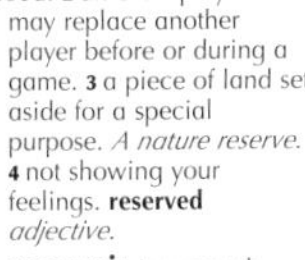

resort

**resolve** *verb* **1** to decide. *She resolved to work harder.* **2** to solve a problem.

**resort** *noun* a popular place, particularly for skiing or swimming. *Aspen is a famous skiing resort.* **resort** *verb* to turn to because your options are limited; to do or go for help, relief, or advantage. *When he lost his bunch of keys, he resorted to breaking a window.*

**resourceful** *adjective* clever at finding ways of doing or achieving things.

**resources** *plural noun* possessions such as wealth or goods. *Oil is one of the country's main resources.*

**respect** *noun* **1** a high opinion or admiration of somebody. *She has great respect for his work.* **2** If you show respect to somebody, you are polite. **3** a detail or particular point. *She's like her mother in every respect.* **with respect to** relating to. *With respect to your order, please find the invoice enclosed.* **respect** *verb.*

**respond** *verb* to reply or react to something. **response** *noun. He made no response to the question.*

**responsibility** (responsibilities) *noun* **1** the duty of having to deal with something and make decisions. Being responsible. *If you borrow my bike, it's your responsibility to keep it locked.* **2** a duty; something for which you are responsible. *Parents have a lot of responsibilities.*

**responsible** *adjective* **1** having the duty of looking after somebody or something; having to take the blame if things go wrong. *She is responsible for keeping her room clean.* **2** trustworthy. **be responsible for** to be the cause of. *Who is responsible for the damage?* **responsibly** *adverb.*

**rest** *noun* **1** not doing anything active; quiet or sleep. **2** a support. **3** the part that is left; the others. **rest** *verb* **1** to stop and relax. *She never rests for long.* **2** to support or be supported. *Rest your head on your knees.* **rest assured** be certain. **restful** *adjective.* **restless** *adjective.*

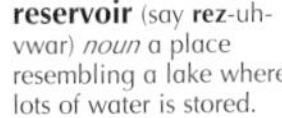

rest

**restaurant** *noun* a public place where you can go to be served a meal in exchange for money.

**restore** *verb* **1** to give back, especially something stolen or lost. **2** to put or bring back as before. *The old church has been restored.* **restoration** *noun.*

Rr

**restrain** *verb* to hold back from doing something; to control. **restraint** *noun.*

**restrict** *verb* to keep within a limit. *She restricts herself to two cups of coffee a day.* **restriction** *noun.*

**resume** *verb* to begin again. *Talks between the two parties resumed yesterday.* **resumption** *noun.*

**résumé** *noun* a summary; a written description of past experience used when seeking employment.

**resurrection** *noun.* **1** the revival of a thing or ideas after disuse. **2** the act of rising from the dead. **the Resurrection** Christ's rising from the dead. **resurrect** *verb* **1** to bring back into use. *I resurrected the old piano from the barn.* **2** to bring back to life.

**resuscitate** *verb* to revive a person from a state of unconsciousness or death. **resuscitation** *noun.*

**retail** *noun* the selling of goods to the public. **retail** *verb* to sell goods. *The camera retails at $100.* **retailer** *noun.*

**retain** *verb* to keep or continue to have.

**retina** *noun* the area at the back of the eye that is sensitive to light.

**retire** *verb* **1** to stop working at a certain age. *My father retired at 60.* **2** to leave a place or room. **3** to go to bed. **retirement** *noun.*

**retreat** *noun* **1** the act of retreating. **2** a quiet, restful place. *We went for a weekend retreat in the country.* **retreat** *verb* to go away or move back, especially when forced to do so. *After a three-day battle, the exhausted enemy retreated.*

**reunion** *noun* a meeting of old friends or family members who have not seen each other for some time. *At the school reunion, Carolyn met her old friends.*

**reveal** *verb* **1** to uncover something so it can be seen. *Her dress revealed a tattoo on her shoulder.* **2** to make known. *He revealed a secret.* **revelation** *noun.*

**revenge** *noun* hurting in return for having been hurt. *Tom squirted water at his brother Jack in revenge for the trick that Jack had played on him.* **revenge** *verb.*

**revenue** *noun* **1** income from any source **2** money paid to the government as tax to meet public expenses.

**reverse** *adjective* opposite in position or order. *The reverse side of the material has lines through it.* **reverse** *noun* **1** the exact opposite. *She always does the reverse of what you expect.* **2** the back. **3** a gear in which you drive a car backward. **reverse** *verb* **1** to go backward. *She reversed the car into the parking space.* **2** to change to the opposite or change around. **reversal** *noun.* **in reverse** in the opposite way from what usually happens.

**review** *noun* **1** a critical opinion in a newspaper or magazine or on radio or television about a book, movie, concert, or play. **2** an inspection or examination. *Hospital practices have been under review.* **review** *verb.*

**revise** *verb* **1** to study facts already learned, especially for an examination. **2** to change or correct something. *He's been so helpful, I'll have to revise my opinion of him.* **revision** *noun. I still have a lot of revision to do.*

**revive** *verb* to come back to life or strength again; to bring back. *A warm drink will soon revive me after that walk in the snow.* **revival** *noun.*

**revolt** *noun* a fight to change a system. **revolt** *verb* **1** to fight against authority. *The army revolted against the dictator it had served and marched on his palace.* **2** to be disgusted. **revolting** *adjective. A revolting week-old banana skin was rotting on the sink.*

**revolution**

**revolution** *noun* **1** a rebellion, especially one overthrowing a political system. **2** complete change of method or of ways of doing things. *The green revolution.* **3** one complete turn of a wheel. **revolutionary** *adjective.* **revolutionize** *verb. Computers have revolutionized office work.*

**revolve** *verb* to turn or keep turning around.

**revolver** *noun* a small gun that does not have to be reloaded after each shot.

**reward** *noun* **1** something given in return for something good or useful you have done. **2** an amount of money given to somebody who helps the police. **reward** *verb. The boy was rewarded for his bravery with a medal.*

**rewarding** *adjective* giving you satisfaction. *Nursing can be a rewarding job.*

**Reykjavik** *noun* the capital of Iceland in the far northwest of Europe.

**rheumatism** (say **roo**-muh-tizum) *noun* an illness that makes joints or muscles stiff and painful. **rheumatic** *adjective.*

**rhinoceros**

**rhinoceros** (rhinoceroses) *noun* a large, plant-eating animal from Africa or Asia with one or two horns on its nose and plated or folded skin.

**rhyme** *noun* **1** a similar sound at the ends of words or lines in poetry, as in "say" and "day," "school" and "fool." **2** a word that rhymes with another. **3** a short piece of writing with rhymes. **rhyme** *verb.*

**rickety** *adjective* not made strongly, likely to break. *The old chairs were rickety.*

**riddle** *noun* a difficult question to which you must guess the answer. **riddle** *verb* to make full of holes. *He riddled the target with bullets.* **riddled with** full of.

rig

**ridiculous** *adjective* silly; absurd.

**rig** *noun* **1** a large structure that is used for drilling for oil or gas. *An oil rig.* **2** the way a ship's sails and masts are arranged. **rig** (rigs, rigging, rigged) *verb* **1** to provide a ship with ropes and sails. **2** to arrange an election or other event dishonestly in order to get the results that are wanted. *The race was obviously rigged.* **rig up** to put something together quickly out of materials that are handy. *The scouts rigged up a shelter for the night.*

**Riga** *noun* the capital of Latvia in the Baltic region.

**rigging** *noun* the ropes and sails of a ship.

**rigid** *adjective* **1** stiff; not bending. **2** strict. *The army has rigid discipline.*

**rind** *noun* the tough outer skin of fruit, cheese, or bacon.

**rink** *noun* an enclosed ice surface for skating.

**rinse** *noun* **1** rinsing with clean water. **2** a liquid dye for coloring hair. **rinse** *verb* to wash something with clean water and without soap.

**riot** *noun* violent or noisy behavior by a crowd, usually in a public place. **riot** *verb* to take part in a riot.

rink

**rip** (rips, ripping, ripped) *verb* **1** to tear quickly. *She ripped her skirt on the fence.* **2** to remove quickly. *He ripped the letter out of her hand.* **rip** *noun.* **rip off** to cheat someone by asking too much money for something. **rip-off** a fraud or swindle.

**ripe** *adjective* **1** ready to be picked and eaten. **2** to be fit for something. *The country is ripe for change.* **ripen** *verb.*

**ripple** *noun* a small wave. *Ripples on the pond.* **ripple** *verb* to make ripples or move in ripples.

**rise** (rises, rising, rose, risen) *verb* **1** to move to a higher position. *The water is rising.* **2** to come up. *The sun rises in the east.* **3** to get up from lying, sitting, or kneeling. **4** to get out of bed. *He rises early.* **5** to get stronger. *The child's voice rose to a scream.* **6** to come up to the surface. **7** to show above the surroundings. *The tower rose above the rooftops.* **rise from the dead** to come back to life. **rise up** to fight against somebody in power. *The people rose up against the dictator.* **rise** *noun* **1** a small hill or upward slope. **2** an increase in number, amount, or value, or the temperature. **3** the act of growing more powerful. *The rise and fall of the Roman Empire.* **give rise to** to lead to.

**risk** *noun* **1** a danger of something bad or unwanted happening. **2** a chance of a loss. **risk** *verb* to take a chance. *I don't want to risk losing my place in line by going back for something I've forgotten.* **risky** *adjective.*

**ritual** *noun* a ceremony or set of actions that is always done the same way. *Religious rituals.*

**rival** *noun* somebody who competes with you. **rival** *verb* to be as good as somebody or something else. *Nobody else's cooking can rival my mother's.* **rivalry** *noun. A great rivalry between the brothers caused big problems for the family.*

**river** *noun* a large stream of fresh water. *The Mississippi River flows southward through the US, eventually reaching the Gulf of Mexico.*

**rivet** *noun* a short nail with a flat head used for holding pieces of metal together. **rivet** *verb* **1** to fasten with rivets. **2** to attract or hold somebody's attention. *She watched the movie, riveted to the screen.* **riveting** *adjective. He gave a riveting performance as Hamlet.*

**Riyadh** *noun* the capital of Saudi Arabia in southwest Asia.

**road** *noun* **1** a specially prepared, hard surface for traffic to travel upon. **2** a method or way. *The road to success is often bumpy.* **on the road** traveling.

**roam** *verb* to wander around.

**roar** *noun* a loud, deep noise like the sound a lion makes. **roar** *verb* **1** to make a loud, deep sound like a lion or thunder. **2** to say or shout something loudly. *She roared with laughter.* **a roaring success** something very successful. **to do a roaring trade** to sell a lot of something in a short time.

**roast** *verb* **1** to cook meat or vegetables in an oven or over a hot fire. **2** to get very hot. *I've been roasting in the sun all day.* **roast** *noun.* **roast, roasted** *adjective.*

**robe** *noun* a long, loose piece of clothing.

**robin** *noun* a small bird with a red breast.

**robot** *noun* a machine programmed to do things automatically. Some robots look and act like a person. *Cars are put together by robots in factories.* **robotic** *adjective.*

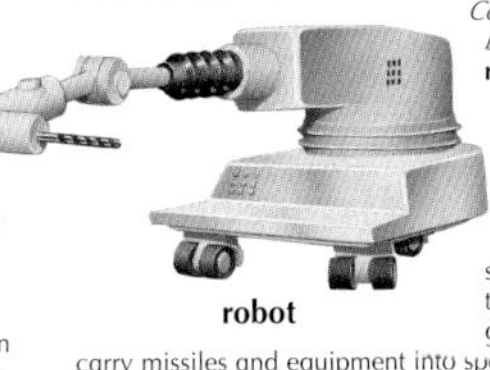

robot

**robust** *adjective* strong. *A robust red wine.*

**rocket** *noun* **1** a machine in the shape of a long tube that flies by burning gases and is used to carry missiles and equipment into space. **2** a kind of firework. **rocket** *verb* to move up quickly. *The song by the popular blues singer rocketed to Number One.*

Rr

**rocking chair** *noun* a chair resting on two curved pieces of wood, on which you can rock back and forth.

**rodent** *noun* an animal that has sharp front teeth for gnawing. Rats, mice, and squirrels are all rodents.

**rodeo** (rodeos) *noun* (say **roh**-dee-oh) a competition in which cowboys ride wild horses and lasso cattle.

**rogue** *noun* a dishonest person, who may be charming.

**role** *noun* **1** an actor's part in a play, movie, or musical. **2** somebody's position in a particular situation. *She didn't enjoy having the role of leader.* **role-play** an exercise in which people behave like someone else.

**rollerblade** TRADEMARK *noun* a boot with a single row of wheels under it for moving fast.

**rollerskate** *verb* to move over a surface wearing rollerskates. **rollerskate** *noun* a shoe with four small wheels fixed under it. **rollerskating** *noun.*

**ROM** *abbreviation* read-only memory. ROM is the memory that cannot be changed in a computer.

Romania's flag

**Roman Catholic** *noun* a member of the Roman Catholic Church, which has the Pope at its head. Roman Catholics believe in the Christian religion. **Roman Catholic** *adjective.*

**Romania** *noun* a country in eastern Europe.

**romantic** *adjective* having feelings about love and beauty, seeing things in an unreal way. Romantic novels and movies are about love and usually have a happy ending. **romantic** *noun.* **romantically** *adverb.* **romance** *noun.*

**Rome** *noun* the capital of Italy in southern Europe.

**rooster** *noun* a male chicken.

**root** *noun* **1** the part of a plant that grows under the ground. *The tree sent down long roots into the earth.* **2** the part of a tooth or hair beneath the skin. **3** the cause or basis of something. *The root of the problem.* **4** in mathematics, a number in relation to the number it makes when multiplied by itself. *The square root of 9 is 3.* **root** *verb* **1** to grow roots. **2** to search through things. *Pigs root around for food.* **rooted to the spot** unable to move.

root

**rose** *noun* **1** a sweet-smelling flower with a thorny stem that grows on a bush. **2** a pink color. **3** the hole-filled nozzle at the end of a watering can, used for watering plants.

**Roseau** *noun* the capital of Dominica in the Caribbean.

**rosemary** *noun* a bush with spiky evergreen leaves used to flavor food.

rosemary

**Rosh Hashanah** *noun* a festival marking the Jewish New Year.

**rota** *noun* (say **roh**-tuh) a list of people who take turns doing a particular job.

**rotate** *verb* **1** to move around a fixed point. *A wheel rotates.* **2** to take turns or come around in regular order. *We rotate the babysitting.* **rotation** *noun. The Earth's rotation is a mystery to me.*

**rotor** *noun* a part of a machine that rotates, especially the blades of a helicopter.

**rough** *adjective* **1** uneven; not smooth or polished. *Rough skin.* **2** not calm, gentle, or polite; using force. *Rough manners.* **3** not exact; without detail. *A rough description.* **roughly** *adverb.* **roughness** *noun.* **rough** *noun* **1** the long grass on a golf course. **2** a piece of writing or a drawing without much detail; not finished. **rough** *verb* to make something untidy. If you rough somebody up, you hit them. **rough it** to live in an uncomfortable way. *Students usually don't mind roughing it for a while on their first trips overseas.* **rough out** to make a quick drawing or plan of something.

**round** *adjective* **1** shaped like a circle or ball. **2** complete. *A round dozen.* **3** going and returning. *A round trip.* **4** all year round. **round** *adverb* **1** in a circle. **2** from one to another; all over the place. **round** *preposition* **1** in a circle. **2** on all the sides of. **3** in every direction or everywhere. **round** *noun* **1** something round. **2** a group or circuit ending where it began. **3** a circular dance. **4** a share given out to everyone. *This round of drinks is on me!* **5** one stage in a game or a competition. *Our team has made it to the next round.* **6** a bullet or bullets from a gun. **7** in golf, playing all the holes once. **8** the state of being round, like a circle, globe, or ring. **roundness** *noun.* **roundabout** not done in the shortest, most direct way. *We got lost and drove a roundabout route into town.* **round-the-clock** all the time. *Paul made us work round-the-clock to get the decorating finished before the new owner arrived.* **round off** not exactly, but to the nearest whole number.

**rout** *verb* to defeat completely, as in a battle. **rout** *noun.*

**route** *noun* (say root) the way you take to get to a place.

**routine** *noun* (say roo-**teen**) the usual, regular way of doing things. *Getting up late upsets my routine.* **routine** *adjective. A routine job.*

**rove** *verb* to roam or ramble.

**row** *noun* (rhymes with go) a line of people or things. *A row of houses.* **row** *verb* to move a boat through the water with oars. *Our team rowed to victory at the Olympics.* **rower** *noun.* **rowing** *noun.*

Rr

**rowboat** *noun* a small boat with oars.

**rowdy** (rowdier, rowdiest) *adjective* rough and noisy. *The twins are rowdy when they are with their cousins.*

**royal** *adjective* belonging to or connected with a king or queen. **royally** *adjective.*

**royalty** (royalties) *noun* **1** members of a royal family. **2** part of the price of a book that is paid to the writer for each copy sold.

**rubble** *noun* broken stones or bricks. *The builders left a pile of rubble.*

**ruby** (rubies) *noun* a red precious stone. **ruby** *adjective. Ruby ring.*

**rudder** *noun* a flat piece of metal or wood at the back of a boat or plane, forming part of the steering mechanism.

ruby

**rude** *adjective* **1** impolite. *It's rude to laugh.* **2** vulgar. *Rude jokes.* **3** unexpected and unpleasant. *A rude awakening.* **4** very simple and roughly made. *A rude shelter.* **rudeness** *noun. Her rudeness is appalling.*

**rug** *noun* **1** a mat smaller than a carpet. **2** a thick blanket, as used outdoors for picnics.

**rugby** *noun* an outdoor game for two teams, played with an oval ball that is kicked or carried.

**rugged** *adjective* **1** craggy and rocky. *A rugged landscape.* **2** rough and strong. *A rugged face.*

**ruin** *noun* **1** destruction. *It will be the ruin of her.* **2** the state of no longer having any money. *My business is facing ruin.* **3** part or parts of a building still standing after the rest has fallen down. *The ruins of a castle.* **ruin** *verb* **1** to destroy or harm. **2** to lose all your money.

**rule** *noun* **1** an order or a law that says what is allowed or not allowed. Instructions on how things are to be done. *The rules of grammar.* **2** power to govern or control. *Under British rule.* **rule** *verb* **1** to govern or control. **2** to decide. *The judge ruled that he must pay a fine.* **3** to make a straight line with a ruler. *He ruled the paper before writing on it.* **as a rule** usually. **rule out** to decide that something is not possible.

**ruler** *noun* **1** a person who rules. **2** a long, flat piece of wood, metal, or plastic with straight edges that are marked with measurements such as centimetres or inches, used for measuring things or drawing straight lines.

**rum** *noun* an alcoholic drink made from sugar cane. *Bananas served with rum sauce are delicious.*

**rumble** *verb* to make a low rolling sound. *Thunder rumbles after a lightning flash.* **rumble** *noun.*

**rumor** *noun* information passed from one person to another that may not be true. *Rumor has it that they are back.* **rumored** *adjective* it is rumored that she is rich.

**rump** *noun* the back part (buttocks) of an animal. **rump** *adjective. I'll have rump steak with fried onions.*

**run** (runs, running, ran, run) *verb* **1** to move quickly on your legs. **2** to take part in a race. *He runs for the school.* **3** to go, travel, or drive somebody somewhere. *The bus runs every hour.* **4** to flow. *Shall I run you a bath?* **5** to move quickly. *A strange thought ran through her mind.* **6** to work or operate. *He left the car running.* **7** to organize, control, or own. *He runs a store.* **8** to stretch or continue. *The road runs through the forest.* **9** to continue to go on for a period of time. *The play ran for a week.* **run away** to leave suddenly. **run behind** to be late ending or starting. **run into 1** to hit a person or thing while driving. **2** to happen to meet or come across. *She ran into an old friend.* **run out** to have used up everything and have nothing left. *We ran out of food.* **run over** to knock somebody or something down when driving. *He ran over an empty bottle.*

**runner** *noun* **1** a person who runs as a sport, as in a race. **2** a thin wooden or metal strip on which something slides or moves. *The runners of a sled.* **3** a messenger. **4** a long strip of carpet. **runner-up** somebody who finishes second in a race or competition.

**runway** *noun* the long strip of hard surface like a wide road on which planes take off and land.

runner

**rural** *adjective* of or like the countryside.

**rush** (rushes) *noun* **1** hurry or hurried activity. **2** a sudden interest or demand for something. *A rush for tickets.* **rush** *verb* **1** to hurry or act quickly. *Don't rush me, I have to think about it.* **2** to move quickly. *He was rushed to hospital.* **3** to get through, over, or into something by pressing forward.

**Russia** *noun* a country in eastern Europe and Asia.

**rust** *noun* a red-brown substance that forms on iron when it becomes damp. **rust** *verb. The bike will rust if you leave it out in the rain.* **rusty** *adjective.*

**rustic** *adjective* connected with the country; rough and simple.

Russia

**ruthless** *adjective* showing no pity; cruel. *He's ruthless in business.* **ruthlessness** *noun.*

**Rwanda** *noun* a country in Central Africa.

**rye** *noun* a grass grown in cold countries, and the grain of that plant which is used for making flour. *Rye bread.*

**sabbath** *noun* a weekly day of rest: Saturday for Jews, Sunday for Christians.

**sabotage** *noun* damage carried out secretly, usually to machines or buildings, as a protest, to weaken an enemy or ruin a plan. **sabotage** *verb. The railroad and bridge were sabotaged by enemy troops.*

**sachet** *noun* (say **sash**-ay) a small, sealed plastic or paper bag containing something. *A sachet of shampoo.*

**sack** *noun* a large bag made of strong material. *A plastic sack.* **2** the amount contained in a bag. *A sack of potatoes.*

**sacred** (say **say**-krid) *adjective* connected with religion; holy.

**sacrifice** *noun* **1** something given to a god as an offering. **2** something you like or value given up for the good of something or someone else. **sacrifice** *verb* to offer or give up something as a sacrifice. *He sacrificed his job to look after his sick parents.* **sacrificial** *adjective. A sacrificial lamb.*

**sad** (sadder, saddest) *adjective* unhappy; showing or causing sorrow. **sadly** *adverb.* **sadness** *noun. Martha wept tears of great sadness.*

**saddle** *noun* a fixed seat on a bicycle or a removable seat that you put on a horse's back for a rider to sit on. **saddle** *verb* to put a saddle on a horse or other animal.

safe

**safe** *adjective* out of danger or free from risk or harm. *Have a safe journey.* **safely** *adverb. They arrived home safely.* **safe** *noun* a strong metal box or cupboard with a special combination lock, used to keep money or valuables in. *The thief discovered the safe behind a picture on the wall and picked the combination lock using a special listening device to hear the clicks.*

**safeguard** *noun* a protection against something unwanted. *She eats a lot of fruit as a safeguard against catching flu.* **safeguard** *verb* to protect.

**safety** *noun* being safe; freedom from danger or harm. **safety pin** a metal pin for fastening things together.

**sag** (sags, sagging, sagged) *verb* to hang down loosely or in the middle, usually because of weight. **sag** *noun.*

**saga** *noun* (say **sah**-guh) **1** a long story of heroic achievement. The first sagas were written about the deeds of Viking heroes in the Middle Ages. **2** a series of novels based on the history of a fictitious family.

**sage** *adjective* wise. **sage** *noun* **1** a wise person. *Three sages came on camels.* **2** a plant with gray-green leaves that is a herb.

**sail** *noun* **1** a large piece of cloth that is attached to the mast of a boat and is raised to catch the wind and make the boat move. **2** the blade of a windmill. **sail** *verb* **1** to travel across the water, to be able to control a sailing boat. **2** to move quickly and easily. *She sailed through the test.* **3** to begin a voyage. *Our boat sails tomorrow.* **set sail** to leave a port.

sailboat

**sailboard** *noun* the board used for windsurfing. *His sailboard went really fast.*

**sailboat** *noun* a boat with sails, powered by the wind.

**sailor** *noun* **1** somebody who can sail a boat. **2** a member of a navy. **3** somebody who works on a ship.

**saint** *noun* a holy person or a very kind and patient person. **saintly** *adjective.*

**sake** *noun* To do something for the sake of somebody or something is to do it for the good of somebody or for the purpose of something. *For heaven's sake, stop arguing with each other.*

**salad** *noun* **1** a mixture of uncooked vegetables, such as lettuce, cucumber, and tomatoes, eaten cold. **salad dressing** a sauce for putting on salads. *This salad dressing is made with oil, vinegar, garlic, and herbs.*

**salary** (salaries) *noun* fixed pay, usually monthly, earned by somebody for work done.

**sale** *noun* **1** the selling of goods for money. **2** a special time when goods are sold in stores at lower prices. **on sale** something on sale can be bought in a store. **for sale** offered to be sold. *The house is for sale.*

**saliva** *noun* the watery liquid that naturally forms in the mouth, also called spit.

**salmon** (salmon) *noun* (say **sam**-un) a large fish with pink flesh eaten as food.

**salt** *noun* a white substance found in seawater, used for flavoring food or for preserving it. Salt crystals. **rub salt into the wound** to make somebody's pain worse by saying something unkind to someone on a subject about which they are already sensitive. **salt** *verb* to put salt in or on food. **salty** *adjective.*

**salute** *verb* **1** to greet a commanding officer. Soldiers salute by raising their right hand to their forehead. **2** to show respect or admiration. **salute** *noun. A salute to freedom.*

**salvage** *verb* **1** to save something that would otherwise be destroyed, so that it can be used again. **2** to rescue a ship or its cargo from loss at sea. **salvage** *noun.*

**salvation** *noun* being saved from sin; the saving of the soul in the Christian religion.

salute

**same** *adjective* **1** not different; exactly alike. *She wore the same dress as me.* **2** not changed. *She still does the same job for him.* **3** a particular one or one already mentioned. *I saw a flash of lightning and at the same moment the tree fell.* **same** *adverb* in the same way. *I don't feel the same about him now.* **sameness** *noun.*

**sample** *noun* a small quantity that shows what something or what the rest is like. *A free sample of shampoo.* **sample** *verb* to test a part of something.

**Sanaa** *noun* the capital of Yemen in Southwest Asia.

**sanction** *noun* **1** permission given to do something. **2** actions taken by countries against a country that is breaking international laws; a punishment ordered when a law or rule is broken. *The sanctions included a total trade ban.* **sanction** *verb* to allow something to be done. *The governor sanctioned the sale of the buildings.*

**sanctuary** (sanctuaries) *noun* **1** a holy place, especially in a church or temple. **2** a place of safety. **3** a place where animals or birds are protected. *A wildlife sanctuary.*

**sand** *noun* a mass of finely crushed stones found on beaches and in deserts. **sandy** *adjective* **1** full of sand. *A sandy beach.* **2** dark blond. *Sandy hair.* **sand** *verb* to smooth or clean a surface by rubbing it with sandpaper.

**sandal** *noun* an open shoe with straps over the foot, worn in hot weather.

**sandpaper** *noun* paper with sand stuck to it, used for smoothing surfaces. **sandpaper** *verb. Please sandpaper the woodwork to smooth off the rough edges.*

**sandwich** *noun* two slices of bread with a filling between. **sandwich** *verb* to put something between two other things. *My travel bag was sandwiched between two big suitcases on the airport trolley.*

**sane** *adjective* **1** able to think normally; not mentally ill or mad. **2** sensible. **sanity** *noun.*

**sanitary** *adjective* **1** concerning the treatment of waste for the protection of public health. *In the Middle Ages, sanitary conditions were very poor.* **2** clean; free from dirt or infection.

**San José** *noun* the capital of Costa Rica in Central America.

**San Marino** *noun* a small country surrounded by Italy. Its capital is also named San Marino.

**San Salvador** *noun* the capital of El Salvador in Central America.

**Santa Claus or Santa Klaus** *noun* children believe that Santa Claus, an old man with a long white beard, comes in a sleigh to bring presents to them at Christmas.

**Santiago** *noun* the capital of Chile in South America.

**Santo Domingo** *noun* the capital of the Dominican Republic in the Caribbean.

**São Tomé** *noun* the capital of São Tomé and Príncipe.

**São Tomé and Príncipe** *noun* a country in the Gulf of Guinea off West Africa.

**sap** *noun* the watery liquid in plants and trees. *Sap rises in the Spring.* **sap** (saps, sapping, sapped) *verb* to weaken somebody's strength or confidence, especially over a period of time.

**sapling** *noun* a young tree.

**sapphire** *noun* a bright blue precious stone.

**Sarajevo** *noun* the capital of Bosnia-Herzegovina in southeastern Europe.

**sarcasm** *noun* amusing, often hurtful things said to mock or upset somebody's feelings, usually by saying the opposite of what is really thought. **sarcastic** *adjective. Your sarcastic tone of voice is not welcome.* **sarcastically** *adverb.*

**sardine** *noun* a small sea fish. *Sardines are an oily fish, good for the heart.*

**sari** (saris) *noun* a long piece of material wrapped around the body, worn by many Indian women.

sari

**Satan** *noun* the devil; an evil power. **satanic** *adjective. Satanic powers.*

**satellite** *noun* **1** a heavenly body such as a small planet, or a human-made object such as a spacecraft, moving around a larger planet. The Moon is a satellite of the Earth. *A weather satellite was sent into space.* **2** a person or country that takes orders from another more powerful one. **satellite dish** a dish-shaped aerial for receiving signals from a space satellite.

**satin** *noun* a shiny cloth made from silk or artificial fibres. *Kate wore a red satin nightgown.*

**satire** *noun* amusing writing used to show the foolishness or badness of people or their ideas.

**satisfy** (satisfies, satisfying, satisfied) *verb* **1** to give enough of what is wanted to make somebody pleased. *Nothing satisfies her; she is always complaining.* **2** to be enough or good enough for what is needed. *One bowl of soup is enough to satisfy my hunger.* **3** to make somebody free from doubt; to convince. *When I had satisfied myself that everybody had gone, I locked the door.* **satisfaction** *noun.* **satisfactory** *adjective* good enough. **satisfying** *adjective* pleasing.

**saturate** *verb* **1** to make very wet. **2** to soak completely so that no more can be held. *The sponge was saturated with water.* **saturation** *noun.*

**Saturday** *noun* the day of the week that comes after Friday and before Sunday.

**saucepan** *noun* a metal cooking pot with a handle.

**saucer** *noun* a small dish on which a cup stands. *Please pass me your cup and saucer and I'll pour you some tea.*

**Saudi Arabia** *noun* a country in Southwest Asia.

**sauna** *noun* **1** a hot steam bath. **2** a room or place where you have a hot steam bath.

**saunter** *verb* to walk in a slow, casual way.

**sausage** *noun* chopped-up meat or soya in a thin, tube-shaped casing. *He had sausage, egg, and bacon for breakfast.*

**savannah** *noun* a grassy plain with few trees. *The African savannah.*

**save** *verb* **1** to make somebody or something free from danger. *He saved my life.* **2** to keep something, especially money, for later use. *Tom has saved enough to buy a new bike.* **3** to make something unnecessary for somebody, so they don't have to do it. *I've cleaned up the kitchen to save you the trouble.* **4** to stop a player from scoring. **save** *noun.*

**savings** *plural noun* money saved, as in a bank. *My savings are under my bed.*

**saw** *noun* a tool with a blade with sharp teeth along one edge, used for cutting wood or metal. *Jason gave me the saw to cut the wood into lengths.*

**saying** *noun* a well-known statement expressing something that most people believe is wise.

**scab** *noun* **1** a dry crust, mainly of dried blood, which forms over a cut or wound. **2** somebody who will not join a strike, an organized refusal by a group to work.

**scaffolding** *noun* a framework of metal poles and boards put up around a building for workers to stand on while building, repairing, or painting a house.

**scald** *verb* **1** to burn yourself with hot liquid or steam. **2** to clean pans or instruments with boiling water or steam. **scald** *noun* a skin burn from hot liquid or steam. **scalding** *adjective. I ran a bath with scalding water and then added cold water to make the temperature right.*

**scale** *noun* **1** a small, flat piece of hard skin that covers the skin of fish and reptiles. **2** a hard layer that forms on the bottom of a kettle, in pipes, or on teeth. **3** a set of numbers, marks, or degrees for measuring. *This ruler has a metric scale.* **4** a set of numbers comparing measurements on a map or model with the measurements in the real world. *The model is to scale.* **5** size or importance in relation to other things. *The party is going to be on a grand scale.* **6** a set of musical notes arranged in order going upward or downward. *Elizabeth plays scales on the piano every day and is improving at them.* **scale** *verb* **1** to remove the scales from fish. **2** to remove from a surface in thin pieces. **3** to climb up. *The climber scaled the rockface.* **4** to make a copy of something so that it is consistently bigger or smaller than the original. **scale down** to make something smaller in size or amount than it used to be.

**scales** *plural noun* a weighing machine.

**scalp** *noun* **1** the skin under the hair on the head. **2** a piece of skin and hair that was taken by American Indians as a mark of victory when somebody was killed. **scalp** *verb* to cut the scalp off a dead enemy.

**scamper** *verb* to run quickly with small, short steps. *The squirrel scampered up the tree.*

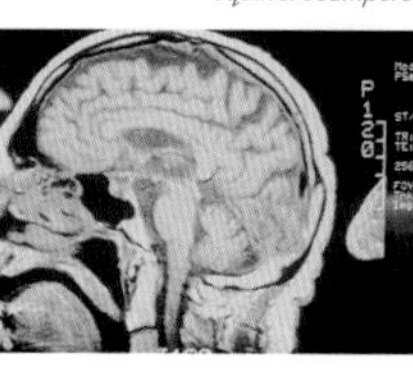

scan

**scan** (scans, scanning, scanned) *verb* **1** to look closely and carefully; to examine. *Mother scanned our faces to see if anything was wrong.* **2** to look at something quickly without reading it properly. **3** to look through information, as when searching the internet. **4** to use special equipment to examine a person or pass an electronic beam over an area in search of something. **5** to count the pattern of beats in each line of poetry. **scan** *noun.*

**scandal** *noun* **1** careless talk; gossip that shocks. *The tabloid newspapers love scandal.* **2** action that shocks or makes people angry. **scandalous** *adjective.*

**Scandinavia** *noun* a region covering the countries of northern Europe: Iceland, Norway, Sweden, and Denmark.

**Scandinavian** *noun* a person from Scandinavia. **Scandinavian** *adjective. Scandinavian languages.*

Scandinavia

**scanner** *noun* **1** a device for putting pictures into a computer. **2** a machine used in hospitals for examining a person by moving a beam of light or X-rays over them.

**scanty** (scantier, scantiest) *adjective* very small; hardly big enough. **scantily** *adverb. Helen and Sarah were scantily dressed in their underwear.*

**scar** *noun* a mark on the skin that is left after a wound or burn has healed. **scar** (scars, scarring, scarred) *verb* to mark with a scar or scars.

**scarce** *adjective* not enough compared with what is wanted; difficult to find. *Fruit is scarce in winter.*

**scarcely** *adverb* hardly; only just.

**scarcity** *noun* a lack or inadequacy, especially of food. *There was a scarcity of bananas during World War II.*

**scare** *noun* a sudden fear; alarm. **scare** *verb* to frighten or make you frightened; to become afraid. *I'm scared of the dark.* **scare away** to frighten somebody so that they go away. **scary** *adjective.*

scarecrow

**scarecrow** *noun* a dummy figure that is dressed in old clothes and put in a field to scare away birds.

**scarf** (scarves) *noun* a piece of cloth worn around the neck or head.

**scarlet** *adjective* bright red.

**scathing** *adjective* to criticize severely. *Her scathing remark made us blush.*

**scat** *an informal exclamation* said to make an animal go away quickly.

**scatter** *verb* to throw or go in different directions.

**scavenge** *verb* to look in garbage for food or other things. *The rats scavenge in trash cans for food.*

**scavenger** *noun* **1** somebody who scavenges. **2** a bird or animal that feeds on waste and decaying flesh.

**scene** *noun* **1** one of the parts of a play, movie, or book. **2** the stage background for a play. *There were only three scene changes.* **3** the place where an event or action happens, or an area of activity. *The scene of the crime.* **4** a showing of anger. *He made a scene in the restaurant when I arrived late.* **5** a view. *She paints mountain scenes.* **behind the scenes** secretly. **set the scene** to prepare so as to convey what is going to happen next.

**scenery** *noun* **1** the landscape and everything natural around you. *When we reached the mountains, the scenery suddenly became more dramatic.* **2** the painted backgrounds used on a theater stage during a play.

scenery

**scent** *noun* **1** a pleasant smell. *The scent of violets.* **2** a liquid perfume you put on your skin to make you smell nice. **3** a smell left by an animal that conveys a message to other animals. **scent** *verb* **1** to detect by smell. *The dog scented a fox.* **2** to feel that something is going to happen; to detect. **3** to put scent on something or fill with scent. *The air was scented with flowers and full of the buzz of insects.*

**sceptic** (say **skep**-tik) *noun* somebody who does not believe things readily. **sceptical** *adjective. I'm sceptical about our chances of winning.*

**schedule** (say **shed**-jull) *noun* a plan that gives a list of events and times for doing things. **schedule** *verb* to put into a plan or timetable. *A scheduled flight to Paris.*

**scheme** (say skeem) *noun* a plan of action or an arrangement. *I like your color scheme better than your furniture.* **scheme** *verb* to make clever, secret plans. **schemer** *noun.*

**scholar** *noun* **1** a person who studies an academic subject and knows a lot about it. **2** a pupil or student who receives money (a bursary or scholarship) to study at a school or university.

**school** *noun* **1** a place for teaching children. **2** the time when teaching is done and you are at school. **3** all the teachers and pupils in a school. **4** a place for the study of a particular subject, especially a college or university department. **5** a group of people who think the same or have the same methods of working. **6** a group of dolphins or fish. **school** *verb* to train. **schooling** *noun.*

**science** *noun* the study of nature, natural things, and the testing of natural laws. If you study science, you might take courses in chemistry, physics, or biology. Psychology is a social science. **scientific** *adjective. Microscopes and thermometers are scientific instruments.*

**scientist** *noun* somebody who studies science or works in one of the sciences.

**scissors** (say **sizz**ors) *plural noun* a tool with two sharp blades, used for cutting things such as paper.

**scoff** *verb* **1** to speak in a mocking way about somebody or something. **2** to eat food quickly and greedily. *Who scoffed the last piece of cake?*

**scold** *verb* to berate or upbraid somebody; to speak angrily. *She scolded the children for misbehaving.*

**scone** *noun* (say skon rhyming with on, or skohn rhyming with bone) a small cake usually eaten with butter.

**scoop** *noun* **1** a deep, round spoon for dishing out soft food such as ice cream. **2** a shovel-shaped spoon for picking up grain, flour, or sugar. *A measuring scoop.* **3** the amount a scoop holds. **4** an exciting news story reported by a newspaper before any other newspapers. **5** a successful piece of business, usually a large profit made from acting faster than others. **scoop** *verb* **1** to lift something or make a hole as if with a scoop. *She scooped out a hole in the sand.* **2** to pick something up with a scoop or spoon. *I scooped some ice cream from the bowl.*

**scooter** *noun* **1** a kind of small motorcycle. **2** a child's vehicle that you stand on and push along with one foot. It has a board fixed to small wheels, and a long handle.

scooter

**scope** *noun* **1** an opportunity; a chance for action. *I wish there was more scope for doing your own mixing in music lessons.* **2** a range or a whole area of action.

**scorch** *verb* to burn something so that it turns slightly brown. *The grass was scorched by the hot Sun.* **scorching** *adjective* very hot.

**score** *noun* **1** the number of points, goals, or home runs made in a game. **2** a written copy of a piece of music for its performers, showing what each person has to play. **3** a piece of music for a movie or play. **4** twenty. *Two score and ten is 50.* When you get scores of something, you get a large number. *Scores of complaints were made.* **5** a reason or point. *He won't let us down; you can trust him on that score.* **score** *verb* **1** to win points in a game or competition; to get a goal, try, or home run in sports. **2** to keep a record of scores. **3** to gain or win success or an advantage. *She is only interested in scoring over her sister at parties.* **4** to mark or cut lines with a sharp instrument. *Score the card to make it easier to fold.* **5** to write a musical score. **scorer** *noun.*

**scorn** *noun* contempt, the feeling that somebody or something is worthless. **scorn** *verb* to show scorn. *She scorns the man who reads only trash fiction.* **scornful** *adjective. She is scornful about boys.* **scornfully** *adverb.*

**scorpion** *noun* a tropical animal with a hard body and a long tail that has a poisonous sting. *Be wary of the scorpion when it arches its tail.*

**Scot** *noun* a person who comes from Scotland.

**Scotland** *noun* a country north of, and bordering, England. Scotland is part of the United Kingdom.

**scorpion**

**Scots** *noun* a dialect of the English language spoken in Scotland. **Scots** *adjective. A Scots writer from Glasgow won the comedy prize.*

Ss

**Scottish** *adjective* from or belonging to Scotland. *The Scottish landscape can be rugged and bleak in winter.*

**scour** *verb* **1** to clean something by rubbing it with rough material. *She scoured the pan.* **2** to search everywhere. *She scoured the papers for information.*

**scout** *noun* **1** somebody sent out to get information or look for talented sportsmen. **2** a member of the Scout Association. **scout** *verb* to go out looking for somebody or something. *We scouted around for a good hotel, but without luck.*

**scowl** *noun* an angry expression on the face. **scowl** *verb* to frown in a show of anger. *He didn't say anything; he just scowled at me.*

**scrap** *noun* **1** a small piece, especially something unwanted, or a small amount. *A scrap of paper.* Scraps are pieces of food that are usually thrown away. **2** waste material, especially metal. **3** a fight. **scrap** (scraps, scrapping, scrapped) *verb* to throw away something unwanted or to cancel a plan or an idea. **scrap heap** a pile of waste, or unwanted things and ideas. *You can put that idea on the scrap heap!*

**scrape** *noun* **1** a scraping movement or sound. **2** damage or hurt caused by scraping. *What made that scrape on the tiles?* **3** a difficult position, usually caused by yourself. *She got into a scrape for not doing her homework.* **scrape** *verb* **1** to remove something by pulling or pushing a knife or other object over it. *He scraped the mud from his boots before coming into the house.* **3** to rub roughly or damage by rubbing. *He scraped his knee when he fell over.* **4** to get or pass something with difficulty. *She scraped through the test.* **scrape by** to get just enough food or money to stay alive.

**scraper** *noun* a tool for scraping.

**scratch** *noun* **1** a mark, cut, or injury made by scratching. **2** the action or sound of scratching. *The dog likes a good scratch.* **scratch** *verb* **1** to rub, cut, or mark with something sharp or rough. *The cat scratched me with its claws.* **2** to rub the skin to stop itching. **3** to withdraw from a race or competition before it starts. **scratchy** *adjective.* **start from scratch** to start from the beginning. **be up to scratch** to be good enough.

**scrawl** *verb* to write untidily. *He scrawled a message on the pad.* **scrawl** *noun.*

**scrawny** (scrawnier, scrawniest) *adjective* thin and bony. *A scrawny pigeon.*

**scream** *noun* **1** a loud cry or noise, either of laughter or caused by pain or fear. **2** somebody or something very funny. *You'd like her; she's a scream.* **scream** *verb* to make a loud vocal noise.

**screen** *noun* **1** a flat surface on which television pictures, movies, or photographs are shown. **2** a computer's visual display unit. **3** an upright frame, usually made to fold, used to divide a room or other area to provide privacy. **4** something that gives protection or hides. **screen** *verb* **1** to shelter, hide, protect, or divide something or somebody. *The trees screened her from view.* **2** to show a movie on television or in a theater. **3** to examine or look carefully at somebody's ability or health. *She was screened for cancer.* **screen off** to make part of a room into a separate area.

**screw** *noun* **1** a metal pin with a spiral groove along its length, used for fastening or holding things together. **2** a turning movement or something that twists like a screw. *He gave it another screw to make sure it was tight.* **3** a propeller on a ship or airplane.

**screwdriver** *noun* a tool for turning screws.

**scribble** *verb* **1** to write quickly and untidily. **2** to make meaningless marks or rough drawings. **scribble** *noun.*

**script** *noun* **1** a written form of a play, film, or talk. *He writes scripts for television programs.* **2** handwriting. **3** a particular system of writing.

scroll

**scripture** *noun* sacred writing.

**scroll** *noun* **1** a long roll of paper or other material, sometimes attached to handles so that it can be easily unwound. Scrolls may contain writing, prayers, or patterns. **2** a spiral design.

**scrotum** (say **skroh**-tum) *noun* the bag of skin that holds the testicles of a boy or man.

**scrounge** *verb* to get something, usually money or food, by asking for it rather than paying or working for it. **scrounger** *noun.*

**scrub** *noun* low-growing bushes and trees or land covered with this kind of vegetation. **scrub** (scrubs, scrubbing, scrubbed) *verb* to clean by rubbing hard, usually with a brush. *She scrubbed the tiled floor with a brush until it shone.*

**scruffy** (scruffier, scruffiest) *adjective* dirty and untidy. **scruffiness** *noun.*

**scruple** *noun* an idea of what is right and wrong that stops you from doing something bad. *He has scruples about playing when he should be working.*

**scuba** *noun* a container of air under pressure, which a diver carries on his back and uses for breathing while swimming under water. **scuba diving** swimming underwater using a scuba.

**sculpt** *verb* to carve or model shapes in clay, wood, or metal. *I am sculpting a head of a monkey in clay.*

**sculpture** *noun* the art of making shapes in wood, clay, or metal, or the shape made in this way. **sculptor** *noun* an artist who makes sculptures.

**scurf** *noun* bits of dry, dead skin in the hair.

**scurvy** *noun* a disease caused by a lack of vitamin C, got by not eating enough fruit and vegetables.

**scythe** *noun* a tool with a long, curved blade on a long handle, used for cutting grass.

**sea** *noun* **1** salty water that covers most of the Earth's surface. **2** a particular area of the sea surrounded by land. *The North Sea.* **3** a large number. *A sea of daffodils.* **at sea 1** on the sea. **2** confused. **sea level** the height of the sea halfway between high and low tide, used for measuring height on land and depth at sea.

**seagull** *noun* a long-winged, web-footed seabird with a loud cry.

seagull

**seal** *noun* **1** a large sea-animal with big flippers instead of legs. It eats fish and lives both on land and in the sea. **2** something fixed to a letter or container that must be broken before opening. *The seal on the package was damaged.* **3** a piece of wax or lead stamped with a design on documents to show that they are official. **4** a small decorative sticker for sealing a letter or document. **5** something made to close an opening to stop gas, air, or liquid from getting out. **seal** *verb* **1** to close something tightly. *To seal an envelope.* **2** to put a wax or paper seal on something. **3** to stop something up or close an opening. *He sealed the cracks with mud.* **4** to make something certain. *We sealed the agreement by shaking hands.* **seal off** to close access, to prevent someone or something getting through.

**seam** *noun* **1** a line of stitches that joins two pieces of cloth together; a line where two edges meet. **2** a long layer of coal or another mineral in the ground.

**search** *verb* **1** to look carefully through a place to find something. *She searched for her purse.* **2** to examine somebody's clothing for something hidden. *They were searched by the police.* **search** *noun.*

**season** *noun* **1** one of four periods of time each year. The four seasons are spring, summer, fall, and winter. **2** the time of year when something usually happens. *The hunting season.* **in season** available and ready for eating. *Peaches are in season.* **out of season 1** not available. **2** not busy. *We usually go to Venice out of season to enjoy the beauty of the place without the crowds.* **season** *verb* **1** to add salt, pepper, or other spices to food to give it a special taste. **2** to leave wood to dry so it can be used. **season ticket** a ticket that can be used whenever you like during a fixed period of time.

Ss

seasons

**seasoning** *noun* salt, pepper, and spices used to season food or give it a distinctive flavor.

**seaweed** *noun* any of a variety of plants that grow in the sea.

**seaworthy** *adjective* in good condition and fit for an ocean voyage. **seaworthiness** *noun.*

**second** *adjective* **1** next in order after the first. *February is the second month of the year.* **2** another or extra. *Many families have a second car.* **second** *adverb.* **second** *noun* **1** a length of time; there are 60 seconds in a minute. **2** a very short time; a moment. *Wait a second.* **3** a person or thing that is second. *I was the second person to arrive at the party.* **second** *verb* to help or speak in support of somebody. *I seconded her proposal because I thought it was a good one.*

**secret** *adjective* **1** not told or shown to anybody else; not known by everybody. *We made a secret plan to escape before midnight.* **secret** *noun* something secret. *I keep my diary secret from my parents.* **secrecy** *noun* the habit of keeping secrets. **secretive** *adjective.*

**secretary** (secretaries) *noun* **1** somebody whose job it is to deal with letters and telephone calls, and arrange meetings and other business affairs. **2** a government minister. *The Secretary of State for Wales.*

**sect** *noun* **1** a group of people who have a religious belief different to the established Church from which they have separated. **2** the followers of a particular philosophy.

**section** *noun* **1** a part of something larger. **2** one of a number of equal parts that can be put together. **3** a cross section. **sectional** *adjective.*

**secular** *adjective* worldly; not religious.

**secure** *adjective* **1** safe; well protected against danger. **2** firmly fixed or certain not to be lost. *She has a secure job.* **3** not worried; happy. *Small children need to feel secure with their parents.* **secure** *verb* **1** to make something safe from harm or attack. *We secured it with with a large padlock.* **2** to get, usually after having made an effort. *We managed to secure two tickets for the concert.* **3** to fix firmly in position. *The shelf was secured to the wall.* **securely** *adverb.* **security** *noun.*

secure

**sedative** *noun* a drug that calms you if you are stressed or helps you to go to sleep.

**sediment** *noun* solid material that sinks to the bottom of a liquid.

**seduce** *verb* to tempt or persuade somebody to do something they might not normally do. *The sales seduced me into buying myself new clothes.* **seductive** *adjective.* **seduction** *noun.*

**see** (sees, seeing, saw, seen) *verb* **1** to use your eyes; to look at something. **2** to visit or meet. *He has to see a doctor.* **3** to understand. *I can see what you mean.* **4** to watch a movie or play. **5** to make sure something is done. *I'll see that dinner is ready.* **6** to imagine or tell what might happen. *I can't see him giving the money back.* **7** to go with somebody; to accompany. *Can you see her home?* **8** to learn something, usually by reading about it. *I see that your team has been promoted.* **see you!** goodbye! **see about** to make arrangements for something to be done. *My brother will see about the tent.* **we'll see about that** perhaps. **see off** to go to an airport or station with somebody who is going on a trip to say goodbye to them. **see through 1** to see the truth about somebody or something; not to be fooled. *He made all sorts of promises, but I saw through him.* **2** to support or help until the end. *He earned enough money in one week to see him through the whole summer.* **see to** to take care of or deal with something.

**seed** *noun* **1** the small, hard part of a plant from which a new plant grows. **2** any of the players ranked among the best at the start of a competition. *The top seeds don't play against each other in the early rounds.* **seed** *verb* **1** to plant or grow seeds. **2** to rank players, especially tennis players, in order of likelihood of winning.

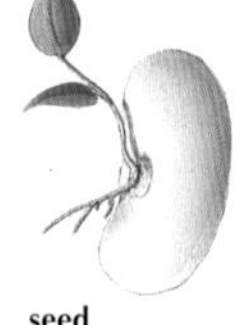
seed

**seedling** *noun* a young plant raised from seed. *The seedlings are in the greenhouse.*

**seedy** (seedier, seediest) *adjective* looking poor, run-down, or uncared for. *He lives in a seedy part of town.*

**seem** *verb* to appear to be; to give the impression of being something. *It seemed a good idea at the time.* **seemingly** *adverb.*

**seep** *verb* to flow slowly through a small opening. *The water seeped slowly out of the cracked bowl.*

**seethe** *verb* **1** to be angry or upset about something. *She was seething with rage.* **2** to bubble as if boiling.

**segment** *noun* one of the parts into which something may be divided. *The segment of an orange.*

**segregate** *verb* to set somebody or something apart from the rest. *It is wrong to segregate people by the color of their skin.* **segregation** *noun. Religious segregation causes wars.*

**seismic** *adjective* to do with earthquakes or sudden shakings of the ground. *Seismic activity.*

**seismology** *noun* the study of earthquakes. **seismologist** *noun* someone who studies earthquakes.

**seize** (say seez) *verb* **1** to take hold of suddenly and forcefully or to take control of. *Panic seized us.* **2** to take by force; to arrest or capture somebody. *The goods were seized by the police.* **3** to take and use something, especially a chance or an idea. **seize up** to become unable to move. *My back seized up as I bent down.*

**self** (selves) *noun* somebody's personality or nature. *She is back to her old self again.*

**self-** *prefix* done by or to yourself.

**self-centered** *adjective* interested only in yourself. *Matilda is a self-centered child, caring little for others.*

**self-confidence** *noun* a feeling of power; feeling able to do things successfully. **self-confident** *adjective.*

**self-conscious** *adjective* embarrassed and nervous because you know or think people are looking at you. *I'm too self-conscious to be a good actor.*

**self-contained** *adjective* complete in itself; not needing anything else. *A self-contained apartment.*

**self-control** *noun* control over your feelings. **self-controlled** *adjective. He exercises self-control and hardly ever loses his temper.*

**self-defense** *noun* an aggressive act or aggressive words used skillfully as a way of defending yourself.

**self-employed** *adjective* working for yourself and not for an employer. **self-employment** *noun.*

self-defense

**self-explanatory** *adjective* clear and needing no explanation.

**self-important** *adjective* having a high opinion of yourself. **self-importance** *noun.*

**self-respect** *noun* a feeling of pride in your own ability and respect for yourself.

**self-sacrifice** *noun* giving up what you want so others can have it.

**self-satisfied** *adjective* pleased with yourself. **self-satisfaction** *noun.*

**self-service** *noun* a system in stores, restaurants, or gas stations where you serve yourself and pay a cashier.

**self-sufficient** *adjective* able to make or produce everything that is needed without outside help. *A self-sufficient household does not have to buy goods from other people.* **self-sufficiency** *noun. Rob and Hazel decided to try self-sufficiency as a lifestyle and bought a farm where they planned to grow all their own food.*

**selfish** *adjective* thinking mainly of yourself and what you want. **selfishness** *noun.* **selfishly** *adverb.*

**sell** (sells, selling, sold) *verb* to give something in exchange for money. **sell out 1** to sell everything so there is nothing left. *The store sold out of umbrellas shortly after it started to rain.* **2** to agree secretly to work for an enemy; to betray. **sell up** to sell everything you have. *I'll sell up and leave.* **seller** *noun.*

**semen** *noun* (say **seem**-un) the fluid produced by the male sex organs that carries sperm for fertilizing an egg.

**semi-** *prefix* half or partly. *A semiprecious stone is not as valuable as a diamond.*

**semicircle** *noun* one half of a circle. **semicircular** *adjective.*

**semicolon** *noun* a punctuation mark (;) used in writing to separate major parts of a sentence with more clarity.

**senate** *noun* **1** the upper house or council in the government of some countries, for example in the USA, France, and Australia. **2** the highest council of state in ancient Rome.

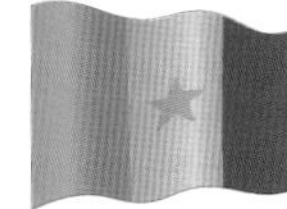
Senegal's flag

**senator** *noun* a member of a senate.

**Senegal** *noun* a country in West Africa.

**senile** *adjective* mentally confused; a disease or weakness of old age. **senility** *noun.*

**senior** *adjective* **1** older in age. **2** higher in rank. **senior citizen** someone over the age of 65. **seniority** *noun.*

**sensation** *noun* **1** a feeling, especially of heat or pain. **2** a state of excitement. *The new movie created a sensation.* **3** a general feeling in the mind that cannot be described. *It gave me a strange sensation to go back to the house I lived in as a child.*

**sensational** *adjective* exciting or shocking.

**sense** *noun* **1** any of the five senses; the ability to see, hear, smell, touch, and taste. **2** the ability to make good judgments and be sensible. *He should have shown a little more sense.* **3** a meaning or explanation. *This word has many senses.* **4** an awareness of something. *She has a great sense of humor!* **make sense** to have a clear meaning. **make sense of** to understand. *Can you make sense of his letter?* **sense** *verb* to become aware of something. *He sensed danger.*

**sensibility** *noun* sensitiveness.

**sensible** *adjective* able to make good decisions; wise. *It was not sensible to go on a long cross-country walk without a map.*

**sensitive** *adjective* **1** easily hurt in your feelings or offended. **2** quick to feel the effect of something; easily affected by something. *My eyes are sensitive to bright light.* **3** being aware of other people's feelings or problems. **4** measuring exactly or showing very small changes. *A sensitive pair of scales.* **sensitivity** *noun.*

**sensual** *adjective* enjoyable or giving pleasure to your body. *Eating and drinking are sensual pleasures.* **sensuality** *noun.*

**sentence** *noun* **1** a group of words that form a statement, question, or command. When you write a sentence, you start with a capital letter and end with a period. **2** a punishment for a criminal who is found guilty in court. *He received a long sentence.* **sentence** *verb* to give a punishment to somebody who is tried in a law court.

**sentry** (sentries) *noun* a soldier who keeps watch. *The sentries outside the Vatican still wear historical costume.*

sentry

**Seoul** *noun* the capital of South Korea in Asia.

**sepal** *noun* any of the leaves forming the calyx of a bud.

**separate** (say **sep**-rut) *adjective* **1** divided; not joined to anything; not shared with another. *She cut the apple into two separate parts.* **2** different. *He gave her three separate reasons for not going.* **separate** (say **sep**-uh-rate) *verb* **1** to keep apart; to be or become divided. *A wall separates our gardens.* **2** to stop living together. *My parents separated when I was eight.* **separation** *noun* **1** separating or being separated. **2** a time of being or living apart.

**September** *noun* the ninth month of the year. September has 30 days.

**septic** *adjective* infected with poison. *The wound has turned septic.*

**sepulcher** *noun* a tomb built of stone or brick, or cut into the rock; a burial vault. *The king was buried in a splendid sepulcher.*

sepulchre

**sequel** *noun* **1** a book or movie that continues a story. **2** an event or situation that follows something else that happened before.



**sequence** *noun* **1** a number of things that come one after another. **2** the order in which things are arranged. *Don't mix up the tickets; they have to be kept in sequence.* **3** a part of a movie when something particular happens. *In the opening sequence, the hero changes into a monster.*

**serene** *adjective* calm and peaceful.

**sergeant** (say **sar**-junt) *noun* **1** an officer in the army or air force who ranks above corporal. **2** an officer in the police force who ranks below inspector.

**serial** *noun* a story with a number of separate parts. **serialize** *verb. The book has been serialized on television.*

**series** (series) *noun* a number of things coming one after another or in order. *A series of TV programs.*

**serious** *adjective* **1** thoughtful; not cheerful, joking, or funny. If something is serious, it is important and has to be thought about carefully. **2** causing worry. *A serious illness.* **seriously** *adverb.* **seriousness** *noun.*

**sermon** *noun* **1** a speech given in church on a religious or moral subject. **2** a lecture or unwanted moral advice.

**serpent** *noun* a large snake.

**servant** *noun* somebody who carries out the orders of another person, usually in their house.

**serve** *verb* **1** to work for somebody, an organization, or your country. **2** to provide with something necessary or be suitable for something. *That old raincoat has served me well.* **3** to help customers in a store or restaurant. *A waitress served us.* **4** to give or offer food to people. *Strawberries served with cream.* **5** to spend time in prison. *He has served three years of his sentence.* **6** to begin a game of tennis by hitting the ball. **serve** *noun* serving, as in tennis. *He has a good serve.* **server** *noun.*

**service** *noun* **1** something that helps people or provides what they need. **2** a job done for somebody. *You might need the services of a lawyer.* **3** the serving of customers in a store or restaurant. *The food is good, but the service is slow.* **4** the repairing of cars and other machines. *I took the car in for a service.* **5** a set of plates and dishes. *A dinner service.* **6** a religious ceremony. *Morning service.* **7** serving in tennis. **service** *verb* to check or repair a car or other machine.

**session** *noun* **1** a formal meeting of an organization. *The court is in session.* **2** a meeting or a time used for an activity. *A recording session.*

**set** (sets, setting, set) *verb* **1** to put somewhere or place in position. *The story is set in the mountains.* **2** to make something official. *He set a price for the sale.* **3** to cause somebody or something to be in a condition. *They set the house on fire.* **4** to prepare something for use or to start doing something. *To set the table.* **5** to harden. *Wait for the glue to set.* **6** to give yourself or somebody else work or a task. **7** to go down. *The sun was setting.* **set** *noun* **1** a group of people or things that go together. *A set of screwdrivers.* **2** a radio or TV receiver. **3** the place where a play or movie is acted. **4** a group of six or more games that make up part of a tennis match. **set back 1** to place something at a distance behind something. *The house is set back from the road.* **2** to delay or make late. *The rain has set back the final.* **3** to cost a lot of money. *How much did the car set you back?* **set off 1** to begin a journey. **2** to make something begin or happen. *Don't set her off crying.* **3** to cause an explosion. **set out 1** to present or make something known. *He set out the rules.* **2** to start a journey. **3** to deliberately start doing something. **set up 1** to place in position. **2** to arrange. *He set up a meeting.* **3** to start; establish.

**setback** *noun* something that makes your position less good than it was before.

**settee** *noun* a sofa. *The children curled up on the settee next to Mother while she read them a story.*

**setting** *noun* **1** the surroundings or place in which something is or happens. *A dark forest is the perfect setting for a fairy tale.* **2** the positions in which the controls of a machine are set. *The dishwasher has three settings: hot, cold, and economy.*

**settle** *verb* **1** to decide or to agree something. *They have finally settled their quarrel.* **2** to become quiet or make calm; to rest. *The medicine will settle your stomach.* **3** to stay in a place or job; to stop being restless. *He finally settled in Canada.* **4** to sink in liquid or come down and cover something. *The snow is settling.* **5** to pay a bill or money owed. **settle down 1** to become quiet or calm. **2** to start living a quiet life. *He got married and settled down.* **3** to sit down and concentrate on something. *She settled down with a good book.*

settlement

**settlement** *noun* **1** a place where people have gathered and built homes, setting up a community. *There was a settlement near the river.* **2** an agreement reached or decision made between two sides. **3** payment of a debt.

**settler** *noun* a person who goes to live in a new country.

**sever** *verb* **1** to break, as by cutting. **2** to part or divide (a relationship).

**several** *adjective, pronoun* a few; not many more than two things or people.

**sew** (sews, sewing, sewed, sewn) *verb* (say soe) to join pieces of material together or make or mend clothing using a needle and thread or a sewing machine.

**sewage** (say **soo**-ij) *noun* waste material from toilets that flows through sewers.

**sewer** (say **soo**-uh) *noun* a large pipe under the ground that carries away sewage.

**sex** (sexes) *noun* **1** the condition of being either male or female; gender. *It is difficult to tell what sex the bird is.* **2** the two groups, male and female, into which people and animals are divided. *The opposite sex.* **3** activity by which people and animals produce young and all the activities connected with this act. **sexy** *adjective.*

**sexism** *noun* the belief that one sex is not as good as the other, especially that women are less able than men.

**sexist** *adjective* showing sexism. *It's simply sexist to say that women are bad drivers.* **sexist** *noun.*

**sexual** *adjective* **1** involving male and female. *The sexual differences between boys and girls.* **2** connected with sexual attraction. **3** connected with the process by which people and animals produce young. *Sexual intercourse.* **sexually** *adverb.* **sexuality** *noun.*

Seychelles' flag

**Seychelles** *noun* a country in the Indian Ocean off the coast of East Africa.

**shade** *noun* **1** darkness under or next to an object which is blocking out the Sun. *We sat in the shade of a tree.* **2** something that keeps out light. *The lamp needs a new shade.* **3** the different forms of a color; how light or dark a color is. *The paint comes in many shades of blue.* **4** a little bit. *There was a shade of fear in his voice.* **5.** a slight difference. *A word with many shades of meaning.* **shade** *verb* **1** to protect something from bright light. *He shaded his eyes with his hand.* **2** to make part of a drawing darker. *She shaded in the background with a pencil.*

**shadow** *noun* **1** a dark shape on a surface made when something stands between a light source and the surface. *I saw his shadow on the wall.* **2** a dark area. *She has shadows under her eyes.* **3** a darkness in a place due to no direct light reaching it. *The valley is in shadow.* **4** a form not as real as it used to be. *She is just a shadow of her former self.* **5** a little bit. *A shadow of doubt.* **shadow** *verb* **1** to follow somebody secretly. *The detective shadowed the man on his journey through the town.* **2** to cast a shadow on something.

**shady** (shadier, shadiest) *adjective* **1** giving shade. **2** dishonest. *Shady dealings.*

**shaggy** (shaggier, shaggiest) *adjective* untidy and rough hair or fur. *The bear had shaggy fur.*

**shallow** *adjective* **1** not deep. *A shallow stream runs past the house.* **2** not showing much thought; not very serious. *She lives a shallow life.*

**sham** *noun* something false pretending to be real. *Her friendliness is just a sham.* **sham** (shams, shamming, shammed) *verb. She shammed interest.* **sham** *adjective.*

**shamble** *verb* to walk by dragging your feet.

**shambles** *plural noun* a place or scene of disorder; a mess. *After the party, the whole house was a shambles.*

**shame** *noun* **1** a feeling of guilt or embarrassment. *He felt a deep sense of shame after he'd been rude to his mother-in-law.* **2** feeling sorry about something. *It's a shame you can't come.* **shame** *verb* to feel shame or make somebody feel ashamed. **shameful** *adjective.*

**shape** *noun* **1** the outer form of something; an outline. *A square and a circle are shapes.* **2** condition. *She looks in good shape.* **take shape** to develop. **shape** *verb* **1** to make something into a particular shape. **2** to develop in a particular way. *A love of acting shaped her whole life.*

**share** *noun* **1** a part belonging, given, or done by a person. *He does his share of the dishwashing.* **2** one of the equal parts into which the ownership of a company is divided. *He owns shares in Southwestern Bell.* **share** *verb* **1** to have or use something with others. *She shares a house with a friend.* **2** to give a portion of something to others; to divide. *They shared the cookies between them.*

**shark** *noun* a large fish with sharp teeth.

shark

**sharp** *adjective* **1** with a fine cutting edge or point. *A sharp knife.* **2** clear to see. *A sharp outline.* **3** quick in thinking, seeing, or hearing; quickly aware of things. **4** having a quick change in direction or steep and sudden. *A sharp bend.* **5** severe and sudden; firm. *A sharp frost.* **6** sudden and loud. *A sharp cry of pain.* **7** sour, fresh in taste. *Gooseberries are too sharp for me, even with sugar sprinkled over them.* **8** a sharp note in music is higher than the normal pitch. **sharp** *adverb* **1** immediately. *Take a sharp left at the church.* **2** exactly; punctually. *We arrived at 3 o'clock sharp.* **sharply** *adverb.* **sharpness** *noun.*

**shatter** *verb* **1** suddenly to break into small pieces. *A stone shattered the windshield and the car veered off course.* **2** to completely destroy or upset. *My hopes of becoming a pilot were cruelly shattered when I was told I was short-sighted.*

**shave** *verb* **1** to cut hair very close to the skin using a razor. **2** to cut or scrape thin pieces off something. *You'll have to shave some wood off the bottom of the door to make it shut.* **shave** *noun. He needs a good shave.* **a close shave** a near accident or disaster. **shaver** *noun.*

shear



**shawl** *noun* a piece of material worn over the head or around the shoulders or wrapped around a baby. *Wrap your new baby in this shawl to keep her warm.*

**shear** (shears, shearing, sheared, shorn) *verb* to cut off the woolen fleece from sheep with a razor.

**shears** *plural noun* a tool that looks like a large pair of scissors used for cutting hedges.

**shed** *noun* a small building for storing things. *A bike shed.* **shed** (sheds, shedding, shed) *verb* **1** to flow out or let something fall. *She shed many tears.* **2** to get rid of or give off. *Snakes shed their skin as they grow.*

**sheep** (sheep) *noun* a farm animal with thick wooly fur. *A flock of sheep are roaming the hillside.*

**sheepish** *adjective* embarrassed, usually because you have done something silly. *He gave her a sheepish look.*

**sheet** *noun* **1** a large piece of cloth, usually cotton, put on a bed over the mattress. **2** a piece of paper. **3** a large, flat, thin piece of glass, metal, or wood. **4** a wide stretch of something thin. *A sheet of ice.*

**sheik** (say sheek, shake) *noun* an Arab chief or prince. *The sheik gave the queen a ruby when she visited him.*

**shelf** (shelves) *noun* **1** a flat board set against a wall or in a cupboard, used for putting things on. **2** a piece of rock on a mountain that sticks out like a wall-mounted shelf.

**shell** *noun* **1** the hard outer covering of an animal, egg, fruit, nut, or seed. **2** the walls of a building or ship. **3** a metal case filled with explosive for firing from a large gun. **shell** *verb* **1** to take something out of a shell. *She was shelling peas.* **2** to fire explosive shells. *The town was shelled during the attack.*

**shelter** *noun* **1** something that gives protection, usually a small building or covered place. *A bus shelter.* **2** protection or being kept safe. *We took shelter under a tree.* **shelter** *verb* **1** to protect somebody or something from harm. *They sheltered an escaped prisoner.* **2** to take shelter.

shell

**shepherd** *noun* a person who looks after sheep. *The shepherd made sure no wolves attacked his flock.*

**shield** *noun* **1** a large piece of metal, wood, or leather that soldiers used to carry to protect their bodies. **2** a badge shaped like a shield. **3** protective cover. *Sun lotion acts as a shield against the sun.* **shield** *verb* to protect. *I shielded my eyes from the windblown sand.*

**shift** *noun* **1** a change of position or direction. *A shift in the wind.* **2** the duration of time that a worker or a group of workers works. *The nurse was working a late shift.* **3** a straight dress. **shift** *verb* to move from one place to another; to change direction. *She shifted in her seat.*

**shifty** (shiftier, shiftiest) *adjective* not to be trusted.

**shimmer** *verb* to shine with a soft light.

**shin** *noun* the front of a leg between the knee and ankle. *Baseball players wear protective pads on their shins.*

**shine** (shines, shining, shone) *verb* **1** to give off light; to be bright. *The sun is shining.* **2** to direct light at something. *Can you shine the flashlight over there?* **3** to be excellent. *He is good at most sports, but he really shines at tennis.* **3** to polish or make bright by rubbing. **shine** *noun* a brightness or polish.

**shiny** (shinier, shiniest) *adjective* looking bright or polished. *Olivia powders her shiny nose each day.*

**ship** *noun* a large boat for carrying people or goods across an ocean. **ship** (ships, shipping, shipped) *verb* to take or send goods by ship.

**shipshape** *adjective* neat and tidy.

**shipwreck** *noun* **1** the loss of a ship at sea. **2** a ship that has been wrecked. **shipwreck** *verb* To be shipwrecked is to be in or from a ship lost or damaged at sea. *The pirates were shipwrecked on a desert island.*

**shipwreck**

**shipyard** *noun* a place where ships are built.

**shire** *noun* a county in Britain.

**shirk** *verb* to try to get out of doing a job. *He is always shirking the vacuuming.*

**shirt** *noun* a piece of clothing for the top half of the body, worn with trousers or a skirt. *Toby wore a satin shirt when he went ballroom dancing.*

**shiver** *verb* to tremble, especially with cold or fear. **shiver** *noun.* **shivery** *adjective. She has a temperature and feels shivery.*

**shoal** *noun* a group of fish swimming together. *We saw a shoal of small fish darting between the rocks.*

**shoal**

**shock** *noun* **1** a strong, unpleasant feeling of surprise or fear. *It was a shock to hear a sudden bang from upstairs when I knew no one else was in the house.* **2** a tremor. *We felt the shock as the train rumbled past.* **3** the effects of electricity passing through the body; an electric shock. *I got an unpleasant shock when I touched the electric fence along the edge of the field.* **shock** *verb* to surprise or upset somebody; to make somebody feel shocked. *I was shocked by the store keeper's rudeness when I asked for the largest size.*

**shocking** *adjective* very bad or wrong. *The celebrity spent a shocking amount of money on clothes.*

**shoddy** (shoddier, shoddiest) *adjective* badly made or done. *Katie produced shoddy work.* **shoddiness** *noun.*

**shoe** *noun* **1** a covering for the feet, usually made of leather with a hard sole. **2** a horseshoe. **shoe** *verb* to put a horseshoe on a horse's hoof.

**shoelace** *noun* a strip of material like a piece of string used to tie up a shoe; shoestring.

**shoot** (shoots, shooting, shot) *verb* **1** to fire a gun or an arrow. **2** to be hit by a bullet or an arrow. **3** to kick or throw a ball at a goal. **4** to move or send quickly in one direction; to move over or through something fast. *The pain shot up his arm.* **5** to put out new growth (shoots) from a stem. **6** to photograph a scene in a movie. *The movie was shot in New York City.* **shoot** *noun* **1** a young growth of a plant. **2** shooting of a movie or still photographs for an advertisement or book. **3** a group of people hunting animals or birds as a sport.

**shore** *noun* the land along the edge of an ocean, sea, or lake. *Let's walk along the shore and look for shells.*

**shortage** *noun* a lack of something; not having enough. *There is a terrible food shortage in Sudan.*

**shortcoming** *noun* a fault or defect.

**shorthand** *noun* a way of writing that uses special signs or shorter forms for words and phrases, so something can be written down as fast as somebody is saying it.

**shortly** *adverb* **1** very soon. **2** in a few words. **3** in a cross way, not politely; impatiently.

**short-sighted** *adjective* **1** unable to see far without wearing glasses. **2** not considering the future effects of something you are about to do or have done.

**shoulder** *noun* the two parts of the body between the neck and the tops of the arms. *She wore a sleeveless dress that showed off her shoulders.* **shoulder** *verb* **1** to take on something, especially a problem or responsibility. **2** to push with the shoulder. *He shouldered his way through the crowd.*

**shout** *noun* a loud call or cry. **shout** *verb* to cry or call loudly.

**shove** *verb* to push roughly. **shove** *noun.*

**show** *noun* **1** a public showing or a collection of things to be looked at. *A Paris fashion show.* **2** a performance in a theater, on television, or in a club. **3** a way of behaving; if something is for show, it is done only to make a good impression. **show** (shows, showing, showed, shown) *verb* **1** to allow or offer to be seen. **2** to be seen easily; to be noticeable. *Any marks show on white.* **3** to demonstrate or make somebody understand something. *He showed me how to use the computer.* **4** to point to a mark or number. **5** to guide. *The waitress showed us to our seats.* **6** to prove or make something clear. *Her grades show that it was worth studying for the test.* **7** to act toward somebody in a certain way. *He shows no pity for the homeless.* **show off** to try too hard to impress people. **show up** **1** to arrive at a place. *Only a few people showed up to the party.* **2** to be seen clearly; be noticeable. **3** to embarrass someone by behaving badly. *"You really showed me up in that shop," said John's mother crossly.* **on show** to be seen by the public. *His paintings are on show at the gallery.* **showy** *adjective* too noticeable; gaudy. *The bride's aunt wore a showy hat.*

**show business** *noun* the business of entertainment. If you are in show business, you work in television, movies, or the theater.

**shower** *noun* **1** a short rainfall. **2** a fall of many small things arriving at the same time. *She was covered in a shower of blossoms.* **3** a device, usually in a bathroom, for washing yourself; it sprays water on your body. **4** a wash under a shower. *I have a shower every day.* **showery** *adjective. It's been showery all day.* **shower** *verb* **1** to fall in a shower. **2** to have a shower.

**show-jumping** *noun* the sport of riding a horse over fences and obstacles.

**shred** *noun* **1** a small piece torn or cut off something. **2** a very small amount. *There is not a shred of truth in what he says.* **shred** (shreds, shredding, shredded) *verb* to cut or tear into small pieces.

**shrewd** *adjective* having common sense; clever. *She is a shrewd businesswoman when it comes to buying and selling.*

**shriek** *noun* a sudden loud, wild cry. *A shriek of laughter.* **shriek** *verb.*

**shrine** *noun* a holy place where people pray. *The pilgrims left offerings at the shrine.*

**shrink** (shrinks, shrinking, shrank, shrunk) *verb* **1** to become smaller in size. *The sweater has shrunk in the washing machine.* **2** to move back, usually in fear. **3** to avoid doing something because it is not pleasant.

shrine

**shrivel** (shrivels, shriveling, shriveled) *verb* to become dry and wrinkled. *Prunes and dates shrivel when they are dried.*

**shrub** *noun* a small bush.

**shrug** (shrugs, shrugging, shrugged) *verb* to raise your shoulders to show that you don't know or don't care. **shrug** *noun.*

**shudder** *verb* to give a brief tremble of fear, cold, or horror. **shudder** *noun.*

**shuffle** *verb* **1** to walk by dragging your feet. **2** to mix up the order of a pack of playing cards before beginning a game. **shuffle** *noun.*

**shun** (shuns, shunning, shunned) *verb* to avoid. *I was hurt when Rupert shunned me in the street, because I knew he had seen me.*

**shut** (shuts, shutting, shut) *verb* **1** to move into a covered, blocked, or folded-together position; to close. **2** to close for a period of time or stop business. **shut down** to stop business or work. *The shop has shut down.* **shut in** to leave or lock in a room. *He shut himself in his room to work.* **shut up** **1** to make a place safe before leaving. **2** to stop talking or stop somebody from talking.

**shutter** *noun* **1** a wooden, door-shaped cover for a window. A shutter can be opened or shut to keep out the light. *Please close the shutters.* **2** the part in a camera that opens to let in light when a photograph is taken.

shuttle

**shuttle** *noun* **1** a train, bus, or aircraft that makes regular journeys between two places. *There is a shuttle service between the sports ground and the college in the center of town.* **2** a pointed instrument used in weaving that carries a thread (the weft) over and under lots of other threads (the warp). **3** a spacecraft used to make a number of journeys into outer space; a space shuttle. **shuttle** *verb* to move or send backward and forward.

**shy** *adjective* nervous, quiet and uncomfortable when in company with other people. *He is too shy to speak up.* **shyly** *adverb.* **shyness** *noun.* **shy** (shies, shying, shied) *verb* to move away suddenly. *The horse shied at the sound of the police siren.*

**Siamese twins** *plural noun* twins who are born with their bodies joined together. *The Siamese twins were successfully separated and grew up happily.*

**sibling** *noun* a brother or sister.

**sick** *adjective* **1** ill; not well. **2** likely to vomit or throw up food. *Going on a boat always makes me feel sick.* **3** angry or fed up. *I'm sick of washing dishes every night.* **4** making fun of misfortune or illness. *William told some sick jokes to his friends.* **sickly** *adjective.*

**sickness** *noun* **1** illness or bad health. **2** a disease. **3** a sick feeling; vomiting.

**side** *noun* **1** a surface of something that is not the top or the bottom. *The side of the cupboard is where the cat sharpens his claws.* **2** one of the two surfaces of something flat. *Please write on both sides of the paper.* **3** the two halves of an area which could be divided by a line in the middle. **4** the right or the left part of your body. *I've got a pain in my left side.* **5** a place next to somebody or something. **6** an edge or border. *She sat on the side of the dance floor.* **7** an upright surface of a building or mountain. **8** a particular position in a discussion, or a group that holds a particular position. *Which side is he on?* **9** a team. **side** *verb* to support somebody's position. *My mother always sides with my brother.* **on the side** as a sideline. *She sells flowers on the side.* **side by side** next to one another. **to be on the safe side** to be prepared in case something happens. **side effect** an effect in addition to the one intended. *This drug can have unpleasant side effects.*

siege

**sideline** *noun* somebody's second or extra job.

**siege** *noun* an operation, usually by an army, to surround a place such as a town or fortress and force it to surrender by stopping food reaching the people inside. *The town was under siege for months.*

**Sierra Leone** *noun* a country in West Africa bordering the North Atlantic Ocean.

**siesta** (say see-**est**-uh) *noun* a rest or sleep after lunch, in the afternoon.

**sieve** (say siv) *noun* a bowl-shaped tool made of wire net or plastic net, used mainly in the kitchen for straining lumps from liquid or soft substances, or rinsing small solids such as rice grains. **sieve** *verb* to put something through a sieve. *Before baking a cake, sieve the flour to remove any lumps.*

**sift** *verb* **1** to put something through a sieve. **2** to examine something carefully. *He sifted through his papers to find the letter.*

**sigh** *verb* to make a sound as you let out a deep breath as a sign of tiredness, sadness, or gladness. **sigh** *noun* the act or sound of sighing. *She breathed a sigh of relief when the job finally came to an end.*

**sight** *noun* **1** the ability to see. **2** the act of seeing something, or something seen or worth seeing. *We went to see the sights of Florence.* **3** something that looks bad or is laughable to look at. *Her hair looks a real sight!* **4** the distance within which things can be seen. *She doesn't let the children out of her sight.* **5** a part of a telescope or gun that you look through to help you aim. **sight** *verb* to see something for the first time by coming near it. *After a month at sea, they sighted land.* **in sight** likely to happen very soon. *A cure is in sight.* **catch sight of** to see for a moment. **know somebody by sight** to recognize somebody without ever having spoken to them and without knowing their name.

**sightseer** *noun* a tourist. **sightsee** *verb.* **sightseeing** *noun.*

**sign** *noun* **1** a mark or shape with a particular meaning. *A dove is a sign of peace.* **2** a movement of the body showing a particular meaning. *Putting your finger to your lips is a sign to be quiet.* **3** a board or notice with a warning or piece of information. *A road sign.* **4** something that shows that something exists or is happening. *A temperature is the first sign of flu.* **sign** *verb* **1** to make a movement as a sign to somebody. **2** to put your signature on a document or form.

**sign language** *noun* a way of communicating, usually with deaf people, by using hand movements.

**signal** *noun* **1** a sound or action that warns, gives a message, or causes something else to happen. *American Indians used smoke signals to communicate over long distances.* **2** a device beside a railroad that uses lights to tell train drivers when to stop. **3** a sound or picture sent by radio or TV. **signal** (signals, signaling, signaled) *verb* **1** to make a sign to somebody. **2** to make something known by indicating with a gesture. *He signaled right, but went left.* **3** to be a sign of something.

**signature** *noun* a person's name written by himself or herself, usually at the end of a letter or document.

**significant** *adjective* meaningful or important. *"significant other" means "partner" or "spouse."*

**Sikh** (say seek) *noun* a member of an Indian religious group, originally from the Punjab.

**silence** *noun* **1** the absence of sound; extreme quietness. **2** not speaking, making a noise, answering questions, or mentioning a particular thing. **silence** *verb* to stop somebody or something from speaking or making a noise.

**silent** *adjective* not speaking; totally quiet. *The library was silent.*

**silhouette** (say sil-oo-**ett**) *noun* **1** a dark shape or shadow against a light background. **2** an outline drawing filled in with black or a cut-out of black paper. **silhouette** *verb. The church was sharply silhouetted against the sky.*

silhouette

**silk** *noun* a soft, light cloth made from fine thread produced by silkworms. *I gave my mother a luxurious silk scarf.*

**silkworm** *noun* a type of caterpillar that produces a silk covering (a cocoon) for its body that is used to make silk.

silkworm

**silt** *noun* fine sand or mud that is carried along by a river.

**silver** *noun* **1** a valuable soft metal used for making ornaments, jewelry, and coins. **2** the color of silver. **3** coins and things made from silver, especially cutlery and dishes. **4** a silver medal, usually as second prize. **silver** *adjective* **1** made of silver. **2** like the color of silver. *Silver paint.* **silver wedding** the 25th anniversary of a wedding.

**simile** (say **sim**-il-ee) *noun* a comparison of one thing with another, using the word "like." "Her cheeks are like roses," is a simile.

**simmer** *verb* to cook gently, just below boiling point.

**simple** *adjective* **1** easy to understand or do; not difficult. **2** without decoration. *Simple food tastes best.* **3** with nothing added. *The simple truth is, she is hopeless at playing the guitar.* **4** without much intelligence or easily fooled. *He's a bit simple.* **simplicity** *noun.*

**simplify** (simplifies, simplifying, simplified) *verb* to make something easy to understand. **simplification** *noun.*

**sin** *noun* **1** the breaking of a religious law or something that should not be done. *Stealing is a sin.* **sin** (sins, sinning, sinned) *verb* to break a religious law or do something that is believed to be very bad. **sinner** *noun.*

**since** *conjunction, preposition, adverb* **1** from that time until now. *I haven't seen her since we left school.* **2** during or at a time after a particular time or event in the past. *He used to play tennis regularly, but has since stopped.* **3** because, as used to state a reason for doing or not doing something. *Since you are too tired, we won't go for a walk along the beach.*

**sincere** *adjective* honest; not false. **sincerely** *adverb. I sincerely hope that they will believe what he tells them.* It is usual to write "Yours sincerely" at the end of a formal letter before your signature. **sincerity** *noun.*

**Singapore** *noun* a city and country in Southeast Asia.

**singe** (say sinj) *verb* to burn slightly.

**singular** *noun* a word that expresses one person or thing. **singular** *adjective.*

**sinister** *adjective* evil or seeming likely to be harmful. *The empty house was a sinister place.*

**sink**

**sink** *noun* a basin with faucets in the kitchen, used for washing dishes. **sink** (sinks, sinking, sank, sunk) *verb* **1** to go down below the surface of water. *The ship sank to the bottom of the ocean.* **2** to go or fall down. *She sank on to the bed with exhaustion.* **3** to get smaller or less. *Prices are sinking.* **4** to become weaker. *His voice sank to a whisper.* **5** to become depressed. *Her heart sank at the thought of retaking the test.* **6** to put money or work into something. *My brother sank all of his savings into a new car.* **7** to make something hard or sharp go deeply into something. *She sank her teeth into the apple.* **sink in** to be or become understood. *Has my advice sunk in?*

**sinus** (sinuses) *noun* a space in the bones of the face just behind the nose. *If you have a cold, your sinuses can get blocked, which is painful.*

**siren** *noun* **1** a device that makes a long, loud warning sound. *Police cars and fire engines have sirens.* **2** a dangerously beautiful woman.

**sister** *noun* **1** a girl or woman who has the same parents as you. **2** a woman who belongs to the same race as you. **3** a nun. **4** a woman who stands up for women's rights and feels very close to other women. **sisterly** *adjective.*

**sister-in-law** (sisters-in-law) *noun* the sister of your husband or wife, or your brother's wife.

**site** *noun* a place where something was or is happening. *A building site.*

**situation** *noun* **1** what is happening in a particular place at a particular time or the things that are happening to you. *The situation looked bleak after the earthquake struck the city.* **2** a job. **3** the surroundings of a place. *Our house is in a beautiful situation.*

**size** *noun* **1** how big or small something is. *The toy dog was the same size as a rabbit.* **2** a set of measurements, as for clothes and shoes. *What size does he take?* **size** *verb* to arrange people or things according to their size. **size up** to form an opinion of a person or thing; to decide how to act after thinking about a situation. *It took me a little while to size up the situation.*

**sizzle** *verb* to make a sound like the sound made by frying food. *The bacon sizzled in the pan.*

**skate** *noun* **1** a boot with a steel blade (ice skate) or wheels (rollerskate), used for skating. **2** a large, flat sea fish. **skate** *verb* to move around on ice wearing ice skates (or on a hard surface wearing rollerskates). *We skated across the frozen lake.*

**skateboard** *noun* a board with small wheels at each end that you ride on for fun. **skateboarding** *noun.*

**skeleton** *noun* **1** the framework of bones in a human or animal body. **2** something forming a framework or an outline. *The metal skeleton of the building was erected.* **a skeleton in the cupboard** something from your past of which you are ashamed. **skeleton key** a master key that opens a number of different locks.

**sketch** (sketches) *noun* **1** a quickly made drawing. *He made a sketch of the castle.* **2** a short description of something. **3** a short, funny piece of writing or acting. **sketch** *verb* **1** to draw something quickly. **2** to give a short description of something with few details. **sketchy** *adjective.*

**ski** *noun* one of a pair of long, flat pieces of wood, metal, or plastic that you fasten to a ski boot so that you can slide fast across snow. **ski** (skis, skiing, skied) *verb.* **skier** *noun.*

**skill** *noun* the knowledge or ability to do something well. **skillful** *adjective. She is a skillful painter.* **skillfully** *adverb.* **skilled** *adjective. A skilled job.*

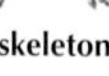

**skeleton**

Ss

**skim** (skims, skimming, skimmed) *verb* **1** to remove cream or other unwanted things from the surface of a liquid. *Skimmed milk.* **2** to read something quickly. *He skimmed the newspaper.* **3** to move quickly along or just above something. *The plane skimmed the treetops.*

**skin** *noun* **1** the outer covering of the body. *Fur coats are made from animal skins.* **2** the outer covering of some fruit and vegetables. *He slipped on a banana skin and broke his ankle.* **3** a thin layer that forms on liquid, especially when it gets cool. *I hate skin on milk.* **skin** (skins, skinning, skinned) *verb* to take the skin off something.

**skinny** (skinnier, skinniest) *adjective* very thin.

**skipper** *noun* the person in charge of a ship or boat.

**Skopje** *noun* the capital of Macedonia in southeastern Europe.

**skull** *noun* the bones of the head that enclose the brain.

**skunk** *noun* a small North American black-and-white animal that gives out a bad smell when frightened or alarmed.

**skyscraper** *noun* a very tall building with many storeys.

skyscraper

**slab** *noun* a thick, flat piece. *A slab of concrete.*

**slack** *adjective* **1** not pulled tight, especially a rope or wire. **2** not firm; weak. *The rules at this school are slack – pupils break them all the time.* **3** not busy or working hard. *Business is slack.* **slackness** *noun.* **slack** *verb* to not work enough; to be lazy. **slacker** *noun.*

**slam** (slams, slamming, slammed) *verb* **1** to shut loudly. *Please don't slam the door!* **2** to push or put down quickly and with force. *He slammed on the brakes.*

**slander** *noun* an untrue spoken statement about somebody that damages their reputation. **slander** *verb* to harm someone by making a false statement.

**slang** *noun* words and expressions used in informal conversation. "Dosh" and "dough" are slang for "money."

**slap** (slaps, slapping, slapped) *verb* **1** to hit somebody or something with the palm of your hand. *Susan slapped Philip's face.* **2** to put roughly or carelessly. *He slapped paint on the walls.* **3** to put down with force. *Robert slapped the book on the table.* **slap** *noun.*

**slapdash** *adjective* careless.

**slate** *noun* **1** a dark gray rock that splits easily into thin layers. **2** a slice of this rock used for covering roofs. **3** a board made from a slice of this rock, used for writing on with chalk. **slate** *verb* **1** to cover a roof with slates. **2** to criticize or attack. *His new movie was slated.*

**slaughter** *verb* **1** to kill animals for food. *The goose was slaughtered for the Christmas feast.* **2** to kill cruelly, especially many people. **slaughter** *noun.*

**slave** *noun* somebody who is owned by (has been bought by) another person and has to work for that person without pay. **slave** *verb* to work very hard, like a slave. *I slaved at cleaning the house all day.* **slavery** *noun.*

**slay** (slays, slaying, slew, slain) *verb* to kill.

**sleazy** (sleazier, sleaziest) *adjective* dirty and unpleasant. **sleaze** *noun.* **sleaziness** *noun.*

**sled** *noun* a seat attached to metal blades, used for sliding down a hill covered in snow and ice. **sled** *verb* to ride on a sled.

sled

**sleek** *adjective* smooth and shiny, especially hair or fur. *The sleek coat of the cat rose and fell as the animal purred on my lap.*

**sleep** *noun* a state of the body when the eyes are closed and the mind is not conscious; a period of sleep. *Most people need about eight hours of sleep each night.* **sleep** (sleeps, sleeping, slept) *verb* to be asleep. **sleepy** *adjective.* **sleepiness** *noun.*

**sleeper** *noun* **1** a person who sleeps. *I'm a light sleeper, so any noise will wake me.* **2** one of a row of heavy beams supporting a railroad track. **3** a sleeping car on a train. *I booked the sleeper to Chicago.*

**sleeping bag** *noun* a warm bag made of stuffed material in which you can sleep, usually when camping.

**sleet** *noun* a mixture of rain and snow; frozen rain. **sleet** *verb. It's sleeting outside.*

**sleeve** *noun* **1** the part of a piece of clothing that covers the arm. **2** a stiff case for a book.

**slender** *adjective* thin; slim.

**sleuth** (say slooth) *noun* a detective; an investigator.

**slice** *noun* **1** a thin piece cut from something. **2** a part or share of something. **slice** *verb* **1** to cut into pieces. **2** to cut off a piece. **3** to cut through something.

**slick** *adjective* **1** well-made and good-looking, but not meaningful. **2** clever, but not necessarily honest. **3** quick and smooth. *The dancers gave a slick performance.* **slick** *noun* a thin sheet of oil floating on water. *The oil slick killed many birds.*

sleuth

**slide** (slides, sliding, slid) *verb* **1** to move smoothly over or on something. *She slid the plate across the table.* **2** to move quietly and quickly, usually in order to go unnoticed. **slide** *noun* **1** the action of sliding. **2** a structure with a slope for sliding down, usually used by children in a playground. **3** a piece of film secured in a square casing. The image on the slide can be projected on to a screen to be seen large, or seen through a viewer. **4** a glass plate, used to hold something that you want to look at under a microscope.

**slight** *adjective* **1** small and thin. **2** not serious. *A slight headache.* **slightly** *adverb.* **slightness** *noun.* **slight** *verb* to treat somebody without respect. **slight** *noun.*

**slim** (slimmer, slimmest) *adjective* **1** thin; not fat. **2** small. *There is still a slim chance of getting tickets for the concert tomorrow night.*

**slime** *noun* thick, sticky liquid, usually unpleasant. *The snail left a trail of slime.* **slimy** *adjective.* **sliminess** *noun.*

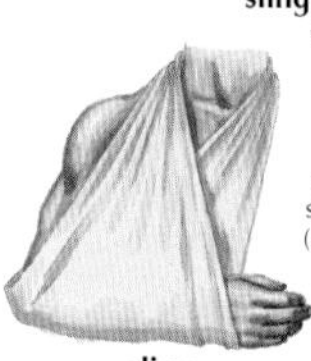

sling

**sling** *noun* **1** a piece of material tied around the neck to support a broken arm. **2** a loop or a device made of ropes and straps for carrying or lifting things. *She carries her baby in a sling.* **3** a strap for throwing stones, like a catapult. **sling** (slings, slinging, slung) *verb* **1** to throw carelessly. *He slung his bag over his shoulder.* **2** to throw with force. *They were slinging stones.* **3** to attach or hold in a sling.

**slip** (slips, slipping, slipped) *verb* **1** to slide and almost fall because you have lost your balance. **2** to move, go, or put something somewhere quickly and smoothly, especially without being noticed. *The girl slipped out of the room.* **3** to put on or take off, especially clothes. **4** to get away, escape, or be forgotten. *His birthday slipped my mind.* **5** to get worse; to fall in quality. **slip up** to make a mistake. **slip** *noun* **1** the act of slipping. **2** a slight mistake. **3** a small piece of paper. **4** a sleeveless garment that women wear under a dress. **5** a pillowcase. **give somebody the slip** to get away from someone who is following you.

Ss

**slipper** *noun* a soft shoe worn indoors.

**slippery** *adjective* difficult to hold or stand on because of being wet or very smooth.

**slipshod** *adjective* careless, slovenly.

**slip-up** *noun* a slight mistake.

**slit** *noun* a narrow cut or opening. **slit** (slits, slitting, slit) *verb* to cut or make a slit in.

**slog** (slogs, slogging, slogged) *verb* **1** to do hard, dull work without stopping. **2** to make a long, tiring journey, walking with difficulty. *Mom slogged back from town with the shopping.* **slog** *noun.* **slogger** *noun.*

**slogan** *noun* a short phrase that is easy to remember, mainly used to advertise something. *A catchy slogan.*

**slope** *noun* **1** a piece of ground or a surface that is higher at one end than the other. **2** a slanting line or direction. **slope** *verb* to incline or to lean to the right or the left.

Slovakia's flag

**slouch** *verb* to stand or move with shoulders and head drooped. **slouch** *noun.*

**Slovakia** *noun* a country in central Europe.

**Slovenia** *noun* a country in southeast Europe.

**slovenly** *adjective* careless and untidy. *The waitress was a slovenly woman in a dirty apron.*

**slow** *adjective* **1** taking a long time or too long; not quick. **2** showing a time that is earlier than the correct time. *My watch is five minutes slow.* **3** not able to understand things quickly; not very active. **slow** *verb* to make or become slower. **slowly** *adverb.* **slowness** *noun.* **slow motion** the slow projection of a movie so that actions appear much slower than in real life. *They showed the goal again in slow motion.*

**slug** *noun* a small, slow-moving animal like a snail, but without a shell.

**sluggish** *adjective* slow-moving.

**slum** *noun* a very poor area of a town, with dirty streets and bad living conditions.

**slumber** *noun* sleep. **slumber** *verb.*

**slur** *noun* **1** an unclear way of speaking in which words run into each other. **2** unfair or bad remarks that could damage a person's reputation. *His words were a slur on my character.* **slur** (slurs, slurring, slurred) *verb* **1** to say words unclearly so they are difficult to understand. *My uncle sometimes slurs his words when he has had too much beer to drink.* **2** to say unfair or bad things.

**sly** (slier, sliest; slyer, slyest are also used) *adjective* cunning and not honest; keeping things secret. *In the story, a sly fox lures the red hen into a trap with his cunning tricks, but the hen escapes.* **on the sly** secretly.

**smack** *noun* **1** a particular taste. *The drink has a smack of lemon.* **2** a sailing boat used for fishing. **smack** *verb* **1** to have a trace of. **2** to hit with the flat of the hand. **3** to open and close your lips noisily. **4** to put, throw, or hit something so that it makes a loud noise. **smack** *adverb. He skateboarded smack into the garden fence.*

**small** *adjective* not big; little in size, weight, or importance. **smallness** *noun.* **small change** coins of little value. **small talk** *noun* conversation about unimportant things; chitchat. *My mother-in-law is only capable of small talk, which I loathe.*

**small-minded** *adjective* petty; thinking in a small way; unwilling to change your mind or listen to others. The opposite of "small-minded" is "open-minded."

**smart** *adjective* **1** neat and elegant looking. **2** clever. **3** stylish and fashionable. **4** quick. *We walked at a smart pace.* **smart** *verb* **1** to feel a sharp stinging pain. *My eyes are smarting from the smoke of the bonfire.* **2** to feel upset, especially about something unkind that is said or done to you. **smartly** *adverb.* **smartness** *noun.*

**smash** (smashes) *noun* **1** the action or sound of something breaking to pieces. **2** a car wreck. **3** a very successful show or movie. *A smash hit.* **4** a disaster in business. **5** a hard overhand stroke, especially in tennis. **smash** *verb* **1** to break noisily into many pieces. **2** to move or be propelled with great force. **3** to destroy or ruin.

**smell** *noun* **1** the ability the nose has to scent things. *Dogs have a strong sense of smell.* **2** something in things that you can detect with the nose. *A smell of gas.* **3** smelling something. *Have a smell of this cheese!* **smell** (smells, smelling, smelt) *verb* **1** to use your nose to discover a smell. **2** to have or produce a smell. If you say something smells, it has a bad smell. **3** to have a feeling or to notice. *She smelled trouble.* **smelly** *adjective.*

**smile** *noun* an expression on the face in which the corners of the mouth turn up, showing happiness or friendliness. **smile** *verb* to express happiness with the face.

**smirk** *noun* an unpleasant, self-satisfied smile. **smirk** *verb* to smile in a self-satisfied way.

**smoke** *noun* **1** gas and small bits of solid material that are seen in the air when something burns. *Smoke from the chimney.* **2** smoking a cigarette or pipe. *He likes a smoke.* **smoke** *verb* **1** to give out smoke. *The volcano is smoking.* **2** to have a cigarette, cigar, or pipe in your mouth and to suck in the smoke and blow it out again. **3** the habit of smoking. *Do you smoke?* **4** to preserve meat or fish by hanging it in smoke. **smoky** *adjective.* **smoker** *noun.*

**smolder** *verb* **1** to burn slowly without a flame. **2** to have strong feelings without showing them. *Her love for him smoldered for many years.*

**smooth** *adjective* **1** having an even surface without lumps or holes; not rough. **2** calm and comfortable without sudden bumps. *A smooth ride.* **3** free from lumps; evenly mixed. **4** very polite; almost too pleasant. **5** pleasant tasting, not sour or bitter. **6** not harsh. *A smooth voice.* **smooth** *verb* to make smooth. **smooth something over** to make a difficulty seem less serious.

**smother** *verb* **1** to die from not having enough air, or to kill by covering somebody's mouth so they cannot breathe. **2** to put out a fire by covering it with something. *He smothered the flames with a blanket.* **3** to cover thickly. *The toast was smothered with butter.* **4** to control or hold something back. *She tried to smother a yawn, but he saw she was bored.*

**smudge** *noun* a dirty mark, usually made by rubbing something. **smudge** *verb* to make a dirty mark on something by rubbing it, or to become messy.

**smug** *adjective* being too pleased with yourself and what you can do. *He had a smug look on his face when he collected his prize.*

smuggle

**smuggle** *verb* to take something secretly into a country or place. *The men from the village smuggled ashore all they could save from the shipwrecked boat.* **smuggler** *noun.* **smuggling** *noun. Smuggling is illegal.*

**snack** *noun* a small, quick meal, especially one eaten between main meals. **snack** *verb.*

**snag** *noun* **1** a problem or difficulty. **2** a sharp part that sticks out and may catch you in passing. **snag** *verb* to get caught on and tear. *I snagged my tights.*

**snail** *noun* a small animal with a slimy body and a shell on its back. **at a snail's pace** very slowly. *Mom walks at a snail's pace.*

**snake** *noun* a long, thin reptile with no legs and a fork-shaped tongue. Some snakes are deadly poisonous.

snake

**snap** *adjective* done immediately. *A snap decision may sometimes be regretted.* **snap** *noun* **1** the action or sound of clicking shut rapidly. *The trap closed with a snap.* **2** a photograph taken quickly; a snapshot. **3** a card game in which one of two players shouts "snap" when he/she sees two of the same cards laid down together. **snap** (snaps, snapping, snapped) *verb* **1** to break. *His patience finally snapped.* **2** to make a sharp sound like something breaking. **3** to bite or catch something with the teeth. *The dog snapped at her ankle.* **4** to say something quickly and angrily. **5** to move or shut quickly with a sharp sound. **6** to take a photograph. *She snapped us at the beach.* **snap at** to take or get something quickly. *We snapped at the chance of spending a week in the sun.* **snap up** to buy something quickly because it is a bargain. *Kate snapped up the dress in the sale.*

**snare** *noun* a trap for catching birds or small animals. **snare** *verb. He snared a rabbit by the edge of the wood and ate it for his supper.*

**snarl** *noun* a twisted or tangled-up thread, piece of wool, or situation. **snarl** *verb* **1** to become twisted and tangled. *Lucy's hair was snarled into knots.* **2** to growl angrily or speak in a low, angry voice.

**sneak** *verb* **1** to move quietly and secretly, trying not to be seen or heard. **2** to take something somewhere secretly. *He sneaked his pet mouse into school.* **sneak** *noun* a person who does or says things secretly and cannot be trusted. **sneaky** *adjective*. **sneakily** *adverb.*

**sneaker** *noun* a sports shoe with a rubber sole; a tennis shoe.

**sneeze** *noun* a sudden outburst of air through the nose and mouth. **sneeze** *verb. I felt a tickle in my nose and had to sneeze.*

**snide** *adjective* unkind remarks that contain indirect criticism. *She made some snide remarks about my friends.*

**sniff** *verb* **1** to make a sound by breathing in air through your nose. **2** to smell something. *The dog sniffed the ground.* **sniff** *noun*. **sniffer** *noun. A glue sniffer.*

**snigger** *verb* to laugh quietly and in a disrespectful way, as about something rude. *The boys whispered rude jokes to each other at the back of the class and sniggered.* **snigger** *noun.*

**snip** *noun.* a short, quick cut with scissors or shears. **snip** (snips, snipping, snipped) *verb* to cut with scissors or shears in short, quick cuts. *I asked the barber just to snip the ends of my hair.*

**snivel** (snivels, sniveling, sniveled) *verb* to speak or cry in a sniffing and whining way.

**snob** *noun* somebody who has little respect for people with less money or power than themselves. **snobbish** *adjective*. **snobbery** *noun.*

**snooker** *noun* a game played on a special table, in which you hit a white ball with a long stick (a cue) and score points each time this ball knocks a colored ball into a pocket at the side of the table.

**snooze** *noun* a short sleep. **snooze** *verb. The dog snoozed in the sunshine.*

**snore** *verb* to breathe noisily while asleep. *Peter claims not to snore, but he makes a funny sawing noise while asleep.* **snore** *noun.*

**snorkel** *noun* a tube through which you can breathe when you swim under water. **snorkeling** *noun. Gordon went snorkeling on the Great Barrier Reef.*

**snort** *verb* to make a rough noise by breathing out through the nose. **snort** *noun.*

**snout** *noun* the nose of some animals. *A pig's snout is ideal for rooting around in the ground.*

**snow** *noun* water frozen into soft, white pieces (flakes) that fall gently from the sky in cold weather and cover the ground, turning it white. *The snow fell thickly on Christmas Eve as we walked to church.* **snow** *verb.*

**snowball** *noun* a ball made out of snow that children throw at their friends for fun. *The snowball exploded on impact, covering Tom in wet flakes.*

**snowflakes**

**snowflake** *noun* a tiny and unique piece of snow.

**snowman** *noun* a figure made of snow, shaped roughly to look like a person.

**snug** *adjective* **1** cosy, warm, and comfortable. *I love being snug in bed, especially when there's a storm outside.* **2** fitting very closely or tightly. **snugly** *adverb.*

**snuggle** *verb* to move into a comfortable position, especially close to another person. *The little boy snuggled up to his mother as she read him a story.*

**so** *adverb* **1** very, to such an extent. *He is so clever.* **2** in this or that way. *He was wrong and she told him so.* **3** also. *My brother has blue eyes and so has my sister.* **4** when agreeing with something that has been said. *"I didn't clean my room." "So I see."* **so** *conjunction* that is why; for that reason. *I missed the bus, so I was late.* **so far** up to now. **or so** about that number. *We've been here for a week or so.* **and so on/forth** and other things like this. *They brought their pens, paints, and so on.* **so long!** goodbye! **so as to** in order to. *She asked us to come, so as to get to know us.* **so what?** I don't care; it's not important.

**soak** *verb* to make or become completely wet. *We were soaked by the rain.* **soak up** to take in liquid. **soak** *noun.*

**so-and-so** *noun* **1** a certain somebody or something that doesn't need to be specified. *She told me to do so-and-so.* **2** a rude or annoying person. *The principal is a real old so-and-so.*

**soap** *noun* a product used with water for washing and cleaning. *A bar of soap.* **soap** *verb.*

**soap opera** *noun* a light television or radio serial, usually about the daily life of a group of people. *I watch the soap opera every week.*

**soar** *verb* **1** to fly without beating the wings. **2** to rise or increase quickly. *Prices are soaring each month.*

**sob** (sobs, sobbing, sobbed) *verb* to cry in gasps. *Linda sobbed all night.* **sob** *noun.*

**sober** *adjective* **1** not drunk. **2** serious and thoughtful; not silly. **3** dull; not bright. *Sober colors.* **soberly** *adverb.* **sober up** to stop being drunk.

**soar**

**soccer** *noun* a game in which two teams of 11 players try to kick a ball into their opponents goal without using their hands or arms.

**social** *adjective* **1** liking to be with other people, friendly. **2** of somebody's position in society or of relations between people. **3** living together as a community. *Social animals live in groups.* **socially** *adverb.*

**socialism** *noun* a political system in which business and industry are controlled by the government, with every inhabitant of a state getting an equal share of that state's money. **socialist** *noun, adjective.*

**society** (societies) *noun* **1** a large group of people in a country who have a particular way of life. **2** a group of people with the same interests. *The folklore society meets every two weeks to listen to stores about the past.*

**sock** *noun* a piece of clothing that covers your foot. *A pair of socks.* **sock** *verb* (slang) to punch.

**socket** *noun* **1** a device, usually in a wall, into which you insert a plug for an electrical connection. **2** a hollow opening into which something fits.

sofa

**sofa** *noun* a soft seat with a back for two or three people to sit on. *I like to curl up on the sofa and read.*

**Sofia** *noun* the capital of Bulgaria in eastern Europe.

**soft** *adjective* **1** not hard or firm. *A soft bed.* **2** smooth to the touch; not rough. *Babies have soft skin.* **3** gentle; not loud or bright; calm. *Her soft voice is a pleasure to listen to.* **4** kind and caring. *A soft heart.* **softly** *adverb.* **softness** *noun.* **soft drink** a drink that is not alcoholic. *Lemonade is my favorite soft drink.*

**soften** *verb* **1** to make or become soft. **2** to become kinder. **3** to make something less terrible or strong. *He tried to soften the news by telling some amusing stories.*

**software** *noun* programs for computers.

**soggy** (soggier, soggiest) *adjective* unpleasantly wet and heavy. *The ground was soggy after the rain.*

**soil** *noun* the earth in which plants and trees grow. *The soil here is very sandy.* **soil** *verb* to make or become dirty.

**solar** *adjective* of or from the sun. If you heat a building with solar power, you make use of the power of the sun.

**solar system** *noun* the sun and all the planets whose motion it governs.

**soldier** *noun* a member of an army. *A Roman soldier.*

**sole** *adjective* being or belonging to only one. **sole** *noun* **1** the bottom of the foot, specifically the part you walk or stand on. **2** the flat bottom part of a shoe. **3** a flat fish. **sole** *verb* to put a sole on a shoe.

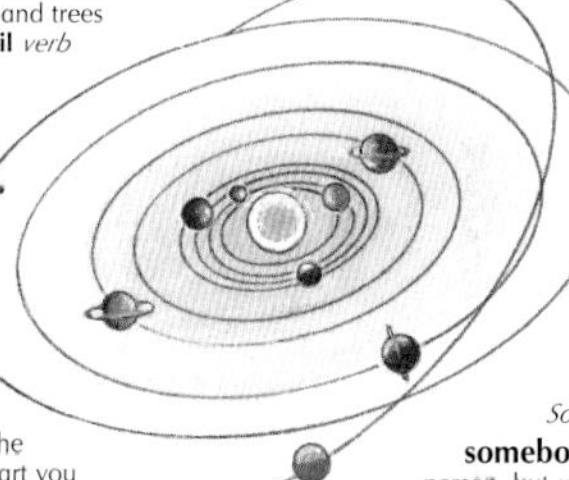
solar system

**solemn** *adjective* **1** serious; not cheerful. **2** formal; in a sincere way. *On his wedding day, the groom made a number of solemn promises to his bride.* **solemnly** *adverb.*

**solicitor** *noun* someone who gives legal advice to his clients and prepares legal documents, but who cannot plead cases in open court, only in a few minor courts.

**solid** *adjective* **1** filled up inside; not hollow; with no spaces or gaps. *Solid gold.* **2** not liquid or gas, but having a shape. *When milk freezes, it turns solid.* **3** of good quality; strong and not flimsy; reliable. *A solid house.* **4** showing complete agreement. **5** continuous; without a break. *I slept for six solid hours.* **solid** *noun* **1** something that is not liquid or a gas. *The baby is eating solids now.* **2** a figure in geometry with length, width, and height. **solidly** *adverb.* **solidity** *noun.*

**solitary** *adjective* **1** alone; without a companion. *I went for a solitary walk to clear my mind.* **2** spending a lot of time alone; lonely. *Bears are solitary animals.* **3** single. *I can't think of a solitary reason for moving.*

**solo** *noun* a piece of music, drama, narrative, or an action performed by one person alone. **solo** *adjective.* **solo** *adverb. He flew solo for the first time.*

**soloist** *noun* a person who plays a piece of music or sings a song alone. **solo** *noun.*

**Solomon Islands** *noun* a country of many islands in the Pacific Ocean.

**solution** *noun* **1** an answer to a question or problem. **2** a liquid in which something has been dissolved. *Bathe your cut in a solution of salt and water.*

**solve** *verb* to find the answer to a problem or puzzle. *Can you solve this riddle?*

**Somalia** *noun* a country in northeast Africa.

**somber** *adjective* dark and gloomy, or serious and sad. *Somber music filled the chapel.*

**some** *adjective* **1** a small number or amount; a few. *Some of the plates are chipped.* **2** somebody or something that is not named. *Some guy asked me the way to town.* **3** a fairly large number or amount. *Aunt Matilda had been living abroad for some years before she decided to visit her family back home.* **4** about. *The river is some 10 feet deep.* **some** *pronoun* a certain amount, number, or part of something. *Some wore red, others pink.*

**somebody** (also **someone**) *pronoun* some person, but not a particular person. *Somebody told me that you were thinking of moving to the country, which is news to me!*

**somersault** *noun* a rolling move in which you bring your legs over your head. **somersault** *verb. Oliver somersaulted across the grass when he heard the good news.*

somersault

**something** *pronoun* a thing that is unknown; some thing. *May I have something to drink?* **something like** a bit like or about. *She got something like $50 for her old bike.* **something to do with** connected with. *The letter has something to do with her new job.*

**sometime** *adverb* at one point in time. *I'll see her sometime next week.*

**sometimes** *adverb* from time to time; not always. *She sometimes walks to school.*

**somewhere** *adverb* in or to a place, but not a known one. *She lives somewhere in Kansas.*

**son** *noun* the male child of a man or woman.

**son-in-law** (sons-in-law) *noun* a daughter's husband.

**sonic** *adjective* of the speed of sound or sound waves. *A sonic boom shattered the silence.*

**sonnet** *noun* a poem with 14 lines.

**soon** *adverb* **1** in a very short time from now. **2** early. *The sooner the better.* **as soon as 1** quickly. *As soon as possible.* **2** at the moment when. *As soon as I get paid.* **as soon** readily or willingly. *I'd just as soon go home.* **sooner or later** at some time, certainly. *Sooner or later, she'll discover the truth about Paula.*

**soot** *noun* black powder left from burning or carried in the air in smoke. *The chimneysweep has cleared the chimney of soot.* **sooty** *adjective.*

**soothe** *verb* to make less angry or less painful. **soothing** *adjective. A soothing throat sweet.*

**sophisticated** *adjective* **1** fashionable and elegant ways; not simple. **2** complicated, with many parts. *A highly sophisticated machine.* **sophistication** *noun.*

Ss

**soppy** *adjective* foolishly sentimental.

**sorcerer** *noun* a man with magical powers; a magician or wizard. *The sorcerer's apprentice.* **sorceress** *noun.* **sorcery** *noun.*

**sore** *adjective* **1** painful or aching. *A sore throat.* **2** upset or angry. *She is still feeling sore about not being invited.* **3** serious, causing worry. *In sore need.* A sore point is something you do not want to talk about because it upsets you. **sore** *noun* a painful place on the body where the skin is infected. **soreness** *noun.*

sorcerer

**sorry** (sorrier, sorriest) *adjective* **1** feeling sadness or pity for somebody; expressing regret. *I'm sorry your dog died.* **2** feeling disappointed with yourself for doing or not having done something, usually said as an apology. *I'm sorry I laughed.* **3** used as a polite way to say that you did not hear or that you do not agree with something. *Sorry, what was the name?* **4** in a bad way; not good. *The house is in a sorry state.*

**sort** *noun* **1** a particular group of people or things that are the same in certain ways; a kind or type. *I don't like this sort of music.* **2** a type of person. *He is not the complaining sort.* **sort** *verb* to put things in order or arrange in groups according to their kind. *I spent all day sorting them into alphabetical order.* **sort out** to tidy, deal with, or put in order. *She tried to sort out in her own mind why she didn't like him.* **out of sorts** slightly ill or annoyed. **sort of** a little; in some way. *Her hair is sort of blond.*

sort

**soul** *noun* **1** the part of a person that is believed to live on after the body has died. **2** a person's thoughts and feelings. *That man has no soul; he is hard and unfeeling.* **3** anybody. *She didn't know a soul at the party.* **4** a style of pop music.

**soulless** *adjective* without feeling or noble qualities.

**sound** *adjective* **1** healthy; in good condition. **2** reliable and sensible. *Sound advice.* **3** deep or strong. **sound** *noun* **1** something you hear or that can be heard. When you turn down the sound on a television, you make it less loud. **2** an idea or impression from something read or heard. *I don't like the sound of their plans.* **sound** *verb* **1** to make a noise or cause something to make a noise. *The siren sounded a warning.* **2** to say what noise something makes. *The rustling of the leaves sounded ghostly.* **3** to seem. *She sounds happy.* **soundly** *adverb. Our team was soundly beaten in the first five minutes.* **sound asleep** deeply asleep. **sound out** to find out what somebody thinks or will do.

**soup** *noun* a liquid food that you eat with a spoon. *A nourishing bowl of soup is nice on a cold day.*

**sour** *adjective* **1** tasting sharp. *Lemons are sour.* **2** not fresh, going rotten. *The milk is sour.* **3** bad-tempered; unfriendly. *She gave me a sour look.* **sour** *verb* to become unpleasant or less friendly.

**source** *noun* a place where something starts. *The source of the river is in the hills.*

**south** *noun* the direction of one of the four main points of the compass. South is to the right of a person facing the rising sun. **south** *adjective, adverb* toward, from, or in the south. *The south wind is warm.*

**South Africa** *noun* a country in southern Africa.

**South America** *noun* one of the seven continents.

**South Korea** *noun* a country in eastern Asia, officially called the Republic of Korea.

**southerly** (say **suth**-ur-lee) *adjective* in or toward the south. *We drove in a southerly direction until we came to the coast.*

**souvenir** (say soo-vun-**eer**) *noun* something you buy or keep to remind you of a vacation or another event. *We bought a miniature Eiffel Tower as a souvenir of Paris.*

**sovereign** (say **sov**-rin) *noun* **1** a king or queen who rules a country. **2** an old British gold coin. **sovereign** *adjective* **1** independent; not under the control of another country. **2** having the highest power in a country.

**sow** *noun* (rhymes with cow) a female pig. **sow** (sows, sowing, sowed, sown) *verb* (rhymes with go) to plant seeds that will grow into plants.

**spa** *noun* a place with a spring of mineral water where people come to be cured of illnesses.

**space** *noun* **1** an empty area in a place. *That desk takes up too much space.* **2** the area beyond Earth's atmosphere where the stars and other planets are found. **3** an empty area or gap in something. *A parking space.* **4** a period of time. *I lost three pounds in weight in the space of a month.* **space** *verb* to arrange things with gaps between them. **space shuttle** a reusable spacecraft that can travel into space and back a number of times.

**spacecraft** *noun* a vehicle for traveling in space. *The spacecraft orbited the Earth.*

**spacesuit** *noun* a suit for wearing in space, with its own air supply.

**spaghetti** *noun* long, thin sticks of pasta that you cook by boiling.

**Spain** *noun* a country in southwest Europe.

**Spanish** *noun* **1** the language spoken in Spain, Mexico, and some South American countries. **2** the people of Spain. **Spanish** *adjective*. *Spanish olives.*

Spain

**spank** *verb* to smack on the buttocks with your hand.

**spare** *adjective* **1** kept for use when needed. *She left a spare key with her neighbor.* **2** free or not being used. *Have you got any spare cash?* **3** thin. *A spare figure.* **spare** *noun* an extra part for a machine or engine. **spare** *verb* **1** not to harm or kill somebody or something; to keep from harming. *Take all I have, but spare the children.* **2** to find enough money or time to give to somebody, or for a purpose. *Can you spare me a minute to help put up these decorations?* **3** to keep from using or spending. *No expense was spared.* **enough to spare** more than enough.

**sparing** *adjective* using or giving very little; frugal.

**spark** *noun* **1** a small particle of burning material that flies up from a fire. **2** a flash of light produced by electricity. **3** a small amount. *A spark of interest.* **spark** *verb* to produce sparks. **spark off** to lead to or be the cause of something. *The discussion sparked off a bitter quarrel between the two families.*

**sparkle** *verb* **1** to shine with a lot of small flashes of light. **2** to bubble. *I love watching Champagne sparkle.* **3** to be lively, bright, and witty.

**sparse** *adjective* small in number or amount; not crowded. *He had sparse white hair.* **sparsely** *adverb*. *A sparsely populated area.*

**spawn** *noun* the eggs of fish, frogs, and some other water animals. **spawn** *verb* **1** to lay spawn. **2** to produce something, especially in large numbers. *The latest fashion show has spawned new ideas.*

spawn

**speak** (speaks, speaking, spoke, spoken) *verb* **1** to say things using your voice; to talk. **2** to know and be able to communicate in a language. *She speaks Italian very well.* **3** to give a speech. *He spoke for an hour.* **speak out** to speak freely about something, especially in favor or against it. **speak up** to talk more loudly.

**speaker** *noun* **1** somebody who is making a speech. **2** somebody who speaks a language. *I'm an English speaker.* **3** a piece of equipment on a radio or cassette player through which the sound comes; a loudspeaker.

**spear** *noun* a weapon used for throwing or stabbing, made from a long pole with a sharp point at one end. **spear** *verb* to make a hole in or catch with a spear or something pointed. *She speared the meat crossly with her fork.*

spear

**special** *adjective* **1** not usual; better or more important than others. *I'm doing it as a special favor.* **2** for a particular person or thing. *Astronauts wear special suits in space.* **specially** *adverb* **1** more than usual; in a special way. *He was specially nice to me because I was ill.* **2** for a special purpose. *A school specially for deaf students.*

**specialist** *noun* a person who has special skills or knowledge in a particular subject; an expert. *A heart specialist is a doctor who treats people with heart disease.*

**speciality** (specialities) *noun* **1** a particular work or study. *Her speciality is French.* **2** fine or best product. *The chef's soup is the speciality of the house.*

**specialize** *verb* to study one subject or know about one thing so that you become an expert on or at it. *Toby's father specializes in racing bikes.*

**species** (species) *noun* (say **spee**-sheez) a group of animals or plants that are of the same kind and are the same in all important ways. *This species of butterfly has become very rare.*

**specify** (specifies, specifying, specified) *verb* to describe or name something exactly. **specification** *noun* a detailed description of work to be done.

**specimen** *noun* **1** a typical thing or example. **2** one piece or a small amount of something that shows what the whole is like. *The doctor took a specimen of blood.*

**spectacle** *noun* **1** a big show or public performance. **2** a strange or silly sight. *Don't make a spectacle of yourself.*

**spectacular** *adjective* grand; impressive. *We had a spectacular view of the mountains from our room.*

**spectator** *noun* a person who watches something, especially a sporting event.

**spectrum** (spectra) *noun* **1** the band of colors seen in the rainbow. **2** a range of different kinds of things, ideas, or opinions.

**spell** *noun* **1** a period of time. *It rained for a short spell.* **2** a quick period of activity or illness. *A spell in hospital.* **3** words that are supposed to have magical powers. *The witch cast a spell on him.* **spell** (spells, spelling, spelled) *verb* **1** to put letters of the alphabet in the right order to make a word or words. *Her name is spelled R-o-s-y.* **2** to mean. *Her silence spells trouble.* **speller** *noun.*

**spelling** *noun* the way a word or words are spelled. *English spelling differs from American spelling.*

**sperm** (sperm or sperms) *noun* the male cell that fertilizes a female egg to produce new life. *Sperm look like minute tadpoles swimming fast.*

**sphere** *noun* **1** a round shape like a ball. **2** a particular area of interest or activity. *The sphere of politics.* **spherical** *adjective.*

sphinx

**sphinx** (sphinxes) *noun* an ancient Egyptian stone statue with the body of a lion and a man's head.

**spice** *noun* whole or crushed seeds from a plant used to add taste to food. **spicy** *adjective.*

**spider** *noun* a small creature with eight legs that spins webs in which it catches other insects. **spidery** *adjective* long and thin. *My grandfather has spidery handwriting.*

**spill** (spills, spilling, spilled) *verb* **1** to accidentally pour liquid somewhere, especially over the edge of a container. *I spilled some milk.* **2** to come out in large numbers. *People spilled out of the park.* **spill** *noun.*

**spin** (spins, spinning, spun) *verb* **1** to make thread by twisting together fibers. **2** When spiders spin, they make a web out of thread from their bodies. **3** to turn around fast or make something go around and around. *The ballet dancer spun around repeatedly on the spot.* **spin** *noun* **1** the movement of going around and around. **2** a short ride in a car or other vehicle. *Let's go for a spin in the country as it's a sunny afternoon.* **spin a yarn** to tell a story. **spin out** to make something last longer.

**spinach** *noun* a vegetable with large green leaves. *Spinach is good for you because it contains iron.*

**spindly** (spindlier, spindliest) *adjective* long, thin, and weak-looking. *The chair has spindly legs.*

**spine** *noun* **1** the row of bones down the middle of your back; the backbone. **2** a sharp point like a thorn on an animal's body or on a plant. **3** in a book, the stiff part running up the middle of the back, to which the pages and covers are attached. The title of the book is usually printed on the spine.

**spire** *noun* the pointed steeple on top of a church or tower. *The church spire can be seen for miles around.*

spire

**spirit** *noun* **1** the essence of a person; the part that is connected with thoughts and feelings; the soul. *She has a good spirit.* **2** a supernatural being; a ghost. **3** liveliness and energy; effort shown. *He keeps the team spirit going.* **4** what something really means, not what it actually says. *Making her pay for her food would be against the spirit of our agreement.* **5** a strong alcoholic drink; whiskey and brandy are spirits. **spirit** *verb* If you spirit somebody or something away, you take them quickly and secretly to another place.

spit

**spit** *noun* **1** a thin, pointed metal rod for cooking meat over a fire. **2** a point of land sticking out into the sea. **3** the watery liquid that is produced in the mouth; saliva. **spit** (spits, spitting, spat) *verb* **1** to force liquid out of your mouth. **2** to rain lightly. **spitting image** an exact likeness. *Evie is the spitting image of her mother.*

**spite** *noun* a wish to hurt or annoy somebody. *She said it out of spite.* **spite** *verb.* **in spite of** despite.

**spiteful** *adjective* being nasty about people you do not like. *A spiteful remark.*

**splash** (splashes) *noun* **1** the sound made when something hits water. **2** a small amount of liquid that has been spilled. *There is a splash of paint on your skirt.* **3** a bright color or effect. *A yellow dress with a splash of red.* **splash** *verb* **1** to hit water or throw liquid around so it flies up in drops and makes a noise. If you splash somebody, you make them wet. *We splashed through the puddles.* **2** to fall or hit in small, noisy drops. *Rain splashed on the window.* **3** to throw liquid on something. *He splashed his face with water.*

**splendid** *adjective* **1** beautiful and impressive to look at. **2** excellent.

**splendor** *noun* impressive beauty. *The utter splendour of the throne room made us gasp.*

**splinter** *noun* a small, sharp piece of wood or other hard material that has broken off from a bigger piece. *I'm trying to get this tiny splinter out of my finger.* **splinter** *verb* to break into small, sharp pieces.

**split** *noun* **1** a cut, tear, or break. **2** the dividing of something. **3** a division between different things. **4** a dish made from cut-up fruit and ice cream. *A banana split.* **split** (splits, splitting, split) *verb* **1** to break, tear or crack. *This wood splits easily with an ax.* **2** to divide into parts; to share. *The children were split into groups.* **split the difference** to agree on a price that is halfway between two amounts. **split up** to separate. *We split up and went our separate ways.*

**spoil** (spoils, spoiling, spoiled) *verb* **1** to ruin or damage something so that it is no longer any good. *The rain spoiled our vacation.* **2** to make somebody selfish by giving them everything they want. *Some parents spoil their children by never saying no.* **3** to treat very well or too well. *I spoiled myself with an ice cream.* **spoils** *plural noun* stolen goods, especially those taken in war.

**spoilsport** *noun* somebody who stops others from having fun and wants to spoil their enjoyment of things.

**spoke** *noun* each of the bars or wire rods that run from the rim to the center of a wheel.

**sponge** *noun* **1** a small sea animal with a body full of holes. **2** a piece of the body of the sea animal, used for washing. **3** a piece of soft rubber or plastic filled with holes, used for washing or padding things. **4** a soft cake. **sponge** *verb* **1** to wash or wipe with a sponge. **2** to live by getting money or things for free without giving anything in return. *He sponges off his friends all the time.* **spongy** *adjective.* **sponger** *noun.*

**sponsor** *noun* a person or business that gives money or help to a person, team, or event, usually in return for advertising a product. **sponsor** *verb* to provide sponsorship for somebody or something.

**spook** *noun* a ghost. **spooky** *adjective. A spooky house.*

**spool** *noun* a round holder or roll on which you wind something. *A spool of tape.*

**spoonerism** *noun* an exchange of the first letters of a pair of words, usually with a funny result. "You have hissed the mystery lesson," is a spoonerism of "you have missed the history lesson."

spool

**spoonful** (spoonfuls) *noun* the amount a spoon can hold.

**sport** *noun* **1** an activity, competition, or game, usually conducted outdoors. **2** somebody who is kind, cheerful, and does not mind losing or being teased. *He is a good sport.* **sport** *verb* to have or to wear something. *He was sporting a bright blue tie.*

**spot** *noun* **1** a small, round mark or a dirty mark. *A blue dress with red spots.* **2** a particular place. *This is the spot where we had a picnic last summer.* **3** a small amount. *A spot of trouble.* **4** a drop. *Spots of rain.* **spot** (spots, spotting, spotted) *verb* **1** to notice; pick out. *Can you spot the mistake?* **2** to rain lightly. *The rain is spotting the sidewalk.* **3** to mark with spots. **spotted** *adjective. A spotted scarf.* **spotty** *adjective.* **on the spot 1** at once. *He was dismissed on the spot.* **2** If you put somebody on the spot, you make them give an answer or make a decision. **in a tight spot** in a little difficulty.

**spotless** *adjective* very clean.

**spout** *noun* **1** the tube or pipe-like opening for pouring liquid from a kettle, jug, or pot. **2** a stream of liquid going upward with great force. **spout** *verb* **1** to stream out with great force. **2** to say a lot in a boring way. *The teacher spouted on about the time he spent in Africa.*

**sprain** *verb* to damage a joint by twisting or bending it. *He sprained his ankle by jumping off a rock.* **sprain** *noun.*

**sprawl** *verb* **1** to sit or lie casually with your arms and legs spread apart. **2** to spread over a large area. *A sprawling town.*

spray

**spray** *noun* **1** small drops of liquid sent through the air. *Sea spray blew off the waves like great galloping white horses.* **2** a special container with liquid in it for spraying. *Hair spray.* **3** a number of flowers or leaves on a stem or branch. **spray** *verb* to scatter small drops of liquid on or over something.

Ss

**spread** *noun* **1** the act or action of opening something out or covering an area with something. **2** the distance or time of spreading. **3** a big meal with lots of food and drink. *Claire put on a magnificent spread for the wedding.* **4** a soft food paste that can be spread with a knife. *Cheese spread.* **5** a number of things, ideas, or interests. **spread** (spreads, spreading, spread) *verb* **1** to open something so that all of it can be seen; to stretch out. *The bird spread its wings and flew away.* **2** to cover a large area or time. *The rainforest spreads for thousands of miles.* **3** to cover something with something. **4** to make or become more widely known, or have a wide effect. *The fire spread to the next building and engulfed it in flames.* **5** to share or divide evenly. *We spread the work over a period of three years.*

**spring** *noun* **1** the season of the year between winter and summer. **2** a coil of wire that goes back to its normal shape after it is pressed. *One of the springs in the mattress has sprung.* **3** a place where water comes up from the ground. *A mountain spring.* **4** to stretch and go back to a normal shape. **spring** (springs, springing, sprang, sprung) *verb* **1** to move quickly and suddenly. **2** to come into being, appear, or be the result of. *Her happiness springs from her lovely children.* **3** to make something happen or known suddenly and unexpectedly. *We sprang a surprise party for him.*

**sprint** *noun* **1** a fast run. *He made a sprint for the bus.* **2** a short race. **sprint** *verb* to run as fast as you can for a short distance. **sprinter** *noun.*

**spruce** *adjective* neat, clean, and smart looking. **spruce** *noun* a kind of evergreen tree. **spruce** *verb* to make yourself look neat. *He spruced himself up to meet his girlfriend's parents.*

**spurn** *verb* to refuse with anger or pride. *He spurned her offer of help.*

**spurt** *noun* **1** a sudden flow or gush of liquid. **2** a sudden increase of effort or speed. **spurt** *verb* **1** to flow out suddenly; to gush out. *Blood spurted from the wound.* **2** to run faster, increasing speed suddenly. *She spurted toward the finishing line.*

**spruce**

**spy** (spies) *noun* somebody who secretly finds out information about other people or countries. **spy** (spies, spying, spied) *verb* **1** to work as a spy to get information. **2** to watch secretly. *He spies on his neighbors.* **3** to notice. *I spied a cookie in your bag.*

**squabble** *verb* to quarrel about something unimportant. **squabble** *noun. Have you finished your squabble?*

**squalid** *adjective* dirty and untidy. **squalor** *noun. She lives in squalor.*

**squander** *verb* to spend money or time foolishly and wastefully. *She squandered her time at college and now she regrets not having studied more.*

**square** *adjective* **1** having the shape of a square with four equal sides and four right angles. **2** forming a right angle. **3** fair; honest. *He wasn't square with me.* **4** even in points, equal, or settled. *I've paid what I owed you and now we are square.* **5** having an area equal to that of a square with sides of the same length. *The room has an area of six square feet.* **square** *noun* **1** a shape with four sides that are all the same length, with four corners at right angles. **2** a place surrounded by buildings that is the shape of a square. *We sat outdoors and drank coffee in the square.* **3** a number equal to another number when it is multiplied by itself, e.g., 16 is the square of 4 (16 = 4 x 4). **square** *verb* **1** to make something square, give a square shape to something, or mark squares on something. **2** to multiply a number by itself, e.g., 6 squared is 36. **3** to pay or settle something. *He has to square his account first.* **4** to match or fit a particular explanation or situation. *His story does not square with the facts.* **a square meal** a good meal that fills you. **a square number** any number that is the square of another number. 4 is a square number (4 = 2 x 2). **square root** a number that equals another number when it is multiplied by itself. 2 is the square root of 4 (2 x 2 = 4).

squashes

**squash** (squashes) *noun* **1** a vegetable similar to a pumpkin. **2** a fruit drink. *Orange squash.* **3** a crowd of people in a small place. **4** a game played with rackets and a small rubber ball that you hit against the walls of an indoor court. **squash** *verb* **1** to press something so that it goes into a flat shape; to crush. *The grapes got squashed at the bottom of the bag.* **2** to press into a small place. *We all squashed onto the bus.*

**squat** *adjective* short and fat. **squat** (squats, squatting, squatted) *verb* **1** to sit on your heels; to crouch. **2** to live in an empty building without permission to do so and without paying rent. **squat** *noun. We lived in a squat for a year.* **squatter** *noun.*

**squeak** *verb* to make a short, very high, loud sound. *Mice and bats squeak.* **squeak** *noun.* **squeaky** *adjective. I have squeaky floorboards in my bedroom.*

**squeal** *verb* **1** to make a long, very high sound or cry. **2** to report a criminal to the police. **squeal** *noun. A squeal of brakes.*

**squeamish** *adjective* easily upset or made sick, especially if something looks unpleasant. *She is squeamish and can't stand the sight of blood.*

**squeeze** *verb* **1** to press from two sides. *He squeezed a pimple on his chin.* **2** to press to get liquid out of something. *I'll squeeze an orange.* **3** to manage to get through or into something. *She squeezed herself into her jeans.* **squeeze** *noun.*

squid

**squid** *noun* a sea creature with a long, soft body, eight arms, and two long tentacles.

**squint** *verb* **1** to look with your eyes almost closed. *She squinted in the bright sunlight.*

**squirrel** *noun* a small, furry animal with a long, bushy tail that climbs trees and eats nuts. *Squirrels gather acorns in the fall and bury them to eat in the winter.*

**squirt** *verb* to force or come out in a thin stream of liquid. *Jessica squirted her water pistol at her little brother.* **squirt** *noun.*

**Sri Lanka** *noun* a country off the tip of India in southern Asia. Sri Lanka was formerly called Ceylon.

**St.** *abbreviation* **1** street. **2** saint.

**St. George's** *noun* the capital of Grenada in the Caribbean.

**St. John's** *noun* the capital of Antigua and Barbuda in the Caribbean.

**St. Kitts and Nevis** *noun* a country in the Caribbean.

**St. Lucia** *noun* a country in the Caribbean.

**St. Vincent and the Grenadines** *noun* a country in the Caribbean.

**stable** *adjective* firmly fixed in position; not likely to fall or change. *A stable relationship.* **stable** *noun* a building in which horses are kept. *There are two horses in the stable.* **stability** *noun.*

stadium

**stadium** (stadiums or stadia) *noun* a sports ground surrounded by covered seating for spectators.

**stag** *noun* a male deer.

**stage** *noun* **1** a period, point, or part in a development or journey. *We divided the journey into three easy stages.* **2** the platform on which plays and musicals are performed. **3** acting in theaters. *A stage production.* If you are "on stage," you are acting. **stage** *verb* **1** to put on a play or perform a show. **2** to organize and hold an event.

**stagger** *verb* **1** to walk or move unsteadily. *The drunk staggered across the street.* **2** to be surprised. *I was staggered that he had died.* **3** to arrange things so that they do not happen at the same time. *The staff staggered their vacations, so someone was always on duty.*

**stain** *noun* **1** a mark that is difficult to remove. **2** a liquid used for darkening or staining wood. **3** a mark of shame or guilt. **stain** *verb* **1** to make a mark on something, usually by accident. *The juice has stained my fingers.* **2** to color wood permanently with a special liquid.

**stained glass** *noun* small pieces of colored glass fitted together to make a picture. Windows in churches are often made of stained glass.

stained glass

**stair** *noun* one of a number of steps between floors.

**staircase** *noun* a set of stairs inside a house.

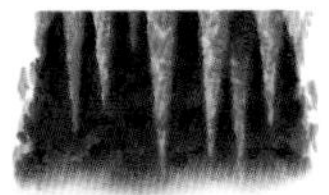

stalactite

**stalactite** *noun* a downward-pointing spike of limestone hanging like an icicle from a cave roof.

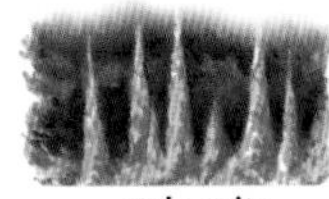

stalagmite

**stalagmite** *noun* an upward-pointing spike of limestone standing like a pillar on the floor of a cave.

**stale** *adjective* not fresh. **staleness** *noun.*

**stalemate** *noun* a situation in which neither side can win. *We had reached a stalemate in our discussions.*

**stalk** *noun* a stem of a plant or fruit. **stalk** *verb* **1** to walk in a stiff, angry, or proud way. **2** to follow an animal or person quietly in order to hunt or catch them. *We stalked the deer across the moor.* **stalker** *noun.*

**stallion** *noun* a male horse, especially kept for breeding. *The princess rode a beautiful white stallion.*

**stamen** *noun* the male part of a flower that produces pollen.

**stamina** *noun* the physical or mental energy needed to do tiring things for a long time.

**stammer** *verb* to repeat sounds of the same word when speaking; to speak with many pauses. **stammer** *noun.*

**stamp**

**stamp** *noun* **1** a small piece of gummed paper with a design on it that you stick on an envelope before mailing it to show that postage has been paid. **2** a small pad with a design or letters on one side which is pressed onto a surface. **3** the mark made by a stamp. *An official stamp on a document.* **4** a mark or sign typical of something. *His songs bear the stamp of youth.* **stamp** *verb* **1** to lift your foot and put it down hard on the ground. *The little boy stamped his foot and shouted.* **2** to walk noisily and with heavy footsteps. **3** to put a postage stamp on a letter or parcel. **4** to press a design or letters onto something.

**stand** *noun* **1** a piece of furniture on or in which you put things. *I put my wet umbrella in the umbrella stand.* **2** a stall or small store where things are sold. *A flower stand.* **3** a position against or in favor of. *She took a stand against scientific experiments on animals.* **4** a position for sitting or standing in a stadium, from where people can watch a game or other event. *We had seats in the stand.* **stand** (stands, standing, stood) *verb* **1** to be on your feet in an upright position. **2** to put or be in an upright position. **3** to remain or stay the same. *My invitation still stands.* **4** to put up with or endure. *I can't stand him.* **5** to be a candidate in an election. *He is standing for President.* **6** to pay for. *Let me stand you a drink.* **stand between** to be an obstacle. *Only one more grade stands between me and a place at college.* **it stands to reason** it makes sense or is likely to happen. **stand by** to be ready to help or take action. **stand for 1** to represent or mean. *GE stands for General Electric.* **2** to put up with; to allow. *She doesn't stand for any nonsense.* **stand out 1** to be easily seen. *Red stands out well.* **2** to be really talented. *He stands out as a real artist.* **stand up 1** to get up. **2** to be accepted as true. *His story won't stand up in court.* **3** to defend. *You must learn to stand up for yourself.* **4** If you stand somebody up, you don't meet them as arranged. **stand up to 1** to resist attack. **2** to stay in good condition. *The carpet stood up well to constant use.*

**standard** *adjective* **1** of the usual or accepted kind. *The standard rules of good behavior.* **2** most widely used or best of its kind. *The standard book on grammar.* **standard** *noun* **1** how good something is; a level of quality, skill, or ability that is considered acceptable. *The school's standard of spelling is very high.* **2** something used for measuring or judging the quality of something. *Different countries use different standards.* **3** a flag of an important person or family.

**stanza** *noun* a verse of poetry.

**staple** *adjective* regular or main. *Rice is the staple food of India.* **staple** *noun* **1** a small piece of wire used for holding pieces of paper together. Staples are pushed through several sheets of paper with a stapler. **staple** *verb* to fasten papers together with a stapler. **stapler** *noun.*

**star** *noun* **1** a large ball of burning gas in space; a heavenly body. **2** a shape, an object, or a mark in which points project from the center. If a hotel has five stars, it means that it is extremely good. *I received a gold star from the teacher for good effort.* **3** a famous actor, sports player, or performer. *A pop star.* **star** (stars, starring, starred) *verb* **1** to have an important part in a play or movie. **2** to mark with a star shape. **starry** *adjective.*

**stare** *verb* to look at somebody or something hard or for a long time. *Don't stare at me!*

**starfish** (starfish or starfishes) *noun* a star-shaped sea animal with five arms.

**starfish**

**start** *noun* **1** the place or time where or when you begin an activity. *Let's make an early start.* **2** a sudden uncontrolled movement. *She woke with a start.* **3** an advantage or an amount of time somebody has over somebody else. *We had an hour's head start over the others.* **start** *verb* **1** to come into being or to begin, especially something you were not doing before. *The baby started laughing when I pulled a funny face.* **2** to take place; to begin. *His music started a new craze.* **3** to set out on a course of action or a journey. *She started as a secretary.* **4** to jerk or move suddenly, usually because you are surprised or frightened. **make a fresh start** to start again from the beginning.

**startle** *verb* to make somebody jump or to surprise someone. *The noise startled him.*

**starve** *verb* **1** to suffer or die from not having any food to eat; to make somebody die from hunger. *Thousands of people starved to death during the drought.* **2** to be very hungry. *"When's lunch? I'm starving."* **3** When you are starved of something, you lack that particular thing and need it very much. *The children were starved of exercise.* **starvation** *noun.* **starving** *adjective.*

**state** *noun* **1** a condition which somebody or something is in. *His state of health.* **2** the government of a country, or a country. *Italy is a European state.* **3** a part into which a large country is divided. *The USA has 50 states.* **state** *verb* to express something in words, especially in a formal way. *The police stated that no charges had been made.*

**statement** *noun* **1** something you state; facts and information given in a written or spoken declaration. *The senator is making a statement later today.* **2** a printed document showing amounts of money paid in, taken out, or owed, usually sent to you by your bank. *I receive a monthly bank statement.*

**static** *adjective* not moving or changing. **static electricity** electricity that builds up or is present in certain things like your hair or nylon.

**station** *noun* **1** a place where trains or buses stop for people to get on and off. *Can you direct me to the bus station?* **2** a building used by a particular service. *A police station.* **3** a company that sends out radio or television programs. *The new radio station plays club dance music all day.* **station** *verb* to put people or things in a certain place for a particular purpose. *The troops were stationed in Iraq for six months to keep the peace.*

**stationary** *adjective* not moving. *The bus was stationary at the red light for three minutes.*

**stationery** *noun* materials for writing, such as paper, envelopes, pens, and pencils.

**statistics** *plural noun* information shown in numbers that can be compared. *The statistics seem to show that test results have been getting better every year in schools.* **statistical** *adjective.*

statue

**statue** *noun* a model of a person or animal in stone, wood, or metal. *The statue of the Little Mermaid (right) is in Copenhagen, Denmark.*

**stay** *noun* **1** a short time spent somewhere. *We had a nice stay in the country over Christmas.* **2** a delay or postponement. *The judge ordered a stay of execution.* **stay** *verb* **1** to remain in the same place or condition. *The weather stayed fine.* **2** to live as a visitor. *She is staying with her brother in Boston.* **3** to last. *The horse stayed the course.* **stay put** to remain in one place. **stay on** to remain in a place or for an extra spell of time. *He stayed on as director for another year.* **stay up** to go to bed after your normal bed time.

**steady** (steadier, steadiest) *adjective* **1** not moving; firm. *The new calf is not very steady on its legs.* **2** not changing; regular. *Charlotte found a steady job.*

**steak** *noun* a thick slice of meat (especially beef) or fish.

**steal** (steals, stealing, stole, stolen) *verb* **1** to take something that belongs to somebody else without their permission. *He stole some money.* **2** to move quietly and secretly. *She stole out of the room.*

**steam** *noun* **1** the hot mist that is produced when water is boiled. *The steam from a boiling kettle.* **2** the power from steam used to drive machines. *A steam engine.* **3** energy. If you run out of steam, you have no more energy. **steam** *verb* **1** to emit steam. **2** to cook in steam, not water. *Do you want to steam the fish?* **3** to travel by steam power. *The ship steamed out of the harbor.*

steam

**steel** *noun* a very strong, hard metal used for making knives and tools.

**steep** *adjective* **1** rising or falling sharply. *A steep slope.* **2** expensive. *Asking $100 for his old bike is a bit steep.*

**steeple** *noun* a tall pointed church tower; a spire.

**steeplechase** *noun* a horse race over jumps, originally run across country over hedges and ditches toward a church steeple.

**stem** *noun* **1** the long, central part of a plant above the ground. **2** the thin part of a plant that has leaves or flowers on it. **3** the long, thin part of a wine glass. **stem** (stems, stemming, stemmed) *verb* to stop something from flowing or spreading. *The nurse tried to stem the flow of blood.* **stem from** to have as its origin; to come from. *Her fear of dogs stems from having been bitten as a child.*

**stench** (stenches) *noun* a very bad smell.

**stencil** *noun* a piece of paper, metal, or plastic with a design or letters cut out of it. You paint over the cut-out areas to transfer the design or letters to a flat surface. **stencil** (stencils, stenciling, stenciled) *verb.*



**stepchild** (stepchildren) *noun* the child of a husband's or wife's earlier marriage. *Mary loved her stepchild as if she were her own.* **stepbrother** *noun.* **stepsister** *noun.*

**stepfather** *noun* your stepfather is the man who has married your mother after your real father has died or your parents have divorced. **stepmother** *noun.*

**steppe** *noun* a vast area of grassland without trees, as in Russia.

**stereo** *adjective* stereophonic; giving out sound, or sound coming from two different places. *Stereo equipment.* **stereo** *noun* **1** a stereo sound or recording. **2** a stereo CD player.

**stereotype** *noun* a fixed idea or typical example of somebody or something. *He is small and thin and does not fit the stereotype of a boxer.* **stereotype** *verb.*

**stern** *adjective* strict. **sternly** *adverb. He looked at her sternly.* **stern** *noun* the back end of a boat.

**stethoscope** *noun* a medical instrument used by a doctor to listen to somebody's heartbeat. *The stethoscope felt cold.*

stethoscope

**stew** *verb* to cook slowly in liquid, usually in the oven. **stew** *noun* a dish of meat and vegetables cooked in liquid.

**stiff** *adjective* **1** not bending or moving easily. *Stiff cardboard.* **2** firm; not runny. *Beat the cream until it is stiff.* **3** not friendly; formal. *The new teacher is stiff with the children.* **4** difficult. *A stiff test.* **5** strong. *A stiff drink.* **stiffness** *noun.*

stile

**stile** *noun* a step on which a person stands to climb over a fence or gate. *Let me help you over the stile.*

**still** *adjective* **1** not moving. **2** silent. **3** not fizzy. *Still water.* **still** *adverb* **1** up to now or up to that moment. *Is he still waiting?* **2** even. *More amazing still, she was able to walk again.* **3** nevertheless; in spite of what has been said. *The children were very difficult; still, she shouldn't have hit them.* **4** even so. *He is not the best baseball player, but he still deserves a place on the team.* **still** *noun* **1** quietness with no activity. *In the still of the night.* **2** a still photograph taken from a movie. **3** an apparatus for making alcohol.



**stimulate** *verb* to make more active or interested in something. *Sunlight stimulates growth.* **stimulation** *noun.*

**sting** *noun* **1** the sharp pointed part of some insects such as bees that can prick a person and cause them great pain. **2** one of the barbed points on the leaves of plants such as nettles. **3** a sharp pain or wound caused by a sting. **sting** (stings, stinging, stung) *verb* **1** to prick with a sting. **2** to feel a strong pain or to feel hurt. *His eyes were stinging from the smoke of the bonfire.* **3** to take more money from somebody than is necessary. *On the ferry they stung us for ten dollars for a coffee.*

**stink** *noun* **1** a bad smell. **2** a big fuss, usually made by complaining. **stink** (stinks, stinking, stank or stunk) *verb* **1** to smell very bad. *The changing rooms stink of old socks.* **2** to be very unpleasant or bad. *That plan stinks.*

**stir** (stirs, stirring, stirred) *verb* **1** to mix something by moving it around with a spoon. **2** to move. *She was fast asleep and is just beginning to stir.* **3** to excite or be touched by something. *The news stirred him into action.* **4** to cause trouble between others, especially by telling stories. *She loves stirring things between friends.* **stir** *noun* **1** the action of stirring. **2** excitement; shock. *The discovery caused a great stir.*

**stirrup** *noun* a metal loop attached by a strap to a horse's saddle for the rider's foot.

**stock** *noun* **1** a supply of goods or other things to be sold or used. *A large stock of food.* **2** a group of farm animals used for breeding or kept for their meat. **3** your ancestors or original family, or a type of animal or plant. *Many Americans are of European stock.* **4** a liquid made from vegetables or meat used in cooking. *Vegetable stock cubes.* **5** the number of shares you own in a company. **6** a garden flower with a sweet smell. **take stock** to think about something before deciding what to do next. **stock** *verb* **1** to keep goods to sell. **2** to fill or supply a place with food or other things.

stock exchange

**stock exchange** *noun* a place where shares are bought and sold.

**Stockholm** *noun* the capital of Sweden in northern Europe.

**stodgy** (stodgier, stodgiest) *adjective* **1** heavy, sticky, and filling, especially food. *I overcooked the rice made it stodgy.* **2** dull and uninteresting.

**stole** *noun* a long piece of material like a wide scarf, worn around the shoulders.

**stomach** *noun* **1** an organ in the body where food is digested. **2** the front part of the body below the waist. *He is doing exercises to get rid of his big stomach.* **stomach** *verb* to put up with, usually something unpleasant. *How can you stomach his insolence?*

**stone** *noun* **1** very hard material found in the ground; rock. **2** a small piece of rock. **3** a jewel. *A precious stone.* **4** the hard seed in the middle of some fruit, such as cherries or peaches. **5** a British measure of weight (1 stone = 14 pounds or 6.35 kilograms). **stone** *verb* **1** to throw stones at somebody. **2** to take the stones out of fruit. **stony** *adjective.* **stone** *prefix* completely. *He is stone-deaf.*

**stoned** *adjective* under the influence of drugs. *Angela gets stoned once a week.*

**stool** *noun* a seat with legs, but without arms or a back. *A milking stool.*

**stoop** *verb* **1** to stand or walk with your shoulders bent forward. **2** to lower or allow yourself to do something. *I wouldn't stoop to thank that woman.* **stoop** *noun.*

**stopwatch** *noun* a watch that can be started and stopped and is used for timing things, such as races.

**storage** *noun* the keeping of things in a special place. *We put our furniture in storage when we went abroad.*

**store** *noun* **1** a supply of something that is kept for later use. **2** a shop, especially a larger one. **in store 1** kept ready for later use. **2** about to happen. *There are lots of adventures in store for you.* **store** *verb* to keep things until they are needed. *The wood is stored in the shed.*

**storey** *noun* a floor of a building. *The apartment block has six storeys.*

**stork** *noun* a tall bird with a long beak and long legs. *There are two storks nesting on the chimney pot.*

**storm** *noun* **1** a very strong wind, usually with rain, thunder, or snow. **2** an excited or angry show of feeling. *A storm of protest followed the election result.* **storm** *verb* **1** to attack or force your way into a place. *The soldiers stormed the stronghold.* **2** to show anger by moving around or shouting loudly and angrily. *He stormed out of the room.* **stormy** *adjective.*

**story** (stories) *noun* **1** a description of real or made-up events. **2** an elaborate lie. *He is always telling stories.*

**stove**

**stout** *adjective* **1** thick and strong. *Stout climbing boots.* **2** rather fat. *He is short and stout.* **3** firm. *A stout supporter of the club.* **stout** *noun* strong, dark beer.

**stove** *noun* a device for heating a room or cooking on. *The woodburning stove gives off a warming glow.*

**straddle** *verb* to sit or stand across something, with one leg on each side of it. *To straddle a horse.*

**straggle** *verb* **1** to grow in an untidy way. *Ivy straggled over the wall.* **2** to move forward slowly behind others. **straggler** *noun.* **straggly** *adjective.* Long and untidy.

**straight** *adjective* **1** going in the same direction; not bent or curved. *Straight hair.* **2** upright. *The picture is not straight.* **3** tidy. **4** honest. *A straight answer.* **straight** *adverb* **1** in a straight line. **2** directly; without stopping. **a straight face** If you keep a straight face, you look serious and try not to laugh.

**straighten** *verb* to make something straight or to become straight. *I straightened my back.*

**straightforward** *adjective* **1** easy to understand or do. *The instructions are straightforward.* **2** honest. *He is a very straightforward person.*

**strain** *noun* **1** the condition or force of being stretched. *The cable broke under the strain.* **2** a state of worry or tension; something that tests you or uses up strength. **3** an injury to a muscle. **4** a tune. *The strains of a song wafted up to where she sat on the deck.* **5** a type of plant or animal. *A new strain of beans.* **2** a quality that develops, or a characteristic. *There is a strain of madness in my dog!* **strain** *verb* **1** to stretch tightly, usually by pulling. **2** to make a great effort. *She strained her ears to hear.* **3** to damage a part of your body. *I've strained a muscle.* **4** to pour something through a strainer to remove liquid. *He strained the peas.*

**strainer** *noun* an instrument for straining solids from liquids; a sieve.

**strange** *adjective* unusual or surprising; not known or seen before. **strangely** *adverb. Strangely, it seems that she did not leave at her usual time.*

**stranger** *noun* **1** somebody you don't know. **2** somebody who is in a place he or she doesn't know.

**strangle** *verb* to kill by pressing on the throat. **strangulation** *noun.*

**strategy** (strategies) *noun* **1** a particular plan to achieve something. *He created a clever strategy to get more money.* **2** the planning of the movements of armies in war. *A military strategy.*

**stratosphere** *noun* the outer part of the air that surrounds the Earth, between about 10 km and 50 km above the Earth's surface.

**stratosphere**

**straw** *noun* **1** dried stalks of grain. **2** a thin tube of paper or plastic up which you suck liquids to drink. **the last straw** the last or latest in a row of unpleasant events. *After a terrible day at the office, losing my purse was the last straw.*

**strawberry** (strawberries) *noun* a soft, juicy red fruit.

**streak** *noun* **1** a long stripe or mark in something. *He has gray streaks in his hair.* **2** a quality of character; a trace. *Phil has a streak of cruelty in him.* **streak** *verb* **1** to move very quickly. **2** to mark with streaks. **3** to run in a public place with no clothes on. **streaker** *noun.*

**stream** *noun* **1** a flow of water smaller than a river. **2** a flow of people or things. **stream** *verb* **1** to flow. *Tears streamed down her face.* **2** to move like a stream or to float in the air. *The sun streamed in through the window.*

**streamer** *noun* a long ribbon or strip of colored paper.

**streamlined** *adjective* smooth and regular in shape so able to move easily through air or water. *Racing cars and powerboats are streamlined.* **streamline** *verb.*

**street** *noun* a road with buildings along the side. **streets apart** very different. *My taste in clothes is streets apart from my mother's.*

**streetwise** *adjective* used to the ways of modern city life. *It's important to be streetwise in some districts of New York, or you run the risk of getting mugged.*

**strength** *noun* **1** the quality of being strong. *Superman has enough strength to lift a truck.* **2** something that gives power; a skill. *Translation is her biggest strength.*

**strengthen** *verb* to make or become stronger. *Please strengthen your resolve to work harder.*

**strenuous** *adjective* using or needing great effort. *I had a strenuous day at work.*

**stress** (stresses) *noun* **1** worries caused by difficulties in life. *She has been under a lot of stress because of her father's illness.* **2** saying a word or part of a word more strongly than another. In the word "bookshop," the stress falls on "book." **3** the force of weight or pressure on something. *The heavy traffic puts stress on the bridge.* **stress** *verb* to give importance to something. *He stressed the need for peace.* **stressful** *adjective.*

**stretch** *verb* **1** to become wider or longer. If you pull a rubber band, it stretches. **2** to spread out or extend over a distance or period of time. *The forest stretches from the mountains to the ocean.* **3** to straighten your body to its full length; to push out your arms to reach something. **4** to reach or be long enough. **5** If a job stretches you, you have to work hard at it. **stretch** (stretches) *noun* **1 the act of stretching or being stretched** *The cat got up and had a good stretch.* **2** an area of land or water, or a period of time. *He spent a long stretch in the mountains when he was younger.* **stretchy** *adjective. Stretchy material.*

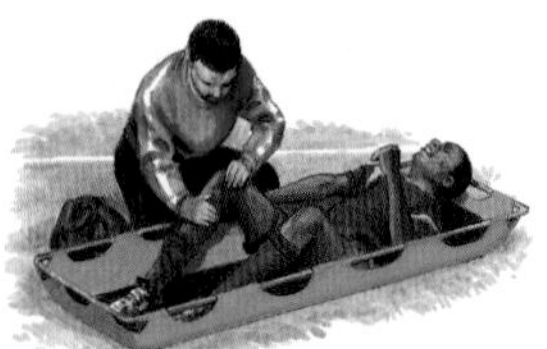

stretcher

**stretcher** *noun* a long piece of cloth fixed between two poles, or something similar, on which a sick or injured person can be carried lying down. *The injured player was carried off on a stretcher.*

**strict** *adjective* **1** firm, making people do what you want. *Our teacher is strict about punctuality.* **2** exact; complete. *The strict truth.* **strictness** *noun.*

**stride** *noun* **1** a long step in walking. **2** If you make great strides, you do much better. **stride** (strides, striding, strode, stridden) *verb* to walk with long steps. *He strode across the lawn to meet her.*

**strife** *noun* trouble between people.

**strike** *noun* **1** a time when no work is done. *The bus drivers are on strike.* **2** a hit. **3** an air attack. **4** finding oil or gold. **strike** (strikes, striking, struck) *verb* **1** to hit somebody or something. *He was struck by lightning.* **2** to stop working for a time, usually as a way of demanding more money or because you are angry about something. **3** suddenly to happen or come to mind. *It struck me that we should have visited him.* **4** to sound. *The clock struck eight.* **5** to find something in a place. *They struck oil in the desert.* **6** to seem. *She strikes me as very intelligent.* **7** If you are struck by something, you are impressed by it. *He was struck by her beauty.* **8** to light or produce a flame. *He struck a match.* **strike lucky** to have good luck. **strike up 1** to begin a friendship. **2** to begin to play music. **striker** *noun.*

stripe

**stripe** *noun* **1** a long line of color among other colors. **2** a band of cloth sewn onto a soldier's or policeman's uniform to show his rank. **striped** *adjective.*

**strobe lighting** *noun* a light that goes on and off very quickly.

**stroke** *noun* **1** a hit or blow. *He cut off the giant's head with a single stroke of his sword.* **2** a movement or action with your arms, as in sports such as golf, tennis, or swimming. *She swims with strong strokes.* **3** a line made by the movement of a pen or brush. **4** the sound made by a clock striking. *He arrived on the stroke of three.* **5** a sudden illness that can cause people to lose the movement in parts of their body. **stroke** *verb* to move your hand slowly and gently over something, especially an animal. **a stroke of luck** being very lucky.

**stroll** *verb* to walk slowly in a relaxed way. **stroll** *noun.*

**strong** *adjective* **1** having power, especially of the body. **2** feeling confident and sure; not easily frightened or upset. *She has a strong character.* **3** not easily broken. **4** having a great effect or taste; not weak. *A strong smell of gas.* **5** a certain number of people. *Our club is a hundred strong.* **strongly** *adverb.* **strong** *adverb. She is old but still going strong.*

**stronghold** *noun* **1** a fortified place. **2** a place where many people do or believe the same thing. *This southern town is a stronghold of Conservatism.*

structure

**structure** *noun* **1** an arrangement of parts; something built. *That bridge is an interesting structure.* **2** the way in which parts are put together or in which something is made. *The structure of a sentence.* **structure** *verb* to arrange or organize. **structural** *adjective.*

**struggle** *noun* a hard fight. **struggle** *verb* **1** to twist, kick, and fight to get free. *She struggled against her attacker.* **2** to make a great effort or fight hard to do something difficult. *The baby struggled to its feet.*

**strum** (strums, strumming, strummed) *verb* to play the guitar by moving your fingers up and down the strings rhythmically.

**stubble** *noun* **1** a growth of short, stiff hair that appears if a man's face has not been shaved for a day. **2** short corn stalks after harvest.

**stubborn** *adjective* having a strong will; not being persuaded to do something you don't want to.

**stud** *noun* **1** a small piece of metal like a nail with a large head, used as a decoration. *A belt with silver studs.* **2** a kind of fastener, usually in two parts that are pressed together, used instead of a button. **3** horses kept for breeding. **4** the place where horses are kept for breeding. **stud** (studs, studding, studded) *verb* to be set with, often as a decoration. *A watch studded with diamonds.*

**student** *noun* somebody who is studying or training, as at a college or university.

**studio** *noun* **1** a room where a painter, potter, or photographer works. **2** a room in which movies or radio or television programs are recorded.

studio

**study** (studies) *noun* **1** the activity of learning about a subject. **2** a subject you learn about or a piece of writing on a subject. *He made a study of Greek philosophy.* **3** a drawing or painting planned as part of a larger picture. *A study of a rose.* **4** a room used for reading, writing, and studying. **study** (studies, studying, studied) *verb* **1** to spend time learning about a particular subject. **2** to look at something carefully.

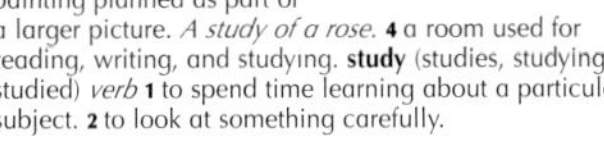

**stuff** *noun* **1** things or personal things. *Take your stuff to your room.* **2** the substance of something. *Try this; it's good stuff for a cold.* **stuff** *verb* **1** to fill something. *She stuffed the pillow with feathers.* **2** to push something quickly and carelessly somewhere. **3** to eat a lot. *The greedy boy stuffed his face with cookies.*

**stuffing** *noun* **1** material used to fill something. **2** a tasty chopped mixture used to fill a roast or vegetables such as peppers. *We like turkey with chestnut stuffing.*

**stumble** *verb* **1** to trip and almost fall over. **2** to stop or make a mistake while reading or speaking. *He stumbled over a difficult word that he was not familiar with.*

**stun** (stuns, stunned, stunning) *verb* **1** to make somebody unconscious by hitting them on the head. **2** to shock. *We were stunned by the news of the President's death.*

**stunning** *adjective* brilliant; beautiful.

**stunt** *noun* a dangerous act that somebody does in a movie or in order to draw attention to themselves.

stuntman or stuntwoman

**stuntman, stuntwoman** *noun* someone who performs stunts in a movie on behalf of an actor, so the actor does not have to take the risks.

**stupid** *adjective* foolish; not clever or intelligent. **stupidity** *noun* being stupid.

**sturdy** (sturdier, sturdiest) *adjective* strong; not easily broken. *A sturdy chair.* **sturdily** *adverb. Sturdily built.* **sturdiness** *noun.*

**sty** (sties) *noun* **1** a place where pigs are kept. **2** (plural sties or styes) a red swelling on the edge of the eyelid.

**style** *noun* **1** a kind or sort. **2** the way something is written, spoken, or performed. *The essay was written in an interesting style.* **3** a superior quality or elegance. *They live in grand style.* **4** a kind of fashion or design. **5** part of a flower involved in pollination. **style** *verb* to design or make in a particular way. **stylish** *adjective* showing superior quality; fashionable. *Stylish clothes.*

**sub-** *prefix* **1** below; under. *Submarine.* **2** subordinate; secondary. *Subsection.*

**subconscious** *adjective* thoughts and feelings of which you are not completely conscious or aware. **subconsciously** *adverb.* **subconscious** *noun.*

**subdue** (subdues, subduing, subdued) *verb* **1** to overcome or bring under control. *He subdued his emotions.* **2** to soften. *Subdued lighting.*

**subject** (say **sub**-djikt) *adjective* **1** having to follow or obey something. *We are all subject to the laws of the land.* **2** liable or prone to. *She is subject to colds.* **3** dependent on. *The plan is subject to approval.* **subject** (say **sub**-djikt) *noun* **1** somebody or something being talked or written about. **2** something studied. **3** in grammar, the word or phrase that does the action of a verb. In the sentence, "The leaf turns red," "leaf" is the subject. **4** a member of a nation that has a king or queen. **change the subject** to talk about something different. **subject** (say sub-**djekt**) *verb* **1** to make somebody experience something. *They subjected him to torture.* **2** to bring under control. **subjection** *noun.*

submarine

**subjective** *adjective* depending on your own taste and opinions.

**sublime** *adjective* grand or of the highest kind. *I think Mozart's music is sublime.*

**submarine** *noun* a ship that can travel under water. **submarine** *adjective. A submarine cable.*

**submit** (submits, submitting, submitted) *verb* **1** to give way. *They had to submit to defeat.* **2** to put forward for consideration. *She submitted her plans to the committee.* **submission** *noun.*

**subscribe** *verb* **1** to pay regularly for something. *He subscribes to several magazines.* **2** to agree. *I don't subscribe to that theory.* **subscriber** *noun.* **subscription** *noun. Please pay your subscription.*

**subside** *verb* **1** to sink lower. *The floods finally subsided.* **2** to become less strong. *Her fear subsided.* **subsidence** *noun.*

**substance** *noun* **1** matter. *Chemical substances.* **2** the main part. *The panel agreed with the substance of the report, but queried some of the details.*

Ss

**substitute** *noun* a person or thing that takes the place of another. *They put in a substitute in the second half and he scored a goal.* **substitute** *verb* to use in place of another. **substitution** *noun.*

**subtle** (say **sut**-ul) *adjective* **1** small and hard to grasp. *A subtle difference between the two.* **2** delicate. *A subtle taste.* **3** clever. *A subtle argument.* **subtlety** *noun.*

**subtract** *verb* to take away; deduct. *Subtract 5 from 8.* **subtraction** *noun.*

**suburb** *noun* a housing district at the edge of a town. **suburban** *adjective.* **suburbia** *noun* the suburbs. *They live in suburbia.*

**subway** *noun* a railroad that runs underground in cities.

**succeed** *verb* **1** to do well. *Kate succeeded in making her two-year-old eat all his lunch.* **2** to come next. *Who will succeed the present captain of the hockey team?*

**success** *noun* **1** doing well; achieving an aim. **2** somebody or something that does well. *The play is a great success on Broadway.* **successful** *adjective.*

**succession** *noun* **1** a series of people or things. *The team had a succession of victories.* **2** following in order. **3** coming next, as to a throne or government office. **in succession** one after another.

**succulent** *adjective* **1** juicy. *A succulent steak.* **2** fleshy. *Succulent plants.*

**such** *adjective* **1** of this kind. *Such people are to be admired.* **2** so great. *We had such fun!* **such-and-such** particular, but not specified. *He promises to come at such-and-such a time, but is always late.* **such as** of the same kind as. *Big cats such as tigers and lions.* **suchlike** of such a kind. *Ghosts and ghouls and suchlike.*

**suck** *verb* **1** to take liquid into the mouth by using your lip and tongue muscles. *She sucked the juice from an orange.* **2** to squeeze something in your mouth. *He still sucks his thumb.* **3** to pull. *The boat was sucked into the whirlpool.* **suck up to** to flatter somebody to gain their favor. *He's always sucking up to his teachers.*

**sucker** *noun* **1** something that sticks to a surface by suction. **2** a person who is easily deceived. *The sucker believed the trickster.*

**Sucre** *noun* the legal capital of Bolivia in South America.

**Sudan** *noun* a country in North Africa.

**sudden** *adjective* happening unexpectedly or without warning. *A sudden storm broke and lightning flashed.* **all of a sudden** suddenly. **suddenly** *adverb.*

**suds** *plural noun* froth on soapy water.

**sue** (sues, suing, sued) *verb* (say soo) to take legal action against somebody. *He sued his employer for damages.*

Sudan

**suede** *noun* (say swade) soft leather with a velvety surface. *Please don't step on my blue suede shoes.*

**suffer** *verb* **1** to feel or experience something bad or painful. *Before the operation, he was suffering badly.* **2** to put up with. *He does not suffer fools gladly.* **sufferer** *noun.* **suffering** *noun.*

**sufficient** *adjective* enough. **sufficiently** *adverb.* **sufficiency** *noun.*

**suffix** *noun* letters added to the end of a word to make another word. In the word "forgetful," "ful" is a suffix.

**suffocate** *verb* **1** to make it difficult or impossible for somebody to breathe. *The fumes almost suffocated her, but she was revived with oxygen.* **2** to suffer or die because you can't breathe. **suffocation** *noun.*

**sugar** *noun* a sweet food obtained from the juices of various plants, especially sugar cane and beet. **sugar** *verb* to sweeten, as with sugar. *Shall I sugar your tea?* **sugary** *adjective*.

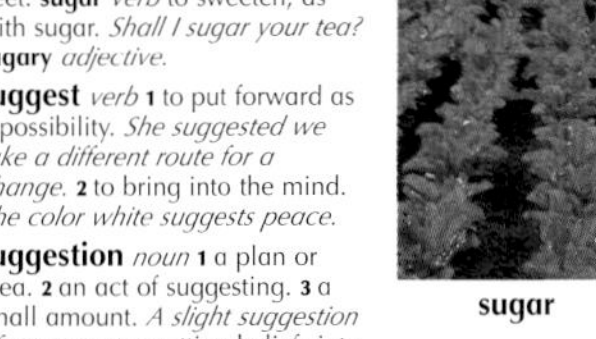

sugar

**suggest** *verb* **1** to put forward as a possibility. *She suggested we take a different route for a change.* **2** to bring into the mind. *The color white suggests peace.*

**suggestion** *noun* **1** a plan or idea. **2** an act of suggesting. **3** a small amount. *A slight suggestion of an accent.* **4** putting beliefs into somebody's mind.

**suicide** *noun* **1** killing yourself deliberately. *He committed suicide.* **2** somebody who commits suicide. **suicidal** *adjective*.

**suit** *noun* **1** a matching jacket and trousers or jacket and skirt. **2** special clothes, such as a spacesuit or swimsuit. **3** one of the four sets of cards in a pack (hearts, clubs, diamonds, or spades). **4** a lawsuit. **suit** *verb* **1** to go well with, or look good on. *That color suits you; it goes with your eyes.* **2** to be suitable or convenient. *Friday doesn't suit me at all.* **3** to adapt. *He suited his style to the audience.* **suit yourself** to do as you want to.

**suitable** *adjective* right for the purpose; appropriate. *Make sure you wear suitable clothes for cold weather.* **suitability** *noun*.

**suitcase** *noun* a case used to hold clothes and other things when traveling. *I packed my suitcase and drove to the airport.*

**sulk** *verb* to be in a bad mood and to show this by being silent. *She hated the party and sulked all evening.* **sulk** *noun*. **sulky** *adjective*. *A sulky pout.*

**sullen** *adjective* **1** silent and bad-tempered. *She gave me sullen looks.* **2** dark and gloomy. *A sullen sky.* **sullenness** *noun*.

**sultan** *noun* a Muslim ruler.

**sultana** *noun* **1** a seedless raisin. **2** the mother, wife, or daughter of a sultan.

**sum** *noun* **1** a total. The sum of 4 and 3 is 7. **2** a problem in arithmetic. **3** an amount of money. **sum** *verb* to find a total. **sum up 1** to summarize. **2** to form a judgment. *He summed her up quickly.*

sultan

**summarize** *verb* to make a summary of. *He summarized what we had discussed in a few words.* **summarizer** *noun*.

**summary** *adjective* **1** brief. **2** without delay or mercy. *Summary justice.* **summary** *noun* a short account giving the main points. *A quick summary of events.*

**summer** *noun* the warm season between spring and fall. **summery** *adjective*. *She wore a summery, short-sleeved dress made of cotton.*

**summit** *noun* **1** the top of a mountain. **2** the highest point. *He was at the summit of his career.* **3** a meeting between heads of government. *The President attended a summit meeting.*

**summon** *verb* **1** to call to appear. *He was summoned to court as a witness.* **2** to call upon. *She summoned him to help her.* **summon up** to build up or gather. *He summoned up all his energy.* **summons** *noun* an official order to appear in a law court.

Sun

**sun** or **Sun** *noun* **1** the star around which the Earth travels and from which it receives light and warmth. *It is dangerous to look directly at the Sun.* **2** light and warmth from the Sun. *She loves sitting in the sun.* **sun** (suns, sunning, sunned) *verb* to be in the sun. *The cat was sunning itself on the terrace.*

**sunburn** *noun* reddening of the skin caused by too much exposure to the sun. **sunburn** *verb* to suffer from sunburn. *She was badly sunburned.*

**Sunday** *noun* the first day of the week, after Saturday and before Monday.

**sundial** *noun* an instrument that shows the time by the position of a shadow on a dial.

sundial

**sunflower** *noun* a tall plant with a large, round flower the size of a dinner plate.

**sunglasses** *plural noun* dark glasses that protect the eyes from strong sunlight.

**sunlight** *noun* light from the Sun.

**sunny** (sunnier, sunniest) *adjective* **1** bright with sunlight. *A sunny room.* **2** cheerful. *She gave me a sunny smile.*

**sunrise** *noun* the rising of the Sun at dawn.

**sunset** *noun* the setting of the Sun at dusk.

**sunshine** *noun* light from the Sun. *We sat in the sunshine and read magazines.*

**suntan** *noun* browning of the skin from exposure to sunshine. **suntan** *verb*.

**super** *adjective* exceptional; extremely.

**super-** *prefix* **1** above or beyond. *Superstructure.* **2** extra large or good. *Supertankers are the biggest ships.*

**superb** *adjective* excellent. *A superb bike.*

**superficial** *adjective* not deep. *A superficial wound.* **superficiality** *noun.*

**superfluous** *adjective* more than enough.

**superior** *adjective* **1** in a higher position. *A superior officer.* **2** better than average. *Superior quality.* **superior** *noun. She is my superior.* **superiority** *noun.*

**superlative** *adjective* **1** of the highest quality. **2** in grammar, the highest degree of an adjective. "Bravest" is the superlative form of "brave." **superlative** *noun.*

**supernatural** *adjective* otherworldly, relating to ghosts or spirits. *He thought there were supernatural forces at work when the jug moved by itself.* **supernatural** *noun.*

**supersede** (say soup-uh-**seed**) *verb* to take the place of somebody or something.

**supersonic** *adjective* faster than the speed of sound.

**superstition** *noun* a personal belief in the special effects of something. Most superstitions are not based on scientific fact. **superstitious** *adjective. Because he is superstitious, he thinks it is unlucky to walk under ladders.*

**supervise** *verb* to oversee actions or work. *The foreman's job is to supervise workers.* **supervision** *noun.* **supervisor** *noun.* **supervisory** *adjective.*

**supper** *noun* an evening meal, especially a light one.

**supple** *adjective* easily bent; flexible. *Athletes who pole vault must be supple.* **suppleness** *noun.*

**suppress** *verb* **1** to prevent from being seen or known. *She tried to suppress a yawn.* **2** to put out of mind. *She tried to suppress her fear.* **suppression** *noun.*

**supreme** *adjective* highest in rank; most important. *The case went to the supreme court.* **supremacy** *noun.*

**surf** *noun* foam made by the ocean breaking near the shore. **surf** *verb* to ride waves on a board. **surfing** *noun.* **surfer** *noun.*

Ss

surf

**surgeon** *noun* a doctor who performs medical operations on patients.

**surgery** *noun* **1** medical treatment involving an operation. **2** a surgeon's operating room or lab. **surgical** *adjective* relating to medical surgery. *Please pass me the surgical instruments when I ask for them.*

**Suriname** *noun* a country in northeastern South America.

**surly** *adjective* bad-tempered and unfriendly. *He had a surly look about him.*

**surname** *noun* a family name. *Jones is a surname.*

**surplus** *noun* an amount left over after requirements have been met. **surplus** *adjective. These items are surplus to government requirements.*

**surrender** *verb* **1** to give up. *The army surrendered after its heavy defeat.* **2** to hand over. *They surrendered control of the company.* **surrender** *noun.*

**surroundings** *plural noun* things around somebody or something. *Our new puppy quickly got used to her new surroundings in a different house.*

**survey** *noun* (say **ser**-vay) **1** a general view. *The book gave a historical survey of the place.* **2** an examination of a property made by an expert before the property is bought by a new owner. **3** a report or plan of an examination of property. **survey** *verb* (say ser-**vay**) **1** to take a general look. *He surveyed the situation.* **2** to examine the condition of something. *They had the house surveyed.* **surveyor** *noun.*

**suspense** *noun* anxious or exciting uncertainty. *The movie was full of suspense.* **keep in suspense** to make somebody wait for important information.

**suspicion** *noun* **1** feeling inclined to believe or doubt something. *His suspicions were confirmed when she was arrested.* **2** a slight trace. *A suspicion of anger in his voice.* **above suspicion** too good to be suspected. **under suspicion** suspected. **suspicious** *adjective. Suspicious circumstances.*

**Suva** *noun* the capital of Fiji in the Pacific Ocean.

**swallow** *noun* an insect-eating bird with a forked tail. *Swallows dart high and low.* **swallow** *verb* **1** to cause to pass down the throat. *Chew your food well before you swallow.* **2** to accept something too easily. *I made up an excuse and he swallowed it.* **3** to overcome. *He swallowed his pride and apologized.*

swallow

**swamp** *noun* waterlogged land, a bog, or marsh. **swamp** *verb* to overwhelm, flood. *The radio station was swamped with letters of complaint.* **swampy** *adjective.*

**Swaziland** *noun* a country in southern Africa.

**swear** (swears, swore, sworn) *verb* **1** to promise something faithfully. *He swore that he would never return.* **2** to make somebody promise something. *He swore them to secrecy.* **3** to use vulgar language. *John was sent off the tennis court for swearing at the referee.* **4** to have great belief in something. *She swears by acupuncture.* **swear to** to be certain. *I couldn't swear to having seen him there.* **swearer** *noun.*

**sweat** *noun* **1** moisture that is given off by the body through the skin. **2** hard effort. *Moving all of that furniture made me work up a real sweat.* **sweat** *verb* to give off sweat; to perspire. **sweat it out** to put up with a difficulty to the end. **sweaty** (sweatier, sweatiest) *adjective.*

**swede** *noun* a yellow root vegetable.

**Sweden** *noun* a Scandinavian country in Europe.

**swell** (swells, swelled, swollen) *verb* to grow larger; to expand. *He swelled with pride.* **swell** *noun* **1** the process of swelling. **2** the rise and fall of the ocean's surface.

**sweltering** *adjective* uncomfortably hot.

**swerve** *verb* to change direction suddenly. *She swerved to avoid the car.* **swerve** *noun.*

swift

**swift** *adjective* quick. *I received a swift response to my letter of enquiry.* **swift** *noun* a small bird with long wings, similar to a swallow. **swiftly** *adverb.* **swiftness** *noun.*

**swindle** *verb* to cheat a person. *He swindled her out of her savings by selling her his fake jewels.* **swindle** *noun.* **swindler** *noun. A notorious swindler.*

**swirl** (say swurl) *verb* to move around quickly in circles. **swirl** *noun* a circular pattern. *The cream left a swirl on the top of my coffee.*

**Swiss** *noun* the people of Switzerland. **Swiss** *adjective. I bought my boyfriend a Swiss watch because they are famously reliable.*

**switch** *noun* **1** a device for turning something on and off. **2** a change. **switch** *verb* **1** to turn on or off. *Don't forget to switch off the lights.* **2** to change. *Sara switched seats with her husband so she could drive them home.*

**Switzerland** *noun* a country in southern Europe.

**swivel** (swivels, swiveling, swiveled) *verb* to turn around. *I swiveled round to look at her when she called out my name, sounding alarmed.*

**sword** *noun* (say sord) a weapon with a long metal blade and a handle.

swordfish

**swordfish** *noun* a large sea fish with a long upper jaw that looks like the blade of a sword.

**syllable** *noun* a part of a word with one sound. "Dog" has one syllable, "ti-ger" and "gi-raffe" have two syllables, and "gor-il-la" has three syllables.

**syllabus** *noun* the program or outline of a course of study. *The chemistry syllabus.*

**symbol** *noun* a mark or sign used to represent something. *The dove is a universal symbol of peace.* **symbolic** *adjective.* **symbolically** *adverb.*

**symbolize** *verb* to be a symbol.

**symmetrical** *adjective* able to be divided into two halves that are exactly the same. A butterfly shape is symmetrical. **symmetry** *noun. Beautiful symmetry.*

**sympathy** *noun* **1** the understanding and sharing of another person's feelings or opinions. *My sympathies go to the widow.* **2** a feeling of pity and sadness for somebody. **sympathetic** *adjective.*

**symphony** *noun* a long piece of music for an orchestra, usually in three or four parts (called movements). **symphonic** *adjective.*

**symptom** *noun* **1** a sign that an illness exists. *He has all the symptoms of measles.* **2** a sign of something. *Symptoms of social unrest.* **symptomatic** *adjective. Headaches are symptomatic of many different illnesses.*

**synagogue** (say **sin**-uh-gog) *noun* the building where Jewish people worship.

synagogue

**synonym** (say **sin**-uh-nim) *noun* a word that means the same or nearly the same as another. "Small" and "little" are synonyms. **synonymous** (say sin-**on**-im-us) *adjective.* "Shut" is synonymous with "close."

**syntax** (say **sin**-tax) *noun* in grammar, the way words are arranged to form sentences.

**synthesizer** *noun* an electronic musical instrument with a keyboard that can make a wide range of sounds.

**Syria** *noun* a country in Southwest Asia.

**syringe** *noun* a device for injecting liquids into the body, also called a hypodermic needle. **syringe** *verb. I had my ears syringed.*

**syrup** *noun* a thick, sweet liquid. **syrupy** *adjective.*

**tab** *noun* a small piece of paper, plastic, or metal attached to a container or a zipper that you can hold or pull. *Pull the tab to open the carton.*

**table** *noun* **1** a piece of furniture with a flat top supported by one or more legs. **2** a list of facts or figures, often arranged in columns. **multiplication tables** a list of numbers multiplied. **tablecloth** a cloth for covering a table. **tablespoon** a large spoon used for serving food.

**tablet** *noun* **1** a small, usually round, solid piece of medicine that you swallow; a pill. **2** a small, flat piece of soap as provided in most hotel rooms.

**table tennis** *noun* a game for two or four people in which small, round bats are used to hit a small ball over a low net strung across the middle of a large table.

**tabloid** *noun* a small-sized newspaper with lots of photographs and short news stories.

**taboo** *noun* something that is forbidden or generally disapproved of by custom or tradition. *Cannibalism is taboo among most people.* **taboo** *adjective.*

tack

**tack** *noun* **1** the saddle, girth, reins, and bridle used to ride a horse; saddlery. **2** a short, sharp nail with a large, flat head. **tack** *verb* **1** to use tacks or small nails to fasten something. **2** to sew something roughly with long stitches before sewing it neatly. **3** to sail into the wind on a sideways or zigzag course.

**tackle** *noun* all the things you need to carry out an activity. *Fishing tackle.* **tackle** *verb* **1** to try to deal with a problem or difficulty. **2** to try to get a ball from another player or bring a player to the ground in games such as football. **tackle** *noun. He made a diving tackle on the opposing player.*

**tacky** *adjective* **1** slightly sticky. *The paint is still tacky.* **2** (slang) vulgar; in bad taste.

**tact** *noun* skill in not upsetting people, especially when a situation is difficult. **tactful** *adjective.* **tactless** *adjective.*

**tactics** *plural noun* the way of organizing or planning things to the best advantage so as to win a game or battle, or to achieve what you want. **tactical** *adjective.*

**tadpole** *noun* a tiny black creature with a round body and a long tail that lives in water and will grow into a frog, toad, or newt.

**tag** *noun* **1** a small paper, cloth, or plastic label. *I sewed a name tag onto Johnny's coat.* **2** a children's chasing game in which someone tries to catch the others.

**tail** *noun* **1** the long part that sticks out at the rear of an animal, bird, or fish. **2** a part that sticks out at the back of something. *The tail of an airplane.* **3 tails** the side of the coin that does not have a head (heads and tails). **tail** *verb* to follow someone closely.

**tailback** *noun* a long line of traffic.

**tailor** *noun* a person whose business is to make clothes, especially men's suits.

**Taipei** *noun* the capital of Taiwan in eastern Asia.

**Taiwan** *noun* a country in eastern Asia.

**Tajikistan** *noun* a country in Central Asia, west of China.

Tajikistan

**take** (takes, taking, took, taken) *verb* **1** to reach out for something and to hold or grasp it. **2** to move or lead to another place. *He took the horse to the field.* **3** to remove. *Who has taken my ruler?* **4** to perform an action; to do. *I'm going to take a bath.* **5** to photograph. *She took my picture.* **6** to swallow. *Take three tablets a day.* **7** to accept. *Take my advice.* **8** to need or require. *It takes half an hour to get to the airport.* **9** to travel by. *Take the bus.* **10** to seize or capture. *The troops took the town.* **11** to choose. *Take whichever one you like.* **take after** to look or behave like. *He takes after his father.* **take away 1** to subtract. *Take away five from nine and it leaves four.* **2** to remove. **take down 1** to remove something that is hanging. *They took down the decorations after the birthday party.* **2** to write down. *He took down several pages of notes during the lecture.* **take in 1** to deceive. *She took me in with her sad story.* **2** to understand. *I didn't take in all you said.* **take off 1** to remove clothes. **2** (of an airplane) to leave the ground. **3** to imitate somebody in an unkind way. **take on 1** to start to employ somebody. **2** to challenge somebody. **take out 1** to remove from a place. **2** to invite somebody somewhere. **take over** to gain control of. **take place** to happen. *Our wedding took place in a church beside the sea.*

**talc** (talcum powder) *noun* a soft, scented powder that you sprinkle on your body after a bath.

**tale** *noun* **1** a story. *A fairy tale.* **2** an untrue or gossipy story; a lie. *She's been telling tales again.*

**talent** *noun* great skill or natural ability to do something really well.

**talk** *noun* **1** a conversation. **2** a short, informal lecture. **talk** *verb* to speak; to use words to express feelings or ideas; to discuss. **talk down** to speak to somebody condescendingly, as if to a child.

**talkative** *adjective* fond of talking a lot. *Are girls more talkative than boys?*

**tall** *adjective* high or of more than average height. *He's a tall man.* **2** having a certain height. *Henry is 6 feet tall.* **tall story** a story that is hard to believe. *He told me of his exciting adventure, but I reckon it was a tall story.*

**Tallinn** *noun* the capital of Estonia in the Baltic region.

**talon** *noun* a hooked claw of a bird of prey.

**tambourine** *noun* a shallow drum with metal disks around the edge that you shake or tap with your fingers.

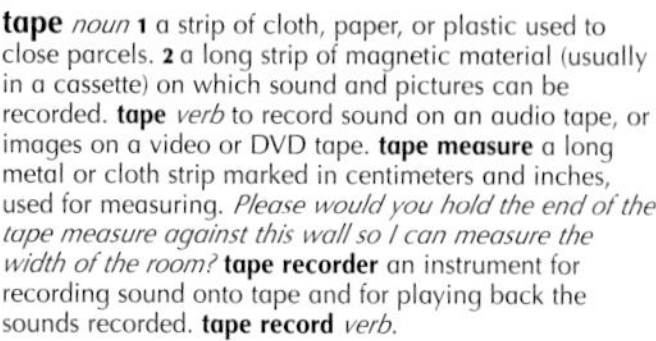

**tambourine**

**tame** *adjective*. A tame animal or bird is not wild and is not afraid of human beings. **tame** *verb*.

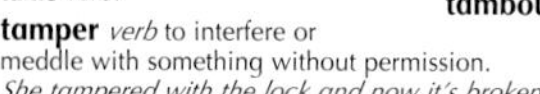

**tamper** *verb* to interfere or meddle with something without permission. *She tampered with the lock and now it's broken.*

**tampon** *noun* a plug of soft material such as cotton wool. *A sanitary tampon.*

**tan** *noun* **1** light brown. **2** (suntan) light brown skin caused by exposure to the Sun. **tan** *verb*.

**tandem** *noun* a bicycle with two seats, one behind the other, ridden by two people at the same time.

**tandoori** *noun* an Indian way of cooking food in a clay oven. *Tandoori chicken.*

**tangerine** *noun* a fruit resembling a small orange with a loose skin and sweet flavor.

**tangle** *verb* to make things such as wires or string into a twisted and confused muddle. **tangle** *noun*. *It took me ages to brush out the tangles in my hair.*

**tanks**

**tank** *noun* **1** a heavy, armored, military vehicle armed with guns. **2** a large container for storing a liquid or gas.

**tanker** *noun* a large ship or truck used for carrying liquids such as oil.

**tantrum** *noun* a sudden attack of bad temper. *Brian threw a tantrum at school.*

**Tanzania** *noun* a country in eastern Africa.

**Taoiseach** *noun* ( Say **tee**-shak) the prime minister of the Republic of Ireland.

**tape** *noun* **1** a strip of cloth, paper, or plastic used to close parcels. **2** a long strip of magnetic material (usually in a cassette) on which sound and pictures can be recorded. **tape** *verb* to record sound on an audio tape, or images on a video or DVD tape. **tape measure** a long metal or cloth strip marked in centimeters and inches, used for measuring. *Please would you hold the end of the tape measure against this wall so I can measure the width of the room?* **tape recorder** an instrument for recording sound onto tape and for playing back the sounds recorded. **tape record** *verb*.

**taper** *verb* to become narrower toward one end. *Church spires taper toward the top.*

**tapestry** *noun* a heavy, woven cloth depicting scenes or designs. In past times, tapestries were hung on walls for decoration or to keep out drafts. *She wove a beautiful tapestry on her loom.*

**tapir** *noun* an animal with a long snout that looks a bit like a pig.

**tarantula** *noun* a large, hairy, poisonous spider. *The tarantula on the wall is as big as my hand.*

**Tarawa** *noun* the capital of Kiribati, a country of many small islands in the South Pacific Ocean.

**target** *noun* **1** a mark that you aim at and try to hit. *He shot an arrow at the target.* **2** an aim or purpose that you are trying to achieve. *We have met our production targets.*

**tariff** *noun* **1** a list of prices, especially for hotel rooms and meals. **2** a tax to be paid on exports and imports.

**tarragon** *noun* a plant, a herb, the leaves of which are used to flavor food.

**tart** *noun* a pastry case (or pie) with no crust on top, often with a sweet filling. *An apple tart.* **tart** *adjective* sharp or sour to taste.

**tartan** *noun* a Scottish woolen cloth with a plaid pattern of different colored squares and stripes.

**Tashkent** *noun* the capital of Uzbekistan in Central Asia.

**task** *noun* a job or piece of work that must be done; a duty. *It's my task to clean the hamster cage each week.*

**taste** *noun* **1** the sense by which you can tell the flavor of food and drink. **2** a particular flavor of food. Food can be sweet, sour, salty, or bitter. **3** the ability to know what is beautiful or good. **tasteful** *adjective*. **taste** *verb*.

**tasteless** *adjective* **1** without flavor. **2** unattractive; showing poor judgment about what is beautiful or good. *Tasteless furniture. Tasteless jokes.*

**tasty** *adjective* having a pleasant taste.

**tattoo** *noun* **1** a permanent colored pattern inked into somebody's skin. **2** a military display of music and marching, usually held at night.

**taunt** *verb* to tease somebody and say hurtful things in order to make them angry. *She taunted him about the size of his nose.* **taunt** *noun*, an insult.

**taut** *adjective* stretched or pulled tight so that it is firm. **tauten** *verb.*

**tautology** *noun* the use of a word that repeats the meaning of a word that has already been used: "a four-sided square," "free gifts," and "a new innovation" are all examples of tautology.

**tawny** *noun* a light, brownish-yellow color. **tawny** *adjective. A tawny owl.*

**tax** (taxes) *noun* an amount of money that people and businesses have to pay to the government to help pay for public services. **tax** *verb. The government taxes our income far too much, in my opinion.* **taxation** *noun.*

**taxi** (taxis) *noun* a car with a driver that you can hire to take you on short journeys. *We took a taxi to the airport.* **taxi** (taxies, taxiing, taxied) *verb* (of an airplane) to travel along the runway before take-off or after landing.

**Tbilisi** *noun* the capital of Georgia in Southwest Asia.

**tea** *noun* **1** a drink made by pouring hot water onto the dried leaves of a tea plant. **2** a light meal eaten in the afternoon or a main meal eaten in the early evening.

**teach** (teaches, teaching, taught) *verb* **1** to tell somebody about a subject and to help them learn about it; to educate. **2** to show somebody how to do something. *Jane taught me how to skate.* **teacher** *noun* a person who teaches, especially at a school.

teacher

**team** *noun* a group of people who work together or who play on the same side in a game. *Our team won the general knowledge quiz.*

**tear** *noun* **1** (rhymes with near) one of the drops of salty liquid that comes from your eyes when you cry. **2** (rhymes with fair) a rip in a piece of fabric or paper. **tear** (tears, tearing, tore, torn) *verb* (rhymes with fair) **1** to pull something apart; to rip. **2** to make a hole in something. *Tina tore her skirt on a nail.* **3** to pull something violently. *Chris tore the wallpaper off the wall.* **4** to move quickly. *The dog tears across the field whenever it sees a rabbit.* **tearful** *adjective.*

**tease** *verb* to annoy or upset somebody by making fun of them for your own amusement.

**teaspoon** *noun* a small spoon. **teaspoonful** the amount that a teaspoon can hold.

**teat** *noun* **1** the nipple or soft, pointed part on a female mammal through which her babies suck milk. **2** a piece of rubber or plastic on a feeding bottle through which a baby can suck milk, water, or diluted fruit juice.

**technical** *adjective* **1** concerned with science and machines and how they work. *We'll need to call in the technical experts to sort out the problem with the computer.* **2** concerned with a particular specialized subject. *Technical jargon is boring to most people.*

**technique** *noun* (say tek-**neek**) a special way of doing something skillfully.

**technology** *noun* the study of technical ideas and the practical use of science in industry. **technological** *adjective. A technological breakthrough.*

**teddy bear** *noun* a soft toy bear.

**tedious** *adjective* boring because dull and long.

**teenager** *noun* a person between the ages of 13 and 19. **teenage** *adjective.*

**teetotaler** *noun* somebody who never drinks alcohol. **teetotal** *adjective. Many Muslims are teetotal.*

**Tegucigalpa** *noun* the capital of Honduras in Central America. Honduras has Caribbean and Pacific coastlines.

**Tehran** *noun* the capital of Iran in Southwest Asia.

**telecommunications** *plural noun* the technology of sending information over long distances by radio, telephone, and television.

**telephone** *noun* an instrument that uses electrical current traveling along wires, or radio waves, to allow you to speak to somebody long distance. **telephone** or **phone** *verb. Please phone me tonight.*

**telescope** *noun* a tube-shaped instrument with lenses inside that you look through with one eye to make distant objects appear bigger and nearer.

**television** *noun* a box-shaped instrument that receives programs which have been broadcast and shows them on a screen as moving pictures with sound.

television

**telex** *noun* a system of sending written messages by means of teleprinters.

**tell** (tells, telling, told) *verb* **1** to pass on information by speaking. **2** to know or recognize. *Can you tell what this is?* **3** to order. *Jeremy told us to be at his house by 9.00 o'clock sharp.*

**telling** *adjective* meaningful and striking. *It was a telling argument.*

**temper** *noun* the mood you are in; how you feel. *Is she in a good temper?* **lose your temper** to become angry.

**temperament** *noun* your personality or the way you usually feel and behave. *She has a calm temperament.*

**temperamental** *adjective* liable to sudden changes of mood; excitable.

**temperature** *noun* **1** a measure of how hot something is. *The temperature has dropped to below freezing.* **2** a fever. *You have a temperature so you are ill.*

**temple**

**tempest** *noun* a violent storm with strong winds. **tempestuous** *adjective. A tempestuous sea.*

**temple** *noun* **1** a building in which the people of some religions, such as Hindus and Sikhs, worship. **2** the flat part on either side of your head between your ear and your forehead.

**tempo** (tempi) *noun* the speed at which music is played. *A fast tempo.*

**tempt** *verb* to try to persuade somebody to want to do something they would not normally do; to entice. *He tried to tempt me to extend my vacation and skip work.* **temptation** *noun.*

**tempting** *adjective* attractive. *It's very tempting to skip classes and go swimming.*

**tenant** *noun* a person who rents the place he or she lives in from someone else.

**tend** *verb* **1** to happen often or usually; to be inclined to. *It tends to be cold at night.* **2** to look after a person or animal. *The shepherd tended his flocks by day and night.* **tendency** *noun. Rob has a tendency to eat too much, and is overweight.*

**tender** *adjective* **1** sore to touch; painful. *The bruise feels tender.* **2** easy to chew; not tough. *The steak is lovely and tender.* **3** loving and gentle; kind. *A tender kiss.* **4** delicate. *Tender seedlings.* **tenderness** *noun.*

**tendon** *noun* tissue that joins muscles to bones.

**tennis** *noun* a game played on a hard or grass court marked with lines, in which two or four people use rackets to hit a ball to each other over a net.

**tenor** *adjective, noun* the highest normal singing voice for a man.

**tense** *adjective* **1** showing excitement, stress, or nervousness. **2** stiff and tightly stretched; taut. **tense** *noun* a form of a verb that shows when something happens (present tense), happened (past tense), or will happen (future tense). **tense** *verb* to tighten or become stiff. *She tensed and flexed her muscles in the gym.* **tension** *noun.*

**tent** *noun* a temporary shelter made from a waterproof material such as canvas or nylon, stretched and supported over poles and held down by ropes.

**tentacle** *noun* one of the long, snake-like limbs of animals such as octopuses and squid.

**tepee**

**tepee** *noun* a cone-shaped tent made of animal skins, grasses, or tree bark, first used by American Indians.

**tepid** *adjective* slightly warm.

**term** *noun* **1** a length of time. *The school term lasts for twelve weeks.* **2** a word or name for something. *ROM is a computer term.* **terms** *plural noun* agreed conditions. *Terms of employment.* **term** *verb* to name. **to be on good terms with somebody** to get along with, to like someone.

**terminal** *noun* **1** a building where people begin or end a journey. *Airplanes for Australia depart from terminal four.* **2** a computer monitor linked to a network. **terminal** *adjective* (of an illness) incurable, liable to cause death.

**terminate** *verb* to stop; to come to an end.

**terminus** *noun* a station at the end of a railroad line or bus route.

**terrace** *noun* **1** a row of houses joined together as a single block. **2** a level area cut out of sloping ground. **3** a paved area next to a building where people can sit.

**terrapin**

**terrapin** *noun* a small turtle from North America. Terrapins live in fresh water.

**terrestrial** *adjective* **1** relating to the Earth rather than to space. *Terrestrial television.* **2** living on land and not in the air or water. *Terrestrial animals.*

**terrible** *adjective* **1** dreadful; causing fear or hardship. **2** bad; unenjoyable. *A terrible movie.*

**terrier** *noun* one of several breeds of small dog.

**terrify** (terrifies, terrifying, terrified) *verb* to make somebody very frightened. *My dog is terrified of thunder.*

**territory** *noun* **1** an area of land, especially land controlled by the government of a country. **2** an area of land where an animal lives and which it will fight to defend. *Wolves roam over a large territory.*

**terror** *noun* great fear.

**terrorism** *noun* the use of violence and threats to obtain demands. **terrorist** *noun.*

**test** *verb* to try out something; to check to see if something works. *I had my eyes tested.* **test** *noun* **1** a set of questions or actions that a person has to answer or perform to find out how much they know or can do. **test tube** *noun* a thin glass container that is closed at one end, and is used in chemistry laboratories to do tests.

**tether** *verb* to tie an animal by a rope to a post so that it cannot move far or escape. **tether** *noun*. **at the end of your tether** to be exasperated and stressed.

**testicle** *noun* one of two small, ball-like glands in a man's scrotum.

**text** *noun* the printed words in a book or newspaper.

**textbook** *noun* a book containing basic information about a particular subject.

**textile** *noun* woven cloth. **textile** *adjective*.

**texture** *noun* the way something feels when you touch it, for example, rough or smooth.

**Thai** *noun* a person who comes from Thailand. **Thai** *adjective*. *Thai silk.*

**Thailand** *noun* a country in Southeast Asia.

**thank** *verb* to tell somebody how pleased you are for something they have given or done for you. *Thank you for my present.* **thanks** *noun* a word we use to say how pleased we are for what somebody has done for us.

**thankful** *adjective* feeling glad or grateful.

**Thanksgiving** *noun* a holiday celebrated in the United States on the fourth Thursday in November. Many people eat turkey on this day and give thanks for what they have.

**thatch** (thatches) *noun* layers of reeds or straw used to make the roofs of some buildings.

**thatch**

**thaw** *verb* to change from being frozen solid to a liquid through warming; to melt. *The ice on the pond is thawing at last.*

**theater** *noun* **1** a building where you go to see plays performed. **2** a room in a hospital where surgeons perform operations. **theatrical** *adjective* connected with plays or acting. *A theatrical costume.*

**theft** *noun* stealing.

**theme** *noun* **1** the principal subject. *The theme of the book is wizardry.* **2** (in music) the main melody. **theme park** a park with different activities and attractions, all based on one particular subject or idea. **theme song** a tune that is often repeated in a movie or musical.

**theology** *noun* the study of God and religion. **theological** *adjective*.

**theologian** *noun* a person who studies theology.

**theory** *noun* **1** an unproven idea put forward to explain something. **2** the rules and principles of a subject rather than the actual practice of it.

**therapeutic** *adjective* being good for the health and mental well-being.

**therapy** *noun* a treatment for an illness without the use of surgery or drugs. **therapist** *noun*.

**therm** *noun* a measurement of heat.

**thermal** *adjective* relating to or caused by heat; using heat. *Thermal energy.*

**thermometer** *noun* an instrument for measuring temperature in degrees Celsius or Fahrenheit.

**thermostat** *noun* a device that automatically switches off radiators and electrical appliances that heat up rapidly (such as irons or kettles) when the temperature has reached a certain level.

**thermometer**

**thesaurus** (thesauruses) *noun* a book that lists together words with similar meanings. In my thesaurus, the words "glow," "gleam," "glitter," "sparkle," and "flash" are listed under the headword "shine."

**thick** *adjective* **1** measuring a long way between two sides; wide, not thin or slender. **2** measuring a certain amount between two sides. *The wood block is 5 inches thick.* **3** dense and closely packed. *Thick, blond hair.* **4** not flowing freely. *Thick cream.* **5** (slang) stupid. **thickness** *noun*. **thicken** *verb*. The opposite of "thick" is "thin."

**thief** (thieves) *noun* a person who steals things. *The thief ran off with my purse.*

**thigh** *noun* (rhymes with high) the top part of your leg, above your knee.

**thimble** *noun* a small, metal or plastic covering that you wear on the tip of your finger to prevent you pricking it when sewing.

**Thimphu** *noun* the capital of Bhutan in Asia.

**thin** (thinner, thinnest) *adjective* **1** measuring a short distance between two sides. The opposite of "thin" is "thick" or "fat." **2** having little fat on your body; slender.

**thing** *noun* an unnamed object that you see or touch. **things** (plural noun) belongings. *Have you packed your things for our vacation?* **it's a good thing** it's lucky. *It's a good thing you arrived on time.*

**think** (thinks, thinking, thought) *verb* **1** to use your mind. **2** to believe; to have an opinion or idea. **3** to remember. **4** to plan or intend. *We're thinking of learning karate.* **5** to admire. *I think a lot of you.* **think up** to invent. **think twice about something** to consider very carefully whether to do something or not.

**third** *adjective* the next after the second. *You're the third person to ask me that.* **third** *noun* one of three equal parts that make up a whole. **third rate** *adjective* of poor quality. *We had a third rate meal at that new restaurant.*

**thirst** *noun* **1** feeling the need to drink. **2** a strong wish for something. *A thirst for adventure.* **thirsty** *adjective.*

**thistle** *noun* a prickly wild plant with purple flowers; the emblem of Scotland.

**thorax** *noun* **1** the middle section of an insect, to which the wings and legs are attached. **2** the chest of a human.

**thorn** *noun* a sharp point on the stem of a plant such as a rose.

**thorough** *adjective* (say **thur**-uh) **1** done well and carefully. *A thorough search.* **2** complete. *A thorough mess.* **thoroughness** *noun. He was famed for his thoroughness.*

thistle

**thought** *noun* an idea; something that you think.

**thoughtful** *adjective* **1** thinking quietly and carefully. **2** considerate and thinking about others. *It was very thoughtful of you to remember my birthday.*

**thoughtless** *adjective* inconsiderate and not thinking about other people's feelings.

**thread** *noun* a long, thin piece of twisted cotton or silk used for sewing or weaving. **thread** *verb* to put thread through the hole (eye) of a needle prior to sewing.

**threadbare** *adjective* (of clothes) worn thin; worn out.

**threat** *noun* **1** a warning that something unpleasant may happen. **2** a possible cause of future harm; a danger. *Each Spring, when the snow in the mountains melts, there is a threat of floods.*

**threaten** *verb* to warn that you may do something unpleasant or may harm somebody. *My brother threatened to hit me if I didn't give him back his bicycle.*

**three-dimensional** *adjective* having depth as well as height and width; solid.

**thresh** *verb* to beat grain from stalks of corn. *The women of the village threshed the grain at harvest time.*

**thrifty** (thriftier, thriftiest) *adjective* not wasteful; careful about spending money. **thrift** *noun.*

**thrill** *noun* a feeling of great excitement and enjoyment. **thrill** *verb. She was thrilled to be chosen.* **thrilling** *adjective* very exciting.

**thriller** *noun* a book, play, or movie with an exciting story about crime and detection.

**thrive** *verb* to be healthy and successful. *The business is thriving.*

**throat** *noun* the windpipe and front part of the neck. *I have a sore throat.*

**throb** (throbs, throbbing, throbbed) *verb* to beat strongly and rapidly.

**throne** *noun* a special seat for a king or queen. *The king's throne was made of gold.*

**through** *preposition, adverb* (say throo) **1** from one side to the other. *The train went through the tunnel.* **2** among or between. *We walked through the crowd.* **3** finished or completed. *Are you through with the newspaper because I'd like to read it before I leave?*

**throughout** *preposition* **1** in all parts. *Throughout the world.* **2** from the beginning to the end; during. *The wind blew throughout the night.*

**throw** (throws, throwing, threw, thrown) *verb* to make something go through the air; to hurl or fling. *Tracy threw the ball.* **throw away** to get rid of something you do not want. **throw together** to put something together quickly. **throw up** (slang) to be sick; to vomit.

**thrush** *noun* a small, brown, garden bird with a speckled breast that sings beautifully.

**thrust** *verb* to push suddenly and with force; to shove. *Doug thrust the heavy wooden door shut with a bang.* **thrust** *noun.*

thrush

**thud** *noun* a low, dull sound made, for example, by something heavy hitting the ground. **thud** *verb.*

**thumb** *noun* the short, thick finger at the side of your hand. **thumb a ride** to hitchhike. **thumbs down** showing that you do not approve. **thumbs up** showing that you do approve. *Our plan got the thumbs up from the boss.*

**thump** *noun* the dull, heavy sound made by punching somebody or something. *I thumped the pillow with rage.*

**thunder** *noun* the rumbling noise you hear after a flash of lightning. **thunder** *verb* to make the dull, continuous noise of thunder.

**thunderstorm** *noun* a storm with thunder, lightning, and, usually, heavy rain.

**thwart** *verb* to hinder somebody from doing what they planned. *He thwarted our plan to leave before lunch by taking so long to pack.*

**thyme** *noun* an herb; a plant with small, aromatic leaves used to flavor food.

**tiara** *noun* a small, semi-circular crown worn by women. *The bride wore a diamond tiara.*

tiara

**ticket** *noun* a small printed piece of paper that shows that you have paid for something, such as a train or bus journey or for a seat in a theater.

**tickle** *verb* to touch somebody lightly on their body so that it makes them laugh or giggle. **tickle** *noun.* **ticklish** *adjective* easily made to laugh when tickled.

**tidal wave** *noun* an exceptionally large wave caused by an earthquake. A tidal wave is also called a "tsunami."

**tide** *noun* the regular rising and falling movement of the sea as it comes toward and goes away from the land twice a day. Tides are caused by the pull of the Moon and Sun on the Earth. **tidal** *adjective.*

**tidy** (tidier, tidiest) *adjective* **1** neat and with everything in its proper place. **2** (slang) quite big. *A tidy sum of money.* **tidy** *verb.* **tidiness** *noun.*

**tie** *noun* **1** a narrow piece of cloth worn around the neck under a shirt collar and knotted at the throat. **2** to come equal in a competition or sporting event. *The score was a tie.* **tie** (ties, tying, tied) *verb* **1** to fasten something with rope, string, or ribbon. *She tied her shoelaces.* **2** to score an equal number of points in a contest. *They tied in second place.*

**tier** (rhymes with near) *noun* one of several layers placed one above the other, as in parts of a wedding cake, or rows of seats in a theater.

**tiger** *noun* a large wild cat from Asia. It has an orange coat with black stripes.

tiger

**tight** *adjective* **1** closely fitting. *These jeans are too tight.* **2** firmly fixed so that it will not move. *The lid is so tight I can't open the jar.* **3** fully and firmly stretched. *Tight violin strings.* **4** having little room to spare.

**tightrope** *noun* a tightly stretched rope along which acrobats walk in a circus.

**tights** *plural noun* a piece of clothing made of very thin material that fits tightly over your feet, legs, and hips; pantyhose. Tights are worn mainly by women, but also by male actors in some historical roles, and ballet dancers.

**tile** *noun* **1** a thin slab of slate, concrete, or baked clay, used for covering roofs. **2** a thin slab of marble or glazed pottery, used for covering floors and walls, as in kitchens and bathrooms. **tile** *verb.*

**till** *conjunction, preposition* until; up to a certain time. *Wait till I get home before opening your present.* **till** *noun* a container for money in a store, with a device that records the amount of each purchase. **till** *verb* to plow and cultivate land.

**tilt** *verb* to slope or lean. *If I tilt the mirror this way, you'll be able to see your haircut better.*

**timber** *noun* wood cut and prepared for building or making furniture.

tidal wave

**time** *noun* **1** the passing of years, months, weeks, days, hours, minutes, or seconds. **2** a particular moment. *What time does the bus leave?* **3** how long something takes or a period in which you do something. **time** *verb* to measure how long something takes. **from time to time** occasionally. **in time** in step with the music. **once upon a time** (a phrase used to begin a story) some time long ago. **on time** not late.

**times** *preposition* multiplied by. *Four times four is 16, two times two is four.*

**timetable** *noun* a list showing the times of classes in a school or the times when trains, airplanes, ferries, or buses depart and arrive.

**timid** *adjective* lacking courage and easily frightened; shy. **timidity** *noun.*

**tin** *noun* **1** a soft, silvery-white metal, usually mixed with other metals or forming a coat on other metals. **2** a tin-coated metal container for storing food or other substances; a can. *A tin of white paint.*

**tinge** *noun* a slight coloring. *I've chosen white paint with a tinge of blue.*

**tingle** *verb* to feel a slight tickling sensation. **tingle** *noun. I felt a tingle up my spine when he asked me to be his date for the dance.*

**tinker** *verb* to fiddle with or make small changes to something with the idea of repairing or improving it.

**tinkle** *noun* a ringing sound like a small bell. **tinkle** *verb.*

**tint** *noun* a light, delicate shade of a color. **tinted** *adjective. Tinted glasses.*

**tiny** (tinier, tiniest) *adjective* very small.

**tip** *noun* **1** the end of something long and thin. *You have a spot on the tip of your nose.* **2** a small gift of money that you give, for example, to a waiter or taxi driver for good service. **3** a place for dumping trash. **4** a useful piece of advice. **tip** (tips, tipping, tipped) *verb* **1** to knock over something so that the contents spill out; to empty. **2** to give somebody a small gift of money for helping you.

**tipsy** *adjective* very slightly drunk.

**tiptoe** *verb* to stand or walk on your toes so that you make very little noise.

**Tirana** *noun* the capital of Albania in eastern Europe.

**tire** *noun* the thick ring of rubber, filled with air, around the wheel of a vehicle. **tire** *verb* to become tired or to make somebody tired and weary. **2** to become bored with something. **tired** *adjective.*

**tiresome** *adjective* irritating; annoying.

**tissue** *noun* the cells that make up a particular part of an animal or plant. *Leaf tissue.* **tissue paper** very thin paper used for wiping or wrapping.

**title** *noun* **1** the name of a book, movie, piece of music, or other artistic work. **2** a word such as Dr, Mrs, or Sir put before a person's name to show their position in society.

**titter** *verb* to laugh in a silly, nervous way; to giggle. **titter** *noun.*

**toad** *noun* an amphibian resembling a frog, but with a rough, warty skin. Toads live mainly on land.

**toadstool** *noun* an umbrella-shaped fungus similar to a mushroom, but nearly always poisonous. *Never touch toadstools, especially red ones with white spots.*

**toad**

**toast** *noun* **1** a slice of bread that has been heated until it has turned crisp and brown. **2** the occasion of several or more people holding up their glasses in the direction of someone and having a drink, following a few words of dedication to that person. *We drank a toast to the bride.* **toast** *verb* to hold up your glass, wish for the success or happiness of somebody, and have a drink.

**tobacco** *noun* the cut and dried leaves of the tobacco plant, smoked as cigars and cigarettes or in pipes.

**toboggan** *noun* a tray-shaped sled without runners. **toboggan** *verb.*

**today** *adverb, noun* **1** this very day. **2** the present time; nowadays. *People live longer today than they used to.*

**toddler** *noun* a child who is just learning to walk. *Toddlers tend to totter when they walk.*

**toe** *noun* **1** one of the five digits at the end of your foot. **2** the front part of a shoe or sock that fits over your toes. **on your toes** ready and alert. **toe the line** to do as you are told. *Imran expected his staff to toe the line.*

**toffee** *noun* a sticky candy made from sugar and butter. *Toffee and pear pie is my favorite pudding.*

**toga** *noun* a loose, flowing garment worn by men in ancient Rome.

**Togo's flag**

**together** *adverb* **1** with another. *She stuck the two pieces together.* **2** at the same time as another. *They arrived home together.*

**Togo** *noun* a country in West Africa.

**toilet** *noun* **1** a large bowl for collecting waste from the body. A flush mechanism uses running water to remove the waste from the toilet and carry it into the main drains of a place.

**token** *noun* **1** a piece of printed plastic or paper that can be used instead of money for buying things. *I got a book token for my birthday.* **2** a small sign or symbol of something. *My boyfriend gave me a silver ring as a token of his love.*

**Tokyo** *noun* the capital of Japan in east Asia.

**tolerate** *verb* to put up with or allow something to happen; to endure. **tolerable** *adjective.* **tolerance** *noun.* **tolerant** *adjective.*

**tomato** (tomatoes) *noun* a round, sweet fruit eaten raw in salads and much used in cooking.

**tomb** *noun* a place where a body is buried; a grave.

**tomorrow** *adverb, noun* **1** the day after today. **2** the future. *Tomorrow's children.*

**ton** *noun* **1** a unit of weight equal to 2,000 pounds or 1,016 kg. **2** (informal) a very large quantity or weight.

**tone** *noun* **1** the quality of a sound or the way something is said. *The piano has a mellow tone.* **2** a shade of color. **3** the condition of a muscle. **tone** *verb.*

**Tonga** *noun* a country comprising many islands in the Pacific Ocean.

**tongue** *noun* the long, soft, pink muscle that moves inside your mouth, tastes things, and helps you talk.

**tonsils** *plural noun* two soft lumps of flesh at the back of your throat.

**too** *adverb* **1** as well; also. *I can sing, too.* **2** more than enough or than is needed.

**tool** *noun* a hand-held instrument or implement such as a hammer or drill that you use to do a particular job.

**tooth** (teeth) *noun* **1** one of the hard, white, bony parts inside your mouth that you use for biting and chewing. **2** one of the pointed parts of a comb or saw.

**toothache** *noun* severe pain in a tooth.

**topic** *noun* a subject to talk or write about.

**topical** *adjective* relating to important or interesting things happening now.

**topography** *noun* the study and description of the landscape's features, such as the position of its mountains, roads, and towns.

**tornado**

**Torah** *noun* a scroll used in synagogs on which are written the first five books of the Old Testament: Genesis, Exodus, Leviticus, Numbers, and Deuteronomy, known as the Pentateuch.

**torment** *verb* (say tor-**ment**) to tease and be deliberately cruel to somebody or to an animal. **torment** *noun* (say **tor**-ment) physical or mental suffering.

**tornado** (tornadoes) *noun* a violent storm with strong winds that spin in a cone shape at high speeds and cause great damage. *A tornado crossed the plains.*

**torrent** *noun* **1** a violent, rushing stream. **2** a flood or heavy downpour of rain. **torrential** *adjective. Torrential rain caused the river to burst its banks.*

**torso** (torsos) *noun* the main part of a person's body, excluding the head and limbs.

**tortoise** *noun* (say **tor**-tuss) a slow-moving land reptile with a hard shell.

**torture** *verb* to make somebody suffer extremely cruel physical or mental pain, often to force them to confess something. **torture** *noun. He was tortured until he revealed the secret way in to the castle.*

**toss** *verb* **1** to throw something carelessly into the air. **2** to move up and down and from side to side. *The boat tossed on the sea.* **3** to spin a coin to see whether heads or tails faces upward.

**total** *noun* the amount when everything is added together. **total** *adjective* complete. *A total success.*

**totem pole** *noun* a large pole carved or painted with traditional symbols of American Indian families.

**totter** *verb* to walk in an unsteady way. *She tottered on her high heels.*

**toucan** *noun* a South American bird with a large, brightly colored beak.

**touch** *verb* **1** to feel something with your hand or with some other part of your body. **2** to come into contact and be so close to something that there is no space in between. **3** to move the feelings. *I was touched by your kind letter.* **touch** *noun* one of the five senses; the ability to feel. **in touch** in communication. **out of touch** not in communication.

**totem pole**

**touching** *adjective* causing a deep feeling of pity, sorrow, or some other emotion. *A touching love story.*

**touchy** *adjective* easily offended or annoyed. *Beth seemed very touchy.*

**tough** *adjective* (say tuff) **1** strong and difficult to damage or break. **2** able to put up with hardships or difficulties. *Arctic explorers need to be tough to survive.* **3** difficult. *A tough test.* **4** hard to chew. *This steak is too tough.* **5** strict. *The mayor is tough on crime.* **toughen** *verb.* **toughness** *noun.*



**toupée** *noun* a false piece of hair worn to cover a bald part of the head.

**tour** *noun* **1** a journey on which you visit many different places. **2** a short trip around one place. **tour** *verb.*

**tourist** *noun* a person who visits different places for pleasure and interest.

**tournament** *noun* a contest of skill between competitors, usually played in heats. *A chess tournament.*

**tousled** *adjective* (of hair) untidy.

**tow** (say toe) *verb* to pull or drag something behind. *The truck towed the car out of the mud.*

**toward** *preposition* **1** in the direction of. *We ran toward the sea.* **2** regarding or concerning. **3** as a contribution. *Everyone gave $2 toward the cost.*

**towel** *noun* a piece of thick, absorbent cloth or paper used to dry things.

**tower** *noun* a tall, narrow building or structure, or part of a building. **tower** *verb* to rise very high. *The chimney towered over the factory.* **towering** *adjective.*

**town** *noun* a settlement with many houses and other buildings such as schools, stores, factories, and offices.

**toxic** *adjective* poisonous. *Toxic waste is dangerous.*

**trace** *verb* **1** to copy a design by placing a thin piece of half-transparent paper over it and drawing over the lines of the design. **2** to search and find where somebody is. *The police traced her to a hotel in Miami.* **trace** *noun* a small mark or amount.

**tower**

**track** *noun* **1** a series of marks left on the ground by an animal, person, or vehicle. **2** a path. **3** a railroad line. **4** a course for horses, runners, cars, or other moving things. **5** one of the pieces of music on a CD. **off the beaten track** remote and not often visited. **keep (or lose) track of** to know (not know) where somebody is.

**tract** *noun* **1** a wide area of land. *The camels crossed vast tracts of desert without stopping to drink.* **2** a leaflet.

**tractor** *noun* a strong vehicle used on farms to pull plows and other machinery.

**trade** *noun* **1** the business of buying and selling goods. **2** an occupation or job that requires a special skill; a craft. *Paul is a blacksmith by trade.* **trade** *verb* to buy and sell; to exchange.

**tradition** *noun* customs, beliefs, and habits that people hand down from one generation to another. **traditional** *adjective. A traditional folk song.*

**traffic** *noun* vehicles traveling along the road at the same time. *The traffic builds up at rush-hour.*

**tragedy** *noun* **1** a sad or calamitous event; a terrible disaster. **2** a play about sad events, with an unhappy ending in which the main character usually dies. **tragic** *adjective. Two people were killed in the tragic accident.*

**trail** *noun* **1** marks left behind by a person or animal as they move through a place. *A trail of footprints in the snow.* **2** a track or narrow path through the countryside. **trail** *verb* **1** to follow a set of marks or clues left behind. **2** to drag or be dragged along the ground.

**trailer** *noun* **1** a vehicle used to carry things, towed by a car or truck. *The truck pulled a yacht on a trailer.* **2** an advertisement showing short extracts from a movie.

**train** *noun* **1** a set of railroad cars pulled by an engine. **2** a series of ideas or events. *You broke my train of thought.* **train** *verb* **1** to learn the skills you need to do something. **2** to teach an animal or person how to do something. **3** to practice and exercise for a sport.

**trainer** *noun* a person who trains or teaches somebody or an animal to compete in a sport. *A horse trainer.*

**traitor** *noun* a person who is disloyal and betrays friends or a country.

**tranquil** *adjective* (say **tran**-kwill) calm and quiet. **tranquility** *noun. The tranquility of a monastery.*

**tranquilizer** *noun* a medicine that is given to somebody to make them feel calm and not stressed. **tranquilize** *verb.*

**trans-** *prefix* across or beyond. *Transatlantic telephone calls. Trans-American highway.*

**transfer** *noun* (say **tranz**-fur) **1** the act of moving a person or thing from one place to another. **2** a design or picture on a small piece of paper that can be moved and stuck to another surface by rubbing or heating. *A transfer of a teddy bear.* **transfer** (transfers, transferring, transferred) *verb* (say tranz-**fur**) to move somebody or something from one place to another. *She transferred her affection to another boy.*

**transform** *verb* to make a complete change in form or nature. *We transformed the kitchen into a bathroom.* **transformation** *noun.*

**transfusion** *noun* injecting blood into a person who has lost a lot of it or needs their blood changing. *He needed a blood transfusion.*

**transistor** *noun* **1** an electronic device that controls the flow of electricity in radios and television sets. **2** a small portable radio that uses a transistor.

**translate** *verb* to change words from one language into another. **translator** *noun.* **translation** *noun.*

**transmit** (transmits, transmitting, transmitted) *verb* **1** to pass something on from one place or person to another. *How are diseases transmitted?* **2** to send out a radio or television program over the air. **transmission** *noun.*

**transparent** *adjective* able to be seen through; clear; obvious. *Clear water is transparent.*

**transplant** *verb* **1** to move a growing plant from one place to another. **2** to perform a surgical operation to put a part of one person's body into the body of another person. **transplant** *noun. The heart transplant was a great success and the man went on to live an active life.*

**trap** *noun* a device for catching birds and animals. **trap** *verb* **1** to catch an animal by using a trap. **2** to corner a person so they cannot escape. *They trapped the wild cat in the alley by blocking off both ends.*

**trapeze** *noun* a bar hanging from two ropes, used by acrobats and gymnasts to swing from and perform skillful movements.

trapeze

**travel** (travels, traveling, traveled) *verb* to journey or move from one place to another. *Speedboats travel fast.* **travel** *noun. Air travel.*

**traveler** *noun* **1** a person who travels regularly. **2** a person who travels from place to place in a mobile home or van.

**trawl** *verb* to fish with a wide net called a trawl net. *The fishing boat trawled the deep ocean for fish.*

**trawler** *noun* a fishing boat that pulls a large net called a trawl net behind it.

**tray** *noun* a thin, flat object with a rim around the edge, used for carrying things such as food and drinks.

**treachery** *noun* disloyalty; the betrayal of people who trust you. **treacherous** *adjective* **1** disloyal. **2** dangerous. *Treacherous rocks line the coast.*

**tread** (treading, trod, trodden) *verb* to walk or to put your foot down on something; to trample. *She trod on the cat's tail by mistake and the cat squealed.* **tread** *noun* **1** the top surface of a step or stair. **2** the raised pattern of ridges on a car tire or on the sole of a shoe that provides grip. *The tread on my trainers provides good grip.*

**treason** *noun* the betrayal of your country, especially by giving away secrets to the enemy during wartime. **treasonable** *adjective. His was a treasonable offence.*

**treasure** *noun* **1** a store of gold, jewels, and other precious things. **2** a precious object such as a painting. **treasure** *verb* to value something very highly or to look after something because it is important to you.

**treasurer** *noun* a person who looks after the money of a club or organization.

**treat** *noun* a rare pleasure; an indulgence. **treat** *verb* **1** to behave toward somebody in a particular way. *She treats me like a servant.* **2** to give medical care to a person or animal. **treatment** *noun.*

treasure

**treaty** *noun* a formal agreement between two or more countries. *An arms treaty.*

**treble** *noun* **1** a boy with a high singing voice. **2** threefold; triple; three times the amount.

**trek** *noun* a long journey, usually on foot and in a remote area. **trek** *verb.*

**tremble** *verb* to shake all over because you are frightened, cold, or excited.

**trench** *noun* **1** a long, thin ditch or channel dug in the earth. **2** a deep depression in the sea bed.

**trend** *noun* the general direction in which things seem to be going and becoming different. *There is a trend for smaller families today.* **set a trend** to start a fashion.

**trespass** *verb* to go on to somebody's land without their permission. **trespasser** *noun.*

**tri-** *prefix* three or three times. *Tricycle, triangle, trilogy, tripod, tripartite.*

**trial** *noun* **1** the period of time when a prisoner is in a law court and when the lawyers, jury, and judge try to decide whether or not he or she has done wrong and is guilty. **2** a test of something to see how well it works.

**tribe** *noun* a group of families descended from the same ancestors who live together and who have the same traditions and language. **tribal** *adjective. Tribal chief.*

**tributary** *noun* a stream that flows into a river or another stream.

**tricolour** *noun* a flag with three bands of different colors, such as the French and Irish flags.

**trifle** *noun* **1** an English dessert made of cake and fruit covered in jelly, custard, and cream. **2** something that is of no importance. **3** slightly. **trifling** *adjective.*

**trilogy** *noun* a series of three novels, plays, or operas that together make a complete work, with the same people or themes in common.

**Trinidad and Tobago** *noun* a country of two main islands in the Caribbean.

**trinity** *noun* **1** a group of three. **2 the Trinity** in Christianity, the Father, the Son, and the Holy Spirit, who together make one God.

triplet

**trio** *noun* **1** a group of three singers or players. **2** a piece of music written for three musicians. *A string trio.*

**triple** *adjective* three times as great or as many. **2** consisting of three parts. **triple** *verb. The tree has tripled in height in one month.*

**triplet** *noun* one of three babies born at the same time to the same mother.

**tripod** *noun* (say **try**-pod) a three-legged support for a camera, telescope, or other instrument.

**Tripoli** *noun* the capital of Libya in North Africa.

**triumph** *noun* (say **try**-umf) a great success or achievement; a victory. **triumph** *verb. Good triumphed over evil.* **triumphant** *adjective.*

**trivial** *adjective* of very little importance. *I phoned Mom to ask her advice about a trivial matter.*

**trophy** *noun* (say **trow**-fee) an award or prize, such as a silver cup or a plaque, given to somebody who wins a game or competition.

**tropic** *noun* **1** one of the two lines of latitude running around the Earth (about 23 degrees north and south of the equator), known as the Tropic of Cancer and the Tropic of Capricorn. **2 tropics** *plural noun* the very warm regions between the Tropic of Cancer and the Tropic of Capricorn. **tropical** *noun. Tropical rain forests.*

tropics

**trouble** *noun* a difficult, unpleasant, or worrying situation; a problem. **trouble** *verb* **1** to cause worry, concern, or distress. **2** to make an effort to do something; to bother. *She didn't trouble to look up when I came into the room.*

**trough** *noun* **1** a long, narrow container used to hold food or water for animals. **2** in weather forecasting, an area of low pressure between areas of high pressure.

**truant** *noun* a pupil who stays away from school without permission or a good excuse.

**truce** *noun* a short period when two sides in a war or dispute agree to stop fighting or arguing.

**trudge** *verb* to walk slowly with determined, heavy steps. **trudge** *noun. The Arctic explorer trudged across the snow for mile after mile.*

**trust** *verb* to believe that somebody is honest, reliable, and truthful, and that they will do nothing to harm you; to depend on. *I trust my husband completely.* **trustworthy** *adjective.* **trustworthiness** *noun.*

**tsar** *noun* (say zar) in former times, a Russian king or emperor. His wife was called the tsarina. Also spelled "czar" and "czarina." *Tsar Nicholas.*

**tuba** *noun* a large brass musical instrument that makes deep sounds when you blow into it.

**tuber** *noun* the round, swollen part of the underground stem of some plants. Potatoes are tubers.

tuba

**tug-of-war** *noun* a contest between two teams who pull on opposite ends of a long rope to test their strength.

tug-of-war

**tulip** *noun* a plant with brightly colored flowers that grows from a bulb in the Spring. *The tulip fields of Holland are world famous.*

**tumble** *verb* to fall down suddenly or to fall and roll over. *Tim's teddy bear tumbled down the stairs.*

**tumbler** *noun* a drinking glass without a stem.

**tummy** *noun* (slang) the stomach.

**tumor** *noun* a lump or growth on the body made of diseased or abnormal cells.

**tuna** *noun* a large sea fish and popular food item. *I love tuna and cucumber sandwiches.*

**tundra** *noun* the vast, treeless plains of the Arctic that remain frozen all year.

**tune** *noun* a sequence of musical notes in a pattern that is pleasant to listen to and often easy to remember. **tune** *verb* **1** to adjust a musical instrument so that it plays the correct pitch. **2** to adjust a radio so that it receives the program you want. **tuneful** *adjective*. **change your tune** to voice a change of opinion.

**tunic** *noun* **1** a tight-fitting jacket, often worn as part of a uniform. **2** a loose, sleeveless garment without a collar.

**Tunis** *noun* the capital of Tunisia in North Africa.

**Tunisia** *noun* a country in North Africa.

**Tunisian** *noun* a person who comes from Tunisia. **Tunisian** *adjective*. *The Tunisian coast is extremely beautiful and is a great tourist attraction.*

**tunnel** *noun* a long underground passage. *My ears popped when the train went through the tunnel.* **tunnel** (tunnels, tunneling, tunneled) *verb* to dig a tunnel.

**turban** *noun* a headdress worn by Sikh and some Muslim men consisting of a long piece of cloth wound around the head.

**turbine** *noun* an engine driven by the flow of water, steam, hot air, or wind pushing around the blades of a wheel or propeller to produce electricity. *Wind turbines.*

turbines

**turbojet** *noun* an aircraft driven by a turbine.

**Turkey** *noun* **1** a country partly in Europe but mostly in Asia. **2 turkey** a large bird reared for its meat.

**Turkmenistan** *noun* a country in western Asia.

**turmoil** *noun* a state of great confusion and unrest.

**turquoise** *noun* **1** a greenish-blue semiprecious stone. **2** the color of the semiprecious stone.

**turret** *noun* a small tower on a castle or the side of a building. *A spiral staircase filled the castle turret.*

**tutor** *noun* a teacher who gives classes to one person at a time or to small groups of people.

**tutu** *noun* the very short, stiff, sticking-out skirt worn by female ballet dancers.

**Tuvalu** *noun* a country of islands in the Pacific Ocean.

**twice** *adverb* two times.

**twiddle** *verb* to turn something around and around in a purposeless way. *He kept twiddling the dials.* **twiddle your thumbs** to have nothing to do.

**twilight** *noun* the time of day when it gets dark, between sunset and night.

**twin** *noun* one of two babies born at the same time to the same mother.

**twinge** *noun* a sudden, short pain. *A twinge of rheumatism caused the old lady to grimace.*

**twinkle** *verb* to sparkle with little unsteady flashes of light. *Stars twinkle in the sky.* **twinkle** *noun*. *He has a twinkle in his eye!*

**twist** *verb* **1** to turn. *To open the door, you must twist the knob.* **2** to wind something around something else. *She twisted her hair around her finger.* **3** to bend and turn in different directions. *The road twisted around the mountain.* **4** to bend something so as to damage it. *She twisted her wrist.* **twist** *noun*.

**tycoon** *noun* a rich, powerful businessperson or industrialist. *A newspaper tycoon.*

**type** *noun* **1** the different designs of letters used in printing. **2** a kind or sort. *Apples and pears are two types of fruit.* **type** *verb* to write something by pressing the keys of a typewriter or computer keyboard.

**typhoid** *noun* (say **tie**-foid) a dangerous infectious disease in which the intestines become inflamed.

**typhoon** *noun* (say tie-**foon**) a tropical storm with violent winds.

**typical** *adjective* **1** the most usual or characteristic of its kind. **2** what you would expect.

**tyrant** *noun* a cruel, unjust, and unkind ruler. **tyranny** *noun*. **tyrannical** *adjective*. *A tyrannical dictator.*

**udder** *noun* the bag-like part of a cow, sheep, or other animal that hangs down between its back legs and from which milk is taken.

**UFO** *abbreviation* unidentified flying object. *Ted thought he saw a UFO in the night sky.*

**Uganda** *noun* a country in eastern Africa.

**ugly** (uglier, ugliest) *adjective* unattractive and not beautiful to look at. **ugliness** *noun.*

**UHF** *abbreviation* ultra-high frequency.

**Ukraine** *noun* a country in eastern Europe.

**Ulan Bator** *noun* the capital of Mongolia in Asia.

**ulcer** *noun* (say **ull**-sur) an open sore on the body, usually having a flow of pus.

**ultimate** *adjective* **1** final; last. **2** beyond which no other exists or is possible.

**ultimatum** *noun* a final offer or warning.

**ultra-** *prefix* beyond. *Ultra-high frequency.*

**ultraviolet light** *noun* light that is beyond the violet end of the visible spectrum, and which makes your skin tan.

**umbilical** *noun* of or near the navel. **umbilical cord** the tube that connects a baby to the placenta inside the mother's womb or uterus.

**umbilical cord**

**umbrella** *noun* something that you hold over your head to keep you dry when it rains. The umbrella's collapsible frame is covered with a round piece of material and is joined to a long handle.

UN flag

**umpire** *noun* an official who watches a game such as tennis and makes sure that the rules are followed.

**UN** *abbreviation* United Nations.

**un-** *prefix* **1** not; opposite. *Uncomfortable.* **2** the opposite of an action. *Undo; undress.*

**unaccustomed** *adjective* not used to doing something. *He is unaccustomed to work.*

**unanimous** *adjective* (say you-**nan**-im-us) of the same opinion; agreed by everybody. *The jury came to a unanimous verdict.* **unanimity** *noun.*



**unassuming** *adjective* modest and not showing off. *The unassuming young man was in fact very talented.*

**unaware** *adjective* not knowing that something exists or is happening.

**unbalanced** *adjective* **1** lacking balance; unfair. **2** slightly insane. *The accident made her unbalanced.*

**unbecoming** *adjective* not suiting. *Molly wore an unbecoming dress that showed off too much of her thighs.*

**unbiased** *adjective* not favoring one side or the other; fair. *An unbiased opinion.*

**uncanny** *adjective* strange, weird, and unnatural. *It's uncanny how Leo always knows what I am about to say.*

**uncle** *noun* the brother of your mother or your father, or the husband of your aunt.

**unconscious** *adjective* **1** not conscious; in a kind of sleep and not knowing what is happening. **2** not being aware of something. *I was unconscious of the difficulties you were in until yesterday.*

**uncooperative** *adjective* making no attempt to help or do things for others.

**uncouth** *adjective* coarse and rough in behavior and speech; rude. *That man's uncouth behavior sets a bad example to his son, who is at an impressionable age.*

**undaunted** *adjective* not discouraged or put off doing something despite setbacks and difficulties. *Susan was undaunted by the harsh traveling conditions.*

**undeniable** *adjective* so certainly true that you cannot disagree.

**under-** *prefix* **1** below; beneath. *Underground.* **2** less than or not enough. *Underdeveloped.* **3** lower in rank. *Undersecretary; understudy.*

**undercover** *adjective* secret. *Undercover activities were common during the World War II.*

**undergo** (undergoes, undergoing, underwent, undergone) *verb* to experience, endure, or suffer something. *She underwent surgery yesterday.*

**undergraduate** *noun* a person studying for a first degree at a university.

**underground** *adjective* **1** beneath the ground. *The subway runs through underground tunnels beneath the city.* **2** acting in secret. *The French Resistance were an underground organization during World War II.*

**underground**

**undergrowth** *noun* bushes and plants that grow near the ground under trees in woods and forests. *The spotted deer browsed in the dappled undergrowth.*

**underhanded** *adjective* secret and dishonest; deceitful. *An underhanded plot.*

**underline** *verb* **1** to draw a line under words to make them stand out. **2** to stress the importance of something. *The accident underlines the need to be more careful.*

**undermine** *verb* to gradually weaken or slowly destroy something. *The damp climate is undermining her health.*

**understand** (understands, understanding, understood) *verb* **1** to know what something means, how it works, or why it happens. **2** to know somebody or something well. *I understand what you feel.* **3** to believe something to be true because you have been told. *I understand that you got married secretly.*

**understanding** *noun* **1** having a knowledge of something and knowing what it means or how it works; intelligence. *He has no understanding of machinery.* **2** sympathy and knowledge of a person. *There's a deep understanding between them.* **3** an agreement. *Perhaps we could come to an understanding about who does what.* **understanding** *adjective* tolerant and kind.

**understudy** *noun* an actor who, in an emergency, can stand in for the actor who usually plays the part. *The understudy for Peter Pan was a great hit.*

**undertake** (undertakes, undertaking, undertook, undertaken) *verb* to agree or promise to do something and to be responsible for it. **undertaking** *noun.*

**undertaker** *noun* a person whose job it is to prepare dead bodies for burial or cremation and arrange funerals.

**underwear** *noun* clothes that you wear next to your skin, under shirts, skirts, and pants. Bras and panties are underwear.

**underworld** *noun* **1** all the criminals and their activities in a city. **2** the place in myths where the spirits of dead people go.

**undo** (undoes, undoing, undid, undone) *verb* **1** to unfasten, untie, or unwrap something that was fixed or tied. *She undid her shoelaces.* **2** to do away with or reverse something that has been done. *Try to undo the damage you have done by saying sorry.*

**undoubted** *adjective* accepted as true; certain. *The play was an undoubted success.*

**undress** *verb* to take your clothes off.

**undue** *adjective* excessive; more than necessary.

**undying** *adjective* never dying or fading. *Romeo and Juliet swore undying love for each other.*

**unearth** *verb* to dig up or find something after searching for it; to discover. *He unearthed some old photos in a trunk.*

**unearthly** *adjective* **1** strange and terrifying, like nothing on Earth. *An unearthly sound of howling echoed across the moor.* **2** absurdly unreasonable. *She telephoned at some unearthly hour of the night.*

**uneasy** *adjective* anxious; not settled. *I feel uneasy in large crowds.* **uneasiness** *noun.*

**uneven** *adjective.* **1** not smooth or flat. **2** not equally matched; one-sided. *An uneven contest.* **3** (of a number) odd and leaving a remainder of one when divided by two. Five and seven are uneven numbers.

**uneven**

**unfailing** *adjective* never failing or weakening; continuous; endless. *You have my unfailing sympathy.*

**unfeeling** *adjective* severe and hard-hearted.

**unfit** *adjective* **1** unhealthy; in poor physical condition. *Justin was unfit and badly needed some exercise.* **2** unsuitable and not good enough. *This food is passed its sell-by date and unfit to eat.*

**unfold** *verb* **1** to spread out by opening. *He unfolded the blanket.* **2** to reveal or gradually make something clear. *The story unfolded gradually.*

**unfurl** *verb* to unroll, spread out, and display something that has been wrapped up. *The soldier unfurled the flag.*

**unforeseen** *adjective* not expected. *Due to unforeseen circumstances, I cannot come.*

**unfounded** *adjective* not based on fact. *Unfounded rumors about the teacher spread through the school.*

**ungainly** *adjective* clumsy and ungraceful.

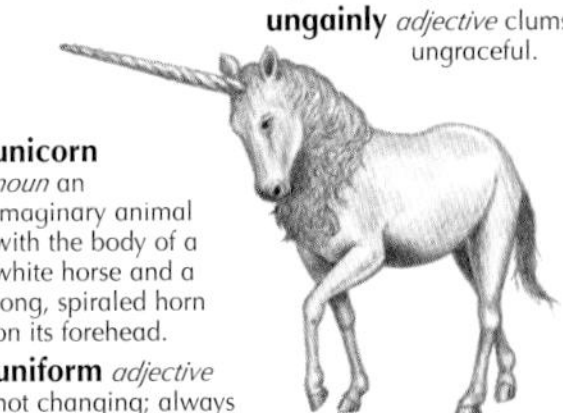

**unicorn**

**unicorn** *noun* an imaginary animal with the body of a white horse and a long, spiraled horn on its forehead.

**uniform** *adjective* not changing; always the same. *The bricks are of uniform size and color.* **uniform** *noun* special distinctive clothes worn by members of a particular group or organization. Nurses, firefighters, and soldiers wear uniforms.

Uu

**unify** *verb* to make several things come together to form a whole and to share a common purpose. *The various Italian-states unified to make modern Italy.*

**unintelligible** *adjective* difficult to understand. *His accent is unintelligible.*

**uninterested** *adjective* showing no interest or enthusiasm. *He seemed uninterested in my news.*

**union** *noun* **1** A trade union is an organized group of workers who discuss with managers any problems affecting workers. **2** the act of joining things together, something united.

**unique** *adjective* (say yoo-**neek**) **1** being the only one of its kind. *His style of painting is unique.* **2** very unusual. **uniqueness** *noun.*

**unison** *noun* **in unison** all together.

**unite** *verb* to join together to form one thing or to do something together; to combine. **unity** *noun.*

**United Arab Emirates** *noun* a country in Southwest Asia, bordering the Persian Gulf and Gulf of Oman.

**United Kingdom** *noun* a country in northwest Europe, made up of England, Scotland, Wales, and Northern Ireland.

university

**United States of America** *noun* a large country in North America, comprising 50 states and one district (the capital, Washington D.C.).

**universal** *adjective* relating to and including everybody and everything.

**universe** *noun* (say **yoo**-ni-verse) the whole of everything that exists, including the Earth, Sun, Moon, planets, and all the stars in space.

**university** *noun* a place of higher education where people go to study for a degree or to research a particular subject.

**unkempt** *adjective* untidy and not well looked after. *The rock musician intentionally had unkempt hair.*

Uu

**unleaded** *adjective* (of gasoline) containing no lead. *This car runs on unleaded gas.*

**unless** *conjunction* if not; except when. *We'll be late for school unless you hurry up.*

**unmistakable** *adjective* distinct and easy to recognize; unlike anyone else's. *Simon's handwriting is unmistakable; I'd know it anywhere.*

unravel

**unravel** (unravels, unraveling, unraveled) *verb* **1** to undo a ball of wool, thread, or string. *The kitten unraveled the ball of wool.* **2** to undo knots or untie woven, knitted, or tangled threads. **3** to solve a mystery or difficult problem.

**unreasonable** *adjective* **1** not sensible. *An unreasonable fear of spiders.* **2** too much, excessive. *Unreasonable demands.*

**unreliable** *adjective* not to be trusted or depended on. *Dad's old car is unreliable.*

**unruly** *adjective* badly behaved; hard to control or rule. *The unruly child would not sit down when told to.*

**unscathed** *adjective* not harmed or damaged. *The horse was unscathed after it fell at the last jump.*

**unscrupulous** *adjective* not caring whether something is right or wrong; having no principles.

**unseemly** *adjective* not suitable for the time and place.

**unsettle** *verb* to make or become unstable and anxious; to disturb. *Thunder unsettles our dogs and cats.*

**unsightly** *adjective* unpleasant to look at; ugly. *Roger has an unsightly scar on his cheek.*

**unsound** *adjective* **1** not in a good condition; unhealthy. *The upstairs floors are unsound.* **2** not based on fact. *I thought her theory was unsound.*

**unstable** *adjective* **1** liable to change suddenly. *She's very moody and unstable.* **2** not steady; wobbly. *The table is unstable because one leg is shorter than the others.*

**unsuitable** *adjective* not right or fitting for a particular purpose. *Slippers are unsuitable for playing sport.*

**until** *conjunction, preposition* up to the time of or when. *She stayed up until long past midnight.*

**untold** *adjective* too much or too many to calculate. *Locust swarms can do untold damage to crops.*

**unusual** *adjective* strange, rare, and unexpected. *My aunt has an unusual necklace made of seashells.*

**unwelcome** *adjective* not wanted. *The phone ringing was an unwelcome interruption to the movie.*

**unwieldy** *noun* bulky, clumsy, and difficult to hold, manage, or move.

**unwitting** *adjective* **1** not knowing and not intended. *Julia made an unwitting spelling error.*

**unworthy** *adjective* not deserving. *Such a ridiculous story is unworthy of attention.* **2** out of character and below the standards expected.

**unwrap** (unwraps, unwrapping, unwrapped) *verb* to remove the covering or wrapping from something, such as a parcel; to open.

**upbeat** *adjective* happy and ever hopeful.

**upbringing** *noun* the way that a child is brought up and told how to behave.

**update** *verb* to add all the latest information; to make more modern. *The website is constantly updated.*

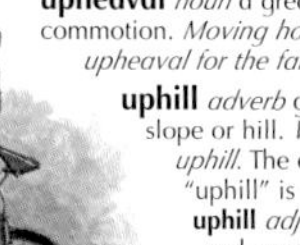

uphill

**upheaval** *noun* a great change; commotion. *Moving house is a great upheaval for the family.*

**uphill** *adverb* going up a slope or hill. *We cycled uphill.* The opposite of "uphill" is "downhill." **uphill** *adjective* difficult and needing a lot of effort. *It was an uphill struggle to survive.*

**upholstery** *noun* the springs, padding, covering, and cushions of chairs and sofas. **upholster** *verb.*

**upon** *preposition* on; on top of.

**upper** *adjective* above; in a higher position. *Your head and chest form the upper part of your body.*

**upright** *adjective, adverb* **1** in a vertical position. **2** good and honest. *An upright person.*

**uprising** *noun* a rebellion or revolt against people in authority.

**uproar** *noun* noisy and angry or excited confusion; a disturbance.

**upside down** *adjective* **1** topsy-turvy; with the top facing down and the bottom facing up. **2** complete disorder.

**uptight** *adjective* **1** (slang) nervous; angry; irritated. *She's always uptight before a test.* **2** prim and conventional.

**up-to-date** *adjective* modern; containing all the very latest information. *Please use the up-to-date map!* The opposite is "out-of-date."

upside down

**urchin** *noun* a poor, shabbily dressed, sometimes mischievous child.

**Urdu** *noun* one of the official languages of Pakistan, also widely spoken in India.

**urge** *noun* a strong desire to do something; an impulse. **urge** *verb* to encourage and try to make somebody do something; to plead. *He urged her to try a little harder.*

**urgent** *adjective* very important and needing to be dealt with at once. *An urgent phone call.* **urgency** *noun.*

**urine** *noun* the clear, yellowish fluid passed from the bodies of animals and humans from the bladder. **urinate** *verb* to pass urine from the body.

**urn** *noun* **1** an ornamental vase. **2** a container for the ashes of a person who has been cremated. **3** a large container for holding and dispensing hot drinks.

**Uruguay** *noun* a country in southern South America.

**USA** *abbreviation* United States of America.

**usage** *noun* **1** a way of using; treatment. *The DVD has been damaged through rough usage.* **2** the usual or customary way of doing or saying things. *British usage is to say "bonnet" for "hood," "wallet" for "billfold," and "windscreen" for "windshield."*

**use** *verb* (say **yoo**-zz) **1** to make something do a job. *She used scissors to cut the cloth.* **2** to consume or take. *Don't use all the hot water.* **use** *noun* (rhymes with juice) **1** the act of using or being in use. *The photocopier is in use.* **2** the purpose for using something. *This tool has many uses.*

**used** *adjective* not new; already owned by somebody. **used to 1** accustomed to. *Brian isn't used to so much exercise.* **2** something that once happened often or that was once true. *We used to swim every afternoon.*

**useful** *adjective* helpful; having a purpose. *Debra gave me some useful hints on essay writing.* **usefulness** *noun.*

**useless** *adjective* of little or no help; having no effect. *It's useless asking him the way there; he's never been before.* **uselessness** *noun.*

**user-friendly** designed to be easy to use and understand.

**usual** *adjective* happening often or most of the time; normal and everyday. *She arrived home at her usual time.* **usually** *adverb. We usually go to the theater to watch a movie on Friday night.*

**utensil** *noun* a tool or container, especially one used every day in the home. *Mother keeps her cooking utensils spotless.*

**uterus** *noun* the womb, in which a baby develops and grows.

**utmost** *adjective* **1** the greatest possible. *It's a matter of the utmost importance.* **2** farthest. *The utmost ends of the Earth.*

**utopia** *noun* an imaginary place where everything is perfect; a paradise. **utopian** *adjective. Sarah leads a utopian existence.*

**utter** *verb* to speak or make a sound with your mouth. *She uttered a squeal of delight.*

**U-turn** *noun* **1** a U-shaped turn that a vehicle makes to go back the way it came. **2** a reversal of plans.

**Uzbekistan** *noun* a country in western Asia.

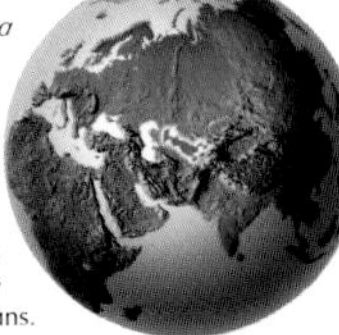

Uzbekistan

**vacant** *adjective* empty, unoccupied, and not in use. *The bathroom is vacant.* **vacancy** *noun* a job that is available. *Are there any vacancies in the company?* **vacate** *verb* to leave. *Please vacate the room by 11 a.m.*

**vacation** *noun* a time that is not spent working or at school; a time to relax and travel.

**vaccinate** *verb* (say **vak**-sin-ate) to inject somebody with a small dose of a disease, such as measles, to protect them from contracting the disease. **vaccination** *noun.*

**vaccine** *noun* (say **vak**-seen) a medicine made from the germs of a disease. A vaccine is injected into people to protect them from the disease.

**vacuum** *noun* space that is quite empty with all gases removed. **vacuum** *verb* to clean with a vacuum cleaner. **vacuum cleaner** an electrical machine that sucks up dust from carpets and floors.

**Vaduz** *noun* the capital of Liechtenstein in Europe.

**vagina** *noun* a passage in a woman's body that leads to the womb.

**vague** *adjective* (say vayg) not clear or definite. *I could just make out a vague shape in the twilight, but I couldn't identify who it was.*

**vain** *adjective* **1** having excessive pride in your appearance or what you can do. **2** useless or unsuccessful; meaningless. *A vain attempt.* **in vain** without success.

**valentine** *noun* **1** a card that you send to somebody you love on February 14 – Saint Valentine's Day. **2** the person to whom you send the card. *Be my valentine!*

**valiant** *adjective* brave.

**valid** *adjective* **1** acceptable. *A valid argument.* **2** legally acceptable. *A valid ticket.* **validity** *noun.*

**Valletta** *noun* the capital of Malta in southern Europe.

**valley** (valleys) *noun* low land between hills, usually with a river flowing through it.

**valuable** *adjective* **1** precious and worth a lot of money, especially something that would be hard to replace. **2** useful; helpful. *Valuable advice.* **valuables** *plural noun* personal possessions of value, such as jewelry.

**value** *noun* **1** the amount of money that something is worth or that it can be sold for; the price. *What is the value of this diamond?* **2** the importance or usefulness of somebody or something. **value** *verb. I greatly value your friendship.*

**valve** *noun* a device on a tube or pipe that controls the flow of a gas or liquid. You pump air into a tire through a valve.

**vampire** *noun* in stories, a corpse that leaves its grave at night to suck people's blood. Dracula is the most famous vampire in fiction.

vault

**vandal** *noun* a person who deliberately smashes and ruins things for fun or through boredom. **vandalize** *verb.* **vandalism** *noun.*

**vane** *noun* **weather vane** a pointer that moves with the direction of the wind and so shows which way the wind is blowing.

**vanilla** *noun* a sweet flavoring for ice cream, cakes, custard, and desserts, made from the seed pod of a kind of tropical orchid.

**vanish** *verb* to disappear; to become invisible. *The bus vanished into the mist.*

**vanity** *noun* being too proud of what you look like or of what you can do; conceit.

**Vanuatu** *noun* a country of islands in the Pacific Ocean.

**vapor** *noun* a gas produced by heating a liquid or solid form of a substance. Steam is water vapor.

Vanuatu's flag

**variable** *adjective* changing or varying a lot; not stable. *The weather has been variable over the past week.*

**variation** *noun* **1** showing variety. **2** something that has changed. **3** differences.

**varied** *adjective* different kinds of. *The presents varied from large and square to small and round.*

**variety** *noun* a collection or number of different things or kinds. *There are many varieties of sheep.*

**various** *adjective* of different sorts; several. *Victor had various jobs after he left school.*

**varnish** *noun* a shiny, transparent liquid that you paint onto wood to protect it and make it look glossy.

**vary** (varies, varying, varied) *verb* **1** to alter; to change constantly. *The weather varies from day to day.* **2** to make different. *I try to vary the restaurant's menu from one week to the next.*

**vase** *noun* an ornamental container or jar for flowers.

**vast** *adjective* very wide; immense. *The vast rain forests of the Amazon stretch as far as the eye can see.*

**vat** *noun* a large container or tub for storing liquid. *There are three vats of wine in the cellar.*

**Vatican City** *noun* an independent city and state within the city of Rome, Italy.

**vault** *noun* **1** a type of arch that supports a roof or ceiling, especially in a church, or a ceiling or roof supported by such arches. **2** a strong underground room, for example in a bank or museum, in which to store valuable things. **vault** *verb* to jump over something such as a gate. **vault** *noun.*

**VDU** *abbreviation* visual display unit; a computer screen.

**veal** *noun* the meat of a calf, used as food.

**veer** *verb* to turn suddenly and change direction; to swerve. *The racing car veered around a hairpin bend.*

**vegan** *noun* a vegetarian who does not use or eat any animal products.

**vegetable** *noun* a plant that is grown to be eaten. Carrots and peas are vegetables. **vegetable** *adjective. Vegetable curry is my favorite dish.*

**vegetarian** *noun* somebody who does not eat meat, only vegetables (and sometimes dairy foods and fish).

**vegetation** *noun* plant life in general, or the plants in a particular area. *Rain forests have lush vegetation.*

**vehicle** *noun* a machine such as a car, bus, or truck that transports people and goods from one place to another on land.

**veil** *noun* a very fine piece of material worn by some women to cover the face or head. *The bride wore a white veil during the marriage service.*

**vein** *noun* (rhymes with pain) **1** one of the tubes inside your body through which blood flows back to your heart. **2** one of the fine lines on a leaf or insect's wing.

**velocity** *noun* speed, particularly the speed at which something travels in one direction.

**velvet** *noun* a material with a soft, thick pile.

**Venezuela** *noun* a country in northern South America.

**venison** *noun* the meat from deer, used as food.

**venom** *noun* poison produced by some snakes and spiders. **venomous** *adjective.*

**ventilate** *verb* to let fresh air move freely through a place. *A well-ventilated bathroom.* **ventilation** *noun.*

**ventriloquist** *noun* a person who entertains by making his/her voice seem to come not from his/her own mouth but from a dummy or some other place.

**venture** *verb* to risk doing something. *"Nothing ventured, nothing gained."* **venture** *noun. Launching the new company was a risky business venture.*

**veranda** *noun* a platform around the outside of a house, usually with a roof; a porch.

**verb** *noun* a word or words in a sentence that describes what somebody or something is doing. In the sentence, "The dog is eating its bone," "is eating" is the verb.

**verbose** *adjective* using lots of words when only a few are needed. "At this point in time" is a verbose way of saying "now."

viaduct

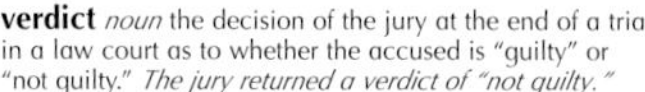

**verdict** *noun* the decision of the jury at the end of a trial in a law court as to whether the accused is "guilty" or "not guilty." *The jury returned a verdict of "not guilty."*

**verge** *noun* the grassy strip of ground along the edge of a road or path. **verge** *verb* come close to. *Jack's behavior verges on rudeness.*

**verify** (verifies, verifying, verified) *verb* to prove by showing the truth of something.

**vermin** *noun* any animal (such as a rat), bird, or insect that can transmit a disease or that damages food crops; pests.

vermin

**verse** *noun* **1** one of the parts into which a poem is divided, usually a distinct group of lines. **2** poetry having rhythm and sometimes rhyme.

**version** *noun* **1** one form or a changed type of something. *A new version of the Bible has been published.* **2** one person's description. *Mary gave her version of the event.*

**versus** *preposition* a Latin word meaning against, often shortened to v. *Boston versus New York. The game we are watching is Atlanta v. LA.*

**vertebra** (vertebrae) *noun* any one of the bones that make up the spine.

**vertebrate** *noun* any animal with a backbone. *Humans are vertebrates.*

**vertical** *adjective* upright; straight up. *The telegraph poles should be vertical, not slanted.* The opposite of "vertical" is "horizontal."

**vessel** *noun* **1** a ship or boat. **2** a container for liquids.

**vet, veterinary surgeon** *noun* a person who is trained to treat sick animals; an animal doctor.

**veto** *noun* the power to refuse to allow something to happen, or such a refusal. **veto** *verb.*

**vex** (vexes, vexing, vexed) *verb* to annoy or worry somebody. *John was vexed by his homework.*

**via** *preposition* (say **vye**-ah) by way of. *We fly to Sydney, Australia, via Rome, Italy.*

**viable** *adjective* likely to be successful; workable. *Building a bridge across the Atlantic is simply not viable.*

**viaduct** *noun* (say **vye**-a-dukt) a long, arched bridge that carries a road or railroad across a valley.

**vibrate** *verb* to shake to and fro rapidly. *The traffic outside makes the windows of our house vibrate.* **vibration** *noun.*

**vicar** *noun* a clergyman in charge of a parish in the Anglican Church.

**vice** *noun* **1** a metal device that grips objects firmly while you work on them with a tool. **2** a weakness in a person's character. *Her only vice is eating chocolate after dinner.* **3** immoral behavior. *Gambling is a vice that is becoming increasingly common.*

**vice-** *prefix* in place of; next in rank to. *The vice president will attend the meeting in place of the president.*

**vice versa** *adverb* the same is true either way or the other way around. *When he wants to eat, she doesn't want to eat, and vice versa.*

**vicinity** *noun* (say viss-**in**-it-ee) the surrounding or nearby area.

**vicious** *adjective* violent; cruel.

**victim** *noun* a person who has been attacked, injured, robbed, or killed.

**victimize** *verb* to deliberately choose somebody to treat unfairly or cruelly.

**victor** *noun* the winner in a competition, game, or battle. *The victor was given a medal.*

**Victoria** *noun* the capital of the Seychelles.

**victory** *noun* success in a battle or contest; a win. **victorious** *adjective. Napoleon's army was victorious.*

**video** *noun* **1** a machine (video cassette recorder) that records TV programs so that you can watch them at another time. **2** a videotape, either blank or containing a recording of a film or TV program.

**vie** (vies, vying, vied) *verb* to compete.

**Vienna** *noun* the capital of Austria in Central Europe.

**Vientiane** *noun* the capital of Laos in Southeast Asia.

**Vietnam** *noun* a country in Southeast Asia.

**vigorous** *adjective* physically energetic, enthusiastic, and strong. *Let's go for a vigorous walk.* **vigour** *noun.*

**Vikings** *plural noun* seafarers from Scandinavia who invaded many parts of Europe between the 8th and 11th centuries. **Viking** *adjective. Viking hordes.*

Vikings

**vile** *adjective* disgusting and very unpleasant; horrible. *A vile smell wafted in from the garbage bins.*

**villa** *noun* a big house with a garden, usually in the countryside or near the sea in Mediterranean countries. In Roman times, a villa was a country house.

**village** *noun* a small group of houses, often with a church, school, store, and bar.

**villain** *noun* **1** a person who breaks the law on purpose. **2** a wicked person, especially in a movie or novel. *The villain of the story was a cruel king.* **villainy** *noun.*

**Vilnius** *noun* the capital of Lithuania in the Baltic region.

**vine** *noun* a climbing plant on which grapes grow. *We picked bunches of grapes from the vine.*

**vinegar** *noun* a sharp-tasting liquid made from wine or malt and used to flavor food and make dressings.

**vineyard** *noun* (say **vin**-yard) a place where grapes are grown for making wine. *A terraced vineyard in France.*

**vintage** *adjective* (of wine) **1** a good example of a particular year. **2** (of cars) made between 1917 and 1930. **3** of high and enduring quality from the past. *Vintage clothes.*

**viola** *noun* a stringed musical instrument that is slightly larger than a violin and produces a lower pitch. *The beautiful mellow sound of the viola reached my ears.*

viola

**violent** *adjective* **1** using a lot of physical force to frighten, hurt, or even kill. **2** sudden, strong, and rough. *A violent storm blew up over the dark Sargasso Sea.* **violence** *noun. I don't like violence on television or in movies.*

**violet** *noun* **1** a small plant with purplish flowers and a sweet smell. *There are violets growing in the hedgerow.* **2** the purplish color of a violet. **violet** *adjective.*

**violin** *noun* a musical instrument with four strings stretched across a wooden frame that you hold under your chin. *Hilary was learning to play the violin.*

**viper** *noun* a European poisonous snake; an adder. *Ian was bitten by a viper.*

**virgin** *noun* a person who has never had sexual intercourse. **virginity** *noun.*

**virtual** *adjective* **1** in practice, but not in name. *The President's wife is the virtual ruler of the country, making all the decisions for him in private.* **2** almost but not completely; not actually said. *The virtual collapse of law and order after the election left the streets in chaos.* **virtual reality** an impression of a real environment in which you can interact, created by a computer.

**virtue** *noun* a particular good quality; goodness. Patience, kindness, and honesty are virtues.

**virus** *noun* **1** a microscopically tiny organism or living thing, smaller than bacteria, that can carry or cause disease. *A flu virus.* **2** a computer program that can damage or destroy data in a computer.

**viscount** *noun* (say **vie**-count) a British nobleman between an earl and a baron in rank. *We invited the viscount and the viscountess to lunch.* **viscountess** the wife or widow of a viscount.

**visible** *adjective* capable of being seen. *From the top of a double-decker bus the whole street is visible.* **visibility** *noun* how clearly you can see. *On foggy days, visibility is poor and you can sometimes see only a few feet ahead.*

**vision** *noun* **1** sight; your ability to see. **2** what you can see or imagine in a dream. **3** great power of imagination and ability to plan. *His vision for the future is that everybody should own their own home.*

**visit** *verb* **1** to go and see somebody or a place. **2** to stay somewhere for a short time. **visit** *noun.* **visitor** *noun.*

**visual** *adjective* relating to seeing and sight. *The visual effect of the computer-generated images in the new movie was stunning.*

**visualize** *verb* to form a picture in your mind; to imagine. *Try and visualize an empty, sun-drenched beach bordered by palm trees, and feel yourself relax.*

**vital** *adjective* essential to life; very important. *Air and water are vital to all living creatures.*

**vitality** *adjective* full of life and energy.

**vitamin** *noun* any one of several substances in food that we need to stay healthy. *Oranges and many other fruits are a good source of vitamin C, which helps keep us healthy.*

**vivid** *adjective* (of colors) strong and bright. *The grass turns a vivid green after rainfall.*

**vivisection** *noun* the use of living animals for scientific research.

vixen

**vixen** *noun* a female fox, a wild meat-eating animal of the dog family. The male fox is called a dog. The young are called cubs.

**viz.** *adverb* namely; in other words.

**vocabulary** *noun* all the words somebody knows in a language. *His vocabulary in Spanish is about 1,000 words.*

**vocal** *adjective* **1** relating to the voice. *Madeleine exercises her vocal cords before singing.* **2** speaking out freely and loudly. *He is very vocal about his beliefs.*

**vocation** *noun* a calling or strong feeling that you want to do a particular job. *Dan had a vocation to become a priest.* **2** a profession or occupation; a career.

**vodka** *noun* a colorless, strong alcoholic drink made from rye that originated in Russia.

**vogue** *noun* a fashion.

**voice** *noun* the sound produced by your vocal cords when you speak or sing; the power to speak.

**void** *noun* emptiness; a huge space with nothing in it. **void** *adjective* having no legal effect; not binding. *Null and void.*

volcano

**volcano** (volcanoes) *noun* a mountain with a crater (hole) at the top through which molten lava from below the Earth's crust sometimes erupts. **volcanic** *adjective.*

**volume** *noun* **1** the amount of space that something takes up or contains. *The volume of water in the lake.* **2** one of a set of books. *A 20-volume encyclopedia.* **3** the loudness of sound. *Turn up the volume so I can hear.*

**voluntary** *adjective* done willingly and not because you have been forced to. *She made a voluntary donation.* **2** done without payment. *She does voluntary work for charity.* **volunteer** *noun* someone who willingly does a job or performs a task without seeking payment.

**vomit** *verb* to bring food or liquid back up from your stomach through your mouth; to be sick.

**vote** *verb* to make a formal choice by means of a ballot or show of hands. **vote** *noun. Please cast your vote now.*

**vow** *verb* to make a serious promise; to pledge. *He vowed to love, honor, and protect his wife.* **vow** *noun.*

**vowel** *noun* a letter that is not a consonant—"a," "e," "i," "o," and "u" and sometimes "y" are vowels.

**voyage** *noun* a long sea journey.

**vulgar** *adjective* rude; offensive; coarse. **vulgarity** *noun. The teacher put a stop to vulgarity in the playground.*

**vulnerable** *adjective* someone or something that is easily harmed because unprotected; weak. *Old people are particularly vulnerable to illness during the cold winter months.* **vulnerability** *noun.*

**vulture** *noun* a large bird of prey that feeds mostly on carrion (dead animals). *The vulture swooped out of the sky and landed on the sheep's carcass.*

**wad** *noun* **1** a thick lump of soft material. *I wiped the wound with a wad of damp cotton.* **2** a tight bundle or pile of paper. *Tim handed me a wad of notes.*

**waddle** *verb* to walk in a clumsy, swaying way with short steps, like a duck.

**wade** *verb* to walk through fairly deep water or mud.

**wafer** *noun* a very thin, crisp cookie that is often sweet. *Chocolate wafers are a favorite snack of mine.*

**waffle** *noun* a light, crisp cake made of batter, the surface of which is formed into a pattern of raised squares. Waffles are very popular in North America. *At summer camp, we eat waffles and maple syrup for breakfast.*

**wag** (wags, wagging, wagged) *verb* to move quickly from side to side or up and down. *The dog wagged its tail with pleasure.*

**wage** (wages, waging, waged) *verb* to carry on a war, conflict, or contest. *The police are waging war on car theft.* **wages** *plural noun* the money paid for work done.

wagon

**wagon** *noun* **1** a four-wheeled cart pulled by a horse or oxen. **2** an open railroad truck for carrying freight. *The train pulled twenty wagons of coal to the coast.*

**wail** *noun* a long, sad-sounding cry. **wail** *verb.*

**waist** *noun* the narrow, middle part of your body above your hips.

**wait** *verb* to stay where you are until something happens or someone arrives; to pause. *We waited 15 minutes for the bus.*

**waiter** *noun* a man or woman (also waitress) who brings food and drinks to you in a restaurant.

**wake** (waking, woke, woken) *verb* **1** to stop being asleep. **2** to rouse somebody from sleep. **wake** *noun* (especially in Ireland) a group of people who stay with a dead body to mourn on the night before it is buried.

**Wales** *noun* a country; part of Great Britain and the UK.

**walk** *verb* to move along on your feet, without running. **walk** *noun. We went for a walk in the hills.* **walker** *noun.* **walk off with** to take something without asking. **walk-over** an easy victory in a competition.

**wall** *noun* a structure made of bricks or stones surrounding a piece of land, or the side of a building or room. **walled** *adjective. A walled garden.* **up the wall** crazy. *The noise is sending me up the wall.*

**wallaby** *noun* a small animal like a kangaroo.

**wallet** *noun* a small, folding case or purse for carrying money, credit cards, and other small documents; a billfold.

**wallow** *verb* **1** to roll and splash around in water or mud. **2** to enjoy something to excess. *She wallowed in everybody's praise.*

wallaby

**walnut** *noun* the edible nut, or the wood, of the walnut tree. Walnut wood is used to make furniture.

**walrus** *noun* a large sea animal similar to a seal with two long tusks.

**waltz** *noun* a graceful dance for two people with three beats to a bar.

**wan** *adjective* pale and tired-looking.

**wand** *noun* a stick that some magicians wave when they perform magic tricks, or that fairies carry in stories.

**wander** *verb* to move slowly from one place to another without going in any particular direction; to roam. **wanderer** *noun.*

**wane** *verb* to become smaller; to lose power. *The Moon is waning tonight.* The opposite of "to wane" is "to wax."

**war** *noun* **1** armed fighting between countries or groups of people; a long period of fighting. **2** a struggle or campaign. *The war against poverty.*

**-ward** *suffix* in the particular direction of. *Homeward; southward; toward.*

**warden** *noun* **1** somebody who is in charge of a college, hostel, or prison.

**warder** *noun* **1** a watchman. **2** a stronghold.

**wardrobe** *noun* a cupboard in which to hang clothes.

**warehouse** *noun* a building for storing goods that are to be sold.

**warfare** *noun* the state of fighting wars.

**warlike** *adjective* hostile and prepared for war.

**warn** *verb* **1** to tell somebody about a possible danger in the future. **2** to advise. *He warned me to go carefully.* **warning** *noun* a notice or statement that warns.

**warp** *noun* **1** the lengthwise strands in a piece of weaving. The warp is crossed by the weft. **2** the thread or wool that you attach to a loom. **warp** *verb* **1** to attach thread or wool to a loom. **2** to become twisted or misshapen through damp or heat.

**warren** *noun* a network of underground burrows or passages in which rabbits live.

**warrior** *noun* a great fighting soldier.

**Warsaw** *noun* the capital of Poland in eastern Europe.

**warship** *noun* a ship armed with guns for use in war.

**was** past tense of "be."

**Washington, D.C.** *noun* the capital of the United States of America.

**wasp** *noun* a yellow and black striped insect that can sting.

wasp

**waste** *noun* **1** things that you throw away because they are broken, worn, or you do not need them any more. **2** not using things in a careful way. *It's a waste to throw away food.* **waste** *verb* to use more of something than you need or to throw something away that could be used. **waste** *adjective. Waste paper.*

**wasteful** *adjective* extravagant; using more than is needed. **wastefulness** *noun.*

**watch** *noun* a small clock that you usually wear on your wrist. **watch** *verb* **1** to look at for some time. *Watch how I do this.* **2** to notice and be careful about something. *Watch how you cross the road.* **watch over** to keep guard or take care of somebody. *I'll watch over the baby while you are out.* **watch out!** be careful.

**watchful** *adjective* always noticing what is happening; alert. **watchfulness** *noun.*

**water** *noun* a clear liquid that falls as rain and that all living things drink to survive. Water is found in oceans, rivers, and lakes. It is made of two gases: oxygen and hydrogen. **water** *verb* **1** to pour water on. **2** to produce tears in the eyes or saliva in the mouth. **3** to dilute. **watercolor** *noun* a painting done with paints (watercolors) that you dilute with water. **water lily** a water plant with flat, round leaves and cup-shaped flowers that float on the surface of water. **watermill** a mill, or a building for grinding grain, which has machinery worked by a water wheel. **water polo** a ball game played in a swimming pool by two teams of seven players. **waterskiing** a sport in which a person skims over the surface of the sea or a lake on skis, towed by a long rope attached to a motorboat.

watermill

**waterfall** *noun* a stream or river that cascades over a cliff or big rock or down a steep hillside.

**waterproof** *adjective* not letting water through. *Take your waterproof coat if you are going out in the rain!*

**watertight** *adjective* closed so tightly or made so that water cannot get in.

**watery** *adjective* full of water or containing too much water. *The soup is too watery for my liking.*

**watt** *noun* a unit of electricity.

**wave** *noun* **1** a moving curved line or ridge on the surface of water, especially the sea. **2** a curl or curved piece of hair. **3** the vibrating way in which energy, such as heat, light, sound, and radio, travels. **4** the act of moving your hand up and down to attract someone's attention or to indicate that you are leaving. **wave** *verb* **1** to move your hand up and down as a way of signaling "hello" or "goodbye." **2** to move something quickly to and fro; to flutter. *The flag waved in the wind.*

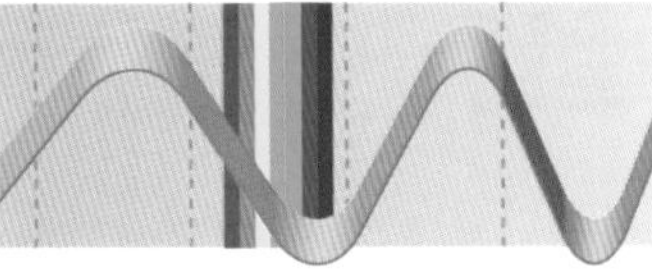

wavelength

**wavelength** *noun* **1** the distance between successive crests of electrical, radio, sound, or light waves. **2** a particular way of thinking or feeling. *Jim and I work well together because we are on the same wavelength.*

**wax** *noun* **1** a solid substance made from fat or oil that becomes soft and sticky when heated. Wax is used to make things such as candles and furniture polish. **2** a similar substance produced by bees (beeswax). **3** a wax-like substance found in your ears. **wax** *verb* to grow bigger. *The Moon waxes and then wanes (grows smaller).*

**-ways** *suffix* in the direction of. *Sideways.*

**weak** *adjective* having little strength or power; easily broken. **weakness** *noun.*

**weaken** *verb* to make or become weak.

**wealth** *noun* **1** a lot of money and possessions; great riches. **2** a large amount. *A wealth of detail.* **wealthy** *adjective* rich.

**weapon** *noun* a device, such as a gun, dagger, or sword, used for fighting.

**wear** (wears, wearing, wore, worn) *verb* **1** to be dressed in; to have on your body. *Do you wear glasses?* **2** to become damaged through use. *I wore a hole in the knee of my pants.* **wear** *noun. Evening wear.* **wear down** to weaken a person's resistance. *She wore him down with her nagging.* **wear off** to fade away or to become less. *The pain is wearing off.* **wear out** **1** to become damaged and useless. *I've been wearing this coat for three years and it's worn out.* **2** to feel tired.

**weary** (wearier, weariest) *adjective* very tired. *You must be weary after your long journey.* **weariness** *noun.*

**weather** *noun* the condition of the atmosphere at a particular time or place, whether it is warm, cold, windy, or rainy. **weather forecast** a report on what the weather is expected to be like in the near future.

**weather vane** *noun* a pointer that moves with the wind and so shows which way the wind is blowing.

**weave** (weaves, weaving, wove) *verb* **1** to make cloth by passing threads over and under other threads. **2** to make items such as baskets by plaiting cane or rushes. **3** (past tense, weaved) to move in and out between people or things. *He weaved through the traffic on his bike.*

**weather vane**

**webbed** *adjective* having the toes joined by pieces of skin. *A duck's webbed feet help it swim better.*

**wedding** *noun* a marriage service.

**wedge** *noun* **1** a piece of wood that is thick at one end and thin and pointed at the other, used to stop things from moving. **2** something wedge-shaped. *A wedge of cheese.* **wedge** *verb. She wedged the door open.*

**weigh** *verb* **1** to place something on scales to find out how heavy it is. **2** to have a certain weight. *Dave weighs a lot more than he used to.*

**weight** *noun* **1** how heavy somebody or something is. **2** a piece of metal of a certain heaviness.

**weird** *adjective* strange; unusual.

**Wellington** *noun* the capital of New Zealand.

**Welsh** *noun* the language of Wales. **the Welsh** the people of Wales. **Welsh** *adjective. Welsh sheep.*

**werewolf** *noun* in stories and folklore, a man who sometimes turns into a wolf, usually at full moon.

**west** *noun* the direction in which the sun sets. The opposite direction is east. **west** *adjective, adverb.*

**western** *adjective* relating to the west; of the west. *Western Europe.*

**Western Samoa** *noun* a country of islands in the Pacific Ocean.

**West Indies** *plural noun* the islands that separate the Caribbean Sea from the Atlantic Ocean.

**whale** *noun* a very large sea mammal that looks like a fish and needs air to breathe.

**wharf** (wharfs or wharves) *noun* a platform or landing place where ships dock to be loaded or unloaded.

**whale**

**wheat** *noun* a cereal crop from whose grain flour is made.

**wheel** *noun* a circular object or disk that rotates around an axle and is used to move a vehicle or to help make machinery work. **wheel** *verb* to push something on wheels. *She wheeled her bicycle up the steep hill.*

**wheelchair** *noun* a chair with large wheels used by somebody who cannot walk easily, if at all.

**when** *adverb, conjunction* **1** at what time. *When does the bus arrive?* **2** at the time that. *When I get home, I will change my clothes.*

**whenever** *adverb, conjunction* **1** when. **2** at every time. *Whenever my grandmother visits us, she brings me a present.* **2** at any time. *Come whenever you like.*

**where** *adverb* **1** in what place. *Where is the dog?* **2** to what place. *Where did you go over the weekend?* **3** from what place. *Where did you find those shoes?* **where** *conjunction* at or in what place. *He went over to the window where there was more light.*

**whiff** *noun* a sudden, slight scent of something. *A whiff of honeysuckle reached us through the open window.*

**whim** *noun* a sudden, and often silly, desire or thought. *On a whim, Richard bought two tickets to Paris and gave one to the delighted Sarah.*

**whimper** *verb* to make a quiet, crying noise because of pain. *The dog whimpered because it had been accidentally shut out in the backyard.* **whimper** *noun.*

**whirl** *verb* to move around and around quickly. *Brian whirled Brenda around the dance floor on New Year's Eve.* **whirl** *noun. A whirl of activity.*

**whirlpool** *noun* a current of water that turns around and around rapidly.

**whirlwind** *noun* a strong wind that spins as it travels over land and sea.

**whisker** *noun* **1** a long, stiff hair growing around the mouth of an animal such as a cat or dog. **2** a hair growing on a man's face.

**whisper** *verb* to speak very quietly using only your breath without vibrating your vocal cords. **whisper** *noun.*

**whistle** *noun* **1** the shrill noise you can make when you blow through your lips. **2** a device you blow to make a sound like a whistle. **whistle** *verb. Jack whistled a happy tune.*

**whizz** (whizzes, whizzing, whizzed) *verb* to move very quickly with a rushing noise. *The racing cars whizzed past.* **whizz kid** *noun* a clever and successful young person. *Dean is a real whizz kid at computing.*

**WHO** *abbreviation* World Health Organization.

**whole** *adjective* the complete and total amount of something. *She ate a whole bag of cookies.* **whole** *noun. Two halves make a whole.*

**wholesome** *adjective* good for you. *Wholesome soup.*

**whooping cough** *noun* a serious infectious disease, particularly of children, that makes you cough a lot and make a terrible noise as you breathe in.

**why** *adverb* for what reason.

**wicked** *adjective* bad, evil, and cruel. **wickedness** *noun.*

**widespread** *adjective* happening over a wide area or among many people. *Widespread flooding.*

**widow** *noun* a woman whose husband has died. *The widow had to bring up her children on her own.*

**widower** *noun* a man whose wife has died.

**width** *noun* how much something measures from one side to the other.

**wield** *verb* **1** to hold and use a weapon or tool. *He wielded an ax.* **2** to exercise power. *Dictators wield complete power in their countries.*

**wigwam** *noun* a dome-shaped tent made from animal skins by American Indians.

**wilderness** *noun* a wild, uncultivated area where nobody or few people live; a desert.

**wildlife** *noun* wild animals and plants in their natural habitats.

**willow** *noun* a tree with long, thin, hanging branches that grows near water.

willow

**willowy** *adjective* tall and graceful like a willow tree. *The fashion model was a willowy young girl.*

**wily** (wilier, wiliest) *adjective* cunning; full of artful tricks.

**wince** *verb* to jerk and make your face look twisted because of pain or fear.

**winch** *noun* a machine with a rope around a turning part, used for lifting things. **winch** *verb* to lift with a winch. *The boat was winched out of the water.*

**wind** *noun* (rhymes with pinned) **1** a strong moving current of air. **2** gases in the stomach that make you feel uncomfortable. **wind instrument** a musical instrument that you blow into to play. *Clarinets, flutes, and trombones are wind instruments.* **windy** *adjective. A windy day.* **wind** (winds, winding, wound) *verb* (rhymes with kind) **1** to bend and twist. **2** to roll or wrap around. **3** to tighten a clock spring. **wind up 1** to end in a place or situation. **2** to tease. *Stop winding me up!*

**winded** *adjective* out of breath through heavy exercise.

**Windhoek** *noun* the capital of Namibia, a country in southern Africa.

**windmill** *noun* a mill (a building for pumping water or grinding grain) that is worked by the action of the wind rotating a set of arm-like sails.

windmill

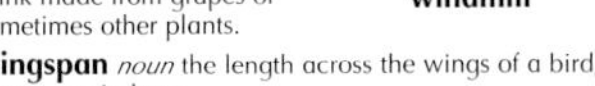

**windpipe** *noun* a tube leading from your mouth to your lungs that carries air to your lungs; the trachea.

**windsurf** *verb* to ride over waves on a special board with a sail. **windsurfer** *noun.*

**wine** *noun* an alcoholic drink made from grapes or sometimes other plants.

**wingspan** *noun* the length across the wings of a bird, insect, or airplane.

**winner** *noun* a person, animal, or vehicle that wins a race or contest.

**winning** *adjective* charming. *Bill has a winning smile, but he doesn't fool me!*

**winter** *noun* the season of the year between fall and spring. **wintry** *adjective.*

**wire** *noun* a thin length of metal that can easily be twisted, used especially to carry electricity and for fencing. **wire** *verb* to put in wires to carry electricity. *The house was wired last year.* **wire** *adjective.*

**wireless** *noun* an old-fashioned word for "radio."

**wisdom** *noun* being wise and having great understanding and judgment. **wisdom tooth** a tooth that sometimes grows at the back of your jaw after the other teeth have stopped growing.

**wise** *adjective* sensible and having a great understanding and experience of something; knowing the right action or decision.

**-wise** *suffix* **1** in the direction of. *Clockwise; lengthwise.* **2** with reference to something. *Healthwise, I'm fine.*

**wishbone** *noun* the V-shaped bone in the breast of birds.

**wit** *noun* **1** common sense; the ability to think clearly. **2** skill in saying things in a clever and funny way. **3** a clever and amusing person. *He's a great wit.* **witty** *adjective. What a witty writer!* **at your wits' end** not knowing how to solve a serious and worrying problem.

**-witted** *suffix* having a particular kind of ability. *Quick-witted.*

**witch** *noun* a woman (often ugly and old) in stories who has magic powers.

witch

**witchcraft** *noun* magic used by witches.

**witch doctor** *noun* a person who is believed to possess magic powers that can cure illnesses.

**withdraw** (withdraws, withdrawing, withdrew, withdrawn) *verb* **1** to take back or take away; to remove. *She withdrew $100 from her bank account.* **2** to go away from. *After the war, the troops withdrew.* **withdrawal** *noun.* **withdrawn** *adjective.* **1** remote. **2** unable to communicate. *She's unhappy and withdrawn.*

**wither** *verb* to dry up, droop and die; to shrivel. *Flowers wither without water.*

**within** *preposition* **1** inside. *A delicious smell came from within.* **2** not beyond. *They were within a mile of home when it started to rain.*

wither

**withhold** (withhold, withholding, withheld) *verb* to hold onto and refuse to give something; to hold back. *He withheld the evidence from the court.*

**without** *preposition* not having; in the absence of. *He made the model dinosaur himself, without any help.*

**witness** *noun* a person who has seen something important happen and so can describe what happened to others, especially to the police or to a judge and jury in a law court. **witness** *verb.*

**wives** the plural of wife.

**wizard** *noun* **1** in stories, a man with magic powers. **2** an expert at doing something. *A computer wizard.*

**wobble** *verb* to move in an unsteady way from side to side; to shake a little. **wobbly** *adjective. A wobbly jello.*

**woe** *noun* great sorrow; misery. **woeful** *adjective. Scarlett gave the soldier a woeful look when she saw what had happened to the town.*

**wolf** (wolves) *noun* a wild animal of the dog family that hunts in a pack. **wolf** *verb* to eat greedily. *Leo wolfed down his dinner before rushing out to play football.*

**woman** (women) *noun* a grown-up female human.

**womb** *noun* a part inside a woman or any female mammal where her young develop before being born.

**wombat** *noun* a small, strong, burrowing Australian marsupial related to the koala.

**wonder** *verb* **1** to ask yourself something; to want to know about. *I wonder what day it is.* **2** to be surprised or astounded. **wonder** *noun* **1** a feeling of surprise and amazement. **2** something so impressive that it causes amazement.

wombat

**wonderful** *adjective* **1** very pleasing; excellent. *What a wonderful day.* **2** marvelous and very impressive. *Emma's grades are a wonderful achievement.*

**wood** *noun* the substance that trees are made of. Furniture is usually made of wood and so is paper. **2** an area (not as big as a forest) where many trees grow closely together. **woody** *adjective. Woody carrots.*

**wooded** *adjective* covered with trees. *A wooded mountainside.*

**wooden** *adjective* made of wood.

**woodpecker** *noun* one of a family of tree-climbing birds with strong, pointed beaks. Woodpeckers use their beaks to peck holes in trees to find insects to eat.

**woodwind** *noun* a group of musical instruments that you play by blowing through a mouthpiece into a hollow tube. *The flute, oboe, clarinet, and bassoon are woodwind instruments.*

**woodwork** *noun* (the making of) things made of wood.

**woodworm** *noun* the larva of a beetle that feeds on wood, leaving small holes in it.

**wool** *noun* **1** the thick hair of sheep and goats, used for knitting and making cloth. **2** yarn made from wool. **wooly** *adjective* made of wool. *A wooly hat keeps your head warm in winter.*

**woozy** *adjective (informal)* feeling weak and unsteady; dizzy.

**word** *noun* a group of letters that mean something. We speak or write words to communicate. **give your word** to promise. **keep your word** to keep your promise. **in a word** to sum up. **word for word** each word exactly as said or written. *I repeated the oath word for word.* **have words with** to quarrel. **word processor** a computer with a keyboard and screen that is used to type letters, write articles, and store information.

woodwind instrument

**work** *noun* **1** the job that somebody does to earn money. **2** the energy you use to do or make something. *Hard work.* **3** something you have made or done. *Works of art.* **work** *verb* **1** to do a job. **2** to use effort to do work. **3** to operate or make something go. *Can you work this machine?* **have your work cut out** to have a difficult task to do. *You'll have your work cut out to finish painting the house before Tuesday.* **work out** to exercise to improve your fitness.

**workable** *adjective* able to be done successfully. *The architect came up with an attractive, workable plan.*

**worker** *noun* somebody who works or who does a particular job. *Factory workers.*

**works** *plural noun* parts of a machine that move.

**workshop** *noun* a place where things are made or repaired, particularly crafts.

**world** *noun* **1** the universe and space with all the stars and planets. **2** the Earth and everything on it. **3** all the things concerned with a particular subject or activity. *The world of music.* **the New World** America.

**worldly** *adjective* in pursuit of wealth and pleasure, rather than spiritual rewards.

**worm** *noun* a small, long, thin creature without legs that lives in the soil.

**worn out** *adjective* **1** too old and no longer in a good condition. **2** exhausted. *You must be worn out after running so far.*

world

**worry** (worries, worrying, worried) *verb* **1** to be upset and uneasy and think something bad may happen. *She worried that she might not be able to find her car in the large car park.* **2** to bother somebody. *Stop worrying me with your silly questions!*

**worse** *adjective* less good or well; more bad, but not as bad as worst. *The weather was bad yesterday but it's worse today.*

**worship** (worships, worshiping, worshiped) *verb* **1** to pray and give praise to God or gods; to take part in a religious ceremony. **2** to love somebody very much. **worshiper** *noun.*

**worst** *adjective, adverb* least good or well; most bad. "Worst" is the opposite of "best."

**worth** *noun, adjective* **1** the value of something or somebody. *That vase is worth a lot of money, so don't drop it!* **2** good or useful. *This job is worth doing well.*

**worthless** *adjective* having no value; not useful. *Worthless ideas.* **worthlessness** *noun.*

**worthwhile** *adjective* useful and important enough to spend time on. *A worthwhile project is always a pleasure for the students to consider.*

**worthy** *adjective* good and deserving respect. **worthiness** *noun.*

**wound** *noun* (say **woon**-d) an injury or bad cut, especially one caused by a knife or gun. **wound** *verb. The soldier was badly wounded in battle.*

**wrap** (wraps,wrapping, wrapped) *verb* **1** to put a cover around or to fold paper or cloth around something. *We wrapped up Dad's present.* **2** to curl a part of your body, such as your fingers or legs, around something. **wrap round your little finger** to be able easily to persuade someone to do something.

**wrapping** *noun* paper or other material put around something to cover or protect it.

**wreath** *noun* flowers and leaves arranged in a circle and tied together.

**wreck** *verb* to destroy or ruin something completely so that it is unusable. *Vandals wrecked the bus shelter.*

**wreckage** *noun* all the pieces that remain after something has been wrecked. *We cleared up the wreckage after the flood.*

**wren** *noun* a very small, brown bird with an upward-pointing tail.

**wrench** *verb* to tug or twist something with violence. *He wrenched off the lid.* **wrench** *noun* a tool used for gripping and twisting things such as nuts and bolts.

**wrestle** *verb* **1** to get hold of somebody and try to throw them to the ground, especially in a sport called wrestling. **2** to struggle. *She wrestled with her feelings after her boyfriend left her.* **wrestler** *noun* somebody who wrestles as a sport.

**wretched** *adjective* **1** sad; very unhappy. **2** poor quality or unpleasant. *The wretched machine won't work.*

**wriggle** *verb* to twist and turn around. *Stop wriggling in your chair or you will turn it over!*

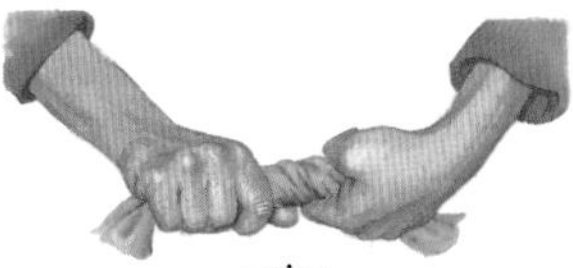

wring

**wring** (wrings, wringing, wrung) *verb* to force water out of a wet cloth by squeezing it. *He wrung out his shirt.*

**wrinkle** *noun* a crease or line in your skin or in cloth. **wrinkle** *verb. Lucy wrinkled her nose in distaste.*

**wrist** *noun* the joint connecting your arm to your hand. *The movie star wore a diamond bracelet on her wrist.*

**write** (writes, writing, wrote, written) *verb* **1** to form words, as with a pen or pencil, on paper. **2** to compose a book, essay, article, or piece of music. **writer** *noun* a person who writes, usually to earn money.

**writing** *noun* **1** anything that has been written, such as literature or poems. **2** handwriting. *He has neat writing.*

**wrong** *adjective* **1** incorrect. The opposite of "wrong" is "right." **2** bad and immoral. *It's wrong to lie.*

**wry** *adjective* **1** twisted; bent. *He gave her a wry smile.* **2** slightly mocking. *A wry remark.*

**WYSIWYG** *abbreviation* what you see (on the computer screen) is what you get (when printed).

# X

**xenophobia** *noun* a deep dislike of all foreigners.

**Xmas** *noun* a short, informal spelling of Christmas. *Merry Xmas.*

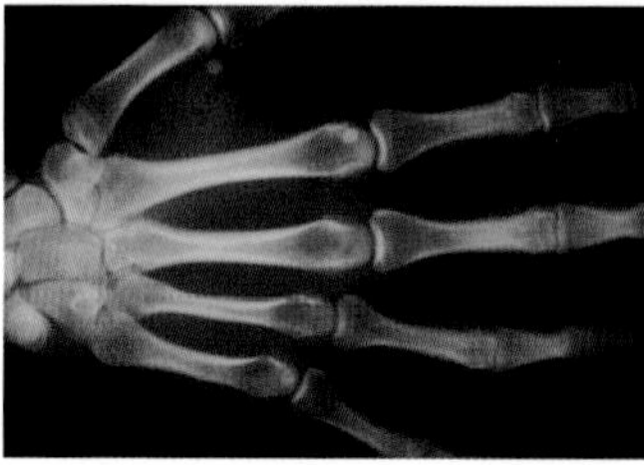

X-ray

**X-ray** *noun* **1** electromagnetic radiation that can pass through solid things. **2** a photograph of a part of the inside of your body made by the effect of x-rays on a photographic plate. This enables doctors to see if any bones are broken or if a part of the body is diseased.

**xylophone** *noun* (say **zy**-luh-**fone**) a musical instrument made of wooden or metal bars ranging in length from long to short. The player strikes the bars with small hammers to make notes.

# Y

**yacht** *noun* (say yaht) a large sailing boat, especially used for racing, or a motor-driven boat used for cruising.

**yak** *noun* a long-haired ox from Tibet and the Himalayas.

**yam** *noun* a tropical vegetable similar to a potato, also called a sweet potato.

**Yamoussoukro** *noun* the capital of Cote d'Ivoire, a country in West Africa.

**yank** *verb* to pull something suddenly and with a degree of force. *Tom yanked the dog's lead.* **yank** *noun.*

**Yaoundé** *noun* the capital of Cameroon in West Africa.

**yap** *noun* the short, high-pitched bark of a small dog. **yap** (yaps, yapping, yapped) *verb.*

**yard** *noun* **1** a measure of length equal to 3 feet or 0.91 meters. **2** an enclosed area next to a building and sometimes used for a particular purpose. *A timber yard.* **3** a garden or lawn next to a house.

**yarn** *noun* **1** wool or cotton spun into thread for sewing, knitting, or weaving. **2** a long and often untrue story.

**yashmak** *noun* a veil worn by some Muslim women to cover all or part of their face.

**yawn** *verb* to open your mouth wide and take in a deep breath when you are tired or bored. **yawn** *noun.*

yashmak

**year** *noun* **1** the time it takes the Earth to travel once around the Sun: 365 days, or 12 months, or 52 weeks. **2** the period of time between January 1 and December 31. **leap year** *noun* a year having 366 days. In leap years, which occur every four years (except at the end of a century), February has 29 days instead of 28.

**yearly** *adjective* **1** taking place once a year. **2** during or lasting a single year. *We renewed the yearly membership fee for the golf club.* **yearly** *adverb.*

**yeast** *noun* a kind of fungus used in making bread, to make the dough rise, and in brewing beer.

**yell** *noun* a loud shout of pain, anger, encouragement, or delight. **yell** *verb.* To utter a loud shout. *Stephen yelled with excitement when he received his grades.*

**yellow** *noun* the color of ripe bananas and lemons. **yellow** *adjective. Yellow roses.*

**yelp** *noun* a sudden, sharp sound of pain or excitement. **yelp** *verb. The dog yelped when I accidentally stood on its tail.*

**Yemen** *noun* a country in Southwest Asia at the tip of the Arabian peninsula.

Yemen

**yen** *noun* **1** the main unit of currency in Japan. **2** a yearning or longing. **yen** *verb.*

**Yerevan** *noun* the capital of Armenia in Southwest Asia.

**yesterday** *noun, adverb* the day before today. *Today is Monday; yesterday was Sunday.*

**yew** *noun* an evergreen tree with dark needles.

**yield** *verb* **1** to surrender; to give up and admit defeat. *He yielded under pressure.* **2** to produce. *How much wheat does this field yield?* **yield** *noun.*

**yoga** *noun* (say yoh-guh) a Hindu system of meditation that exercises the body and mind, using breath-control, physical exercises, and focused concentration.

**yogurt** (also **yoghurt**) *noun* a thick liquid food made from soured milk. *Greek yogurt is delicious with honey.*

**yoke** *noun* a wooden bar with two pieces that fit around the necks of a pair of animals to keep them together so they can pull a plow or heavy load. **yoke** *verb.*

**yolk** *noun* (rhymes with oak) the yellow part in the middle of an egg.

**Yom Kippur** *noun* a Jewish holy day at the start of the Jewish New Year in mid-September. It is a time of fasting and prayer.

**yonder** *adjective, adverb* (old-fashioned) over there. *The bench is under yonder tree.*

**young** *adjective* not old; having lived or existed for only a short time. **young** *plural noun* the offspring of animals. *The young of cows are called calves.*

**youngster** *noun* a young person.

**youth** *noun* **1** the time when a person is young. *He was a gymnast in his youth.* **2** a young man. **3** young people in general.

**youthful** *adjective* **1** young. **2** having the qualities of being young; relating to the young. *Her youthful enthusiasm belied her age.*

**yo-yo** *noun* a toy made of two disks with a deep groove between them, around which a long string is attached and wound. You can make the disks spin up and down the string as it unwinds and rewinds.

**Yule** (in full, **Yuletide**) *noun* the Christmas period.

# Z

**zodiac**

**Zagreb** *noun* the capital of Croatia in southeast Europe.

**Zambia** *noun* a country in southern Africa.

**zany** (zanier, zaniest) *adjective* funny in an odd kind of way. **zanily** *adverb.*

**zap** (zaps, zapping, zapped) *verb* to strike or attack something suddenly in, for example, a computer game. **zap through** to skip quickly from one to another, for example, music tracks on a CD or TV programs.

**zeal** *noun* enthusiasm; determined eagerness.

**zebra** *noun* an African animal like a horse with black-and-white stripes on its body. *A herd of zebra roamed the plain, well camouflaged in the long grass.*

**zenith** *noun* **1** the sky directly overhead. **2** the highest point; the peak or summit. *The pop group's fame reached its zenith when they made a world tour.*

**zero** (zeros) *noun* nought; the name of the figure 0.

**zest** *noun* **1** enthusiasm; great enjoyment. *A zest for living.* **2** the outer peel of a lemon or orange.

**zigzag** *noun* a line that sharply bends one way and then another like the letter Z. **zigzag** *verb. The path zigzagged up the hillside.*

**Zimbabwe** *noun* a country in southern Africa.

**zinc** *noun* a hard white metal used in alloys.

**zip** or **zipper** *noun* a long, narrow fastener with two rows of teeth that can be made to lock and unlock by sliding a tab up or down. *Zip up your coat!*

**zither** *noun* an ancient musical instrument with strings that are plucked.

**zodiac** *noun* (say **zoh**-dee-ak) a belt of the sky through which the Sun, Moon, and planets move and which astrologers divide into twelve sections, each with its own symbol or sign and name. The twelve names of the zodiac are: Aries, Taurus, Gemini, Cancer, Leo, Virgo, Libra, Scorpio, Sagittarius, Capricorn, Aquarius, and Pisces.

**zombie** *noun* **1** in stories, a dead body that is brought back to life. **2** a person who does not seem to be aware of what is going on, and is dull and apathetic.

**zone** *noun* an area that is made separate for some special purpose. *A no-parking zone.*

**zoo** *noun* a place where wild animals are kept for people to look at and study.

**zoology** *noun* (say zoo-**ol**-ogee) the scientific study of animals. **zoological** *adjective.* **zoologist** *noun.*

**zoom** *verb* **1** to move very quickly. **2** to focus a camera quickly from long distance to close up. **zoom lens** a camera lens that can be made to focus quickly on close-up things and then faraway things.

# Some general spelling rules

(But always remember, there are lots of exceptions to most rules!)

## Nouns

To make a noun into a plural noun, you normally add "s"—

road, roads; cake, cakes.

But if the noun ends in –ch, –s, –ss, –sh or –x, you add –es—

ass, asses; church, churches; bush, bushes; bus, buses; mix, mixes.

**This church is one of many churches.**

Nouns ending in a consonant plus a "y" lose the "y" and add –ies—

baby, babies; copy, copies.

Many nouns ending in "o" generally add –es—

cargo, cargoes; hero, heroes.

Plurals that do not follow these rules are shown in the dictionary—child, children; mouse, mice.

Some nouns are always plural in form:

Scissors, shears, oats, clothes, pajamas, trousers, measles, spectacles.

Some nouns have irregular plurals—

man, men; mouse, mice; woman, women; goose, geese; foot, feet; tooth, teeth; ox, oxen.

Some nouns are both singular and plural in form—

Fish, sheep, deer.

**deer**

## Adverbs

Adverbs are usually formed by adding –ly to the adjective—

odd, oddly; amazing, amazingly; quick, quickly.

But if the adjective ends in –ll, just add –y—

dull, dully.

If the adjective ends in –le, drop the –le and add –ly—

simple, simply.

If the adjective ends in –ic, add ally—

historic, historically.

(A notable exception is public, publicly.)

Adverbs that do not follow these rules will be found in the dictionary.

## Adjectives

To most adjectives of one syllable, you normally add –er to make a comparative—

near, nearer; fast, faster (Anne can run faster than her sister).

And you add –est to make a superlative—

nearest, fastest (Andy is the fastest runner in his class).

**He ran fast, but not faster than the fastest runner.**

If the adjective ends in –e, just add "r" or "st"—

simple, simpler, simplest.

With some short adjectives ending with a consonant, the consonant is doubled—

red, redder, reddest.

With adjectives of more than two syllables, use "more" and "most" for the comparative and superlative—

careful, more careful, most careful. (He's the most careful person I know.)

Adjectives that do not follow these rules are shown in the dictionary, for example—

bad, worse, worst; good, better, best.

## Verbs

To make the present participle, past tense and past participle of most regular verbs, you add –ing, or –ed, or –d—

talk, talking, talked; pray, praying, prayed.

If the verb ends in "e," the "e" is dropped and –ing, or –ed are added—

tame, taming, tamed.

The final consonant is doubled when a short word ends in a consonant—

chat, chatting, chatted; slam, slamming, slammed.

## I before E

"I before e except after c" is a good general rule, but only applies if the "ie" in the word is pronounced "ee." So, it is "ie" in words such as field, believe and siege, and "ei" in words such as ceiling and receipt.

Some exceptions are: either, neither (which can be pronounced "ee"), seize, weird, protein, Keith, Neil.

Words like eight, deign, reign and neighbour are spelled with "ei" because they are not pronounced "ee."

## Apostrophies

The possessive form of a noun is shown by writing 's at the end—

the boy's book; the children's house; Charles's bike.

When a plural noun ends in "s", add an apostrophe after the "s"—

The girls' mother.

**The jester's hat looks good on all the jesters' heads.**

## Each other or one another

Use "each other" for two—the two boys helped each other.

Use "one another" for more than two—all the children helped one another.

## Double negative

"I never said nothing" is incorrect if what you want to say is "I never said anything." But it is correct if what you want to say is "At no time did I ever say nothing."

## What's wrong?

Can you correct the mistakes in these sentences?

1) Was you angry with me?
2) The cat is eating it's supper.
3) Im to busy to see you.
4) He drunk all the milk.
5) He dances good.
6) You could of said you wasn't coming.
7) Lie the book on the desk.
8) The cacti needs watering.
9) This is the widower of the late Mrs Jones.
10) Calm down and don't get so historical.

(Answers: 1) were; 2) its; 3) I'm; 4) drank; 5) well; 6) have; 7) lay; 8) need; 9) no "late"; 10) hysterical.)

## Guess my definition

In this game, you read out the definition of a word and ask your friends to say what the headword is. For example "a soft, yellow food made from cream and milk". (The answer is "butter.")

## Matching sounds

Try to match the words that sound the same: beat, him, thyme, cymbal, steal, knight, meddle, bear, see, two, symbol, steel, beet, bare, time, night, sea, medal.

## Hidden words

Take a long word like 'measurement' and see how many other words you can find within it. (The word "drawing," for example, contains: draw, raw, win, wing, in.)

## Odd ones out

Which are the odd ones out in these groups:

1) cod, trout, whale, herring, shark.
2) car, lorry, van, airplane, motorbike.
3) orange, apple, lamb, plum, cherry.

## Backword

The word "evil" becomes "live" if you spell it backward. Can you think of any other words that do this?

## Sounds right

Think of a phrase or sentence that uses all these words:

1) roar, croak, neigh, bellow.
2) crash, clang, bang, thud.

## Code words

This code hides a simple sentence. All you have to do is read down the first column and then up the last column to find the message "Thanks for the presents."

| | |
|---|---|
| T E N S | S I D E |
| H U R T | F O U R |
| A V O N | O L O P |
| N I N E | R U S E |
| K I S S | T O S H |

## In alphabetical order

Put these words in alphabetical order:

1) crown, cruise, crane, crow.
2) live, lamb, loose, letter, likely.
3) dragon, donkey, dust, dinosaur, deaf.

## Chain words

A game to play with several people. Using the last two letters of the previous word make another word, e.g., reserve, vest, street, etiquette, telescope, pedal, alone, negligent, entire, and so on.

## Sets

Think of a single word for each of these sets of words:

1) aluminum, brass, bronze, iron, zinc.
2) plaice, cod, herring, trout.
3) chair, sofa, bed, table.

## Scrambled words

See if you can make new words from these words (e.g. the eyes—they see).

angered, astronomers, evil, funeral, nameless, night, nuclear, orchestra, organ.

(Answers: enraged, moon-starers, veil, real fun, maleness/lameness, thing, unclear, groan.)

## Changed

Take two words of the same length and link these two words together by putting in other words, each different from the next word by one changed letter. Here, for example, is how you could change "head" into "tail"': HEAD HEAL TEAL TELL TALL TAIL.